An Unfinished History of the World

HUGH THOMAS is a historian living in London. His principal work has been in the world of Spanish studies: for example, *The Spanish Civil War* (1961, revised edition 1977), *Cuba or the Pursuit of Freedom* (1971) and *The Conquest of Mexico* (1993). He has, however, also published a history of the causes of the Cold War, *Armed Truce* (1986), a biography of John Strachey (1973) and some polemical literature: e.g. *Europe: the Radical Challenge* (1973), as well as several novels. The last three of these were *Havannah* (1984), *Klara* (1988) and *I, Montezuma* (1995). *The Spanish Civil War* gained the Somerset Maugham Prize in 1962, and *The Unfinished History of the World* the first National Book Award for History of the Arts Council in 1980. Hugh Thomas was chairman of the Centre for Policy Studies 1979–89 and was given a peerage as Lord Thomas of Swynnerton in 1981.

HUGH THOMAS

An Unfinished History
of the World

PAPERMAC

First published 1979 by Hamish Hamilton
Revised edition published 1981 by Pan Books
Revised edition with new epilogue published 1989 by Pan Books

This revised edition with new epilogue published 1995 by Papermac
an imprint of Macmillan General Books
Cavaye Place London SW10 9PG
and Basingstoke

Associated companies throughout the world

ISBN 0 333 62799 7

1 3 5 7 9 8 6 4 2

A CIP catalogue record for this book is available from
the British Library

Phototypeset by Intype, London
Printed and bound in Great Britain by
Mackays of Chatham plc, Chatham, Kent

this book is dedicated to
Rómulo Betancourt

Contents

Book One
The Foundations of History

Book Two
The Age of Agriculture

Book Three
The World Transformed

Book Four
Our Times I: Industrial Triumphs

Book Five
Our Times II: Absolutism and Democracy

Book Six
Our Times III: Wars of Our Time

Contents

Book 5b
Our Times III: Wars of Our Time

List of Maps

List of Maps

Preface to the 1980 Edition

This book is a revised edition of *An Unfinished History of the World* published in what I now regard as draft form in London in 1979. I have made substantial additions, subtractions and rearrangements in it. I am grateful to all who pointed out errors, inconsistencies and ambiguities in the first edition. The notes have been abbreviated.

H.T.
Cafaggiolo, Italy
3 September 1980

Preface to the First Edition

The main purpose of this study is to provide a short history of the world arranged on thematic, rather than chronological, lines. I wrote it principally because I had spent a great deal of time investigating specialised subjects and thought that I should like to consider the background against which those occurrences had taken place. At the end of the book I have allowed myself to be drawn into a discussion of the crisis which appears to affect the world in the last quarter of the twentieth century. My suggestion is that the best way of dealing with these difficulties is to place them against their historical roots.

It will become evident that the 'world' mentioned in the title is not so large as some would expect. There is more here about Tuscany than Tobago. Sir Henry Maine wrote, in his one famous book *Ancient Law*: 'It is difficult for a citizen of Western Europe to bring thoroughly home to himself the truth that the civilisation which surrounds him is a rare exception in the history of the world. The tone of thought common among us all, our hopes, fears and speculations would be materially affected if we had vividly before us the relation of the progressive nations to the totality of human life.' I have tried to keep that caution in mind. Still, it is obvious that it is Western Europe with North America which, since the fifteenth century at least, for good or evil, has provided the world's dynamism. Even the 'vulgar Marxism' which attracts so many students from poor parts of the world is a European product. I can still hear Professor Fernand Braudel explaining to some astonished students at the University of Reading his theory that the Mediterranean was a sea which 'psychologically' surrounded Brazil. North America is also a Europe-over-the-water. That this era of European dominance may one day come to seem a short one, lasting from about AD 1400 till 1945 (or perhaps 1973), is possible. Modern statesmen, such as Charles de Gaulle or Jean Monnet, who, in contrasting ways, have sought to regenerate Europe since the Second World War, may come to resemble the later emperors of Rome whose titanic efforts to resist decay were destined to failure. On the whole, I think that catastrophic interpretation of the future of Europe premature, not because of our greater self-confidence but because it is hard to see new ideas on the horizon which could effectively challenge ours in a free encounter; and because the West still has leaders with a sense of its historic past. The world's demoralisation, wrote Ortega y Gasset at the end of the 1920s, derives from the demoralisation of Europe. Despite decline of Europe's political power, that still seems to be true. There is also here within consideration of Europe a certain emphasis on the role of Britain, since, in the critical two hundred years after 1700, that country was associated with more innovations than any other.

This book is an unfinished history. I have cut out a few chunks of rock and given them certain shapes, and I present them to the reader as if to say 'this is how a history of the world should be shaped, in my opinion, if such a book could, in fact, be written'. The shapes are these. First, I have tried to bring together what seem to be the most interesting elements in the pre-history of the world and to notice how the age referred to by anthropologists as the age of hunters was, slowly, transformed into an era when agriculture began to affect the cultivable regions of the world. Such divisions in time are more comprehensible than the 'stone' age, the 'neolithic' age or the 'bronze' age. In Book II, I discuss the 'age of agriculture' in the hope that a fresh look at the history of so long a time may be found by treating it as if it were a single epoch. I justify this by the suggestion that, to most people, those years were really the age of grain, or the age of rice rather than the age of Egypt, Rome or chivalry. Book III discusses the intellectual transformation which occurred in Europe between the Renaissance and the Enlightenment. The forward movement which then characterised European life derived from a reinvigoration of ideas formulated during antiquity but snuffed out after the conquest of the Mediterranean world by a Roman despotism. In Book IV I discuss the industrial era, and in Book V I notice how, and consider why, the innovations concerned have not as yet resulted in the creation of Utopia. Book VI discusses the problems of the present, and speculates how the liberal heritage of the West can be preserved.

A book of this sort is an adventure for its author. Having written several books about modern times, I wished to consider our relation to antiquity; and, having spent a great deal of time in other books discussing armies, anarchists and governments, I desired to consider, for a change, such often neglected topics as the history of brandy, of the thermometer and of the radish.

I need to make a number of acknowledgements: first, to the historians whose works I have pillaged in order to write this book.

Secondly, I thank Marjorie, Virginia and Lorenzo Scaretti for making available to me for so many summers at Il Trebbio an incomparable place in which to work. So many travellers passed through the valley beneath and so many exemplary men have lived at, or been to, Il Trebbio, that anyone with a historic sense can be forgiven if, from time to time, they persuade themselves that, though remote, they are living at the heart of civilisation. If some can picture Lorenzo de' Medici walking under the pergola with Politian or Luigi Pulci, his country neighbour, others can as easily imagine Dante plotting in the neighbourhood with the Ubaldini, Giotto walking with his sheep, Becket, Montaigne or Boswell travelling past, or Hannibal or Totila the Ostrogoth or General Mark Clark (with the 84th Indian division) preparing their armies. Amerigo Vespucci spent a summer or two at Trebbio as a child, escaping from the plague. In this 'folding of the Apennine', as Matthew Arnold put it in a line of *Thyrsis*, it is possible to approach that 'undisturbed, innocent, somnambulatory' reflection which, according to Goethe (who once spent a rather uncomfortable night in the valley, too, at Ghiereto), is essential for the production of anything worthwhile.

I am also grateful to Anne Somerset, who worked as a research assistant in the last stages of the book, who is responsible for the accuracy of many of the statements which I venture to make, and who typed, retyped and, on occasion, retyped again and again sections of the book; to my wife Vanessa, who also typed and retyped page upon page and made innumerable helpful suggestions as well as reading the proofs: to Cass Canfield Junior, of Harper and Row, always enthusiastic; to Christopher Sinclair-Stevenson, of Hamish Hamilton; and to Lord Gladwyn, Daniel Johnson and Phyllis McDougall for their kindness in reading sections of the book in manuscript or in proof.

H.T.
1 April 1979

Maps

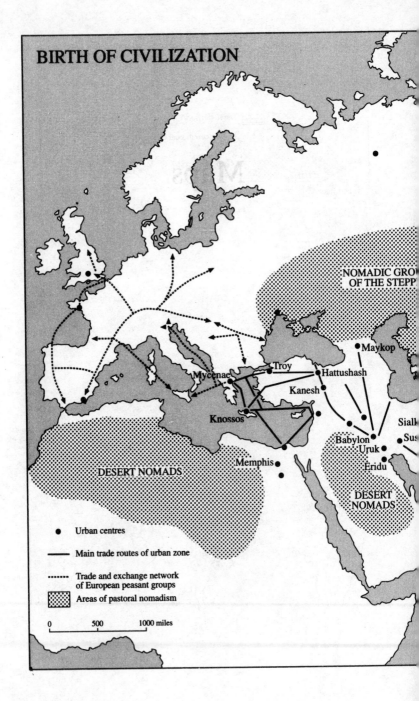

BIRTH OF CIVILIZATION

NOMADIC GRO
OF THE STEPP

Maykop

Troy
Hattushash
Mycenae
Kanesh

Knossos
Siall
Babylon
Sus
Uruk
Memphis
Eridu

DESERT NOMADS
DESERT
NOMADS

- Urban centres

—— Main trade routes of urban zone

------ Trade and exchange network
of European peasant groups

Areas of pastoral nomadism

0   500   1000 miles

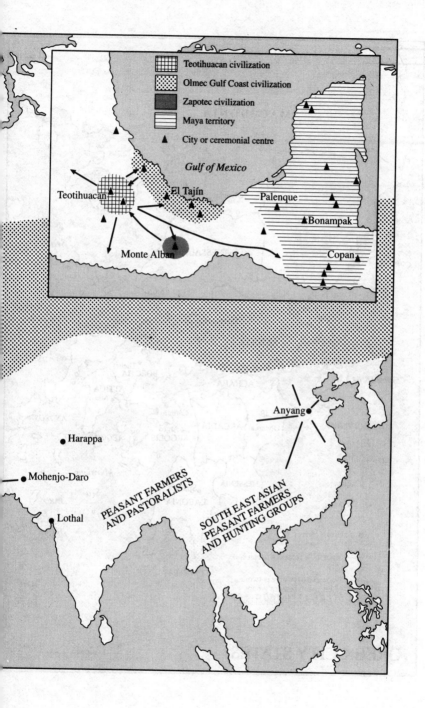

Teotihuacan civilization

Olmec Gulf Coast civilization

Zapotec civilization

Maya territory

▲ City or ceremonial centre

Gulf of Mexico

Teotihuacan

El Tajín

Palenque

▲Bonampak

Monte Alban

Copan

Anyang●

●Harappa

●Mohenjo-Daro

PEASANT FARMERS AND PASTORALISTS

●Lothal

SOUTH EAST ASIAN PEASANT FARMERS AND HUNTING GROUPS

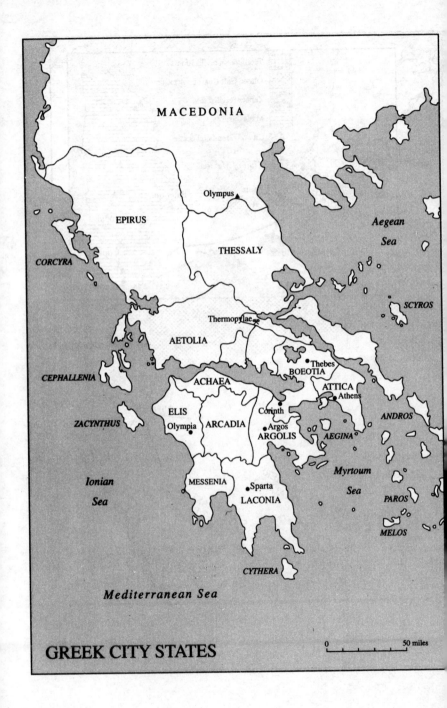

GREEK CITY STATES

SWISS CONFEDERATION

HUNGARY

DUCHY

Como

DUCHY

OF

OF Milan

Verona Venice

Turin

SAVOY

Pavia

M. OF Padua

MANTUA

SALUZZO

MILAN

Po

DUCHY OF GENOA

REP. OF
FERRARA

Pola

VENETIAN REPUBLIC

Genoa

D. OF MODENA

Bologna

DALMATIA

REP. OF
LUCCA

Arno Florence

Rimini

Pisa

FLORENCE

Urbino

Siena

Assisi

REP. OF
SIENA

Tiber

Adriatic Sea

ELBA
(to Naples)

CORSICA
(to Genoa)

Rome

KINGDOM

Capua Benevento

Bari

Naples OF

Salerno

Taranto

NAPLES

KINGDOM
OF SARDINIA

Tyrrhennian Sea

Cagliari

Palermo

KINGDOM OF
SICILY

ITALY IN THE 15TH CENTURY

Mediterranean Sea

0   200 miles

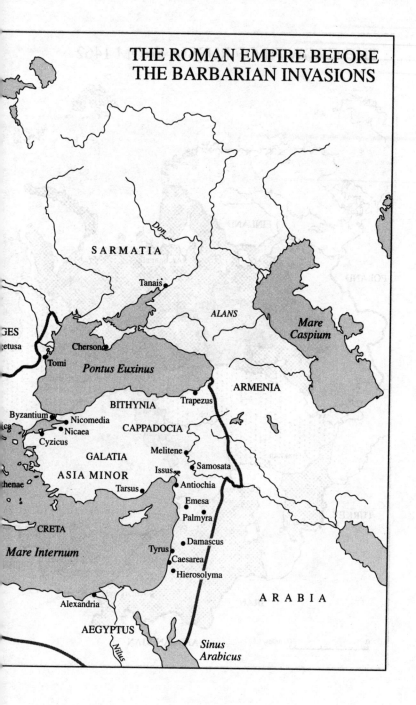

THE ROMAN EMPIRE BEFORE
THE BARBARIAN INVASIONS

SARMATIA

Don

Tanais

ALANS

Mare Caspium

GES

getusa

Chersona

Tomi

Pontus Euxinus

ARMENIA

Byzantium

Nicomedia

BITHYNIA

Trapezus

Nicaea

CAPPADOCIA

Cyzicus

GALATIA

Melitene

ASIA MINOR

Issus

Samosata

chenae

Tarsus

Antiochia

Emesa

CRETA

Palmyra

Mare Internum

Tyrus

Damascus

Caesarea

Hierosolyma

ARABIA

Alexandria

AEGYPTUS

Nilus

Sinus Arabicus

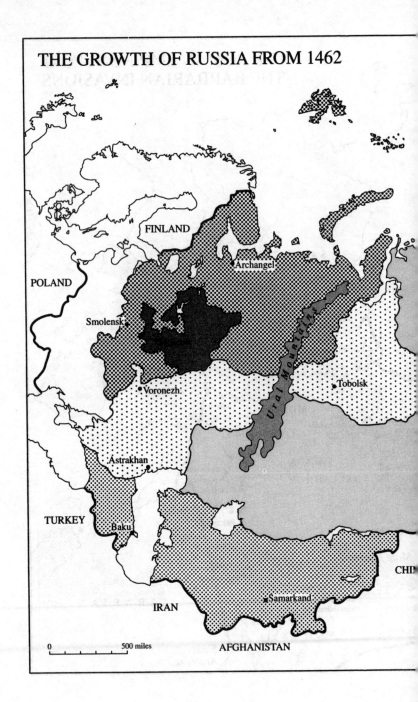

THE GROWTH OF RUSSIA FROM 1462

FINLAND

POLAND

Archangel

Smolensk

Ural Mountains

Voronezh

Tobolsk

Astrakhan

TURKEY

Baku

IRAN

Samarkand

CHI

0   500 miles

AFGHANISTAN

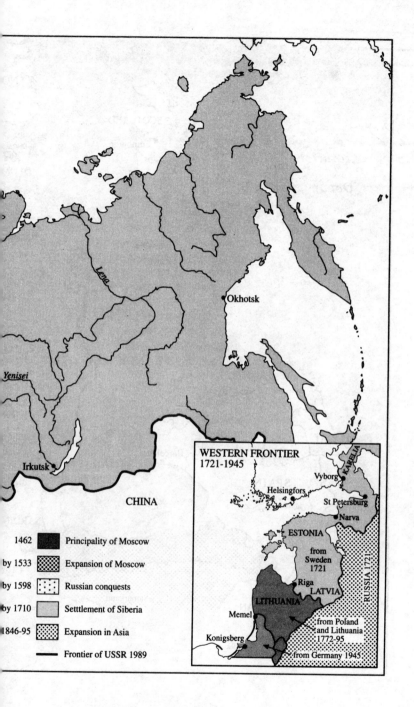

Okhotsk

Lena

Yenisei

Irkutsk

CHINA

WESTERN FRONTIER
1721-1945

KARELIA

Vyborg
Helsingfors
St Petersburg
Narva

ESTONIA

from
Sweden
1721

Riga
LATVIA

RUSSIA 1721

LITHUANIA
Memel

from Poland
and Lithuania
1772-95

Konigsberg

from Germany 1945

1462		Principality of Moscow
by 1533		Expansion of Moscow
by 1598		Russian conquests
by 1710		Setttlement of Siberia
1846-95		Expansion in Asia
———		Frontier of USSR 1989

EUROPE CIRCA 1520

SWEDEN

kholm

Baltic
Sea

TEUTONIC
ORDER

RUSSIA

Danzig

Vistula

POLAND

Oder

Dnieper

HUNGARY

Danube

Black Sea

OTTOMAN
EMPIRE

Constantinople

OTTOMAN
EMPIRE

ic Sea

Mediterranean Sea

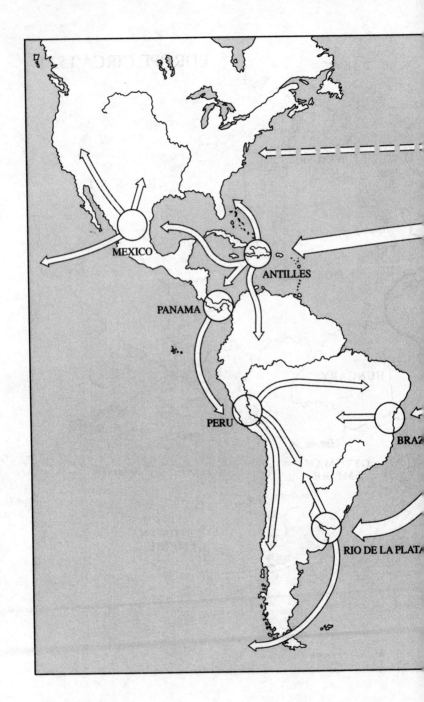

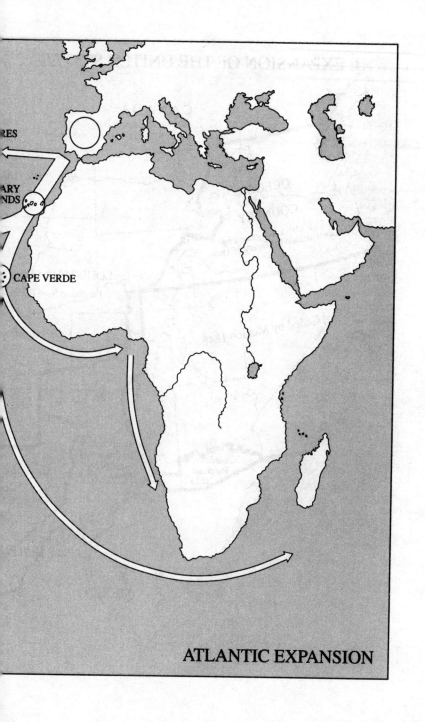

RES

ARY
NDS

CAPE VERDE

ATLANTIC EXPANSION

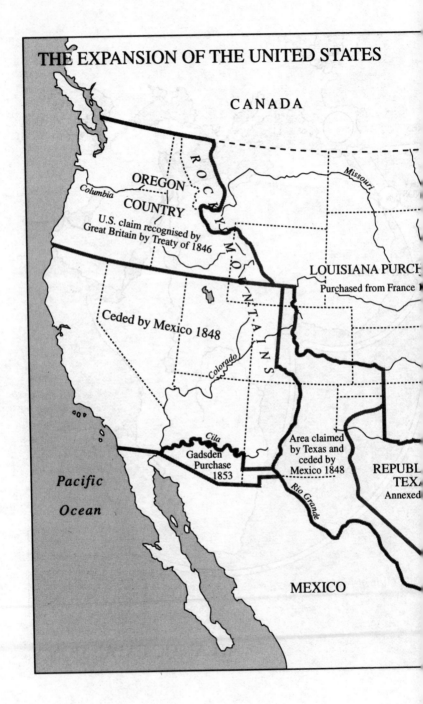

THE EXPANSION OF THE UNITED STATES

CANADA

ROCKY MOUNTAINS

OREGON
COUNTRY

Columbia

U.S. claim recognised by
Great Britain by Treaty of 1846

LOUISIANA PURCH

Purchased from France

Missouri

Ceded by Mexico 1848

Colorado

Cila

Gadsden
Purchase
1853

Area claimed
by Texas and
ceded by
Mexico 1848

REPUBL
TEX
Annexed

Rio Grande

Pacific

Ocean

MEXICO

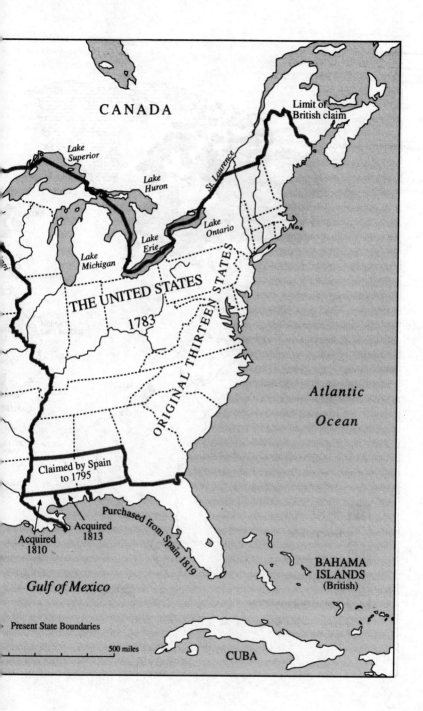

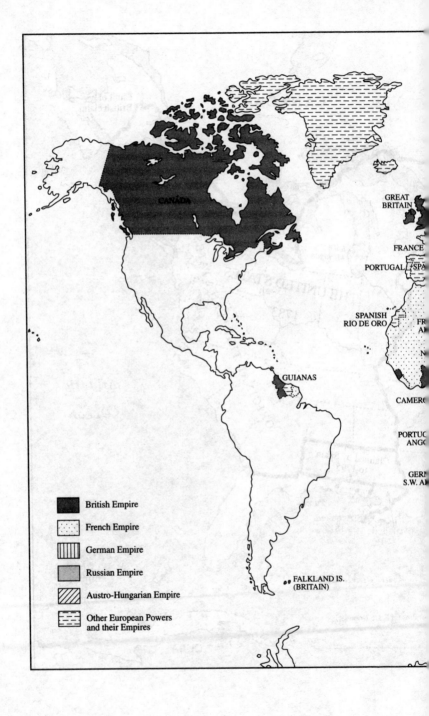

GREAT
BRITAIN

FRANCE

PORTUGAL SPA

SPANISH
RIO DE ORO

FR
A

N

CAMERO

PORTUC
ANGO

GERN
S.W. A

CANADA

SPANISH
RIO DE ORO

GUIANAS

FALKLAND IS.
(BRITAIN)

British Empire

French Empire

German Empire

Russian Empire

Austro-Hungarian Empire

Other European Powers
and their Empires

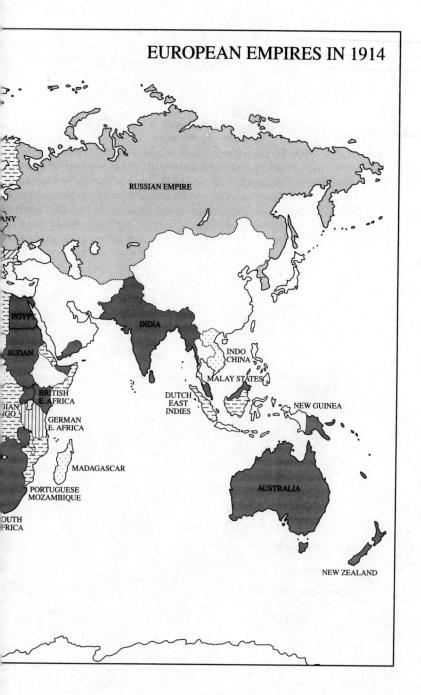

EUROPEAN EMPIRES IN 1914

RUSSIAN EMPIRE

ANY

EGYPT

SUDAN

BRITISH
E. AFRICA

GIAN
NGO

GERMAN
E. AFRICA

MADAGASCAR

PORTUGUESE
MOZAMBIQUE

OUTH
FRICA

INDIA

INDO
CHINA

MALAY STATES

DUTCH
EAST
INDIES

NEW GUINEA

AUSTRALIA

NEW ZEALAND

Book One

The Foundations of History

The investigation of a single detail already requires profound and very penetrating study . . . [But] historical research will not suffer from its connection with the universal. Without this link, research would become enfeebled, and, without exact research, the conception of the universal would degenerate into a fantasy.

von Ranke

1

The Birth of the World

Geschrieben steht: 'Im Anfang war das *Wort!*'
Hier stock ich schon . . .

(It is written: 'In the beginning was the *word!*'
Here I am stuck already . . .)

Goethe, *Faust* Part 3

Genealogy has its satisfactions, but how disconcerting to those who worship ancestors to find that, in the direct male line, men derive from, in ascending order, a monkey, a newt, a sea-lily and a bacterium. The legend that the Earl of Northumbria in Shakespeare's *Macbeth* was descended from a fairy bear seems, once the principles of evolution are accepted, only mildly misleading.

Life, however, is the first ingredient to take into account. The solar system of which the Earth is part is now known to be a galaxy of 100 billion stars in an archipelago of galaxies comparable to ours, adrift in space. The Universe apparently began 15,000 or 20,000 million years ago as a result of an explosion which propelled all the galaxies away from each other. The nearest galaxy to our own is two million light years away. Our galaxy and the Earth came into being almost simultaneously, following the contraction, by rotation, of clouds of dust, between 4000 and 5000 million BC. The Sun was a concentrated core at the centre of this rotation. The planets formed around pieces of débris.

No one suspected until recently that the Earth and the Universe were so old as this. In the seventeenth century, James Ussher, archbishop of Armagh, spoke of the world as being created in 4004 BC. The French naturalist Georges Buffon, in the eighteenth century, thought that the world might be 'at least 70,000 years old'. In 1755 the philosopher Kant speculated that it might be 'a million, or even millions of, years old'. But the timetable now regarded as correct was discovered in 1935 by an inspired astronomer, Edwin Hubble, of Missouri. The considered study of the skies, however, began long ago in Babylon where much data were gathered and analysed, by relatively advanced mathematics.

The Earth's crust wrinkled for a long time, creating mountains.

Seas were caused by the further condensation of vapours. The sea
and the land were once absolutely divided in a planet which thus
had one ocean and one continent, but the latter, known to geologists as Pangaea, split into the present continents about 2000
million BC, leaving two-thirds of the globe now covered by water.
Much movement of land, however, continued afterwards. The
creation of the Channel, which divides England from Europe, and
the Bering Straits, which cut off Asia from America, was the
product of later commotions. India was separated by sea from
northern Asia for a time before 45 million BC, as was, till about
2 million BC, North from South America. Africa was once as
close to South America as is North America. The Mediterranean
became a desert about 6 million BC and a stretch of water a
million years later, while the Black Sea was once the arm of a
great ocean, which included the modern Caspian and Aral seas.

Those early years of the Earth belong to chemists, not to historians. For a historian, it is enough to know that a metallic core,
3,750 miles wide, came into being within the Earth – mostly liquid
iron and nickel, though solid in the centre. Between that core and
the Earth's crust, a 'mantle' of iron and magnesium 1,875 miles
deep took shape. The crust, of diverse composition, varies between twelve to thirty miles in depth on land, and only four miles
under the sea.

Before the coming of anything recognisable by the name of
'life', many fundamental matters had been decided: the Earth
began to rotate clockwise, creating westerly winds; some latitudes
were already cold, some hot; the tilt of the Earth's axis had
created seasons; mountain ranges affected climate; and seasons
had begun to be differentiated.

Life, in the form of bacteria and micro-organisms, began about
3500 million BC, or perhaps a little earlier. The first plants, descendants of bacteria, grew in seas. Their immediate descendants
were worms (which came into being about 1000 million BC);
shellfish; jawless fish; scorpions; and vertebrate fish, which were
living by 450 million BC. The worms were the first living things
which, unlike their predecessors, plants, had to seek food from
outside themselves: plants make for themselves the chemical elements which they need in order to survive. From the vertebrate
fish descended reptiles, large and small. Some of these were dinosaurs, pleisosaurs or ichthyosaurs, the ancestors of turtles, liz-
ards and snakes. Other extinct reptiles, known as therapsids,
resembling the duck-billed platypus, could walk on two feet and

had teeth. Whether they had fur, warm blood and laid eggs is obscure. From them, nevertheless, the mammals descended, at first being small and insect-eating, weighing less than twenty pounds, comparable to lemurs, bushbabies, shrews or squirrels. These ancestors of the successful animals of the world today lived side by side with the dinosaurs, who dominated the world for 150 million years.

The eclipse of the dinosaurs about 65 million BC was probably due to an as yet unidentified climatic change which destroyed all large animals along with, it seems, about three-quarters of all species then extant. Mammals survived since, apparently, they were still very small. But they had multiplied their species. Primates, the direct ancestors of men and monkeys, had appeared. So had insects and birds, while most flowering plants had assumed something like their present shape.

About 30 million BC an animal was born which is believed to be a common ancestor of man and ape. Those species diverged between then and about 5 million BC. The date is a matter of dispute. Some anthropologists believe that men were different from apes by 20 million BC. Others put the date nearer 4 million BC. At all events, between 10 and 5 million BC, the ancestors of men were still living in trees. They were herbivorous. Then, or perhaps a million years later, ancestors of men began to walk upright, as their usual mode of locomotion, and to carry things in their arms. By then, too, man was beginning to be carnivorous – a differentiation from other primates which was caused by a shortage of nuts, berries and fruit. That, perhaps, was also the main reason for the descent from the trees, though our closest relative among the other primates (the African chimpanzee) also lives on the ground, and though the chimpanzee can use objects such as stones with agility.

There were soon more differentiations from other primates; the more subtle possibilities of man's use of his hands; and his greater fertility. There are minor differences in sexual behaviour between humans and apes and, while chimpanzees and gorillas mate only during the female's ovulation, women, like female gibbons, can do so at any time. Gibbons, like most humans, live customarily in monogamous families, while male chimpanzees and gorillas seek to establish harems of females, which they try to dominate until overthrown by a younger rival. All the apes, however, are biologically close to men, and an almost political sense of cooperation can be discerned in monkeys, though, unlike men and birds, they do not as a rule cooperate in the pursuit of food. Chimpanzees seem, though, to share food on the rare occasions when they eat meat. On the whole, apes eat vegetables or fruits, and do so on the spot. Some regard the cooperative search for game as the determining one in human evolution from apes.

The distinctive characteristic of human beings, however, derives from the size of their brains. That may have followed man's change to an erect posture. The human brain needs a large skull and a large cortex. It is not the size of man's brain alone which has been responsible for his place in the world; porpoises and whales have larger ones. Even so, the brains of men's ancestors doubled in size between about 3 million and 1500000 BC from 450 to 900 cubic centimetres. Those bipeds were making stone tools and were hunting animals by 2500000 BC. By 1500000 BC, the stone tools had begun to be flaked on both sides, perhaps to cut up elephants and mammoths, which could not have been eaten without some such implement.

Subsequently, after the beginning of both hunting and the making of stone tools, man's brain developed to its present approximate size of 1,400 cubic centimetres. The history of *homo sapiens* proper begins, or indeed of what anthropologists now call *homo sapiens sapiens*. This seems to have occurred at some time between 150000 BC and 90000 BC, but it may have been more recent still. The main races of men probably made crossings at different times of the 'threshold' from a more brutal to a more sapient state[1]. Where the line was first crossed, and by whom, is unknown. Probably it happened in several continents at much the same time. Perhaps the decisive change causing the brain to grow further was made possible because the early tools already in use enabled their users to enjoy, as we would now put it, a better standard of living.

The differences between *homo sapiens* and *homo sapiens sapiens* were considerable: for example, the first, who in the past was often known as 'Neanderthal man' (from the fossilised remains found in the Neander valley in Germany in 1856), had a brain the same size as modern man, but differently shaped. Most of the tools of *homo sapiens* which survive derive from flakes of flint. *Homo sapiens sapiens* has a less tough skull than his predecessor. His tools were slender and sometimes already shaped for ritual uses. Harpoons, needles, awls, complicated weapons and long voyages all followed fast, or at least fast in comparison with what had gone before. In comparison, *homo sapiens* pure and simple seemed closer to his immediate predecessor, to whom the name *homo erectus* is now given. That *homo erectus*, remains of which were found in Java in the 1890s and subsequently in Africa and China, had frontal lobes which were not well developed, and his brain was small. His jaws and teeth were larger than modern man's. Even so, he used a stone axe. He used caves for shelter and even had fire, about 150000 BC, in both Hungary and China, first for keeping warm, giving light, and sharpening sticks at the ends to ward off enemies.

The change occasioned by the coming of *homo sapiens sapiens* may have been inspired by language. No doubt men were never silent. Apes communicate with one another, if without language. Even simple tools must have needed speech for them to be made well. But the use of clear speech constituted a decisive change, making possible a whole range of activities previously unthought of. Among primates without language there are no religions, no politics and no works of art. Speech is the main element of cohesion among human beings, even among the few primitive tribes that have survived[2]. But its origins are a mystery.

Thirty families of languages have been identified as existing in historic times. They embrace 2,500 main languages and dialects[3]. But many languages avoid classification: when the Europeans discovered Australia, 500 tribes were found there, each with 500 to 600 members, and each one with their own tongue of several thousand words. Europe must once have been the same. In South Africa the differences were even greater when the Europeans arrived: some tribes there spoke different languages among the men and women. Probably many people talked to each other effectively by whistling languages, such as the finger-aided, articulated Silbo, which survives on the Canary island of Gomera, and, in a slightly different manner, at Oaxaca in Mexico and at Ansó in the Pyrenees. Some think, with Carleton Coon, that the 'social requirements of a group of hunters made speech necessary'[4]. Possibly the first languages were without parts of speech, with most phrases and thoughts expressed by a single word. Was speech a single invention by a single tribe and did others imitate it imperfectly? Over 20,000 years two sister languages may be expected to deviate and to lose all semblance of relationship. But if all language derives from a single mother tongue, the original separation would have been many tens of thousands of years before 20000 BC. Thus more than one breed of men probably discovered speech independently.

*

The questions posed by all these happenings go to the roots of the problems of human life and of history: what caused the deviation of man from animals? What was (and is) the cause of evolution within life? What inspired life? What caused the occurrences which themselves led to the birth of the Earth and of the solar system? Was it a 'spark from heaven', as Matthew Arnold put it[5], which caused the beginning of life? If the 'man monkey' became man because of a mutation in a single person, causing a change in the size of the brain, is there any reason to suppose that that mutation was caused by God, or a god, or some other extraterrestrial 'creative agent', in Lewis Mumford's phrase[6]? Was there some fortunate cross-breeding? Did life originate at some time or has it, in some way, here or elsewhere, always existed, as J. Z. Young posed the question[7]? Were there precedents for life on Earth or elsewhere? Was life on Earth brought by meteorite, or even by design, as some have argued, from another planet? Or from another solar system? Did God wind up the Universe and then leave it to its own devices, as once suggested by a Christian bishop, Nicolas Oresme, at about the time that the clock was invented?

These questions have not been solved satisfactorily by geologists or chemists any more than they have by theologians and philosophers. Since the questions are open, they give grounds for hope, or fear, of the existence of God and of the validity of religion but scarcely give proof of the greater closeness to truth of one religion than another. The sceptical may take comfort from the realisation that religion (which itself, in a sense, 'evolved' from nature worship and polytheism to monotheism) began when the early history of the Earth was unknown. But even the sceptical must accept that no system so intricate as that of life has occurred by chance. Sir Isaac Newton proved that the force which causes a stone to fall is the same as that which keeps the planets in their path. But that does not divorce the Universe from a spiritual order. Even the agnostic scientist Laplace, who told Napoleon that 'il n'avait pas besoin de cette hypothèse-là' (that is, religion), agreed with Newton that the way that the planets revolved in the same direction round the Sun was unlikely to be a matter of chance.

The relation of the Earth with the Sun was known to the Greeks in classical times. Thus Aristarchus of Samos wrote, about 250 BC, that 'the Earth (and other planets) revolve round the Sun in the circumference of a circle, the Sun lying in the middle of the orbit'. He calculated, fairly exactly, the relative distance from the

Earth of both the Moon and the Sun (because of these insights he, like Galileo later, was persecuted). Astronomy was thus started on the right path but little more was done for 1,800 years, even if Eratosthenes of Alexandria, who died in 194 BC, calculated the circumference of the Earth at 24,650 miles (it is 24,875).

Similarly, man's evolution from animals was guessed by Anaximander of Miletus who, in the sixth century BC, saw that the structure of fish resembled that of humans, and argued both that men were descended from animals and that life began in the sea or in slime. The members of Pythagoras' colony at Croton forswore eating the flesh of animals since they too believed men to be related to them. That idea was also held by many African tribes who knew apes at first hand. But it was a point of view unacceptable to Christianity and Islam, and apes were rare in countries which adopted universal religions. Between Anaximander and Darwin, the only major scientific work achieved in biology was that undertaken in the eighteenth century by the Swedish master-classifier, Carl von Linné (Linnaeus) who divided the two million or so different living things (800,000 plants; 800,000 insects; 400,000 animals) into species. Earlier, in the seventeenth century, the English chemist Robert Boyle, 'the father of chemistry and the uncle of the Earl of Cork', had recognised the true nature of the elements to constitute the simplest form of matter. Another Englishman, John Dalton, had established that every element consists of its own variety of atom.

Evolution continues. The teeth and jaws of human beings become smaller as cooking rids them of the gastronomic troubles of early man. Alterations in glands, brain and reproductive organs occurred during the age of the hunters. The movement of the Earth's crust also continues: India is pushing against Asia, so is Italy against northern Europe. These things cause tremors such as those which brought the great Chinese earthquakes in Tang Shan in 1976. The Universe is presumably continuing to expand.

Kant, who first argued that the Earth might be millions, rather than just thousands of years old, thought that the factor most distinguishing men from animals was an intuitive awareness of an inner moral law embodying Reason. Conduct, he believed, is to be judged in respect of whether it can be regarded as motivated by Reason. The test for an act should be, can the principle implied by it be applied universally? Unless it can, the act cannot be disinterested. Was that categorical imperative always present? Did

such concepts follow automatically from the increase in the size
of man's brain? Did they have any effect before hunting, while
man was still in the trees, and when the making of a stone axe
was as remote from his capacity as is our capacity, as a rule, in
the twentieth century, to envisage an infinite universe? How early
did it, for instance, become evident that 'man rarely remains in
his customary level in . . . critical circumstances: he rises above
it or sinks below it' (as Tocqueville said, comparing men to nations)[8]? When did man first appreciate the truths remarked on by
one of the characters in Malraux's *Les Noyers de l'Altenburg*? 'We
know we have not chosen to be born, that we will not choose to
die. That we have not chosen our parents. That we can do nothing
against time'[9]. Were 'the timid . . . always cruel', as Gibbon
argued[10]? 'I have been specially disgusted with Rousseau since I
went East', said Napoleon. 'Savage man is a dog'[11]. But did
'savage man' have any connection with an Egyptian of AD 1800?
Did early men of 2 million BC – 'protohuman hominids' as those
who study them in the crevices of the Rift valley speak of them
– forage and hunt as baboons do today? Was there a division of
labour then between men and women? (Doubtless the factors of
females having repeated pregnancies of nine months, and the
habit of a carnivorous diet, did indeed begin an allocation of tasks
along lines which have dictated the behaviour of humans ever
since.)

Any comment on pre-history must also notice the critical invention, in the twentieth century, of a technique for dating ancient
remains based on measuring the carbon within the object concerned. This brilliant method was devised by Willard Libby, a
chemist from Colorado, during the 1940s. It has two limitations:
first, dating of objects older than 40,000 years is almost impossible
since carbon dies; second, the samples needed are large. Doubtless new methods in future will remove these deficiencies. Various
other methods of dating fossils and meteorites have also been
devised which have enabled even the most remote dates mentioned in this chapter to be roughly confirmed.

This book is a study of history. There is one desirable corrective
to any undue parochiality, however, about the development of
our own species. There are two million species living on the Earth.
But those two million species represent far less than one per cent
of the species that have ever lived, the rest being now extinct.
Though man is now in control of the Earth, his era of dominance
is measured in terms of thousands of years in comparison with the

millions during which the dinosaur held sway. Though this book lays emphasis on the part played by men in history, the reader should not forget that one of the most beautiful of creatures, with an exquisitely made apparatus for feeding off human blood, is the most dangerous of all the 3,000 types of mosquito: the *aedes aegypti*. The future could belong to it.

2

Hunters

There seems no reason to doubt that man found himself and
emerged as a dominant species first and foremost as a hunter.

Grahame Clark, *World Prehistory*

Most of man's time on Earth as a human being has been passed
as a hunter. This hunting, which lasted until at least about 10000
BC, is held to have been based on the stone hand axe which gave
to the era its Greek name: 'palaeolithic' or 'old stone' – a word
invented, along with 'neolithic' or 'new (that is, polished) stone',
by Christian Thomsen, a Danish pioneer archaeologist, in 1836.
Those who lived in the age of hunting might, however, have been
surprised to have been thought of as people of a 'stone age', for
many of their weapons, as well as their houses, boats and bridges,
were made of wood, which did not survive so easily as stone. The
yew lances found at Clacton (England) or Lehringen (Saxony)
suggest the nature of the age of hunters as much as do the stone
axeheads in museums all over the world. 'Well may ours be called
a wooden century,' wrote a pioneer of America in the nineteenth
century AD, pointing to the houses, bridges, fuel, pins (instead
of nails) and latches of wood which marked his days, thereby
marking a continuity rarely interrupted, before the twentieth century, among pioneering peoples. Still, the stone axe made possible
the cutting and shaping of wood. Other stone implements permitted the scraping of skins for an early version of clothes and
also the cutting of meat for better food. As with most great
innovations, no one can decide whether stone implements were
invented in several places independently, or whether there was an
original centre, from which the idea radiated. Common sense
suggests a diversity of invention. Further, the surviving stone axes
show not only a definite pattern of improvement, but also that, in
some countries at least, early hunters went to great lengths to get
good stone.

The stone from which the early hunters made their tools naturally varied: granite, basalt, quartz, obsidian and flint were all
used. Large numbers of these ancient tools have been found and

many names have been given to them from 'hand axe' and 'chopper', to 'flaked axe', 'blade' and 'scraper'. Most of those names are inadequate. Microscopic traces of wear have recently been analysed to show more accurately the purposes of those ancient implements. 'Butchering', woodworking, working on hides, cutting material other than wood such as reeds or bracken have been identified. The old 'hand axe' turns out to have been used as much for cutting meat as wood. 'Scrapers' were concerned with dressing hides[1]. 'Blades' began the age of spears, arrows and harpoons, their handles being later decorated with beads, stone, bone, antler or ivory (obtained from mammoths, then widely dispersed in the northern hemisphere). There were also, by then (say 30000 BC), special tools for special activities – for example, for engraving designs and for working bones or antlers. The 'late stone age man' and the 'late hunter' were busy with perforation, with awls; with rubbing or polishing; and with the shaping of antlers. Needles of bone were already in use, as were spades of mammoth bone, spoons of mammoth ivory and clubs of antler, from reindeer.

Some hunting tribes survived a long time. Some still do so, in artificial circumstances. Australian aborigines, San ('bushmen') in South Africa, Eskimoes, some hunters of northern Siberia and some tribes of southern Chile are characteristic representatives either still in existence or in being until very recently. Some South American Indians in tropical regions might also still be called 'hunters'. The San people of South Africa live normally in packs of one large family strong but, sometimes, in gatherings, of up to a hundred. None of these peoples is now isolated. Some live nomadically, without much clothing but use pottery as well as basket-work. The Kwakiutl Indians of British Columbia led, until the twentieth century, an elaborate but primitive cultural life, built around fishing. Their boats, of great cedar trunks, survive. Most of the North American Indians, now settled or extinct, lived in the fifteenth century AD much as they did in 10000 BC. The 50,000 or so Eskimoes now living reached Alaska or Greenland between about 100 BC and AD 1200. Their tents of caribou or sealskin; their permanent winter villages and temporary snow summer houses; their boats, kayaks and dog-drawn sledges of wood; their methods of hunting seals, caribou, foxes, ptarmigan, with weapons and hooks (of stone, antler, driftwood and latterly iron); their movements during the seasons; their clothes of caribou hides and fur, and their knives of antler or whalebone – are indications not only of adaptation to circumstances but of a society older than most others, even if the primitiveness is mitigated by modern implements.

Another picture of life in a human pack can be guessed from what the Europeans saw when they began to colonise Australasia. In Tasmania about AD 1770, between 2,000 and 4,000 people ranged over 25,000 square miles in bands of fifty, sheltered from the weather by windbreaks, using chipped stones as tools, and wooden clubs and spears (the tips hardened by fire) as weapons. Tasmanian hunters rarely stayed in one place, though they lived on the coast, avoiding the rain forest of the interior. Good hunting needs space: to be sure of food, hunters in Tasmania had to live at a density of no more than ten people to the square mile. Many tribes of Brazilian Indians were, when discovered by the Spaniards or Portuguese, like the Tararya tribe of the Rio Grande region, still in the seventeenth century semi-nomadic hunter-gatherers, 'great runners and people for whom roots, wild honey and field-mice were an important supplement to the usual peccary, deer and other game'[2].

The species of animals killed by early hunters ranged widely from elephant and rhinoceros to horse and deer, depending on the part of the world. Bone harpoons made fishing as rewarding as killing animals. Fishing was also often done by building dams in rivers. Hunters knew the usefulness of cords and threads (for fastening, binding and sewing, using needles of horn or bone) and they made baskets.

Hunters evidently often killed each other, both thoughtlessly and by design, within and outside the tribe. Many were cannibals, or, at least, ate the brains and marrow of the bones, if not the flesh, of their enemies. About 15000 BC, the bow and arrow were invented, in central Asia – a great improvement on both the axe and the stick, in the hands of a skilful archer. Hunting man had some sort of boat from which to fish. He may not have had the sail, but he had the oar by about 20000 BC. Hunters had a more varied diet than most non-humans now surviving and perhaps even than some modern peoples too.

Modern man descended from early hunters at different times, in different places. The wonder is as much that there are not more sub-species of man, white, black, mongoloid, as that there are more than one.

The colour of skin and climate are connected. Black skins keep the body cool and protect the skin from sunlight better than white ones. But there is little differentiation of colour among American

Indians or Chinese peoples. Black was, for a time, believed to be
the original colour of man, with other colours arising through
mutation. Now some argue that the original colour was yellow.
Such ideas do not seem to be firmly based. Some such changes
may have been caused by variations in climate. The Earth is
known to have been warmer at the time of the eclipse of the
dinosaurs, in 50 million BC, than it is today, and more of it was
covered by forest than is the case now. By 25 million BC the
climate was cooler. Much of the Earth was then covered by grass:
a condition which favoured the evolution of the horse, among
other animals.

The different races of men arose as a result of gradual genetic
diversification following widespread colonisations of new territories during the 'final glacial circle' – that is, the last ice age –
between 60000 and 10000 BC, when a great deal of now inhabited
land was under ice. Climate determined (though presumably did
not alone inspire) ethnic characteristics. Blond, fair-skinned
people survived in cool conditions. Dark skins did well in hot,
non-forested regions. Yellow skins prospered in tropical rain forests. Eskimoes probably gained their flat noses through the need
to mitigate the temperature of the air before drawing it into their
lungs.

At all events, as everyone knows, pink, sallow and pale-skinned
people gathered eventually in the northern hemisphere. Black and
dark brown people lived in the tropics (in Africa and South-East
Asia but not, to begin with, in tropical America). Yellow, brown
or mongoloid people were to be found in Central Asia and Malaysia, Japan (after 7500 BC), Australasia, parts of Polynesia and
the Americas, both North and South (inhabited as far south as
southern Chile by 15000 BC). The Earth was thus colonised,
almost completely, by roaming tribes, save for some islands which
could only be reached later by skilful seamanship (New Zealand,
Mauritius, some Caribbean islands, Hawaii and some Mediterranean islands). The existence of a land bridge of flat tundra up to
700 miles wide between Siberia and Alaska between about 17000
BC and 8000 BC has now been well known for two generations.
Across it, the indigenous Americans, and many animals, crossed
from Asia. With great skill, the direct ancestors of modern Australoids crossed the forty miles of open water separating Indonesia
and New Guinea before 35000 BC – the first maritime colonisation. Recent archaeology in Soviet Central Asia shows that hunters were established there as early as 250000 BC, and perhaps

before – the earliest known adaptation to those harsh, semi-arid conditions.

During this long era, while man was establishing his primacy over other animals, most of the characteristic human habits and qualities must have come into being, including the beginnings of family life; humour, art and love; and attitudes to disease and to education. Hunting people must have known which wood was the toughest, and which the most supple, much better than most twentieth-century people. They naturally knew animals well, and their seasons for breeding. They knew plants, and their uses as poisons as well as foods and drugs. Tribes sometimes depended on single herds of animals and pursued them from cool to warm places, according to season, as shepherds later led sheep in that fashion. Though hunting man did not read or write, practise agriculture or manufacture anything for profit, most of the human virtues and vices, as they are normally reckoned to be, must have existed by 20000 BC.

Most tribes of early man were probably no more nomadic than the Indians of North America, the Scythians, or the Huns of Central Asia, before they attacked westwards. That is, they had regular hunting grounds, from which they were only displaced by stronger tribes who attacked them. Within those hunting grounds, there were regular stopping places, in caves or artificial dwellings scooped out of soil, huts of poles and skins held together by mammoth bones and, later, by mud walls. In size, such tribes varied. Perhaps there were some tribes larger than those 500 to 600 strong met by Europeans when they got to Australia. Perhaps the average was twenty to forty: 'Fifty would be the limit,' wrote Carleton Coon[3]. These groups would consist essentially of a few families in which perhaps five or six adult men would hunt and the rest would depend on them. While the males hunted, the females would be gathering plants, cooking (by roasting in pits) or looking after children – though boys went hunting as assistants to their fathers. The long childhood of humans emphasised the desirability of a permanent union between man and woman greater than among other animals. A low density of population perhaps kept down epidemics. But there was high infant mortality. Expectation of life was well under thirty years, and few would attain the age of fifty.

On death, hunters were, towards the beginning of historic times, buried, sometimes in a cave, with the limbs flexed to save space (and so economise the effort of digging graves) or to ensure against the dead man's return as a ghost. The beginning of regular burials suggests respect for the transitoriness of life – the earliest recognition, perhaps, of 'human nature's eternal and indestructible metaphysical need', ultimately articulated by religion, as Burckhardt put it[4]. Thus, even before the age of agriculture, man believed in some deities, subscribed to some magic, perhaps even had hope of life after death: what else, otherwise, is to be made of the burial place found in Uzbekistan, where a dead child of the era of hunting was surrounded by a ring of goat horns, pushed downwards into the earth floor?

The first record of man being anxious to conserve the memory of the dead dates from 70000 BC and, from 15000 BC, men began the habit of leaving prized objects in graves. Sometimes the dead might be buried in the fur of the skins which they had worn in life, perhaps sprinkled with red ochre to preserve them; and, the nearer to historic times the burial, the more likely it would be that the bodies would be accompanied by ornamental objects, such as shells or jewellery, of ivory, horn, snails' shells or the vertebrae of fish. Objects found in those ancient graves give ample support to the remark of Bernard Berenson that in the fear of death all the arts have their roots[5].

The first aesthetic act of all was the making of stone axes with an elaboration beyond functional needs: patterns of geometric shape, for example, or herringbone patterns, criss-crosses and chevrons. Figurines of mammoths, of other animals and of women began soon to be modelled from clay – particularly of women – for use in graves. Those 'Venus figurines', which robustly emphasise breasts, thighs, buttocks and pregnancy, if rarely heads, legs or arms, are the earliest artistic creations yet found. They have been discovered in the western Pyrenees and south-west France, on the Italian Riviera, in Bohemia and the Ukraine, made from clay, by hand, of course, but nevertheless fired in heat to ensure a finish. Artists in caves also used the unevennesses in rocks, marks of drips and stalagmites, as elements in elaborate, perhaps magical paintings. Those artists relied primarily on their fingers, but also employed branches, and brushes of fur or feather. Unusual powers of observation were needed for such art: qualities which made for better hunting and helped to lead to agriculture in those areas which were then good for grazing animals.

Both trade and mining should be associated in a primitive form with life before agriculture. Stone was exchanged and sought in remote places. Mining for flint was carried out in Europe at least

by 10000 BC and those who dug out flint also found the red
mercury ore cinnabar to serve as a pigment. The iron oxide ochre
was mined elsewhere for the same purpose. The volcanic glass
obsidian, white marble and fossilised seashells were sought before
agriculture had begun in the Balkans. The 'mining' concerned
meant the digging of shallow pits and trenches. The husbandry of
minerals thus probably proceeded that of animals and plants.

Clothes also should be given a date of origin in the days of the
hunter. They enabled human penetration of the colder and drier
zones of the Earth. The bearskin enabled survival in freezing
temperatures. Sewing and tailoring of a primitive sort improved
fitting between the human frame and the animal skin or fur. This
enabled even Arctic lands to be penetrated by ancient hunters.
No doubt this led to a rapid increase in population.

Most primitive communities which survived into historic times
also had a marked if incomplete idea of equality and freedom
within the group concerned, combined with exclusiveness, suspicion and prejudice towards the outside. Thus, though no one in
such tribes married a sister or a brother, or a father or mother,
they usually did marry distant cousins. Prohibitions on exogamy
gave these people their coherence. There was sometimes no chief
in such tribes, sometimes no explicit authority. The most experienced people might guide the community, but they often did not
have the power to rule it. Common ancestors would be likely to
be worshipped. Kinship, genealogy and myth were usually matters
of concern. All older people might be regarded as parents: all
children, a communal responsibility.

Some German tribes in being in Tacitus's day also lived in a
rough state of democracy. Primitive tribes described by Herodotus
did the same. There are signs too that, in the early days of
Babylon, the villages had their affairs ordered by councils of
elders, rather than by despots.

Beyond these things frequently common to 'primitive' peoples,
there was, and is, a wealth of diversity. Among some tribes it
might be permissible to marry aunts, while some can marry only
aunts on the mother's side. Some communities recognise matrilinear descent, in order to maintain purity of blood. Inheritance
through the sister's son, as practised by the Ashanti monarchs of
West Africa, was a well-known custom in many communities.
Patrilinear and matrilinear communities appeared early on, each
with distinct characteristics.

Was this, we wonder, the golden age described by the most

influential of modern philosophers, Rousseau: 'While the Earth was left to its natural fertility and its immense forests whose trees were never mutilated with the axe, it could afford, on every side, both sustenance and shelter for every species'[6].

Or was Rousseau's less famous contemporary, Vico, more accurate when he saw these early men as 'like the Cyclops Polyphemus, in the Odyssey, fathers of primitive families, despotic, savage, violent, ferocious, able to survive only by means of the most terrifying discipline, by enforcing absolute obedience'[7]?

The fears and practices of South American Indians in historic times support Vico. In Brazil in the sixteenth century, Corupira, a gnome with upturned feet, was the lord of the secrets of the forest. He protected game and thwarted men. He and his outrider Macachera are even said to survive.

There is nothing of which to be sure. Such evidence as there is can be arranged to persuade oneself that hunters lived in a near-anarchist paradise. Jean Jaurès described the 'open field in mediaeval agriculture as constituting primitive communism'. Early communal living in tribes, in competition with each other, might be made to seem like a small capitalist enterprise. Naturally, there is no certainty that there was religion: yet it is easy to imagine hunting men enjoying a primitive worship of Sun and Moon, and a general flight of the whole tribe into the bushes at a clap of thunder. There must have been political cooperation: careful planning to secure the right food at the right time. Among hunting people who survived into historic times in America, even each species of game was believed to be ruled by a spiritual leader – some great white beaver, for example, who ruled over all beavers. Similarly, hunters themselves had to regulate their killing to prevent over-hunting. Thus political life also has an ancestry older than agriculture.

3

Farmers

Tillers of the earth have few idle months
In the fifth month their toil is double-fold.
A south wind visits the fields at night;
Suddenly the ridges are covered with yellow corn. . .
They lost in the grain-tax the whole of their own crop.

Po Chii-I (AD 806)

The decisive changes during the age of the hunter were probably decided by alterations of climate. Long 'ice ages' succeeded false dawns of warmth. Much of the life of man as a hunter was passed in the last ice age. The sea was then about 600 feet lower, as a rule, than it is now. Arabia, the Gobi Desert, North Africa and the Sahara were less dry. Both England and Japan were linked to the continents near to them. Asia and America still met over the Bering Straits as did Asia Minor and the Balkans, over the Bosphorus. The Adriatic was dry. But, halfway up England, the Arctic began. That embraced northern Germany, northern Russia and nearly all Canada.

The 'retreat' of the last 'ice age' occurred because of the shrinking of the polar ice cap, between 12000 BC and 6000 BC. This caused geographical as well as climatic changes which led, in turn, to all sorts of opportunities, including agriculture and, in the end, to settled political systems. It also cut off, through the narrow strait of deep water between Java and Bali, the Australasian fauna and flora from the Oriental. So the Australian aborigines were isolated and had no contact with the rest of the world until the Chinese investigated their coastline in the fifteenth century. The sea also rose to cut off Britain from Europe, Scandinavia from Germany and Russia from Alaska. But many places in the north of the Earth were opened up for settlement. Forests of oak, elm and alder in Central Europe took the place of the open grazing lands formerly occupied by reindeer. The peoples of Central Europe turned from hunting reindeer to fishing, as well as to more varied forms of hunting, while those of the Near East probably racked their brains in order to find a way of surviving in their established habitats. Many doubtless died, others emigrated. Perhaps we can see, in Herodotus's story of a people whom he knew as the Psylli, a distant memory of that lost time: 'The Psylli, a people of North Africa, had all their water ponds dried by the South West wind. They declared war on the wind, went out to the desert to meet it where it came from, and were buried in it by heaps of sand'[1]. That time saw the origin of the myths of the golden age and of the Garden of Eden: a time in the past when food was abundant, and no effort was needed to live. Afterwards, 'man could only eat by the sweat of his brow'[2]. The change of climate as well as over-hunting led to the extinction of large game, such as mammoth. That in turn caused a drop in population. Some tribes died out, defeated by the need to find new game day after day. Others returned to the berries and fruits of the days before hunting, or intensified the search for fish or molluscs. Perhaps the reindeer, which gave horn and bone as well as meat and moved, then as now, in herds hundreds of thousands strong, was already half-domesticated. That probably gave men ideas as to what they might do with other animals if they could be captured. (Reindeer had been drawn to man as much as man to them, because of their taste for the salt that they found in human urine.)

Agriculture probably began with the domestication of the dog about 15000 BC, an event characterised by the formation of regular packs for hunting in which man and dog collaborated. Dogs, descended from wolves or dingos, were taken by the first invaders of America with them, not as completely domesticated animals (the remains of the earliest domesticated dog in the Americas seems to come from Idaho, about 9000 BC). Early dogs were mostly used as sheepdogs, the many varieties of modern dog being bred much more recently. Perhaps some kind of stock keeping had preceded this, for that could be done by nomads.

Robust historians in the past felt confident enough to speak in terms of an 'agricultural revolution' occurring between about 12000 BC and 7000 BC but it is eccentric to speak thus of changes which extended over several thousand years. The invention of agriculture is a phenomenon like the Renaissance: its beginning is not where it seemed to be fifty years ago. Furthermore, every year a new discovery gives evidence of earlier agriculture than was once considered likely. The presence of large peas, beans, cucumbers and water chestnuts has, for example, been held to prove that cultivation of those vegetables began in Thailand and Burma about 9750 BC. South-East Asia, China, India and Africa are less well studied for these matters than is the Near East, where

it is customary to regard agriculture as having been conceived.
China, in particular, although populated by early man, has few
traces of human life, except in Manchuria, between 'Peking man'
of 450000 BC and 2500 BC, when what had seemed an empty
land began to support a large and busy population. But new
archaeology may find earlier traces of pastoral endeavour there.
Still, by 13000 BC, wild wheat fields, brought about by warm
winds previously unknown, were beginning to be harvested by
permanent settlements of farmers in what is now southern Turkey,
eastern Syria and northern Iraq. At first the wild wheat would
merely be regularly cut and not sown; and then it would be
regularly planted also. The wheat concerned was emmer wheat,
an ancestor of modern wheat which, along with rye (originally a
weed of the early wheat fields), barley, oats, millet and spelt,
grew wild in the eastern Mediterranean. There, too, it was domesticated. That meant encouraging the cross-breeding of the
tougher tamed plants whose grains have to be regularly sown,
since, unlike wild ones, they do not disperse automatically[3]. Like
many modern plants (and other things), domesticated wheat
would die out soon if not tended by man, for domestication means
not simply a 'taming', but a genetic change in order to make the
plants concerned better suited for man. (Wild animals can be
tended, but that is not the same as domestication.)

Other agricultural innovations included weeding; digging soil
with a hooked branch or an antler; the use of fire to complete the
clearing of a tract of land and to fertilise it – the idea being spread
by seeing the effect of accidental fires; and the use of a flint-
bladed sickle, perhaps with a bone handle, with which to cut the
harvest, though, in the earliest days, the harvest was accomplished
by pulling out stalks by hand. Still, grooved hafts of bone in which
short pieces of flint were mounted, and adapted from ancient
weapons, were being used near the Nile, for reaping by 12000
BC. At that time they were probably for cutting harvest grass that
grew wild; whether that is so or not, the sickle certainly preceded
cultivation.

From pictures of a later time, it is possible to guess roughly
what an early harvest was like. The reapers formed a line, cutting
the corn and laying the cut sheaves on the left. Their neighbours
did the same, but left the sheaves to the right. Others bound the
sheaves, which would then be spread on the threshing floor, the
tips towards the centre. The grain would be trodden out, to begin

with by men, a few thousand years later by animals. The corn would then be ground by pestles. By the time of the first dynasty in Egypt (3100 BC), the sickle haft had been improved by being curved. It was then made of wood, though it retained its cutting edge of small flints till about 2000 BC.

In this style the Near East, particularly Egypt, began its long history as a granary to the Mediterranean. The grain would be boiled in a pit, beaten into a paste and mixed with water to make the first flatbreads, perhaps baked with a crust. Ancient Iraqi civilisation had a barley flatbread made from paste, spread out and cooled on a hot surface – it is still so eaten there. These heavy early breads might be eaten with sesame oil, fish or sauces. The grinding played a large part in these undertakings, since, while corn can be kept for a long time, flour cannot be.

Did agriculture begin in one or two places, lead to the establishment of villages, and then become diffused over the whole earth, being early seized upon by weary hunters who had been seeing their game die and were anyway glad not to be going on their travels again? Or did it occur at the same time in many places? In the valleys of the Tigris and Euphrates, the Nile, the Indus and the Yellow River, perhaps the Mekong or in Central America? Caution suggests a diverse origin, though it is indeed 'hard to accept', as Christopher Wrigley put it, 'that men should have lived for tens of thousands of years during which the idea of putting seeds or tubers back into the ground should have occurred to no one, and that it should then have occurred to several people independently'[4]. Yet many things were learned independently in America and in the Old World, at a time when there was no contact between the two. The dog was domesticated in both the Near East and in the Americas at the same time and maize was planted in both places, without agricultural pioneers from one world playing a part in the achievement of the other. By all accounts, the radish was separately domesticated in many places. Then the whole process of agricultural innovation was stretched over thousands of years. If agriculture radiated as an 'idea', perhaps even in a world without very good means of communication it would have developed faster than it did in practice.

Agriculture was achieved probably by a slow migration of cultivators. Primitive cultivation with hoes exhausts the soil, ignores rotation of crops and fallow, and necessitates the constant clearing and sowing of new ground. When one neighbourhood was farmed, the village probably moved on slowly into what had previously been bush. Hence the lengthy delay in passing on the new techniques.

Five rivers (the Nile, the Euphrates, the Tigris, the Indus and the Yellow River) were if not founts at least the foci of early agriculture. Cattle may have crowded towards these rivers because of climatic changes. The muddy deltas were good places to discover that nutritious plants could be deliberately sown. Possibly, planting began in places where game or wild fruits were short. The Euphrates and Tigris, admittedly, lacked an alluvial plain. The agriculture which grew up between those rivers was dependent on the timing of the thaw high up in the Armenian mountains and the spring rainfall. Hence, perhaps, the intricacy of the politics there. All the same, ancient Iraq had a high productivity: 200 grains grown to one sown. In Egypt and in China, the deposit of mud left by the rivers could be cultivated again and again without treatment.

The ancient valley of the Nile was, unlike Egypt today, a land of marshes in which papayrus, sedge and rushes grew to more than a man's height. The wadis teemed with Barbary sheep, wild oxen and wild asses. The annual flood continuously changed the lie of the land while fish, wild boar, hippopotami and large flocks of water-birds supplied much game.

The main Egyptian crop continued to be wheat, the early Chinese crop was millet (rice did not appear till many generations later, being a native of south China or Indo-China and grown best in the Yangtze valley) while, in Iraq, six-row barley was more common. The earliest crops in the Indus valley were various kinds of barley and wheat. Recent work suggests that settled agriculture in Baluchistan had begun by 6000 BC. Though some semi-horticultural agriculture was practised in the Americas also by that date (beans, squashes, chili peppers, gourds), the earliest maize was cultivated in Mexico between 6000 and 5000 BC.

The tools of this early agriculture need a little further investigation. Thus the foot-plough was no more than a stick put into the ground and pulled towards the cultivator. It has been in use in the twentieth century AD in the Scottish highlands but would have seemed primitive in the twentieth century BC in Egypt. A Peruvian plough, the same instrument of the Andes, made of hard wood and sharpened by fire, is still in use. Early ploughs were little more than hoes, but harrows and rakes, in much the same form as modern ones, were eventually introduced. The foot-plough became, about 7000 BC, a two-man plough, in Egypt at least, with one man pulling on a rope in front, and a second man pressing the plough's point into the ground. A cross-beam gave this plough more sophistication. But eventually the use of animal power transformed matters.

Reindeer may have been ridden occasionally, or milked, as they still are in Lapland. The much maligned wolf probably taught man many different ways of rounding up cattle. Perhaps wild goats hovered near the new agricultural settlements in the hope of finding grain till they invited capture. The 'omnivorous goat' must have been used to clear scrub soon after the extension of agriculture away from the natural gardens of the river valleys. Goats also provided milk, hair and a waterproof skin for use in clothing, whether or no those benefits were realised before the control of breeding started to ensure more productive strains. Then, even before agriculture, nomads had herded sheep for meat, for milk and for skins: since, long before the invention of spinning and weaving, sheep were recognised as being able to provide a good natural covering. Pigs were domesticated in several places, at much the same time. It is possible that they, like goats, took some initiatives in securing their own domestication. Once villages began to be formed, the shining virtues of the pig must have become quickly apparent, for it can provide abundant supplies of meat and fat (and bristles as well as skin) and be kept in restricted places. Pigs are as good as goats at destroying undergrowth. They soon became the staple domestic animal of China.

All these animals were taken in a domesticated form throughout the Old World, including Africa. In the Americas, the still nomadic tribes continued an unrelenting war against wild animals, much as Europe and Asia had done before 10000 BC: mammoth and giant sloth were still being hunted in 6000 BC but the destruction of all large types (except reindeer) was complete by 5000 BC and the cultivation of crops was, perhaps in consequence, beginning.

All these early domesticated animals were used for a time as beasts of burden. Even sheep were made to tread in the seed sown by shepherds in Egypt. But they only made a minor impact on how the harvest was gathered, in comparison with cattle, whose domestication was the most important step taken by human beings in their exploitation of the animal world. This apparently occurred in Turkey, Macedonia and Greece about 6000 BC. The innovation seems to have taken a long time to be carried elsewhere. Egypt and Iraq did not have cattle as beasts of burden before 4000 BC; Central Africa not before 3000 BC, north-west Europe not before 2500 BC and China only by 2000 BC. (From the beginning, China used cattle for traction, hardly at all for milk; in Africa, cows were mostly used for meat.) At least by 2500 BC, there were different breeds: humped cattle in India and Iraq, piebald in Egypt and among the lake dwellings of Switzerland and Denmark. Many theories, some beguiling, explain differences between the fighting bulls of Spain, the hornless Angus, and the white cattle of Italy. In that first society of which there is a detailed memory, namely Egypt, there were certainly two types of cattle: lean cattle, with powerful horns, living on grass, used for the plough, with bulls for heavy loads: and the other, *bos africanus*, for meat. The Americas had no cattle till AD 1492 – in effect, no reliable beasts of burden apart from the lazy llama.

Agriculture began on light soil where the early scratch plough had worked well. The first cattle-powered version of this in Egypt (as in the Yellow River delta in China) was pulled by two cows, even though the plough itself was little more than a stick. In Sumer, a heavier stick was dragged diagonally across the earth, throwing up loose soil at the sides, and there too a stone-edged plough was first used, with a yoke binding the animals firmly to the shaft. But even that more powerful method of cultivation was inadequate for the heavier soils of northern Europe. Agriculture came late there, and hesitantly. The castration of the bull, and his conversion into the ox, which has played such a part in agriculture, followed in the Near East about 4000 BC, probably in one of the cities of northern Iraq. That too seems to have followed only very slowly in northern countries.

Several more animals were employed in agriculture between 2000 BC and 1000 BC. First of all, the ass (of African origin) began to be in regular use in caravans for trade between Iraq and Egypt. The North African dromedary was also put to the same purpose by 1600 BC in Palestine. The process was assisted by the invention of wheels, in use in Iraq as early as 4000 BC, and employed for ox-carts only a few hundred years later, both there and in Egypt. Wheels were used in China by 2000 BC.

Finally there came the domestication of the horse, though that word seems inappropriate for the early use made of that animal on the plains of the Russian steppe, where hunting tribes were long celebrated as bold riders. Their constant practice 'had seated them so firmly on horseback', wrote Gibbon of some of their descendants, that 'they were supposed to perform the ordinary duties of civil life there . . . even to sleep without dismounting'[5]. But though in the steppe men learnt how to ride horses, all the earliest pictures of domesticated horses show them drawing light carts or chariots, rather than being ridden. By 2500 BC, for example, carts were in use in Turkestan; in Macedonia and Troy by 1800 BC. By 1700 BC chariot-borne nomads or hunters able to make use of this superior equine technology were sweeping regularly towards the settled communities. The spoke (four were normal to begin with, six later) seems to have been invented at the same time. By 1500 BC the horse chariot had become a decisive weapon of war, just as 3,000 years later horses with mounted soldiers were effectively used against the Aztecs and Incas.

Horses reached north-west Europe slowly, perhaps not before 1000 BC, presumably already domesticated. The horse was probably taken to Greece about 2000 BC and to India about 1500 BC by the first Aryan invaders, in the shape of a pony. In China, the ox-cart was at any rate known by 2000 BC, and the horse and cart, or chariot, not much later, though the 'horses' were small Mongolian ponies with heavy heads, or even 'half asses' comparable, no doubt, to the true wild horse which existed till recently in Mongolia. Not till much later did the Chinese use the larger, more graceful, smaller-headed horses, the expedition to obtain which from Central Asia is commemorated in the legend of the heavenly horses of Ferghana: an emperor needed horses to carry him to Heaven. Once again the Americans had to wait for Columbus and Cortes to see a horse which they could use: for the few which had come with the earliest emigrants had died out, probably eaten by men about 5000 BC or so. The earliest American camel came to a similar end.

Early horses were ridden and driven without saddles, stirrups or horseshoes and, though they had from early on primarily a military use, and a use for transporting the great, they were eaten too. Mares' milk and blood were drunk extensively in central Asia – indeed, in some circumstances are drunk there to this day. On the other hand, the use of horses for traction was rare, for the heavy harness used for oxen throttled horses. No one had the ingenuity to think of a different method until someone did so in China in the third century AD.

These cattle, carts, asses and horses began by revolving round a wheat civilisation in Egypt; a barley one in Babylon; a millet one in China; and a mixed cereal one in India. In the Americas, maize would subsequently establish itself almost as decisively, in the few areas where there were settled communities.

The merit of those staples was that, unlike fruit, meat, berries and all other food known till then, the grain so obtained could be stored for a long time. The effect of this on the stabilisation of societies can easily be imagined.

Beyond the borders of the few agricultural regions, however, nomads continued their old existence, constantly attracted by the prosperity of the settled peoples whose land they sometimes laid waste and sometimes sought to capture. At that time – between 10000 BC and 2000 BC – the majority of the five to ten million people in the world were still nomads. They included in 2000 BC the ancestors of the Greeks, Romans and Indians, the 'Aryans' living near the Caspian Sea, who lived by rearing cattle and who talked a version of ancient Sanskrit which was the ancestor of Hindustani as well as of Greek. For a long time, too, even 'settled' agricultural kingdoms had uncertain borders; as suggested by the Indian practice that where a horse was permitted to wander at will, the king claimed all the land over which it wandered.

For hundreds of generations, settled agriculture was indeed established in only a few limited regions. Thus in Central Asia, among the forests of what is now Russia, the agricultural technique which lasted into the sixteenth century AD (and till the twentieth in the north) was half-nomadic: having made a clearing in the woods, the peasants set the undergrowth and stumps on fire. Ashes left after the fire were rich in potash and lime. The soil so treated yielded several good harvests. After it ceased to do so, the peasants would move to another part of the forest and there put into effect this 'slash-burn' method anew. Much of the world lived thus until the Industrial Revolution. Many nomads approached the age of industry without the recollection of a long, settled agriculture. The abundance of wild life was a determining factor in the food supply of most of the world in AD 1750; certainly so in AD 1500. Nor should one forget 'the many primitive peoples who', as Karl Wittfogel put it, 'endured lean years and even long periods of famine, without making the crucial changeover to agriculture, and who thus demonstrate the immense attractions of non-material values when increased material security can be attained only at the price of political, economic and cultural submission'[6].

The gypsy and the bandit have a place in history. Nomads constantly battered at the doors of settled communities, often forcing an entrance, capturing the states concerned, as the Mongols captured China in the early thirteenth century AD, but, as a rule, were absorbed by the vanquished. Indeed, in many remote places, such as the Tibetan plateau, shepherds still move their herds of yaks from one area of sparse grass to another, even if they have ceased to menace China. The Scythian, Pecheneg or Hungarian nomads who threatened Western Europe in the ninth century, and the Mongols who for so long menaced both China from the west and Russia from the east, have as much claim to represent continuity in history as the owners of a Tuscan villa. In mediaeval France, Marc Bloch tells us, semi-nomadic men of the forests prowled round the edges of the *grandes domaines*: huntsmen, charcoal burners, gatherers of wax and wild honey, dealers in wood ash or simply woodmen – men who were from the beginning more traders than agriculturalists. The white pioneers in the American Midwest depended in the 1830s for their subsistence on 'the natural growth of vegetation and the proceeds of hunting'. So, too, did their Indian opponents. In western Spain, in the early twentieth century, the typical peasant was still the *yuntero*, a landless man with a team of mules which he would graze on common land. Even in France in the nineteenth century a few regions belonged to hunters. Those who lived from the forest always opposed the extension of the land under the plough. Even in Europe and other major agricultural regions there were only modest additions to the acreage under cultivation between prehistory and the Middle Ages (c. AD 1050–1300), and then afterwards only sporadically and in special areas (England during the days of the early enclosures, Tuscany in the fifteenth century) Most agricultural revolutions after 1300 till the twentieth century were concerned with a better way of using existing soil, not with cutting down more of the greenwood.*

All the early agricultural revolutions must have had major consequences for the populations of settled regions. The domestication of cattle, for example, must have been the prime cause for the gain of one hundred per cent in the population of the Near East which is believed to have occurred in the thousand years between 5000 and 4000 BC. On the other hand, the nomadic peoples must have remained the same in number as they had always been.

---

* The last hunting people are the fishermen of the twentieth century. Their time may soon be up.

4
Gods

Who went with Duke Mu to the grave?
Now this Yen-hsi
Was the pick of all our men
But as he drew near the tomb-hole
His limbs shook with dread.
That blue one, Heaven,
Takes all our best men.

Book of Songs, tr. Arthur Waley

Ancient societies were held together primarily by religion. That had in the beginning three main characteristics. First, a widespread worship of the sun as the chief among influences for fertility. Second, a concern with death. Third, a gradual evolution from polytheism to monotheism.

The sun was more important to farmers than to hunters. Sacrifices were made to it all over the world, from the horses offered by the Parsees to the cattle offered, after testing to see if they were clean, by the Egyptians. The temple of the sun at On (Heliopolis in Greek) had a priestly class well established before the unification of the Egyptian kingdoms. But there also survived there, from earlier days, animal gods, such as the beasts of Anatolia. Possibly hunters usually worshipped animals or rivers, and those were ousted by the sun when the latter became needed to ripen crops.

The connection between death and religion now seems normal, though perhaps, in modern times of secular funerals and neglect of ceremonial, it may cease to be so. Still, when the expectation of life was shorter – perhaps thirty years as a maximum in both agricultural and nomadic societies in 5000 BC – it was natural to be concerned by mortality. The worship of dead ancestors was as universal as the worship of the sun.

In Jericho in the earliest days of its history, about 7000 BC, the dead were buried under the floor, while skulls had their features restored by plaster and were buried separately from the bodies. Later, in the great days of Ur (about 2700 BC to 2500 BC), the tombs of the famous, above all of kings, were vast rooms. Such monarchs' deaths might be followed by suicide, on the tombs themselves, of their courtiers: perhaps ten or twenty of them would drink a cup of poison and die forthwith, to be covered by the king's horses and then by earth. Others, in ancient Iraq, preserved their dead in honey. In Egypt, even before the unification of the kingdom, bodies were buried in the sand of the desert, in which rainless land they would be preserved for thousands of years. From about 3500 BC onwards royal and rich families among the Egyptians embalmed their dead. The numerous mummies now in museums all over the world commemorate a respect for death and the past combined. At the same time, everyone from kings to paupers took great trouble with their tombs: the kings built their pyramids long before they were old men and, as dynasty succeeded dynasty, pyramids became grander, brick giving way to stone. Even as early as the third dynasty, the gods of the dead claimed 'the greater part of Egypt's resources', according to Pierre Montet[1], the pyramids being lined by tiles, filled with pictures, alabaster, gold, resin and silver. Each pharaoh took up his residence near the site chosen for his tomb, where, during most of his lifetime, work on the pyramid and temple continued. Thus, till about 1500 BC, there was no capital in Egypt. It was a country whose government moved regularly each generation[2].

These entombments were religious acts of the first importance. The pyramid was not really a tomb. It was the home of the king who himself, if generously provided for, would not only be immortal but would ensure that all who had worked for him would live for ever. Life after death would be a 'perpetual domain', another, even more immobile Egypt from which hail, locusts, epidemics, invasions, robberies and famine would have been removed. The individual would live there with his ever youthful wife, his ever gambolling children and his staff of scribes, stewards and craftsmen, each man retaining the rank which he had gained in life. Thus the Egyptians, who for the first time devised the intoxicating idea of immortality, organised their entire society around the hope of it: an aim which was not made more realisable by the humidity of the tombs, which ruined silver and bronze and which caused much of the elaborate leather and linen used to rot. Still, if it was accepted that the soul was immortal, the society which accepted it, however hierarchical, had to look on individuals in a new light. If the soul were assured, to have to worship the king was a small price to pay. Souls of the wicked in Egypt were supposed to pass into the bodies of animals and only return to human life, for another chance, after they had traversed every species, a journey believed to last 3,000 years. The Egyptians also believed in some oracles, such as that of the goddess Latona, but that form of worship did not interest many people before the classical age of Greece.

For a long time Egypt was alone in maintaining this interpretation of life and death. Collective burials, associated with commerce or mining, continued throughout the Mediterranean, in caves or in orifices specially cut in rocks, between 4000 and 1500 BC. The rulers of Mycenae were placed in circular vaults. The kings of ancient Ethiopia were embalmed, painted to resemble the living and placed in a crystal pillar specially hollowed out. Scythians, by 1000 BC, were being buried in chambers roofed by timber, themselves deep inside grass-covered barrows, their rulers being embalmed and accompanied to the grave by wife, chief servants, horses, clothing and family possessions. Ordinary people, says Herodotus, were permitted to avoid a massacre of those dimensions by giving the corpse a banquet[3]. The tombs of early rulers of Japan were, it seems, buildings up to eighty acres in size.

While most bodies, therefore, were buried, there were variations: the Massagetae, a people of Scythia who had wives in common, were killed when they grew old, and the bodies were boiled and eaten. Only if people had died of disease were they buried, an eventuality which caused much wailing. Among the Indians, in some tribes the flesh of the dead was removed but the bodies were buried. The Romans' predecessors as masters of central Italy, the Etruscans, were buried in tombs so elaborate as to persuade some scholars that they were more obsessed than others by death or by life after death. Later – to carry this analysis into more modern times – the Romans were first cremated, and then buried. Augustus changed the system back to cremation, for he feared the effects on health of the by his time overcrowded common burial pits.

The idea of an immortal soul, meantime, stole, like a ghost in its own right, through the Mediterranean. The desire of innumerable early religions for such a hope is summed up in a quotation in Greek on a flat gold leaf found near Catanzaro in southern Italy: 'In Hades, thou wilt find on thy left a spring and, near the spring, a white cypress. Go not near. Thou wilt find another spring, an icy spring, that hath its source in the lake of Mnemosyne and, before it, thou wilt see guards. Then shalt thou say to those guards: "I am a son of earth and the starry sky, but I come of a race of gods, as ye know: my lips are parched, I am dying of thirst: oh hasten, give me to drink of the icy water of the lake of Memory." And they will allow thee to drink from the sacred source and, when thou has drained each drop, thou wilt reign with the other heroes"[4].

In the early days of the age of agriculture, all accepted the religion, and the view of the purpose of life, of the tribe of whom they were members. Not only priests but kings, civil servants and craftsmen looked on the existence of the gods and goddesses adopted by their peoples at some remote time as the explanation of life. Religion and race went together. A member of the Massagetae did not contemplate becoming a worshipper of Jehovah. He believed in his people's gods just as he accepted the rule of his monarch. Naturally, no individual could call in question in Egypt a hierarchy of authority which culminated in a living god. Not only each tribe but very often each family had their own gods and their own religion. Many walls of Çatal Hüyük, for example (8000 BC), were so richly decorated as to suggest that they were shrines. Their number and small size suggest that they were domestic in character: shrines built for the intimate worship of gods conceived of as ancestors, or ancestors as gods, long before the age of full-time priests in public temples. Only the establishment of cities and of organised communities limited the number of gods, or at least demoted many belonging to individuals.

By 3000 BC the ordinary people of Sumer, as of many other prosperous agricultural communities, believed that they depended upon deities who were the owners of the soil. To secure the favour of the deities, they paid tribute to the priests. The priests of ancient Israel were more differentiated from temporal rulers than were those of Egypt; and, indeed, the Iraqi states were closer to theocracies, which in turn necessitated careful planning.

The revenues gained in old Iraq were used to provide the gods (doubtless the priests) with feasts, an ample supply of beer and specialist craftsmen. The earliest temple yet unearthed, at Eridu, not far from Sumer (of about 3500 BC), a direct ancestor of the church and mosque, with a long central hall and an altar, had large flanking chambers for grain, while the earliest writing, at Uruk, dealt with the grain accounts of the temple there. The characteristic form of ancient Iraqi architecture was the artificial mound, called a ziggurat or temple tower, the tower of Babel being the best known, that of Ur the best preserved example.

As the generations passed, these religions became associated with epics, prayers, myths, incantations, hymns, songs, dances and rites, as well as a panoply of gods arranged in uncertain, sometimes changing, hierarchical order. Most settled societies had fertility cults of one sort or another, the maintenance of production being a matter of preoccupation and antedating consideration of what happens after death. Ladies of heaven, gods of vegetation, fish gods, moon gods, water gods, gods of wisdom, love and war, all made their appearances in Iraq, anticipating comparable myths in other countries: thus in Sumer about 3500 BC, Iranna, goddess of love and of war, set off to conquer the nether regions. While she was away, 'the bull sprang not upon the cow, the man impregnated not the maiden': a prefigurement of the exploits of both Persephone and Baal (who descended into the underworld for seven years).

The Mayas, like the men of Stonehenge, were concerned to propitiate the gods at the right moment. Hence their meticulous concern with punctuality, their calendars and their huge temples. In Bolivia there was Tihuanaco, a goal of pilgrimages for many miles around, built much later it is true but with its area measuring 3,280 feet by 1,471 feet and its central place given to the sun of a comparable nature to the gods of Egypt. Maize too had the status of a god in Mexico.

The Incas in Peru ruled over a state which recognised the Sapa Inca as a descendant of the sun and thus as divine. The combination of religious and temporal power in the person of a divine emperor also characterised Rome after Augustus, while the emperor of China, 'the son of Heaven', played the critical part in all the great religious ceremonies.

Despite the great innovation earlier noticed which was implicit in Egyptian religion, what struck contemporaries about the gods of Egypt were their riches and their number. The god Amon at Thebes owned a tenth of Egypt, for example, including 433 gardens, 46 workshops, 83 ships, 65 little towns and 400,000 beasts. On Amon's estates 90,000 men worked. If other gods were less well off, the diversity was astounding. The forty-two provinces of Egypt each had a separate deity. So did the smallest city. Most gods had innumerable cults. The forms in which the Egyptian gods were worshipped later shocked Romans: 'What monsters are revered by demented Egypt?' asked the poet Juvenal. 'One part worships the crocodile. Another goes in awe of the ibis, which feeds on serpents. Elsewhere, there shines the golden effigy of the long-tailed monkey. But the size of the religious buildings of Egypt could only astound. The great temples (usually a rectangular walled enclosure of unbaked brick, sometimes 300 yards by 1,500) and the sacred gardens and orchards were as surprising to foreigners as the large, parasitical staffs of the temple headed by shaved, circumcised and bemasked priests, men without any moral code save to respect the tradition into which they had been born. The great pyramids to which attention was rightly paid by all observers, ancient and modern, were each made of over two million blocks of stone averaging 2½ metric tons in weight, and employed in their building 4,000 masons for twenty years continuously as well as 100,000 men for three months' work a year for the same period.

China was an exception to these developments. Though the settled communities on the Yellow River and beyond were brought together under the Shang dynasty (after about 1500 BC) or under their mythical predecessors, the Hsia, neither the early agricultural societies nor the monarchies which succeeded them established a very elaborate religion. Sacrifices might be made to the king's ancestors or to the gods of the soil. Questions might be asked of gods as to, for example, where a traveller should stay on a journey or whether the harvest would be good or bad but the replies to such questions were usually only 'yes' or 'no', 'lucky' or 'unlucky'. The sky god T'ien was the supreme being later worshipped by the emperor as chief priest and believed to control the universe. From an early time the idea developed in China that the harmony of the universe was controlled by the balance of the forces of nature: wet and dry, female and male, moon and sun – yin and yang. But the place of gods in society was less than it was in the West, and there was no priestly bureaucracy. Why did China have no dominant religion? Perhaps because kings, priests and ordinary people knew that benefits derived from hard physical effort to maintain the irrigation canals, rather than waiting (or praying) for rain. So the beautiful painted pottery and silk of the earliest days in China were not necessarily created in honour of a special deity. Nor, at the earliest stage of their history, can much be said about the ancient Indians, preoccupied as the cities of Iraq were by a mother goddess and by sacred trees. In America the Mayas, concerned with a nether world which seemed 'a blood curdling vision of smoke and fright' seemed equally superstitious.

Even the Etruscans, otherwise so intelligent, still sought, as late as the fifth century BC, the interpretation of the will of the gods in claps of thunder, lightning, the flight of birds and livers of sheep.

By that time such ancient forebodings, and indeed such a diversity of gods, had ceased to have a determining hold over the imaginations of a few richer peoples. For, in several such societies, the notion of a single god had been conceived, about 1500 BC. Most early agricultural societies usually had, besides a miscellany of minor deities, one who was allowed precedence: for example, Enlil, the deity of Nippur, as of the atmosphere and of the earth, was accepted as the dominant god of Iraq, identified in Babylon as Marduk, and as Bel (Baal) or Lord in neighbouring Iraqi cities. The people of Eridu worshipped Enki, lord of the earth but also of the sweet waters for he 'had founded his chamber in the deep'. About 1400 BC the Pharaoh Amenophis IV tried to abolish all the minor gods of Egypt and to establish the sun in a place of overweening importance. Animal representations of deities were banned, and revenues of all gods were directed into a single royal treasury. These moves failed because of the attitude of the well-entrenched priests, the earliest clash between Church and state and won by the former, whose livelihood as well as its traditional customs were threatened by the king's decrees. But among a then nomadic tribe, the Jews, which had fled from Iraq precisely because its leaders had rejected the gods there, and then emigrated to Egypt, the cult of a single god, Jehovah, began to flourish not long afterwards. The implications were momentous and will be discussed in a later chapter.

Though religion provided the frame of all old societies, government and law cannot be omitted in any consideration of what held the most primitive of them together.

5

Kings and Waterworks

I now accept that the settled and just management of society by a progressive oligarchy is probably the best we can hope for.

R. H. S. Crossman, *Diaries* 1967

In all ages whatever the form and name of government, be it monarchy, republic or democracy, an oligarchy lurks behind the façade.

Sir Ronald Syme, *The Roman Revolution*

The most civilised nations of modern Europe issued from the woods of Germany; and in the rude institutions of those barbarians we may still distinguish the original principles of our present laws and manners.

Gibbon, *Decline and Fall of the Roman Empire*

By 3000 BC most settled communities were establishing semi-religious authoritarian monarchies, whose rulers already customarily succeeded their fathers, and whose purpose, even if no longer explicitly admitted, was to ensure that ploughing was regularly done and to make military arrangements to prevent nomadic hunters from seizing the harvest when it was in. Assemblies there may have been in the cities of the earliest days of Iraqi agriculture. But there was evidently no sense there of a will of a majority. Those assemblies probably continued deliberation until practical unanimity was attained. This lasted a long time, and in any emergency monarchical power was sought, and that tended to be confirmed. Kingship always had in ancient Iraq a limited tenure. But the threat of emergency was never absent, and concentrated authority became the rule once cities began to argue with others over drainage, supplies, transit and irrigation.

Irrigation was a main function of these kingdoms. For most of them depended not on rainfall (it was believed in antiquity to have rained only once in Egypt, on the day that the country was invaded by Cambyses, King of Persia) but on water from rivers or wells, which had either to be allowed to flood the fields, as in Egypt, or to be artificially, intelligently and regularly diverted.

The preparation and maintenance of these hydraulic systems needed disciplined, hard-working and cooperative men. Small-scale irrigation can be managed by independent peasants but, if rivers have to be manned and floods taken advantage of, a large administration is desirable. Hence one reason for the early Chinese despotism, whose first ruler, Yu, the founder of the Hsia dynasty, is supposed to have risen to his kingly rank (sometime between 2200 BC and 1980 BC) from the position of supreme hydraulic functionary[1]. The kingdom of lower Egypt – though not Egypt of the Delta – was also made into a single unit because a change of climate forced the nomadic tribes about 5000 BC to move close to the Nile and depend absolutely on it for water. Menes, the founder of Memphis and the mythical first king of the first dynasty, is said to have thrown a dike across the western part of the valley of the Nile, compelling a branch of the river to rejoin the main stream, thus reclaiming fifty miles of valley[2].

In historic times the construction of reservoirs, tanks, canals and wells was looked upon as one of the most important of the functions of government in India, with careful distribution and measuring of water[3]. Irrigation is still the most time-consuming single item in the farmer's calendar in both China and India. Probably the same was true in the past of Babylonia, the lake area of Mexico, Maya Yucatan, and of all countries dependent on rivers whose overflow, properly handled, brings fertility and life and whose unchecked waters leave devastation in their wake. 'The dikes,' Karl Wittfogel points out, 'have to be repaired in the proper season so that they will hold in times of inundation; and the canals have to be properly cleared so that the water will be satisfactorily distributed'[4]. Doubtless the history of despotism cannot be wholly written as a footnote to that of irrigation. All the same, irrigation necessitated, and made for, a source of central authority in a way which agricultures dependent on rainfall do not.

6

Figures and Alphabets

The inventions of language and writing were presumably the essential tools, if we may so call them, with which all the others were produced and led to the Bronze, Iron and Machine ages.

J. Z. Young, *An Introduction to the Study of Man*

1

To carry out these arrangements, as well as to invent the windlass, pulley, crank and lock with a key, all complicated beyond the dreams of hunting man, the pioneer agricultural kingdoms also needed adequate methods of calculating, accounting, reckoning, recording and, finally, writing. As Gordon Childe put it, 'When a society has possessions in greater numbers than it can use immediately, it needs numerals'[1].

The citizens of the towns of what is now Iraq were responsible for the fundamental innovations. There, the first calendar and the first, hieroglyphic, script were devised. There too were worked out the first system of numbers and the first system of weights and measures. In the schools of ancient Iraq, multiplication, division, square and cube roots, algebra and geometry were all taught. Those schools knew of the theorem, now called after Pythagoras, by 1700 BC and were close to quadratic equations – reaching, indeed, a level of mathematical achievement rarely found elsewhere until the Renaissance. This ancient Iraqi mathematics used both a decimal and a sexagesimal system. So far as the first system was concerned (invented because we have ten fingers), they employed the 'place-value' system, which modern Europeans also use – by courtesy of the Hindus and Arabs, it is true – whereby the value of the symbol depends on its position relative to other symbols. Thus '5' equalled (and equals) '5' when thus written and '50' when in front of a '0'.

Some of the cities of Iraq used the sexagesimal system. It is for that reason that, in mathematics and chronology, the circle is divided into 360 degrees, the hour into 60 minutes, the minute into 60 seconds, while the day has 24 hours. The ancient Iraqis knew that the value of π was 3 1/7, while the inhabitants of Israel about 1000 BC believed it to be exactly 3. In all these matters the

Egyptians learned from their neighbours and altered their systems for their own benefit. They used the decimal system but only that. Units were indicated by strokes and 10s, 100s and 1,000s by signs. They multiplied and divided by 2, occasionally by 3, but used hardly any higher table. They used fractions in a primitive way. Their system of 'unit fractions' was adopted by the Greeks and Romans, and greatly delayed progress in mathematics. On the other hand, the Chinese had a good understanding of ordinary fractions, which they were using effectively at the time when their history begins to be separable from myth. The Hindus, who were in touch with China from an early time, had a more elaborate version and it was from them that Europe, through Islam, gained the use of the modern fraction, as of other mathematical innovations.

Still, much could be done with Egyptian mathematics. The Great Pyramid of Gizeh, built about 2900 BC, demonstrates the Egyptian mathematical achievement. Its base is a perfect square. The sides run exactly north to south and east to west. All the surfaces have the same slope of 50°, being built of stones so well fitted that it is impossible to insert a blade between them.

The Iraqis in 4000 BC, meantime, had made the day when the moon was full, as well as the day of the new moon, a day for religious ritual: thus there were 'moondays' on the 1st or 28th (or 29th) of every month. Later, half 'moondays' also became feast days. But this lunar month does not, unfortunately, coincide with the solar one. Sumer therefore replaced the lunar calendar with a solar one. That remained inaccurate. For a time, a year of twelve months each of thirty days was used, but every six years there was a thirteenth month, occasionally a fourteenth one. This irregularity was adequate for Iraq, but the Egyptians, desiring greater accuracy, in order to know precisely when the flood of the Nile was going to reach them, devised a calendar with twelve months of thirty days each, plus five extra days. In the end, the Egyptians worked out their calendar by reference not to the rising of the Nile, which was occasionally unreliable, but to Sirius, the Dog Star, which rose every year at dawn at the same moment on the same day. The discrepancy with the true year, as it is recognised now, was slight.

Perhaps the Egyptians' mistakes were due to their belief that the earth was flat and the sky a table held up by four pillars, while the stars were supposed to revolve round a celestial pole. Also, they worshipped, rather than studied, heavenly movements, and their geometry was based on surfaces and volumes, not on lines.

More accurate than either of these two peoples were the Mayas, who a little later but entirely independently employed a full-time priesthood to collect astronomical facts and predict the future by mathematics based on the use of an arrangement of knotted strings. The settled Indian societies of old Central America all had calendars, but the Mayas had the best one devised about 360 BC. They knew that the year was a little more than 365 days. Indeed, the later Mayan calculation of a year of 365·2420 days was closer to the modern evaluation of 365·2422 days than the Gregorian one – which was 365·2425[2].

Mayan civilisation was able to make these calculations so well because they had developed the use of the zero. They divided their year into nineteen months – eighteen of twenty days each, and one of five. Their metrical system was vigesimal. It seems likely that the Mayas derived their system from the Olmecs, a people who lived to the north of them but who did not create an elaborate civilisation apart from their skill with figures.

Mayan priests owed their influence to their control of the calendar and to their ability to predict everything, from full moons to eclipses. Their temples were established with astronomical considerations in mind: the shrine of Uaxactun, for example, built about 328 BC, was so laid out that anyone standing on the steps of the largest pyramid could, at the Equinox, see the sun rise in the dead centre of the main temple.

2

Ancient Iraqi civilisation also devised the first hieroglyphic script, about 3500 BC. This occurred, apparently, at the city of Uruk and was soon copied elsewhere. Numerals, pictographs and ideographs were inscribed by a sharp reed pen on clay tablets. No transaction was regarded as having validity unless it was recorded on these tablets. About 1,500 separate signs were used, mostly abstract and mostly still undeciphered. The tablets which can be read record business transactions by the temples and sales of land. The simplest were no more than tallies with a few numerals. Others bear the impressions of cylinder seals to identify parties, or witnesses to the transactions recorded. Probably this invention did not seem at the time as sensational an event as it may now appear. The illiterate brain is, after all, capable of great feats of memory, of calculation and of wise judgement. Also, it may be that accounting, at least, if not a form of writing, antedated the inscriptions at Uruk[3]. Writing may have been a development of reckoning. By about 3000 BC, at all events, the end of the reed used to inscribe the tablets had begun to be shaped like a wedge, for which the word is *cuneus* in Latin – hence the usage 'cuneiform'.

The language in which this momentous innovation was embodied was Sumerian, a difficult tongue, without much relation to others then known. Later, Akkadian became the lingua franca of ancient Iraq, despite its six hundred written signs, being succeeded later still by Aramaic, the spoken language of a greater number of cities than Akkadian. Aramaic later began to use an alphabet, of twenty-two letters, an idea which was devised by some Semitic people – were they the Jews? – about 2000 BC. A linear form was in use in Crete and Mycenae by about 1400 BC in order to express Greek.

The Egyptians had by then their own hieroglyphs, copied from Iraq but not slavishly. Each hieroglyph was with them a separate ideogram and, in the hands of their best scribes, a different work of art. That continued to be the handwriting of priests for many generations. Soon, a simpler 'hieratic' Egyptian came to be used in secular documents. The Egyptians took no steps towards an alphabet (though pen, ink and papyrus were employed on the Nile from 3000 BC), perhaps since, in the beginning, they only needed (or their priests only wished them) to record the yearly height of the Nile's flooding, the genealogy of Memphis's priests and the names of kings. Papyrus, a reed which grew in the Nile, was, nevertheless, soon in demand throughout the eastern Mediterranean, because, when the pith was cut into strips laid across one another, dried and stuck together, a roll of something similar to writing paper could be formed. Ink from lamp black was first used upon it.

The Egyptians realised the inconvenience of having a gap between priestly and written language. A 'demotic' tongue was eventually devised (in the fifth century BC). That simply added another layer of language, for both the two previous tongues survived. A subsequent form, Coptic, demotic Egyptian with a Greek alphabet, had a brief heyday.

Indian writing, during the civilisation of the Indus and much later in the Aryan era, had connections with that of Iraq. It would be reasonable to assume that it reached India as a result of commerce. But the idea of ideograms came to the Chinese, apparently independently, in the form of signs engraved on scapular bones of sheep or shells of turtles, as a means of asking questions of

Heaven. Probably by 1500 BC, certainly by 1200 BC, the Shang dynasty had a script of some 5,000 ideograms, though only 1,500 of them are readable. With modifications, this script became the basis of modern Chinese, which has always remained faithful to ideographic, as opposed to alphabetic, script. The Chinese also had figures by 1200 BC.

Chinese ideographs are not, and never have been, representations of sounds. They stand for ideas which every reader can pronounce according to his dialect. In its earliest days, Chinese was inscribed on bamboo slabs with a stylus. Thus the earliest Chinese literature is badly preserved, if indeed it is preserved at all.

The Chinese 'characters' were ill-designed for a polysyllabic language such as Japanese. But since it was the only available system, the Japanese adopted it and added a syllabic auxiliary script which enabled them to render adequately the cases and tenses of their language. But that is to anticipate. It did not occur till well after AD 600.

In the Americas, writing came later still. In the Mayan regions from Mexico to Honduras, and nowhere else before AD 1492, hieroglyphs in a vertical pattern, sometimes combined with numerals, were introduced by 600 BC. The oldest American system, Zapotec, appeared in the lovely valley of Oaxaca, about three hundred miles south of Mexico City. The Mayas' hieroglyphs have been as yet incompletely translated.

An alphabet, once acquired, did not necessarily survive conquest: when Homer spoke of a letter being entrusted to a traveller, writing was a dim memory in Greece. The idea, known in Mycenae, had died out. Thus, Dr John Chadwick points out, Homer described writing as something 'almost magical'[4]. Like the Phoenicians (who carried the alphabet of twenty-two letters back to them), the Greeks of the classical age began by writing from right to left but, when they developed the simpler Ionic script, they were already writing from left to right. From Greece the alphabet was taken to the Etruscans in Italy and thence passed, substantially altered, to the Latins. By then, writing was being used to tell stories as well as to render accounts of what was owing. In 2100 BC the poem of Gilgamesh, King of Uruk, was written down. A novel is believed to have been written by Simibet, in Egypt, not much later. Mythological poems of ancient Phoenicia date from 1400 BC, the song of Deborah from 1150 BC. The biographies of David and Saul, included in the later biblical Book of Samuel, are held to be of much the same date. A thousand years before Christ, therefore, the long history of written literature, and even history itself, had begun. The famous classical books of Chinese literature (including the Book of History), revered by Confucius and known, quoted and studied by generation after generation of Chinese scholars, were probably composed between 1000 and 700 BC.

Appendix: Major alphabets other than those discussed

1 'Cyrillic' was devised in the ninth century. It is called after a native of Thessalonia, St Cyril, the apostle of the Moravians. For many generations, St Cyril was supposed to be the author of this script but that is now contested. At all events it was an alphabet of thirty-eight letters based on the Greek Liturgical Uncial (large, unjoined letters) with special signs for all Slavonic letters. Though not used in Moravia or by the western Slavs because of their conquest by the Latin Emperor, it was used by Russian and other orthodox Slavs from the tenth century.

2 Arabic is an alphabet deriving from ancient Aramaic. Writing in Arabic survives from the fifth century BC. Aramaic was much the most famous of northern Semitic alphabets.

3 The Latin alphabet, a derivative of Greek, was in use in Italy by about 500 BC. Its shipment was the work of Greek colonies in southern Italy.

4 Persian: like Arabic, the Persian alphabet derived from Aramaic.

5 Korean: this was not developed till the fourteenth century. It was, and is, a simple practical alphabet which gradually displaced the Chinese characters over the centuries since.

7
Laws and Tablets

The state without law would be like the human body without mind . . . The magistrates who administer the law, the jurors who interpret it – all of us in short – obey the law in order that we may be free.

Cicero, *Clu*, liii, p. 146

Government arose for three reasons: to assist the community concerned to provide defences against enemies; to preserve the religion of that community; and to provide law. The third of these actions became more important still, at least while the communities were at peace.

The earliest codes of law which have survived seem more like the rules of a game than anything which we now speak of as law: but, as Professor Huizinga has pointed out, law is an attempt to give to life the rhythm and the predictability of a game: and games, as everyone now recognises, are not superficial things[1]. When a king died in Persia, before the Achaemenid line, there was, according to tradition, five days' anarchy to show people the advantage of having kings and laws. That did not mean that kings were supposed to be subject to laws. But it was appreciated by priests, noblemen, 'elders', merchants and rulers that the knowledge of law could not be confined to the king and so kept secret. Codes of law, from an early time, were therefore made known by being carved on stone in a public place. In this respect, kings in Greece and those in Babylon behaved similarly. The codes were conceived of as deriving from deities. The making of law, the central function of the modern state, was foreign to primitive communities. In the ancient Mediterranean, these codes of law were intended to clarify old customs, themselves conceived as unalterably decided.

Such codes could not be promulgated before the coming of writing and perhaps the evolution of writing was connected with the beginning of the codification of law. At all events, in ancient Iraq collections of laws were common by 2000 BC. Perhaps every city in that congeries of city states had one. In Ur, for example, in 2100 BC the code makes it plainer than any surviving pot or

45

pyramid that the human beings of that time would be recognisable to modern man: 'If a man has broken another man's bones, he shall pay one mina of silver,' the code specified, and went on, 'if a man has hired an ox and damaged its eye', he would have to pay half its price. Other laws made provision for inheritance, prevention of cruelty to children, illegitimate children and property. Judges were professional, and court procedure was carefully worked out, as were rules for the treatment of witnesses, testimony on oath, rules for a clash of evidence (including trial by water; though, more logically than in Europe, the guilty person sank, the innocent floated).

The precious intellectual achievement of a rule of law had not yet been achieved. The laws of Hammurabi of about 1750 BC, which purported to be handed down by the god Shamah, however, show that it was realised that if, for example, the requital for a murder were left to the family of the murdered person, a long vendetta might follow. To replace that by a system in which the state was the impartial arbiter was an achievement as great as the invention of pottery. The people of ancient Iraq seem already to have known that 'when justice is both certain and mild, it is more efficacious'[2], in Tocqueville's words. Another sign of their individuality is that, as soon as law began to be written down, personal names were also recorded. Perhaps, indeed, the name, in the form which we know it, as well as writing, is a consequence of law (Herodotus knew of only one African tribe, the Atarantes of Morocco, who used no names at all)[3].

In contrast with Iraq, the ancient Egyptians had no code of laws, and no professional lawyers. They did, however, have contracts, wills, decrees, judges, reports of proceedings, and punishments. The Indians – in the Indus valley or in the early days of Aryan dominance – were also slow to develop legal institutions. Kings, chief priests and elders of the community concerned acted as judges in accordance with custom.

8
Pots, Mines and Cloths

As the advantages of copper over stone for tools and weapons
became apparent, communities had to enter trade to secure it, and
therefore had to produce extra foodstuffs or other natural products
to pay the traders.

Kathleen Kenyon, *Archaeology in the Holy Land*

1

The settled societies of the early agricultural age were held together by further innovations: pottery, for example, which had
been anticipated by wooden vessels which had the same original
aim of carrying water, and by the clay ornaments of the late
hunting era. Probably the first pots were merely clay-lined baskets.
Clay beads, bricks made from clay and clay for mortar anticipated
the use of clay for pottery.

Pottery proper was devised, as were numbers and the alphabet,
in Iraq, where clay vitrifies easily and forms a hard product difficult to break, even with a hammer. Monochrome pottery was
being made by 7000 BC, painted by 6500 BC and, within a few
hundred years after that, all the ancient cities of Iraq boasted
decorated bowls, drinking flasks, and cylinder seals carrying patterns, fired in well-built kilns whose temperatures already reached
800° centigrade. By 4000 BC the Egyptian potters knew that a
glaze could be put on pottery by treating it with sand, potash and
soda, and that they could make the colour blue by adding salts of
copper. About 3000 BC, at Uruk (Erech in the Bible), the potter's
wheel was devised, making it possible to do in two minutes work
that had previously taken several hours. Perhaps it was invented
at the same time as the brick mould. By 2000 BC the wheel had
been so improved that it could be turned by the foot or a stick.
Henceforth a professional potter was normal, being closely connected in Iraq with early metallurgists. This wheel was carried
through Europe, Africa and the East but it made slow progress:
it did not reach southern Britain till about the time of the birth of
Christ. In China, it may not have developed till about 1600 BC
and modern scholars consider that that development was independent of any shipment of ideas from the Near East.

By a coincidental development to which, perhaps, inadequate attention has been paid, pottery was also invented in the Americas. The American peoples did not achieve the potter's wheel, it is true, before Columbus and the Spaniards took it there in the fifteenth century AD. (The Aztecs had wheels in toys, but did not use it for any other purpose. It was as gunpowder was to the Chinese: a means of diversion.) All the same by 4000 BC pottery was being made in Mexico, Columbia and Ecuador. Beautiful painted pottery was being made by the Mayas by 3200 BC. The work there was more laborious than in the Near East, since pots had to be built up from coils of wet clay as they still are sometimes in the Old World. Between 300 BC and AD 500 the art of pottery reached a great height in Moche, Paracas and Nazca in Peru, with the depiction of portraits on earthenware jugs, elaborate sculptures and finely painted vases. Ancient Peru certainly had solved all the technical problems of modelling, kiln-baking, glazing and colouring.

All early pottery was developed alongside brickmaking. Bricks were shaped in moulds and fired in the sun, afterwards in kilns. In consequence, early houses seemed little more than large pots – as Sir James Jeans put it[1]. Before the wheel, after all, potters made both houses and pots with their hands.

2

An activity which complemented pottery was spinning. That began with the use of vegetables such as reed, palm fibre and esparto grass. The making of baskets, ropes and matting has a continuous history since about 6000 BC in Egypt. Hemp was also used in China before records began (say, 4000 BC). By 3000 BC flax was established in Egypt providing the main material for clothing. The fibres of that carefully cultivated crop were soaked and spun, a stick being used, to avoid entanglement, subsequently as a spindle, with a whorl or weight on top. Less important was the distaff, for holding the fibres ready to spin. The loom was invented about 5000 BC, providing a frame on which threads were stretched parallel to form the warp, to be crossed at right angles by the continuous woof. As with pottery, the New World independently, though later, worked out the art of spinning and weaving, making use both of its own cotton and the wool of alpaca and llama. Though fleeces continued to be worn without spinning – Herodotus spoke of 'Fair Libya abounding in fleeces'[2] – wool was regularly used in the eastern Mediterranean by 3000 BC.

Sheep (and wool) were taken from the Near East to India, thence further east. Cotton was carried from India to Egypt. It seems not to have been known in China till AD 700. But two out of the four usual types of cotton were native to the New World. Elaborate and finely woven cloths were thus made in Mexico and Peru from cotton long before the coming of Columbus. The colour of the weaves of Nazca, in Peru, for example, were striking in comparison with all products of the Old World just as its pottery was. Red and black dyes were available from the *bixa* shrub or the handsome hardwood tree, jagua. Their dyes included red, from the cochineal insect, and purple, from the *purpura* mollusc. Pigments were mixed to obtain a most elaborate variety of tones. So in all the more settled polities of pre-Columbian America, cotton clothes were worn – if only as skirts for married women. Many slept in cotton hammocks – one of the great American inventions. Even messages were conveyed in Peru by strands of cotton with knots in them named *quipus*. The distance between knots might indicate time. Earlier, a coarser cloth had been made in Mexico and perhaps elsewhere from the fibres of the maguey.

In the Far East, China developed the use of silk, from silkworms feeding from white mulberry trees, before historically recorded time begins with the Shang dynasty. Did this 'sericulture' begin in the time of the legendary Emperor Fu-shi, about 3000 BC? That is now thought unlikely. Another mythical emperor, Huang Ti, was supposed to have encouraged the silkworm about 2630 BC, since he believed silk clothes would enable him to escape from frost. By 1000 BC, at all events, China had carefully drained vast regions for mulberry plantations on which the silkworms fed.

The significance of these developments was that, thenceforth, the use of clothing was no longer confined to those who could scrape skins effectively. It is hard to think of a more important change. Its effect upon population must have been most beneficial even if, in hot countries, the earliest clothing was merely a 'lower garment' and a cloak.

3

At the same time as pottery was first used, mines, and smelted and hammered metals, had already begun to affect commerce, agriculture and war.

Stone was mined, and traded, as has been seen, before anything else. Thus many axes have come to light at sites far away from where the stone of which they were made derives. On the other hand, tribes needing Cornish or Cumbrian stone probably merely went to seize it. Was salt also a 'primordial narcotic', sought by agricultural man from the beginning? Perhaps, since the Chinese began taking brine from deep wells in Szechwan from the earliest days of settled life[3]. The most important object traded in ancient Iraq was obsidian, a dark, volcanic, rock-like bottle glass carried from the mountains of Asia Minor by river. It was used (as by the Mayas in Yucatan) for knives or spearheads, before copper was mined for the same purpose.

Metal has usually to be separated from other elements with which it is organically combined. That was done, to begin with, by burning charcoal at a high temperature in a furnace in which the right circumstances were achieved for, first, reducing the metals to their elementary state and, second, achieving a chemical reaction in order to secure the separation of all extraneous matter. Metal came soon to be worked into objects, either by shaping it with the anvil, heating it if it was needed to be soft; or by melting it, so that it could be poured liquid into a mould, there given a rough shape to be finished again with a hammer when dry. These processes were first learned in Asia Minor between 6000 and 4000 BC, before writing, that is, and long before the domestication of the horse.

The business of mining was carried on with copper much as it had been with flints, to begin with, but ambitious vertical shafts and horizontal galleries began to be dug into the deposits where copper was known to be. Digging through stone was assisted by heavy mauls swung on a rope or by antlers used as picks. Sometimes dry stone walls were made. Depth of excavation was given a maximum by the availability of fresh air.

Copper was man's first abundant metal and tools made of it gave rise to almost as many basic transformations as the adoption of agriculture. Agriculture was merely a matter of recognising how useful to man certain natural activities could be. The processing of metal called for a deliberate effort to cause a radical change in the natural state of affairs.

Mining began in Western Asia but by 4000 BC smelting of copper was being carried on in the Balkans and, by 2500 BC, in Spain and the Aegean.

Copper much improved the quality of all tools both for mining itself and for agriculture. In the great days of Babylon, about 2000 BC, copper was being traded from there to Africa and Asia in great quantity. By 1500 BC also the coppersmiths, perhaps by accident, had discovered that if, while copper is being melted, molten tin or lead or antimony is poured in, the ensuing mixture, bronze, will be harder than, and, above all, remain sharp longer than, stone.

Bronze further improved both tools of agriculture and weapons in war, and the minute supplies of tin possessed by Asia Minor were, in consequence, for many years regarded as fifty times more desirable than, say, silver. The prayer of the wife of the Bolivian tin miner, Patino, 'Lord, may it be tin not silver' when a seam was discovered in the nineteenth century AD, was perhaps foreshadowed in 1500 BC. Tin was also discovered in northern Europe and exported to Babylon from there. (Flints from Britain also had a market, dug up from thirty-foot mines between 3000 and 2000 BC.) Iron was forged by 2500 BC, also in Asia Minor. That final elimination of waste which enables iron to become steel, with its sharper edge and greater durability, was embarked upon there too about 1400 BC.

Among the founders of metallurgy, the Egyptians should not be forgotten. They had no iron, no copper and no tin, but they did have gold and, from 4000 BC or the earliest days of the united kingdom, the goldsmiths of Memphis (a famous clan of dwarfs), the scribes who weighed their products, the bellowsmen who heated the open fires through pottery pipes, and the men who poured the liquid gold into moulds or hammered it on the anvil were exporters-in-chief of ancient Egypt even if they were not essential in the economy. The Egyptian state was strong and settled, commerce was an affair of state and more cautious than the trade of Babylon. It was that which, in the end, made it easy for Greek merchants (following in the steps of the Phoenicians) to capture the trade of Egypt, as they later captured that of much of the eastern Mediterranean by the time of Herodotus.

These metallurgical developments reached India and China, through traders, within a few hundred years of their achievement in the Near East. A copper knife dating from 3000 BC has been found recently in China. There was much bronze in China by 1200 BC, for example, but used only, it seems, for war and ritual, not agriculture. Ironworking has also been, for a long time, associated with the disintegration of the Chou dynasty about 500 BC and steel has been associated with the victory of the Ch'in. Once again, as with pottery, the balance of evidence seems to suggest that the Chinese developed these arts independently.

Copper and its working were also invented in pre-Columbian

America, and the use of gold and silver for manufactured objects was widespread in both Mexico and Peru. The legend of El Dorado of Columbus's time confirms the leadership of that region for goldsmithery. Those ancient American Indians also mixed gold with other metals to make alloys, and pounded gold to make sheets or threads of a fineness comparable to anything in the Old World.

9

Cities, Trade and Slaves

And Hiram King of Tyre sent messengers to David & cedar trees
and carpenters and masons; and they built David a house.

1 Kings v, 2

When at home a slave had to be either at work or asleep.

Plutarch, *Cato*

1

The birth of agriculture, paradoxically, by modern considerations,
saw the birth of the city. The widespread yield of cultivated over
wild crops, and the greater possibility of storing the fruits of them,
made it safe for more and more people to enjoy the benefits of
'urban' life.

What were they like, those early 'cities' primarily of farmers,
set up around the fields of wheat or millet in 8000 BC? Probably
simply overgrown villages, a collection of mud huts, 'baked mud
and baked reeds, comparable to a beaver's nest', says Lewis Mumford[1]. Such no doubt was Jarmo in northern Iraq, which in 7000
BC had a population of 150; such also perhaps were Çatal Hüyük,
in Turkey, and Jericho which, about 6800 BC, had populations of
2,000, living in houses with walls of baked mud and reeds, floors
of beaten mud and roofs of carefully plastered branches. Houses
were recognisable as such – more than mere shelters. By then,
other villages in the Near East had rectangular houses with several
rooms, stone foundations, clay ovens with chimneys, even clay
basins in the floor. A thousand years later unbaked brick had
become the characteristic building material in Iraq, being used to
make a typical Oriental house, its rooms grouped round a courtyard. By 4000 BC such places had cobbled streets and circular
temples: the architects had mastered the principle of the vault.
Those architects used stone, which was rare in Iraq, for doors,
fireplaces and drains. By 3000 BC some cities boasted 50,000
people or even, as in the case of Ur, perhaps twice that (in 2200
BC). Around the temples, movable property in the form of objects
beyond what could be carried on the person were gathered in

53

street markets, hence stimulating artistic as well as technological innovation.

Sumer, the most famous of the early cities of Iraq, was a town of thick, walled, windowless mud huts. Rooms were fitted together to suit the site, rarely with a master plan but with low doors and common walls. It had, like many cities of ancient Iraq, some town planning for military purposes on a gridiron pattern. One can compare those cities with a more primitive settlement, Çatal Hüyük, which had no streets, only a series of rectangular houses contiguously interspersed by courtyards. The walls in Çatal Hüyük were of the same dried clay as they were in Sumer, but the houses were bungalows with flat roofs and no doors. Entry was through holes in the roof. The rough lamps used by hunting man, an open stone container for animal fat, including a wick of twisted dried grass or moss, had given way to lamps of metal or pottery. The oil used was probably the olive oil or sesame oil as was used for cooking.

In Egypt, houses were more often built with wood than they were in Iraq. The public buildings there were, however, using stone by 2500 BC. The capital of Egypt was then surrounded by a stone wall while the palaces had columns and colonnades. By then, already, the essential characteristics of city life had taken form: walls, streets, blocks of houses, workshops, an organised market, the temple and its precinct, the administrative area. To construct these things out of unbaked clay, or mud, or wood or stone, copper tools of an elaboration not surpassed until the Renaissance were devised. There were also pull-saws and bow-drills, as well as glue (made by boiling down bones, skins and hooves), useful not only for shaping buildings but also for making boxes, chair frames and tables. Some ancient cities, such as the first version of Troy (c. 2300 BC), had walls of sun-dried bricks twelve feet thick. Stone in Egypt was cut from cliffs in great courses by masons using wedges, and was taken away by a large force of labour. All blocks could be dressed and squared by hand, and big buildings could be built: the Great Hall of Karnak at Thebes, for example, measured 329 feet by 170.

Settled life came into existence in regions which were, during much of the year, uncomfortably hot in the day and cold at night. It was early realised, however, that thick walls could act as both insulators against, and reservoirs of, heat. Curved roofs had similar effects, as did a limitation of the number of windows, the growing of plants in courtyards, and narrow streets.

The early houses of temperate zones, such as Europe, differed since there was less need for heavy walls in houses and also less of a demand for city walls since, among other things, there were no irrigation works to be defended. Houses were more often, and earlier, individual units, often round. There were also peoples who lived on platforms of timber in the middle of lakes. Crete, meantime, had two-storey houses from 1700 BC – a typical house being supported by stone piers, with frames of timber, facing inwards onto courtyards approached by cloisters. The Cretans had staircases probably before anyone else did. Mycenae, more exposed to attacks from pirates, was surrounded by limestone fortress walls, the light coming through high windows.

All these urban achievements were far from the felt tents, wool-pile rugs and waggons of the Scythian nomads and others who constituted the most serious threat to all these societies. But they were close enough to the cities built, from adobe bricks, by the Nazca and Moche people of ancient Peru, though many villages of Central America and the Caribbean before Columbus remained loose and formless clusters except for a central open space[2]. The arch did not reach America before Columbus but the Mayas did have a form of vaulting to support their roofs. Two legs of the vault were drawn close together until the space could be bridged by capstones.

Trade in stone, obsidian, perhaps finished clay objects, preceded agriculture. Malachite, turquoise and dyes for cosmetics were among the earliest objects exchanged. Hard stones for grinding grain, as has been seen, were always sure of markets. Such trade and markets must, to begin with, have been arranged by pedlars, working on sufferance of states. Some early peoples – Hittites, Egyptians and Mycenaean Greeks – left their trade to be organised by officials, while in ancient Iraq private entrepreneurs were involved from the earliest times. From at least 2000 BC a type of currency in the form of silver rings or bars was in existence among Iraqi merchants. Cowrie shells served the same purpose in Asia and the East.

As the generations passed, political control in Iraq passed from Ur to Sumer, from Sumer to Assur, from Assur to Nineveh and from Nineveh to Babylon, but trade continued regardless, the ships being improved and the donkey caravans becoming slowly better organised. Though the Bible recalls the military achievements of Tiglath Pileser and Shalmaneser, it neglects the trade which brought Assyrians cotton from India and silver from Cilicia, and which may have caused the wars. Assyrian merchants had, for example, established their own quarters in numerous cities of Asia Minor by 1950 BC, regulating the traffic of copper, ensuring the departure of the caravans, making their Akkadian tongue a lingua franca throughout the Middle East and using Akkadian cuneiform to record transactions. Baskets, carpets and other textiles were sold before 3000 BC along the Euphrates and by then commerce had begun between Iraq and Egypt. Sargon of Agade in Iraq spoke of ships full of goods being moored outside his capital, in 2370 BC. A caravan route employing 200 donkeys, travelling twelve to fifteen hours a day, was soon in being between Armenia and all the cities of Iraq.

Egypt was more favoured agriculturally than were the cities of Iraq. Limestone was available from the mountains near by for its lavish building schemes (including the pyramids). But some imports were sought, all the same; particularly timber. Egypt went to Byblos in Syria for trees, to Lebanon for cedar, later to Crete for olive oil, and in exchange sold salted fish, flax and papyrus, ox hide and rope, alabaster and lentils – and gold, a state monopoly.

2

Among the earliest of commodities exchanged for profit were slaves. It may be that slavery, like politics, anticipated agriculture. But the earliest societies seem, in fact, not to have relied on slave labour. More important in such societies was the forced labour demanded of the people themselves. Thus neither the economy of the earliest days of Iraq nor that of China employed slaves on a large scale. But, though slaves were always rare in China, that ceased to be so in the Near East by about 2000 BC at latest. By then Egypt, for example, was importing large supplies of slaves from 'Nubia' or Syria and even re-exporting them to Iraq. Thenceforth, most references to agriculture or to large-scale building in antiquity must imply the employment of slaves. The King's Chamber in the Great Pyramid of Gizeh (2900 BC) was roofed by fifty-six slabs of stone, each weighing 54 tons. Slaves in thousands were responsible for moving them, as they were for building other great works of ancient Egypt which survive to puzzle, as well as to impress, the visitor with their grandeur.

Long before that, slaves had begun to be imported to Iraqi cities as objects of commerce, and so a process began which, in one form or another, has continued ever since. Female slaves in particular were sought for work in Iraqi spinning workshops. Soon, too, slaves who had for a time all been the property of the state could be bought by private persons. Eventually, many households in Iraq had three slaves each[3]. That pattern was copied elsewhere.

Most slaves began as prisoners of war, or were slave girls procured by raids into the hills from among nomads, but they were subsequently often bred in captivity. People also became slaves because of debt or hunger, or were sold as children by poor parents. Sometimes, too, people might be seized by creditors to become slaves. Even on occasion, they might sell themselves. Crimes were sometimes punished by enslavement.

These early slaves of the Near East were rarely members of an unbreakable caste, for they could often work their way to freedom. A free woman might marry a slave; and slaves could acquire property. Slavery, it seems obvious, did much to mingle races.

10

A Short Introduction to War

God of the silver bow! thy shafts employ,
Avenge thy servants, and the Greeks destroy

Chryses's prayer, *The Iliad*, Book I

Contact between all these ancient peoples came from war as well as from commerce; and war, from the beginning, played a decisive part in establishing states. The city states of Iraq came into being when several tribes wished jointly to guarantee their defence as well as their production of food. Doubtless that was the case in Egypt too. The unification of both was secured by force and, in Egypt, the fighting (about 3000 BC) is thought to have lasted for many generations. Still, it may be that the earliest forms of war were throughout the world much like a kind of sport, such as indeed it still seemed to Robert Louis Stevenson when he went to the South Seas in 1888: not often very destructive, an encouragement and outlet for energy. Sophisticated weapons changed all that.

Antler and stone axes assisted hunting tribes against each other, as well as against animals and trees. Bows and arrows, like slings and lances, preceded the sowing of the first wheat seed by the first farmer. Afterwards, copper axes were used for war as soon as they were used against scrub oak, sloe, hawthorn and wild acacia. By 3000 BC war had assumed a familiar shape. Iraqi kings organised their men in the form of a phalanx, while Egyptians preferred the horde, relying on pastoral tribes living near them to do the serious fighting on their behalf. In Egyptian practice, a day would be fixed for the battle rather as if it were a lawsuit. The fighting would be postponed if the enemy were not ready, and it was formally accepted that the gods would give victory to the better army. Such forms were sometimes followed in ancient China and in the European Middle Ages. But how to apportion the value of a good army, or a good weapon, was as hard then as at any later time. Thus the long bow and arrow, introduced from Central Asia, is held to have given the Semites of Akkad their victory about 2500 BC over the lance-carrying soldiers of Sumer, while the triangular bow, helmet and coat of mail are regarded as having helped them to defeat Egypt about 1200 BC[1].

The horse and two-wheeled chariot allegedly developed by the Milani, a tribe of Asia Minor, were used to decisive effect by the Hittites and Kassites, who conquered Iraq about 1500 BC. Subsequently, the Assyrian Empire at its grandest depended on the battering ram and the siege engines, perfected by Rome, as well as on a method of organisation whereby every able-bodied man knew that he was liable to be called up to serve, and whereby engineers, officers and shock troops each knew their allotted tasks as if they constituted regular professions. Later, Babylonian kings had large standing armies which fought continuously for years. Organisation, technology, courage and good leadership, as much as good luck, contributed to victories then as now.

Bronze weapons' superiority over those of copper and stone was great, perhaps comparable to the advantage given by gunpowder. Iron and steel followed. The Hittites won victories for many years because of their possession of iron weapons, the secret of which the royal smiths kept to themselves for as long as they could. But even now none will say that the victories of the numerous sea-raiders which caused such upheavals in the Mediterranean about 1200 BC were due primarily to the use of special weapons.

The importance of war in the foundations of history is shown by the fact that the earliest epics of almost every country deal with a conflict of one sort or another. The longest poem in the world, for example, the Hindu *Mahabharata*, revolves round the struggle at Kurukshetra between the Kauravas and the Pandavas over land-rights, and is set in the fertile but strategic region north of Delhi. In this and every other epic, the story told is essentially how the foundations of the kingdom concerned were established by war and the heroism of legendary warriors. The end is usually happy: 'the Pandavas ruled long and peacefully. They finally renounced the kingdom . . . and went to the City of the Gods in the Himalayas'[2]. Only the Chinese thought of their first monarchs as sages, rather than as warriors.

Book Two

The Age of Agriculture

The doctrine that our remote ancestors had simple law dies hard. Too often, we suppose that, could we get back to the beginning, we should find that all was intelligible, and we should then be able to watch the process whereby simple ideas were smothered by technicalities. But it is not so. Simplicity is the outcome of technical subtlety – it is the goal, not the starting point. As we go backwards, the familiar outlines become blurred: the ideas become fluid and, instead of the simple, we find the indefinite.

F. W. Maitland, *Domesday Book and Beyond*

During the ten thousand years between the birth of agriculture and the Industrial Revolution, the three most important changes were, first, an increase in the population of the world; second, an increase in the acreage of land placed under the plough; and third, the growth of a number of communities in which it was accepted that the individual might have rights as well as duties.

One should not overestimate the land cultivated.* Even in 1870 only a quarter of the German Empire was under the plough. Similarly, the mind's eye, when looking at the past, should not imagine a countryside of cultivated prairies. Rather it should imagine a field cut out, on high scrubland or perhaps out of a forest; or a group of small fields, possibly protected by some defensive structure against bandits or marauders, as was the case in Africa until recently.

The third change occurred among certain European peoples which depended on rainfall to water their crops, lived in cities and were influenced by Greek thought and by Christianity.

It should be realised too that, while a history of a sort can be fashioned for Australasia, Africa and America before 1500 or 1750, the population of the world was concentrated around the Mediterranean and in Asia, with some increase in northern Europe.

* *A population of 750 million (such as the world had in 1750) would need about 1,200 billion acres to support it.*

11

The Masters of the Old World

To the world when it was half a thousand years younger, the outlines of all things seemed more clearly marked than to us. The contrast between suffering and joy, between adversity and happiness, appeared more striking. . . . Every event, every action, was still embodied in experience and solemn forms which raised them to the dignity of a ritual. For it was not merely the great facts of birth, marriage and death which, by the sacredness of the sacraments, were raised to the rank of mysteries; incidents of less importance, like a journey, a task, a visit, were equally attended by a thousand formalities; benedictions, ceremonies, formulae . . . we at the present day can hardly understand the keenness with which a fur coat, a good fire on the hearth, a soft bed, a glass of wine, were formerly enjoyed . . . Then again all things in life were of a proud or cruel publicity. Lepers sounded their rattles . . . Every order and estate, every rank and profession, was distinguished by its costume . . . The contrast between silence and sound, darkness and light, like that between summer and winter, was more strongly marked than it is in our lives. The modern town hardly knows silence or darkness in their purity nor the effect of a solitary light, or a single distant cry.

J. H. Huizinga, *The Waning of the Middle Ages*

Of the four major innovating societies, a stable despotism was eventually established in China. Whether or no the Hsia or the Shang, or perhaps even the Chou, were the first historical dynasty, hereditary monarchy certainly managed China from about 1000 BC onwards. Though not always able to resist conquest, China could usually absorb her conquerors. Under the Han dynasty, after 202 BC, Chinese landowners consolidated their claims on the peasants, as the state did upon the landowners who became bureaucrats. But Confucianism restrained the systematic misuse of power. Hence a political structure which enabled the Chinese monarchy to expand throughout the valley of the Yellow River, and then south to the Yangtze. Neither landlord nor tax official under the Han dynasty demanded so much from the peasant that he could not survive.

Chinese agriculture continued to depend on the methodical

cultivation of a single crop, rice; a fixed system of water supply; and strong defences, such as the Great Wall of the third century BC, behind which a network of roads and canals could be constructed to ensure good harvests and the swift carriage of imperial orders.

About half the area of modern China was probably under some kind of loyalty to the Chinese monarch as early as the Chou dynasty; later the area gradually grew, despite a long period of confusion between 400 and 200 BC. During that confusion seven Chinese states fought each other. The victory went to the Ch'in, based in what is now Shensi province. From that family the West derives the name 'China'.

Egypt survived as an independent state till its conquest by Persia in 525 BC but, after vicissitudes, continued recognisable as the old Egypt till it fell to Rome in 30 BC. Thereafter, Egypt constituted the richest part of the Roman Empire, and its method of despotism contributed a great deal of the style to the Empire which was established by Augustus on the ruins of the old Roman Republic. Egypt also marked the history of Africa indelibly: the Sudanese principality of Kush, for example, with its capital at Meroe, copied Egypt's political system and till the first century AD carried on a vigorous trade with the Mediterranean world. Other African monarchies copied Kush and others them, the torch of the pharaohs thus being passed on continuously: even perhaps by the same families, since it has been suggested that the royal family of Kush, themselves descendants of Egyptian rulers, established a new government, after the fall of their original fief, in the region between Lake Chad and the Nile.

The cities of Iraq became the basis for the Assyrian and Babylonian empires before being conquered by Persia in 539 BC. They were by far the richest part of the Persian Empire, which itself survived till conquered by Alexander in 331 BC at the battle of Gaugamela. That battle handed over most of the Near East to European rulers till the coming of the Arabs in the seventh century AD. For them, too, the region survived as a granary and a centre of government for many generations, until the depleted irrigation works were allowed to fall in at the time of the Mongol invasions in the thirteenth century.

The civilisation of the Indus valley, meantime, spreading a thousand miles along the river and several hundred on either side, particularly along the coast, became the focus for a congeries of Indian monarchies established in imitation of it, along other rivers.

From the start, in what Mortimer Wheeler called its 'exacting and minatory environment', it traded, thereby acting as an essential geographical link with the West and China[1]. True, the 'Aryan' invaders who fell upon India about 1500 BC, as they did upon Greece and Asia Minor, emerging from pasture lands near the Caspian Sea which they had exhausted, were ethnically different from the founders in the Indus civilisation. But though the manner of their victory led to the unusual system of segregation known as 'castes', the survival of several ancient gods and goddesses from the Indus valley suggests that the Aryans were partially absorbed by those whom they conquered. That in turn led to the establishment of tribal monarchies, which were gradually institutionalised to form the basis of ancient Indian society, whose unique feature remained the castes which, in the words of a modern Indian historian, Romila Thapar, 'localised many of the functions which would normally be associated with a truly oriental despotism'[2]. The subsequent political history of India is partly the history of dynastic power, partly that of village councils and guilds, and partly that of castes and how they interacted.

By the fourth or third century BC these different political manifestations had been overtaken by imperial authorities which, under the Mauryas or the Moguls, lasted in one way or another, feebly or forcibly until the Europeans came.

As for the Mayas in Yucatan, their ancient civilisation based on the calendar and the irrigation ditch continued in, latterly, a degraded form until the fifteenth century. They did not, however, evolve a unified empire and remained an agglomeration of city states comparable to those of the early days of Iraq.

Outside these founding civilisations, many peoples sought successfully to emulate the forerunners. Most of them also strove to achieve predictability of crops by insisting on despotic monarchies whose ambitions were to plan the economy with care. But in the wet northern regions of Europe and Asia, where agriculture could be organised without hydraulic arrangements, many of the customary freedoms and much of the mobility within hunting tribes survived.

However agriculture was organised, no serious change in the way of living of these peoples and the neighbours who imitated them occurred till after AD 1700. Until then a majority in every settled community were concerned with tillage. Opportunities for barter and exchange were exceptional, and arose primarily in connection with the exploitation of natural products of woodlands and wastes. In that respect, 'the needs of most people were indeed equal', as the Orwins* put it. The kings, noblemen, courtiers, priests of this religion or that, knights, artists and craftsmen were a small minority, all supported by workers on the land. The men who made history were, Gibbon says, enabled to survive by eating the produce which was 'the result of the patient toil of the husbandmen'[3]. The fields, which produced these fruits so successfully over so many generations, were literally the work of men's hands. Even the fields of Europe represent the subjugation of nature by men after a long struggle, 'often with inadequate weapons, and at a cost impossible to measure', again in the words of the Orwins[4]. The pioneering process of clearing the land by girdling, cutting and burning trees, the planting of corn amid the stumps of dead trees, was still a major endeavour in the nineteenth century AD. So was the business of turning treeless prairie into wheat fields. The history even of Rome was an elaboration on the theme of how the minority who lived in towns fed themselves by the labour of the majority who did not.

Change was modest. The Egyptian priests of the sun would not have found themselves immediately at home at the court of the Sun King, Louis XIV, nor among the Aztec worshippers of the sun conquered by Cortes. Yet they would have recognised, in those polities, the absolute dominance of religion, as well as the unquestioned agricultural basis of the absolute and hereditary monarchy. True, such priests might have been baffled by the change towards mystical, as well as intellectually inquisitive, religion which occurred about 500 BC (leading to Zoroastrianism, Buddhism, Confucianism, the Eleusinian mysteries and ultimately Christianity). Perhaps they would have been astonished at the ease with which Jehovah, the god of the Jews, had inspired an international religion (though not one recognised by Jews) long after Moses had led his band of followers out of Egypt. But all Egyptians would have been at home with the plough, the sickle and the ox, as well as the wheat, barley and fruit whose cultivation occupied the majority of men in AD 1800 as in 1800 BC; as with the vast peasantry, which still in AD 1800 constituted between eighty and ninety-five per cent of the population even of Europe[5]. They would have recognised the roles of the great estate and the small farmer, the tenant and the landless labourer, the vineyards

* C. S. and C. S. Orwin, authors of The Open Fields, a great work of historical investigation into English agricultural economics.

and the wine, and though the plough would have differed from the one with which they were familiar, they would perhaps have understood more than we would today a society in which 'agriculture, in the great majority of the provinces . . . may be considered a huge factory for the manufacture of corn', as it was expressed by the commissaries of the provincial assembly of Orléanais in 1789[6]. They would, too, have recognised a world in which, normally, little happened: 'from the beginning of the sixteenth century, agricultural life in the province of Córdoba was slow, sulky life, without accidents, without emotions, a life without history', as Díaz del Moral, the historian of Spanish anarchism, put it[7].

Furthermore, the changes that did occur in these agricultural societies continued to be caused, like the beginning of agriculture itself, primarily by natural phenomena or by climate. The wet warm climate of the Ganges always had a pervasive effect on Indian history, enabling the establishment, on the large plain, of strong, unitary kingdoms. In Spain, only forty per cent of the soil has ever been cultivable: the rest is mountainous or barren. So the 'cruel winters and the burning summers', wrote Claudio Sánchez Albornoz, '. . . uneven and uncertain rains, limited fertility of the majority of the soil . . . have hardened the . . . peasantry forced to suffer the inclemency . . . during millennia'[8]. The lack of a frontier has been the deciding feature of Russian history: indeed, 'Russia *is* the frontier', wrote Tibor Szamuely[9]. Russian farmers must confine livestock indoors two months longer than European farmers; while the network of navigable waterways, poor soil in the north, vagaries of rainfall (heaviest where it does least good), as well as the belt of fertile black earth (250 million acres) deriving from humus (vegetable mould) have been the main motors of Russian history. The black earth area has always produced seventy per cent of Russian wheat, though, over the course of its recorded history, Russia has averaged one bad harvest out of every three. The 'barbarian' invasions of the Roman Empire in the third and fourth centuries AD perhaps derived, Joseph Needham speculated, from the 'progressive or cyclical dessication' of the Gobi and steppe regions where the Huns, Goths, Saxons, Franks, Mongols and Vandals had, presumably, previously cultivated their flocks in peace[10].

Some too have alleged that declining rainfall about 250 BC was the explanation for the end of the rural simplicity (and discipline!) which characterised the life of early Rome. Since there was not enough rain to maintain adequate water in the rivers, pools and marshes were formed which became breeding grounds for mosquitoes. They brought malaria. When the rain came again, in the late second century, the character of the countryside had already changed, and the vine and olive had been introduced into the best fields of Italy, causing Rome to depend on imports of corn for her bread – hence the grain imported, the trade from Egypt, with its despotic tradition, the free loaves, the crises of the last hundred years of the Republic and the establishment of the Principate.*

The clarity of Greek light obviously influenced Greek art, and perhaps explains the clarity of Greek philosophy in ways which historians who primarily interest themselves in the 'economic and social forces which underlie the history of peoples'[11] may overlook. The fourteenth century AD in Europe saw the beginning of a cold wet period, caused by a small advance of the glaciers. Heavy rain ruined innumerable harvests as well as the English vineyards of the early Middle Ages, and fishing replaced agriculture as the chief economic activity of northern countries such as Scandinavia and Iceland. Some have called the centuries after the fourteenth the 'little ice age'. The first English economic historian, Thorold Rogers, 'never noticed, in any earlier century, such a continuity of dearth as there was from 1630 to 1637, from 1646 to 1651, from 1658 to 1661 and from 1693 to 1699, in each case inclusive'[12]. The winters of 1709 and 1740 were arctic in intensity in Europe, and were followed by very cold springs and summers: Saint Simon paints a chill picture of Louis XIV's courtiers pressing their noses to the windows of the Château at Versailles, shivering, waiting for the news, which they rightly suspected of being bad, from the battle of Malplaquet: a contest which occurred in early September. In 1316, 1675 and 1816, Le Roy Ladurie wrote, 'all Europe spent the summer round the fire'[13]. Doubtless there were compensations. Long cold winters encouraged more people than just the men of Iceland to stay at home and read, and more than just the Scots to listen to family prayers: 'Snow and cold weather can . . . help to explain the high degree of literacy in Alpine populations,' says Professor Cipolla[14]. The hailstorm of 13 July 1788 devastated the harvest of that year in France, helping to cause the famous shortages of 1789; while the earthquake of 1756 in Lisbon caused men to question the idea of progress. 1816 was the worst summer ever recorded in northern Europe: there was

* Discussed at length on page 73.

frost in July. There was scarcely a harvest at all. The consequence was famine, the last major such event in the northern hemisphere until the government-inspired dearth of Russia in the 1930s.

About some natural occurrences or climatic changes there will always be speculation. Were the lake villages of Central Europe of 500 BC built because of the rise of the lakes themselves, and was that rise the result of the cold spell of that era? And was the decline of the Maya civilisation explicable by changes in the weather? Did the earthquake on Thera about 1500 BC really smash the Minoan fleet and thus also the 'first empire which built its fortune on the waves'; or was it some other natural disaster? Did the first civilisation of the Indus valley collapse because of an excessive flood from the great river, a failure in hydraulic arrangement which China, Egypt, Babylon and the Mayas managed to prevent?

These speculations border on tautology. Civilisation began in river valleys. Both Egypt and Babylon depended on seasonal floods to bring back fresh soil, to irrigate and to fertilise the land. Copious spring rains had the same effect. But rivers were everywhere, till the age of railways, the motors of both commerce and (through the waterwheel) industry. The modern industrial age even began, in the eighteenth century, with the creation of false rivers: canals. The absence of long inland waterways, wrote Geoffrey Blainey in *The Tyranny of Distance*, explains much of Australia's early history. 'L'Angleterre, c'est une île,' said Michelet, as if that explained all. Nor is a geographical explanation of history, such as was favoured by Montesquieu (and more recently, indirectly by Fernand Braudel[15]), particularly new: in the fifth century BC, one follower of Hippocrates attributed the mildness of Asiatics to the tamer conditions in which they lived, and the capacities for endurance and high spirits of Europeans to their hard struggle for existence. Madame Curie, on return from a visit to Spain, said that if she had been born in Andalusia she would never have invented radium, a judgement which overlooked the unpromising atmosphere for medical research in Madame Curie's own birthplace, Warsaw. Two points can be made: first, weather has had a greater effect in countries which have depended on rainfall and less on those which have had to establish hydraulic administrations; second, as many have been stimulated to achievement by the harshnesses of geography as have been bowed down by them. The Attic Greeks are a good example of that. Who would have thought it likely that so many achievements of civilisation could be begun in the Iraqi desert between two rivers, with a hot climate, where there was no building stone, no minerals and no timber (save palm trees)? Yet Sumer and Babylon triumphed over those deficiencies because the soil was fertile, because there were spring rains and hence there was water for irrigation if it could be organised, and because the rivers gave access to valuable stone and metals in remote highlands. Israel, Rome, Venice and the Netherlands, as well as Athens and Sumer, responded to natural deficiencies with resource.

The question as to how far the different civilisations discussed here knew of or were in touch with each other may have been perplexing the reader. The answer to this can be explicit in relation to the Old and the New World: no connection between them existed before the end of the Middle Ages. The Near East and India were, however, in touch from the earliest days. On the other hand, China was largely isolated – even from India, by the Himalayas and by the steppes of Central Asia. The beginning of any real contact must be dated from the time of the Emperor Wu, who reigned from 140 till 87 BC. His wars with Central Asian nomads led him into the pursuit of the large Central Asiatic horse which could carry an armed horseman – unlike the Mongolian pony, the only horse bred in the steppes north of China. Eventually he secured this horse by means of a most adventurous expedition against Bokhara. From Bokhara, the Chinese learned of the existence of Greece, Persia and later of Rome. The famous viceroy Pan Chao advanced to the Caspian Sea with 70,000 men, and envoys went to the Mediterranean. Later, Roman envoys went to China. Both land and sea routes between the East and the West came to be used for trade – Roman glass and gold were exchanged for Chinese silk. But this contact should not be overestimated. By the time the Arabs conquered the lands between the two old civilisations of the Mediterranean and China, the trade had fallen away. The Han dynasty collapsed in AD 221 and afterwards an 'age of confusion' ensued. This era has become the subject in China of innumerable legends and folk tales. But it was of importance only in the field of literature, and not that of commerce[16]. Contact between China and Persia, and China and India, nevertheless continued. Pilgrimages were made by Chinese Buddhists to India; a Nestorian church was established in the T'ang capital, Ch'ang-An; the last pre-Muslim Persian king died in Ch'ang-An while Arab traders established communities in Chinese ports – two mosques being built, one at Canton, one at Ch'ang-An. They are still in use.

12
Master Crops

Quetzalcoatl, the Plumed Serpent . . . brought corn to men, turning
himself into an ant in order to steal it from the ants who had hidden
it. Thus men were the sons of Quetzalcoatl . . .

Frederick Peterson, *Ancient Mexico*

The lucky grains were sent down to us
The black millet, the double-kernelled,
Millet pink-sprouted and white.
Far and wide the black and the double-kernelled
He reaped and acred . . .

Origin-Legend of the Chou tribe (c. 900 BC)

('He' is Hou Chi, 'Lord Millet'.)

1

The first crop of the world in terms of importance has been, for
many centuries, rice. It still provides the main diet for six out of
ten people in the world. Its likely original home was South-East
Asia but it is not clear who domesticated it first. Perhaps the
Chinese were responsible, between 2000 and 1500 BC, though
rice is known to have been grown, wild, in Thailand about 3500
BC. To begin with its cultivation was limited to one harvest a year
instead of the two or three which make the modern rice field
almost a factory. But even one harvest of rice needs to be grown
in muddy water constantly in movement. Clear water attracts
mosquitoes, and stagnant water does not give enough oxygen.

Rice, since time immemorial, has been grown in nurseries, to
begin with. The small plants reared there are transferred to grow
in soil which, when well manured, gives a higher yield than wheat
fields. Rice is both land-intensive and labour-intensive: fallow is
never needed. Hence there has never been a rotation of crops.
Rice has never had its centre in the oldest focus of Chinese
agriculture, the estuary of the Yellow River valley, for there grain,
millet and wheat have been the characteristic crops. Rice has had
its centre in the plain of the Yangtze River. It is there that most
of China's canals were dug.

71

The Chinese developed their classic pattern of agriculture between 1500 BC, by which time rice was certainly domesticated, and 500 BC, when their system of canals was firmly established. Millet, wheat, buckwheat, sorghum and barley continued to be grown, but the Chinese did not leaven bread (partly because they did not have the vine) and unleavened flatbread is most unsatisfactory if eaten continuously. There was never much beef in China and, while some emperors 'ate only game', pigs continued to be the main livestock. The scarcity of both cattle (except for the invaluable water buffalo) and horses meant that, in China, human excreta has always played as large a part as animal manure in fertilising fields.

After its success in China, rice was cultivated everywhere in the Far East, in the Philippines, Indonesia, Malaya and Japan (though not till 100 BC), displacing millet and usually helping the establishment of sober societies, ruled by authoritarian monarchs. India also began to grow rice, which, with some wheat and other grain as well, became the staple crop there too. All these agricultures depended primarily on irrigation, not rainfall. All concerned observed that rice harvests fail less often than harvests of wheat, providing that the water supplies are properly managed.

The threat posed by famine in the age of agriculture justified, in most minds, disciplined despotisms.

The first Chinese Empire was established around the need to ensure these supplies of food: the centre being the city of Hsiao-T'un (Anyang), a city carefully laid out in zones, the quarter of the palace and that of the artisans being easily distinguished in their present state, with rectangular houses of wood on terraces of beaten earth, pitched or gabled roofs supported by stone, and sometimes with bronze bases. From this city, the Shang dynasty about 1200 BC probably ruled a stable state, dominating a series of village communities. How that half-mythical dynasty gained power is a mystery, though presumably it was by force – or by the manipulation of real, or imagined, fears of war. Its more historical successors, the two Chou dynasties and afterwards the Ch'in, established their rice-powered state with meticulous attention to maintaining regular supplies. The security which this ensured must have been the main explanation for the rise in the population of China so steadily in comparison with the dramatic declines and uneasy recoveries in such countries as Egypt or ancient Iraq.

The history of societies dependent on grain was more complicated. Consider some examples from the history of the Mediterranean in classical days. In the days of the Mycenaean kingdoms, Greece had a good supply of wheat and barley, presumably because its population was so small. In the fifth century BC the cultivable acres of Greece were given over to vineyards and olive farms whose produce was exchanged with the 'barbarians', above all those who lived in the Ukraine, for grain of numerous types. Athens's empire was created out of the need to guarantee her supply of grain. The silver from the mines of the Laurium financed the navy which ensured the grain. The ensuing economic problems resulted in the quarrels within Greece and the instability of the political system there. Why did Athens fall? asked Maurice Bowra, and answered, because she was too poor, the alliance which she directed was too diverse, her gods were overthrown by more profound cults and her science turned sterile. 'Athens fell because she depended on corn from the Black Sea,' he went on, 'and, when cut off, she had no choice but surrender'[1].

Even more restless was the history of grain in Rome. Italy about 500 BC was a land of small farms, though the cultivated area might not have been greater than the 'built-up area' today. As noticed before, the landscape was without the olive, the vine or the cypress, as well as the tower and the bell, those characteristic sights of historic Italy, all of which were subsequently imported. A few rich proprietors might have had as many as 200 acres of fields, but even seventy acres was unusual, and probably over half the farms of the tribes of Italy were of five acres or less. This majority of the farmers grew wheat or barley, reared goats and pigs, perhaps a flock of sheep and, if rich, owned a pair of oxen or mules. Slaves were fewer than free labourers. Most Romans until 300 BC were farmers, working from their houses in the city or living in small, semi-fortified villages in the neighbourhood. The city of Rome was supplied by its own farmers. The disciplined way of life of early Rome was underpinned by a simple agricultural self-sufficiency.

The conquests by the Romans in central Italy led to the formation of a state domain, *ager publicus*. Out of this conquered territory large estates began to be formed. Legally all those estates were supposed to be less than 500 *iugera* (333 acres) but that rule was often broken.

In 232 BC the then consul Caius Flaminius tried to carry out a programme to encourage prosperity by establishing allotments for poor farmers on conquered land, including land farmed by rich landlords. The Senate was hostile, believing in the sanctity of private property, above all of their own by now large estates, and vetoed the plan. Flaminius ignored them and took the matter to the Assembly of the Roman people where his father, a senator, in the name of paternal authority, dragged him from the platform. But the law was passed. Instead of prosperity the era of demagoguery began. The government, to keep the price of bread low, encouraged the import of grain. They began to demand that commodity from all conquered enemies. This they distributed free or at a subsidised price, beginning a characteristic Roman food policy – learned from the East, for Egypt had a custom of giving away free boiled meat to the poor in a field outside cities known as 'the Table of the Sun'; in 1064 BC, the Emperor of China had set up a store of grain to be sold cheaply if the harvest were bad. Thereafter more and more Roman farms abandoned corn for vines, olives, horticulture and pasturage.

These changes were encouraged by a temporary one to a less rainy climate. (The olive, a native of the east Mediterranean, had been known in Greece for a long time, but was not seen in Italy before 400 or 300 BC.) All these new crops were best grown on large estates, often on a mixed farm. Small farmers frequently gave up the struggle (and went into towns) or were forced into the hands of usurers. The owners of large estates preferred to employ slaves rather than free men, despite the difficulties which slaves always caused. The influx of destitute farmers to the city of Rome in turn worsened that city's grave problem of food. These events led to the political crisis of Rome in the first century BC.

In the early part of that century, the price of grain in Rome rose: pirates on the sea were interrupting supplies between Africa and Italy. The Senate approved provisions of free grain but even the Roman economy could not afford to issue them indefinitely. The tribune Gabinius proposed that a command should be conferred on Pompey in order to put down the pirates. The Senate opposed the idea for fear of what Pompey would do with that command afterwards. The 'mob' thereupon stormed the Senate, and the 'people' confirmed Pompey's appointment. That by itself lowered the price of grain. The price fell further when Pompey beat the pirates off the sea in three weeks. Ten years afterwards prices of grain were again rising. Cato, who was by then consul, distributed subsidised grain, as did his enemy Clodius, the unscrupulous tribune who was the Roman agent of Pompey and Caesar during the years of their alliance. In a few years, a further crisis brought Pompey to supreme power. But his reluctance to force recalcitrant suppliers to give up the grain that they were hoarding (some of them were his own old soldiers settled on new land) turned the populace against him. The scarcity continued and led to the overthrow of the Republic.

After the civil wars, Augustus introduced a distribution of grain to 300,000 citizens. This *annona*, the characteristic item of social security aid to those whom Gibbon described as 'lazy plebeians', was eventually changed by Alexander Severus to the provision of loaves[2]. Thereafter, all free men were eligible for tickets for loaves and the distribution continued, despite the failure of the imperial government to prevent both the sale and the inheritance of tickets. Other free issues from time to time at Rome included oil and pork. Wine was sold at subsidised prices. 274 public bakeries produced both free bread and the loaves put on sale. About AD 350 there were 120,000 daily recipients of six half-pound loaves in Rome, 80,000 in Constantinople where Roman practice was copied. Most of the grain used in these free issues, as well as the rest of Rome's needs, came from far away.

If Varus's famous legions had beaten the Germans in AD 9, the history of Roman grain would have been different. For there, as Tacitus put it, 'corn was the only produce required from the earth'. But the corn of Germany stayed beyond Rome's reach. Sicily and Egypt, and other parts of North Africa, remained the granaries of Rome, supplemented by Britain and Romania.

The collapse of Roman authority brought the civic munificence of the Empire to an end though Pope Gregory the Great revived the *annona*. In the meantime, a population used to free distribution had no more idea how to look after itself than a domesticated wheat could survive without cultivation. The reduction in the size of the Roman population to under 100,000 in AD 800 from a million in AD 400 was principally caused by famine, itself a consequence of the end of the free supplies of bread.

From the early Middle Ages onwards, in Europe, civic authorities intervened in matters affecting the supply not only of grain but of all food. The regulations recalled the rules of Rome and might suggest to the unwary that something like a modern state then existed. In France, for example, inspectors searched pigs' tongues for ulcers held to cause leprosy. In mediaeval Venice, fish was taken to a single place to be valued and examined. Several

Italian cities employed inspectors who checked against the sale of underweight loaves of bread. There was scarcely a town of importance which did not have what Venice described as its grain office, which controlled not only grain and flour but also sales of loaves. In Venice itself, flour could only be sold in two places: near St Mark's and on the Rialto. The Doge was informed of the level of stocks and, if he discovered that the city had reserves sufficient only for a year or for eight months, he would investigate. In England, the Assize of Bread of 1266 stipulated weights, consistencies, prices and colours of bread which have remained in being ever since. In 1390 the authorities of London were doing what the Emperor of China had started to do in 1000 BC: buying quantities of grain to relieve the poor during the dearth, keeping large reserves. Similarly, Philip II of Spain was kept 'minutely informed of the variations in the weather from seed time onwards'. It was not just an economic matter, 'for' Braudel reminds us 'famine, real famine, when people died in the streets, was still a reality'[3].

In the sixteenth century the small size of the area devoted to the production of grain meant that the Mediterranean world, despite its brilliance, was always close to famine. That dictated politics and war. As late as 1660, London, the richest city in Europe, was so short of food that 50 out of 250 people in a prosperous parish died of starvation. The last great European famine was that in Andalusia in 1882. The Balearic Islands could scarcely support their cities till the eighteenth century. There were numerous crises of subsistence in France in the seventeenth century, resulting in local famines which, on occasion, trebled the normal death roll. In short, famine was characteristic even in purportedly rich places till the age of modern transport, which enables food to be carried from place to place quickly: 'And great was the famine in the land,' runs a chronicle of 1192 in Castile or, 'and people were dying of hunger . . . and the famine in the kingdom was severe until the summer . . . and they were eating the animals and the dogs and the cats and even the boys that they could steal', runs another chronicle, from Andalusia of 1213[4]. Very often in history, deaths were attributed to 'plague' when starvation would have been a more exact name. In the eighteenth century in northern Spain, an average meal was still 'a little bit of black bread accompanied either by some kind of milk or some vile vegetable but, all in all, in such small quantity that there are those who get up from the table satisfied once in life'[5]. Flour made from acorns is said to have supported Spaniards in three-quarters of the Iberian peninsula before the Romans came.

Famine apart, winter diets in wheat-powered continents in the age of agriculture were bad. It was that, rather than the cold, that made winter a difficult time. Salt bacon, dried fish, bread and dried peas gave no protection against scurvy. Manors and monasteries had herb gardens, orchards and vineyards and some villagers had plots on which they could grow a few vegetables. But vegetables were usually neglected, out of a belief that meat gave strength and passion – an illusion from nomadic life. The Tartars, for example, with their diet of raw horse flesh, scoffed at bread eaters – 'those who eat the tips of weeds'. Mediaeval Europe was more carnivorous than it had ever been before, since the countryside remained open with huge pastures. Rich Englishmen may have eaten two or three pounds of meat a day, often raw. The meals eaten by people at a time of carnival were very different, in all countries, from ordinary meals.

3

Agriculture in the Americas, meantime, came to be based on maize and, to a lesser extent, on potatoes until the coming of Columbus. Maize is a crop as bounteous in its returns as rice and gives less trouble. Its grain is edible even before it is ripe. One grain of maize sown can produce a hundred grains in the following harvest, even in dry soil, more in well-watered land. Not much weeding is necessary. Two harvests are possible with irrigation. Grown on the edges of lakes or on the terraces of the Peruvian Andes, maize became, over many centuries, the staple food of the Americas, often eaten with tomatoes, peppers or fish. Maize was well established by 1000 BC. The Toltecs believed later that it had been brought, with other signs of material and spiritual progress, by the mysterious white god Quetzalcoatl, who was supposed to have stolen it from the god of the underworld.

The Spanish chronicler Oviedo described how in his day – say 1510 – in Central America seven or eight grains of maize would be placed in a hole in the ground made by a pointed stick and repeated after a pace. The Indian women ground the maize in a concave stone by means of another round one which they held in their hands, and added water to make a dough very like the basis of white bread. It was normally eaten hot and kept only a few

days after cooling. There were, however, many types of maize
and many methods of preparation: in Mexico the end-product
resembled an omelette more than a loaf.

Potatoes, indigenous to the Andes, were grown on high land
everywhere between Chile and Colombia before 1492. They never
competed with maize and were regarded as a substitute for it in
land above 11,000 feet, where maize cannot grow.

Bread was also made, in that remote America before Columbus,
from the tapioca plant, manioc or yuca, the roots of which were
grated, squeezed free of juice and boiled. The pulp was sieved
into cakes and cooked, on a griddle, to become 'cassava bread'.*
Indigenous to Brazil, tapioca was also cultivated in North America
and the Caribbean for many generations before the Spaniards
arrived. It is easy to grow. The Spaniard Las Casas wrote that in
many cases about two acres of land cultivated with it would yield
150 to 175 loads of cassava bread, and that a single load could
last a person for a month. The poisonous roots were grated,
drained of juice and baked into an unleavened flat bread which
kept for months. Another American plant was the sweet potato,
of various types.

From these and other plants, wines and beers of all sorts were
made: wine from pineapples, palm tips and mamey fruit, and beer
from maize, yuca and potatoes were all produced with as much
care as in the Old World. This beer from maize was made by
soaking the grain until it swelled and sprouted; it was then boiled,
taken from the fire and allowed to stand – it was ready to drink
after a day, at its best in four days and spoiled in a week.

Another bread was made in the Americas from the palm-like
zamia, by grating the stems of that plant, shaping the pulp into a
ball and leaving it in the sun, till it began to ferment. It was then
flattened and baked. Meantime, early Californians had a diet of
obscure molluscs, groundnuts, avocadoes, chili peppers and some
game such as guinea pig or duck. The guinea pig later on was to
be seen running in and out of houses in Peru in the days of the
Incas, combining edibility with fearlessness.

The Aztec peasant's food was porridge from maize as a beginning to the day, perhaps sweetened with honey and red peppers.
More important as a staple was an omelette made of dough from
a dried crushed kernel of maize, boiled with water, charcoal and

---

* Cassava is an old Caribbean Indian (Taino) word and bread from it for a long
time formed the main diet of poor people of all races living round the Caribbean.

lime, with other skins added, and probably often eaten with tomatoes and chili peppers. The Aztecs used no cooking oil from seeds. Their main meat was game (though they sometimes ate small dogs that did not bark), and they continued to eat insects and other forms of life long ago dismissed from the tables of the Old World: tadpoles, larvae, winged ants, white worms, newts and iguana. Turkey, muscovy duck and avocado also played a part in their diet, both being indigenous to the Americas. In the valley of Mexico, Spanish observers marvelled after 1492 at the system of dikes created to keep brackish water from flowing into sweet-water areas, and at the elaborate terraces and well-faced canals[6].

Now, societies based on maize needed control of water as much as those based on rice. Hence in America irrigation canals were constructed to divert water which, as in China, derived from sources other than rainfall. Hence too, the foundation of 'hydraulic monarchies' necessitating disciplined work by large labour forces.

By 3000 BC most settled communities were establishing semi-religious authoritarian monarchies, whose rulers already customarily succeeded their fathers. Assemblies there may have been in the cities of the earliest days of Iraqi agriculture. But there was there evidently no sense of a will of a majority. Those assemblies probably continued deliberation until practical unanimity was attained. In any emergency monarchical power was sought, and that power tended to be confirmed. Kingship always had in ancient Iraq a limited tenure. But the threat of emergency was never absent, and concentrated authority became the rule once cities began to argue with each other over drainage, supplies, transit and irrigation.

4

Fish also played a part in supplementing all early diets, whether based on rice, wheat or maize. Drying, salting, smoking, as well as accidental preservation by frost, made fish a major item of commerce. Salmon weirs and millponds were maintained to enable Christians to fast in style on Wednesdays, Fridays, and in Lent. Monasteries kept stew ponds and large breeding ponds. The Portuguese lower classes in the 1520s were thought by the Venetian ambassadors to live largely on cooked sardines. Many made money from buying or selling fish. Thus, German merchants of the Hanse in the Middle Ages made fortunes from salted herring

– which lasted a year, provided the gutting had been done well. Subsequently, in the fifteenth century, the Dutch introduced fifty-fathom nets for fishing at night, particularly off the English coast – one cause of the later Anglo-Dutch wars. Cabot's discovery of cod off Newfoundland gave New England its first major export, and supplied the British navy with salted fish for two hundred years.

Fish was more taken advantage of in the New World than in the Old. Vast numbers of different varieties of fish were to be found in the rivers of Brazil, for example, and the aboriginal inhabitants devised effective methods of preservation by cooking it in its own fat, over a slow fire, slicing and sealing it in earthenware jars. Turtle was equally important; 'a culinary complex itself', says Freyre, in old Brazil[7]. All the island and coastal peoples of America fished, sometimes in *canoas* (their word – hence canoe), sometimes by floating calabashes, usually with nets, occasionally by the use of *barbasco* – a general name for a fish stupefaciant.

5

All ancient peoples developed alcoholic drinks. Pride of place should be given to wine although through the ages more beer has been drunk – as is the case today.*

The wild vine flourished in the Caucasus. It was there, probably, that it was first brought into domestication. Disseminated by birds, it was widely distributed early on: as all Christians recall, Noah, a 'husbandman', had not only a vineyard, but made himself drunk. Vines were grown in Egypt by 4000 BC in the delta of the Nile, and wine was used as part of the rituals for Osiris. Vineyards became common, the grapes were pressed by dancing, and wine made in a way that did not change much until the twentieth century. Doubtless to begin with a drink for the rich – the Egyptian poor drank beer† – wine later became popular, perhaps under the influence of Greece or of Crete. In both countries, the vine was extensively cultivated, the wine being differentiated by place and year in the modern style. It began to be exported. The Greeks

* World wine production in 1978 was reckoned at 294 million hectolitres (Italy the largest producer), and beer at 801 million hectolitres (the USA the largest producer).
† The ordinary Egyptians used the foam of beer, it seems, rather than yeast to leaven their bread by fermentation, but unleavened flatbreads survived a long time in the ancient Middle East, not only for use in the Jewish Passover.

kept wine in large pots and, when exported, placed it in goat or pig skins, or clay amphorae.

These exported Greek wines were prevented from going bad by treatment with resin or by the addition of vine ash and other spices. Thus most of the wine exported by the Greeks was fortified: 'a sherry type'. About AD 100 the wooden barrel, with metal hoops, was introduced by the 'barbarian' Celts, to whom the Greeks exported a great deal. Barrelled wine kept better than did wine in amphorae. The barrel was an important Northern contribution to the life of the South. Most early wine drinkers made their wine strong and diluted it to drink. Only Scythians drank it pure.

At the time of Christ, Italy was reckoned the best producer of wine. France was then held to be too cold a place for grapes to ripen properly there. But vines need only an annual average temperature of 22 degrees centigrade. So the French vineyards were founded, in the days of the Antonines. The conquest by the Arabs of the eastern Mediterranean meantime ruined the estates where the vine had begun its history – it was forbidden to Muslims traditionally on the ground that some of Muhammad's generals had been found drunk on the battlefield. One caliph of Muslim Spain nevertheless ordered the destruction of vineyards; and he was overthrown. (Wine was sold freely in Spain under Islam, lending support to those who, like Claudio Sánchez Albornoz, argue that Muslim Spain was at heart Catholic and Latin.) Mediaeval Europe regarded the heavy drinking of wine as a most knightly action. The *Chanson de Guillaume*, for example, has a couplet which runs: 'And drinks of wine a gallon at two gulps: Pity the men on whom he wages war'[8].

Vines were much planted in France in the Middle Ages, particularly when new granaries in Germany were opened up by expansion eastwards in the twelfth century. Frenchmen turned many wheat fields over to vines, and exchanged wine for cheap grain. On the other hand, wine was as important in Christianity as it had been in the Egyptian ritual: without wine, there could be no mass nor, until the chalice became reserved to the priest alone in the thirteenth century, no communion for the faithful. Christianity considered wine to be essential for its mysteries and took it wherever it went, even to countries such as England where it had never been before. The South of Europe, however, continued to produce most of the wine and the North bought it. So a substantial trade followed. The bottles and corks now so associated with the wine trade were not used before the seventeenth century and were not common till the eighteenth. It was also only then that special vintages began, the expensive ones sometimes owing their fame to the routes which they took more than to the quality of wine concerned. The preservation of wine for long periods was, however, impossible before the exploitation of the great cork forests of Spain.*

Consumption of wine in the late agricultural age in wine-drinking countries might be 100 litres per year per person, as was characteristic of Valladolid in the sixteenth century. A similar figure has been quoted for Paris on the eve of the Revolution. Before the age of purification of water, the drinking of alcohol was the best way to swallow liquid without being poisoned. Tea, chocolate and coffee were not known, save in the regions where the plants concerned were indigenous: tea in China, and of a different sort in the Andes; coffee in Abyssinia; chocolate in Mexico. The Indians had soft drinks – the juice of mangoes and limes, sugar cane and rose-hip juice – but fruit juices in Europe were rare and, in northern Europe, where the orange and lemon were unknown, never met with. Milk could be found, but the scraggy cows of the age of agriculture were needed for ploughing, not milking, and the thin milk available was often foul, though watery whey was drunk widely. Milk in towns was as unhygienic as water was, probably being responsible for scrofula. Cattle in many towns were diseased and usually kept in bad conditions. Other peoples arranged alternatives. The Mongol armies drank the blood of their horses: half a pint every tenth day could be taken from each animal through a vein – and every horseman had eighteen mounts. Blood, it was said, had the merit of not needing to be cooled, nor did it involve transport costs. Other primitive herdsmen also drank blood: the Arabs drank camels' blood before the coming of Islam, while the Irish drank cows' blood mixed with milk, in the seventeenth century; the Masai do the same in the twentieth. Many nomads also made wine (kumiss) out of fermented mares' milk, and similar alcoholic juices have been concocted out of the milk of camel, tiger, deer, dog, yak and sheep.

Various forms of beer were also drunk from the earliest time. Technically, it was ale: it was without preservative herbs such as

---

* A line of Horace's makes clear that the properties of cork were known in antiquity, but it does not seem as if it was much used until the seventeenth century.

hops, which were not introduced till the late Middle Ages, at least in Europe. In ancient Iraq, forty per cent of the grain in some cities went on the manufacture of beer. A workman at Sumer might receive about 2·2 pints a day, and officials might get five times as much. Indeed, beer was sometimes used in Sumer in lieu of wages and probably evolved from bread-making there. (It was discovered early that bread made from sprouted grain, or malt, which had been dried, and then pounded, kept better than bread made from ordinary flour.) Both ancient Iraq and Egypt had numerous types of beer, some strong. In the end, Babylonians found that they did not have enough barley to feed their population with beer as well as bread and so took to wine as Egypt had done. Tacitus found the Germans drinking strong beer (which some have mistakenly supposed to be gin), and the Chinese had as many beers as they had crops. Peasants in Russia were brewing *kvass*, beer made from rye, from the Middle Ages onwards. Most beer was brewed domestically: something which could be done by any peasant family, though beer was sold in mediaeval Europe and was an early target for government regulation. Then there was cider, which apparently began to be made in the Basque country, for there the cider apple is apparently indigenous.

6

One distinguishing mark between European and other diets – here ancient Egypt, like other Middle Eastern civilisations, should be classed with the East – was the number of prohibitions in civilisations other than the European, sometimes associated with early attempts at hygiene. Egyptian priests were not permitted to eat fish, and not supposed even to look at beans. During the New Kingdom, pork was forbidden to priests: a legacy, it is said, from the Hyksos kings, who were believed to be of Semitic stock. Both Jews and Arabs, from the earliest days, were equally forbidden to eat pork – a characteristically nomadic view, it has been suggested, since the pig is an animal of a static culture. India gave the best example later of such bans. There, the list of impure items by AD 500 included: any meat cut with a sword; all carnivores; locusts, camels, and sour rice; any dish which had been sniffed; while when food had been eaten from an earthenware dish, the latter was to be broken and not used again. By AD 200 each Indian meal was supposed to consist of thirty-two mouthfuls. By then the inelegant custom had arisen whereby the wife waited on, and did not share the food of, the husband.

Perhaps, as so often, regulations give an indication as to what was not done, rather than what was. A characteristic meal in India between AD 500 and 1750 for a labourer might have been no more than milk and *ghi* (purified butter), some half-cooked vegetable to give it flavour, barley porridge mixed with a mustard stalk, and some fruit – all washed down with half-fermented water, in which the barley had been boiled. On the other hand, the rich ate as well in India as Trimalchio, the great gastronome, in Rome; and on all ceremonial occasions, even for poor people, elaborate meals were sought, including oxen, goat and sheep, and every spice, washed down by intoxicating wines made from honey. From the earliest days, herbs and spices were regularly imported into Asia from what is now Indonesia.

The basis of food during the age of agriculture was remarkably similar to that of today: wheat, rice and maize (with latterly potatoes) have been the dominant food crops of the last six thousand years, including the last two hundred. On top of that, first, peoples became accustomed to crops which were indigenous in other parts of the world – even the Chinese depended on rice, which did not originate on the Yellow River. Secondly, they became used to crops which were grown a long way from where they were consumed. A good example of this is to be seen in respect of wine. Apart from those generalisations, the picture is one of imprecision. Certainly diets can be estimated, for example, for Venetian sailors of the early fourteenth century, who had rations of two pounds of bread, an ounce of cheese, three pounds of salted pork, washed down with a quarter litre of wine – or, every day, between 4,530 and 6,470 calories. A sixteenth-century 'man of property' in England might eat per day an ounce of cheese, 1½ pounds of meat, a pound of bread, six ounces of herring, a quart of ale; or for a Polish peasant at the same time, also a day: four ounces of cheese, nearly two pounds of bread, four ounces of herring, three litres of beer, two ounces of butter, three ounces of 'husks' and an ounce each of peas and eggs[9]. But it is impossible to know how typical these estimates were, and how far such official diets were fulfilled: a similar official one for the British soldier in the First World War was rarely put into practice. How many people lived only on hard-boiled eggs as did the Florentine printer, Piero di Cosimo[10]? According to Vasari, he cooked fifty at a time and ate them one by one when he was hungry. Don Quixote's habitual diet was 'a stew of hash more beef than mutton most nights, boiled bones on Saturdays, lentils on Fridays, a young pigeon as a Sunday treat'; on that he spent three-quarters of his income. Was that characteristic? And how often would he have had that 'portion of badly soaked and worse cooked salt cod with some bread as black and grinning as his armour'? A few impressionistic recollections from literature give as likely a picture of what food in the age of agriculture was like as statistics do: thus Montaigne said that at the Crown Inn at Lindau he enjoyed a 'double headed' cabbage, of which they made soups all the winter, broths without bread and rice eaten from a big pot: 'There was great abundance of good fish which they serve up with the meat course: they disdain trout and eat only the roe . . . plenty of woodcocks and leverets . . . stewed plums, pear and apple tarts . . . sometimes, they serve up the roast first and the soup at the end, sometimes the other. The only dessert they have is pears, apples, which are very good, walnuts and cheese'[11].

13
Techniques

We always get back to the same questions: who was talking about gear wheels in −1st century Bactria? Did the Roman-Syrian merchant Chin Lun who visited China in +226 happen to take an interest in cartography. . . ?

Joseph Needham, *Science and Civilisation in China*

The history of the age of agriculture can be made to seem merely an elaboration on the history of the plough. The first 'scratch' plough, as has been seen earlier, was an enlarged digging stick or downward pointing spike, drawn by men to begin with, then later by two oxen attached to it by a pole. The triangular 'share' of this plough did not, as a rule, turn over the soil, and left a wedge of earth undisturbed between the furrows. Cross-ploughing – sometimes more than once – was therefore necessary. The consequence was a fairly square field. Cross-ploughing also breaks up soil well and brings more stones to the surface. In ancient Iraq, the first time a field was ploughed it was to break up the ground; the second time, a funnel often was attached to the plough to ensure an even distribution of seed.

It was soon realised that the wooden, often oaken, blade worked better if protected by a hard edge: so the Egyptians began to use a flint edge. Later, bronze and iron shares were used. The Romans had many iron ploughshares. Other peoples used pebbles skilfully wedged into holes in the wood. A bough of a tree with an iron tip was used in Britain before Caesar landed. That was also employed by the ancient Germans. This primitive plough was still to be seen in France in 1913, in Russia till 1930 and in other places in the Mediterranean and the East till even later, particularly in places where it is dry.

The Chinese, meantime, had about 1000 BC developed a curved 'mouldboard' to overturn the sliced sod. Used continuously for the cultivation of rice thenceforward, it was not, however, known in Europe for another 1,400 years.

Actually, the scratch plough (as has been seen) was not very effective in northern Europe, with its heavy soils and wet summers. So agriculture, when it was taken north, was till about AD

500 confined to drained hillsides or plateaus, with light soil. The teams of two oxen or mules used for ploughing in classical times were also too weak for heavier work.

The corn of Greece and Rome was grown on soil which grew worse, being scorched by drought in summer and drenched by a rain in winter which washed away the nutrients. Conditions were further worsened by the denuding of hillsides by woodcutting. The soil was held neither by dead leaves nor by dry roots. Hence the poverty of Greece which about 650 BC led quickly to debt once coinage had been introduced, and subsequently to the establishment of colonies. Cattle were scarce; so, therefore, was manure. The yield of Roman corn was poor, 4 grains to 1 sown compared with 200 to 1 in Babylon.

During the first century AD a bigger plough began to be used (perhaps invented in France) for heavier soil. It was usually pulled by as many as eight oxen. This had several advantages. It was easily moved from field to field. Ploughmen could regulate the depth of the furrow. But, for effective and economically worthwhile operation, it needed peace, stability and predictability. So it did not come into general use, even in northern Europe, until re-introduced, modified, by the Slavs about AD 600. This mediaeval heavy plough, the Slavs' only contribution to human improvement until the Russian novel of the nineteenth century, had three new elements: a knife-like iron blade in front of the plough – the coulter, which slashed vertically into the ground; a ploughshare in the form of a blade which cut horizontally through the ground at grass roots; and a mouldboard, like that devised in China, which turned over the soil or turf on to one side. This plough was sometimes set on wheels and it was drawn by a team of oxen, sometimes four, sometimes eight in number. It coped well with heavy soil and permitted the clearance of forests more easily than the simpler, old ploughs. Soil was thrown up with such force that cross-ploughing was not necessary, with a consequent saving of labour. Since these fields were usually ploughed clockwise, with the sod turned over inwards to the right, they came to look like a long low ridge, assuring a crop on the crest even in wet years, and one in the trough or furrow in the driest. The old squarish fields gave way generally to long ones.

The disadvantage of this heavy plough was that it needed a team of oxen to pull it and, while it did well on large estates, it was too unwieldy as well as too expensive for small holdings. Poor farmers, therefore, had to work in cooperation. Sometimes this had the effect of assisting the creation of large estates, sometimes it led to something close to cooperatives. The heavy plough encouraged the process by which manors created from virgin land in northern Europe were divided into common fields, themselves divided into strips, usually about 220 feet by 20 feet, and divided one from another in a disorganised manner.*

In many parts of the world this plough was never used. African agriculture remained based upon the scratch plough till the twentieth century, as did that of most of Asia and America until after 1492. In Africa's case, the unavailability of a good animal for traction was the main reason: oxen did not live long in the tropics. Indeed, the most powerful kingdom of South-West Africa before the Portuguese arrived there – Congo – knew only the hoe and the axe and no plough, though its farmers practised shifting cultivation and rotation of crops (principally millet, beans and sorghum)[1].

In the Americas, land was cleared by the girdling of trees, and occasionally felling – with stone or shell axes. Digging was done with a pointed and flattened heavy stick. The agricultural technique which most interested the Spaniards when they reached the Caribbean in the 1490s, and which plainly by then had a long history, was the heaping of earth into round, knee-high mounds several feet wide, to provide loose and well-aerated soil for root crops such as manioc or potatoes. Apart from the spade, the most frequent agricultural tool was the *macana*, a wooden broadsword with a cutting edge on both sides used as a machete and also as a knife – occasionally for digging, too.

The use of the heavy plough of northern Europe accounted for the increase of food and, therefore, of population in Europe during Carolingian times and, thence, at one remove, for Viking expeditions. It also led to the extension of arable land throughout Europe between the eleventh and the fourteenth centuries, and to the transformation of the Po valley from marshes and forests into the flat prosperous plain which it now is, with its drainage regulated (as a result of the initiative of the Benedictine and Cistercian monks). Perhaps too the Crusades and the expansion of religious orders in Europe may be explained by this growth of population and hence by the new plough.

Within a few hundred years, too, the efficacy of this plough had been enhanced by changes in the energy driving it: the horse

---

* See page 104 below.

became a competitor of the ox. There again, northern Europe differentiated itself from the rest of the world.

The horse, in a previous chapter, was shown as drawing chariots effectively for war, and being ridden chiefly for hunting. Apart from bits and bridles (known before 1000 BC in Europe), the only aid to horsemanship was the spur. Light horseshoes became common in the Mediterranean about 100 BC, when the Gauls and then the Romans adopted iron shoes. Though the Greeks had a saddle cloth of sorts, the earliest saddle in the West seems not to have been seen earlier than the first century AD, though it may have been used by 'barbarians' in Central Asia long before that[2].

The discovery of the stirrup transformed the history of the horse and of war. Spears needed no longer to be thrown, but could be held securely as lances and rammed home. Horsemen became the directors of the battlefield. Hence the equestrian knight, symbol of chivalry. In 732 Charles Martel held the Arabs at the battle of Tours, his cavalry equipped with stirrups[3]. A century later Charles the Bald, summoning his tenants-in-chief to the feudal host, ordered that they should attend mounted. Horses were by then being bred to be as big as possible. By 900, nomadic tribes and settled monarchies alike used stirrups, though not always iron ones: the Sassanids who crossed the Oxus about then with 10,000 horses were, Gibbon tells us, 'so poor that their stirrups were made of wood'[4]. (Horses were never cheap: in the time of the Cid in Spain, about AD 1000, a horse cost the equivalent of fifty oxen[5].)

The consequence was the organisation over the next generation in much of Europe of 'feudalism'.* Under this intricate system, nobles held land from kings in return for military service and sub-tenants held land from nobles on the same understanding. Anyone who could not, or would not, fulfil his new military obligations forfeited his grant of land. So the households of lords became schools in which boys were trained in chivalry, the creation of a 'self-conscious cosmopolitan military caste aware of its solidarity and soon aware of its traditions', as Marc Bloch described it, kept in good morale by *chansons de geste*, and trained by tournaments to keep fit. These knights wore heavy armour and bore pennons, shields and hereditary arms to enable recognition. Entry into knighthood (as in crafts or priesthoods) became a rite, often enacted in church, perhaps after a long vigil of prayer, with

* The word was invented in France about 1720.

swords blessed, the Church accepting knightly oaths. Horses were carefully trained and, as Persian horses had been, were protected by mail. Each knight was the captain of a small team of squires, grooms and servants, together with several horses, rather as a bullfighter is the 'sword' of his *cuadrilla*[6].

The idea extended at first no further than the Carolingian Empire. The Anglo-Saxons knew the stirrup. But they did not recognise its military use. Harold and his men rode horses with stirrups but dismounted to fight, while William's charged. After his victory, William established in England a horse-powered autocracy based on knights' service. Byzantium, Islam and other societies copied Europe, as did the Germans eventually (though the ceremonies of initiation for knights derive from ancient German practice). The wars of the Reconquista in Spain were fought, on both sides, by cavalry with stirrups: for example, the Almoravides in 1094 were said to have had 150,000 horse and only 3,000 foot.

Last among Europeans to become aware of the need for a professional class of cavalry were the Italians: in mediaeval Florence, armies still consisted of footsoldiers, and (as in modern Europe) all able-bodied citizens could be called upon to be soldiers at a moment's notice. No horses decided a battle in Italy before the battle of Montaperti (1260) outside Siena (where Manfred and the Siennese Ghibellines were able to inflict a great defeat on the Florentine Guelfs because of their judicious use of a few German cavalrymen)[7].

This apotheosis of the horse had important agricultural consequences. Sometime in the late ninth century heavy horseshoes of iron, like the light Roman ones but stronger, followed the stirrup into Europe from the East. They reached Byzantium by 900, by 950 they were habitual in the West for long journeys and by 1000 they were already cheap enough to be afforded by peasants.

The heavy horseshoes meant that hooves could stand up to hard terrain. The size of the horses bred for war (the *destriers*) made them competitive with oxen in agriculture, if only a new harness could be found which, unlike the yoke, did not press against the horse's windpipe and jugular vein. Another weakness of the old yoke was that the drawing came at the withers: too high for maximum effect. So, even with new shoes, horses could not be used for ploughing, nor harrowing, nor even heavy hauling.

At some time in the early Middle Ages, also from the Central Asian source whence all great equestrian innovations have come, far on the windy plains of the steppe, the modern horse-collar arrived. If its coming was unrecorded, its effect was great. It allowed the horse to pull as hard as the ox. But the horse can move faster, and is stronger, than the ox. It can cover twice the ground the ox can and can work two or three hours more a day. The question of speed was decisive in making farmers turn to horses in northern Europe, for the weather there is temperamental, and the success of the crop depends on taking maximum advantage of a good opportunity. This change, together with the use of shafts attached to the breast-band, and of traces to link teams of animals, enabled a series of major agricultural changes in northern Europe. In the twelfth century ploughing from Kiev to Normandy was usually done with horses, while in the Mediterranean, oxen continued, with lighter ploughs. At the same time the wagoner and the carter carrying goods by horse assisted the revival of the mediaeval European economy.

These changes were less marked elsewhere. China devised the horse collar, but did not use horses to agricultural advantage because water buffaloes seemed more appropriate for rice farming than horses. In the Americas there was no plough before AD 1492. Indeed, there were no metal tools at all, save for a few bronze instruments among the Incas. In Africa horses were always expensive, since like oxen they did not like tropical circumstances; in the sixteenth century horses were costing three times as much as slaves in Central Africa: the decisive reason surely for Africa's continuing slow development.

The horse helped the beginning of a real rotation of crops in Europe. It had been long known that crops would exhaust the soil if the same ones were grown on it year after year. Only Egypt with its fertile loess had been able to avoid all forms of rotation. Civilised countries of antiquity, such as the Roman Empire, had used a rotation of two years: one year grain, one year fallow. Occasionally the field not in use for wheat might be used for pasture. Though both Greeks and Romans observed that peas and beans restored exhausted soil, they did not make a habit of alternating them with other crops. Many believed that beans contained the souls of the departed.

The main agricultural improvement of mediaeval Europe, so far as crops were concerned, was the substitution in many places of a rotation of three crops for one of two. That was probably inspired by the increase in size of fields and estates, as more and more forests in Europe fell before the axe. As with irrigation, the great abbeys were among the first to adopt the change. Thus often

in mediaeval northern Europe good land was divided into that
which grew spring corn, winter corn such as oats (for horses) and
fallow; while in the South corn and fallow continued to take turn
and turn about. In northern Europe peas and beans began to be
grown regularly alongside the oats, imparting desirable acids to
the soil. Later on, in Flanders, cereals and fodder alternated,
while Dutch fields began to have five years of crops, then five
years of pasturage.

These changes in methods of cultivation were not complemented by changes in methods of harvesting. Corn was, from its
first appearance, cut by a sickle, one of the oldest and most
continuously used tools of all. When gathered, it was threshed by
a wooden flail or trodden out on an earthen threshing floor by
oxen or horses. After threshing, the grain was separated from
chaff by being tossed in the air, the wind carrying the chaff away.
All these usages, which began in the Near East in its golden age,
continued almost unchanged everywhere till the nineteenth century AD, and in many places, even in Europe, survived till the
twentieth.

The grinding of grain also early developed the principles which
characterised it till the nineteenth century, between a fixed and a
rotating stone, though refinements were added (grooves, for example, incised in both stones by the miller or by an itinerant
craftsman; while the texture of the stones themselves was often
considered important). At first Egypt and Babylon employed a
small bun-shaped stone for use on large saucer-shaped stones, for
grinding. This was replaced in Egypt by the 'saddle quern', the
best maker of flour for thousands of years: a miller sat at one end
of a rectangular slanted stone and pushed a rubbing stone backwards and forwards. This was in use among the Celts in Britain,
for example, at least by 300 BC. Later the rubbing stone was
made square to permit the grain to trickle through a slit to the
grinding surface, so saving the trouble of lifting up the stone
whenever another handful of grain was needed.

Though there were a few professional bakers in ancient Egypt,
most people made their own bread until the Roman Empire. The
full rotary motion made possible by driving donkeys or mules
round a mill gave the professional baker in Rome an advantage
over the housewife, thus enabling large-scale and semi-mechanical
grinding. By 100 BC in Rome bakers were becoming millers, the
millers mass producers. Such rotary querns were widespread in
Europe by about 200 BC, to judge from remains from Celtic Britain.

The millers were pioneers in other ways. They were, for example, the first to make use of that most important piece of machinery, the watermill, which had been apparently developed in Pontus in the first century BC, the same time that it was devised in China – a simultaneity that suggests a closer connection between the two regions than is usually realised. The earliest type of mill used an axle which was horizontal in China, and vertical in the West. The lower end of the axle had a wheel immersed in a stream. The upper end passed through the lower millstone and was fixed directly to the upper stone, which it turned.

This mill, mostly used for the grinding of corn, could only work well with fast-flowing water. In the first century BC the Roman architect Vitruvius designed a vertical 'undershot' waterwheel which connected the wheel's horizontal axle with the vertical axle of the stones, so permitting faster rotation. The idea was influenced by the Persian *noria* or *saquiya* by which pots were arranged round the circumference of a wheel, turned by a man or an animal, and dipped into water. Within a hundred years a mill of this sort would presumably have been in wide use in Rome had it not been for the availability of slaves. By the end of the Roman Empire in the fourth or fifth centuries the more powerful 'overshot' wheel also existed, both in the Mediterranean world and in China, but neither civilisation showed much imagination, to begin with, in applying the device to an industrial process. These wheels were kept for grinding corn, and that they did well. For example, a wheel at Arles in late Roman days had sixteen overshot wheels, which ground three tons of corn an hour. Chinese waterwheels, on the horizontal principle, perhaps an extension of the rotary quern, were often constructed and, in India, waterwheels for irrigation were 'a familiar part of the rural landscape' by about AD 650[8].

There were further innovations in the Byzantine era. Some experiments were made with tide mills. Still, only in the tenth century AD was there any serious use of watermills for activities other than the grinding of corn (probably the first use other than grinding corn was on the Serchio near Lucca)[9]. But from then on there was such use, encouraged by the Cistercian monks, so that soon (and until the nineteenth century) there was scarcely a village between Moscow and the Atlantic which did not have its wheel, used for an increasing diversity of actions. The wheel could lift and tilt hammers used in forging, pump bellows for ovens, launder, saw, crush olives, full cloth, and reduce paper to pulp, pigments to paint and malt to beer. Domesday Book records already nearly 6,000 mills in England at the time of the Norman Conquest. There were said to be 60,000 watermills in France in the sixteenth century – and 500,000 in Europe on the eve of the Industrial Revolution[10]. Among the first acts of Columbus in his new colony of Hispaniola in 1493 was the building of a watermill to grind cane, and that was soon followed by others to cut wood and grind sugar cane. In 1534 a mill was set up in Paris for polishing precious stones, but it was soon taken over by the King for use as a royal mint, to produce 'milled' coins. Probably the biggest wheel of all was established in France at Marly to feed the fountains of Versailles, generating seventy-five horsepower. But by then the age of agriculture was already in its dying days.

Just as commerce began in earnest when obsidian was carried down the Euphrates to Jarmo in Iraq about 5000 BC, so the waterwheels of mediaeval European towns made the rivers into real engines of prosperity for a whole era. A Cistercian monk recalled that 'the river enters the abbey as much as the well, acting as a check, allows. It gushes first into the corn mill, where it is very actively employed in grinding the grain under the weight of the wheel, and in shaking the fine sieve which separates flour from bran. Then, it fills the boiler . . . to prepare beer for the monks' drinking . . . it is now drawn into the fulling machines . . . its duty now to serve in making their clothing [by] lowering the heavy hammer and mallet* . . . [next] the river enters the tannery, where it devotes much care and labour to the materials for the monks' footwear; then it divides . . . and passes through various departments, cooking, crushing, watering . . . or grinding . . . At last . . . it carries away the refuse'[11]. Every river, indeed, in the age of agriculture was a river of life. The ancient Egyptians depended so much on the Nile that it was worshipped in innumerable guises, above all as Hâpi, depicted as a well-nourished man with huge breasts hanging over his chest and a vast belly bulging over his belt. Hâpi seemed to be dead much of the year, when nature in Egypt was exhausted, the trees being grey with dirt and only a few vegetable plots being kept alive with the greatest difficulty. Then in June the river would rise again, driving forward mud and debris which coloured the water green. The rising water could be seen at Aswan about 7 June, it was at Cairo about the 17th and in the delta two days later. The green Nile had by then turned

* 'To full' is to beat or tread cloth in order to cleanse or to thicken it.

red as the river spread over the banks to cover the countryside, and in September the whole valley would seem a shallow lagoon between deserts, the towns becoming little Venices, joined by causeways. Sebeh, the crocodile god, was often seen by the pious. The protection of causeways and walls became the main work, though pilgrimages would be undertaken to holy places. The cultivable area was divided into rectangles varying between 1,000 and 40,000 acres and they were fed with water, by sluices, so as to be flooded to a depth of three to six feet. The water was then drained off back to the Nile by a system of canals when, in October, the Nile began to shrink and return to its 'normal' bed[12].

These two periods in Egypt, *perit*, when the river was going out into the fields, and *shemu*, when it was withdrawing, were actually the first well-identified seasons, the river being thus the father of the calendar as well as of many other undertakings, both industrial and agricultural, in the age of agriculture. Aside from any industrial use, water of course played a decisive part in agriculture everywhere. For example, 1,500 tons of water are needed to grow a ton of wheat, 4,000 tons of water to grow a ton of rice and 10,000 tons of water to grow a ton of cotton fibre[13]. The availability of water seemed a generation ago to be the decisive element in all agrarian productivity and land reform. A traveller looked at, for example, west Valencia in Spain to see weed-choked crops on rocky hillsides, badly pruned mulberries, olives caught by frost and mean, terraced wheat. Only a few miles away lay the richly irrigated coastal plain which has given five crops every two years for hundreds of years because, it seemed, it had a good system of irrigation. Vines, carobs, rice, fruit, all flourished – in the thirteenth century as today. The worship, almost, of water has thus good credentials. An automatic device to raise water, the *shaduf*, enabled the vines, date palms, flowers and vegetables of Egypt to be watered as early as 2000 BC. A continuous chain of buckets was in use in the Hanging Gardens of Babylon to water the flowers there. Wells lined by rough stone and with a rope pulley existed in Egypt by 1500 BC, while water was being conserved by damming as early as 1300 BC on the Orontes in Syria.

Only wind is comparable to water. Yet the windmill has a less interesting history than the waterwheel. Originating in China or Afghanistan, perhaps derived from the revolving bookcases of China or the wind-driven prayer wheels of Central Asia, windmills by the tenth century were being used in Persia for irrigation and for grinding corn. There was a Western copy of this by 1180, in

England. It was once held that these windmills were brought back by the Crusaders, but there were no windmills at that time in the Holy Land. The earliest mills turned horizontally and they continue thus in China, but a vertical wheel was used in Europe in the thirteenth and fourteenth centuries.

For a time windmills were believed to have an advantage over waterwheels, for they could not be stopped by freezing and could be built almost wherever needed. But Mediterranean people found waterwheels more reliable. Windmills thus took a long time to reach central Castile, where they were still a novelty in the days of Cervantes. Hence Don Quixote's surprise at seeing them looking so white against the parched earth. By the fourteenth century in Holland, however, tower windmills had been devised, with their bodies built of stone or brick and their sails adjusted to the tops of the buildings. Many of these were used for pumping water as well as for grinding corn. Holland, whose flat land was specially good for this type of energy, at one time had 8,000 windmills. The average strength of a windmill was the same as that of a watermill – five to ten horsepower.

The plough, the ox, the horse, the waterwheel and the windmill, the water buffalo and the irrigation ditch: these were the motors of the age of agriculture. Yet a lack of technology, pure and simple, is not the only reason for unproductive agriculture. Gunnar Myrdal, in his famous study of the causes of poverty in the twentieth century, *Asian Drama*, singled out other explanations for change and underdevelopment, health and ill-health in a country's economy. The character of ownership, the type of lease, the political system, seemed to him as important as the availability of a tractor or the existence of a farm-to-market road. If that analysis be true of the present century in Asia, it must have been so of most of the world in the past. The next chapters, therefore, discuss the way that land was held in an age when most of the populated world was managed by landowners.

14

Landlords and Labourers

The fourteenth century peasants had been at once more oppressed and better cared for. The great seigneurs may have sometimes treated them harshly, but they never abandoned them to their own devices.

Alexis de Tocqueville, *L'Ancien Régime*

1

The small portion of the world being farmed in the days of classical antiquity was being looked after by, in a rough ascending order of status: slaves, who could be sold at will by a master, though their rights, like their duties, differed from era to era and from place to place; serfs, or labourers who, though more free than slaves, had their freedom of movement constrained by law or custom; labourers, paid in kind or cash for a set piece of work or a set number of hours; modest farmers, owning their own land, perhaps able to employ one to two labourers, and whose livelihood depended on their own work and that of their family; farmers, some rich, some poor, who rented land, sometimes for money, sometimes by some form of sharecropping; small properties; and great estates, some in private hands and some, in the East in particular, maintained more or less as state farms on which special groups of serving men, slaves or forced labour were from the earliest days employed (though most of the land even in those despotisms was farmed by smallholders). Still, the characteristic economic and social holding of the age of agriculture was the large estate: not because of the charms of country life in agreeable circumstances, so well and so delightfully chronicled from the time of Horace onwards, but because of its political significance. All landholding was for several hundred generations a political form, but none more so than the great estate.

In Egypt, in the Middle East in antiquity, in China and India, in Rome and feudal Europe, the large estate was what it had been in mediaeval France and would be in nineteenth-century South America: 'a unit both territorial and social'[1] in France, according to Marc Bloch, or a 'social and political organisation, a means of control, the basis of the ruling oligarchy' in nineteenth-century

South America, according to John Lynch[2]. The great estates of
Andalusia, which for so long provided Castilian noble families
with their revenues, continued the same under Romans, Goths,
Arabs and Christians – latifundia growing wheat, olives or barley,
or breeding bulls, and run by a bailiff. Of tyrants, kings, princes
of the Church and nobles between 2000 BC and AD 1800 it might
have been said, as it was of General Rosas in Argentina in the
nineteenth century, 'Who was Rosas? An owner of land. What
did he accumulate? Land. What did he give to his supporters?
Land. What did he take from his enemies? Land'[3]. Along the
Ganges, everyone noticed, the landowners were, from the time
of the Aryan conquest, the potential traders as well as rulers,
since they had both leisure and capital.

Where if anywhere can the great estate be most 'typically'
found? In eighteenth-century Ireland, where 'landed property,
being rooted in conquest, was free from all manorial obligations?
Where entails were so common that an estate rarely came into
the market?' Nowhere, says Elie Halévy, had the formation of
large estates been carried so far[4].

There, certainly, the evils of 'absenteeism' were seen most vividly. For there, without any attachment to the soil, the landlords'
thought was to extract, with a minimum of trouble, the maximum
amount of money from a population very different to themselves.
The estates were run by agents who received a percentage of
revenue from the estate and who oppressed in the name of their
employer the cultivators of the soil. That, however, may be too
harsh a generalisation. Not all great estates were so ill run. Surely
a more characteristic example might be found in the Roman Empire when the great estate, the *fundus*, an enterprise usually called
after some long-dead owner (for example, 'Fundus Claudius'),
would be divided into tenancies and a home farm, ancestor of the
feudal demesne farm which, in many places, survived till the
present – in, for example, the 'administration cane' land of the
Latin American sugar estate of the twentieth century. Large estates, such as that of Pliny the Younger at Tifernum in Tuscany,
with its 3,000 acres, would employ a big slave population and also
much casual labour. In France and in other outlying parts of the
Roman Empire the estates of the early centuries were a continuation of an earlier system, going back to the days of the Celts,
since 'all points to the conclusion that the Gallo-Roman aristocracy was a caste of village chieftains, drawing part of their incomes
from dues owed by their peasant subjects', the regime itself having

its origin in an ancient tribal system, and the change from clan
leadership to seigneurial authority being, for Marc Bloch again,
'relatively simple', comparable to what happened later in mediaeval Wales[5].

In similar circumstances mediaeval Germany was a country
which seemed not unlike Africa in the nineteenth century, 'where
the Chief was only just becoming Lord'[6]. Similarly, though the
life of an estate in Europe might be interrupted (and land not
cultivated) during a time of civil war, or invasion by nomads in
the fifth and sixth centuries, or as a result of the marauding
Vikings and Magyars in the ninth and tenth centuries, or the
Hundred Years' War of the fifteenth, there was very often continuity. The great estates of Rome passed, without much change
in type of farming, though with change of ownership, from the
Empire to the Middle Ages. Some of them were made over as
gifts to the Church. Some dominant mediaeval families may have
had a connection with leading Roman subjects of early Frankish
kings but, if so, the direct line of descent was broken: no blood
connection seems to exist between mediaeval landowners and the
holders of land under Rome[7].

When the Germans occupied the Roman Empire, they seized,
or were given, substantial sections of the land (about two-thirds
of the acreage in France, half of the forest), so that a new race of
German (that is, Frankish) landowners held the old Roman estates. But the estates themselves did not change much in shape,
nor, Henri Pirenne argued, was the area of cultivated land increased[8]. Such estates retained their old characteristics: demesnes
or home farms, tenant farmers owing services and dues, and
territorial intermixture of demesne land with that of tenants. But
'the constant unrest, the habitual resort to force, the insecurity
which impelled everyone to seek a protector . . . the abuse of
power fostered by the absence of government . . . all combined',
wrote Bloch, 'to draw an ever-increasing number of peasants into
the hands of seigneurial subjection'[9]. The anarchy at the end of
the Carolingian state, for example (and of the time of the Vikings), gave many vassals the chance to seize outright lands which
they had received as temporary grants, particularly those 'counts',
originally 250 to 350, who had been intended as a bureaucracy to
begin with but who, from the saddle of the big horses of mediaeval
Europe, made themselves the captains of feudalism. Afterwards
the enfeebled monarchs could only confirm the titles or continue
the process – arms, titles, exemption from taxes granted in return

for knightly service. In the fiefs so created, the lord was king. Feudalism imposed obligations on all: the Earl of Stafford could not refuse his duties to the King; was he, in an absolute sense, no freer than the serf? All had some freedoms in the age of agriculture, some more than others. Most people had fewer than their ancestors had in the age of hunters.

Everywhere feudalism had different forms, with different effects. In England, it was installed by the plan of William the Conqueror; and assisted the growth of the monarchy. In Germany, feudalism prevented the survival of a central monarchy. Spain's feudalism proper was confined to Catalonia, which Charlemagne reconquered from Islam; elsewhere, the military orders, the availability of Muslim slaves, the royal grants of latifundia, made landholding in Spain more Oriental in character than northern European. In France the system lasted a long time, preserving its inconveniences and privileges, more than the benefits, due to royal interventions. The National Assembly after 1789 'totally abolished' the feudal regime; among the duties of those who hold the Légion d'Honneur is the task of combatting 'any enterprise tending to re-establish the feudal regime'[10]. But the end of feudalism often meant the end of obligations by landlords (to the king, as to the serf), without freeing the labourers. Thus, after the wars of independence in South America, the latifundium* was a refuge against chaos, much as the early mediaeval fief was. Yet the great private estate of the nineteenth century rarely imposed irksome duties on landlords. Similarly, the Thirty Years' War enabled Junkers in Prussia to establish local despotisms over peasants, who were often Slav in ancestry. The government of England in the eighteenth century seemed, perhaps was, a committee of landlords. Landowners were the richest class in England till at least the 1870s[11] and financed much of politics as if it were one more private interest, only a little more important than their stud-book. In the nineteenth century, indeed, the large estate was probably at its most powerful (as in some ways was the hereditary monarchy): a tamed labour force was available to work at low wages for a lord who had few feudal limitations on his ownership and often still had real privileges.

The word 'feudalism' is not one which can be exactly used anywhere save in Western Europe. But Japan's feudalism cer-

* Never precisely a feudal enterprise.

tainly was close to Western Europe's while in India, in the early Middle Ages, a system existed in which the monarch granted the income from certain lands to certain tenants, whose responsibility was to provide levies. Equally, the Chinese system of landholding was for several hundreds of years before the Han unification based on the work of peasants who, in return for protection, did work on their lord's estate. Tribute was passed 'from rank to rank', ultimately reaching the imperial court where noblemen were expected to serve certain sojourns. Later, both Indian and Chinese ranks acquired a hierarchical flavour, not unlike Western ranks of nobility (except that the Chinese lords were learned and they themselves carried out what religious duties were necessary, in the absence of a priestly class). Later – but not much before the fall of Rome in the West – the whole system gave way to one in which officials rather than noblemen ran new territories and old ones as well.

The Chinese system after the formal achievement of an empire under the Ch'in dynasty in about 200 BC avoided feudal concessions. Instead there were 'commanderies' – posts of responsibility and honour which were filled for life by appointed officials.

Feudalism was a word also used with great confidence by Gilberto Freyre to describe the *casa grande* which dominated old Brazil for several hundred years: 'fortress, chapel, school, workshop, house of charity, harem, convent of young women . . . hospital . . . and bank'. Even on the cattle ranches of Rio Grande, there was a custom, according to one traveller, Nicolão Dreys, of ringing a bell loudly across the countryside to advise the travellers wandering near by that they could come to the lord of the manor's table then being spread'[12]. Certainly the *casa grande* was 'an entire economic, social and political system'. So indeed was its predecessor, the system adopted by the Portuguese monarchs of dividing Brazil between the Amazon and the São Vicente into a dozen hereditary captaincies, under lords proprietor (*donatorios*) whose lands varied in width from 100 to 30 leagues and were of an indefinite extension into the interior – estates which were exceeded in size in the history of European colonisation only by the large *prazos* of Mozambique, which sometimes took eight days to cross.

This is an oversimplification of the diversity of the 'Great Estates': how can one begin to compare, it will be asked, the estancias of South America, with their hundreds of head of cattle (original grantees in the Spanish Empire were entitled to 74 cattle, or 666 sheep, on an estate of a league* square), even with the farms in the same places based on manpower before the Spaniards introduced their cattle-powered agriculture? The tangle of rents, mortgages, tenancies and entails cannot, it will be said, be so simply dismissed. And what, anyway, is a 'large' estate? 130 or 250 acres would have been considered a large enterprise even for a monastery in mediaeval France and so would five acres in the rich Valencian huerta. The biggest estate in fourth-century Attica, apart from one exceptional case, was sixty or so acres. The large farms of the early Roman Empire – Pliny's 3,000 acres have been mentioned – seem on a different scale. In Domesday England, a large manor such as that at Staines in Middlesex, with its six watermills, fish weir, meadow for twenty-four teams of oxen, wood for thirty pigs, was 2,280 acres while the manor of Leominster (Hereford), held by Harold's Queen Edith and her family, accounted for nearly 10,000 acres. Yet the management of a great estate the world over has many similarities with others like it. Absentee and resident landlords, even bailiffs and *fattori*, even sharecroppers, the differences are of emphasis, not of fundamental purpose. Whether the estate was a part of the one-fifth or so of France owned by the Church in 1789, or whether it was run by the Templars, estates owned clerically were much the same, too, in character. Japan's warrior landlords also resemble England's tenants-in-chief and their problems in the fifteenth century were not unknown in Europe; a self-contained agricultural unit, producing all it needed, making its own tools and weaving its own cloth, met in Japan, as in Europe, problems deriving from the rise of commerce, and the growth of industries: problems which were posed in comparable terms in both places.

The great estate was, it is desirable to appreciate, the characteristic form of landholding until well into modern times. For example, in Mexico and throughout the Spanish Empire, the estates given to the conquistadors as *encomiendas* passed from generation to generation and became the basis for the large Mexican ranches which survive to this day, though by the nineteenth century the original great grants had been divided. Along with the cultivation of the three major crops – wheat, rice and maize – the large estate gives an essential continuity to agricultural history, and hence to history itself.

* About three miles.

2

Almost always the type of farmer who suffered most was the tenant farmer. How many types of lease there are! Ranging from those with services to those merely specifying years, a lifetime, twenty-one years or, as often in Ireland, a lifetime and twenty-one or some other number of years! Very often the relation between landlord and tenant has been the worst in human affairs, with the farmer having no inducement to refrain from exhausting the soil as the end of the lease drew near. Some landlords have sought to turn tenants into labourers.

3

A system of tenancy popular with landlords for six hundred years in Europe, and still found in most parts of the world is sharecropping, or *métayage* (*mezzadria*). By that the tenant, in return for a free house and plot, and perhaps implements, surrenders to the landlord a half, a quarter or another fraction of the crop. Established in Roman times, the system was common in French vineyards and also in central Italy, whose astute financial leaders realised that it was a good defence, in an economy in which money was becoming common, against inflation. There were Italian states where all those who leased land were obliged to employ that type of lease. Subsequently, *métayage* became widespread in Europe and for several generations seemed the ideal manner of running an estate. But there were usually some difficulties. It was not clear how permanent the leases so obtained were, and the system did not absorb technological change very easily. Still, in many parts of Italy, a system which had its roots in Rome and was first apparently practised formally in the seventh century by the Benedictine abbey of Sta Fiona, on Monte Amiata in Tuscany, lasted till the 1960s, when a combination of new and expensive machinery and the demand for labour in the cities destroyed it.

In France, *métayage* accounted for half the territory in 1789, above all in the centre and south. Stripped of feudal adjuncts, the system survived since the lord or proprietor could not gain his share of the produce without contributing his share of the working capital. But by the end of the nineteenth century, in France it had become simply the curiosity of certain provinces. The same was the case in Germany, where it had once been common, especially in wine-growing districts.

The system has been used outside Europe too. Thus, in the US South, after the collapse of the slave-powered cotton plantations at the end of the civil war in 1865, sharecropping was considered the best way of ensuring labour to produce cotton: though the bargain was a harsher one than normal in Europe, for in order to receive half the crop the cultivator, usually a freed slave, had to bear the cost of all fertilisers, the baling and the ginning.* The region where this system of cultivation has worked best in modern times seems to have been in the Basque provinces. There, very often, the owner has lived in the nearby town, the rainfall is regular, relations between tenant and owner are good, and contracts are often oral. Hence the Basque country, till the twentieth century, was the 'satisfied area' of Spain, almost the only place in the country where there was no social problem[13].

It is difficult to avoid a word or two about what seems to be on the surface a different type of cooperative, namely the system known as the common (or open) field, which for a thousand years dominated northern Europe and still exists in a few isolated pockets. That system implied farming in common with three main elements: first, an arable area, growing corn, divided into three large fields, in one of which at any one time winter grain might be growing; spring corn and some vegetables might be in another field; while the third would be fallow. Each of these large fields, however, would be divided into strips representing a day's labour with the heavy plough, or 22 yards by 220 yards, that is, an acre in size, and the different plots would remain permanent freeholds, regardless of the crop. Treeless, hedgeless, cut up by balks and mere-stones into furlongs, gores and headlands, these open common fields were 'very ugly things' to look at, in William Cobbett's recollection[14].

Secondly, there would be an area of meadowland, allocated among the community as the ploughland had been, each family having a strip on which to grow an annual crop of hay. Finally, there would be wasteland (a common much like the open field during the fallow season), used for permanent grazing or for the possible expansion of the area under arable farming if the population should grow. On this waste land there might also be an area of wood, useful for firewood, acorns, beech-mast for pigs and so on. There might also be, in the nearby village, a mill, a pond or a bog, where some would have the right to cut peat. On the common, custom often enabled weavers to spread cloth to dry after dyeing and squatters to establish huts.

* Ginning means the removal of seeds of cotton by a gin (engine).

It was the first of those three tracts which was of the most importance, since it had other uses than simply the production of grain. At any time other than when there were crops growing on it, for example, livestock could graze there, leaving behind invaluable manure for the future.

Now this system lasted in much of France, England, Germany and to some extent Spain for 500 years or more in one form or another. It had interesting consequences. First, the proper functioning of the system required the disciplined adherence to it of every member of the community. Second, the right of common grazing on the stubble after the harvest made it impossible for any individualist to try to grow an extra crop. The farmer was thus so closely dependent on his neighbour that he could do little without his help or assent. His lands were so mingled with those of others that the traditional 'peasant's memory' was needed to recognise what belonged to whom. No fences could be set up, save where a strip abutted on to the common way, since that would have interfered with grazing. The parcelling-out meant that cultivation had to be in common, even if the crop went to an individual owner. Within what might seem on the surface a collectivist employment and control of land, however, individual rights were strictly maintained. Finally, villages in the economy of the common field were compact, with few isolated homesteads.

The system outlived the conversion of the villages into towns: the peasantry of Wiesbaden brought ploughs and dung carts to and fro across the town daily as late as 1845. Even Berlin had its three fields in 1819.

Land in Russia, until the Revolution of 1917, was also mostly held communally though not in fields comparable to those of Western Europe. Scattered villages characterised Russia, not great estates, and the villages were often divided from one another by waste. Each village, as a rule, divided its land into sections according to the quality of the soil and its geographical ease of access. Every household claimed small strips of land corresponding to the needs of its adult members (the strips were usually nine to twelve feet broad, several hundred yards long, the shape and size certainly being similar to the strips in the West) and one man probably had some thirty to fifty such strips. From time to time, perhaps every ten years, the village would re-divide the strips, an action often unpopular and usually having to be underwritten by the local authorities. These villages were run by a council of heads of family. Meantime within every family, work was also traditionally done in common, since the father was usually assisted till his death by sons and grandchildren. This 'joint family' was also often unpopular, particularly in modern times (probably due to over-population) and, in the generation between the emancipation of the serfs in 1861 and the Revolution in 1917, many Russian peasants broke away from their families, though as a rule remaining within their village.

For a generation or so, these old cooperative agricultural farms seemed the hope of Russia: Alexander Herzen looked on the commune as 'the one lightning conductor – free from the taint of capitalism, from the greed and fear and inhumanity of destructive individualism', upon which a 'new society of free self-governing human beings might be built'[15]. Such hopes were in the end falsified.

Common fields of one sort or another existed nearly every-where, in both the Old World and the New, since peasants without animals can be easily coordinated into something close to teams, even when they work irrigated fields with a digging stick and even when they are working with ploughing teams on separate fields. The exception to the general frequency of the use of open fields was India. There, after the Aryan conquest about 1500 BC, land began by being owned by the village and farmed in common. But with the decline of tribal units, land was divided between families and thus outright private property came into being at an early date. Because of a multitude of hindrances in the development of a free market, poverty and handkerchief-sized plots, that system survived many generations though today much of India is owned by large-scale farmer-capitalists.

How these intricate types of common farming began has been an interesting subject for argument. In Russia the origins of the system have been endlessly debated[16]. In Europe the system is held to have derived from the type of cultivation carried on by the Germans before they invaded the Roman Empire. Each year the leading men of a tribe would meet and decide (as was later done at a court leet in England) which part of the land recently cleared should be ploughed, and planted with what. By the time of Tacitus (AD 100) land was already being divided up between individuals, and the frequency of division had declined. But when new lands were conquered or new waste cleared, the process would begin again. The size of the strip would be decided by the action of the plough. Naturally the land for cultivation would be adjacent to the settlement concerned and, upon that, the men of the community would go to work. By the end of the working day each would have ploughed one or more strips, according to the nature of the soil. Next day the labourers would move on, to set out and plough the section beyond the first day's work. In the end all would have land ready for sowing in strips, equally dispersed, so that, in theory, all would have the same opportunities, the same share of the different sorts of soil and the same hopes of avoiding climatic disaster.

In a typical village of old Europe a farmer's year might be: about 15 October the winter sowing of wheat would be finished, and the livestock grazing on the wheat stubble in the second open field of the three would be driven off. There would then be twelve days of ploughing. This land would lie untouched and exposed throughout the winter. The farmer would concern himself then primarily with his cattle, which would be quartered near, or inside, his house. Ditches, fences or implements would be mended and corn threshed. In March there would be spring sowing. The stocks of winter food for the livestock (as for humans) would be finished while the cattle would be tethered on the commons or waste in April immediately that there was any sign of grass. That month and the next, the farmer would be occupied with sheep and lambs, cows and calves, and be beginning to plough the fallow ready for the autumn wheat's sowing. At the end of June the grass in the common meadows would be ready for the hay harvest in which, after the swathes had been cut with scythes, women and children would share. That work would be finished by the beginning of August, when the 'aftermath' on the by then harvested meadow would be open for common grazing (and manuring) till October. The corn harvest would follow. Young and old would repair to the cornfields, the men cutting the corn with sickles, the women and children binding the staves and building them into stooks. Finally the corn would be stacked in barns and threshed there during the winter, the grain obtained being ground in a watermill or a windmill.

Even when there were no open fields, something similar occurred, with religious and festive rites differing from country to country. Of course, there were local deviations (the harvest in northern France being in July, in England in September and in the South earlier). The French system of uniting all the stock into a common herd for grazing on stubble was, for example, not usual in England. The division of land into small farms, themselves split into parcels, was nowhere more elaborate than in Spain where, by the end of the age of agriculture, a farm in, say, Guadalajara probably averaged twelve to forty acres, split into fourteen to twenty parcels. With all such harvests, there might be a combination of the efforts of many different sorts of landowners, some being rich, some not. For example, at Laxton, a village in Lincolnshire, in England, the lord in the thirteenth century derived his living partly from his demesne farm of 250 acres, partly from his strips scattered among those of the tenants and partly from services on three 600-acre open fields. Four hundred years later, in the same village, the lord's strip was larger but there were no services (or rents) due to him any more. The open fields were smaller too than they had been in 1232. On them, there were still innumerable strips in every shape, two freeholders having land of over 600 acres, most having enterprises under forty acres in all (and divided up). The farms concerned, even the smallest, were busy with a mixture of arable and animal husbandry. Animals were needed for a variety of purposes, but to feed them was a major undertaking. The scarcity of manure was the chief reason for what would now seem the low yield of wheat, and lords sometimes asked for pots of human excrement as part of their dues.

4

Every major project of agriculture in the Near East and Mediterranean in antiquity depended upon slaves. So did both those industrial undertakings which depended on agricultural products, and those mines whose products were concerned to improve agriculture as well as to furnish weapons for war. On the other hand, slaves were not much employed in those projects in agriculture which depended on irrigation. There, as has been suggested before, the population would be more likely to be subject to various forms of forced labour. In the Mediterranean world, the Mycenaean kingdoms were perhaps a touchstone of the general character of slave labour in the region about 1400 BC. There were many slaves there, especially female ones, some working in the textile industry or for bronzesmiths, and many in private households. Some were captured in war, most were bought (suggesting already that the traffic in slaves was the largest single commercial item). Families and children of slaves were permitted to keep together. Much later the slave population of Athens was decisive in enabling it to continue as a city of commerce. Chios, the first Greek democracy, was also the first Greek city to import large consignments of slaves from the 'Barbarian East'. Previously the slaves had come from the Scythian or Slavic North. By then, slaves were cheap: they cost no more to buy than a year's expenditure on their upkeep. It thus seems clear that the economic problems of a slave trade had been resolved: Greece needed slave labour, Asia (or the peoples on the northern coast of the Black Sea) could provide the slaves.

The people who in the end established their rule over the ancient world, the Romans, had, to begin with, no slave estates. Was that, as some have suggested, the reason for Rome's success over Carthage, by then a bloated state with her plantations filled with disgruntled slaves from all over the Mediterranean? If so, Rome later fell into Carthage's bad ways. The campaigns of conquest from the third century BC onwards brought territory to Rome but, even more, waves of slaves who went to work on new plantations in Italy: 25,000 slaves were gained from the capture of Agrigentum, 60,000 from Marius's victory in Germany, 150,000 from the capture of Epirus and, it was said, two million, from Pompey's victories in Asia. By then Delos, the island which had been the greatest colony of the Athenian Empire, had become the slave emporium of the civilised world. 10,000 slaves a day were sold there, according to the geographer Strabo. A special dock was built for the purpose. Even numerically these undertakings rivalled the market in slaves in the West Indies in the eighteenth century.

This slave population transformed Roman society. Slaves, to begin with, made millionaires out of the great commanders. Caesar was poor when he went to Gaul but he returned rich from the booty of slaves which he had acquired. After his victory at Alesia in 52 BC he gave one slave each to his legionaries. As occurred in Russia in the Middle Ages, or in Africa in the eighteenth century, the profits available from trading in slaves sometimes led to war to replenish markets. Captured slaves weighed down armies. Furthermore, the availability of this labour force made possible, more than anything else, the creation of plantations (particularly in Sicily and south Italy) which were worked by gangs of slaves, as were the similar estates of colonial America. The racial mixture of Rome was slowly transformed. Anyone who was not a Roman citizen could be enslaved and, though certain races were favoured on the assumption that they provided the best workers, there were no specific slave races, to the Roman mind. But innumerable slaves were freed for good service. Masters in

Rome constantly spurred on their slaves to work hard by offers of bonuses with which they could buy their freedom. Sick slaves abandoned by their masters were also often freed, while the slaves of the Emperor became men of immense, if perilous, eminence. The eunuchs who managed the later Empire in the East were often slaves. Their power derived from their control of imperial audiences and, with weak rulers (of which there was no lack), they thereby could direct the Empire. All imperial slaves had opportunities to better themselves. After centuries of manumission eighty per cent of Roman families had, in the second century AD, once been emancipated from slavery[17].

Roman slaves were often able to secure that they were well treated. Many had hours of recreation during the afternoon, and might have found the week of forty hours in the twentieth century irksome. It was accepted that slaves had souls. They were allowed to worship the souls of their predecessors. Magistrates were bound to consider complaints laid by slaves against the injustice of masters. The killing of slaves was considered to be murder.

The character of Roman slavery, as of Rome, was changed by the end of the wars of expansion. Roman slaveowners 'were reduced', Gibbon wrote, 'to the milder, but more tedious, method of propagation'[18]. Many landlords converted their estates to leasehold or employed labourers when the slave prices rose. By the late Empire, in consequence, Roman slaves were working mostly in domestic service rather than on estates. Some masters of estates in the late Empire comforted themselves (as did the owners of West Indian sugar plantations later) that slaves worked badly in comparison with free men. After all, the death of a slave meant the loss of capital. That reflection did not prevent the decline of the Roman economy.

Nor did slaves vanish with the coming of Christianity, despite the Roman Church's dogma that all members of the human species were potentially members of *societas Christiana*. Throughout the Dark Ages, slave families continued in Europe. Slaves continued to be brought from the Levant or Slavic Europe. But the collapse of commerce after the Arabs captured the seas prevented a flourishing trade. There were, too, many diversities of treatment among those who were slaves during the Dark Ages in Europe. Some *servi* were looked upon as human cattle in their master's house. Some were, in effect, 'tenant slaves', living like free tenants though unable to participate in judicial assemblies or be summoned to the army. We hear in Maitland's *Domesday Book and*

Beyond of a king of Sussex giving land and '250 slaves' to a supporter[19]. But slaves in mediaeval Europe often had a cottage and yard of their own, even if the duties demanded of them were constant. Vikings looked on slaves as the richest plunder and, with those whom they caught, they turned their own scarcely cultivated plots into slave plantations – as if the slaves were trained agronomists. The Viking realm in Russia, the monarchy of Rurik, was also built up on the sale of slaves to Islam through the Khanates of Kiev. That active mediaeval sale of slaves (in Russia, in Sicily, perhaps above all in Islamic Spain) resulted in the accidental use of the word *esclave* or 'slav' becoming a vernacular synonym for the Latin *servus*.*

By the late Middle Ages, because of the increase in Europe's population, this European slave trade had almost died out. Only a few domestic slaves remained. The Black Death revived a demand for them when labour was hard to come by. In the fourteenth century Florence authorised the import of slaves, provided that they were infidels. By the end of the century in that city, Iris Origo wrote, 'hardly a well-to-do household [was] without at least one slave: brides brought them as part of their dowry; doctors accepted them . . . in lieu of fees'[20]. The persons concerned were often girls (Circassians, Tartars, Greeks or Russians) bought in Ibiza or Majorca. But they were slaves hired to wash plates or to carry wood to the oven, not to work on farms. Their economic contribution was modest, though, in the Balearic Islands, their agricultural work continued. Northern Europe had by then forgotten slavery, though it was nowhere explicitly condemned. In Byzantium, on the other hand, the shrinking Empire until its fall had slaves much as Tuscany did, while every year from the Middle Ages till 1700 the Crimean cavalry would sweep into Russia in pursuit of young Slavs for the big markets of Asia.

Asiatic slavery in the Middle Ages was comparable to what it had been in Rome. Slaves were employed as manual labour in large enterprises, such as mines, draining marshes, on fleets. In Islam, Bernard Lewis explains, the growth under the Abbasid caliphate of many rich capitalists with 'considerable liquid capital

---

* Slav derives from *slovo*, a word to signify (in Slav) people who can speak as opposed to *nemtsy*, dumb people – a word also used for 'German'. The Slavs, a nomadic people of cattle grazers, lived in the third century AD between the Vistula and the Oder, with little political organisation, and first began to migrate in the sixth century eastwards towards Russia and southwards to the Balkans, being pressed by the Avars whom they later absorbed.

at their disposal led to the purchase of slaves in large numbers in agriculture'. Most of these were Negro, chiefly from East Africa. They were treated harshly. That led to numerous revolts, including a famous quasi-religious revolt in the ninth century which began among the slaves working on the salt flats east of Basra. For a time, the rebels controlled a great deal of southern Iraq and south-west Persia. But the main basis of production in Islam was by free, or semi-free, peasants. Most Muslim slaves were used as domestic servants or in the army. The military slaves, the Mamluks, many of Slav or Christian origin, in the end formed a powerful military caste, almost dominating the state, as the Emperor's house slaves had dominated Rome.

The overthrow of the Caliphate, weakened by excessive taxation and overspending in Baghdad, was partly due to a rebellion of Turkish slaves. From the ninth century the caliphs used those slaves extensively, since their bowmanship and horsemanship were unrivalled in Asia, and since, once converted into a palace guard, these slaves were loyal to the persons of the caliphs. Ultimately one Turkish tribe, the Seljuks, from among whom many slaves had continuously been taken, entered the Caliphate as conquerors, accepted Islam and came to dominate the Empire. They did not abolish the Caliphate, however. Having become Muslims, the Seljuks allowed it to survive, much as the Goths permitted the Western Empire to flicker on till AD 476, leaving it to be destroyed only by the Mongols in 1258. With their successors, the Ottomans, the vast slave household (*Kullar*) of the Sultan, including the civil administration from the grand vizier downwards, the standing army of janissaries (infantry) and *sipahi* (cavalry) as well as the harem, was the real government of the Empire[21].

There were few slaves in the Chinese empires. Instead, all owed labour to the emperor or lord. The canals which irrigated the fields, which allowed for the communication between provinces and which really unified the country were mostly built by forced labour. To widen the canal between the Yangtze and the Huang Ho valley about 5,500,000 workers, including all commoners between fifteen and fifty, were concentrated under the control of 50,000 police in the seventh century AD. They were workers in a classic system of *corvée*. Nor were slaves numerous in ancient India but they existed, both in mines and in domestic service, and also in the service of the guilds. In the *Arthashastra*, a treatise on government of about 300 BC, it was said that a man may be either a slave by birth – that is, of low caste status – or by selling himself, or by being captured in war, or as a result of a judicial punishment.

The history of slavery has been written often but, understandably, in a mood of anger that such a thing could have occurred in the past for so long. Some of the best historians of it in the West Indies, for instance, have been its most polemical critics. What seem to be needed are, first, a considered study of the economic significance of the traffic in slaves in Mediterranean antiquity when it was evidently the most important item of commerce for so long; and second, the role of domestic slavery as a means of providing a career open to talented people, which contrasted with the Oriental *corvée*. Perhaps it was this role of slavery as an institution, which like the Catholic Church provided to the clever the chance to rise, that explains the acceptance of the principle of slavery by that Catholic Church itself.

5

An intermediate position between slave and hired labourer was filled by an individual known as the serf. This person had equivalents in many societies. Typical was the serf of the late Roman Empire, who was chained by law to his holding, as was his son after him. Otherwise, he was free to do as he wished. Subsequently, in the Middle Ages in Europe, the position altered. A serf, though he inherited the Latin name *servus*, a slave, was free except that he could not change his lord. He was attached to a man, not to a holding. True, some masters like the abbot of Vézelay thought that his serf was 'mine, from the soles of his feet to the crown of his head', while in mediaeval England a man was permitted to kill his serf with impunity ('if a man slay his serf, his is the sin, and his is the loss'[22]). Equally, serfs were as a rule discouraged, in mediaeval Europe, to marry out of the circle of those serfs dependent on the lord in question. That ensured that the lord kept control of the children. Marriage outside the circle necessitated permission and payment. Serfs could sometimes buy their freedom, while the sale of serfs was a means of obtaining money: after the battle of Poitiers in 1356 some French knights sold freedom to their serfs in order to raise their own ransoms.

At the end of the Middle Ages repeated enfranchisements, the growth of an economy based on wages and a series of unprecedented difficulties (such as the Black Death) giving rise to shortage of labour, caused the decline of Western European serfdom, though it survived in some places until the nineteenth century. In

Eastern Europe, however, where the land was cleared more slowly, where the economies were less dynamic, where even the three-field system had scarcely begun before the fifteenth century (with lower yields from the crops) and where new land was still being sought, the bonds of serfdom were increased. In 1417, towns in Prussia agreed to hand runaway serfs back to their masters, and Prussian landowners were given the right to have fugitives handed back to them in 1494. Much of Russia's population, too, was turned into serfs instead of tenants between 1550 and 1650. The monarchy in Moscow was then emerging as the master of the country, and the conquests of land in the hands of Tartars were opening up immeasurable opportunities for those peasants who could escape from Muscovy. Until then peasants could move where they liked, provided that they were not in debt. The Tsar, concerned about receiving what he considered his share of taxes, introduced a statute of serfdom in 1649 which bound serfs to masters, and slaves and serfs were then, as it were, merged under the name of the latter. That system lasted till 1861. Elsewhere in Eastern Europe serfdom lasted nearly as long. The average village was 'servile' in 1750 in east Germany. Serfs still owed their masters heavy services and payments in kind and, in most German states in 1788, peasants were not allowed to leave their lord's estate. Even the Duke of Savoy, the King of Denmark and the princes of west Germany did not formally abolish serfdom before 1770, and the King of Prussia only embarked on abolition in 1807.

Not everything generally supposed about the evil condition of serfs in the past is true. Thus a Russian serf lived in his own house, not in a barracks, and the produce of his labour was his own. Serfs could not leave their village without permission. Otherwise, they probably had better standards of living than Scottish or Irish peasants of that day, and they were certainly more free than slaves in the West Indies or in the US.

6

The small farmer, the private peasant, the family with three acres and a cow, have a mythical position in the history of agriculture. The sterling virtues of independence characteristic of such people along with their self-reliance and austerity are held to have given some of the greatest states their most valiant men. At the time, many regretted the conversion of Rome from a land of resourceful small farmers to one of great estates. Others point approvingly to the small size of the farms of Attica, or recall the 'bold peasantry'

of England. Ernest Renan thought that the 'shrewd' peasants of
Normandy incarnated human virtues. Whether he would also have
thought that the peasants of the valley of the Ganges were such
admirable freeholders, though they had been so for many generations, seems improbable, for all his knowledge of the Orient. The
truth is that smallholders have often been the most narrow-minded
of those who have made any contribution to agriculture. With
enterprises less than forty acres in size, and tending to fragment
further because of the birth of too many sons, constantly on the
verge of being degraded into dependent tenancies and indebted
to larger landlords, such smallholders have been too poor to be
able to introduce technological improvements.

The essential distinction in the European Middle Ages was that
between those who could afford a plough team and those who
could not. Sometimes smallholders without a plough might (as in
northern Spain) create cooperative ventures for themselves; or
they might commend themselves to lords, seeking protection without conceding deference. On the whole the small peasant occupies
a more important place in what people have thought about agriculture than in what really happened. The 'yeoman' is more a
figure in literary than in economic history and his virtues are more
sung in poetry than in practice. He is also less frequent than
literature would suggest. Thus in Spain in 1797 only twenty-two
per cent of all those involved in farming owned their own land[23].
This compares with approximately one-third of the Spanish labour
force who at the time were day labourers – men who, under most
versions of feudalism, secured some benefits but did not do so
under the system which replaced it.

Of course, there were exceptions to this rule. For example, the
distribution of the lands of Visigothic noblemen in Spain by the
Arab conquerors to the soldiers of the army of the faithful created
a new class of smallholders who, according to Bernard Lewis,
'were largely responsible for the agricultural prosperity of Muslim
Spain'[24]. Similar claims have been made for the smallholders of
the Ganges, the tobacco farmers of Cuba and so on. In most
instances these prosperous smallholders were, however, men who
devoted themselves to intensive labour on a single crop in exceptional circumstances. Many, such as the Arab smallholder of
Almería, were primarily concerned with producing a crop, such
as silk, for manufacture.

7

Throughout history paid labourers have played a part in work on large estates. But except in special circumstances most labourers had *some* land. They worked for wages because their land, or their fathers' land, was too small to keep a family. That land might be tiny, but it was there. The landless labourer of Andalusia and Estremadura makes an important contribution to the history of rural protest in Spain but, as an individual in agricultural history, he was rare.

It will be asked, but what of the history of rural unemployment? In mainly agricultural countries today the numbers of unemployed are usually not registered and many who are dependent on a wage from agriculture are often underemployed. Agriculture, by the nature of its activity, has always created some seasonal unemployment. Many families have lived all winter from what they have managed to secure during the harvest. Hence, there were always, through the ages, peasants' revolts: crushed, rarely publicised, often not even recorded, there were always challenges to authority, however constituted. In Fuenteovejuna in 1476 the land had been given by King Enrique IV of Castile to the knightly order of Calatrava. Their local administrator or *comendador* was Fernan Gómez de Guzmán who entered the city as into a conquered town. In 1476 the entire people, led in this instance by their mayor and aldermen, assaulted the palace of the *comendador*, whom they threw out of the window and killed. A few weeks later a judge came. He asked: 'Who killed the *comendador*?' 'Fuenteovejuna,' came the answer, one which inspired a legend, as well as a play by Lope de Vega.

In the last generation the history of peasants' revolts has for the first time begun to receive attention. It is desirable to be reminded that the old world of agriculture seethed, under a surface of rhythmic serenity. Fugitive serfs, robbers and fugitive slaves have a place in history. In all probability the best of us have them among our ancestors. The tiny armies of mediaeval Europe have doubtless attracted too much attention in the past. The longbowmen and their successors the crossbowmen were not machines. Yet the old regimes maintained themselves, and the poor remained patient; the poorer they were, the more resigned.

15
Crops and Cloths

Just as there was an orderly system for supplying abundant clothing for the armies, so also wool was distributed every two years to all the subjects and *curacas* in general, so that they could have clothes made for themselves and their wives and children.

Garcilaso de la Vega,
Royal Commentaries of the Incas, Book V, Chapter VIII

Agriculture, in the past as today, is not always concerned with the production of food. Many crops have always been grown, even by the most primitive peoples, to produce raw materials for textiles and so provide clothing.

Clothes in the age of agriculture began by depending on the rough furs and skins of the age of hunters. But dressed skins (leather) and sheep's wool played an increasing part, followed by linen, silk and cotton. Even in hot and prosperous countries, the use of hides and fur, however, never died out: the Japanese had a *jimboar*, or leather overgarment painted on the back, for wearing outside, at the time of the Renaissance. Fur was less expensive than cloth was in mediaeval Florence. Both leather and fur have had long and prosperous histories.

Textiles, including the vegetable fibres, linen and cotton, have been turned into fabric by four processes, all of them known from 4000 BC: the cleaning and straightening of the fibres to make a roll of parallel strings; spinning, to create thread; weaving, to make the fabric; and finishing – bleaching, dyeing, fulling and pressing. All those processes were done by hand until the eighteenth century, though mechanisation had affected finishing before that. Of the commodities concerned, wool is the most interesting to consider in detail.

Wool has been a commodity of value since at least the days of Crete, whose 100,000 sheep were one of the sources of its wealth. Then, as under Rome, spinning was carried out at home on a spindle stick. On the other hand, weavers were professional people from the earliest days. Even the poorest bought clothes ready made. The weavers of the ancient Mediterranean bought yarn from private spinners and sold cloth either direct to clients or to merchants. There were a few weaving factories. The importance of sheep and their wool in antiquity is suggested by the investigation of a sheep's liver being, in both Babylon and among the Etruscans, a means of finding the will of God.

Already under Rome certain wools had special clients. Thus the fineness of the fleece of sheep raised on the meadows of the Channel coast had been noticed, and Tournai had by AD 400 a factory for making the imperial army's cloaks. Afterwards Friesian cloaks made Flanders famous: Charlemagne gave Haroun al Raschid a *pallia fresonica*. By the thirteenth century Flemish workshops, directed by 'capitalist entrepreneurs', as Pirenne put it[1], had come to be considered without rivals for the fineness of their weaves and the beauty of their colours. In that basic element of mediaeval commerce in Europe, the wool trade, Flanders played the main part.

From the thirteenth century in Europe the disentangling (carding) of wool was done by a pair of wire-toothed brushes, the wool being worked from one hand to another, that task having been previously entrusted to a teasel, a member of the thistle family (*cardus*). Combing, as an alternative to 'carding', with metal teeth mounted on horn and a wooden handle allowed the comb to slip more easily through the wool. Then the spinning wheel came. Like most major mediaeval innovations this was invented in China, being apparently tried out in Germany in 1280 (at Speyer) for the first time in Europe. It doubled productivity, though spinning continued to be mostly carried out at home, occupying days when there was no work on the land for wives and daughters. Afterwards a horizontal frame loom was devised, a great help to weavers. Finally the fulling mill was invented, with power-driven mallets, driven by waterwheels. These new things seem first to have been tried in Italy.

Four European peoples depended for their wealth in the late agricultural age on wool: those of Flanders, England, Tuscany and Castile.

To begin with, English shepherds supplied the Flemish weavers. Then, after the Norman Conquest, Flemish artisans crossed the Channel and taught the English how to use wool. Eventually wool became 'the sacred staple and foundation of our wealth', in Andrew Young's words, though uttered long after it had ceased to be so.

This industry became increasingly well known in mediaeval Europe. Most of the work was done in scattered villages, a loom being placed in the main room of the cottage, the spinners helped by hand cards for carding, by distaff and spindle. Often this peasant worker would have clipped his wool from his own sheep. He would need water to remove the grease from the cloth, while a tub or two of dye and water would be placed at the door. Fulling and teasing might be done for a fixed payment at one or other of the many publicly maintained watermills. The industry was often a family concern: the father might sit at the shuttle, his wife and daughters at the spinning wheel, while a son might be doing the carding. Such a family might have an acre or two of land on which there would be a cow for milk, some chickens and perhaps a horse to fetch the wool from the shepherd unless there were family sheep also. The horse would take the carded wool to the fulling mill, where after a careful inspection it would be sold to a merchant whom the peasant might have known before and who might go direct to the peasant to place orders.

This type of long self-sufficient factory-family, which was also a world, eventually came to an end in Europe because of specialisation. Some families began to undertake spinning only, and some bought several looms. Some weavers allowed themselves to get into debt, and merchants would lend them money on the security of their looms. Sometimes those merchants would end up owning everything which the weaver possessed. The process known as 'putting out' meant that the weaver became more a workman, less a part-farmer. In some cottages, the 'sweating of labour' would, at the end of the age of agriculture, be worse than in a factory. Sometimes specialisation was insisted upon by those peasants who preferred spinning to digging and, like those who produced wooden tools such as scythes, hoped to concentrate upon it. Often, too, weavers would have enough work in their wool business to keep them from agriculture except during harvest.

Being one of the oldest industries, wool was more regulated than any other. Innumerable English Acts of Parliament, for example, laid down rules about length, breadth, weight of pieces and so on. Most of these rules were made to ensure quality. Most peoples in Europe employed quite a large number of wool inspectors to this end. These rules were, by the eighteenth century, an obstacle to all improvement in conditions of work. Colonies dependent on England were not allowed to produce wool. Ireland was prevented from developing a wool trade of her own. Only finished cloth was allowed to be exported (to prevent people from

copying) and almost every government banned the export of live
sheep.

The history of wool in Italy differed substantially from that in
England. There, the streams and rivers running into the Arno,
between Florence and the sea, gave such places as Prato and
Lucca the chance to act as purveyors of cloth to Venetian merchants. In Prato well-built canals provided water for fulling and
dyeing. Tuscan wool workers all developed their own speciality:
weavers, carders, spinners, dyers, wool-sellers, wool merchants
and yarn dealers were separate careers. By the thirteenth century
all were embraced in guilds led by the merchants. The poorest
group were the washers and carders (*i ciompi*, from the clogs that
they customarily wore). Above them were the other grades,
mostly women who, though employed by merchants, were working in their own homes, as in England. By that time the best
merchant sold Tuscan wool only to the poor, since it was rough.
The best cloth, on which Tuscany became rich and so financed
the Renaissance, was bought raw from Spain, Minorca, Africa or
England, particularly from the Cotswolds. Thus the shepherds of
Burford and Northleach made their contribution to the revival of
commerce, and the great barns of the Cotswolds helped to create
the fortunes of the Bardi, the Medici and the Frescobaldi.

The wealth of Florence was thus based on the import of raw
wool and the manufacture of finished wool. This achievement of
an economy based entirely on commerce had no precedent in the
ancient world nor in the East. The experience gained in this
commerce led to the establishment of the Florentine banking
families and, indeed, to the whole paraphernalia of modern finance, with its double book-keeping ('the Italian method'), and
trading associations which led to modern companies, shares, representatives abroad, sleeping partnerships and credit systems.

Finally among the wool trades of the Middle Ages that of Spain
deserves notice, since it derived from the exploitation of a single,
especially desirable breed of animal, the *merino* sheep, with white
curly wool, introduced into Spain from Africa by the Muslims (its
late discovery may have been due to its poor capacity for providing
mutton)[2]. But the semi-annual sheep migrations along fixed routes
which characterised the history of Spanish wool were known under
the Goths, probably under the Iberians. Indeed, the keeping of
sheep in the Mediterranean had for hundreds of years a similar
pattern of life, almost always causing quarrels between herdsmen
and husbandmen. Rome had had a special praetor to look after

the routes. Those practices were not interrupted by the fall of Rome. Mediaeval monarchs in both Italy and Spain merely sought to codify old rules. Spain in the Middle Ages had a more pastoral economy than any other country in Europe. On its broad grasslands, herds not only of sheep but of pigs and wild cattle grazed. This geography fitted better than did arable farming with the background of a 'perpetual crusade', which Macaulay spoke of concerning the Spanish Middle Ages[3], and shifting frontiers. The migratory cycle of sheep in Estremadura and south Castile during the winter, in the northern mountains during the summer, coincided with the alternation of winter peace and summer fighting. Shepherds made their way from Christendom into the land of the Muslims even in the earliest days. By about 1400 Spain was exporting raw wool all over Europe, especially to Tuscany, while English exports had dropped there. For Spain wool had become the 'indispensable source of royal revenue'. The Spanish state sought, in the words of the historian of the Spanish wool trade, Julius Klein, a 'carefully planned policy aimed persistently at one definite purpose, the export of those raw materials for which the greatest quantities of gold and foreign commodities could be secured in return'[4].

The Spanish wool trade was thus an export business, but there was no native cloth industry. King Ferdinand tried to found one by introducing detailed regulations for guilds, even prescribing a form of 'putting out system', à l'anglaise, establishing standard grades, weights of wool and so on, but all to no avail. Foreign merchants even took over the selling of the wool with royal permission and, in the middle of the so-called 'golden century' of Spain, the Genoese secured a monopoly of the export trade of wool (as of the sale of slaves to the Spanish Empire). Vast quantities were sold too to the Spanish Empire, while the woollen blanket, or *serape*, replaced the old *manta* of cotton or vegetable fibre of pre-Columbian America.

The Spanish failure to exploit a great natural resource must be attributed to one of the Spanish institutions which, like many such, was a mixed blessing, despite its fame: the Mesta. Its history not only reveals much about the economic failure of the Spanish people in the sixteenth century but also explains perhaps why the Latin American peoples have not benefited more from the advantages of having been a part of the European community of commercial nations.

The Mesta (the word derives either from *mezclado* or 'mixed'

– mixed that is, with strange flocks; or from *mecht* meaning winter encampments in North Africa) was a guild of sheepowners which arranged movements of sheep from summer to winter quarters, from north to south, along numerous well-defined sheepwalks. The Mesta protected the sheep from landowners who enclosed rights of way. It ensured the marking of the sheep. It organised herding. It arranged the policing, and fixed the rests, for 2·6 million sheep in 1479 and, in 1526, 3·4 million, who moved about 200 or 300 miles up and down Spain. The Mesta had its first letter of privilege in 1273 and it survived, latterly shrunken, till 1839. The daily march was sometimes fifteen miles, the average five miles and travel usually took a month. The southbound journey was made to coincide with the fiestas in the towns concerned and with harvest time.

Now, anyone who paid sheep tolls could join the Mesta, and such a person would not have to possess any specific number of animals. Far the largest number of sheep in the Mesta belonged to farmers who themselves led a few hundred sheep down the route, though there were also grandees who employed a bailiff to lead their 30,000 sheep for them. Meetings of the Mesta were regularly held, in a democratic manner, several hundred people being present (a tenth of those entitled to attend), though in the end the richer landowners took over the organisation. Women sheepowners had all the rights that men had.

The Mesta was a protected organisation and was given every subsidy and political advantage that it desired by the Crown. The Crown did all that it could to encourage the sale of wool abroad. This centralisation of management hampered severely the birth in Spain of free enterprise. Spain, indeed, by insisting on governmental control of marketing, was behaving more like the Islamic despotisms that the Christians had conquered than a modern European society, such as Tuscany, to whom she was selling the wool. Every effort was also made by the Crown to extend pasturage at the expense of husbandry. Attempts by landowners to improve agriculture, even in the *vegas* of Granada and Murcia, were either forbidden or choked by taxes. 'Seldom, if ever, had the agrarian life of a nation been held in so firm a grip, or been made to follow so strictly the single-minded purpose of a determined administration,' Julius Klein concluded, adding that it 'was not unlikely that the Mesta pressed the Kings to expel both the Moors and the Jews'[5], who by then were more concerned with crops than with livestock. The history of the Mesta is, therefore, one of how a governmental organisation dominated the main raw material of Spanish clothing in the later stages of the age of agriculture. Its static character helps to explain why wool was not the material which would in the end determine the manufacturing age in its earliest stages – neither in Spain nor elsewhere in Europe. That role was played by cotton. The example of the Mesta was also decisive in the way that the Spaniards managed their trade with the New World after 1492, as will be seen.

Almost as important in commerce as wool was silk, mostly produced on mulberry trees by silkworms,* the great discovery of the Chinese in the earliest times. The Chinese retained their monopoly of the manufacture of silk, by reeling, till about AD 300, when the Japanese discovered, or stole, the secret of the process. They were followed by the Indians. Long before that caravans had begun to go regularly west from China to Syria along the famous 'silk road', a path which lay along the south side of the Tien Shan mountains as far as Kashgar, and then crossed into Persia by Kashgar, Ferghana and Samarkand. The journey took nearly 250 days. Ten or twelve ships also went east from Suez every year. In China and, later, Japan, officials wore silk in public as a matter of course. In the Western mind, China was so associated with silk that the Greek and Roman names for China, Seres, indicated the cultivation of that commodity.

In the Mediterranean world, silk clothes were confined to begin with to women. From the time of the reprobate Emperor Heliogabalus onwards, in AD 237, men came to like them too. The Emperor Aurelian complained that a pound of silk was sold in Rome in his day for twelve ounces of gold. The drain of gold in Rome in the later Empire was caused by an insatiable appetite for silk.

In the days of Justinian, in the sixth century, the Chinese secret reached the West. Some silkworms' eggs were smuggled to Byzantium. From then on Chinese silk lost its unique position. There were enough people in the West who could acquire knowledge of silk-growing to ensure that Mediterranean merchants could produce a silk equal to that of China in quality. The Byzantine state, however, maintained a monopoly of silkworms on the mulberry trees for about 500 years. Only when merchants from Genoa and

* Some wild silk has been produced for many generations in China, and also in Assyria, Syria and the Aegean, by worms feeding on the oak. The product was not precisely a silk since it was not made by reeling (the cocoons were collected after the moths had emerged) but by combing and spinning.

Venice took over the finances of Constantinople, after 1204, was Italy able to become a manufacturer. Lucca became the first Italian capital of sericulture. Other cities soon rivalled it. Muslim Spain also made silk, particularly in Almería, then a great industrial city, which boasted 5,000 looms. The mountains behind, the magical Alpujarra, were covered with mulberry trees, and many Berbers were attracted to settle there. (Silkworms like a light airy climate, but dislike noise and bad smells: the smell of fried fish apparently causes them to die.)

The two main vegetable fibres of the age of agriculture were linen and, less important, cotton. Linen from flax was extensively cultivated in Egypt. Herodotus believed that all Egyptian clothing was linen, whether it was the upper robe and short kilt of the men or the long robe of the women; priests wore a leopard skin over their linen dress. (But many ordinary Egyptians and some priests wore cotton.) Used for linseed oil, sails and cordage, as well as for clothing, linen was grown all over Europe in the Middle Ages. It was the most important vegetable fibre in the West till the eighteenth century and was the only Western crop to find a market in Peking. No great technical development affected its processing between the days of ancient Egypt and the Renaissance, save for a machine which broke up the tissues. Linen was popular for underclothes for hundreds of years, from the time of the richer Greeks to that of the merchants of mediaeval Tuscany. When Dr Johnson wrote that 'Kit Smart had no love of clean linen', he was referring to underclothes[6]. Still, for the majority in Europe as in China underclothes were unknown till the thirteenth century and, to a great extent, till the nineteenth. Only manufacturing industry could produce clothes in large enough quantities to make any real impact on the scabies, tinea and other skin diseases which derive from lack of cleanliness.

Cotton was indigenous in Burma and Sind; in Egypt (as tree cotton); and in the West Indies (in its 'sea island' form). Egyptian cotton was a poor product and no match for Burmese cotton, which was widely worn in India in the fourth century BC. Alexander's armies carried that latter plant to Greece where it began slowly to be cultivated. Under Rome it was cultivated extensively, particularly in Malta. The Muslims took it to Spain and, mixing it with a linen warp from Egypt, it became well known in mediaeval Europe as 'fustian' (from the Cairo suburb of Fostat). This, together with locally grown cotton, was used in mediaeval Europe as an alternative to wool when wool was in short supply.

Sea island cotton was cultivated in the Americas long before Columbus arrived there; and cotton cloth (and some other cloths made from vegetable fibre) was much used, in fine weaves, in many places before 1492, and constituted a major item in assessments of tribute at the time of the Spanish conquest. In China mandarins wore silk in public but cotton in private, while ordinary Chinese people, for thousands of years, simply wore at work a long white cotton shirt gathered at the waist.

From early on people wished to have their clothes coloured if they could. The importance of colours in the symbolism of chivalry is well indicated by J. H. Huizinga, in his *The Waning of the Middle Ages*: the symbolic meaning attached to blue and green was so marked and peculiar as to make them almost unfit for usual wear. Blue signified fidelity; green, amorous passion; yellow meant hostility; grey or brown were both colours of sadness; white and red meant gaiety. There were many other combinations[7]. Hence the importance of dyeing, one of the most complicated of the early chemical processes, since the days of ancient Egypt.

It was known early that cloth would take colours more deeply and permanently if treated with the salt known as alum. In classical days that was gained from numerous volcanic regions of the Near East, and by the thirteenth century from Yemen, but after the fall of Constantinople in 1453 the West was cut off from those ancient sources. Then large deposits were discovered at Tolfa in the Papal States, the exploitation of which was entrusted by the Pope to the Medici family. Another deposit was discovered near Volterra, a find which led to Lorenzo de Medici's brutal attack on that then independent city. As to the dyes themselves, all then had an animal or vegetable origin – yellow from saffron, weld or fustic, while green and black both came from mixtures, particularly making use of indigo or of woad, grown throughout Europe. Purple came, for a time, from Tyrian purple, a brilliant dye derived from a crustacean found on the coast of Syria. The secret of making it, however, was lost after 1453. Red derived from the madder plant, cultivated near both Rome and Avignon, the two papal cities of Europe. Later, that was supplemented by the discovery by Europeans of cochineal, a product of the Americas made from the dried bodies of dead insects on Mexican cactuses.

These processes are a reminder that techniques may be used for thousands of years before the scientific principles behind them are recognised. The trading of these cloths over thousands of miles in difficult conditions recalls too that the desire for comfortable clothes and even the subservience to fashion and the elaborate treatment of raw materials are among the most deep-rooted of human attitudes, influencing profoundly agriculture, commerce, war, technology and methods of government. The manufacture of cloth was the chief industry of the age of agriculture, and in the end innovations in it indeed led to the transformation of the world.

16
Population and its Slow Growth

Few persons in the old world ever found themselves in groups
larger than family groups and there were few families of more than
a dozen members (including the extended family of uncles, etc.).
There was no object in England larger than St Paul's or London
Bridge.

Peter Laslett, *The World We Have Lost*

A good estimate of the numbers of the 'very rare food-gathering
biped' that man seemed to be about 2 million BC is 100,000[1]. At
the birth of settled agriculture, there were perhaps already five
million people in the world. The figure might have been 100
million at the time of the first dynasty in Egypt, due to the increase
of the area under crops made possible by the taming of cattle.
Perhaps there were about 200 million by the time of the birth of
Christ and 500 million about AD 1500[2].

None of these figures can be expected to be accurate. But the
population of the world was higher in the sixteenth century than
it had ever been before, and the most recent increase had been
the fastest. Population has not grown to modern levels by a steady
process. There were setbacks. The best known of these is what
happened in the New World after the arrival of the Spaniards.
According to good estimates Mexico had before then a population
of about twenty-five million.* That population fell to six million
by 1548 and by the end of the century was only 1,350,000, of
whom 100,000 were Spaniards. Mexico's population only recovered to its levels of 1492 in the mid twentieth century. Probably
the population of Peru began to fall before the Spaniards conquered it, since smallpox preceded Pizarro there.

The history of Egypt is another example of irregularity: the
population at the time of the Middle Kingdom (1991–1570 BC)
was perhaps four million, much as it was in AD 150. It fell to
three million by AD 550 and was less than two and a half million
between 1600 and 1800. It had probably grown back to seven
million by the time of the British occupation in 1882 and is perhaps

* There is, however, a less catastrophist view of Mexico's population in 1500.

127

now forty million. China experienced a similar decline and recovery, on a larger scale, between the first century and the sixteenth century AD.

Most of the great peoples of the past around which conventional history is constructed had what would now seem small populations, at the time of their greatness. Ancient Babylonia perhaps had four to five million in 2000 BC, Egypt (as noticed above) also had four million at that time. Greece in the fifth century BC had perhaps two million, and the city of Rome in Caesar's day a maximum of a million. Germany had four million at the time of Otto the Great, France five million under Charlemagne. Italy had between five and ten million during the lifetime of Leonardo. Spain attained seven million under Ferdinand and Isabella; England had three million under Elizabeth I and nearly eight million at its zenith, in the eighteenth century.

The populations of the East were always larger: India perhaps had a population of thirty to forty million in 300 BC, China sixty million in the first century AD. The comparative size of those populations, and the inability of the people concerned to create anything in the way of free institutions, shows the folly of supposing that large numbers are a benefit in themselves.

Often, peoples which have been invaded have attributed their ill luck to the supposed number of their enemies. In that way did the Mediterranean peoples explain their defeat at the hands of the Celts and Germans. The romanised Germans of Charlemagne's time said the same of the Vikings. Their grandchildren spoke thus of the Hungarians. In most cases such expeditions were, however, not caused by 'pressure of population'. They were mounted by 'small numbers of warriors seeking booty', as Marc Bloch put it[3].

The question which needs to be answered is: why did not the population of the world increase faster? At, for instance, the rate that it is increasing in the twentieth century? After all, the world's population may have been 250 million in AD 1. If so, it took 1,500 years to double. But it rose from 500 to 1,000 million between 1500 and 1825: a mere three hundred and twenty-five years. It doubled again in the hundred years between 1825 and 1925; and yet again, in fifty years, between 1925 and 1976, from 2,000 million to 4,000 million.

The first thing to be said is that the expectation of life did not rise between the era of Neanderthal man and the eighteenth century AD. It was 29 years in the Stone Age, and perhaps did

well to average between 25 and 30 between 1700 and 1750.*
England between, say, 1300 and 1750 was exceptional in having
an average rising to 35 years. In comparison, in the late 1970s the
expectation of life was believed to be 71 in Europe, 62 in Latin
America, 56 in Asia and 48 in Africa. Asia, Africa and Latin
America thus have a life expectation a third higher than that of
Europe before the eighteenth century. Sweden is today apparently
the nation with the highest expectancy of life (75 years): Guinea
the lowest (27 years) – that is still below that of Neanderthal man.

A rise in the birth rate, not a fall in the death rate, seems to
have been the cause of the rise of the population during the
eighteenth century, and perhaps that was usually the case before.
In the sixteenth and seventeenth centuries a birth rate of 35 per
1,000 was normal in Europe[4]. In the eighteenth century, that rose
everywhere. By 1800 most European countries had a birth rate of
40 per 1,000 (France was 33 in 1802, Russia over 50 in the 1860s).
The highest figures for birth rates in recorded series for European
countries all occur at different times: Austria being 43 per 1,000
in 1820, Germany averaging 40 between 1872–79, Britain reaching
36 in 1878 and Italy reaching 39 in 1836. Now these figures are
often exceeded in the 'Third World' today. Few African countries
have a birth rate under 40 per 1,000. The Latin American birth
rate is 38 to 40 per 1,000, while India, Indonesia and China
average respectively 43, 48 and 33[5].

Why did these high figures for birth rates begin to be achieved?
Was it the coming of better medicine, or some other changes in
the character of disease? A better climate and hence, for that
reason, better food? An end of civil wars and other improved
arrangements for public order? Or other factors, contributing to
a revival of optimism? In the nineteenth century (figures for earlier
times are not reliable) the highest rates of birth coincide with
times of self-confidence in the country concerned: France had its
highest birth rate in the year of the Peace of Amiens, 1802;
Germany, in the year immediately after the formation of the
Empire, 1871; Russia, in the year of the emancipation of the serfs;
Italy, in the year of reunification; and so on. The same has been
true of other countries in the twentieth century.

* The expectation of life for anyone who had already reached 30 years in the
seventeenth and eighteenth centuries seems to have been another 22 to 26 years
in England, which meant that a man's death usually coincided, as Lawrence
Stone pointed out, with the marriage of his eldest son (perhaps making an
inverse causal relation between the adult mortality and the age of marriage).

From these modern instances, it is necessary to go back further and ask again, what prevented the birth rate from being higher? First, there were attempts in the past to limit births by contraception. For example, there were contraceptive benefits in the requirements of Lamaist Buddhism that every family should contribute a son to one of the great monasteries. Tibet also practised for hundreds of years a system of polyandry which also restricted births. The Chinese employed abortion and infanticide before Christ, and sought, if they did not achieve, a contraceptive pill in the seventh century AD. Ancient Egypt, concerned to maintain the family, also wished to keep the population stable. Paste made from crocodile dung used as a pessary, honey and natron (a carbonate of soda) placed in the vagina and medicated tampons of lint dressed with tips of acacia were all apparently used in the seventeenth or sixteenth centuries BC. Soranus of Ephesus in the second century BC discussed different methods of contraception, including recommendation of 'abstention from coitus at times which we have indicated'. It is thus foolish to suppose that the very idea of contraception is a modern one.

It seems obvious, also, that despite the Church, the king, the hope of having young people to look after the old and the need of hands in the harvest, many families throughout the world often in the agricultural past limited their number by, for example, *coitus interruptus*, postponement of marriage, abstinence, abortion and infanticide. Henri II's law shows that abortion must have been sufficiently practised for it to be legislated against.* There were doubtless also many who would have liked to have said to their sons-in-law what Madame de Sévigné, in the seventeenth century, said to hers: 'Listen to me, son-in-law, if, after this boy's birth, you do not give my daughter a rest, I shall assume you do not love her [and] . . . take her away from you. Do you think that I gave her to you to be killed?' When the son-in-law obeyed, she wondered: 'Do I owe this to his temperance or to his real affection?' Careful investigation of families in the days of the Renais-

---

* Henri II of France insisted on *déclarations de grossesse* (that being tantamount to saying that the government wished the child to be born), and the parishes in England were ordered to collect vital statistics by Thomas Cromwell in 1538, in order to establish information about descent needed to maintain rights of inheritance firmly. But that system was not thoroughly maintained and it was not until the nineteenth century that it could be said to be so: a good example of the length of time that it often takes human societies to implement ideas even when they know them to be good ones.

sance has shown that fewer families had a large number of children than is often believed. After all, the age of agriculture was an age of peasants, who have at least one inducement to limit children: to avoid the division of properties. In France, by the eighteenth century, children were also already competitors with other luxuries which were then available. Perhaps women's desire to keep their figures, in an aesthetically aware society, played its part. Perhaps that had been the case in Egypt, Greece and Rome before. The use of wet nurses shows that maternity was not always chic.

No doubt *coitus interruptus* was the most common method of contraception used, since no foreign body placed in the uterus could have been hygienic – though the importance of hygiene was unknown. Since this practice is held to require self-control, the early decline in the rate of French growth of population has been attributed to greater self-control among the French. French historians, however, doubt that: 'L'unique problème est celui du "pourquoi" et non celui du "comment",' wrote Pierre Chaunu,* 'parce que le "comment" les singes anthropomorphiques le connaissent . . . et les sociétés primitives sont celles qu'ont été les plus efficaces . . . les recherches sous ma direction en Normandie montrent que la diffusion d'un certain malthusianisme latent dans les campagnes Normands se situe . . . dès 1730–40 . . . il s'agit d'un problème de motivation, et non pas de technique'[6]. Such devices as there were seem to have been more used against disease than against conception.

Probably the most obvious way in which population was limited in the past is illustrated by the history of infant mortality. Statistics will presumably never be found which explain this accurately for the remoter past. The main points to notice, however, are first that before the eighteenth century there was never any alternative to breast feeding and, second, that here as elsewhere there was no knowledge of hygiene. Mothers and nurses, therefore, poisoned children in thousands. Some knowledge of what happened can be gleaned from the experience of the eighteenth century itself.

Where possible, the rich then were in the habit, in Western Europe as elsewhere, of turning over their babies to wet nurses. That necessitated, in the families of the upper class, care in the

---

* Pierre Chaunu has recently used his great prestige as a demographic historian to appeal for more births in the advanced world, particularly in France.

choice of nurse, since it was thought that a child's character would thereby be influenced. Nevertheless, many wet nurses were inadequate. Babies were passed from one to another and then, in the end, were often distressed to return to the real mother: 'Who has not seen these banished children,' asked Cobbett, 'when brought and put into the arms of their mother, screaming to get from them and stretching out their little hands to get back to the arms of their nurse?'[7]

As for the poor, whenever they could, they turned over their unwanted children, legitimate or illegitimate, to foundling hospitals to which, even in 1750 – perhaps particularly in 1750 – thousands of children were sent. On the eve of the French Revolution forty per cent of births in France were believed to be *enfants trouvés*. A majority of such children died. An American historian, William Langer, commenting on these events of only 150 years ago, wrote: 'In the light of available data, one is almost forced to admit that the proposal seriously advanced at the time that unwanted babies should be painlessly asphyxiated in small gas chambers* was definitely humanitarian.' 'The survival of the wet-nurse in France, into the eighteenth century, ensured a high rate of infant mortality,' wrote Lawrence Stone, another historian of the modern family. In pre-Columbian America the lack of milk from animals meant that mothers had to nurse their children till three or four years old. That must have decreased feminine fertility even if it may have helped the children.

The slow growth, and occasional decline, of population in the age of agriculture worried most societies. Homosexuality was widely rendered illegal essentially for that reason, as in Babylon. Europe and the Mediterranean were influenced in respect of population by Christianity and Judaism and by God's reported adjuration to Adam and Eve 'to be fruitful and multiply'. Indeed, most societies had policies towards population one way or the other. (It is left to the modern democratic state, otherwise so much of a busybody, to have no policy on the subject, except those it by implication adopts on behalf of the 'Third World'.)

The golden age of Greece, for example, had unambiguous attitudes. The discrepancy between Genesis's 'Be fruitful and multiply' and the Greek anxiety about overpopulation could not have been wider. The Greeks had too many people for their supply of food from 700 BC onwards. Hence, their colonisation of the

* Gas was invented about 1800.

Mediterranean, their reliance on wheat from the Black Sea, and the proposals of Plato for an ideal city, of 5,040 people. Aristotle merely wanted to keep population stable. He thought that over-population would increase the poorer classes, not the intelligent ones, lead the city to anarchy and, afterwards, to despotism. Plato considered population on eugenic grounds: 'nuptial inspectors' would ensure that the best wedded the most beautiful. These views (which had no successor till the twentieth century AD) were held against a background in which abortion or abandonment of children were usually permitted. The only difference among the Greek states was that in Sparta (where, uniquely in history, it was provided that no member of the ruling group should be able to identify his children or parents) it was the state which would decide whether a child would be permitted to survive; while, in Athens, that duty was the responsibility of the father.

These stony-hearted policies, along with a public cult of homosexuality, were successful. By the second century BC, Greece was short of men. Polybius complained that people were preoccupied by money and food and wished neither to marry nor to have children. The kings of Macedon passed a law trying to persuade their subjects to breed. Sparta changed its laws to give a bias against bachelors. It encouraged the wives of old men to have children by others. In vain; the decline of population and of Greece continued apace.

The Romans carried out censuses from about the sixth century BC, and for the next five centuries their population rose, encouraged by a flow of slaves captured in wars and by the frequency of marriage by girls from the age of twelve onwards. But by the time of Augustus fashionable families practised a cult of childlessness. The first Emperors had few or no children: Gibbon recalled that, of the first fifteen Emperors, Claudius was the only one whose taste was 'entirely correct' in sexual matters[8]. Old Roman law had given unlimited power to the *paterfamilias*, even to the extent of permitting him to expose newborn children on rubbish dumps if they were not desired – earlier, even to kill or to sell a child.

From the first century AD the state encouraged the population to grow. Laws were passed which obliged the young to marry. The continuous flow of slaves and other non-Roman immigrants seemed to make no difference: the population declined. Celibates suffered loss of inheritance: again, to no avail. Gibbon wrote, 'Pious maids who consecrated their virginity to Christ were restrained from taking the veil till their fortieth year. Widows under

that age were compelled to form a second alliance within five
years by [the threat of] the forfeiture of half of their wealth'[9]. To
kill a child was proclaimed to be the same crime as parricide.
Probably Septimus Severus' law of AD 212 proclaiming all citizens
of the Roman Empire to be free and equal was decreed with one
eye on the size of the population. But, as previously in Greece,
these laws were to no avail. All who write of the decline of Rome
notice the shortage of men for armies, and the deserted
farmlands[10].

The coming of Christianity seems, despite its message that marriage was, as with the Jews, intended for the procreation of children, to have exacerbated Rome's problems in this regard. For
the Church exalted virginity, condemned adultery, insisted on the
maintenance of marriages (however badly they were working and
however unequal the partners were in age) and extolled monasticism. Some fathers of the Church (Tertullian, Origen) condemned marriage as impure. Meantime, the burden of taxation
meant that 'the horrid practice of exposing or murdering the new
born infants' became ever more frequent. The importance of the
eunuch was symbolic. Soon afterwards the Western Empire fell.

The subject of population, like most things of the mind, was
not raised in a new form till a thousand years later, although St
Thomas Aquinas had made clear that in his view 'any carnal act
which could not result in generation is unnatural'. The humanist
Leone Battista Alberti, in his *Treatise on the Family*, written in
Florence in 1432, agreed and suggested that the state should
honour those with large families. Luther, Muhammad and Machiavelli said the same. Bodin in Paris in the sixteenth century
argued that 'il n'est ni force ni richesse que d'hommes'. Juan de
Mariana, Vauban and Frederick the Great thought the same.

On the whole, the intellectual climate during most of the age
of agriculture was one where most religions encouraged large
families. The Greek and Roman experience was exceptional in
this matter, as in others. Most people were encouraged to marry
and people were more afraid of the population dying out than
growing too fast. In the eighteenth century, just when the world's
population was beginning to leap forward at an unprecedented
pace, the cleverest men believed that the world was less populated
than it once had been. Montesquieu wrote, in his *L'Esprit des
Lois*, 'il y a à peine sur la terre la dixième partie des hommes qui
y étaient dans les anciens temps. Ce qu'il y a d'étonnant, c'est
qu'elle se dépeuple tous les jours. Si cela continue, la terre ne

sera plus dans deux siècles qu'un desert'[11]. The Abbé Raynal thought in 1781 that it would be odd if the USA could support a million people[12]. David Hume was of much the same view.

A typical family in the world of agriculture is no doubt impossible to define. Was such a thing to be found in India, between the Aryan and the European conquest? There, the family was often a large one, generally extending over several generations with sons and their families living in the patriarchal centre. Early marriage was unusual, most people had some choice in their mate, but a wife had to practise a symbolic self-immolation at the death of her husband, and among the upper classes of central and east India later a real sacrifice (*suttee*) – the first instance of which is believed to have been in AD 510. The Indians banned any incestuous relationship very strongly. Polygamy and polyandry were known but monogamy was more usual. The position of women was subordinate, even if, as often in old societies, idealised in literature. The only women who had any real freedom in India in its golden age were those who became Buddhist nuns, prostitutes or actresses. Yet to know what happened in this model family, in truth, it would be necessary to ask an endless number of questions comparable to those posed by Burckhardt in his chapter on morality in *The Civilisation of the Renaissance in Italy*: 'Was the marriage tie really more sacred in France during the fifteenth century than in Italy? What eye can pierce the depths in which the character and fate of nations are formed? in which even those intellectual capacities which, at first sight, we would take to be primary are, in fact, evolved late and slowly?'[13] Literature tells something of the realities of the past, but poetry and novels even of the same period give different pictures. Still, some truths emerge: 'Among the Massagetae, wives were held in common,' said Herodotus, 'but the Egyptians, like the Greeks, had only one wife'[14]. In mediaeval Europe girls were often really nuns in their own house. Despite immense varieties some facts stand out:

First, the world was managed, and most families, by people who would now be regarded as young men.

Second, the more primitive the society, the larger the group: Marc Bloch tells us that 'vast kindreds' or 'patriarchal families' characterised Europe till the sixth century AD at least, and only slowly did the idea of such clans begin to count less and individuals or small 'nuclear' families count more[15], though none of those professionally concerned in demographic history would agree as to when that began to be so.

Third, what Gibbon calls the 'iniquity of primogeniture' was a comparatively late development, even among monarchs and noblemen.

Fourth, a great many children, certainly many more than today, found themselves, because of early deaths, without either their fathers or mothers fairly early on in their childhoods[16].

Fifth, about half the population at any one time were probably under age: approximately the percentage of a country such as Venezuela today. But there was only rarely a school. Dr Laslett adjures us, therefore, to 'imagine our ancestors in the perpetual presence of their young offspring', some of whom were of course working, even if that merely meant hovering around the loom[17].

It is tempting to regard population and its growth as a key to human history. After all, the numbers concerned in the age of agriculture were much smaller than they are today. Time and again 'population pressure', a useful if vague expression, has been given as the explanation for this or that occurrence. The inflation in Europe in the sixteenth century was caused by the import of gold and silver from South America, it was once, it seemed, proved by Earl Hamilton. But that argument forgot the growth of European population. Have not those who attributed the Russian Revolution to the First World War forgotten the increase of population in Russia since 1861? On the other hand, much of history was a time of slow growth of population. There were also setbacks due to disease, war and famine, as the next chapters will try to show.

17

Diseases and Doctors

There is alas simply no way to decide whether the division between the two main branches of the Protestant movement would have taken place anyway or whether that important phenomenon did take a decisive turn when Luther and Zwingli bade one another a hasty adieu in 1529 in order to escape the 'sweats'.

W. H. McNeill, *Plagues and Peoples*

When King David of Israel committed what to Jehovah seemed the disgraceful crime of making a census, he was offered a choice of three punishments: war, famine, and disease. He chose disease.

The part of disease in restraining the growth of population in the age of agriculture is obvious. What the killing microbes were is more difficult to decide: could the disease which devastated Athens in the fifth century have been measles – a measles in its prime, newly arriving amid a population lacking immunity or powers of resistance, as suggested by W. H. McNeill[1]? What were the plagues which carried away thousands in Rome during the second and third centuries AD? At that time, after all, smallpox and measles were not recognised as being separate things, and the name of leprosy was given in the past to many skin infections. The word 'plague', too, was attached to anything from influenza to dysentery.

In the absence of knowledge of the epidemics, the effect of disease on history can scarcely be studied. But some general comments are worth making. First, maladies which had been mastered by those who lived with them for generations gained new leases of life when travel made possible their rebirth in new continents. Hunting man met fewer diseases than modern man. Though peripatetic, he came into touch with fewer centres of bacteria. He adjusted himself to those local illnesses which he and his ancestors had long known. A good example of that was the way in which the natives of the Caribbean and northern South America became immune to the only serious disease of that continent, syphilis. The legends of old Cuba before Columbus, for example, were full of tales of heroic canoers finding the cure for that disease in remote jungles.

Travel and commerce, however, since 1492 have spread all diseases world-wide. Man has been a more effective carrier than rats. Irrigation, which from the early days of Sumer was the hallmark of civilised agriculture in the West, encouraged the mosquito and the diseases that it carries. Similarly, when the explorer Orellana led his Spaniards down the Amazon, they met no fever of any sort: within a hundred years such a journey would have been most risky, for yellow fever prospered in the New World as well as did malaria. The former was taken there in 1648 from West Africa, no doubt in a slave ship. It ruled the countries of the Caribbean as firmly as did any viceroy. Hookworm sprang from fertilised fields. Larger, and more, cities meant more rats. More rats meant more plague bacilli in the fleas on the rats' backs. Indeed, diseases such as measles, mumps, smallpox and influenza depended on the large populations of settled agricultural man. They derived from modified versions of diseases which affected animals and are probably about 6,000 to 8,000 years old.

Secondly, some diseases have been created by man. For example, gas gangrene, the worst complication to affect a patient suffering from a gunshot wound, naturally had no history before the dissemination of firearms in the sixteenth century.

A third consideration is that the lives of great diseases are controlled by elements not fully known but comparable to those of civilisations. This seems particularly to be so in respect of plague, the epidemic which caused more distress than any other malady in history and which, because of its unmistakable symptoms, even in literature, can be more easily chronicled than any other. It is an exemplary tale and worth a diversion.

There are two plagues: bubonic, caused by bites of fleas and resulting in large tumours, or buboes, in the groin or the armpit and pulmonary plague, transmitted by spit or breath. Most plagues in history were bubonic plagues.

With this illness, *xenopsylla cheopsis*, the flea feeds on the blood of an infected rat and takes into itself a quantity of plague bacilli. These lodge in the forestomach of the flea which becomes blackened by a solid mass of bacilli. When a flea feeds, the blood does not pass to the stomach but goes into the hole made by the flea's bite. The bacilli flood the hole with regurgitated blood, whether it be that of a man or another rat.

The rat concerned is the black one, *rattus rattus*, which originally came from India. The disease itself may have been endemic there for thousands of years. It was apparently unknown in Europe before 300 BC. Perhaps it was brought to the Mediterranean by Alexander's army. The opening of a regular land route to the East (ensured by Alexander) made possible the transmission of a disease whose incidence in the West was partly a consequence of Mediterranean man's desire for silk and spices. Even so, the 'plagues' of Rome may not have been such. The first unquestionable incidence of plague in the West was the epidemic which affected Constantinople in Justinian's day: 10,000 were dying from bubonic plague there in 542. The sporadic return of this disease was a cause of the subsequent weakness of the Eastern Empire (as of the Persian one too), so helping the easy victories of the Arabs in the seventh century. About that time the plague was first seen, apparently, in China. It returned there again and again. Half the population of Shantung was said to have died from it in the 760s.

The plague then became quiescent for reasons as obscure as those which caused its later revival. Did it revive as a result of the slave trade from the Black Sea to Italy? Was it transmitted by the Tartars, who in 1346 were besieging the Genoese in their fortified trading post at Kaffa in the Crimea, and who threw their infected corpses over the walls into the town? At all events, the plague swept into Europe: 'It began,' wrote Boccaccio, 'both in men and women with certain swellings in the groin, or under the armpit. They grew to the size of a small apple or egg . . . These spread all over the body. Soon after . . . black or purple spots appeared on the thighs or any other part of the body . . . most people died within three days . . . most of them without fever. Some thought that moderate living would preserve them. They formed small communities living entirely separate from everybody else. They shut themselves up in houses where there were no sick, eating the finest food . . . [while] others thought the sure cure was to drink and be merry'[2].

Whatever evasive action was pursued, a third of Europe's population died, two-fifths by 1400. Poland escaped, but no other country in Europe did. The Near East lost many too. The loss of population in Europe and the Mediterranean was not made up for a century or more. Economies declined. Farms were abandoned. Labour was short. Prices rose. Thousands were ruined. At the first suspicion of a recrudescence of plague, the rich fled to their country houses. Magistrates and prelates abandoned their duties. It seemed, therefore, that the poor suffered worse. The psychological reaction was curious: flagellants beat each other furiously

to propitiate God's supposed wrath, while some accused Jews of
spreading the disease. The optimistic Christianity of the thirteenth
century gave way to mysticism. Painters depicted the dance of
death, instead of the serene pastures loved by Giotto. The failure
of Church and Bible to have anything effective to say encouraged
lay scepticism and, perhaps, the use of the vernacular in literature.
The cult of St Sebastian grew, since the world saw itself as being
dealt terrible blows by unseen arrows. The plague in England
even led to a statutory policy for wages – the 'Statute of Labourers', which sought to fix wages at or near the rates prevailing in
1346. In the event, the shortage of labour made wage-labour more
attractive, and in the west of Europe most escaped from feudal
restrictions in consequence.

The plague returned often to Europe between then and 1750.
It is especially remembered in England in 1666, but that was only
one of several visits, and not the worst. Spain suffered a terrible
visitation of plague between 1647 and 1654, probably the most
severe catastrophe in her modern history: half Seville died, giving
Cádiz the chance to restore her ancient position as the greatest
trading city of the Spanish south. Plague was taken to the New
World and the outbreak there of 1576 nearly destroyed the native
population of Mexico. Italy suffered in the seventeenth century,
and again in 1743. Russia suffered severely in 1709 and 1720,
while 90,000 died in 1720 in Marseilles and near by (including all
the policemen, most public servants and thirty-two out of thirty-
five surgeons). Then, though there continued to be epidemics in
Egypt, and though a million died of the plague in India in 1895,
the bacillus withdrew, as it were, from Europe and it has not been
seen since. Why? Did the black rat find the new stone houses of
absolutist Europe less friendly than the wooden ones of feudalism?
Was the black rat overthrown in a civil war of the animal world
by the brown or grey rat? Did people wash more? Were the
quarantine arrangements begun in Venice which ensured the insulation of Marseilles in 1720 really effective? None of these
explanations is satisfactory: Italians had stone houses in the fourteenth century, and plague can be passed on by squirrels as well
as by rats. Whatever the reason, despite occasional panics (the
steamship was believed likely to bring back plague to Europe
from China in the 1870s), the life of the plague, in Europe at
least, simply came to an end.

It was not till long after the plague ceased to be a menace that
its cause came to be known. A connection with rats was suspected,

it is true, but the part of the flea was not realised. Only in 1898 did Paul Louis Simond suggest that the flea might be the transmitter. Only in 1914 was that hypothesis proved.

When plague disappeared, other diseases took its place. A roll of succession comparable to a list of monarchs could be devised showing that bubonic plague was followed (in Europe at least) in the eighteenth century as the reigning malady by smallpox (though that had been known, in a minor way, since the days of Justinian), in the nineteenth by tuberculosis – briefly challenged by cholera – and in the twentieth by heart diseases, cancer and, as a cause of death, accidents in cars. Leprosy, the malady *par excellence* of the early Middle Ages, never re-established itself in Europe after the Black Death.

These diseases did not have such devastating effects, both in terms of numbers killed and of psychological disturbance caused, as did plague.

The eclipse of plague was not secured by doctors, nor by an international medical programme. It died. Its death coincided with a general improvement in climate, which itself did much to revive a spirit of optimism in European affairs. Perhaps the increase in the world's population in the eighteenth century is directly related to both the climate and the optimism, as much as to the better health.

Similar brief histories to that of plague could be written about other diseases, such as malaria or sleeping sickness. Each could be defined in its way as a history of the world. For example, malaria: Known once as 'ague', and deriving its modern name in English from the false assumption that it derived from the bad air, *mal aire*, of Italian swamps – particularly 'bad night air' – malaria was known in antiquity and was accurately described by the great Greek physician Hippocrates. Many African tribes knew that the disease was carried by mosquitoes. But that view was not recognised as true by Europeans till the nineteenth century. (A Tuscan proverb argued that 'the best remedy against malaria is a well-filled stewpot'.)

Though Hippocrates knew of malaria, and Alexander the Great is believed to have died of it,* it is not evident that it was a serious disease before the late Roman Empire. In the last years of that undertaking, the shortage of manpower and the prevalence of invasions led to the neglect of the drainage in Rome and of the

---

* He may also have died of drink.

once developed irrigation in the farmland of the Campagna. The stagnant water afforded an opportunity to the mosquitoes which remained there for 1,500 years, making malaria the characteristic disease of the region, and being the main cause of the decline and depopulation of Rome for so long. (The draining of the marshes was, however, begun by Pope Pius VII in the eighteenth century and completed by Mussolini in the 1930s.) The population of Rome had grown from about 130,000 in '508 BC to 750,000 in 70 BC, and reached over a million during the third century. It fell back to 700,000 in the days of Constantine the Great and numbered a mere 35,000 in 1050, before rising to 100,000 by 1600, 160,000 by 1800, 300,000 by 1880 and only reaching a million again in the time of Mussolini: the life of the holy city was probably determined more by malaria than by any other factor. Alexander Borgia died of it, and so did Dante.

Every time that malaria is mentioned, Africa should come back into the discussion. That continent has been so influenced by the disease that it might well have been called after it. The frontiers of existing countries there derive from the desire of both Arab and European conquerors to base their colonies on the coast. Malaria also ensured that, while Africa could be circumnavigated by a European, in 1487, it was not till 1853–56 that it could be crossed by one: Livingstone. Malaria prevented a Portuguese conquest, or even much penetration, of Central Africa till the nineteenth century too.

The history of both plague and malaria recalls that, before the nineteenth century, little serious contribution was made to the relief of the disease by either medicine or doctors. Certainly population did not increase because of what was done in that respect before the nineteenth century.

Of course, there have been doctors and surgeons for many generations. Some may claim that those generations of experience were essential to the medical achievements of the industrial age. That seems dubious. The benefits of surgery were equally modest till the nineteenth century.

The earliest medical or surgical activity was the trepanning of skulls. It occurred as early as 7000 BC. To relieve pressure on the brain, or to let out devils? Perhaps both. At all events, in ancient Iraq, the piece of bone cut out was often prized and hung round the neck as an amulet. Bones of remoter times have often shown signs of disease though not of surgery. The Chinese, perhaps as a result of information passed from the West, used trepanning to cure blindness caused by tumours.

Ancient Babylon and Egypt both had doctors and doctor-gods, and Ningizzida, son of the god Ninazu, was the first, it seems, in Babylon to have been identified by a rod of entwined serpents. In Egypt, doctors were often priests. Epidemics had goddesses. Many diseases were held to be the work of demons. All doctors in Egypt were specialists: there were no general practitioners. Both Babylon's and Egypt's doctors were served by innumerable instruments and prescriptions, most with magical or semi-religious qualities. The laws of Hammurabi in Babylon named punishments for doctors who failed to cure diseases. In its heyday Babylon cultivated 250 medicinal plants, used 150 mineral substances and bred animals for medicinal purposes. Emetics were used to sicken demons. Tablets which survive preserve many diagnoses: 'If a man's body is yellow, if his eyes and his face are yellow, and if his skin is flabby – it's jaundice'[3]. Egypt was well known throughout the ancient world for its good doctors, and great families of surgeons were established – nearly all professions became hereditary – who, among other things, opened abscesses and stopped bleeding by cauterisation, using adhesive plaster on wounds. Though they possessed many recognisable implements, including an early scalpel, they did not amputate.

In Greece, medicine showed to begin with no advance on Egyptian and Babylonian practice, though the art of bandaging was apparently developed there. An important change came with the great Hippocrates of Cos, who in the fifth century BC devised his famous method of taking and keeping notes on patients. He also invented the clinical lecture and the bedside instruction and insisted that doctors had to behave honourably: an idea embodied in the Hippocratic oath which binds doctors always to work for the patient's benefit, not to give deadly drugs, not to misuse their position, and to keep silent about what they may learn in the course of treatment.

These rules were challenged by Hippocrates' contemporary, Plato, who thought that doctors should not only concern themselves with the prolongation of life but should consider the interests of the state. Despite many generations of incompetent doctors, the Hippocratic idea was not seriously challenged by physicians until the twentieth century when, in both Communist Russia and Nazi Germany, Plato's ideas were partially put into effect.* Even in democracies, doctors have been known to break their oath of secrecy about what they have learned from patients. Doubtless there have been instances of physicians refusing to treat patients (or insisting on so doing) before the twentieth century. It is hard to think of previous occasions when such malpractice became a governmental policy.

Many books were attributed to Hippocrates, but only his aphorisms remain: for example, 'Life is short, art is long, opportunity fleeting, experience fallacious, judgement difficult'; or, 'Those naturally very fat are more liable to sudden death than those that are thin.' Hippocrates' studies of actual cases were also without parallel, like many Greek innovations, till the seventeenth century AD. Other Greeks too did great things in medicine. Herophilus, in the third century BC, for example, dissected a human body in public, and recognised the brain to be the centre of the nervous system. Erasistratus of Chios, a grandson of Aristotle, about the same time, thought that disease was caused by excess of blood, a truly disastrous error. (He was said to have discovered, by the motion of the pulse, the love which the Emperor Antiochus had conceived for his mother-in-law, and was rewarded with a large sum.)

Rome, on the other hand, was uninventive in medical matters. But the Empire did develop an effective system of medical organisation, based principally on greater attention to sanitation. Imperial Rome had numerous public lavatories, drainage was good, and the first hospitals were created, beginning as private nursing homes in doctors' houses. The Emperor Vespasian in the first century AD gave doctors a salary at the public's expense for the first time. The Roman army took care to secure an adequate supply of doctors. Otherwise, Rome's contribution to medicine would merit the neglect that its method of imperial succession also deserves, were it not for the extraordinary figure of Galen, who died in AD 200 and who was the most influential doctor of all time.

Galen is a good example of a strong character whose most important ideas were all wrong. His energy, learning and friendship with the humane Emperor Marcus Aurelius gave him a great reputation in his lifetime and control over the imagination of medical Europe for a thousand years. As a student of anatomy, Galen knew where the bones are in the human frame, though he

* See below, page 571.

knew animals better than he did men. There was little he did not know about muscles, and so he may be considered as the founder of experimental physiology. But he was ignorant of the brain and of the vascular system. He thought that blood was made in the liver. He believed that suppuration was an indispensable part of healing, and in the 'miraculous' powers of certain substances. He and his followers endeavoured to heal wounds by constant interference, such as changing bandages, an error not finally dismissed until the twentieth century. Galen lived at a time of decreasing rationalism and an increasing desire to believe, whatever the absurdity of the belief. He and his school brooked no criticism and, unfortunately, conquered the medical schools of the Roman world. (Ptolemy, who re-established the Earth at the centre of the Universe, did the same for astronomy as Galen did for medicine.*)

The era known in the West as the Dark Ages was specially sombre in respect of the study of medicine. Byzantium kept what books it could. Few read them. The Nestorians, chased as heretics from the Eastern Empire, translated many Greek medical books into Syriac and subsequently they were re-translated into Arabic. But in the West of Europe, monks relieved patients as best they could, innocent of theoretical knowledge, and worshipped St Cosmas and St Damian, two patrons of 'medicine' murdered under Diocletian. Some trepanning was done with a thong-drill and a few recollections of the advances made during the pre-Christian era survived in remote, if pagan, valleys. Princes and priests alike meantime often treated leprosy, with brutality.

That disease had previously been confined to the East. It reached France and Britain in the sixth century (though some still claim that it was brought to Europe by the Crusaders). Lepers were isolated, declared legally dead and often excluded from the Church – an impious act of cruelty for which the Bible gave no justification. 20,000 leprosaria were founded outside mediaeval towns in Europe, in which the shattered, white-faced patients, many of them only suffering (at least at the beginning) from chicken-pox, were forced to await a lingering death. These centres of isolation were almost the only medical innovation of the Middle Ages. They had, in the end, some good effects: the arrangements for quarantine used with success for plague derived from the

---

* This is perhaps unfair to Ptolemy who did list 1,022 stars and made serious contributions to astronomical movements and to optics. His *Almagest* also seemed a breath of fresh air when translated into Latin from Greek about 1160.

special landing station where Venetian lepers were forced to wait for first a *trentaine*, then a *quarantaine* (forty days) in the open air.

One improvement to man's physical life does, however, date from the Middle Ages: spectacles, without which subsequent intellectual life would be hard to imagine, were in use in a primitive form from the fourteenth century onwards (perhaps devised by Roger Bacon in England), making a substantial if unacknowledged contribution to the revival of learning.

While Europe slept and America lived a dream of innocence free almost of disease, Islam was at work. Arabic Spain, for example, knew the old Greek books on medicine and made use of them. A school of medicine was established at Salerno, then a strong principality, near Naples, and derived much vigour from military contact with the Arabs. A few old Greek books were translated into Latin. Salerno also taught the desirability of a balanced diet and revived memories of Hippocrates. Public dissection began again. A few adventurous monks went to Spain to bring back the secrets of Graeco-Arab medicine to northern Europe. Though sometimes branded wizards, they persisted. Thus a Renaissance in medicine began in the end. But still the impact of medical science on life and death remained slight. It is hard to believe that population was much affected one way or the other by those ancient scalpels.

The medicine of China before the Industrial Revolution seems to have been at every point more successful than that of the West. That was because of the use of acupuncture, which from an early time enabled the Chinese to be more ambitious in cautery. I-Ching also wrote: 'In China, there are more than 400 different kinds of herbs, minerals, stalks and roots, most of which are excellent and rare in colour and taste . . . thereby, we can control any disease and control the temperament.' In treatment, we hear, 'I-Ching relied largely on abstention from food'[4]. Europe, which learned so much from the East during the Middle Ages, never considered the use of acupuncture as a means of securing the patient's insensitivity to pain. Chinese medicine, on the other hand, remained almost as unchanging in its character as did China in its methods of irrigation, being based on a series of special principles formally laid down, including an elaborate way of listening to the pulse and the use of mineral drugs.

The Indians included medicine from an early time in their curricula of education. It was practical. It suffered no special setbacks during what Europeans speak of as the Middle Ages but remained as static as the system of castes, except for the beginning of work in veterinary science. On the other hand, the Indians of old America before 1492 used a large number of herbs, leaves and food as medicaments. Carima cake soaked in water for children who had worms, cashew juice before breakfast for the 'conservation of the stomach', the bud of the embaiba tree for wounds and tobacco leaves for diseases of the sexual organ were among innumerable recipes listed by Gabriel Soares in a sixteenth-century Log Book[5].

These considerations deal with the regular practice of medicine. In most of the world, Europe included, the age of agriculture was a time when disease was looked upon as an evil presence which could be exorcised – by witch doctors, charmers, wizards, witches or even kings. English wizards, for instance, in the sixteenth century told their clients to dig holes in churchyards, boil eggs in urine and tie staves, salt and herbs in cows' tails. Money retrieved from the offertory of a church was held to have magic power. Magic in the age of agriculture had other uses: for example, detection of thieves, as love philtres, to give foreknowledge of rebellions or pursuit of treasure. In the rational days of the nineteenth century these ideas were dismissed as dangerous fancies. But today the role of suggestion, faith in therapy, the power of ritual as well as the concept of psychosomatic disease have been, rightly, reconsidered. In the late seventeenth century a French doctor had a patient who was convinced that he was possessed of the devil. The doctor called a priest and a surgeon, while equipping himself with a bag containing a bat. The patient was told that a small operation was needed, the priest offered a prayer and the surgeon made a modest cut in the man's side. As the cut was made, the doctor allowed the bat to fly up and cried, 'Behold, the Devil is gone.' The man was cured. Possibly more people throughout the world were effectively cured in this manner in those days than as a consequence of the weak working of a weak science.

18

Swords and Soldiers

Crassus was in the habit of observing that nobody should be called rich who was not able to maintain an army on his income.

Sir Ronald Syme, *The Roman Revolution*

The second of the evils supposed in the Bible to have been linked to the limitation of population was war.

Now, in the age of agriculture, people died because of war less in battle than as a result of marauding armies. In a contest as long-lasting as the Hundred Years' War between England and France, the devastation of crops was more destructive than the killing of men. Men also died from disease contracted in war, or from the consequence of crowding tired, ill-fed men into a small space, a fertile ground for microbes. How appropriate that Clausewitz, the greatest writer on war, should have died from cholera in 1831 when stationed on the German–Russian frontier! Cholera also carried away, in the same epidemic, not only Clausewitz's chief, Field-Marshal Gneisenau, but the commander of the Russian army across the river and Hegel as well. (That first great European outbreak of cholera seems to have been brought back from Bengal, where it had been endemic and destroyed, on its slow way, eighteen per cent of the population of Cairo and thousands of Muslims on the way to Mecca. Nobody then knew that cholera was caused by a bacillus which can live a long time in water.*) At the same time, large armies have often preserved peace, even if at a price. The history of war is, therefore, not the history of killing by violence; and the Great Condé perhaps was statistically right to suppose that 'one night in Paris' would 'make up for the losses at the battlefield of Rocroy'[1].

The violence of savage peoples was, and is, expressed in head-hunting, assassination, man hunts and predatory expeditions, caused by fear, religion, hunger and cruelty. Can such killings be dignified by the name of warfare? No: the idea of 'warfare' applies when, as J. H. Huizinga put it, a 'special condition of hostility solemnly proclaimed is recognised, as distinct

* For cholera see page 582.

from individual quarrels and family feuds'[2]. This definition has not always been carried out even by modern peoples who believe themselves civilised. Still, in African communities a fight over the succession to the chieftainship was traditionally a permanent feature of life. To men of the Stone Age, war was not the business of a few select people. It was the occupation of every adult male, whose aim was to kill enemy males and to abduct the women and children. In some respects, people of the twentieth century have returned to a condition where discrimination between victims is impossible: slaughter is now on total lines. That sort of war must have been one reason for the failure of population to rise as fast as it might between at least the coming of agriculture and the birth of Christ. The Bible, the Homeric poems, Herodotus and almost every work which gives useful historical evidence are full of terrible wars to the death, heroes being always successful warriors, successful nations being always those successful in battle. Death in action was considered the noblest way to die throughout most of history.

What have been the causes of war? Overpopulation has often been considered one likely reason. But overpopulated China remained many years at peace, and the American Indians, who occupied vast territory per head of population, were usually at war. The barbarian conquests in late Roman days were carried out by small but fierce tribes from places where the density of population was low. Even in 1939, Germany had less pressure of population than Poland, and Italy had a lower birth rate than Ethiopia did when the former attacked the latter in 1935. The German desire for *Lebensraum* was more an excuse for, than a cause of, the Second World War. In general, wars seem, like crime, to have been caused by the desire of the undisciplined to seize the goods of the comfortable.

Very often the audacious have had such confidence in their weapons that they have believed victory to be theirs for the asking. Thus, to begin at the beginning of recorded history, the weapons in the Mycenaean age were, like those of the European 'Hallstatt culture', made of bronze: swords (just invented), double axes, spears and javelins. Armour was sometimes made of bronze too, but also of leather, heavy linen (surprisingly good against swords) and shields of ox-hide, with metal bosses. Chariots were then more often used for taking warriors to battle than in the fight (unlike the use to which the Hittites put their equipment). Cavalry was not much used, since the horses of that time were small, unshod animals with no proper harness and whose riders had no stirrups. These Mycenaean forces seem to have been prepared for use against seaborne raiders but, as with other peoples, once an effective array of weapons had been achieved, it cost little to begin wars on slight excuses. The seduction of Helen was a good example of that.

Innovations in technology were almost always decisive in their early stages. The battering rams and siege engines devised by the Assyrians, perfected by the Romans, were decisive in sieges. The Hittites retained their knowledge of the secret of how to make iron till their empire fell apart, but thereafter that precious information soon spread – to farming also. (Ploughshares and sickles, as well as sword and dagger blades, were soon being made out of iron all over the Near East.) The Persian conquests (of Assyria, Babylon, Media and Lydia) were achieved by mounted bowmen and camels from Bactria. The 'long lances' of Scythia were thereby shown to be ineffective. The decisive battle between the Persians and the Lydians was won by the former, since according to tradition the latter's horses did not like the smell of the Persian camels. Cyaxares, King of the Medes, was the first man, according to Herodotus, to give any real organisation to an army, dividing the troops into companies and forming distinct bodies of spearmen, archers and cavalry, who before that time 'had been mingled'[3]. This innovation probably preserved more life than it destroyed. The crossbow, invented in China during her 'feudal wars', was the decisive instrument in securing the Han dynasty's victories against Mongol nomads.

The numbers involved in these armies were large in proportion to the populations even if estimates of Xerxes' force by Herodotus resemble the exaggerations by Spanish chroniclers of the sixteenth century in the New World. Sparta, the great military power of Greece, after the eclipse of the cavalry of Thessaly was a state in arms rather than a strong country with a good army. She had 5,000 warriors of the officer class, 5,000 shepherds and 35,000 'helots'. Both Greece and Persia were in the end reduced by Alexander's 35,000 men, a force adequate to conquer half the world. The Roman army at Cannae was said to be 50,000 to 80,000 strong, while the Roman army at its zenith in, say, the second century AD included thirty legions each of about 12,500 – or about 375,000 to 400,000 men in all. It seems a small force with which to preserve peace in the age of the Antonines. The monarchies of the Middle Ages in Europe, however, never approached such figures: the King of France commanded the largest army in feudal Europe at Crécy: 12,000 men. That number of Berbers was enough to conquer Spain for Islam in 711. The First Crusade gathered only 25,000 to 30,000. The German Emperor's great offensive against the Turks in 1467 numbered a mere 18,500.

In comparison, Oriental armies seem almost modern: Haroun-al-Rashid once conducted a summer campaign in Persia with, apparently, 135,000 regular soldiers, while under the Sung dynasty, it is said, China had trained several million men. In the long 'time of the warring states' in China there is frequent mention of a hundred thousand heads being cut off.

Even so, wars fought with these weapons could not have much effect either way on the history of population. Casualties of a few hundred young men were not decisive for a country's survival. Once peoples became regularly concerned with the enslavement of a population which they conquered rather than their annihilation, the direct effects of war became modest. The indirect effects nevertheless remained.

This point is made by the slightest consideration of how these armies actually fought. Sometimes the parties (as in mediaeval China and ancient Egypt) might put their disputes to a representative test: Chalcis and Eretria fought by terms of a contract in which rules were laid down beforehand in the temple of Artemis. Time and place for the battle were specified, and so were the weapons. A code of honour had grown up too. Even Xerxes of Persia, according to Herodotus, refused to act 'like the Lacedaemonians who, by killing the heralds, had broken the laws which all men hold in common'[4]. All the evidence is that from an early stage regularly instituted states endeavoured to keep to certain rules in the actual battle. They looked after captives, if not as laid down in the Hague Conventions of 1899 and 1907, infinitely better than, say, the Germans and the Russians treated captives on the eastern front in 1941–45. Only after battles was violence likely to be uncontrolled. The existence of rules to which all states within a certain civilisation adhered of course made the attacks by outsiders, 'barbarian hordes', all the more feared.

Sieges, on the other hand, really were often devastating to civilians: in the Peloponnesian war, Sparta built two walls round Plataea, one against the besieged, one against any relief force, the two lines being sixteen feet apart[5]. Such devices were intended to 'reduce' the populations concerned and often they did so, causing innumerable civilian deaths. When sieges ended in the besiegers' victory, the besieged were often 'put to the sword'. Such actions, even when carried out by peoples such as the Greeks who were more thoughtful than most, resulted in innumerable killings. Thucydides ascribed the breakdown of order and of democracy to the demoralising effect of war: 'Greek states lived on so bare a subsistence rate,' Maurice Bowra wrote, 'that a long war had a devastating effect . . . machinery for enforcing law was undermined by the absence of men on foreign service . . . and [also] more violent politicians came to the fore'[6].

From the fourth century BC onwards, for eight hundred years, large, organised armies were the decisive political influences in the Mediterranean world. First, there were the phalanxes of Macedon, the secret of whose success was that cavalry, for which northern Greece had long been renowned, was for the first time linked with infantry rather than scattered. The infantry abandoned heavy armour for greater mobility and greater ease in using the long lance in battle. Once Greece had been reduced by Philip, the Macedonian armies in Asia were sustained by an irresistible Greek fleet. Alexander, it is said, was also the first to use a torsion catapult to despatch arrows and stones, at the siege of Tyre in 323 BC. That was a great innovation, marking the beginning of an era in which such catapults would give attack an advantage over defence.

The history of the Roman army, however, is so important in the history of war that it deserves a diversion. For the Roman army was, to begin with, the state, inseparable from it and with no other institution comparable to it, each class within the state being obliged to play a military part, even more than was the case in Sparta. Thus before entering the *cursus honorum*, the career for the leaders of Roman political life in the Republic, at twenty-eight years of age, a man had to have served ten campaigns. All magistrates and politicians were thus ex-soldiers. On the other hand, the rank and file of the first Roman army were farmers, who returned home at the end of the season's campaigning. That military basis for many years gave Roman life its coherence, and the recollection of that arrangement cast a shadow over the careers at least of the European nobility till only recently.

War followed war throughout the third and much of the second century BC. Rome succeeded in dominating and absorbing the peoples of the Italian peninsula with this army, but thereafter large-scale foreign operations and Mediterranean-wide diplomacy seriously strained the old constitution, with its principle of annual office and colleges of electors.* War, for example, forced a change in the law which prevented a man being a consul more than once in ten years. The establishment of the proconsulship, which led to the achievement of great power by Caesar and Pompey (and hence to the Empire), began with the desire for a commandership-in-chief, a post first filled by Scipio Africanus for ten years[7].

A century later, Marius, in the war against Jugurtha, found that out of the old classes in the census there were no citizens willing to fight. But there were innumerable extra *classi*: the proletariat of the city, ex-slaves, ex-captives, men from non-Roman peoples, men Celtic in origin and men never normally conscripted. Marius made of them a volunteer but professional army. Henceforward soldiers ceased to expect to go home to their farms. A breed of men was born who knew only the Legion and its eagle.

The new legionaries extended the Empire. But there was not enough money with which to pay them. Hence their loyalty turned towards individual generals, who promised them rewards provided that they won. Hence, the Roman civil wars, which finally ruined the old constitution and killed thousands of potential fathers of families. Peace was only achieved when Augustus decided to give smallholdings in Italy to thousands of his, and his great-uncle's, soldiers, at the cost in many cases of long-established smallholders. Augustus also paid his men a cash bounty equivalent to tl...teen years' wages, a sum raised by sales and inheritance taxes.

The imperial task of the Roman army afterwards was to preserve peace, with these professional cadres, in the territories which the Republic had won. The main strength (sixteen legions†) lay on the Rhine and Danube. The next most important army was that constituted by the legions on the Euphrates. While Egypt, Africa and Spain had one legion each, Britain had three. Italy at that time was held by 20,000 men. This entire standing army was composed of volunteers at eighteen who served for twenty-five years. After that, they would receive a grant of land or a gratuity, but land, the best asset, was almost always preferred. Recruitment became local. Soldiers were theoretically not allowed to marry, but usually did so, so that in the end it seemed as if soldiering was becoming an hereditary calling. Equally characteristic of Rome during this defensive era were the famous fortified cities, whose ruins are so often visible, established in the form of a

* See below, page 184.
† Each of about 12,500 men.

square or quadrangle big enough to hold 20,000 men, the prae-
torium or general's quarters rising in the centre above the straight
streets constructed on a gridiron pattern, a symbol both of Roman
power in the provinces and of military power in guaranteeing that
authority. Over these years authority in the Roman Empire
moved, indeed, to those defensive barracks: the old capital became increasingly a shell. The true capital was wherever the belligerent Emperor kept his headquarters.

The wars against Picts, Germans and Parthians were the only
interruptions in the triumphant administrative achievements of
the early Empire. But at the end of the second century the main
question in Rome became one of how to control the controllers
of the peace. This is an occurrence which, subsequently though
not before, affected many armies, particularly effective ones.
Usually such events have led to destructive civil wars, affecting
both population and national confidence. In Rome the difficulties
arose from the growth of the imperial guard (the nine praetorian
cohorts stationed at Rome and in certain Italian towns, which had
been founded under Augustus). After the death of Caligula in
AD 41, the 'praetorians' frustrated a patriotic move on the part
of the enfeebled Senate to revive the Republic. In AD 69 the
guard gave the Empire to Otho who, however, lost it in four
months. After the serene era of Vespasian and then of the Antonines, the guard dominated the Empire for ninety years, from
193 to 280, killing Pertinax, auctioning the Empire to Severus
Julianus and murdering two imperial candidates from the Senate
in 238. Meantime, other armies had their imperial candidates and
pretensions; for, from AD 68, as Tacitus put it, it was known 'that
elsewhere than at Rome an emperor might be created'[8]. In the
second century the Empire was in consequence disturbed by a
continuous civil war between the army of the East and that of the
Danube, the Senate in Rome customarily bowing to the wishes of
whichever proved stronger.

These disputes were the first occasion when military force unrelated to properly constituted power became the determining
factor in a political system. After the fall of the Roman Empire
this concept of military intervention in politics became again of
minor importance until the collapse of the European empires in
the nineteenth and twentieth centuries, when military politics like
that of the praetorian era were revived: 'the caprice of armies
long habituated to frequent and violent revolutions might even
raise to the throne the most obscure of their fellow soldiers'[9].

Gibbon's contemptuous words characterise the history of Africa, Latin America and Asia after the European empires had withdrawn: old customary loyalties bound men no longer, but neither did imperial ones.

As the political power of the Roman armies increased, their military capacity declined. That also has been a mark of modern political life: the more political the army, the less professional and the less effective they have been militarily, since, as Gibbon put it in respect of the late Roman Empire, 'the relaxation of discipline, and the disuse of exercise, rendered the soldiers less able and less willing to support the fatigues of the service; they complained of the weight of the armour which they seldom wore; and they successively obtained the permission of laying aside both their cuirasses and their helmets'[10]. The consequence was the introduction of barbarians into the Roman armies: 'every day more universal, more necessary and more fatal' and the 'most daring of the Scythians . . . found it more profitable to defend, than to ravage, the Roman provinces'[11]. The consequences included the breakdown of order, the pessimism and decay which characterised the second half of the Roman Empire and the decline in the birth rate.

The end of antiquity will always be, as it has been for two or three centuries, a fit subject for meditation by reflective historians. The role of war in causing it cannot be forgotten: the final collapse in the eastern Mediterranean, and the end of Mediterranean commerce as it had been known for generations, was occasioned by the great Arab victories. But among the causes of the failure of population to grow faster, the place of war figures less greatly, at least directly, than may seem to have been the case at first sight. Great armies have been as often as not the instruments to preserve civilisations.

Meantime, the main offensive forces between the third and the fourteenth centuries AD were constituted by Central Asiatic hordes. Sometimes relying on well-armed horsemen, sometimes being a whole tribe in arms, wave upon wave of these aggressive nomads fell on Europe, the Near East and China. Even the Arab invasions paled into insignificance in comparison with those of the Mongols. The Mongols captured most of Russia and all China and were repelled only by Japan in 1281 – because they were land warriors who could not manage maritime fighting.

19

The Religious Frame

Heaven made the sovereign for the sake of the people.

Hsun Tzu, c. 250 BC

1

The age of agriculture could not conceive of life without God, or gods. Religion was the chief common factor among all peoples of whom there is record, whether well-established monarchies in Asia or Stone Age tribes in Brazil. Religion adapted itself to the demands and the timetables of agriculture. Almost every people at one time or another attributed great authority to the part of the sun. Indeed, the sun has probably been worshipped more consistently than any other deity. Never perhaps was the sun more passionately worshipped than it was by the Aztecs in Mexico two thousand years after that primitive religion had been eclipsed in most of the Old World. 'In their days of triumph,' wrote Ignacio Bernal, 'they [the Aztecs] had to go on bearing the terrible burden of keeping their god, the sun, alive. Every evening, as the sun sank behind the mountains in the west, came the terrible doubt: would it reappear tomorrow? During the night would it defeat its enemies, be able to fight off the tigers and other terrors that would attack it? . . . Unfortunately for the neighbours of the Aztecs the only nourishment acceptable to the sun was human blood'[1].

Worship of the moon, the stars, comets, rivers, seas, streams and animals survived into modern times, as well as occasional worship of the sun. Still, the most striking development in the age of agriculture was the gradual growth, 'development' perhaps would be a better word, of religions which aspired not to be more than the sum of beliefs, traditions and hopes of a mere people, but which were put forward as a complete explanation of human life and history, and refused to be tied to the destiny of a simple people. One of the most remarkable facts in history is the way that these magnificent visions began to emerge at the same time (give or take a century or two) in the Mediterranean world, in India and in China.

The Egyptians, as has been seen earlier, seemed to be making some steps towards these ideas in the days of the Middle Kingdom. But it was the Jews who first conceived in definite terms of a personal and unique deity who had founded the world.

Judaism received about 1200 BC a formal theology from Moses, who led the Jews out of Egypt, first to Mount Sinai and thence to Canaan, a beautiful territory halfway between Babylon and Egypt, whose inhabitants had previously worshipped numerous gods at open-air shrines. The priestly hereditary class of Judaism, descended from Moses' brother Aaron, could inspire political and religious deference among the 'Children of Israel' since (as in Babylonia in many cities) for a long time there was no monarch, only a succession of 'judges'. But the revelation of the idea of the transcendence of God was not confined to a few holy men but made manifest to the people. Religion, law and politics held the people together (largely by oral teaching, for it was a long time before Moses' law was written down). At Mount Sinai, the different groups were bound into a legal community by a 'covenant' with the God Jehovah, who was assumed to be the Jews' supreme commander in war, as well as the world's creator and judge. The exceptional legal position of Jehovah distinguished the Jews from their neighbours, even if the laws proclaimed on Jehovah's behalf by Moses and his successors derived in part from Hammurabi and other legislators of old Iraq. Among many substantial conceptions attributable to the Jews, and passed on to Christianity, was the sense that law was a concept which, originally given by God, bound rulers as well as ruled. Another was the dangerous, if inspiring, one that the Jews were a specially chosen community.

The Jews were a tiny people. They had no desire to export their religion to others. It remained for the combination of Judaism with certain aspects of Greek thought to provide the intellectual preparation for the victory of the universal religion of Christianity.

The Greeks of classical times had many deities, whose characteristic was that, like the deities of Iraq whom the Jews had rejected, they fought, quarrelled and did not die. There was a master god, Zeus, brought by the Aryan ancestors of the Greeks from the Caspian Sea whence they originally came, while the other gods were indigenous to pre-Aryan Greece. In Greek religion, there was no orthodoxy, there were no sacred books, no order of authority, nor a clear link between the rumbustious gods of Zeus' court, with their magnificent good looks which never faded, and the Delphic, Dionysian, Eleusinian, Orphic and other mysteries. The Greeks in the classical age lived in a religious maelstrom. Many attributed all passion, rain, witty thoughts or qualms of conscience to the gods. All saw the gods as self-sufficient and, above all, successful beings, the memory of whose extraordinary achievements glittered across the Mediterranean like swords in sunlight. With these gods men might be friendly, but they must never insult them: when Actaeon saw Diana naked, he was torn to pieces by his own hounds.

The Greeks did, however, share with the Jews (unknowingly) a sense of 'destiny, vague, but sure', even if that destiny was not revealed, at least not in Homer. They believed in some ultimate order of 'necessity' or of 'fate' to which even gods (as well as great men) had to conform. They thought that poetry, the first art of literature, and indissolubly linked with music, was the 'voice of a man who had a god to prompt him'[2]. The Greeks were anxious to establish where man fitted in the universe. They sought a harmony defined as 'keeping to one's place'. Finally, they allowed themselves to speculate about the chances of religion having a rational basis. That was a great step forward in freeing the intellect from superstition: 'When it comes to the gods, I am unable to discover whether they exist or not,' wrote Plato, 'or even what they are like in form. For there are many things which stand in the way of this knowledge – the obscurity of the problem and the brevity of man's life'[3]. When it came to the point, too, the religious authority to which the Greeks paid in the great days most attention was the Pythia, the priestess of Apollo at Delphi, who considered that most troubles could be settled by common sense.*

The Greek philosophical imagination anticipated every problem of religion (though not every experience) and drew some of its inspired thoughts from Egypt (though nothing directly from the Jews). Thus the Greek community at Croton in southern Italy thought that the body was a temporary prison of the soul, while Pythagoras, the inspiration of that colony, believed not only in immortality but in the transmigration of souls, an idea which he had learned from Pherecydes of Scyros (who died in 515 BC). Further, 'like the Italian painters of the Renaissance who painted again and again the familiar stories of the Bible, Greek tragedians told again and again familiar myths', using religion as a lens

---

* Professor Fontenrose of the University of California has analysed 615 preserved responses deriving from the whole corpus of classical literature.

through which to glimpse all the problems of the world, fostering thereby, as Maurice Bowra put it, 'a new spirit of enquiry into the visible world . . . a desire to understand things exactly'[4].

At much the same time, equally thoughtful visions began to be glimpsed in other parts of the world, drawing men away from animal or weather gods, towards more mystical beliefs. Thus the Aryans who went to India – and perhaps that connected them with their distant Greek cousins – sensed forces around them which they could not control, and which they invested with divinity. These forces, they believed, could only be propitiated by sacrifice. Such views were commemorated in the Rigveda, a long collection of sacrificial hymns (*Veda*), dedicated to the gods of the Aryans, written down by priests, about 1000 BC. Later, a sect of poets, in the *Upanishads*, a mystical version of the *Vedas* (about 600 BC), taught that the soul could escape from the suffering inherent in earthly life by the realisation of its identity through an impersonal, if cosmic, soul. The doctrine of rebirth to a higher level, ensured by former acts (karma), was also conceived. These ideas were welcomed by traditionalists on the grounds that they gave a sacred sanction to the system of castes.

India between then and the fourth century BC was as reflective as, if less stimulating than, the same epoch in Greece. Parsya argued that life could be organised best by the acceptance of four vows: to injure nobody; not to steal; to be truthful; and to possess no property. Another prophet, Mahavira, who was almost an atheist, added non-violence, chastity and rigid asceticism to those, and so founded Jainism. The Jains, for example, believed in the transmigration of souls: if one lived well one would be reincarnated in a higher state; if badly, lower; even insects may have been, and may again become, humans. That meant that it was desirable to avoid eating anything, in a fruit or vegetable, which might be alive. Hence the Jains' vegetarianism, and the evolution of a concept, shared by Buddhists, that cows (always prized by Aryans) were sacred. Meantime, the serene Siddhartha, the Buddha, about 500 BC, taught that meditation, morality, altruism and personal religious experience could lead to Nirvana, or a peaceful release from the continuous cycle of birth and rebirth. He also put forward an early version of the idea of the social contract for the origin of the state.

These views did not overturn the system of castes nor the old religions of India. The castes divided society completely and, though Buddhism and Jainism supported the lower castes, the priests, the brahmins, continued skilfully to use the new ideas to underwrite the old castes. The combination evolved into Hinduism by the third century BC, the original framework being modified to allow the birth of a new generation of gods: Shiva, the god of destruction, change and rebirth; Vishnu, a god of sacrifice, the preserver, embodied on earth by the hero Krishna; Rama, the spirit of conjugal devotion; and Brahma, the creator, the Indian equivalent of Zeus or Jehovah, though less important, save for his alleged role in founding the castes. These revisions leading to modern Hinduism were embodied in the *Bhagavad-Gita*, written about the first century AD, which prescribed that every man should act according to law, regardless of the consequences. About the second century AD the peoples of South-East Asia came to be influenced by Hindu culture, probably as a result of Indian traders' visits to countries which were still barbarous: Burma, Thailand, Malaya, Indo-China, Sumatra and Java. Buddhism followed.

Numerous other sects survived and prospered, sometimes splitting or coalescing, though occasionally, as exemplified by the case of Asoka in the third century BC, a great king might arise who was affected by one of India's beliefs (in his case, Buddhism) and that belief would dominate the peninsula for a time. All these new religions coexisted, however, with India's more ancient beliefs. Buddhism, indeed, became the dominant religion of Asia, establishing outside India a magnificent network of monasteries and convents, which became the direct stimulus for hundreds of years of sculpture, poetry, architecture, education and sceptical reflection.

A similar intellectual vitality characterised China about the same time. Many philosophers were able to obtain a hearing and to record their views. They were consulted by kings and noblemen. The absence of priests prevented conformity. Philosophers recalled the golden age of the Five Sages and planned how it could be restored. The mythical Lao-Tzu preached that man was part of a harmonious universe governed by law and that he could find his best ethical guide within himself. Example was all, teaching useless. Mo Ti argued that self-discipline, clear thinking and the accurate use of words were the only guides to correct action. He suggested that a benevolent paternalism was the only hope for effective government. Confucius (born about 550 BC) also taught the virtues of clear thinking which, with self-discipline, he believed could lead the superior man to correct action in all his relationships: above all, the good landlord would treat his peasants well. Loyalty, filial piety, respect for antiquity and observance of the old chivalric code was the foundation on which everything should rest. A man of royal descent, Confucius gave enthusiastic support to the Chou emperor as representative of the only unifying factor which he could see in society. His hero, however, was Yu, the legendary founder of the equally legendary Hsia kings, who ate simple food and dressed poorly, even if he had built irrigation canals to the public benefit. Mencius, who lived about 320 BC, more specifically urged monarchs to pursue the public welfare.

When the Ch'in dynasty established itself, in the third century BC, a 'golden age of Chinese philosophy' was inaugurated. All the thinkers associated with it lived in a society rendered stable by the firm rules needed for the production of rice, but whose people had only a feeble attachment to its old gods – perhaps because Chinese prosperity was due to human endeavour in hus-banding water rather than, as occurred in the rainy West, to the emptying of the heavens. The Chinese Empire was for many centuries managed by Confucian scholars with a remarkable de-gree of tolerance of Buddhists (received in China traditionally in AD 65), Taoists (followers of Lao-Tzu with some elements of Buddhism) and others including, later, Muslims and Christians. Buddhism was the only important foreign influence in China. But despite the inherent difficulties, the sacred books of Buddhism were translated into Chinese. Though Confucianism remained the philosophy of the Chinese governments, Buddhism became the religion of most Chinese. The intellectually minded were alarmed at the contradictions between the two. Most Chinese accepted both at different times.

Buddhism arrived a little later in Japan. There the native religion – Shinto, 'the way of the gods' – has been as long-lasting as its national dynasty. Shinto constitutes a pantheon of gods made up by forces of nature, well-known natural sites and past heroes. Japanese gods were conceived as vague, impersonal forces. Their rituals paid much attention to cleanliness. Buddhism was able to grow well in such circumstances though its success in Japan owed much to the promotion of Prince Shotoku, a power behind the throne in the seventh century AD.

The movement towards intellectual religion was also experi-enced in Persia, where about 660 BC Zoroaster refined the religion previously prevailing in Persia out of all recognition. The world, he believed, was a battleground between good and evil.

Good men were those who obeyed the good god Ohrmazd, lord of wisdom. If they did so, they would after death cross the Bridge of the Requiter to Paradise. Evil people, on the other hand, would fall off the bridge and be interned indefinitely in the 'House of the Lie'.

These powerful and simple interpretations captured first Bactria, then Media (Zoroaster, whose name meant 'rich in camels', was a Mede) and, in the end, Persia itself. The great Achaemenian kings of Persia were Zoroastrians. The 'barbarians' of Greek history were led by men whose religion was in many ways as close to Christianity as was their own religion and, through the heresy of Manichaeism, affected Christianity directly. Indeed, a kind of 'vulgar' Zoroastrianism has had the longest life of all religious ideas.

The religion practised officially by the people who came to dominate the most civilised part of the Western world, Rome, was less reflective. There, from the earliest days until the fourth century AD, priests, augurs, keepers of the Sybilline books and vestal virgins maintained watch over the flight of birds and the sacred fire, predicting the future and imposing on the past a patina of gravity, not always justified by the events so embalmed.

'The deities of a thousand groves and of a thousand streams', representatives of 'every virtue and every vice, exercised a pantheistic authority' over nature, while 'the various modes of worship . . . were all considered by the people as equally true, by the philosophers as equally false; by the magistrates as equally useful'[5]. Thus Gibbon summed up Roman religion. No doubt Mars, the god of war, and then Jupiter, the father of the gods, once exercised a real authority over Romans but, by the time when they began to write of them, the hold of the gods was as modest as that of the river wizards over China; they were used principally to inaugurate magistrates. The diversity of deities increased when Rome managed to conquer so much of the settled agricultural world in the West. The conquerors brought law, but unlike the European conquerors of the world in the sixteenth century they had no universal religion to propagate. Indeed, the religion of Rome could be, and was, easily assimilated to the Greek, of which it was originally an offshoot.

Rome also accepted without difficulty the sacred springs and trees of Britain and Gaul, the heavenly goddess of Carthage, Baal in Syria and, in Egypt, the vast paraphernalia of temples, animal gods and professional priests. Mithraism, the worship of Isis,

Stoicism, Judaism and Platonism all flourished under Rome, after their fashion. Their idiosyncracies were protected by law. Thus a Jew could not be sued on the sabbath and was not pressed to serve in the army, since he could not there obey the law of Moses. This tolerance had been practised by the Achaemenian emperors of Persia and was the mark of all 'empires' in the ancient world. A cult of the Emperor himself began, it is true, in the time of Augustus, but for many generations its function was to provide an excuse for athletic festivals. Those were held throughout the Empire, with a devotion to ancient custom but with less religious feeling than in many courtly ceremonies of conventional piety. Waves of mysticism, however, occasionally swept the Roman Empire: Domitian established a cult of Isis, while Hadrian's friend Antinous set up a cult of Diana. Diocletian, who restored the Empire, believed in Mithras. Hence his persecution of Christianity when he heard that Christians in the army were insulting the old gods.

After centuries of toleration, cynicism, agnosticism, mild polytheism, pessimism and a cult of the Emperor which fell short of that constructed for the Pharaoh, the Roman Empire in the third century AD constituted an easy conquest for Christianity. The ground for the acceptance of that faith had been prepared, regardless of the question of the divinity of Christ, by the blending of mysticism with Roman wisdom and with a long-term optimism embodied in the idea of the immortality of the soul.

2

Christianity had a radical and new conception of human destiny. With Pythagoras and the citizens of Croton, Christians believed, from the beginning, that the body was a prison. Life on earth was a preparation for Heaven. Christians also accepted the Egyptian concept of immortality and considered both the end of the world and the Kingdom of Heaven to be imminent. Where Christianity differed from other religions was in the place that it gave to the individual, the human being who, even if his spirit were the only thing that counted, had full responsibility for his own fate, regardless of the demands of temporal power. A second element was the attention which it paid to the care for the poor, humble and sick. In place of numerous deities too, there was only one paternal God. Christians were ordered to follow a special rule of life, consisting of the eating of a common frugal meal, baptism by water and acceptance of the idea that answers were provided to all questions in a series of sacred books. But above all, the humane but austere character of the Redeemer, Jesus, son of God, born in Nazareth in what now seems to have been 6 BC, presented a major contrast with saviours in previous religions.

The Church also proclaimed that 'ideas should rule the world. It nourished in men's minds the conception of an absolute truth and a universal law, and, along with these, the notion of a superior virtue . . . it preserved the tradition of a cosmopolitan and democratic society in which all are called and in which the lowest and the humblest could be raised to the government of mankind'. Kings were not irresponsible. They were also governed by law[6].

In the first and second centuries AD Christians were more unpopular in the Roman Empire than were the Jews. They were said to practise ritual infanticide. They appeared positively to enjoy insulting old gods. Still, the tolerance of Rome prevailed for many generations. Two Jewish teachers, St Paul and St Peter, seemed an improbable threat to the established gods, even if they had been executed by Nero. The Christian religion was also, to begin with, confined to Greeks and to urban merchants. The landowners and the peasants remained pagan. Innumerable other mystery religions competed for the minds of Romans: Mithraism and Manichaeism, Egyptian and Syrian cults, many old, some new. Greek was the language of the Church of Christ till the fourth century, though Christians went East as well as West – even to India, where the apostle Thomas is supposed to have founded the Syrian Church in Malabar before being killed in AD 68.

Persecutions under Rome were sporadic. They were due to working-class agitation against Greeks as much as anything else. About AD 250 they became more frequent, perhaps because of the need to find scapegoats for so many disasters. The Emperor Decius ordered everyone to worship the old gods. Perhaps that was one of the things that inspired St Anthony, an Egyptian peasant, who died about AD 350, to organise a group of Christians in collective worship, so beginning the monastic movement, carried further, perhaps on Buddhist inspiration, by St Martin of Tours. Meantime, the organisation of the Church by bishops controlling dioceses, choosing priests and deacons, excommunicating and baptising, had begun. The bishops were elected by the clergy, and by the general body of Christians in the diocese.

Only a small percentage of the Empire could have been Christian before 300. The Christians were an active, restless, determined minority. What distinguished them from the followers of other religions was their self-confidence, self-sacrifice, hard work, austerity, determination and selfless care for the sick at a time of increased numbers of plagues. They acquired particular following in the countryside, unlike the other mystery religions of the time. They also showed a unique willingness to challenge the temporal order in the name of a higher authority which was not specifically political.

The triumph of the Christians was immediately preceded by the violent persecution organised by the Emperor Diocletian, who declared Mithras to be the protector of the Empire in AD 307, and who expelled the Christians first from the army (in which the cult of Mithras was strong) and then from the civil service. Next, on the prompting of the pagan Galerius, he closed the churches, confiscated books of scripture and banned religious meetings. Numerous Christians were executed – the figures reaching to eighty-three people martyred in Palestine between 303 and 313.

Ten years later the Emperor Constantine became a Christian because he saw, on one of his marches, with his own eyes, 'the luminous trophy of the cross placed above the meridian sun' and inscribed: 'By this, conquer'. He did conquer, at the subsequent battle of the Milvian Bridge, but his Christianity perhaps derived more from calculation or from 'superstitious liking for a symbol which had brought him luck than out of moral conviction'. Still, once he had committed himself, he did not retreat. Constantine favoured Christians in the army and bureaucracy, endowed the Church with estates, buildings and allowances of corn, and legalised bequests to it. He empowered bishops to make slaves of Roman citizens and permitted any party to a civil suit to transfer his plea to a bishop's court. These actions transformed the history of Christianity.

The income of the Church had originally depended on the faithful's first-fruits of their harvest or freewill offerings. Now the situation was changed, though there were difficulties in resolving the dividing line between a bishop's personal and ecclesiastical income.

For the time being, the pagans suffered inconveniences only (confiscations of lands and of treasures from temples), though they were forced to ban sacrifices. But once Christianity had become official it spread fast. After many centuries in which the world had seemed free from magic, miracles began again. Chapels began to be built over the tombs of dead holy men. Their anniversaries were celebrated and they themselves were worshipped as if they were minor gods. Their relics (if they could be found and identified at all plausibly) were venerated. Saints were held to protect especial cities as old gods had done. Pictures began to be painted depicting the saints, at the right hand of God. Further privileges for Christianity were introduced by Constantine's son, Constantius II. The Church was rendered immune from poll tax. Even gravediggers were excused taxes. It was accepted too that clergy could only be tried by bishops. The Emperor Julian, Constantius's cousin, sought to restore paganism but, though he revived the Empire, he died too soon to be able to do much for the crumbling pantheon of old gods. About thirty years later Theodosius, the last great Emperor, put the question to the decayed Senate whether the worship of Jupiter or of Christ should be the religion of Rome. The Senate was full of aristocrats who doubtless preferred Jupiter. They were cowed by Theodosius's known preferences. The Senate voted Jupiter out and Christ in: a rare example of religious change occurring after pacific debate. Thereafter, with a few exceptions, such as the Pantheon in Rome and the temple of Venus in Carthage, the Church of Christ took over the old buildings of the old religion. The temples were usually destroyed and their stones used for churches. The Pythia, the voice of the god Apollo at Delphi, was formally closed down in 391. In Egypt, Archbishop Theophilus not only destroyed the idols and the temples, but ruined the priests. He burned the great library of Alexandria, the greatest collection of books in antiquity.

All these developments put the Jews in a peculiar position: they were at once indispensable, but at the same time a burden, to the triumphant belief. From the consequent ambiguities Judaism has never escaped[7].

Unfortunately the Church's triumph did not lead to harmony. Even Constantine had found, at the first congress of the Church, that his new religion was rent by controversies. The followers of Bishop Arius argued that, God being indivisible, the Son must be a being later in creation than the Father ('There was a time when He was not'). Bishops of Rome soon claimed primacy over other bishops. Even within Rome, within thirty years of Constantine's death, fighting and bloodshed broke out between the followers of two rival candidates to the Papacy. In the East fanaticism burned in a hundred minor controversies. All the time, though, the Church increased in size, numbers, riches and influence. Monasteries and churches dotted the Mediterranean world. Doorkeepers, singers, funeral attendants, gravediggers and male nurses counted as clerics. All had incomes and privileges. Pagans were excluded from posts in the government and in the law. Compared with these changes the eclipse of the Empire in the West seemed a minor occurrence.

Though the spirit of humanity was always latent within the Church, Gibbon was speaking little less than the truth when he said that in the first century of the legalisation of the Church, 'a boundless intolerance of all divergences of opinion was united with an equally boundless toleration of all falsehood and deliberate fraud that could favour conventional opinions. Credulity being taught as a virtue and all conclusions being dictated by authority, a deadly torpor sank upon the human mind which, for many centuries, almost suspended its action'[8]. Even the design of churches of the early Middle Ages needed no invention, being based on pagan temples or Greek basilicae. Some argued later that the expensive edifice that the Church had become was a critical reason for the collapse of the Empire itself. Gibbon sourly commented that even the 'vices of the clergy' were then 'far less dangerous than their virtues'[9].

The most interesting characteristic of those days was the spread of monasticism, including the phenomenon of the anchorite or hermit. Some holy men reduced themselves to the level of animals. St Simeon Stylites considered that he could serve God best by sitting for thirty years on the top of a pillar sixty feet high. Monasticism, nevertheless, when coherently articulated by St Benedict of Norcia (who founded Monte Cassino in AD 529), led to the revival of the Church. The monks of the early Middle Ages in Benedictine monasteries resembled colonists, isolated in a hostile world, thrown on their own resources, village states of literacy in a rural countryside. Christianity became increasingly a rural religion as town life, independently, became less secure.

A few individual Christians stand out against a confused backcloth of divided loyalties, uncertain power, and authority depending upon nostalgia: for example, the first 'four fathers' of the Latin Church. The first of these was St Jerome, the great translator of the Bible from Greek into Latin – 'the Vulgate'. A hater of cities (and thereby typical of the character of Christianity at that time) and a persistent advocate of monasticism, Jerome had decisive importance because of his austere but magnificent literary style which dominated the writings on government as upon Christianity for centuries, holding together Christian kingdoms as nothing else.

Second was St Ambrose, the aristocratic Archbishop of Milan, who influenced the Emperor Theodosius, and who wrote *Duties of the Clergy* which, if based on Cicero's *De Officiis*, was for centuries the only generally available work on ethics. Then St Augustine, Bishop of Hippo, wrote *The City of God* to argue, correctly, that the decline of the Roman Empire was not the fault of Christianity. In so writing, he also introduced a breath of Greek philosophy and even of Manichaeism into Christianity. He was on good grounds to point out that the decay of classical science had begun long before Constantine made the Empire Christian. The ideas of original sin, salvation through grace and a predestined universe either derived in their mediaeval form from him or were embellished by him.

A fourth early father, Gregory (who died in 604), was the first Pope to be an administrator. He began a Christian revival based on austere practice (celibacy, fair elections to bishoprics and effective law), honest accounting and rational administration in the city of Rome. Gregory was able to establish for the first time that the Bishop of Rome was head of the Western Church. With financial help from Byzantium, he seemed to have the powers of a new Emperor in the West. Many of Gregory's innovations affect the Catholic Church in the twentieth century: for example, the organisation of parishes, the timing of festivals, the order of processions and the character of sacerdotal clothes. His innovations in administration were to make possible the later mediaeval claims by his successors that the Pope of Rome was superior to the Emperor.

The generally low intellectual level and slavish respect for custom of the Church at that time were, in the first place, due to the ambiguity of the relations between Church and state at a moment of weak temporal authority. It was also something that the powers of politics and of religion could be distinguished. To render to God what was God's and to Caesar what was Caesar's was not fully acceptable even under Rome: Caesar was expected to come first. Gregory the Great represented what Hobbes described the Papacy to be: 'the ghost of old Rome sitting crowned upon the grave thereof'[10]. For many generations afterwards the Catholic Church assumed implicitly that it was the Empire.

3

Into a demoralised and divided Christian world, the Arab invasions thrust like an arrow. The Arab tribes, many of them living as collective entities, led by a sheikh without authority, had, before Muhammad, the same simple worship of the sun, moon and stars, attended by rich priests, as other peoples had at a primitive stage. The new religion grew out of the rivalries of Mecca and Medina, two prosperous market towns run by oligarchies, where some Christian Greeks and Jews traded spices. From those foreigners, Muhammad derived some of his ideas.

Muhammad preached a religion which, in theory, seemed close to Christianity, emphasising a single god, the last judgement and the efficacy of prayer. Regarding himself as the last of the prophets as well as the secretary of Allah, Muhammad played the part of a new Christ. He was a personage of decisive political importance in his own lifetime and one, as Gibbon put it, 'distinguished by the beauty of his person, an outward gift which is seldom despised except by those to whom it has been refused'[11]. There was more belief in fatalism among his followers than in any Christian writing, however, even than in the works of St Augustine and of Calvin, while the duties of Muslims were both more precise and more numerous than those of Christians (reciting the profession of faith; attesting the mission of Muhammad; saying five daily prayers; fasting in Ramadan; going on pilgrimage to Mecca; taking part in war when it was proclaimed to be holy). Muslims had also to turn five times a day in the direction of Mecca. Their hands had to be clean. They had to go to the mosque on Friday. They were not supposed to drink wine; and they had to give a tenth of their income to charity. Muhammad himself is a rather mysterious being. Was he illiterate, as Muslim tradition suggests? Did he pass his early life in commerce? Did he really have eleven wives, ten of them widows? Such matters are obscure. All that can be said with certainty is that he was half a warrior and half a prophet who, when his ideas were rejected in his native city of Mecca, organised the neighbouring people of Medina and some poor Meccan *émigrés* under his own leadership, to become the core of an army of conquest. He went to Medina on that city's invitation to resolve their internal squabbles. He left it as its ruler. With him, there was no dilemma between religious and temporal power nor, indeed, between civilian and military power. Church, state and army were one. Bernard Lewis says that he revived and redirected currents that already existed among the Arabs of his time, and that 'his career was the answer to a great political, social and moral need' for 'a higher form of religion' than that which the Arabs had had before then[12]. But he himself only conquered a small territory in Arabia. His successor led the faithful into Iraq. In ten years of unrivalled conquests, Omar, the first caliph (the word meant 'the deputy to the prophet'), conquered Egypt and Syria (Jerusalem fell in 638) from the Byzantines and Persia from the Sassanids. The Byzantine armies were overstretched, badly led and wracked by disease. They had been fighting the Persians for three centuries. Both sides in that conflict were an easy prey to the Arab horsemen.

A century after Muhammad's death the Muslims had pressed the Eastern Empire into Asia Minor, conquered all the fertile territory which lay between Morocco and the Indus, occupied Bokhara and Samarkand, overwhelmed Spain and penetrated France. A Muslim fleet, built after a brief Byzantine reoccupation of Alexandria had shown the caliph the importance of sea power, controlled the Mediterranean after 655. Well did the great Belgian historian Henri Pirenne argue that these events more than the German invasions marked the real end of the Graeco-Roman civilisation. It was not that the Arabs imposed their culture on those whom they vanquished. For it was only after Islam received a mixture of Persian thought that it was a culture at all. The Christian sects in the Middle East survived intact under Arab rule. Islam was essentially a military empire to begin with.

What caused this expansion? Overpopulation? Religious self-confidence? Desire for glory? Doubtless a mixture of all three. The conquerors were not holy men but generals whose religious interest on the whole was modest. The desire for glory was as important a motive as any. After all, the conquerors took over only state lands and lands of the enemies of the regime in countries which they conquered. They did not interfere in previous religions provided their leaders paid tribute. The old subjects of the Byzantine Empire found the charge light. Bernard Lewis claims that the Christian populations of Syria and Egypt preferred the rule of Islam to that of orthodox Byzantium[13]. The Jews may have thought the same. Much to the surprise of the Arabs, many of these Levantines became Muslims. Indeed, they began to contribute to what Islam became. Christian churches also remained open in Al-Andalus, the Muslim kingdom in southern Spain[14]. Nor did Islam stifle scientific enquiry. Hence the preservation of chemistry; hence the early universities; hence the persistence of the craftsmanship of antiquity; hence the skill with which the caliphs made use of men of many nations and faiths. Hence indeed the intellectual and commercial superiority of the Arab world in the ninth and tenth centuries, particularly in Spain. There the spirit of Muslim toleration was seen at its best. There music (elsewhere condemned) was prized. There, there were numerous marriages at every level, the royal one included, between Christian and Muslim: would any Christian king of 880, other than a Spanish one, have sent his son (as Alfonso III sent the future Ordoño II) to be educated at a Muslim court? This tolerance even survived a disdain on the part of Spanish Muslims for the 'polytheists' of the North, even survived the semi-sacred character of the Caliph of Córdoba. Under the cloak of Islam, too, the ancient Near Eastern peoples began to speak Arabic and, in the end, particularly after the Turkish conquests gave both Arabs and Levantines a new common master, to think of themselves as Arab, united in religion if in nothing else by the fact that the Koran remained liturgically Arabic.

Neither the tolerance towards different creeds expressed by Islam, nor its role in preserving the memory of classical knowledge, should permit any neglect of its autocratic nature and its denial of the right of individuals to seek their own destiny. The fatalism which predestination inculcates stifled the Arabs' capacity for individual initiative. The concept of a holy war such as that waged by Muhammad is the reverse of humane. Muslim punishments were, indeed are, harsh. Redemption by good works scarcely existed in the Muslim mind, which was also encouraged to concentrate on a sybaritic picture of what Heaven might be for those who were just: 'For them are prepared gardens . . . they will be covered with gold bracelets, and shall be clothed in green silk and brocades . . . Youths who will continue in their bloom forever shall go round to attend them with goblets and beakers and a cup of flowing wine . . . They shall not hear therein any vain discourse or any charge of sin but only the salutation "Peace! Peace!" ' In the Bible and the Christian sacred books, the precise nature of Heaven is left to the decision of God the lawgiver, and neither the diet nor the quality of the staff are so lovingly described.

Furthermore, Islam remained a state religion; the caliph was the head of the cult. None of the sects, neither Sunnis nor Shi'ites, nor the derivatives of those into which Islam soon became divided, engaged in a serious struggle to limit the power of the Muslim state. Indeed, the idea would have been incomprehensible. Nor were there many political innovations in the way that the caliphs exercised power. They ultimately moved their capital to the Persian village of Baghdad, and they drew inspiration from old Persian customs of relying on governors to manage revenue. They used Persian Muslims as civil servants and were anxious like the Sultans in Delhi to display, deliberately exaggerated, the difference between ruler and ruled.

Disputes multiplied within Islam from then on, but it is difficult to see any points of abstract principle at stake. As with early Christianity, issues of sect, personality and people became inextricably interwoven, traditions grew, vendettas flourished. Zoroastrianism also lingered on in Persia and constituted the background to the heresies leading to the establishment of autonomous principalities in the east of the Islamic Empire. But peasants' hostility to taxes, noblemen's reluctance to become peasants, slave resentments and ambitions of governors who knew that they were indispensable as collectors of taxes all played a part.

None of this affected Islam's attitude to commerce. Indeed, the conversion of so many of the Middle Eastern peoples to Islam stimulated their trade. By the eleventh century, for example, first the Arabs and then Muslims of Indian origin dominated the seaborne trade of the Indian Ocean. Muslim trading colonies grew, their merchants were granted the right to build mosques, religious teachers followed, and the followers of Islam spread their creed from the Swahili coast of East Africa to the spice islands of Indonesia – Sumatra, Java and Bali – usually cooperating cordially with local merchants. The militant methods pursued in the west of Islam were no more successful, if more commonly chronicled[15]. These conquests of commerce repeated those carried out by Hindu merchants in the second century AD.

4

The Christian Church challenged temporal claims. In the early Middle Ages the Church was a legal class, protected by its own law and courts, but not primarily a social class. It drew members from all sections. There were, of course, divisions within it: monks; priests, who were permitted to marry until the eleventh century, with dynasties of priests being as common as they had been in Egypt; prelates, equal in authority and riches to great lords, and some of them as adept in war as in peace. All these persons' relations with civil authority were ambiguous. Some would have liked to have dispensed with civil power altogether. After all, as Walter Ullmann put it, 'for the greater part of the Middle Ages, government and its underlying principles were controlled first and foremost as integral parts of applied Christian doctrines[16]. But churches needed armed, if usually barefoot, soldiers to protect them. Other churchmen, from the grandest to the poorest, were appointees of the barons, who also sometimes constituted themselves abbots. When they did not do so, there was often an open sale of offices. Kings meantime claimed frequently to be descended from pagan gods, but desired ritualistic coronation and soon were found claiming miraculous powers. They were often advised by clerics: between the eight and thirteenth centuries all the chancellors of France were clergymen. Not till the fifteenth century did professionals begin to supersede ecclesiastics.

The ideology of this mediaeval Church was amateurish, somewhat illiterate, Manichaean, with many nature rites and much magic. Many still believed that the end of the world was close: 'the fear of Hell was one of the great social forces of the age', Marc Bloch remarked[17]. Here there was some agreement between Christian and Scandinavian conceptions of the end of the world. For ancient Scandinavian tradition believed that three years of extreme moral degeneration would precede the 'world catastrophe'. The doctrine was much the same as Bishop Otto of Freising's idea of a forty-two-month reign of Antichrist before the day of judgement.*

The intellectual and moral revival of the Church of Rome in the Middle Ages began when a pious duke of Aquitaine founded in 910 the monastery of Cluny in Burgundy. The aim was a reforming organisation within the Church under the Papacy. Cluny and its daughter houses stood for the celibacy of the clergy, an end of lay influence over clerical appointments (particularly bishops), an end of the sale of ecclesiastical offices, an abandonment of work in the fields and, as a substitute, prolonged services. These ideas came to dominate not only Cluny's own network of monasteries which regarded Cluny's abbot as their leader, but many other Benedictine houses. Their ideas assisted the Church's integrity but the inclination of the Abbots of Cluny was to restrict what little classical learning that remained: Abbot Odo saw Virgil, the most famous classical writer during the Middle Ages, as 'a beautiful vase full of vermin'. 'My grammar = Christ,' said Peter

---

* In Norse lore the twilight of moral powers was the twilight of gods, Ragnarok, which denoted not the consequence but the cause of the end of the world. The gods and heroes assembled by them in Valhalla fall in the battle against the powers of night. Afterwards comes the world conflagration, whereupon a newborn world emerges with a rejuvenated race of men and a new supreme god[18].

Damian, who introduced flagellation into the hermitage of Fonte Avellana about 1043 and believed that a monk's role was to mourn, not to study.

Among the monasteries affected (in architecture and behaviour) by the Cluniac reformation, the most important were those along the route to the shrine of St James at Compostela where the cult of that saint had become, in Américo Castro's words, 'a positive creed' against Islam, after his legendary appearance on a white horse at the battle of Clavijo in 822. The pilgrimage of so many to Santiago made León and Castile turn their eyes to France. French knights in turn animated the Reconquista. Indeed, the main line of the Spanish kings in the late Middle Ages derived from the French Capetians through that Count of Burgundy who 'liberated' Portugal and founded a kingdom there. The first bishop in reconquered Toledo (1085) was French.

Cluny was a remarkable achievement. It offered an 'exalted daily round', the companionship of noble buildings and distinguished men, the daily recital of the Bible in regular sequence followed by elaborate rituals: what Sir Richard Southern described as 'a majestic life, perhaps superior to any form of Christian life, before or since', while the lovely hills along the valley of the Grosne in Burgundy lay behind. The abbots themselves also moved on a grand scale, respected among kings, dukes, popes, even emperors[19].

Somewhat earlier, the divisions between Western and earlier Christianity, which had dogged the Church since the collapse of the Western Empire, broke into the open. It was claimed in 754 by 338 Eastern bishops that all visible symbols of Christ were blasphemous. The worship of images would lead to paganism. The controversy inspired a severance between the Greek Orthodox and the Roman churches. Long expected, the chief curiosity was the ground of the dispute, since the slant-eyed beauties who passed for the Virgin Mary on ikons continued to play a greater part in the imagery of the East than any other portraiture in any other branch of the Christian family. Behind the dispute, too, lay a difference in attitude to temporal power: the Byzantine emperors had a truly Oriental view of the Church as a branch of the national bureaucracy; the Western Church, long independent of imperial control, regarded itself as superior to all temporal power just as, as they put it in a dangerous metaphor, the head is to the body.

Eventually, the ideas of Cluny, in the persons of Popes Leo IX and Gregory VII, reached Rome, causing the bitter, if intellectual, controversy over episcopal investiture. Though forced to concede defeat in some arguments with the Emperor, the Popes were effective in renewing the Church. Their victory was marked by the Crusades, called for in 1095 by Urban II (previously Abbot of Cluny) and by the movement to build the 'Gothic' cathedrals begun after the monastery of St Denis in 1137 (Cluny had been started in Romanesque style). These great churches both calmed and inspired the spirit, though (in keeping with Cluny's tradition) they gave grounds for dreams, not speculation. In Gothic churches, music sounded well but words rang out no more than they do in opera. Mediaeval Christians were thus offered an aesthetic but not an intellectual experience. The Gothic movement was slow to mature: the pointed arch, enabling cross-vaulting and leading to great new heights to the naves and choirs, did not appear till the thirteenth century. But when it did, the mason entered upon his golden age, with much work in the limestone or sandstone quarries.* In the meantime, there was a ban on the sale of offices. Laymen, kings and squires were excluded from the choosing of churchmen, while bishops were henceforth, in theory, selected by a college of canons. Clerical marriage was also banned, for the first time formally, though higher clergy had usually restrained themselves from such unions.

The papal administration which grew out of this reformation was a competent one and influenced modern government in a variety of important ways. An expert staff ensured fast correspondence. Papal legates maintained obedience and contact. Popes held regular courts of justice. In cathedrals a common life comparable to that in monasteries was established by canons and, particularly in England, many cathedrals were turned outright into the churches of Benedictine monasteries. From the twelfth century cathedrals were asked to provide masters to teach poor scholars and clerks, and as an unsuitable accompaniment to this educational reformation a catalogue of miraculous stories spread across

---

* As a rule, the mason was the director of a mediaeval building, being concerned with every important structural problem from the counterpoise of buttresses to the design of the tracery. 'Minor' matters such as carpentry, slating, glazing and plumbing were all incidental. Masons filled the countryside with stone castles instead of wooden ones. Countess Albereda of Bayeux was so pleased with the mason who built her castle that she had him executed to prevent him building another. The person of the 'architect' remained anonymous as a rule till the Renaissance.

Europe – particularly those about the Virgin Mary, who until then had played a minor part in such tales.

The Crusades, embarked on in a mood of religious frenzy but sustained partly for commercial benefit, also brought back many new objects of veneration: the Crown of Thorns, the Holy Blood, a part of the True Cross and the skull of John the Baptist. Military orders too were founded, international like the Templars and the Hospitallers, or local, like the Teutonic Knights or the Order of Calatrava, fusing the ascetic life with the life of combat and powerful enough to dominate kingdoms. Alfonso I of Aragon even named the Hospitallers and the Templars heirs to his kingdom. Never had the Church militant seemed more determined: 'God has fixed a day for you to be at Edessa:* there the sinners will be saved who hit hard and who serve him in his need.' It was as if, as one song of the Crusades put it, God had organised a tournament between Heaven and Hell. Another revival of the time of the Crusades was the statue. Sculpture had vanished from Europe after AD 500, but the Europeans who reached Palestine and the Near East in the train of the Crusaders could see the statues of the past for themselves. Before 1100, life-size saints reappeared in the recesses of great churches. The Popes meantime sought to achieve, through the mediaeval *sacrum imperium*, a political armature, with the See of Rome as its real centre.

The recovery of the Church was continued by the foundation in the eleventh century of the Cistercian order which in the days of its English founder, Stephen Harding, aimed at a return to the simple life, as prescribed by the then half-forgotten St Benedict. Founded in 1098 at Cîteaux, like Cluny in 'watery Burgundy' amid vines and sheep, the white-habited 'Cistercians' grew fast in numbers so that, as a result of the leadership of St Bernard of Clairvaux, there were 500 houses by 1200. The return to the manual labour which Cluny had scorned enabled the Cistercians to make a greater mark in cattle-, horse- and sheep-breeding than they did in theology. The export of English wool by the Cistercians was a determining element in the English economy. Lay brothers were recruited to do the heavier work in the fields, while the abbots remained in loose touch with Cîteaux, whose lord was the spiritual commander of an enterprise which was to the colonisation of East Europe what the East India Company would be to India.

* The principality of the Norman crusader Bohemond, which was captured by the Turks in 1144.

The Franciscans and Dominicans, grey and black friars, followed in the early thirteenth century. They spread at a rate at least comparable to the orders based on Cluny and Cîteaux. These friars had as their chief purpose the preservation of the mediaeval city for the Church and the defeat of the numerous heresies which seemed so attractive to many in the prosperous thirteenth century. St Francis and his followers advocated the beauties of humility and devotion, seeking to live the life of Christ and preaching in simple, large churches to big audiences who sang cheerful hymns written in the vernacular. His followers were to possess nothing and to beg when they could not work. They were priests appropriate to the age of troubadours, wooing My Lady Poverty with good humour. The Franciscans used oratory, for the first time, as a means of making propaganda for the Church, an approach made possible by the revival of cities where large audiences could be found. As J. H. Huizinga wrote, 'the modern reader of newspapers can no longer conceive the violence of impression caused by the spoken word on an ignorant mind lacking mental food'. The Franciscan friar Richard, for example, preached in Paris in 1429 during ten consecutive days. He began at five in the morning and spoke without a break till ten or eleven. When he finished his tenth sermon 'great and small wept as touchingly and as bitterly as if they were watching their best friends being burned'.

The Dominicans were also devoted to preaching (they were commended originally by the Pope as 'Friars Preacher'). Their founder's passionate hostility to the Albigensian heresies, and his success in destroying them, secured for the Dominicans control of the newly founded Inquisition (1233), an institution intended to ensure intellectual conformity throughout Christendom. The Dominicans thereafter had a great influence on the subsequent history of education. Large churches, such as Santa Maria Novella, Santa Croce and even the Duomo (built by the guild of wool merchants) in Florence, made a marked contrast with the great Gothic cathedrals contemporaneously spreading over northern Europe. In Dominican churches, as in Roman law-courts, the words of the orator were meant to be heard. Both these orders might under other circumstances have become heresies. Instead, they became the most reliable first line of defence of a Church determined to maintain unity even if it had to persecute.

Mediaeval Europe was a firmly Christian society; movements of dissent, like that of the well-organised Albigensians, never questioned the essential truth of the Christian revelation. Petrarch, whose work so inspired the Renaissance, was a fervently Christian writer. Wicked princes were explained away as bearing the mark of the Antichrist, whose dreadful empire would precede the coming of the Kingdom of God. Frederick II, Stupor Mundi, is said to have suggested that Christ, Moses and Muhammad were imposters: he was almost alone to do so in the thousand years between 400 and 1400.* He also raised the question of whether he was, legally or technically speaking, the owner of the possessions of his subjects; to receive the answer 'no'. It was that legacy of independence which Christianity so contributed to the 'liberal heritage' of the West. It was perhaps characteristic that it was left to the prince who doubted the validity of Christianity to seek intellectual justification for tyranny. Yet the various questions raised by the movements of dissent – doubts about transubstantiation or whether it was permissible to study pagan works – led the way to a revival of scepticism which would destroy the unity of Christianity.

The desire to keep scepticism at bay was the chief motive for the Church's interest in the universities. Those schools grew round some prominent teacher – Ivrenius, a teacher of Roman law, the inspiration in the twelfth century of the first university, Bologna; or Vacarius, who taught the same subject a little later, to inspire Oxford. When these institutions began, they were as peripatetic as were the Dominicans. But they soon became fixed in one place and have been a permanent part of the intellectual world ever since. At much the same time friars ceased to be respected for their poverty and became popular, because of their wealth. Saint Francis's austere ideas were even described as heretical in 1322. It is said that upon being told that a certain Parisian doctor had entered a Franciscan monastery as a friar Saint Francis exclaimed: 'These doctors, my sons, will be the destruction of my vineyard.' At all events, after innumerable arguments, divisions and schisms, by 1500 the friars were large and prosperous landowners and the Church itself seemed once again corrupt, luxurious, murderous, even, according to Burckhardt, 'satanic', and practically secular[20].

Further, while the basic tenets of religion were rarely contested anywhere, Europeans, at least, had an almost equal reliance upon the idea of a fixed universe in which the four elements – earth, air, fire and water – were maintained in ceaseless permutation by the distant but predictable movements of the universe. That went

---

* Though Moses was portrayed as a sorcerer in some Mystery plays.

for the majority of educated people. The uneducated majority had a variety of magicians and fairies in whom to place their trust from time to time. The prophets in the minds of many people in mediaeval England, for example, were not confined to those mentioned in the Old Testament. They included Merlin, whose prophecies were reissued in manuscript in the fifteenth century to justify the claims of one participant or another in the Wars of the Roses. People also believed in the Devil. The early Hebrews attributed evil to the existence of rival deities. But the triumph of monotheism made it necessary to explain why there should be evil in the world if God were both omnipotent and good. So the notion of Satan was a necessary complement to that of God. 'Possession' by the Devil survived as a fairly common complaint. Hobgoblins were believed in by children throughout the world. Thus among the Hebrews there was Lilith, a horrible hairy monster reputed to roam at night in search of children. Other devils were said by the Greeks to steal children too.

Another belief which survived the days when organised religion dominated society was that in spirits and ghosts, superstition and magic, demons and chiromancy, sorcery and alchemy. Towards the end of the age of agriculture, theism, or deism, Platonic mysticism and even a kind of revived paganism all revolved in the minds of the seekers after truth. Some branches of Christianity and other religions collaborated, in practice, with these beliefs. Thus the mediaeval Church used the lives of saints in one form or another to find a method to prophesy the future and control it. Over 500 miracles were associated with St Thomas à Becket at Canterbury, while local saints, prayer and sacraments were invoked in ways that often suggested magic more than faith.

Religion and ritual, religion and ceremony, religion and carnival all went together: many European Christians worshipped the Virgin Mary as they might have worshipped a goddess of fertility. Dr Huizinga speaks of 'the extreme saturation of the religious atmosphere' in the late Middle Ages. A Corpus Christi procession in Portugal in the fifteenth century, for example, would include guild banners and ensigns, dancers depicting emperors, apostles, devils, saints and rabbis, with some dancers performing a Jewish dance, clowns making faces, a serpent of painted cloth with men underneath, blacksmiths, carpenters, gypsies, moors; St Peter; stonemasons carrying toy castles; St John surrounded by shoemakers; Temptation represented by a dancing girl; St George on horseback; Bacchus sitting on a hogshead; a Virgin on a donkey;

St Sebastian surrounded by robbers – 'the whole of Portuguese life', Gilbert Freyre commented approvingly[21].

Another concept which made its appearance during the age of agriculture, in one form or another, was honour. Europeans like to suppose that this was a combination of Christianity and feudalism but, though it played an essential part in both, the roots of the idea of honour must be sought among the Hindus of the Mahabharata and in Japan, in Persia or Greece. By the fifteenth century it meant as much to Europeans as religion did. Guicciardini, the historian of Italy, wrote: 'He who esteems honour highly succeeds in all that he undertakes, since he fears neither trouble, danger nor expense.' Burckhardt suggested that in his day 'the decisive rule of conduct' for cultivated Europeans was 'a sense of honour' – that 'enigmatic mixture of conscience and egotism which often survives in modern man after he has lost, whether by his own fault or not, faith, love and hope'[22]. The same sense of honour informed mediaeval chivalry: 'If my children are honest and brave,' Marshal Boucicaut's father is supposed to have said, about 1380, 'they will have enough; if they are worthless, it would be a pity to leave them much'[23].*

In the south and east of the Mediterranean as in all South Asia, Islam remained the dominant creed. Except for Moorish Spain and the Balkans, no Islamic territory has been lost to that religion. In Islam, as in the West, a universal empire survived in theory long after its regions were in effect separate kingdoms. As in Christianity with Latin, Arabic kept together the ethnically divided peoples who subscribed to the creed. Pilgrims went to Rome (or Jerusalem) or to Mecca because of the collapse of the political unity which had made those holy places the hearts of great communities embracing continents. Islam's legacy to the technical and intellectual revival which began in Europe in the late Middle Ages, and affected the globe, was a different one from Christianity's in three clear ways: first, a good Muslim knew that people who supported other religions, even ones comparable to Islam, were likely to burn in Hell whatever happened; second, Islam was more fatalistic; third, the theology, wrote Bernard Lewis, was 'determinant, and authoritarian, demanding the unquestioning

---

* Jean le Meingre, surnamed Marshal Boucicaut, fought at the Christians' defeat at Nicopolis and was taken prisoner at Agincourt. An admirer wrote a book about him which made him out as the mirror of true chivalry.

acceptance of the Divine Law'. A book, Bernard Lewis continued, in Islam was 'often presented not as an individual and personal creation of the author but as a link in the chain of transmission'. Hence, when the era of Muslim expansion came to an end it was easy for Islam to go to sleep, as it were, and to remain in an intellectual torpor which was to last till the nineteenth or twentieth century when it and other ancient faiths met the modernising challenges of the West[24].

20

Laws and Governors

Step by step, as the power of the state waxes and the self-centred and self-helping autonomy of the kindred wanes. Private feud is controlled, regulated, put, one may say, into a legal harness.

Pollock and Maitland, *History of English Law*

Has not everything been done under constraint?

Peter the Great

1

The essence of ancient government was that it provided the law of the peoples concerned. The complexity of government depended upon the complexity of law. Governments conceived themselves as having some responsibility for the preservation of the customs and traditions of the people, though to a great extent religious leaders concerned themselves with that task.

It has been earlier noticed that many ancient governments busied themselves often with codes of laws but not all: Chinese statesmen were always averse to any kind of codification of law, even their philosophers believing that each case should be judged on its merits and that the abstract should be avoided. In the eighth century AD there was, nevertheless, some codification of Chinese criminal law on a modest scale. But civil law remained little used, on the ground, argued Joseph Needham, that 'a genius for compromise had long been characteristic of private and commercial life' in China.

The beginning of a philosophical attitude to law is to be found as with many other things of the mind in Greece during the sixth or fifth century BC. It was not simply that in Greece, particularly in Athens, people felt intellectually imaginative enough to speculate on any subject. After all, speculation might lead anyone anywhere. The decisive matter is that the Greeks realised that men had risen from brutish levels. They attributed that, not to any abstract idea of progress, evolution or any other vague force, but to law. Secondly, they made comparisons with the law practised by themselves and by barbarians, whose laws they regarded as being based on the whim of an irresponsible barbarian ruler. Their laws, they thought, protected their lives and property, and enabled them to plan their lives as they wished. The Greeks were wrong to dismiss the laws of Babylon as worthless (much less the law of Moses, of which they do not seem to have heard), even to set them on a par with the unwritten customs of, say, the Scythians, but they were right to argue that (as with China and ancient Mayan society too, had they known it) in Persia or Babylonia 'the ruler's will had the force of law' (as the Roman legist Ulpian would later formulate it). The Greeks fully appreciated the paradox that they obeyed laws 'in order to be free', as Cicero (and later, in slightly different terms, Goethe) put it. The explanation of this change was political. The kings in Athens and in other Greek communities had given way to largely commercial oligarchies. So the states concerned required a concept of law other than that which was the command of the lawgiver.

Greek law, though reflecting the will of the gods, gave much attention to the question of how people should behave in relation to one another. Justice was conceived of as indicating, in Maurice Bowra's words, 'a natural tendency to obey the rules of a civilised society and as giving every man his due'[1]. The word was considered one of the four cardinal virtues (along with courage, wisdom and temperance). The Athenians, according to Thucydides, respected laws 'whether they are actually on the statute book or belong to that code which, although it is unwritten, cannot be broken without acknowledged disgrace'[2]. In Athens, too, knowledge of the law was part of the business of being a citizen, since in litigation each man had to plead his own case. Though litigation was rife in the fifth century BC, advocacy was not a professional activity. That meant that there were great advantages if a man could acquire a detailed knowledge of the law, in order to be able to plead effectively before a jury of 500 persons.

In modern life many languages (including English) leave an ambiguity between laws which describe regularities of nature and laws which are prohibitions or commandments. These two kinds of law in the twentieth century have hardly more in common than the name. But in ancient societies, including the Greek, that was not the case.

The consequence of these attitudes in Athens was the achievement of a democracy which, whatever its shortcomings, was direct, not representative. This was possible because the population was small. All power was vested in the open-air meetings of all male citizens held on the Pnyx. 45,000 were entitled to attend. One-tenth of the total population, that is, perhaps 4,000 to 5,000 people, customarily went to the meetings. A council of 500 was selected by lot to judge what needed to be judged, while the assembly elected ten generals to defend the state. There was no permanent officialdom – a unique occurrence. Power was 'judicial and administrative'. But the administrative was a tiny part of the business transacted on the Pnyx. Nor was legislation needed. The laws had been dictated by Solon long before. The 'legislature' was much more of a jury than a parliament.

In the Italian peninsula, a system prevailed which to begin with had certain similarities to the Greek one. Etruscan kings were elected for life by a consultative assembly, and the election was confirmed by a council of elders, an anticipation of the Senate of Rome. In Rome, as in Athens, there was to begin with a democracy, not direct like the Athenian one, not so 'representative' as those which modern large states have achieved. The propertyless poor were less powerful than their numbers would have ensured in a full democracy but they did have a vote on critical occasions as a 'century' in the so-called *comitia centuriata*. In addition, the power of the executive, in the hands of consuls, was limited to one year. A 'dictator' could be named, but only in an emergency, and only for six months. Weighted voting gave patricians advantages over plebeians, but the plebeians could impose changes such as the provision of 265 BC that no one should be elected to the same magistracy twice (a law subsequently altered). Roman democracy had many other qualifications but the essence of it was that it was complex. The gradual simplification, decay and ruin of ancient complexities led Caesar to the Principate, an eventuality ensured by the use of violence in the so-called *comitia tributa*, the public 'committee of clans', and by the exploitation by Caesar's great-nephew Augustus of the fear of renewed anarchy in Rome.

Against this background Roman law began as did Greek or Babylonian Iraqi law, but the subsequent development was different. Inscribed, according to tradition, by the decemvirs on the famous twelve 'tables' with the intention of making clear what the rules of the people were, the law was continuously modified, from the earliest days until the time of Justinian. Even so, law in Rome was a slave to its code. The most just complaint could not, and never did, move the judges, unless permitted by the praetor, whose task was to introduce some consideration of equity. Motives could not be discussed in Roman courts. As early as the time of

Caesar there were complaints about the law's pedantry. Further, while in the beginning Roman trials had been held, as in Greece, in front of large gatherings, laymen proved incapable of dealing with cases when law had become refined. Thus a profession of 'juriconsults' grew up. Latin literature is full of impressions of how they worked: 'the clients from the country flocking to the great man's antechamber in the early morning and the students standing around with their notebooks to record his replies', as Sir Henry Maine described it[3]. Roman magistrates remained amateurs. They were assisted by assessors who were professional.

Some historians of Rome give the impression of an Empire increasingly riddled with restrictions. Rome seemed more litigious than law-abiding: already in the first century AD the Emperor Vespasian was wondering how the system could cope with the flood of suits, criminal and civil, which occupied the time of the hot and crowded courts. Legal practice, too, left much to be desired: the injured party, not the state, was supposed to bring the guilty to the dock. On the other hand it is evident that, in their speculation as to whether or no there was a law of nature, Roman lawyers devised the then original and now fundamental concept of the equality of citizens (if only citizens) before the law. Marcel Reinhard is right to argue that the Romans were administrators before they were conquerors, jurists more than administrators.

The law of Rome had become obscure by AD 500. It could be established only from a vast array of sources: the works of classical legal writers, imperial decrees, decrees of prefects and edicts contained in many thousands of volumes which, says Gibbon, 'no fortune could purchase and no capacity could digest'[4]. By the later Empire, too, the municipal courts had faded away, and the court of first instance was the provincial governor's. Later, minor cases were dealt with by a specially appointed *defensor civitatis*, while Constantine took the bold step of empowering bishops to decide civil cases at the behest of both parties. The bishops gave a cheap and consequently popular service. Around these courts grew a tradition of scholarship and practice which, particularly after the eclipse of the Empire, profoundly marked the political as well as the legal evolution of Europe.

Essentially, the Roman law that we know is Justinian's. In his day an effort was made to make the law consistent. But his 'Digest', 'Codes' and 'Novels' were, in the end, unsuccessful. 'Instead of a statue cast in a simple mould, by the hand of an artist,' wrote Gibbon, again, 'the works of Justinian represent a tessellated pavement of antique and costly, but too often of inconsistent, fragments'[5]. The chief element which survived the subsequent untutored age was what Gibbon refers to as the 'exclusive, absolute and perpetual domination of the father over his children', and, indeed, over his wife. But behind that and other concepts was the idea that the law derived from certain clear, well-defined principles and not from custom: the main contribution of Roman law to the modern world, and indeed to the 'Latin' way of thinking.

Under the Empire, Rome was transformed from a democratic republic of jurymen to something close to an Eastern despotism, echoing Alexander's or the Pharaohs' systems. The victory over Egypt completed a process which had originated with Scipio Africanus's conquest of Carthage. Egypt influenced Rome. In Egypt, the Roman Emperor was looked upon as an absolute monarch. He was served by a prefect himself served by the surviving large staff of the Pharaohs. Between the first and the fourth centuries Rome took upon itself many Egyptian characteristics, political and administrative. From Egypt came the theocracy of Caligula, the idea of a large bureaucracy, the idea of separating civilian and military power; from Egypt too came both the grain to feed Rome and the largest quantity of taxes paid in the Empire – for it was the richest province. The bureaucracy established itself because the senatorial class ceased to serve as competent administrators. The Emperor Gallienus sought to extend the Egyptian model formally to the rest of the Roman Empire. The Illyrian Emperor Aurelian wore a diadem and golden costume, with precious stones, copied from the Persians. The Emperor in the late Empire was absolute, making all appointments down to those of provincial governors and dominating the law. When the villainous Emperor Commodus sentenced Appianus, an Egyptian priest of Alexandria, to death for rebellion, the latter protested. The following exchange then took place:

> Commodus: 'Do you realise whom you are addressing?'
> Appianus: 'Yes, a tyrant.'
> Commodus: 'Not so, you are speaking to the Emperor.'
> Appianus: 'Certainly not. Your father, the divine Marcus Aurelius, had every right to call himself Emperor because he cultivated wisdom, despised money and loved what was good. But you have no such right since you are the antithesis of your father. You love tyranny, vice and brutality.'

This meant that Rome was at the end of its history as an Empire rather similar to the kingdoms of the East. Thus, the Persian Empire of the Achaemenian dynasty was also a bureaucratic state, in which provincial governors and satraps were not aristocrats but high officials. The Persian bureaucratic tradition was indeed one of the most continuous of Middle Eastern institutions, affording, after AD 650 as before, invaluable service to the Caliphate as to the Sassanids. Naturally, Persians interpreted Islamic law according to their own judgement. Equally, the unified Chinese Empire, established by the Ch'in dynasty after 220 BC and essentially preserved ever since, was a bureaucratic form of government. Holders of estates which might have deserved the name of 'feudal' beforehand all vanished. The nobility had to live in the capital, and the country was divided into thirty-six (later forty-one) prefectures. Everything was standardised, merchants discriminated against, roads and walls meticulously built for defence and for supervision.

Similar developments, though on a more modest scale, can be glimpsed in Africa. There were in that continent during the age of agriculture a large number of monarchies looking back institutionally at a remote remove, as suggested before, to the Egyptian monarchy. These states were as a rule run by a king who, says J. D. Fage, 'led a life sedulously secluded from the common people: he gave audience from behind a curtain; not even the most intimate of his courtiers might see him eat and drink'. Such monarchies, numbering anything from a few thousand to over a million in population, were almost always based on the hereditary position of the king, and the bureaucrats around him were also nobles, a bureaucracy without paper, reading and writing, but one in which power was exercised by officials who held office by the king's pleasure, could be dismissed at will and who as a rule managed such external trade as there was as a royal monopoly[6].

A good example is the ancient kingdom of Congo in the fifteenth century before the Portuguese came. There the king theoretically enjoyed absolute power but, in practice, he had to pay a great deal of attention to noblemen, of whom the most important were the governors of five of the six provinces into which the kingdom was divided (the sixth was run personally by the king). Neither king nor subject would ever have disputed the power of tribal law, all paid much attention to the medicine man. Various states to the south and east intermittently looked on the Congo kings as their lords and gave tribute to them[7].

The development in India, from complex institutions based on custom to a simpler system based on personal power, is comparable, superficially, to the evolution of political power in Rome. Among Aryan invaders the original chiefs seem to have been elected as leaders in battle. Those chiefs assumed privileges associated with kingship. Their power, to begin with, was often restrained by tribal assemblies, such as a council of elders and a general assembly of the tribe. Some tribes were directly managed by assemblies, just as Athens was by the meetings on the Pnyx.

Gradually, partly as a result of alliances between priests and rulers, partly as a result of the growth of administrative systems, kings became hereditary, the assemblies' powers diminished and finally monarchs became regarded, or caused themselves to be regarded, as divine. Some semi-democratic republics, however, did survive a long time, especially in hilly regions, in the foothills of the Himalayas or in the Punjab. Meetings of heads of families discussed laws and elected leaders. One day perhaps these institutions will seem almost as worthy of as careful a study as those of Greece. They were, however, always coincident with monarchies in which the usual simple rules of absolute government survived and which, in the end, prevailed everywhere, resulting in something like an imperial system by about 250 BC under the dynasty of the Mauryas. Those monarchs set up a monarchy, a regime whose chief interest is that it created a system of secret police agents within the nation whose mission was to gain information. This system declined for the reason that many great polities do in the end – excessive taxation – but left behind in India both a desire and a memory of empire which it never lost. Nor was the memory of general assemblies of the populace lost. Thus, within the empire of the Pallavas about AD 800, assemblies of villages, of guilds and of professional groups were held annually and representative committees of those assemblies – a modern touch – met more often. In that regime, indeed, it was possible to detect again the glimmerings of what promised to be a democratic life, sometimes under the supervision of an official, but sometimes not.

Such developments are not detectable in China, though the absence of historical evidence for anything which happened there before about 1200 BC may hide a multitude of virtues. At all events, hereditary monarchy continued to be the rule in China throughout the age of agriculture. Monarchs were only overthrown by other monarchs, even if some of them might, like the founder of the Han dynasty, be of modest origin and others, like the Mongols, be outsiders. The requirement for a Chinese emperor to marry outside his own family and the refusal to countenance marriage with foreign barbarians caused unions with families of officials which, as a rule, led to many difficulties. The difficulties which such marriages caused the Han dynasty, for example, were never solved: save by the Emperor Wu Ti who did resolve the matter by having the family of the officials put to death. Wu then embarked on a reign of unparalleled military success, both against Central Asiatic nomads and to absorb the southern sections of what is now China itself.

In the end, however, the 'consort dynasties' caused the temporary destruction of the united empire. After two hundred years of confusion and civil war the T'ang dynasty re-established the empire. That family's second representative secured the reduction of the military aristocracy by devising his famous system of examinations for entry into the civil service. It produced a class of officials dependent on the emperor. It destroyed Chinese feudalism and made the Chinese state into the bureaucratic structure which is so well known.

Precisely the opposite occurred in Japan. There, from the time of the formation of the kingdom, a single royal house has ruled. There have been practically no attempts to displace it. But as a rule the power of the emperor has been modest. Instead, consort families such as Fujiwara held the authority like Carolingian mayors of the palace. Eventually, the latter title became the Shogun,* 'the generalissimo and supreme commander' after the great victories in the Gempei war in the twelfth century of the great general Yoritomo. In time these consort families fell from power; the emperor remained. Neither consort families nor emperor broke the power of aristocratic landlords and the Chinese system of government by examinations never took hold. Very often the empire itself was held by a child, while abdicated ex-emperors held much authority.

The general rule, however, seems to have been, in the age of agriculture, that settled communities evolved from diversity to simplicity, often from some degree of government by consultation towards government by decree. Kings remained supreme magistrates as well as commanders-in-chief and high priests but increasingly, particularly in rich and stable societies, that is particularly

* Short for Seiidaishogun – 'barbarian-subduing great general'.

in what would have seemed in modern language to have been the advanced countries. Yet, beyond the settled communities, among nomads or, even, more primitive agrarian monarchies such as 'the ancient Germans' (while they were still 'ancient'), more free practices survived. Lord Acton, in a fanciful passage in his Essay on Liberty, recalled that Tacitus pointed to the Germans of the first century AD 'with a vague and bitter feeling that to the institutions of these barbarians the future of the world belonged'. Their kings, when they had kings, did not always overrule their councils. They were sometimes still elected. They were sometimes deposed. They were also sometimes bound by oath to act in obedience to the general wish. As among the early Babylonians – and the later Vikings – they enjoyed real authority only in war[8]. Modern historians agree that among the matters resolved by the Magna Carta by the King of England was that 'authority should be subject to law which the community itself defined'[9].

Nor should the role of size be forgotten. A Greek city might be able to be governed by an assembly of all its citizens. But China under the dynasty which established the empire there, the Han, was much larger than any Western nation state. There was no means of consulting the whole population even if anyone had wished to do so. Thus it seems that in those days monarchy was the only possible form of government in China. No sage ever questioned its validity. The isolation of China, although penetrated by commerce, was sufficient to prevent ideas of representational government ever being carried there. Even if they had been, the Chinese would not have been much interested in the theories of those whom they held to be barbarians.

2

The courts, armies and such other political apparatus of many of these ancient states were financed by taxation. This included poll taxes on citizens, often payable in kind and often collected by headmen in villages, who were in countless countries the most important political and judicial local personages, but also by other tax farmers. It included customs such as the twenty per cent demanded on all goods which crossed frontiers in the Roman Empire; and inheritance taxes such as the five per cent in the Roman Empire paid on wills worth more than 100,000 sesterces, other than by direct heirs. There were also indirect taxes such as the excise of one per cent demanded in all Roman markets. Income derived also from loot in war as well as from profits from national enterprises such as mines. Nearly all these taxes and ways of raising money survive. But most taxes were on spending. Income tax as such was not conceived of till the fourteenth century in Italy but, from Babylon to China, from India to Aztec America, all despots sought their percentage of every crop, which is much the same thing. According to Genesis xlvii, 24, a fifth of all produce in Egypt was owed as a tax to the pharaoh. The revival of the Japanese monarchy under the Tokygawa Shogun in the fifteenth century was based on an exact survey of every rice field which took fifteen years to complete. Every peasant had to pay his tax direct to the government, not to the landlord.

The share of produce paid by the producer was, indeed, the distinctive tax of the age of agriculture as income tax is of our age. In India in the earliest days the king alone co. ..l sanction clearance of waste and took a percentage, usually a sixth, of the crop as a tax. The Muslim and Ottoman empires also acquired the habits of simple confiscation of goods under the guise of poll taxes and of using provincial governors as tax farmers, who often in effect became rulers, rendering a purely formal homage to the caliph, whose function was reduced to giving formal and often retrospective approval to things done in their name.

Almost everywhere people who had no money had to serve certain days of labour, as was the case in Egypt during the Middle Kingdom, and the more efficient despotisms had recourse to censuses to ensure that that service was performed, from the earliest days of agriculture. Such censuses might be accompanied, as in Rome under Diocletian, by a careful estimate, as in a budget, by the appropriate authority of how much money would be needed in the coming year, how many horses and uniforms, say, or how many recruits needed for the army.

Could it be, as is clearly implied in the work of the best of modern historians of Rome, Rostovsteff, that overtaxation of the Roman Empire was the chief reason for its collapse? That beguiling theory omits the fact that many other large, overtaxed despotisms, such as the Chinese Empire, lasted a long time despite their fiscal systems. The French doctor Bernier, who lived in both the Ottoman Empire and the Mogul Empire in the seventeenth century, noticed that there was 'little encouragement to engage in commercial pursuits', since tax-hungry despots had the 'power and inclination to deprive any man of the fruits of his industry'. So anyone who managed to acquire wealth sought to conceal it for fear of confiscation on arbitrary grounds[10]. But, Bernard Lewis explains, 'one of the primary causes of economic decline' in the caliphate 'was undoubtedly the extravagance and lack of organisation at the centre'[11].

To turn from those powerful despotic monarchies to a consideration of nomads or feudal Europe, or any other society where the paraphernalia of government was modest, is like turning from something like the present system of the state to that of ancient Greece. Yet even in feudal Europe men were not living in prefiscal innocence. Pepin, Charlemagne's father, for example, confirmed the application of the Mosaic principle that lords and estates should pay a tenth part of their harvest to the Church – a principle which often meant that those lords, who controlled the local churches, took the 'tithe'. One principle of the Gregorian reform in the eleventh century was the provision that tithes should be ensured for the Church – the monasteries and chapters of cathedrals, rather than the village priests. Hence the accumulation of sacks of grains in tithe barns up and down Europe. Kings also collected a poll tax, the *geld*, to pay for their battles against the Vikings, and the Normans in England maintained it, even though they were really the Viking danger institutionalised. Domesday Book was considered to be a 'geld book' by the great Maitland and it clearly had many fiscal uses even if modern mediaevalists frown on so simple a judgement[12]. Yet it is the modest incidence of taxation which strikes the student of mediaeval Europe as being so remarkable – tiny in comparison with the Caliphate or the Byzantine Empire as well as with Rome or the modern state. The only way that the Carolingians, for example, could raise money effectively was through profits on their own lands, from tributes from conquered peoples, from booty and from a few tolls on the roads from the insignificant commerce. Only in the late thirteenth century were the most powerful kings of the Middle Ages, those of France, able to institute a regular tax, the *taille*, for which the authority of their people was not needed and which was used to finance an expensive army.

In the Roman Empire there were always distinctions in the income of the state which never occurred in such simple despotisms as those of the Tartars. This income was divided into *res privata* (crown lands gained by confiscation, or old royal lands, such as parts of Cappadocia, and much scattered property in towns and agricultural land which was let and which paid for the general purposes of the state); *res summa* (customs duties on frontiers, taxes, fines); and special levies for wars or emergency. After the

Empire became Christian under Constantine, the Church also limited imperial authority. The Senate, though impotent, was influential. Emperors who defied it seldom died in their beds, Professor A. H. M. Jones pointed out[13]. The secretariat of Roman Emperors was also small and for a long time, despite Egypt's influence, personal. Magistrates, such as prefects of the city (in control of the urban cohorts or police and the corn supply, water, etc.), and the governors of provinces only slowly established secretariats of any size. From the time of Constantine civil servants increased in numbers and pretentiousness. They began to wear uniforms and to hold ranks in fictional regiments. Many were corrupt, pedantic and rapacious. Bureaucratic offices also became hereditary – a rule which in the end applied to workers in royal mints, weaving and dyeing factories, gold mines and to town councillors. Yet even in the fifth century the numbers of men working for the Emperor were infinitesimal in comparison with those of the present day, never exceeding 40,000 in both parts of the Empire,* and private property was guaranteed.

3

For much of the age of agriculture, monarchs lived in their kingdoms as great landowners did on their estates, conforming to the customs of the property accepted by their ancestors, relying on their stewards, sons or chaplains for advice, seeking to enlarge their estates by marriage or, occasionally, conquest, fighting their cousins if they had unfairly taken their inheritance, sometimes lapsing into senility or vice and, therefore, temporarily leaving the running of affairs to brothers or scheming uncles. Kings' wars were often, even in the seventeenth century, as Albert Sorel put it, 'a kind of armed lawsuit'[14]. A king's court was a lord's household somewhat enlarged. In both, all dined together, privacy was non-existent, rooms such as libraries were few (only in the seventeenth century did the idea of the great hall begin to vanish in England, and lord and lady begin to dine apart). The King's property in England in 1100 resembled that of a lord of the manor in an open field,† an enterprise dotted about the shires, some in bad soil, some in good, disorganised and not centralised but often giving a substantial revenue; and, in Eastern despotisms as in Western monarchies, the ruler was usually the largest landowner.

* Excluding 375,000 in the army.
† See below, page 543.

The King of Prussia personally owned nearly a third of his kingdom as late as 1750. Yet there were differences, not always evident to the observer nor even to the man who worked there, but profound, as will be seen.

The question of inheritance, of estates as of kingdoms, for example, varied. Consider again mediaeval Europe. Sometimes the lord of an estate would decide which of his sons, or, occasionally, daughters or other relations, would succeed him. Sometimes the sons themselves would decide which of them was the best. Primogeniture only slowly became the rule in most European countries after the Carolingians, though there was no trace of it in ancient Roman practice. For many generations petty lords continued to practise common inheritance and common cultivation. Sometimes, if a lord were defeated whilst fighting to extend his lands, he might be succeeded by an enemy; or the king, or other superior political authority (or a bishop), might grant the lands concerned to a new tenant, in return for certain obligations. In England under the Anglo-Saxons land was still being given to office holders, the title to which soon became hereditary. But the main difference between the West and the East was that, once possessed of an estate, an English lord became a person of local significance, unlike his Oriental contemporary, who remained usually at bottom no better than a civil servant and could be dismissed at a moment's notice.

Here then there were in the era of feudalism in Europe certain fundamental differences between customs prevailing in the West and those in the East. Feudal Europe was poorer than Islam or India or China. Its monarchies had smaller armies. It was less quick to make use of innovations. But it had ceased to be nomadic. It was a congeries of settled communities within which noblemen, bishops and, already, merchants existed in their own right. Indeed, they had, or had obtained, rights. In their own localities they were the masters. No matter that this relative freedom derived from the universal, apparently irremediable, recognised and regretted weakness of the central authority. It led to fundamental differences in the end. Properties in feudal Europe were still granted, and granted by kings not against an obligation to pay something (that was a secondary matter) but to do something. Such obligations in much of mediaeval Europe were sealed by a physical act of homage, hands submitted together, to the master: he who proffered hands made a declaration as a man. The chief would then kiss his subordinate, and on the mouth. This act had happened among the Germans before the fall of the Roman Empire, but during the Carolingian era, as in India under the Gupta dynasty, an oath might be made, on the Gospel or on relics. Later still, the obligations were extended in, for example, Normandy and England to cover an obligation to hold, at the disposal of the superior, a prescribed number of knights and men. The vassal himself would as a rule decide how this service was to be fulfilled. He could, as some princes of the Church preferred, keep his vassals on the demesne and so, though having to provide for their board and lodging, maintain the estate intact; or, more usually, he could let out estates to them. But in feudal society in its purest form, such as the kingdom of Jerusalem, tenure was dependent. Everyone who held land held it of someone else, though only rarely were there more than a few men between king and peasant, in the hierarchy of holdings: 'Four townsmen hold of Hugh de Lacy, who holds of S. de Furneaux, who holds of the Count of Brittany, who holds of the King'[15]. Such obligations would ultimately be commuted into rents.

Oversimplicity usually begets deception. Yet even in the age of agriculture there were never more than three types of monarch: first, despots, symbolised by the personality of Frederick II, Emperor and King of Sicily, who sought, in Burckhardt's phrase, to transform 'the people into a multitude destitute of will and of means of resistance'; who 'centralised . . . the whole judicial and political administration'; who collected taxes 'by those cruel and vexatious methods without which . . . it is impossible to obtain money from Orientals'; who crowned his 'system of government by a religious inquisition'[16]; and who regarded everything within the state as his own property – just as Wang Mang, the usurping Hsin emperor of China in the first century AD declared the entire land of the country to be the property of the state. When Rijkloff van Goens, the Dutch envoy to the Sultan of Mataram in Java in the seventeenth century, suggested to that monarch that he might encourage the trade of his people so that they could both become richer and pay higher taxes, the Sultan replied, 'My people, unlike yours, have nothing which they can call their own, but everything of theirs belongs to me.'

Second, there were rulers who regarded themselves as the trustees of a series of laws and customs by which they themselves were bound, even if gradually. Sovereignty over vassals and fiefs became the means whereby the kings of England, France, Portugal and Spain gradually succeeded in establishing sovereignty over territory. In the differences between the two sorts of rule lay the foundations of the different types of modern state. The combination of fief with vassalage, or feudalism, is unique to Western Europe. The feudal lords of Europe were able to establish a degree of independence of, and separation from, the monarchy because the monarchy lacked the means, on the whole, to prevent them. The efforts of Frederick II were unsuccessful. Thus there emerged out of feudal Europe one of the strongest forms of private property known to mankind. The great estates in the European West came to be, unlike such enterprises elsewhere, grand outposts of resistance to central power. In the East, and that included Russia, the central power looked on the great estate as, as it were, one of its own dependent branches.

Third, there were those monarchs who, like the kings of the powerful mediaeval state of Cambodia ('Kambuja' originally, but latinised by French missionaries), were regarded as living gods. Kings of Cambodia had not only to govern, but to protect religion. They were chief priests as well as chief magistrates. Their capital, the magnificent city of Angkor Thom, was planned to render homage to these ideas. The religion concerned was first Hinduism, especially the cult of Shiva; second, Buddhism. Their domains included Thailand, Laos, south Vietnam and parts of Burma and Malaya.

The coming of a society which respected the independence of the individual conscience can be traced to developments in certain parts of the Mediterranean and Western European society during the age of agriculture. It is still confined to a few parts of the world, and despised in others. The reasons for this transformation during the agricultural age can, first, be attributed to feudal landholding; second, to the memory of Athens; third, to Christianity and the emphasis laid in Judaism upon law; and fourth, to the growth of societies of merchants who, though oligarchic, managed to gain independence of agricultural monarchies. Gradually, as a result, the belief grew that people's representatives had a right to choose their governments.

The part of religion in the transformation is the most important of the elements concerned. Religion has often been, and is still often, an impediment rather than an encouragement to independent enquiry. Enlightened scepticism is the impulse towards the study of truth. Yet the background to that is a recognition of the uniqueness of the individual soul. The emphasis by the Greeks on the world of the spirit was a forerunner to Christianity. But their agnosticism prevented such speculation becoming an accepted attitude of mind. Large societies will always demand some complete explanation of past, present and future such as is contributed by religion. It was the achievement of Christianity to make possible an intellectual culture which not only gave to its followers the security of such a general interpretation but, through the idea of personal salvation, gave encouragement to individual responsibility. Self-reliance as well as self-denial, Lord Acton pointed out, is 'written as legibly in the New Testament as in the *Wealth of Nations*'[17], and the concept of modern political representation was clearly worked out in mediaeval ecclesiastical law.

Book Three

The World Transformed c. 1450–c. 1750

And new Philosophy calls all in doubt,
The Element of fire is quite put out;
The Sun is lost, and th'earth, and no man's wit
Can well direct him, where to look for it.

John Donne

The word 'Renaissance' was apparently invented by the French nationalist historian Jules Michelet, in 1840. The idea of treating the thousand years following the fall of Rome in AD 410 as a self-contained unit of historical time was that of Flavio Biondo in the 1440s. The expression 'Middle Ages' was invented by the German Christoph Keller, in the seventeenth century. These labels have not been rejected, yet each generation of historians throws the origins of the Renaissance back earlier while economic historians often date the end of the Middle Ages in the seventeenth century. In this book, those ideas and discoveries are discussed which, in the last few centuries of an age when most men and women lived on the land, led to an 'industrial age' – a phrase which really means an age of machinery and mass production – and to an international society.

21

The Renaissance in Europe

It is well to observe the force and virtue and consequences of discoveries. These are to be seen nowhere more conspicuously than in those three which were unknown to the ancients . . . namely, printing, gunpowder and the magnet. For these three have changed the whole face and state of things . . . the first in literature, the second in warfare, the third in navigation.

(All three derived from China.)

Francis Bacon, *Novum Organum*, Book I, aphorism 129

The word Renaissance implies the recovery of the achievements of Rome and Greece and, in the process, some changes in the society which developed in consequence of the quickening of the human spirit that followed. This was a European phenomenon. No such reinvigoration occurred in China under the Ming dynasty. Yet China had a few generations earlier seemed far more innovative a society than Europe. Certain factors, speculated upon by Joseph Needham in many learned volumes, made Chinese mediaeval society more favourable to the application of science in early times than European.

As has been shown, China knew the blast furnace and cast iron nearly 2,000 years before the West. She knew of paper and gunpowder in the early Middle Ages, while her irrigated agriculture was sophisticated long before the plough had reached much of Europe. She established a united state of one people long before the nations of Western Europe did. Her rulers and civil servants were less superstitious than those of the West. Her population was 200 million, in comparison with which France, the most populous state of the West, had probably no more than fifteen million. Is the explanation of Chinese decay that industrial development, in its first stages at least, needs the energy of entrepreneurs, rather than old dynasties of bureaucratic noblemen? Is the explanation to be sought in the culture of China, whose distinguishing feature was that no one can learn to read Chinese by himself: he has to be taught? Did the rhythm of a successful but disciplined society, based on the cultivation of rice, prevent sustained enterprise? Did the low status of craftsmanship prevent a Chinese industrialisation in the sixteenth century? Perhaps the critical point is that China, like most Eastern despotisms, was an efficient bureaucratic empire turned towards the past. Families rendered tribute to ancestors who had established stable village communities for intensive cultivation.

Most great Chinese innovations occurred before the T'ang dynasty devised its famous system of recruitment of civil servants by examination. A frequently hereditary class of artisans assured to those communities such manufactured goods as were necessary. Commerce was local where it was not based on the family. Both the Chinese and the Japanese policies of isolation and exclusion were deliberately designed to keep merchants in a lowly place – despite the establishment of a good deal of commercial freedom under the Sung dynasty (AD 960–1279). Muslim and European merchants traded with the monarchs, not the people, and kept to their ghettoes. No independent cities established themselves even in the chaos following the eclipse of the Mongol Empire. The Chinese naval expeditions of the early fifteenth century to the Persian Gulf, Africa, Malaya and perhaps Australia under the inspired leadership of Cheng Ho were never pursued and were less concerned with the spirit of enquiry than with a desire to defend the despotism; perhaps undertaken out of uneasiness lest a deposed nephew, known to be in the South Seas, reappear from thence to claim a disputed throne.

The Renaissance in Italy, on the other hand, took men infinitely further into the realm of ideas than the Romans (whom the men of the *quattrocento* in Italy sought to emulate) had dared to venture. The recovery of antiquity took a form which Rome herself would have despised or misunderstood. Romans were great lawgivers, engineers, administrators, soldiers and mechanics, but they did not excel in the realm of abstract thought. Theirs was the world of affairs. That applied also to those whom Romans prized in the Greek world. Aristotle, for example, was good at biology, but bad at anything which needed experiment: observation was his speciality.

What was it, China aside, that caused these changes to occur primarily in 'ce petit cap du continent Asiatique' which Paul Valéry liked to call Europe[1]? Marc Bloch believed that the comparative immunity of Western Europe from invasion (since the Vikings and Hungarians) played a great part. He recalled the Russians and Chinese, overwhelmed by the Mongols; the Indo-

Chinese, crushed by Khmers; East Europe, never free of the Turks and 'steppe people'. But what of the Japanese? The Aztecs? Surely insulation could not be the only explanation for the European Renaissance? Otherwise the Tasmanians might have invented the wheel. Nor was Europe wholly isolated.

The European Renaissance was far from being a matter of a number of artists such as Brunelleschi or Michelozzo going down in the *quattrocento* from Florence to Rome in order to copy ruins. That comment in no way reflects on the quality of classical copies, such as Brunelleschi's Santa Maria degli Angeli, and Michelozzo's chapel in the church of Santissima Annunziata, nor on the seriousness with which artists of the Renaissance took their work. But the recovery of urban life, the revival of scepticism, the retrieval of the histories of Livy and the rediscovery of art had all begun in the eleventh or the twelfth centuries, had caused a commercial reinvigoration in the thirteenth century and had only been interrupted in the fourteenth century by disease and its consequences.

The element of recovery in this Enlightenment was decisively important. It did not take the shape only, nor even primarily, of a recovery in art. For example, the seventeenth-century French mathematician Pierre de Fermat was the founder of the theory of numbers. Fermat was inspired by Diophantus of Alexandria, whose *Arithmetica*, written in the days of the Antonines, was rediscovered in the sixteenth century. Fermat's experience was typical of all leaders of thought during the Renaissance. His work depended on a classical model, though he excelled his mentor in breadth of understanding[2]. Orators, preachers and professors studied Cicero, Quintilian and the imperial panegyrists, and no accomplishment was 'more highly esteemed than the power of improvisation in Latin'[3]. Students of herbs in the sixteenth century studied Dioscorides' *Materia Medica*. There was a rediscovery of technology long forgotten or abused. Thus mediaeval man had tended to look down on mines and mining – as if it were a rape of the soil. The pick was held to remove the irreplaceable soil from God's earth. But in *De re metallica*, in the sixteenth century, Georgius Agricola called the miners' profession 'higher than that of merchants'.

Admittedly, in technology, the process of recovery had begun long before the days of what has come to be called the Renaissance. For example, the potter's wheel had been lost in Europe after the fall of Rome. It was revived in the ninth century. Thereafter pottery (which had never declined in China) gradually recovered its ancient quality. True porcelain had begun to be made in China at Wen-chou in Chekiang about AD 400 when it was found, probably by accident, that a crystalline white mineral, feldspar, could be incorporated in the body of the pottery to create a glaze, so making possible the pottery known as 'stoneware'. By 900 this art had been perfected in China and the famous jade green ware of the T'ang dynasty began to be exported. Stoneware also began to be made in the Rhineland after 900, and a salt glaze was begun in the fifteenth century.

Another critical change at the time of the Renaissance was that people knew where they were more accurately. That was not only because of the discovery of America nor of spectacles (in the thirteenth century), nor because of the invention of the telescope about 1600 (probably in Middleburg in the Netherlands)*, but also because of the coming of the clock to Europe in the fourteenth century. Earlier, there had been a great vagueness about time, which even affected dates: when precisely *was* the year 1000? How old was the king? As for the hours of the day, waterclocks were rare. They froze in winter in the north of Europe, though elaborate striking waterclocks had been known in the Near East for a long time: the great Mosque of Damascus had one by at least 1186. Sundials, on the other hand, known in China from the first century BC, were unsatisfactory because they depended on fine weather. Hour glasses were not much used, since the sand enlarged the opening through which it flowed.

But after the invention of the counterpoise clock in Germany no European city felt proud of itself unless it had an elaborate public clock, with angels, planets and prophets 'marching and countermarching', often attached to churches, sometimes to town halls[4]. Among the first clocks were those of Strasbourg (c. 1354), Wells (c. 1375–80), Salisbury (c. 1386) and Rouen (1390). These clocks had only an hour hand. A minute hand followed, about 1400, and a second hand, about 1550, though the minute hand took a long time to come into general use: the clocks depicted in Brueghel's paintings of about 1550 have only one hand. The pendulum was devised by Galileo in 1581 (on seeing a lamp in Pisa) but it only began to be generally used in 1641. It was not till 1670 that the great Dutch scientist Christiaan Huygens invented the grandfather clock. Portable clocks had been invented in the fif-

---

* Galileo exploited this brilliant idea, and made a modest telescope to observe the sky in 1608, but there seems little doubt that the inventors were Dutchmen.

teenth century. Jewel bearings began to be used about 1700 and small watches, as we know them, came into general production about 1750.

As important in telling people where they stood was the adoption of the Gregorian calendar, which was more accurate than the old Julian one.

Not least among the consequences of the voyages of the sixteenth century was the beginning of accurate geography. Maps were known in China in the first century BC. But the people of the Mediterranean in the Middle Ages knew little more about the world than Herodotus had done. He had not realised that there was a sea border to the north of Europe. A Catalan atlas of 1375 had given India its proper shape, and some Egyptian and Greek maps were locally accurate. But no one knew the extent even of the three then familiar continents – Europa (named after the daughter of King Agenor seduced by Jupiter), Asia (called after the daughter of Oceanus) and Africa, a word used by Romans to designate Tunisia, probably deriving from a lost tribe, the Aourigha, of Berber origin, driven by the Carthaginians into the desert.

After the sixteenth century cartography improved enormously. The great Mercator, whose real name was Gerhard Kremer, a Flemish mathematician who spent most of his life at Duisberg under the protection of the Duke of Cleves but who was employed by the Emperor Charles V in his military campaigns, made the first modern map projections. His maps were the first to be known as an atlas, a word taken from one of the Titans whom Greek legend made a son of Asia. It is thus appropriate that the greatest of Renaissance popes, Pius II (Aeneas Sylvius), should have been a keen geographer as, indeed, was Petrarch, the first true reviver of learning in mediaeval Europe, in the judgement of John Addington Symonds[5]. It is equally appropriate that the works of the historian of antiquity who was the most conscious of geographical matters, namely Herodotus, should also have been revived at the time of the Renaissance. Herodotus was not a direct inspiration. But, as Arnaldo Momigliano suggests, the new historians did as Herodotus had done: they travelled, 'questioned local people, and went back from the present to the past, by collecting oral traditions'[6]. The first Latin translation of Herodotus was done about 1452 by Lorenzo Valla, the librarian of the Vatican who proved that the gift of temporal power by Constantine the Great to the Papacy was a fraud: a good augury.

The system of 'Arabic' numbering which the Abbasid Empire took from India, meantime, quickly passed into general use in the Muslim world and reached Europe through Spain. Adelard of Bath, the great translator, first used arabic numbers, with its invaluable use of the zero, in his translation of Al Khwarizmi's *Algebra* in the early twelfth century, and Leonardo of Pisa, in his *Liber Abaci*, in 1202 asserted that the arabic system was better than the Roman one. It took some time before that method passed into general European use. But by the fifteenth century it was general, and a great assistance to clearer thought.

Renaissance man is also recognisable in innumerable small ways to his modern descendants. The autobiography of Benvenuto Cellini, for example, is the work of a modern man, respecting himself more than God, pope or duke, avowedly out for himself. Even the exaggerations – his personal killing of the Constable de Bourbon, his escape from the Castello San Angelo – are similar to boastings of men of the modern age. Burckhardt believed that the Florentines of the fifteenth century were 'the pattern and the earliest expression of modern Europeans generally'. A few jokes of the Middle Ages amuse us, it is true, but from the days of the Renaissance humour becomes much more recognisable. Wit, as long dormant in literature as style, reappeared as a weapon even in theological disputes. In the *Decameron* of Boccaccio, Madonna Oretta was bored by someone telling her a long story and going back to the beginning: 'Sir,' she remarks, 'your horse trots too roughly. I beg you to allow me to go on foot.' The discussion of humour at Urbino as imagined by Castiglione would not seem out of place in the twentieth century: 'On three counts I have to go to Bologna,' said Giacomo Sadoleto, a learned jurist. 'The three counts are Count Ludovico de San Bonifacio, Count Ernesto Rangole and the Count of Pepoli,' interposed Professor Filippo Beroaldo. 'Think how generous he is,' said Niccolo Leonice, of an aquaintance, 'for he gives away not only his own things but those of others.' Thus the jesters, fools, parodists and satirists of antiquity were revived as much as the dome of the Pantheon.

The individuality of the Renaissance was also expressed in the resumption of the use of a surname as well as a personal name – a habit which had existed in Rome but been forgotten by commoners. (In Herodotus's day the custom had already existed of taking the father's name to distinguish a man from others with the same Christian name; and some took a matronymic.) In the twelfth century in France it was common to add a nickname, or perhaps a second Christian name, to the original single name. By the thirteenth century the second name, whatever its form, began to be hereditary in grand families. But the process was slow: in Burgundy, for example, people took their mothers' names; new branches of a good family might take a quite new name. Servants and slaves sometimes took the names of their masters.

Only in Western Europe and in China did the surname at first evolve. Elsewhere people were known by given names with the addition of 'son of so-and-so'. That form is still visible, particularly in Wales where the placenames which served as the basis for many surnames in the past in England next door were too long, Celtic and unmanageable. In China that form is exceptionally rare. Chinese surnames were almost always taken from places, professions or ranks. For example, Wang, the word for king, was taken by the large number who were serfs on royal lands. These usages date from very early in China; from, indeed, the foundation of the unified empire in the third century BC.

These personal names reflect too the fact that henceforth great personages strove to ensure their survival by means of portraits. Artists painted self-portraits, donors and princes were depicted as saints or gods, sculptors successfully transmitted memories of themselves beyond the grave.

Finally, as a counterpart of the Renaissance's revival of Roman customs, the women of the sixteenth century were as independent as those of the first – if not more so. The sixteenth century saw the beginning of the modern recognition of women's individuality as expressed in the lives of Isabella of Castille, Vittòria Colonna, Caterina Sforza, Isabella Gonzaga, Elizabeth of England and even poor Mary of Scotland. Francis I of France relied for advice on his sister Margaret of Angoulême, author of *Mirror of a Sinful Soul* (published in 1531), while Charles V was successfully represented in the Netherlands by *his* sister, Margaret of Austria. The most successful treaty was the Ladies' Peace of Cambrai in 1529 between Margaret of Austria and Francis I's mother, Louise of Savoy; it ended, G. R. Elton said, 'a whole phase in the history of Europe'[7]. Margaret of Parma and Renée of France, at the court of Ferrara, were also very influential. Even in the Americas, Father Cardim, travelling in Brazil at the end of the sixteenth century, was 'amazed to find "great ladies" in Pernambuco'; 'creative maternalism', says Freyre, 'played an essential part in old Brazil'[8]. Neither the Portuguese nor the Spaniards found Amazons; but Saint Teresa of Avila and Sor Juana Inés de la Cruz were worthy competitors. All these noble souls are commemorated in the characters of the heroines who dominate so many of Shakespeare's plays. Nevertheless, even these achievements were anticipated earlier in China where the Empress Wu had reigned as sovereign for many years; she even conquered Korea in the late seventh century AD.

22

The World Opened Up

They brought the harp, the guitar, the violin and the trumpet, as well as written music. Many instruments were known to old America as to old Africa but all the music was remembered not inscribed. Innumerable variations of music followed.

Gilbert Freyre, *The Mansions and the Shanties*

The most astonishing change brought about in the days of the Renaissance was the opening of the whole world to European shipping. This was an innovation beside which the Reformation, for example, seems at first sight a minor matter local to Christianity in Europe.

This new era began when the Portuguese, under King Diniz the Worker, about the year 1300, started, with Venetian and Genoese expert advice, to finance long sea journeys. The best-known of his descendants, the mysterious stay-at-home Henry the Navigator, sent out many expeditions after 1418 to discover the African coast, perhaps with the intention of propagating religion, perhaps to find a route by sea to Ethiopia as well as to Guinea, though his motives are hard to be certain of. Probably he thought that he could turn the western flank of Islam. At the end of the fifteenth century Columbus was beginning to set off for America, and within twenty years the Europeans were to be found everywhere: Europeans of every origin. Willem Bosman, author of an account of Guinea at the end of the seventeenth century, described the role of the Portuguese discoverers and conquerors as that of 'setting dogs to spring the game which, as soon as they had done, was seized by others' – the Spaniards, the Dutch, French and English being the greater beneficiaries.

The technological base for these journeys were the stern-post rudder, the astrolabe, the magnetic compass, new sails and ships with three masts.

Mediaeval ships in Europe, like those of antiquity, mostly hugged the coasts. Only exceptionally were they out of sight of the land. Merchant ships of that era, Braudel pointed out, were more like travelling bazaars than the great destination-conscious vessels of the nineteenth century. They stopped almost daily to

209

buy and to sell, daily renewing their supplies, and dropping into small ports a day's voyage apart[1]. Usually powered by oars, they might put up a square sail with which they could make headway given a fair wind. No such ship could do anything against an adverse wind, though the square sail gave stability on large ships. Even the most powerful ships had a sailing season limited to the months between April and November. Few could expect to survive the effects of the wind in the winter on the sea. No ships of the ancient world, even those which regularly at the summer solstice set off from Myos-Hormos, the port of Egypt on the Red Sea, to sail to Malabar (in forty days), were larger than about 330 tons, the average being between 60 and 130 tons, while Pliny wrote that in his day a large merchant ship was fifteen tons only.

The rise of Islam transformed communications in both Africa and Asia. The Arabs conquered Persia by AD 652 and their first embassy to China was in 651. In 758 Arab pirates looted Canton. Later in the eighth century they reached Malaya. About that time the great Muslim general al Hajjáj al Thadafí even contemplated the conquest of China. Within the next few centuries much of North Africa also became part of the Islamic world, to begin with as part of the Caliphate under governors, who made themselves independent. Some of them, in North Africa, were able to reconstruct something of the economic life which they had inherited from Rome. The ships which made possible such a revival were powered by a triangular sail which despite its name of 'latin' (lateen) effectively challenged the old Roman square sail, since with it a vessel could beat into an adverse wind.

Northern Europe had mediaeval innovations too. Indeed, in the end, their ships proved the best when they had to face a sea more turbulent than the Mediterranean. The Viking ship, a 'deckless masterpiece of joinery', as Marc Bloch described it, had a keel, a steering oar with a tiller, a square sail and thirty, or sometimes even sixty, oars a side. In the twelfth century the Scandinavians also developed the cog: a clinker-built* ship with a square sail, a development of the 'round ship' of North Sea trade. The Vikings, like the Arabs, began as pirates and ended as merchants. They wished to seize the wealth of the prosperous South, not to destroy it. Their most remarkable accomplishment was the establishment of their commercial sites for the better carrying on of the slave trade in the Varangian state in Russia.

---

* External planks overlapping downwards and fastened with copper nails.

Gradually, along all the rivers of Europe up which the Vikings sailed in those incomparable vessels, commerce was reinvigorated. Cloaks from Flanders began again to be exchanged for wine at fairs at Lille or Ypres or in the other, increasingly prosperous cities of the Low Countries. The Venetians increased their contacts, which had never been wholly dropped, with Byzantium. Genoa copied them. Venetian ships began to challenge the Islamic command of the Mediterranean from the early eleventh century by making use of the Arabs' own seamanship.

Before the end of the thirteenth century Genoese merchants organised regular sailings between Italian ports and the North Sea. They did that largely by making use of the stern post rudder, by which a helmsman could manage the rudder at the rear of the boat rather than the middle. This had been devised in China before 1100. The Arabs then introduced to the western Mediterranean both the astrolabe* (originally Persian), and the magnetic compass (originally Chinese), whose needle was allowed to float on a straw but by the late thirteenth century was already on a pivot. The first sea chart dates from about that time too. During the next few generations Mediterranean merchants began to use vessels with three masts, with a square sail on their main mast but triangular ones on the other two. Then, in the fifteenth century, northern European ships began to use this type of vessel. They were thereby enabled to face the Atlantic with greater confidence, since they could meet an adverse wind but at the same time expect to receive stability from their square sail.

As important was the sea quadrant (invented about 1456) by which the sailor measured the elevation of the pole star by a plumb line passing over an engraved scale. That transformed sailing at night. The combination of these changes enabled captains to envisage for the first time the great adventure of long journeys without sight of land.

The country which first made use of these innovations in seamanship and boatbuilding was, as indicated earlier, Portugal. Portugal was a thin slip of a country founded by commoners during the Second Crusade. With a population of a million in the fifteenth century, Portugal managed to escape the stagnation and civil war which characterised much of Western Europe in the fifteenth century. Indeed, the mercantile forces were powerful enough to

---

* An instrument which enabled a ship's position to be determined from calculating the height of the sun.

dominate the monarchy. Portugal's great achievement was the carrack (*nao*), the characteristic modern sailing ship of the age of discoveries. In addition to the stern post rudder, this light-gunned round-bodied vessel had its tiller in the hull. The forecastle had high bows. A later version was the galleon, which was more heavily gunned and was longer and narrower, with more modest superstructures. But the distinction between the two was often blurred. Most were about 400 tons in burthen.

With these ships the Portuguese discovered a larger world than anyone in Europe previously thought existed. They brought Africa, America and Asia within reach of European commerce, conquest and colonisation. Already in 1418 the Portuguese had reached Madeira. In 1427 Diego de Sevilla found the Azores. (The Canary Isles were 'discovered' by a few merchant adventurers from Spain in 1402–05.) After great struggles, a Portuguese ship rounded the difficult West African Cape Bojador with its very high winds in 1434. That was the turning-point in Portugal's and Europe's discovery of Africa. In 1444 Nuño Tristam reached the Senegal river and began to bring back slaves from there – another turning-point in Europe's history. In 1445 Dinis Dias rounded Cape Verde; and the Cape Verde Islands off it, previously uninhabited, were colonised between 1456 and 1460.

In 1469 King Afonso leased the Guinea trade to a private entrepreneur, Fernão Gomes, with the stipulation that he carry forward the exploration a hundred leagues a year. He did so: Guinea and the Gold Coast were reached in 1470. The Portuguese established their fort at El Mina in 1482. In 1484 Diego Cão reached the Congo River, and in 1488 Bartolomeu Dias rounded the Cape of Good Hope, in search of the legendary kingdom of Prester John which was believed to lie behind the realms of the Moors. Nine years later Vasco da Gama left with four ships to chart the route to India round southern Africa. The Spaniards, meantime, completed their conquest of the Canary Isles in 1496, after a bloody war.

By then European ships had reached America. Portuguese and perhaps English fishermen looking for cod had skirted the Great Banks at least by 1480. Even earlier the Vikings had settled parts of Greenland, and one of them, Leif Ericsson, was driven on to the coast of Newfoundland, where he settled about AD 1000. Thorfinn Karlsefni and three ships also spent three winters in the Americas between 1003 and 1006. Where were their shadowy 'Helluland' and 'Markland'? Labrador and Cape Cod? At all events, Norsemen knew the Americas, if only Labrador, between then and about 1350. After the Latin translation of Ptolemy's *Geography* in 1410 the sphericity of the earth, which had never been forgotten, also spread in scientific circles. Columbus heard of the idea as a young man.

Christopher Columbus was the son of weavers in Genoa. He began to make journeys by sea about 1472. He went to England, Portugal and Madeira, and perhaps on an early Portuguese journey to Guinea. His enthusiasm commended him to Queen Isabella of Spain, whom he met through her confessor at La Rábida near Palos (Huelva) in south-west Andalusia. He gained financial support both from the Queen (as a private investment) and from merchants in Cataluña and Valencia. He set off to find a westward route to India. The expedition was composed of people from Palos and the neighbourhood. He went with three caravels of 280, 140 and 100 tons respectively. This journey opened up a new world to Europe as well as the old one to America. Burckhardt wrote: 'of the discoverers of ancient lands, Columbus alone was great but he was very great because he staked his life and expended a vast power of will upon a hypothesis which gives him a rank among the greatest philosophers. The confirmation of the spherical shape of the earth was a premise of all subsequent thought'[2].

Columbus's four journeys (1492, 1493, 1498 and 1502) led to the European consolidation of the Americas – first Hispaniola, then Cuba, Puerto Rico and Jamaica, and finally the mainland, beginning at the isthmus. Other Italians followed Columbus, in the service of kings of other nations, and Columbus's second journey was financed by a Florentine, Juanoto Berardi. John Cabot, another Genoese, soon reached Newfoundland and Brazil in 1498 (in the service of the King of England), while Amerigo Vespucci, a Florentine and agent of the Medicis in Seville, discovered the Amazon. He got as far down the coast of South America as the Cape of São Roque, with Alonso de Ojeda (in the service of Spain). In 1500 Pedro Cabral, a Portuguese sailing to India from Lisbon, in the wake of Vasco da Gama, landed apparently by mistake in Brazil, which he at first named Vera Cruz, then Santa Cruz (it was subsequently given its traditional name because of the abundant red dyewood – brazilwood – carried from there to Europe in the first thirty years of the sixteenth century).

In 1501–02 Vespucci sailed along the Brazilian coast at least as far as the Rio Grande. His Christian name was soon given to the continent. He was a subordinate to the Portuguese admiral Goncalo Coelho, but Vespucci's letter *Mundus Novus* about what he had seen was widely read. Some monks at Saint Dié in Lorraine were in 1507 preparing a new edition of Ptolemy's *Geography*. Their leader, Martin Waldseemüller, interpreted Vespucci's letter as indicating that he had discovered a fourth continent and boldly put the name 'America' on the map.

During the next few years the Portuguese also smashed the Muslim monopoly of trade in the Indian Ocean with great speed and complete ruthlessness. The commercial lure was spices. In Europe fresh meat was difficult to find in winter. Dried meat was not very succulent unless spiced. The market for spice was thus potentially large. It was captured by establishing a few fortified harbours to serve as entrepôts. This era began with the governorship of Francisco de Almeida, and then of Afonso de Albuquerque. Under Almeida, Portuguese forts were set up in East Africa at Sofala and Mozambique in 1505 and 1507. Then at the battle off Diu in 1509, one of the world's decisive engagements if ever there were one, Almeida destroyed the Muslim galleys by the skilful use of light sailing ships manned with guns. Against them the old galleys of the East, like those of Venetians and Turks, with no artillery and no iron used in the building of their hulls, were no match. That began the era of European domination for the next four centuries – or rather of Western European domination. The mounting of cannon on the upper as well as the main deck by the French in 1506 was the fundamental innovation which destroyed the old art of war at sea based on ramming and boarding.

This victory was followed by Albuquerque's capture of 'Golden Goa', which shortly became Portugal's chief trading port of the Indian Ocean. He next captured the Muslim principality of Malacca (in 1511), giving to Portugal the major distributing centre for Indonesian spices (cloves, cinnamon, mace, nutmeg) and pepper, as well as a naval base which controlled the entry into the Java Sea and the South China Sea. China had by then withdrawn from an interest in expansion. In 1515 Albuquerque captured Ormuz, the gate of the Persian Gulf, and reduced the Shah of that island to the rank of a puppet. Though he failed to capture Aden, and so never established Portuguese control over the Red Sea, the three strong ports of Goa, Ormuz and Malacca were soon followed by some forty fortified coastal settlements in the arc between Mozambique and the Moluccas, stretching up to Nagasaki in Japan, giving Lisbon domination of a part of the world which was itself divided among many petty rivalries and whose rulers were technologically unaware. Meantime, in 1513 Jorge Alvarez, a Lisbon captain, put into Canton and in 1542 Antonio da Mota, also from Lisbon, reached Japan. Eastern trade was transformed.

Until then the Mamluk beys, who governed Egypt, had kept prices of pepper and other Eastern spices high by insisting that the annual consignment be small. After 1509 a Portuguese thal-·assocracy blocked the Egyptian trade, which had mostly gone through Venice, and opened their own more effective commerce. Thus European power began in the East.

Meanwhile, in 1513 Balboa crossed the isthmus of Panama to discover the Pacific, while in 1519–22 an expedition led on behalf of Spain by, first, a Portuguese, Fernão de Magalhães (Magellan), and then a Basque, Juan Sebastián del Cano, circumnavigated the globe, going westwards. In 1519 Cortes embarked on his astonishing journey to Mexico, and in 1536 Pizarro conquered Peru. Those were the only two centres of settled empires in the Americas, and over the other tribes and principalities the Spaniards and Portuguese – the latter based in Brazil – had established a ruthless suzerainty by 1550.

The Spaniards also established themselves in the East, following Magellan's journey round the world. They founded a permanent settlement at Cebu in the Philippines and in 1571 founded Manila. Their first Spanish governor-general of the Philippines offered to conquer China for Philip II, an offer which was wisely rejected. Actually, the Philippines always had closer connections with Spanish America than with Asia.

These journeys and the conquests which ensued changed the course of history. The Portuguese conquerors in particular showed extraordinary mobility: 'Individuals of worth, warriors, administrators, technicians, were shifted about by the colonial administration in Lisbon like pieces on a backgammon board . . . from Asia to America and thence to Africa,' commented Gilberto Freyre. They found in the East a marvellous accumulation of wealth and a long tradition of trade; and in the West a population of aborigines still virtually in the age of polished stone. The conquests on both sides of the world were brutal but no one opposed them at home. The long wars with Indian tribes in Brazil and South America took their toll, the fighting with other Europeans

began immediately and there were years of disputes between
Spain and Portugal as to where the Pope believed the line dividing
them should be.

From the sixteenth century there were always regular sailings
between the Old and New Worlds, as there were also between
the European and the Eastern ports. The journey round the
world, including a stay at Goa or Manila to repair the ship, lasted
a year and a half under the most favourable circumstances. The
voyage round the Cape of Good Hope to India took six to eight
months, as did the crossing of the Pacific from Manila to Acapulco, though the return journey from Acapulco and Manila often
took less than three months with a following wind.

From Europe to the Indies ships sailed from Spain in convoys,
so as to combine defence and navigation. From 1543, ships were
forbidden to leave Spain for the Indies with less than ten vessels
in the fleet. The fleet outwards left every May, taking a week to
reach the Canaries, and then the crews would bid farewell to
Europe at Tenerife, with its towering cone. Then, for perhaps
forty days (Columbus took thirty-three days from the Canaries to
the Bahamas), they would see nothing of land till they crossed the
Windward Islands, close to the wild, rocky island of Dominica.
Thereafter there would be Santo Domingo, Vera Cruz and
Nombre de Dios, sometimes Havana. The fleets would usually
sail from Seville (though from 1492 till 1500 also from the ports
of the Río Tinto, Palos and Moguer). That established an effective
monopoly of control. (The Río Tinto ports were silted up by 1500.
Málaga and Cartagena were concerned with the Italian trade.
Ships from Corunna and Bilbao had to go a long way south to
Portugal to pick up favourable winds.) Only Cadiz could really
have been a rival to Seville, but Cadiz was more exposed, both to
pirates or enemies and to winds. So Seville both imported and
re-exported, though it was a far from ideal spot. Few great ships
could be launched there. The services of maintenance for big ships
were poor. The harbour was small. Ships above a certain draught
could not cross the bar at Sanlúcar fully loaded. Thus wine destined for the Americas was put on board at Cadiz. Passengers
often embarked at Sanlúcar. Yet Seville was the centre of the
bureaucracy and remained the seat of a school of navigation
founded by Vespucci.

In the Americas, Vera Cruz, Nombre de Dios and Acapulco
came to life only when the fleets sailed in. The captains-general
came down from the hills to take over the towns. When the fleets

left, those cities returned to being shanty towns sunk in malarial torpor, housing a few officials only. The Atlantic fleet would stand well to the north, out of the winds, before the Atlantic crossing began. The captains would seek a westerly wind near Bermuda and then run down to the Azores. After 1562 the fleets would always meet at Havana and there pick up a naval escort to help them cross the Atlantic free from pirates. The Pacific fleet was smaller but also important.

The Portuguese were less rigid. Their trade with both Brazil and the East was carried on from a score of ports. Their Eastern trade was entirely maritime: they made no attempt to conquer territory. Their ships sailing back from Brazil eventually, after 1648, did receive a naval escort (at Bahia) but outward-bound ships never did. On the journey eastward Portuguese ships were forbidden to stop anywhere between Goa and Lisbon. But in the seventeenth century it became common for homeward-bound Indiamen to touch at a Brazilian port, usually Bahia, on one excuse or another – a call which became a settled habit after 1690 when gold was discovered in Minas Gerais[3]. Later they began to stop at Delagoa (from Goa) and Angoa (to Goa).

The ships themselves increased in size. In the early sixteenth century large carracks or galleons of some 1,600 tons were built by ambitious European monarchs, with heavy cannon bristling. But these large vessels, with four or even five masts, large forecastles and deckhouses, proved ineffectual in war. The battles of the late sixteenth century were won by smaller vessels. Thus the Spanish Armada was composed of 132 vessels of which the largest was 1,300 tons with about thirty bronze guns, and the opposing English fleet of 197 vessels had as its largest an 800-ton ship carrying fifty-five guns. In the seventeenth century the largest ships, such as Portugal's *Padre Eterno*, the *Royal Charles* or the French *Saint Philippe*, were between 1,500 and 2,000 tons. Spanish 'galleons' such as those used to carry treasure from America were several decks high, with several rows of oars, some worked by several men. From the sixteenth century onwards Portuguese ships were often made in India, from the teak forests on the west coast which many believed to be superior to European oak. Other vessels were made from Brazilian hardwoods.

Meantime, the smaller caravels of 100 to 150 tons continued to be employed in, for example, the Brazilian trade; and while the ships which went east from Portugal had first to establish their dominance over the Muslim fleets, there was no such competition in the New World from the *canoas* of the Caribs nor from the large balsa barks of the Peruvians. For no American before 1492 knew anything of seapower or seamanship. Numerous though those ships were, they did not travel fast. For example, the news of the successful rebellion of the Portuguese against the Spaniards in 1640 took over two months to reach the capital of Brazil (the King* was proclaimed on 1 December 1640; the Viceroy in Bahia heard the news on 15 February).

Of course, whether or no the colonisers were Jesuit priests who wished to found a holy republic of 'Indians domesticated by Jesus' (like those of Paraguay), or families which soon established near-feudal dominance over thousands of acres, or soldiers of fortune, adventurers, merchants, exiles, 'near Christians' (that is, Jews), shipwreck victims or mere traffickers in parrots, the ships to the New World brought men, and a few women, to begin a new life and to found a new society: probably about 110,000 Spaniards and Portuguese in the course of the sixteenth century.

Nor were these oceans confined to Portuguese and Spaniards. The English and the French began to prey on the Americas very early in the sixteenth century, and the Portuguese decision to occupy Brazil permanently may have been taken to avoid a major French intervention there. Tropical rivers were the scene of continual wars. Then in the late sixteenth century the Dutch appeared. The Dutch victory over Spain had been made possible by skill at sea. Thereafter the heirs of those victorious sailors in Europe burst into their maritime era. 'Companies of Afar' were founded, merchants previously content with selling in Europe found a new world. The Dutch first sailed to the Spice Islands in 1594, the first large fleet bringing back spices came back in 1599 – the total profit being over 400 per cent. In 1619 the Dutch occupied Jakarta in Java (Batavia), and Malacca in 1641[4]. In 1667 they conquered the Celebes. Though less successful in displacing the Portuguese in Brazil, the Dutch dominated Eastern trade in the late seventeenth century. Their main route to the Spice Islands was to sail to the Cape of Good Hope (where they established a 'victualling station' – the foundation of South Africa – in 1652) and then due east 3,000 miles to the north of the 'Roaring Forties' before turning north-east along the west coast of Australia. Dutchmen such as Abel Tasman sailed round that continent and con-

---

* The King, João IV, is credited with having composed the tune of the hymn 'Adeste Fideles'.

sidered it valueless. Meantime, far to the west and north, the
English drove out the Portuguese from Ormuz in 1622, handing
it back to Persia, where it declined – to revive as a name for naval
significance only in the 1970s.

The Dutch East and West India companies were in effect cartels
which had monopolies, so far as the Dutch were concerned, of
trade with two distant parts of the world. The East India Company, with its charter in 1602, received a monopoly in trade and
navigation east of the Cape of Good Hope and west of the Straits
of Magellan, for example. Both companies were empowered to
wage war, build forts, enlist military and naval personnel. Both
were self-perpetuating oligarchies drawn from the leading merchants of the main cities of the Netherlands. They aimed at profit
but, especially in the case of the West India Company (incorporated in 1621), profit by war, not peace. Others emulated them.
The wars of Europe were thus world wars in miniature thereafter.

23

Commerce Revived

But see! Each muse in Leo's golden days,
Starts from her trance, and trims her wither'd bays,
Rome's ancient Genius, o'er its ruins spread,
Shakes off the dust, and rears his rev'rend head.

Alexander Pope, *Essay on Criticism*

The innovations of the Renaissance might have been ineffective, comparable to the innovations of the Hellenistic age, if European commerce had not been able to market the goods which invention and improvements in communication made possible. For, Paul Mantoux wrote, the progress of commerce and industry had become so interwoven that 'it is difficult to discover on which side a new development started, progress in industry seeming impossible unless preceded by progress in commerce'[1]. Holland, in the seventeenth century, became the leading commercial country in the world. But it traded few Dutch goods. Everything was carried everywhere by the Dutch, regardless of make. England also became a great commercial country long before she was an industrial one. The transformation of the old hierarchical society into one where men could begin to shape their own life, with the chance of choosing between different forms of profession and consumption, was therefore associated with the growth of commerce, the increase in the use of money and an elaboration of the ways that both commerce and money were manipulated.

Money had existed in one form or another for many generations and in almost every type of society. Almost everything under the sun has been for a time used as money – beans of the cacao tree in ancient Central America, seashells off the Canary coast, cowries in both China and on the Gulf of Guinea, cows in India, beer in Sumer, salt in Senegal, on the Niger and in Abyssinia, copper bracelets, horses, chickens, cylinders cut from coral (in Etruria), dried fish (Iceland), furs (Russia), tobacco, grain, sugar and cocoa. In Canada playing-cards would be used for money in the eighteenth century, nails were still being used in Scotland in 1775, while Japan used rice in the seventeenth century. In colonial Brazil an Indian slave, a 'piece', took the place sometimes of money; debts were paid and provisions were acquired with them. African slaves later took their place. But the money mostly respected through history has been coinage of gold, silver and copper – and latterly, though not till well into the age of industry, nickel, other base metals and paper (paper was used as money in China from the ninth to the fourteenth century, and then abandoned, since it brought inflation).

The concept of metal as a means of exchange is ancient. It was apparently developed in both the Far and the Near East independently. Silver was used in ancient Iraq as a standard of value, without any metal changing hands. The price of an object about 2000 BC in Babylon might be stated in silver but be paid for in cloths, bronze objects or beer. The first silver coins appear to have been struck by the Hittites about 1500 BC. They were well supplied with silver, which was also used as a medium of exchange by those Assyrian merchants who for a long time dominated commerce. Coins were later used by the Lydians, another people of Asia Minor, the traditional 'inventors' of money. Their kings stamped a lion's head as a badge on ingots of electrum with a standard weight. From Lydia the idea of stamped coins passed to Greece, many of whose towns soon after 700 BC were minting silver, particularly at Aegina where silver pieces were given heads of turtles, each with a given weight. It also seems possible that coins, or round pieces of metal, officially stamped as a token for a value, may have been used by the Chinese as early as that.

Long before this, gold and silver had begun to be admired, worked and prized for aesthetic reasons. The discovery that gold can be plated thin to cover stone or wood was made by Egyptians before the establishment of the Egyptian state. Most of the gold of Egypt passed through the hands of pharaohs for a time and much of it was immobilised in tombs, though robbers from the earliest times sought to break them open. Babylon also acquired, even if it did not produce, a great deal of gold, while Crete was the home of men of legendary skill with that metal. There was, however, a legend that even Minos came from Egypt. Gold was certainly carried to the east Mediterranean from Spain, the Danube, perhaps Central Africa, and even Ireland, long before 1000 BC. A gold goblet was said to hang from a chain on Hercules's bow. To the Greeks the beauty of gold, with its brightness and permanence, was indissolubly linked with the gods, whose palaces, thrones, chariots, lyres, arrows and armour were all said to be made of it. The fact that gold is as malleable as lead and can be beaten when it is cold added to its appeal. The gods of Greece themselves were said to be 'golden' because of the divine light shining from them, and the legendary time when men were closest to gods was known to the Greeks as the golden age.

The Greeks chose silver as their currency for they had plenty of it in the silver mines of Laurion and never had enough gold, though King Croesus of Lydia sent 7,500 pounds of it to Delphi (one reason for the prestige of that sanctuary in a gold-less land). Currency created inflation immediately. Instead of borrowing grain, peasants started to borrow money in order to buy it at high prices. To repay the loan the peasant either had to raise the cash or to hold on till the market revived. Either way he was in a weak position. The Athenians, meantime, realised the importance of having a gold reserve to back their silver currency. Thus Pheidias made the chryselephantine statue of Athena so that 2,000 pounds of gold could be taken off it in an emergency. Alexander's conquest of Persia caused gold to be more plentiful in Greece. Not only did he conquer Persia but he also captured remote, rich sources of gold in the far east of that empire which even the Achaemenians had not touched. The subsequent Hellenic age was, therefore, characterised by an unprecedented quantity of gold objects for personal use – hammered, cast, engraved, embossed or applied with paste on to glass. Even so, most commercial transactions continued to be by barter.

Rome began its rise to prosperity almost without gold, on the fringe of the Greek silver world. That changed when she conquered the Etruscans. The Etruscans had brought their gold techniques from Lydia to Etruria. Their goldsmiths had in particular developed filigree. Other Roman conquests in the south of Italy and afterwards in the Val d'Aosta caused Roman reserves to stand at 4,000 Roman pounds in 218 BC. That hoard quadrupled by the end of the third Punic War. But the reserves remained reserves: for many generations the Romans, like the Greeks, kept their currency silver (in the silver *denarius*.) There was, under the Republic, little gold in private hands. The use of silver as the day-to-day currency also meant that the Romans had as much need for silver as for gold when they sought their war indemnities.

Yet Rome had a gold coinage before the end of the Republic (the *aureus*). In the early Empire there was a lavish display of personal gold and vast spending of it on luxuries from India, as the Roman gold coins found in India prove. Spain had by then become the main source of Roman gold. The Roman coinage was of a high quality to begin with but by the third century AD was debased. Silver ceased to be used. The Empire tried out a coinage of bronze and copper. By that time the precious metals of the Empire had been converted into plate or jewellery. Inflation and monetary instability ensued, and those familiar things characterised the crisis in the Empire of the third century AD, as much as civil war did. That era was the only time before the sixteenth century when the use of money was so widespread as to make the shortage of it a serious inconvenience or even a misery for more than a minority of people. Otherwise, the majority lived on their own produce, served their masters according to their status and rarely saw a coin from one year's end to another.

The later Roman Empire was given financial stability, in the end, by Constantine, who obtained gold by robbing the pagan temples in the name of his conversion to Christianity. Constantine issued a gold *solidus*, seventy-two of which were held to equal a pound of gold. That 'solid' object (also known in Constantinople as the 'Byzant') remained unchanged in weight and purity well into the Middle Ages. Constantine's silver *milliarensis*, of which twenty-four were supposed to equal one *solidus*, was less successful, and later abandoned. Afterwards, the collapse of the administration in the West left the mines for these precious minerals without skilled labour, guards, transport or a central market. Mine shafts were abandoned to floods, and looting was rife. Even so the Visigoths, Burgundians, Merovingians and Anglo-Saxons all operated mints, producing gold coins which, like their political pretensions, feebly, slavishly and badly echoed Roman practice. Thus the Merovingians had a *sou*, instead of a *solidus*, and a *denier*, for a *denarius*. New gold could not be obtained, but old coins could be melted down and used again – enough to permit a gold coinage theoretically to limp on.

Paradoxically the economic revival of AD c. 700 in Western Europe led to the disappearance of the gold currency. Gold was scarce in the Carolingian Empire because of a revival of Byzantium backed by an ambitious pure gold currency. The currency of Charlemagne was, theoretically: £1 or *libra* (*lira*), a pound's worth of gold. That was equivalent to 20 *soldi* (sols), or shillings, of silver. Each *soldus* was worth 12 copper *denarii*, pence or deniers. In practice, gold was not current, and a silver penny, or denier, later became the only real coin. Charlemagne tried to ensure that his coins should only be coined in the royal mints. But his son Louis the Pious allowed certain churches to coin money. In England the King was not so ambitious: 'No one is to coin money except in a port,' decreed Athelstan, but that word included many inland towns². Minting continued anarchic and English *denarii* had many different alloys and weights. That comment could be made about many primitive countries whose coinage seems at first sight to be sound.

The Caliphate, on the other hand, always had both gold and silver coins, the gold being brought from as far away as the Niger and Senegal. Timbuktu became in the early Middle Ages 'a city of gold' linked by camel to the Mediterranean, to which spices, gold, slaves and ivory were carried in bulk. El Andalus, or Moorish Spain (independent from the Caliphate by the mid eighth century), also had an elaborate money economy, with silver-plated *dishemes* minted early and gold *dinars* minted in the eighth century. Those currencies were the heart of an economy which was as superior in the volume of its trade to Western Europe as was its ostentation and culture.

By the late Middle Ages, however, the repeated ravages of Turks and Mongols, as well as the caliph's own extravagances, had caused the collapse of the main Islamic polity and the virtual return in the Near East to subsistence agriculture and to barter. But, by then, large numbers of Arabs (perhaps they were Persians) had settled in Chinese and other Eastern ports. Their descendants played a part in the Chinese imperial administration. Chinese merchants visited Baghdad. From the East, Islam had imported silk, paper, porcelain and a little steel, not to speak of arabic numerals, from India. The commerce and finance of the time of the Abbasid caliphs developed banking, a system of cheques and letters of credit, and loans (including loans made to governments) on a scale which seems not to have been equalled under Rome and which directly led to Italian emulation: after all, most of the bankers were Jews or Christians because of the Muslim ban on usury. Arab conquests in Sicily, as well as the prosperity of Egypt under the Fatimid caliphs, made Italy very close again to the eastern Mediterranean.

The European gold currencies revived, as did commerce and banking generally, after the Crusades. The Italian cities who financed the latter soon had enough gold to produce the florin – in Florence – in 1252, the *janarius* in Genoa the same year and other coins in Venice and elsewhere. Even England, in 1330, had a florin. Probably this mediaeval currency was made from Arab gold melted down, though by then there was some new gold mining in Europe, especially in Hungary. The Serbian monarchy of Stephen Dushan also mined silver successfully, enabling that state to be quite strong for a few generations. The Bohemian silver mines were opened in the fourteenth century.

By that time several major alterations had occurred in the way that Europeans, especially Italians, managed their commercial transactions. Everything seems to point to the Crusades as being the 'motor' of the changes. Thus the Crusades offered, as has been suggested earlier, great opportunities to merchants, principally Italian merchants. Such merchants of the twelfth century were usually men who could write, could use a system of credit and operate internationally. Perhaps a majority of early merchants were children of non-free parents. Their meeting places were fairs: St Denis (actually known from 629); the six fairs of Champagne; Foggia (which sold the pastoral products of southern Italy); and Danzig (a great fair from the mid tenth century, where grain was exchanged for saffron from Armenia, cattle from Moldavia, cloth from England); and, in England, there were important fairs at Stourbridge, Winchester, Beverley, Greenwich and Boston. Though other associations of merchants were founded (for example, that of the merchants of the Hanse who linked England and the Low Countries with the Baltic and Scandinavia), the trade of the Middle Ages was dominated by Italians. Merchants were soon found directing most of the Italian cities which had managed to escape, during the wars of the Guelfs and Ghibellines, from direct control by either the pope or the German emperor. Those cities may have thought that they were operating 'in the name of God and profit', in the closing words of letter-writers from Prato of the fourteenth century, but the latter motive seems often to have been strongest.

These merchants devised the beneficial customs of underwriting and insuring bills of lading, and providing separate letters of advice. In the footsteps of the Italians came the Jews (whose exclusion from Spain in 1492 amounted to the expulsion of the business community of the country) and the Armenians (whose dispersion for commercial reasons in the sixteenth century lost them for ever the chance of achieving a national state)[3]. But the concept of the company, the share, the capital market and the stock market, began in Italy in the thirteenth or fourteenth century. Indeed, the 'company' – the word in most European languages derives from an association of those with whom a man breaks bread (*con pagne*, signifying 'with bread') – owes its origin, in the form that it is now known, to innovations undertaken at the time of the Crusades in Italy. Men had, of course, often sought profit before. Indeed, they had always done so. But it seems doubtful whether they associated it in any form comparable to the modern company before the age of the Crusades, or elsewhere than in the Mediterranean. Werner Sombart suggested dating 'the birth of modern capitalism' to 1202, when Leonardo of Pisa's *Liber Abaci* appeared; that did educate merchants in double-entry book-keeping. But before the coming of printing few really benefited.

The history of the company is considered in a later part of this book. In the course of the Renaissance and seventeenth century, however, there were formed, for the first time, several chartered companies, such as the Dutch and the English East India companies and, in the Portuguese Empire, the Brazil Company, formally incorporated in 1649. These companies fitted out fleets, provided arms and were open as a rule to all to become shareholders; in return the Crowns concerned afforded them monopolies of trade in certain zones, perhaps with exceptions (the slave trade, for example).

The second important development was the birth of modern banking. This cannot in itself be attributed to the Crusades. For, after all, the Crusades themselves were financed by banks. But the renewed contact with the eastern Mediterranean brought Italian financiers into contact with those Christian or Jewish money-merchants who handled the financial arrangements within the disintegrating Muslim world. At all events, there were in the thirteenth century in Italy three classes of traders in money: first, petty moneylenders; second, money-changers who dealt in the exchange of currency, precious stones and bullion; and, third, bankers who were also merchants. Among these last, Amalfians, Venetians and Pisans were the oldest established and Florentines the newest and later the most energetic. Buying wool, making and selling woollen goods, these Italians began to operate on so large and so international a scale that they soon became moneylenders to kings; and not only to kings. With Peter's Pence and other ecclesiastical taxes pouring into Rome in the late Middle Ages, the question of who held the papal account was a matter of great importance: for example, the Pazzi family's conspiracy in Florence in the fifteenth century would not probably have got under way if that family had not already secured the transfer to themselves of the papal account from the Medici. By the mid fifteenth century, at all events, Cosimo de' Medici was sitting in his office in the Via Larga in Florence at the headquarters of an international bank with branches in Rome, Milan, Geneva, Bruges, Ancona, Pisa, London and Avignon, trading in almost every known luxury and necessity, on the general principle, as John Hale says, of 'spreading risks through diversity'[4].

A third development, whose connection with the Crusades is less obvious, was the beginning of a tendency throughout mediaeval Europe, particularly in England, for all lords to turn their feudal dues into rents and to realise their incomes in cash. Merchants in new towns encouraged this, and labourers in times of labour shortage such as occurred in the fourteenth century encouraged it too.

It is easy to compare the financial system reviving the West with the failure of the Chinese, otherwise so inventive, to develop adequate banking arrangements. The individual merchants in China under the T'ang dynasty were the only source of credit. All emperors and bureaucrats were frightened that capitalists might accumulate fortunes. On the other hand, emperors in China did not mind bureaucrats accumulating riches, however they did so. Paper money was introduced into China about AD 910; but the efforts of an inspired reformer, Wang An Shih, a minister of finance under the T'ang dynasty (he died in 1086), to introduce taxation in money, rather than in grain, failed[5]. In that failure, a reflection of innumerable signs of stagnation within old China, is to be seen one more reason why China did not profit from her technological superiority. It is something which remotely recalls the relation of technologically imaginative Europe and the commercially more ingenious USA in the twentieth century. In ancient India and China usury and the lending of money, the exchange of goods for cash and manufacture, all occurred so as to rival in sophistication anything which happened in Europe till the thirteenth or fourteenth century. But in any rich country the state was strong enough to control prices to limit profits by merchants even if they were reasonably independent men or even, as occurred in the Mauryan Empire about the third century BC, to fix the percentage of profit. Now for the first time, in Italy, an undoubtedly rich region, states were controlled by merchants, and not vice versa. Even the German emperors and Spanish kings depended on merchants, either Italian or from the Low Countries, to finance their wars.

Commerce, like mining and pottery, had an American history

before Columbus. When the Spaniards reached Mexico they found there a class of small-scale, private professional merchants. Throughout the Central American mainland, markets were held in which pottery, salt, bricks, pearls and gold objects were all traded as if at a Spanish *feria*. There were also exchanged in Mexico cotton goods from Yucatan, marble or alabaster, copper axes and bells from Michoacan, as well as weapons of obsidian. The great market at Tenochtitlan greatly impressed Cortes, and he observed how every crop or product seemed to be there exchanged, with grains of cacao, grains of gold, dishes of tin and gold dust carried in the quills of feathers as a form of currency. There was the great contrast between Mexico and Peru – for in Peru no one sought money. In Cuzco there were no merchants and no market[6].

In India by that time, independent merchants also existed after a fashion. But, like the merchants used by the Tsar in Russia, their status was always inferior. They were often more the ruler's commercial agents than they were capitalists, even though some of the Muslim merchants seemed more like the latter. Perhaps for this reason the astute Spanish jurist Vitoria would have preferred an empire based on commerce rather than on conquest since he thought that commerce was as effective as conquest in spreading the Gospel.

The discovery of America – appropriately by a Genoese: Genoa was the leading financial centre in the sixteenth century – gave Europe access to vast new sources of gold and silver.

Columbus and all his successors were absolutely preoccupied by the search for gold, and in the end, after many disappointments, Balboa found the way to it in large quantities in Colombia. Before that, the native population of most of the Caribbean had been enslaved and worked to death to produce quantities of the ore which did not exist. In Cuzco too, the Incas had accumulated such vast stores of gold as to render the Spaniards berserk: where else could they see a garden composed of gold flowers?

Both Aztec and Inca goldsmiths had been expert in casting gold. They used silver with it to produce a polychrome effect 'more magnificent than exquisite', as the historian of gold C. H. V. Sutherland put it[7]. Old Mexico had innumerable gems. Little survives, for most went into the Spanish melting pot. Atahualpa's offer to fill a room with gold to secure his ransom from Pizarro was fulfilled with plates of gold. The gold was then boiled down. In all, 750,000 pounds of gold were sent from Spanish America to

Spain between 1492 and 1600, of which at least ten per cent became royal property. This gold was so great in quantity as to offer many opportunities, above all to the Spanish economy, but also to the rest of Europe. It also provided disturbances, adding greatly to the inflation begun by the discovery of silver in Bohemia. The price level in Spain rose in the sixteenth century 400 per cent, partly as a result of the import of these and other precious metals, though partly also because of an increase in population and because of spending on war by the government. The import of precious metals, however, enabled all European countries of any importance to have a gold currency, which in turn allowed, in the prevailing circumstances of reliance on gold, a vast expansion of the credit available to both states and private people. Indeed, the significance of the Spanish inflation of the sixteenth century, meticulously chronicled by Earl Hamilton, is that it was the first monetary crisis in a Europe becoming used to transactions in cash, and on a scale larger than the inflation of the late third century. (The attribution of the rise in prices in the sixteenth century entirely to the import of gold and silver now seems extravagant to most careful students, since the large-scale exploitation of the silver mines of Potosí in Peru and Zacatecas in Mexico did not begin till after the beginning of the inflation.)

The gold of America offered great opportunities to the brilliant Renaissance goldsmiths, of whom Cellini was supreme. But it also caused kings to default on debts. The long-term effect of the coming of American gold was to inspire a major, beneficial and decisive shift in the character of commerce towards private merchants. Hence the foundation of the first great banks: the Bank of Palermo (1551), the Banco della Piazza di Rialto (1587), the Banco di S. Ambrogio (Milan, 1593), the Monte de Pietà (Naples), Santo Spirito (Rome) and in the seventeenth century the Exchange Bank of Amsterdam (founded 1609) and the Bank of England (1694)[8].

The immediate effect of the import of precious metals was to invigorate the economy of Holland; for Antwerp, then of course a Habsburg possession, was the port selected by the Spanish kings to act as their market. That and the fact that the Portuguese had also chosen Antwerp in 1504 as the market for their Eastern spices made it a city of vast wealth. It succeeded Genoa as the commercial centre of Europe and remained so till the Habsburg bankruptcy of 1557. (It was also the first centre of opposition to the Habsburgs in the 1560s and refugees from Antwerp helped to invigorate the new Dutch economy after the rebellion.) Antwerpers in Amsterdam really built up the Netherlands[9].

The supply of gold from the Americas also made possible a vast expansion of trade with the East which had almost died since the fall of Rome. The golden *cruzado* of Portugal, the São Tomé minted in Goa and the *Moeda* (moidore) too, revived contact with the East as effectively as if it were a renaissance of the *aureus* of old Rome. The production of spices in Asia and the demand for them in Europe doubled during the second half of the sixteenth century: pepper above all. The Portuguese also secured at Macao a monopoly of trade between China and Japan – a trade of Chinese silk for Japanese silver bullion. Macao and Nagasaki thus were for generations the centre of a European trade as profitable as it was substantial.*

The mining of these ores declined in the depressed seventeenth century. But the second silver age in the eighteenth gave to Spain apparently inexhaustible supplies of silver, from Mexico. Brazil became a great gold producer after the discovery of the metal in Minas Gerais in 1694. That province's baroque capital, Ouro Preto, seemed later the most prosperous city in the world. Once gold had been found in Minas Gerais there was a gold rush of epic proportions, the first such to occur, the local Indians being killed, expelled or enslaved. King João V of Portugal became one of the richest European monarchs while explorers looking for gold carried out feats of endurance as important as Livingstone's travels in Africa. Among the fields they discovered was the fabulous if remote one on the Cuiaba river – which had its gold rush in 1719. Despite the 3,000-mile river journey into the centre of the continent it necessitated, it was this which made the gold moidore of the eighteenth century one of the most popular coins in circulation.

In the sixteenth century Europe was productive too. Silver was found in Bohemia at Joachimsthal, in the valley of the river Thaler, in such profusion that the word 'thaler' was given to a

---

* Eventually the trade passed from Portugal to the Dutch, who also established themselves in Nagasaki. To silk and minerals, the seventeenth century added Chinese porcelain. The impetus was given by the Dutch capture of two Portuguese carracks containing 'china' in 1602. Much was taken to Holland thereafter and re-exported. Over three million pieces of Chinese porcelain were shipped in Europe in Dutch East Indiamen, and millions were also transhipped to Batavia for disposal in Eastern markets. This led to Dutch imitations. See below, page 324.

new Bohemian coin: hence, at one remove, the better-known word 'dollar', a contribution to the world's vocabulary for which Bohemia has not always been credited.* Meantime, Genoese, Flemings, Germans and Portuguese (Jews) had so established themselves as to dominate Spanish commerce by the late sixteenth century. Companies of Flemings could be formed to defend Cadiz against Drake in 1590. The Dutch trade in Cadiz reinforced Amsterdam as Europe's major money market. A stream of French artisans into Spain became so great as to cause popular outbreaks against them.

Banking developed late in England. Private persons for a long time were happy to entrust their money to merchants, merchants to goldsmiths of Lombard Street. The notes issued by these men began in the mid seventeenth century to take the place of cash in some transactions. The first Bank of England was simply a group of people who had agreed to lend £1,200,000 to William III at eight per cent. In return they received the title of corporation and the right of receiving deposits, discounting commercial bills or doing, that is, what the Exchange Bank of Amsterdam or the Bank of St George at Genoa had already been doing for some time. That bank not only issued the first bank notes in England but, more important (paper money played little part in the ordinary life of most people till the nineteenth century), guaranteed the price of gold at £4 4s 11½d per ounce, at which price it remained till 1914. Although that stability was only made possible by the increase of production of gold during the next two centuries (about seven times more gold was produced in the eighteenth and nineteenth centuries than was produced in the sixteenth and seventeenth) it meant that for the first time gold was established as the key commodity in international trade. Thereafter, too, for 200 years every reputable bank issuing a bank note had enough gold or silver in its vaults to make it convertible on demand: the root of an unparalleled public confidence.

Three other aspects of the revival and reinvigoration of European commerce in the course of the Renaissance need to be noticed. First, the new states of Italy, or rather Venice, embarked upon the modern science of statistics. Feudal states knew only the catalogues of rights and possessions and tended to look on production of goods as fixed. But Venetians began to reckon men

---

* The Spanish *dólar* was the best known silver coin in the newly independent colonies in the 1780s and hence was adopted as the currency of the US.

from the early sixteenth century in souls, not hearths, and the speech of the dying Doge Mocenigo in 1423 gave something like a statistical account of the resources of Venice, almost in the style of a modern annual of statistics. Florence was soon even more sophisticated.

Second, the same Italian states began to develop a rational administration of taxation which made mediaeval Europe seem amateur, though as a result, by the end of the sixteenth century familiar complaints were heard: 'all states of Europe groaned under taxes in the late sixteenth century', Braudel tells us, and in Florence, considered 'a model of administration', the burden of taxes was so great that in 1582 it led to an exodus of population[10].

Third, the combination of better communications, new forms of trading, banking and an increase in goods made possible the creation of a new method of financing trade and investment. This was the market in prices, stocks, shares and commodities. Was it the invention of Jewish refugees from Spain, Huguenots or sober Dutch burghers? Whoever is to be credited with this remarkable work of Renaissance art, it was created in the Netherlands, principally at Antwerp, in the early sixteenth century on the basis of what Dutch merchants had learned in Italy, particularly in Venice and Florence.

By the mid sixteenth century speculation on 'grain futures' was current in Amsterdam. In the early seventeenth century herrings, spices and whale oil were also objects of speculative trading. Pure financial speculation in shares of companies began in Amsterdam about then too – the one major innovation of the Dutch, for everything else they did was an improvement on Italian practice. The idea took on 'like a rocket' (in the words of Violet Barbour) in London, though not before the 1690s. Brokers, men whose whole life was spent dealing in shares, came into being. It was already observed in the early seventeenth century that, 'without possessing shares, or even a desire to acquire any, one can carry on a big business in them . . . the seller so to speak, sells nothing but wind, and the buyer receives only wind'[11].

This, like so much else, was the achievement of merchants who fled from Antwerp after its fall to the Spaniards in 1585. It began a new custom of managing commerce which played a decisive part in financing the Industrial Revolution. It only began to falter to any marked extent when governments took to intervening regularly in markets during the First World War and after the collapse of the Russian market in 1917. In the meantime, public and private loans and foreign investments came to be more and more important in economic life. The financial network founded by the Dutch was far from a narrowly national one. The Dutch East and West India companies were, as it were, large trusts based on Amsterdam fortunes. Even in the Dutch revolutionary war, merchants of Amsterdam traded with Spain, as they did with Britain in the Anglo-Dutch wars. The famine which struck France in 1709, after the terrible harvest, was relieved by Dutch grain carriers, even though Holland was at war with France. In the twentieth century tourists in search of art travel in numbers superior to the population of all Europe in the fifteenth century to see the 'great cities of civilisation', Venice, Florence and Amsterdam. How few realise that the works of art before which they stand delighted were themselves made possible by a financial revival as remarkable as anything recovered during the Renaissance!

24

Slow Journeys by Land

In the south go by boat, in the north take a horse.

Chinese proverb

'Sit in thy cell and thy cell shall teach thee all things
The monk out of his cell is a fish out of water'. . .

The Blessed Antony, in Helen Waddell, *The Wandering Scholars*

One means of communication which did not improve during the
Renaissance was travel by land. The changes of the Renaissance
were carried out by men of cities, private merchants who, however
rich, were not the masters of great labour forces, and by small
rather than large states – Florence, Venice, Portugal, the Netherlands, England; not France, the German Empire, Russia or the
Ottoman Sultanate. The roads of antiquity had been the achievement of despotisms and as a result had enabled the ruler's messengers to travel fast, rather than assist merchants to seek profits.
Thus the freedom-loving Greeks had bad roads. Their streets were
undrained, even if they did prepare a wheel rut to help carts and
chariots, particularly on the way in and out of mines and quarries.
Their charioteers were prized, the Cyreneans in particular being
noted for their skill at chariot driving, but chariots were a useful
assistance in war rather than a help to trade. In Egypt, Herodotus
considered the great road which carried the stones of the pyramids
to be scarcely inferior to the pyramids themselves. But that road
was a road for slaves, not for free men. Long before the era of
Herodotus the Near Eastern roads of tyranny had been brought
to their best by the Assyrians, whose provincial governors remained in day-to-day touch with their lords through professional
messengers. These travelled along post roads by horse or mule,
exchanging steeds at specific places – thus originating a system of
imperial control which lasted till the nineteenth century AD. They
were in particular used and extended by the Persians, whose
empire was consolidated by good roads. These constituted the
glory of the Middle Eastern public service until the Arab conquest
in the sixth century AD. Thereafter the increasing use of horses

and camels rather than wagons, and the collapse of the Caliphate, caused them to fall into disuse.

A few bridges were also built in the ancient Near East. Most of them were decorative (the 36-foot wide bridge at the palace of Minos, for example, or the bridges of Nebuchadrezzar at Babylon, resting on a hundred brick piers) or were used for aqueducts. Fords usually served the purposes of modern bridges. Xerxes carried his army across the Hellespont by joining about 700 ships, anchoring them and tying them to land. Planks were then laid across, then brushwood and then earth.

For a few hundred years the trade routes to India by land were as good as those achieved by sea. They ran through Afghanistan either via Kabul or Kandahar, and then through Persepolis or Susa. Within India elaborate roads had been built by that time and Afghanistan linked India as well as the Hellenic world with Kashgar and China along what became known as the 'old silk route'. Along these roads soldiers and missionaries travelled as well as merchants.

Such a judgement could not have been passed on the famous system of Roman roads. The concept of good roads reached Rome through the Etruscans. Perhaps they brought the idea from Lydia. Such Roman improvements as there were were based more on hard work than original thought. The ground was dug up and set with stones. The middle part of the road was raised to allow drainage and topped with gravel. Bridges, however, were built by the Romans with stone for the first time (for example, the fine bridge still in use at Rimini). Main roads were driven by them to run straight from city to city, with little account taken of hills or obstacles. There were major and minor post stations every ten or twelve miles along the main roads. Each station kept horses, vets, ostlers, surgeons, cartwrights, carriages and wagons. The upkeep was maintained by provincial taxes. The horses (whose average life was four years) were provided by a regular levy. Each station was managed by a retired official from the imperial service. Inspectors paid regular visits. Expensive though the system was, particularly in the outer provinces, it enabled travellers on horseback easily to travel 100 miles a day. There was also a wagon post which provided ox wagons with two pairs for heavy goods. In the outer Empire pack donkeys and camels were maintained. There were in all 54,000 miles of Roman roads, a network of communications which maintained the Empire, enabling the legionaries to march their 10,000 paces a day or sometimes more. Still, on those roads, civil servants had priority and the bulk of internal Roman trade went by the sea or rivers. It was always cheaper to ship wheat from Syria to Andalusia than to carry it from south to north Spain overland. Inland, the life of the Roman Empire consisted of the provisioning of little oases, 'drops of water on a drying surface', as Peter Brown put it[1].

The eclipse of the Roman civil service meant the end of the roads and posts. Armies of barbarians travelling in caravanserais could force services from captured towns on old post routes. No one else could. Those who travelled to Rome in the early Middle Ages on pilgrimage would stop at monasteries or at large, half-empty castles, taking with them bedding and cooking-things. Inns were as risky as that where Theseus was nearly murdered by Procrustes. The Arabs travelled by horse or in caravans of camels, 'ships of the desert' as they became called, and so did not need the roads: the role of the camel had earlier also been destructive to the old Roman civilisation of northern Africa. Introduced into the region by Septimus Severus about AD 200, that animal was thereafter mastered by nomads of the desert, who used it to raid the old pleasant cities and gardens of the Mahgreb and then return into the pathless desert[2]: a means of communication which favoured banditry rather than administration or commerce.

In the Middle Ages both the caliph and the emperor of China had roads which made the poor horse-tracks of Europe seem most inferior. Marco Polo described the Emperor's secretariat receiving despatches from places ten days' journey off in one day and one night. In the nineteenth century the postal service of China would have 2,000 express stations, 30,526 horses and nearly 50,000 foot messengers, with about 70,000 service personnel. Probably that reflects the state of affairs earlier too. But these elaborate services were used less as a means of communication than as one of control by the government.

Some quickening of transport on land in Europe came with the horseshoe and the carthorse in the eleventh century. Peasants could then think of selling their surplus, if they had one, at a fair or market. Previously such a thing was as unthinkable as in those countries of Africa or South America in the twentieth century where there are no roads from farm to market, where motor traffic is impossible and animals of traction unavailable. Some other technical improvements of wagons, such as the pivoted front wheel (and perhaps the brake), derived from the early Middle Ages. Most Roman vehicles, except post-chaises and ceremonial

chariots, had been two-wheeled. But by the twelfth century a
four-wheeled *caretta*, capable of carrying heavy loads, very slowly,
was in being. By that time 'international' travel by road had
recovered. Priests or monks went from northern Europe to Rome,
took back with them the idea of Romanesque architecture and
indeed often took back craftsmen from Italy. By the fourteenth
century Chaucer could write that every April people longed to 'go
on pilgrimage' – which would not have been safe a hundred years
before.

Reliance on the horse meant that seasonal interruptions of
communications were due less to bad weather than to difficulties
of obtaining forage: Carolingian *missi* never began their tours of
inspection till the grass had grown; armies waited till the hay was
cut. Mediaeval journeys 'internationalised' several peoples. Hungary, for example, lay on a land route to Jerusalem which the
destrier had made an alternative to the pirate-infested seas (though
Richard Coeur de Lion found it had its risks too). Frederick
Barbarossa was received in Hungary by a king, Bela III, not
unlike himself in habits. Bela's queen was Margaret, a sister of
the King of France and widow to the heir apparent of England.
A Frenchman wrote the first history of Hungary. Meanwhile the
builders of Gothic cathedrals also threw bridges across many of
the rivers of Europe. Not far away in Asia the Mongol Empire,
which from 1279 till 1350 embraced all China and most of Russia
(except for Novgorod) and even approached Budapest, was kept
together by horsemen capable of riding at the Roman pace of a
hundred miles a day for days on end, thus maintaining the tradition of good communications and despotism till the dawn of our
own times.

In the European Renaissance further changes making for good
communication inland are hard to discern. The wheel, it is true,
was improved by making it concave. Coaches in towns appeared
in the late fifteenth century:* Luther travelled to the Diet of
Worms in one in 1521. Neither invention made any contribution
to long-distance transport till roads were improved to bear the
latter delicate innovation. Roads in the sixteenth century in Europe consisted of tracks a yard wide, satisfactory enough for horse-

---

* The coach was an Hungarian invention, the word deriving from Kocs, a town
  between Raab and Buda. The key to this innovation was a body suspended on
  straps, with a bogie. The front axle was attached to the chassis by a pivot, a
  device revived for war in the fifteenth century.

men, alongside which flocks and walkers had sometimes beaten out footpaths.

The only innovation of the Renaissance in respect of transport was, however, seen in the Americas. One of the many groups of llama tenders who lived in the highlands of the Andes, the Incas, had in the fifteenth century established a monarchical system, and constructed a network of fine roads for couriers, partly made of stone, partly raised on causeways if they crossed marshes or rainy regions, partly built of earth but always well marked. Rivers were crossed by monkey bridges made from cables of plaited agave fibre, or floating bridges, or pontoons of reeds. Up and down the Andes, too, went caravans of llamas, bred as beasts of burden though they could only carry a hundredweight and travel fifteen miles a day. These were the only important domestic animals of the Americas before 1492, and they were quite inadequate for, then as now, they decided for themselves what they would carry. Though their wool was too coarse to be spun, it could be used for fibres.

The Spaniards and Portuguese on horses conquered America, mules sustained the conquest. The arrival of the horse gave North American Indians, Chilean Araucanians and Brazilian Guaicuru a beast of burden which served them well in war; as well, in the end, as it did the Europeans. With the horse came the blacksmith and with him the anvil and the forge; leatherworking joined iron-working as a new craft for America. The introduction of the mule provided, within only a few years of the Spanish conquest, essential links between Vera Cruz and Mexico, Lima and Cuzco, Panama and Nombre de Dios. Without those animals the gold and silver of the new continent would never have reached the Caribbean, much less Spain. The owners of the convoys later financed the production of cotton and coffee, being pioneers of early South American capitalism. In the eighteenth century, Braudel estimated, South America was a continent powered by two million mules, though in the Argentinian pampas as in North America, ox-carts were used, and in the mines of Brazil slaves carried the gold.

The Indians whom the Europeans conquered were capable of long and sustained journeys: for example, the great expedition of the Tupinambá tribe away from the coast of Brazil at Pernambuco across the continent to escape the Portuguese. To their dismay, they met Spaniards on the other side of the continent, near the headwaters of the river Madeira. They retreated back to the island of Tupinambarama on the Amazon, where they remained till they met the Portuguese again in the 1630s. Other Indians provided the Portuguese with the skilled manpower which gave Brazil its later shape, as a result of countless long expeditions. Nor were the Spanish conquistadors behindhand in walking; Alvar Núñez Cabeza de Vaca walked naked from Florida to Mexico in three years between 1533 and 1536.

In Europe the French began the revival of communication by land. Grants for new roads and state coaches were agreed by Louis XIV in 1664. A series of *pavés du roi* began to underpin the communications within what was already the most centralised state of Europe. In the mid eighteenth century an *École des Ponts et Chaussées* was set up. The engineer Trésaguet was in the 1760s beginning his famous system of roads of three layers: foundations, contours hammered in, small hard stones on top.

Equally famous was the French government's lack of compunction in seizing all the private land which it needed for roads and tearing down all the houses which stood in its way. The French Department of Highways was fascinated by the straight line, carefully avoiding existing roads if they showed the slightest deviation from this ideal rectitude. By 1789 France had achieved a good system of stone roads radiating from Paris. The idea was beginning to be copied in Spain and inspired the use of long-distance coaches in both countries. These French roads were also inspiring Catherine the Great and Joseph II in Russia and Austria. Britain had in the eighteenth century what seemed on the map an elaborate system of communications, with an endless series of well-established roads. But most such roads were impassable. The only good ones were those which still had some Roman stones left. The parishes were responsible. They were incompetent. Carts sometimes took five hours to travel ten miles or were held up for a day or more by floods. In the seventeenth century the different regions of England were thus cut off one from the other. A North Road, with a turnpike, was begun in 1663, but the tolls were unpopular. The rebellion of Bonnie Prince Charlie, in 1745, proved the need for better roads for strategic purposes: the bad going had made the concentration of the royal army difficult and a network of turnpike roads on the French pattern was financed, also on the French pattern. Those roads were still far behind French ones, which were anyway being further improved, as the Revolution drew nearer, by the great eighteenth-century bridge-builder Perronet. The last of his bridges was begun in 1787 and ended in 1793. The earliest users were the mob assembling for the execution of King Louis XVI: some of the stone used was taken from the Bastille, the symbolic fortress of the old regime of the agricultural age.

Armies did not travel any faster after the Renaissance than they had done before. Napoleon's army moved no faster than Caesar's. Few armies covered more than thirty miles in twenty-four hours before 1850 and the coming of railways. But 120 miles a day were then covered on the sea in good weather. The truth is that until the invention of the internal combustion engine in the 1880s the road played a minor part in war, in ideas and in commerce.

25

A Real Revolution: Printing

I began to fall into the habit of reading them [romances of chivalry]
. . . and it seemed to me that it was not wrong to spend many
hours of the day and night in such vain exercise, though concealed
from my father. I became so utterly absorbed in this that if I did
not have a new book [to read] I did not feel I could be happy.

Saint Teresa de Jesus

Communications are not simply a matter of journeying. The pen
since the fourteenth century has often been mightier than the
horse. That was due to printing. If any innovation deserves the
word 'revolutionary', printing is it.

Until the fifteenth century AD the best way to communicate
with many people was either by oratory or drama: at all events,
the spoken word. Some tried to improve on this. Atticus, Cicero's
friend, sought to found a business by getting slaves to make copies
of books. In Rome, authors hoped for a public reading in a private
house. Augustus and Claudius encouraged that. Hadrian built a
special 'Athenaeum' for it. The Romans also made several contributions to the art of printing, for they cut patterns out of
wooden blocks and stamped them in plaster. They were prevented, probably, from going any further in respect of printing,
not only through lack of technological invention, but through the
absence of a cheap material on which to print. The Egyptians had
used papyrus, but that was in short supply. The ancient Babylonians had had pressed seals but no papyrus. The Greeks based
their life on oral communications. There is no evidence of private
reading then being a regular practice.

The Romans substituted parchment (specially treated goat- or
sheepskin) for papyrus, an invention originating in Pergamum,
which had devised it when Ptolemy Epiphanes banned the export
of papyrus in order to try to check the growth of a library which
could be a rival to that at Alexandria. The Church adopted parchment, then lawyers did. The custom began of folding a rectangular
sheet to form pages and then binding them together as a 'volume'.
The early Christians invented the idea of the modern book. But
since 200 quarto pages of parchment would require the skins of

twelve sheep or more goats, the material on which writing was done was sometimes more valuable than what was written on it.

The Chinese had had paper since AD 105.* They made it from decayed vegetable matter and kept the method of making it for a long time a secret. In the ninth century an Arab expedition took some Chinese papermakers prisoner at Samarkand. The secret of paper then passed to the West. Arab paper manuscripts survive from the ninth century. By AD 1150 there was a paper industry in Moorish Spain, probably in Morocco and Sicily. Thence the idea was taken northwards, though the Arabs used rags instead of the fibre of vegetables. Játiva, the native city of the Borgia family, some miles south of Valencia on the border of Al-Andalus, had a paper mill using cotton and linen by 1150. It was first turned by hand, then by wind and water. By 1200 there was another such mill in France, and one at Fabriano in the Italian marshes about forty miles north-east of Assisi by 1300. A watermill was employed to tear rags to shreds.

Meantime, the Chinese had devised a method of real printing. That was a result of the Buddhist expansion about AD 500 to 700. The Buddhists felt the necessity for the endless repetition of famous names. Textbooks by the thousand were needed for the public examinations. It seems that the first block printing known is that of a Buddhist charm of about AD 770 done in Japan from wooden blocks. That type of printing did very well and was widely distributed in China. The British Museum owns a Chinese scroll, the Diamond Sutra dated AD 868. It contains a large pictorial woodcut. Several hundred years later, under the Sung dynasty, as a result of a demand for scholarly works by provincial civil servants starved of literature in remote posts, the Chinese devised printing with movable type in the modern manner, about 1040. The idea spread in the East. Since the languages of the East were ideographic, the type could only be made for words, not letters. Still, a currency in paper was devised, making use of printing; and Marco Polo observed, in the thirteenth century, the Chinese block printing of playing cards. These were soon copied by the West. Punches were also devised for marking metal by goldsmiths and silversmiths. By 1410 Jan van Eyck was using oil paints which adhere to metal and so enabled engravings.

Printing proper came when a movable type was devised which

---

* The date for the invention of a Chinese paper-like substance has been pushed further and further back – as far as the first century BC.

could be used repeatedly, combined at will, removed easily and which produced uniformity of lettering. Type had to be available in large numbers even for a single sheet. They were needed by the thousand for a whole book. To obtain them, casting in replicas was devised. A single letter cut in high relief on a steel punch was then struck into a slab of copper to provide the intaglio, or matrix (female die), of that letter in reverse. Any number of replicas could be cast by pouring molten lead into them. Was it Johann Gutenberg, the goldsmith of Mainz, who first did this? Or Johann Fust, his financial partner? Or Peter Schöffer, a German inventor also, from Gernsheim, north of Wörms? Or Procope Waldfogel, at Avignon? At all events, by 1448 a printing office had been established by Gutenberg and Fust at Mainz, with type made from an alloy of lead, tin and antimony. They settled down, with Schöffer's help, to produce the Vulgate Bible in St Jerome's translation. The first scientific work, Pliny's *Natural History*, was published in 1469. The proof reader made much the same marks as he does today, against thick black Gothic letter type to begin with, and then Roman type after 1467, in Strasbourg. Italics were devised by Aldus Manutius in 1501 in Venice. The ink used was much the same as now: an oil-bound liquid made by grinding linseed oil with lampblack or powdered charcoal. (Probably the linseed oil derived from its use as a varnish by Flemish painters.) The composing was completed by locking up the lines and the spaces, inking them and then pressing them on paper.

By 1500, 40,000 editions of books were in being, at 200 to 300 an edition: about ten million books.* Printing presses had been set up throughout Europe, the first books being printed in Venice (as indicated earlier) in 1469, in Paris in 1470, in Florence and Naples in 1471, Spain and the Netherlands (at Aalst and Leuven) in 1473 and Cracow in 1474. Few changes had such dramatic consequences. Reading was transformed from being a special privilege to be a democratic opportunity for all. Pope Sixtus IV founded the Vatican Library to house the new flow of books, and others followed suit. By 1500 it was hard to remember the days when enlightened princes might keep thirty or forty *scrittori* employed or when Cosimo il Vecchio in Florence hired forty-five men to copy, in the beautiful Italian hand of the day, 200 books

---

* *Incunabula*, a book from the time when printing was in its swaddling clothes, dates as a word from 1639 when the word was used in that sense by Mallinckrodt, dean of Münster. Some early editions rose to 1,000 copies.

for the library at the Badia of Fiesole – or when the great book-collector Poggio might pass thirty-two days copying the works of Quintilian, which he had found in the Benedictine abbey of St Gall. It was no longer only the rich who could aspire to possess books. Even the first news-sheets were published before 1500. Such broadsheets were often seen during the next century. By the end of the seventeenth century printed news-sheets had become, as Keith Thomas says, 'an indispensable feature of London life'[1], and the same was soon true of the Netherlands and Germany. Books became in the sixteenth century things for entertainment as well as instruction – a transformation as great as any in human history.

The printing press soon crossed the Atlantic. Small presses were established in Mexico in 1539, in Lima in 1583 and the Philippines in 1593 (though the Portuguese were still banning presses in Brazil in the eighteenth century). During the sixteenth century 200 million books were printed, and in the seventeenth, publishers were printing between 500 and 2,000 copies of a book. For a few best-sellers such as the tales of chivalry which so went to the head of the Spanish nobility, and that of Don Quixote, they printed as many as 4,000: the best and most successful of these romances was probably *Amadis de Gaul* by Garci Ordóñez de Montalvo, published in 1508 – but *Carlomagno and the Twelve Peers of France* of 1525 ran it close. Such immensely successful books not only influenced the conquistadors in their imaginative searches for El Dorado, or the Fountain of Eternal Youth, but helped as much as any religious book to hispanise South and Central America. Books were sometimes printed in Indian languages before they were in European ones. Printing affected the Spanish expeditions to the New World from the beginning: it has been repeatedly asserted that Columbus was stirred to his dreams by reading in Seneca's play *Medea* a prophecy that a 'new sailor' would discover a new world beyond Thule. Ovid too was much read, especially the *Metamorphoses*, by the conquistadors.

Hence the origin of so many of the geographical names in the new continent: California, a craggy island which occurs in the sequel to *Amadis de Gaul*, *Sergas de Esplandian*; Patagonia, which is to be found in *Primaleon*; while the first Spaniards who descended the Amazon river in 1542 brought back reports of Amazons, and the conviction grew that they existed near the river that now bears their name in a new world brought to the European readers most vividly by such writings as Vespucci's *Mundus No-*

vus, a letter which had thirty-six imprints in five languages[2]. (Had it been left to Vespucci, this 'New World' would not have been called America.) Columbus's first letter about his first journey was similarly widely distributed, in 1493. It was this literary background which formed the essential intellectual basis for one of the greatest human achievements: the incorporation of South and Central America into the body politic of the Latin empires of Portugal and Spain. Those empires were not concerned merely with temporary economic aggrandisement and political prestige, but with the establishment of their homeland's own institutions, culture, religion and language – a task which for all its shortcomings was ultimately established; the printed books which poured into those areas from the conquest onwards contributed in great measure to the achievement.

The discovery of America by Europeans, of course, does not owe everything to the printing press. Earlier chapters on navigation would alone disprove that. But a case can be made for thinking that the Reformation in the Christian Church, with all its intellectual consequences, could only have occurred after the invention of printing.

Christianity had already divided into an Eastern and Western branch by the eighth century. Within the Western branch there had been numerous heresies, partly social protests, which in the end were quelled (the Albigensians, Lollards and Hussites). Now the increasing availability of the Bible, the wide circulation of religious polemics and the realisation of the differences between the Church's practice and its intellectual foundations transformed Western Christianity. The editions of the Church fathers and the Greek text of the New Testament translated by Erasmus of Rotterdam made evident in 1516 the shortcomings of basic ecclesiastical writings. Erasmus's *Praise of Folly*, published in 1511, satirised all institutions, especially the Church.

The conclusion of that work – an exhortation to the reader – expressed Erasmus's hope that the Bible might be translated into all languages – a plea which was rapidly answered. Polyglot Bibles were produced by presses in Alcalá, Antwerp, Paris and London – nine languages in the London Bible of 1657. There was an immediate political consequence: the prevailing organisation as well as the temporal pretensions of the Papacy were shown to be gravely out of line with the original ideas of the primitive Church.

The basic Lutheran doctrines of justification by faith alone, *sola fide*, and the priesthood of all believers were an essential corollary of the diffusion of printing. Had it not been for printing, the Church would have been able to crush the Reformation as it had crushed the Albigensians – despite 'the spiritual crisis'. The Elector of Saxony was able to protect his protégé Luther as the Count of Toulouse was not able to defend the heretics of the twelfth century, since the printer's block, if not the pen, was shown to be mightier than the sword. Luther's translation of the Bible, completed in 1534, did for German what St Jerome's had done for silver age Latin. His earlier great treatises – *The Address to the Christian Nobility of the German Nation*, *The Babylonish Captivity of the Church* and *The Library of a Christian Man* – were sold in great numbers to 'a wide public' (only *The Babylonish Captivity*, addressed to scholars, was written in Latin), as were the books, pamphlets, sermons and letters published at the rate of a piece a fortnight. Between 1517 and 1520 Luther's thirty publications sold well over 300,000 copies. Woodcuts helped the propagation of the new gospel. Calvin's *Institutes*, whose first edition appeared in 1536 when he was twenty-seven years old, were incessantly read by all who desired Protestantism but did not want to hand over authority to secular monarchs – the first consequence of Lutheranism. Haemstede's *Book of Martyrs* (published at Antwerp in 1559) and Guy de Bray's *Confession* – an open letter to King Philip II (1561) – formed the religious climate for the Dutch revolt against Spain[3]. A battle of pamphlets over the efforts of John Pfefferkorn to destroy Jewish books championed by John Reuchlin, the leading hebraist, led to the first popular satire, *Letters of Obscure Men* (1515 and 1517) in which the monkish defenders of 'tired traditions' were exposed very successfully.

It may seem perverse to attribute the series of intellectual disruptions known as the Reformation to technological causes. There was a demand for something more holy than the Roman Church in Germany. In particular there were profound tremors of mysticism and millenarianism. Yet the outpouring of religious tracts which characterises the sixteenth and seventeenth centuries in Europe cannot be imagined without the presses which, readily, long before newspapers became general, printed everything which came to them. The history of religious persecution in the seventeenth century is above all the history of printed tracts. 'Protestantism,' wrote Elie Halévy, 'is a book religion . . . from every Christian worthy of the name, it demands a knowledge of the Bible'[4]. The Reformation in Scandinavia – a country never fully assimilated to Mediterranean Christianity – was inspired by the

Swede Olaf Petri, the Dane Taussen and the Finn Michael Agricola, all of whom produced an unceasing output of writing.
Printers and publishers were frequently centres for obscure religious movements. The most recent historian of printing, Dr Elizabeth Eisenstein, points out that Catholic Christianity was
peculiarly vulnerable to the revolutionary effects of typography.

The Counter-Reformation was also much assisted by the
presses: the first book printed in the Americas was appropriately
the *Doctrina Breve* for the use of priests. The first dated printed
product from Gutenberg's workshop was an indulgence.* The
men of imagination who carried out the conversion of the Indies,
the most remarkable achievement of the modern Church, could
not have performed their task without the accompaniment of
thousands of copies of that work. The great open chapels in which
the 'spiritual conquest' of the Mexicans was completed were a
long way from Seville[5]. But the *Doctrina Breve* linked them all.
The most successful institution of the Counter-Reformation was
probably the Society of Jesus and its most extraordinary achievement was the Jesuit campaign to establish missions in Brazil and
Paraguay. Many cloistered jungle mission villages were founded:
a society kept together by reading and writing, in which *The
Spiritual Exercises* of St Ignatius played the decisive part.

The Portuguese Crown's right to act as patron of the Roman
Catholic missions in vast regions of Africa, Asia and Brazil, the
Padroado, was also made possible by the written word. From the
earliest days of the colonisation of Brazil the Jesuit school vied,
in cities such as Bahia, with the plantation houses and city mansions for control over children, women and slaves, emphasising
from the beginning the intelligent child with a literary bent. It was
The Spiritual Exercises which gave Matteo Ricci, the founder of
the Jesuit mission to China, 'one of the most remarkable and
brilliant men in history', as Joseph Needham refers to him, his
successes at the Chinese court in the latter days of the Ming
dynasty[6]. Equally, the visit of St Francis Xavier to Japan in 1549
carried books (as well as fire-arms). It was Jesuits who introduced
the first printing press with movable type to India and perhaps to
Japan, while the Indians in the seventeenth century were able to
treat as a proverb the saying 'the nib of a Jesuit's pen is more to

* 'When . . . Johann Luschner printed at Barcelona 18,000 letters of indulgence
for the abbey of Montserrat in May 1598 this can only be compared with the
printing of income tax forms,' wrote a historian of printing, S. H. Steinberg.

be feared than the point of an Arab's sword'[7]. The Jesuits' peda-
gogical manual *Ratio Studiorum*, given final form in 1599, unaltered till the nineteenth century, ensured the serious and
disciplined if formalistic and conservative education in schools and
universities henceforth. How appropriate that the founder of the
order, Saint Ignatius, should have acquired the habit of study
from reading 'vain treatises' – romances, no doubt – while recovering from a wound to his leg after the siege of Pamplona in
1521!

The age of printing did not prevent the seventeenth century
from being, in Europe and European dominions, the great age of
sermons: the pulpit was the greatest medium of communication,
but printing enabled the greatest sermons, such as those of Antonio Vieira, the Jesuit missionary, to live long beyond the day of
preaching.

The most curious aspect of the Reformation admittedly was
that it occurred when, thanks to the rediscovery of antiquity and
the reinvigoration which that gave to painting, the Church of
Rome was served by the most gifted artists. Painting, however,
was a product of illiteracy. The Church could impose dogmas,
relate legends and stimulate devotion, without submitting anything to critical enquiry. Religious paintings were hung in churches
less as ornaments than as tools of evangelism. Printing posed a
challenge, therefore, to the 'propaganda by sight' upon which
preachers had relied for so long[8]. In Victor Hugo's *Notre-Dame
de Paris* a scholar deep in meditation in his study gazes first at the
first printed book which has come to his hands, and then at the
cathedral visible through a window: 'This will kill that,' he says.
Printing also raised a fundamental question about the need for an
institutionalised Church: if all could understand the Bible what
need was there of a middleman, so to speak, between God and
man, in the form of a priest? Yet, while painters turned away
from the grotesque improvisations of the early Middle Ages, they
secularised their subjects more than their patrons realised. They
transformed every scene, religious or not, into a pageant. Saints
became humble scholars. St Ursula looked as if she were a village
girl, the Virgin Mary, an ordinary mother, while the spectators of
the Crucifixion looked as if they were uninterested.

The Reformation gave, of course, also a religious justification
to the local disputes between the Holy Roman Emperor and the
German princes. It divided Europe at a time when some of its
peoples had established order at home and were interested in

long-distance trade. It caused the decline, into innumerable parts, of half the European population, so that each Protestant could be said to be able to found his own Church. It also inspired the Counter-Reformation, which caused a rebuilding of learning in the Catholic Church as imposing as that in the Protestant. Thinking independently about the headship of the Church led to thinking independently about the nature of politics, science, art and learning. The country which the Neapolitan adventurer Francesco Caraccioli (not Voltaire, as is often supposed) believed to have a hundred religions and only one sauce – namely, England – was in the forefront of all forms of intellectual adventure during the seventeenth century.

The Reformation also increased the gulf between those who believed that one should find one's way to God by intellectual endeavour and those who thought that all such effort was pointless or heretical since, in the words of Muhammad (and some Andalusians), 'it is written' (*estaba de Dios*). It also began the dissolution of social bonds which, after the collapse of others such as loyalty to neighbourhood and family, would cause eventually a major social crisis. Some indication of the shape of the future was given when Protestant churches abandoned the confessional, since the personal confession and interrogation of every layman had been a most 'compulsive system of social discipline'[9]. Even the Church of Rome introduced a private confessional box after the Counter-Reformation whereas, before, confessions were public. It was not that Protestantism represented scepticism while Rome and the Counter-Reformation spelled prejudice. For example, Nicolaus Koppernigk (Copernicus), a Catholic Pole working at the episcopal palace at Heilsberg, agreed with the long-dead Aristarchus of Samos that the sun, 'as if sitting on a royal throne, governs the family of stars which move around it'. The Pope (to whom Copernicus dedicated his book) was not at first critical. But Luther and Melanchthon were hostile. Copernicus's disciple Giordano Bruno believed the universe to be infinite and so 'nobody can be said to be in the centre of it'. He was burned for his attitude towards transubstantiation and for attacking the Pope, rather more than for his astronomical arguments. Servetus, who anticipated Harvey's theory of the circulation of the blood, was burned at the instigation of the Protestant Calvin.

Another consequence of printing was the beginning in the sixteenth century of a concern for self-education which has never ceased. Before printing, few were in a position to teach themselves anything. Subsequently, it has been usually accepted that, in the words of Doctor Johnson, 'you can never be wise unless you love reading'[10]. Few such opportunities were open without printing. Nor were they open in China, where despite the serenity of the life the character of the script still prevented the exploitation of the invention of movable type, already achieved in the eleventh century. But in Europe politicians, artists, leaders of opinion, even soldiers, now read voraciously. Libraries came into being in every 'gentleman's residence', and one of the great forms of art, the novel, was soon born. In these libraries a gentleman in the sixteenth century might find editions of More's *Utopia* (printed in 1516), Machiavelli's *The Prince* (1532), Vives' *On Education* (1531), Ascham's *The Scholemaster* (1568), Sir Thomas Elyot's *Boke of the Governor* (1531), Antonio de Guevara's *Diet of Princes* (1529), Erasmus's *The Christian Prince* (1516), Castiglione's *Book of the Courtier* (1528) and then, a bestseller of the 1570s, Abraham Ortel's first popular world atlas, *Theatrum Orbis Terrarum*, published in 1570 in Antwerp. Another great success in Antwerp was Christopher Plantin's publication – subsidised by the Papacy – of a Bible in the original languages along with the Latin text. Soon printing began to be used for other, political, non-religious purposes; for example, Richelieu in the seventeenth century employed publicists to gain the support of 'public opinion' for his truculent foreign policy and that work was carried out by the production of books: *Considérations Historiques sur la Généalogie de la Maison de Lorraine* or other such titles sought to prove the French right to new provinces; while the first patriotic utterances of German literature belong to the humanists of the time of Maximilian I. A copious flow of books on strategy began in the sixteenth century too.

Dutch printers were peculiarly important. In the seventeenth century the export of English and German Bibles printed in Holland was 'almost a major industry', wrote C. R. Boxer, and French writers banned in France made the most of the Dutch freedom to print what they liked. By the end of the seventeenth century there were probably more books printed in the Dutch Republic than in all other European countries together. During the eighteenth century the Netherlands became the chief publishing centre of the Enlightenment.

After the sixteenth century there were few technical innovations in printing for several hundred years, though the letters in a press could wear out. One exception was engraved books, of which the first was Bettini's *Monte Santo di Dio*, published in Florence in 1477. Etching was invented in Augsburg in 1505 and drypoint etching in 1528. Printed images followed printed books. These included maps, designs for houses and medical illustrations. A book of dress patterns published in the 1520s made 'Spanish fashions' popular throughout the Habsburg Empire, from Lima to Brussels. The illustrated book, with its woodcuts and elaborate drawings, came to be seen in all courtly houses. Engravings played an essential part in communicating ideas in the late seventeenth century, particularly ideas of architecture and science, and particularly architecture in the Americas, whose eager practitioners carefully studied treatises, textbooks and illustrations to the general benefit.

The standard of printing decayed in the seventeenth century, but the rate of output of books and pamphlets increased and, in the eighteenth, the consumption of paper tells its own story. In England, for example, paper charged with duty totalled 2·5 million tons in 1713 and 12·4 million in 1800. By that time there were numerous semi-newspapers: in 1760, even forty provincial journals in England. Within a few years of the beginning of the Industrial Revolution, Tom Paine's *Rights of Man* sold in tens of thousands and Byron's *Corsair* could be sold in an edition of 10,000 on publication. It could soon be fairly said in London that, in Lewis Mumford's words, 'the swish and crackle of paper is the underlying sound of the metropolis'[11]. Ideas could immediately be communicated to large numbers of people, provided they could read, and the availability of books was the greatest stimulus to people to teach themselves to read. The majority of the population could eventually be shown the existence of general as well as particular issues. The modern world was thus born. Appropriately the old one can be said to have ended when the portrait of King Louis XVI engraved on paper money enabled an alert republican to halt the fleeing monarch at Varennes.

26

City Life

Cosimo de' Medici to Santi Bentivoglio who had lived as a wool merchant in Florence, though the heir to the Bentivoglios of Bologna:

'Weigh well, young man, this matter which you must consider: wherein resideth, to the philosophic mind, the greater advantage: the delights of a private citizen's estate, or the pleasures which the government of a city can afford?' Santi hesitated and, on the advice of Nero Capponi, chose Bologna.

Stendhal, *Journey to Italy*

1

The Renaissance revived the idea of living in cities. Partly that was a consequence of the revival of Greek learning and writings. The Greeks had seen the city state as the natural unit for society. They believed that such states did not exist in their time (between 900 and 400 BC) among other peoples, and considered this a sign of their Persian opponents' barbarism. The city state seemed to the Greeks a natural development of family and of village. Even Plato and Aristotle, so far-sighted in so many things, saw the city state as the desirable, even the logical, end of political development. Neither foresaw the multinational empires of the future, though Aristotle was the tutor of Alexander. A sense of self-sufficiency was the main characteristic of Greek cities. There was naïvety in that view: Athens expanded and, had she not been thwarted, her empire might have grown as did that of Rome, a city state originally populated by urban farmers which established Mediterranean unity. Nor did the Greeks recognise that, in ancient Iraq, the most remarkable achievements had occurred when that society was concentrated in cities as independent as, and for longer than, those of classical Greece.

The Greek cities were of special interest to the Italians during the Renaissance: contemporary Italy seemed a reincarnation of the Greek world. Italian cities, like Greek cities, were in every sense of the word close to the country. Their inhabitants usually had nearby estates or, if poor, gardens of vegetables, and their streets were full of sheep, straw and hay, cattle and pigs. Zimmern

252

in *The Greek Commonwealth* wrote: 'Greek civilisation is in a sense urban, but its basis is agricultural and the breezes of the open country blow through Parliament and the market place'[1]. About three-quarters of the Athenian burghers owned some land in Attica. In the fourteenth century in England, Trevelyan wrote, 'the English town was still a rural and agricultural community as well as a centre of industry and commerce'[2].

Around the cities of the Renaissance, throughout Europe, a great number of festivals, Mystery plays, processions, pantomimes, illuminations, carnivals, balls, boat races and games came to occur regularly, symbols of continuity with rural life, of interplay between religion and paganism and art and religion beside which our modern festivals are shadows, without ritual significance. This was a reminder of the fact that the birth of agriculture coincided with, and was made possible by, the village and the city perhaps at the same time, built for defence as well as for occasional commercial exchange. In this respect, James Mellaart, discoverer of Çatal Hüyük, warns us to avoid thinking that cities developed out of villages: 'the reverse seems far more logical'. Agriculture was built round the fortified group of homesteads and had nothing to do with the isolated farmhouse which constitutes the idea of 'the country' to many minds in the twentieth century[3].

The Roman Empire, in the mind of the Renaissance, represented an urban achievement: a mosaic of cities which governed their surrounding hinterlands. All Roman citizens belonged to a city, even if they lived elsewhere. Some Roman imperial cities were commercial (for example, Carthage, known after its eclipse as a centre of cheap woollen goods), or semi-colonial (such as Trier and Arles). All had the same magistrates, prefects, curators of aqueducts and of drains, managers of ports, taxation, amphitheatres, baths and public services.

The idea of the city suffered during the Dark Ages. Even the Christian Church derived its strength from the countryside. Nevertheless, that Church had based its diocesan boundaries on those of Roman cities. That held together the municipal tradition. Bishops' power increased as states' power decreased. Some cities survived with habits barely interrupted in the Byzantine Empire, even when conquered by the Arabs. Perhaps Italy never lost the idea of what urban life could aspire to. Elsewhere, towns consisted of little more than groups of clergy attached to the cathedral or the urban monasteries, together with a few students at the ecclesiastical schools and some artisans needed for the cathedral's upkeep. There might be weekly markets and an annual fair. At the city's gate, a toll might be levied, there might be a mint within the walls and there would be huge granaries. Bishops had temporal as well as spiritual power, judicial as well as police activities. It was they who kept up the walls against both Vikings and Saracen pirates, or against other bandits. Kings and noblemen seemed purely rural beings, inhabiting remote castles.

The way that cities declined and managed to revive in Europe is exemplified by the history of Florence, which afterwards did much to revive civilisation, not just urban life. Florence, founded as a Roman camp about AD 50, was laid out in a square (not now distinguishable) and surrounded by a wall (still visible) like other Italian cities. Florence recovered from long decline as a result of the Crusades. It was a good stopping place on the Arno at the crossroads on the way from Rome to Bologna and from Pisa and Genoa, and near the foot of several passes across the Apennines. Municipal life began following the death in 1115, without heirs, of Matilda, Grand Duchess of Tuscany. Florence, like other cities, was then able to pursue its independence between Pope and Emperor. For a time a general assembly of citizens was the source of political power. That came to mean an upper stratum of 150 merchants. If noblemen with estates near by (such as the Ubaldini in the Mugello) had joined forces, they could have prevented the emergence of an oligarchic but independent Florence. But they did not. Had Florence, like Pisa and Lucca, been in a plain, or like Siena and Arezzo, on a height, the feudal nobility might have settled inside the walls. But they preferred to remain outside, on fortified mountains near by. Thus the distinctive character of Florence: its lack of old nobility, its *grandi* being merchants.

Long civil wars followed during the twelfth and thirteenth centuries, the Pope, the French and the Emperor by proxy taking part, despite the intellectual revival associated with Giotto (born 1266) and Dante (born 1265). The heroes of the latter were anyway imperial nobles such as the Cardinal Ottoviano degli Ubaldini who confessed, 'I lost whatever soul I had in the Ghibelline cause'[4]. Florence experimented with annually elected consuls and then had a system of eight priors who ruled for two months, living, while they did so, all together in the town hall. The subsequent papal victory in the south of Italy did not alter these Florentine liberties. They in turn were accompanied by the commercial boom based on manufactured, coarse woollen cloth and wool itself imported from the north and locally refined.

Meantime, political control, as in some other free Italian cities, was accumulated by the craft guilds (in Florence's case the seven major guilds and fourteen minor ones). A form of organic oligarchy lasted till about 1530, though the Medici family established an informal mastery before that, and though there were difficulties with mercenary commanders-in-chief (*condottieri*). The rebellion of the lowest-paid wool workers (the *ciompi*) in 1378 threatened to create a genuine democracy, but this system was one of rule by merchants through guilds – nothing like a syndicalist state managed by workers. Indeed, from 1378 onwards single men without official position (Maso degli Albizzi, Gino Capponi, Niccolo da Uzzano and then Cosimo de' Medici) dominated the town and the enlarged province of which it was the centre. The Florentine constitution continued to be based on the principle of distrust to prevent power being concentrated in too few men for too long. But, in the end, the Medici gained political control, in order to protect their bank. By then families such as the Medici constituted, in effect if not in name, a new aristocracy: 'A gentleman can be made with two yards of cloth,' Cosimo de' Medici remarked presciently[5].

The struggles between rich and poor in Florence were a rehearsal for the 'class struggles' of the nineteenth century. In Florence towards the end of the fourteenth century, according to Werner Sombart, 'We meet the perfect bourgeois for the first time'[6].

These developments were accompanied by the elaboration of new political thought: taking Roman law as the basis of law, such scholars as Bartolus of Sassoferrato argued that every ruler in his own city was the equivalent in authority of the Emperor[7].

The house of a merchant in Tuscany in about 1400 consisted of twelve to fourteen rooms if he were a successful man. Its roof would be tiled and the windows would have small, heavy, wooden shutters. It might have glass, which though rare was a luxury (in 1332 a Franciscan included glass in his list of luxuries which had drawn God's wrath on the city). By the sixteenth century glass had become cheap and easily available (it had been used for decorative and solid objects in the Mediterranean from 2500 BC). There might be a loggia on the side of the house for entertaining, with a vaulted ceiling. Perhaps there might also be a fireplace, a modern luxury recently devised in France, usually of stone and set against the wall with a chimney. A chimney would probably be the main decorative element in the room, being much prized. Since few recalled Roman systems of heating, it was also the only refuge in a cold house (in Europe until the twentieth century it was often desirable to wear furs, if you had them, inside the house during winter). A Florentine merchant might also have warming pans, as well as *scaldini*, little jars containing charcoal which one might hold when cold, on the knee or in the hand. For light, there might be horn lanterns, wax torches on long poles, tallow candles and brass oil lamps – identical to those of Rome – in which olive oil burned.

The walls of such a house might be hung with French serge or linen, perhaps a carpet. Carpetings for floors were rare, though not unknown (in the thirteenth century the carpets used by a Toledan bishop travelling to London were a curiosity). The bed of the master of the house would be the most important piece of furniture, often curtained and canopied, with a mattress perhaps covered with striped French cloth. Pillows, sheets and blankets were already in use. Most rooms would have large chests as their only furniture, being used for baggage as well, in which clothes, linen, jewels, furs would lie (the cupboard was a later device), and a truckle bed for servants to sleep on. By then, in rich families, dining rooms were beginning to be separate from kitchens, as they had started to be in monasteries because of the scale of the preparations, while the use of the common table for all the household was dying. Servants, after the Renaissance, would everywhere have their meals separately below stairs.

Even rich men's dining rooms would be barely furnished in Florence at the turn of the fourteenth and fifteenth centuries. They contained a table five yards long, with only one glass as a rule from which all would drink (as with a loving cup) and then pass on. There were no forks save for serving and few spoons. Most people brought and used their own knives. Benches would be far more common than chairs, which were regarded as rare, honorific items till at least the sixteenth century. Kitchens would have a wooden sink, a safe for dry meat, cauldrons, and pots and pans still familiar in the twentieth century.

The coming of the chair as a piece of furniture for every day marks the Renaissance in Europe as much as anything else. The turner and the joiner who made this furniture with wheel-lathes, pole-lathes or mechanical saws worked in oak till the sixteenth century when all sorts of other woods, from walnut to beech, elm to pine, began to be used. Joiners were not independent of carpenters till the Renaissance. The Renaissance also revived the plane, known to Rome but forgotten for centuries. With these tools, benches gave way to stools, stools to chairs, in Italy first but afterwards everywhere in Europe. For the joinery of the Italians spread. France was a centre of fine work by the sixteenth century and was preparing, even then, to surpass Italy. By the seventeenth and eighteenth centuries chairs were as important in the lives of any who could afford them as they are today, fortunes being made by those who marketed or designed them.

Furniture and panelling were two of the household uses of wood. No means of heating, though, existed apart from firewood. All carpenters' tools derived from wood, as did spinning wheels, wine presses, ploughs and navies. (Was Europe's power attributable to her great forests? Braudel once asked; was Islam's eclipse due to her lack of them?) The demands for wood in late mediaeval Europe are hard to imagine. Most of the supply was floated down the rivers. Every fleet needed a forest to build it, so all mercantile nations required access to the Baltic and to the pine trees grown there, for their masts. The quantity of wood meant a continuous danger of fire in mediaeval and Renaissance towns. As early as 1276 Lübeck issued an ordinance enforcing fireproof ceilings, London in 1189 gave privileges to those who built roofs of tile and in 1212 ordered thatched roofs to be whitewashed to resist the fire better. Even so, fires happened often and spread easily once they had begun.

These cities of the Renaissance all began to have paving again. In this, they copied the cities of Moorish Spain, for Córdoba, capital of Al-Andalus, with its half million inhabitants (and 300 mosques, 80,000 shops and workshops) had paving from the ninth century. Paris laid down slabs of stone to guard against the dust in 1185, Florence in 1240 and London in 1280.

As early as the thirteenth century the land around prosperous towns, particularly in Italy, was beginning to be built upon, as it had been in the days of Rome. The slopes of the hills near Florence filled with villas, and the Venetians began to design their beautiful, if melancholy, houses on the Brenta. Such houses took advantage of the better water and air in a well-chosen spot in the country, and often served as a place to escape the plague. The construction of such houses indicated confidence that their owners would not be disturbed by bandits or barbarian noblemen from the hills; the Medici villa at Cafaggiolo was the first example of a house where castellation was decorative. These innocent beginnings would lead in the end to suburbia, the commuter, and their attendant *grandeurs et misères*.

The cities of the Renaissance were in many ways impractical. Alberti's treatise on city planning in the fifteenth century in Florence took no account of cannon. Fortifications played little part in his consideration. But gunpowder would sound the death knell of free cities as it did of chivalry. A typical Russian city of the seventeenth century was neither a priestly nor a commercial place but a 'military and administrative outpost, run by the state, where a few government buildings were set amid a rambling agglomeration of low wooden houses, churches and bazaars set in vegetable patches with wide but unpaved streets and unregulated river banks'[8]. Such would characterise many cities of the future. Moscow in 1700 had 16,000 households of which no less than 7,500 were lived in by officials of the state, and 1,500 by clergy.

Nor was the scale of Renaissance cities such as to anticipate the difficulties of modern megalopolises. Naples, with 300,000 people, was the largest Christian city in 1600. London had 200,000, and Paris and Moscow 150,000. No other European city was of this size except Constantinople, still a distended monster with over 700,000 people, and none approached the size of Rome at its height nor some of the Chinese cities: Yangchow, capital of South China in Marco Polo's day, had a million to a million and a half inhabitants in 1280. Lisbon, the capital of the country which changed the world, had a population of 40,000 about 1450; the next largest city in that kingdom, Oporto, numbered 8,000. No other city of Portugal boasted then more than 3,000 souls.

Nor did any European city of the Renaissance, for all the attention paid to antiquity, approach the arrangements for drainage and water supply which had been worked out by the ancient Iraqis and Romans. Ancient Babylon showed a knowledge of elementary drainage and there were both sewers and cess pools; even main drains leading to the river. In Assyria, palaces had lavatories and bathrooms superior to those which exist in the twentieth century in half the world. Water might be procured by wells or aqueducts. Sennacherib brought water to Nineveh along a 300-yard aqueduct and a six-mile canal to water his orchards. Calah had wells ninety feet deep, one of which could yield 5,000 gallons a day in 1952. Similar conditions existed in Mycenae: water reached flushing lavatories and bathrooms, through terracotta pipes, and vanished through sloping gutters. Later the Greeks used aqueducts and devised the siphon to carry water in pipes over heights. Their contemporaries, the Etruscans, paid a greater attention to drainage than any other early people: thus the *cloaca maxima* in Latium, built in the sixth century BC, was so large that it seems as if they had some inkling that that group of villages would become the capital of a million people. Though most Romans collected their excreta in jars or pots which they carried downstairs to empty into a vat at the foot of the stairs to be emptied by manure merchants, or to be taken to a cess pool, and though urine was often poured out of top windows, Rome was more hygienic than many cities of today because of the number of her pipes for drainage, themselves due to the availability of cheap lead. Rome was supplied by twelve aqueducts carrying water along underground courses. These fed the 1,352 fountains – of the fourth century AD – from which most people drew their water, and the 1,000 public baths in which the Romans spent the better part of their leisure, not only bathing but indulging in sports, cultivating physical fitness and beauty (large baths had hot and cold air rooms, swimming baths, tubs and, from the Empire onwards, mixed bathing). Other Roman cities had less elaborate aqueducts and some (at Segovia or Pont du Gard) survive. The Romans were adept tunnellers; the tunnel which took water to Rome from Lake Fucino, in the Apennines, stretched three and a half miles: the longest in the world till the railway tunnels of the 1870s. For Romans living in the old capital, the fall of the Empire dated from the moment when the public slaves no longer maintained such things and when the fountains ran dry.

The world took many generations to recover Rome's standards. That was one reason for the small size of Western cities. Another was the difficulty of provisioning cities larger than a few thousands. William Dunbar, in a famous poem, spoke of London as 'the flower of cities all'. But where could a nation with more than one London get its meat, game and grain, in a community still largely pastoral? Constantinople in Dunbar's day ate 300 to 500 tons of grain a day, thereby necessitating the constant use of the Ottoman fleet and the command of the Black Sea, for access to the Ukraine.

Some comparison can be made between the sophisticated cities of the Old World and those of pre-Columbian America. There, houses often formed a random cluster around an open space on which the great house of the chief, or *cacique*, might be built. The open area would be a place of assemblies and festivities. Villages in, say, Cuba or Hispaniola in the 1490s might house about a thousand to two thousand people, all living in twenty to fifty multi-family houses, with, of course, agricultural plots near by to feed all concerned. Houses in that society would be simply sleeping places except for the house of the chief, who would hold there the mummies of his ancestors, perhaps masked in gold. But Tenochtitlan and Cuzco were great cities, as Teotihuacan, Uxmal and Palenque had once been. The main Spanish contribution to the New World was thus not the city, for that was known. It was, as German Arcienagas put it, 'the village . . . with its priest and church, its mayor and town hall and gentleman's houses of adobe and tile. The village became a new stage for celebrations . . . a show window . . . a market where all news is known. The village became for the peasant the essential school, and club. Only the lorry [truck] has wrought as great a change'[9].

The grandeur of some American cities held the Spaniards spellbound. Bernard Díaz del Castillo said that the movement and noise in the latter ought to be compared to Constantinople, and Cortes reported that the main square there was twice that of Salamanca. A great political centre where market-places brought people from the entire country, and where both civil and religious ceremonies were performed and sacrifices conducted, Tenochtitlan may have been larger than any European city except for Paris, Naples, Venice and Milan. Cuzco's population, on the other hand, probably did not exceed 50,000.

Still, the cities captured by the Spaniards were pale shades of the great places which had vanished in one part or another of the Americas before. Thus Teotihuacan, north of Mexico City, reached a population of 200,000 between AD 350 and 650 and set up a strong central administration. Between AD 650 and 700 it was plundered and destroyed: how we do not yet know. It left a great legend whose influence did not end with the Spanish conquest.

2

Several developments in European cities occurred as a prelude to industrialisation: carriages effectively arrived as a means of urban transport; and it became appreciated that a column of men can only be led in martial order through a straight, flat street. The great Palladio wrote: 'The ways will be more convenient if they are made everywhere equal; that is, there will be no place within them where armies may not easily march'[10]. That comment from Europe's greatest architect meant that there would be no more street battles in higgledy-piggledy towns between townsmen and apprentices. Along the boulevards of the new Rome, inspired by Vitruvius but reconstructed by Bramante, according to Sixtus IV's master plan, or the new Paris begun by Henri IV, or even the new London (fortunately prevented by civil war from being fully palladianised by Inigo Jones), the glittering uniforms of the new absolutist states of post-Renaissance Europe could swagger, inspiring respect and fear. Was it instinct or design that caused public opinion in London to refuse Wren's grand plan for the rebuilding of London after the Great Fire, which devastated 436 acres of London and gave England's greatest architect such a unique opportunity? Would liberty have survived if he had had his way and he had made London one of the world's most beautiful cities? Perhaps, since a pattern had already been set whereby in England great noblemen regarded their town house as a *pied à terre* (in a square as favoured by Jones) and their country houses as their real home. In France, on the other hand, noblemen, in their detached Parisian *hôtels* looked on the country as a place of disgrace. In that attitude they were copied by the rest of continental Europe.

Most European towns began in the sixteenth century to cease to have just one or two functions (commerce, defence or government). They were becoming again, as they had been in antiquity, centres of living for tens of thousands, including many who, like the Neapolitan *lazzaroni*, the most famous beggars in Europe, were there simply to pick a living where they could. There had been little point in being a thief or a beggar in the country, for the people there were too poor. But in Naples or in Amsterdam (proof that the growth of a post-mediaeval city need not raise intolerable problems of design) or London and Paris, there were enormous opportunities for the shiftless. The age when the city became a lure for everyone ambitious, rich and poor, honest and dishonest, had begun again.

Then, during these last generations before industrialisation, the urban house of the West, if not the city, attained the character it retained till the transformations wrought by air-conditioning and central heating in the twentieth century. Rooms were differentiated. The pantry began to differ from the kitchen, the dining room from the drawing room (a room for conversation, meeting, reception, 'withdrawing'). Doors, previously narrow, opening inwards and letting one person through at a time, became double – a sign of self-confidence. Even impoverished Germany had glass in its windows in the sixteenth century. A curved chimney shaft was found to prevent smoke more effectively than a straight one and the better draught gave more heat. Heat was helped too by the cast-iron stoves, often manufactured in England, often decorated elaborately as in Germany or bare in France, but used in most places from Russia to the Atlantic. In these rooms, mahogany panelling began too to be introduced from the West Indies and South America, a fine wood so hard that it could only be worked by steel tools of the best quality. It was that which led to the finest achievements of the rococo age, with cabinet-making in the hands of Boulle, Chippendale, Sheraton and Hepplewhite. A major change in European building materials also occurred. The sandstone and limestone quarries of France were opened to enable stone houses to be built like the Roman ones, for endurance, in place of wood. In England, brick took over from wood. Other European nations copied one or the other. This process, complete by the end of the seventeenth century, caused another great change in the character of northern European peoples. It marked them out even more from dwellers in the wood and bamboo houses of China and the East in general (good against earthquakes). The felt tent of the nomad seemed further away than ever.

Urban achievement at its height seemed to be expressed, to many travellers in the seventeenth century, in the home of mahogany, the Spanish imperial cities of the New World. Officials, planters and priests lived in cities, themselves planned on classical principles, with fine municipal buildings and splendid palaces. Already in the late sixteenth century Mexico City astonished visiting Englishmen. It was much larger than Madrid or Seville or indeed any Spanish town and was not fortified because it was far inland. Enemies could only come over the sea. Other Spanish American cities were similarly undefended, unless indeed they were on the sea as were Havana or Cartagena. In some ways, those bureaucratically run imperial cities seemed more 'modern' than those of Spain itself. Seventeen cities, and a third of the villages of Spain, were still under seigneurial jurisdiction about 1800, while Spanish American ones ran themselves with oligarchic merchants as municipal councillors.

Urban life in the eighteenth century seemed, from one point of view, to be at its height. A decline in crime made going out safer.

A network of communications provided by good messengers ensured swift delivery of everything from state papers to love letters. The cities were small enough for people to be able to walk out from them into the country. This same small size enabled the give-and-take of casual conversation between acquaintances who met by chance. Hence Dr Johnson's famous comments on the charms of London. On the other hand, the life of the city as a work of art, as a self-conscious achievement complete in itself, was in decline. In the seventeenth century cities such as Genoa still had vast financial empires (Genoa succeeded Antwerp as the centre for the redistribution of Spanish silver as well as of silk and spices from the East) and Venice remained rich. By the eighteenth century they had ceased to be so. Some cities survived as states (including, indeed, both Genoa and Venice till 1798) but the 'nation states', Britain, France and Prussia, were by then determining events. Even Florence had become a satrapy of the Habsburgs. By Louis XIV's time the torch even of fashion had passed from Italy to France.

German cities, particularly, suffered in the eighteenth century. Many were independent still. But they were not well placed to take part in world trade; the Treaty of Westphalia gave foreigners control of many German rivers, and in many places it confirmed in power oligarchies determined to prevent craftsmen from playing the part in town government which they had in the late Middle Ages[11]. The Thirty Years' War physically ruined many old cities. England dominated Germany's woollen industry and supplied Germany with manufactured goods through merchant adventurers. Even the Hanse was dissolved in 1669. All the northern German cities, save Hamburg, lost importance. Hamburg was for a time an exception to the general decay in Germany. Its trade increased after the fall of Antwerp to the Spaniards. It became, as Antwerp had been, a centre of refuge for exiles of all sorts. Hamburg had the first coffee house and the first masonic lodge in Germany. A Dutch bank was effectively founded in 1619. In the fifteenth century it seemed as if German painting, German scientific invention and German trade might grow in importance. By the eighteenth century that was plainly not to be for another hundred years and it then did so under the inspiration of the country-minded Junkers rather than of city fathers.

Those who live in great cities have usually enjoyed higher incomes, better access to schools, doctors and professions linked to literacy than those who live in the country. Magistrates have been more exposed to challenge by opinion and hence fairer. Cities have been also more impersonal than villages. In the country the tyranny of local opinion and lack of tolerance towards deviation is normal. In the city 'no man there marketh another's doings', as a traveller said of Venice in the sixteenth century. Eccentricity and individualism were thus easier there.

Still, as in respect of the discussion of landholding, the pursuit of a rule begets deception. In Italy in the Middle Ages, for example, there were many towns run by despots who sought to organise the population as if they were their servants. In comparison with these towns feudal domains, like those of Charles the Rash of Burgundy, seemed dominions of consent.

The link between urban growth and freedom of conscience was often tenuous. But agricultural communities were always governed by landowners. Urban ones needed a different organisation. In the East the cities of India and China were used as administrative capitals by all-powerful rulers. In the West, more particularly in Europe, the cities grew into the market-places for ideas as well as for commodities.

27
Gunpowder Wars, Gunpowder States

Mars was the midwife of the Dutch Republic.

J. H. Plumb,
Introduction to C. R. Boxer's *The Dutch Seaborne Empire*

The sixteenth century was that of Leonardo and Erasmus but it was also the first century of gunpowder. The origins of this commodity, like that of other characteristic things of the Renaissance, are to be found in the Middle Ages and not, primarily, in Europe.

In the late seventh century AD, Callinicus of Heliopolis (Syria) devised a fireball, made of naphtha or liquid bitumen, which when mingled with sulphur and pitch and hurled at the Arab armies besieging Constantinople in AD 716–18, helped the Greeks to victory. This 'Greek fire' was not a direct ancestor of gunpowder. But its success resulted in experiments with other combustible powders and liquids. The older Greek 'artillery', based on twisting of hair by torsion and used by the Romans, was inadequate for northern Europe, for it worked only in dry summer campaigns; otherwise the fibre lost its elasticity.

Once commerce revived, many clever ideas came to Europe from the East. The first of these was the *huo p'ao*, known in Europe as the 'trebuchet' and used in China by the eleventh century AD. This tilting engine for throwing missiles by the use of weights began to be used in Europe by the early twelfth century. By that time a hand weapon for throwing Greek fire was being used in Byzantium. It also seems that, from the ninth century, the Chinese were using saltpetre, sulphur and crushed charcoal, thrown by catapults to cause an explosion, in order to frighten demons. The humane and intelligent Sung dynasty in China were overthrown in 1126 when their capital K'aifeng fell to invaders from the north who apparently used gunpowder for the first time. A tube to throw spears, not just fire, was in use in China in 1232 (at the siege of Loyang). In 1252 something close to a rocket was being used in Cologne. Saltpetre, known as 'Chinese snow', was in use for war in Egypt by then.

The critical invention in these matters was the combination of the right mixture of ingredients to make true gunpowder, with the realisation that, if it were made to explode in a tube, a ball of stone or iron might be ejaculated. Greek fire had resulted in the elaboration of copper tubes strong enough to contain the explosion. Metallic guns were used in both India and China by about 1275, spreading thereafter to the rest of the East. Perhaps the Philippines saw gunfire before France did.

Gunpowder was in use in Flanders by 1314, at Metz by 1324 and in a bronze gun near Florence by 1326. King Muhammad IV of Granada attacked Alicante with artillery in 1331. Cannon balls took longer to be invented but iron shot was being made at Lucca by 1341. England had two calibres of gun firing lead shot by 1346, and cannon balls were being made at Toulouse by 1347. Petrarch speaks of gunpowder as common about 1355. Cannon were in use in China by 1356, and played a decisive part in the wars of the rebellious Ming against the Mongol emperors between that date and 1382, although they seem not to have been used in India till taken there by the Portuguese in the sixteenth century. In 1389 cannon were first used in a decisive battle, at Kossovo, causing Serbia to become a vassal state of Turkey.

These early cannon were inefficient. Even at Kossovo they were unwieldy and difficult to manage. The guns were wrought-iron or bronze monsters, either welded into crude tubes and strengthened by iron hoops, or, if bronze, cast direct by craftsmen who knew the art from making bells. The shot was small. The gunpowder was loosely mixed, and that retarded the explosion. These guns were of most use on ships – a consequence of navies' mobility; in 1377 the first naval battle with artillery occurred, off La Rochelle: a Spanish naval victory over England, in which twelve Castilian galleys destroyed thirty-six English ones[1]. Even so, the Venetians had bowmen as their main naval armament till 1450.

Actually, till about 1450, when mobile artillery was devised, drawn by oxen in Italy or mounted on gun-carriages drawn by horses in France, the new developments had little effect. Swords, charges and archery were still deciding wars till the mid fifteenth century, and castles remained invulnerable. Then, gun-founders altered their techniques. They ceased their concentration on increasing the size of guns, which were useful only in sieges, and movable only with great difficulty. (The crowning achievement of that era had been the great brass cannon made for Sultan Muhammad II by the Hungarian gunmaker Orban to throw large stone thousand-pound balls into Constantinople. It needed 60 to 140 oxen to pull it, 100 men to manipulate it and two hours to load it. It cracked and never worked properly.) Even so, other such guns helped the Turks batter down the walls of Christian cities which had resisted them for years and French versions helped Charles VII of France to drive out the English at the end of the Hundred Years' War.*

Still, the impact of gunpowder was not appreciated till King Charles VIII of France's 'first modern army' invaded Italy in 1494. It included batteries of light mobile bronze field artillery, firing iron cannon balls rather than stone ones. They destroyed every castle they aimed at. The battles of Ravenna (in 1512) and Marignano (in 1515) were won by superior artillery. These opened a new age in warfare. Heavy siege artillery with gunpowder (firing at 900 paces and distinguished from field artillery) meant that cities could no longer rest peacefully behind stone walls, secure in the knowledge of their invulnerability before horsemen. Nor could independent-minded barons. Field artillery was decisive at Belgrade in 1521, at Mohács in 1526 and in Ivan the Terrible's conquest of Kazan and Astrakhan during the 1550s. The first two of those victories gave the Turks much Christian artillery, to their advantage later. Thereafter the European states depended for survival on foundries such as Spain's at Málaga (established in 1499) and Medina del Campo (established in 1405), or those at Innsbruck, Venice and the Tower of London.

These state workyards, in which individual craftsmen collaborated, were helped by the growth of central European metallurgy which, in the end, gave Germany an advantage over Renaissance Italy. The casting of iron for the first time in west Germany in the fourteenth century transformed European iron technology and further developed the methods of warfare which were to dispense with castles, chivalry and the Renaissance in Italy as well, inaugurating the modern state, with its clearly defined frontiers, internal order, and strong institutions[2].

These developments are likely to be deplored by those who, like anarchists, see in the modern state little but evil. But still the new state of the sixteenth century, modest in its pretensions compared with its descendant of the twentieth, had beneficial effects. It removed men from fear of barons and marauding armies and probably helped the growth of population as much as the eclipse of the plague. It is hard to feel nostalgic for the internecine wars of the Italians before mobile artillery, immortalised though the

* Hand-guns as well as cannon were used by the French in the 1450s.

fights between the Oddi and Baglioni of Perugia may be in the paintings of the young Raphael (who observed the combats as a pupil with Perugino): the terror, bloodshed, treachery and murder involved made even conquest by a foreign power seem a blessed release[3]. The *Pax Medicea* in Tuscany did seem to Giovanni Rondinelli in 1583 a good end to the 'old days' of the Florentine Republic when that city had been filled with towers, castles and 'violently quarrelling factions'[4]. The same might be said of France, at the time of the Hundred Years' War, a time of continual struggle in which, while the losses in battle were slight, armies, public and private, mercenary and monarchical, lived for years on or off the local inhabitants, committing thefts and acts of indiscipline and creating a culture of war from which the country took generations to recover.

The use of cannon and shot fired by gunpowder was the most striking adaptation of any invention by a society which did not itself have the original idea. War, the preservation of governments, riots and crimes have all been transformed by gunpowder. The knight in armour, the Ritter of the Middle Ages in Germany, the rules of war, the distinctions made between *guerre couverte* (private war) and *guerre publique* (public war between states), not to speak of *guerre mortelle* (when the populations in vanquished territories could be 'put to the sword'), all vanished for good or evil – though the French knights' great days had been in decline since their decimation by longbowmen at Crécy in 1346. Also in decline henceforth were the professional mercenaries, Swiss or German, who had in mediaeval Italian wars come to look on war as a tactical exercise in which the aim was to capture an enemy's army, not to defeat him by expensive battles: *condottieri* were sometimes suspected of settling beforehand what was to happen; even of arranging beforehand to draw the game. Such sportsmanship soon vanished, the Swiss being defeated by the French at Marignano in 1515, their 'solid phalanxes of pikemen' being no more the master of the field, even if mercenary captains lasted until well into the seventeenth century – the greatest of them all, the Czech nobleman Wallenstein, being murdered on the brink of establishing a kingdom. The most successful army of the fifteenth and sixteenth centuries, however, was a national one, nationally led and financed, that of Spain: an army of infantrymen not cavalrymen, with noblemen sometimes in the ranks and carrying hand-guns. They dominated Europe from the defeat of François I in 1525 till their own eclipse at Rocroy in 1643, despite the fear that Europe was then at the mercy of the dynamic Ottomans, poised in the sixteenth century to defeat the Habsburgs in Hungary. (The Ottomans, though they reached Vienna, were in the sixteenth century more raiders than occupiers.)

In the sixteenth century cannon were still individuals, and often had names. They were made differently one from another. Their expectancy of life was short. Bells were often melted down to make them. The best guns were German or Venetian, and German ones were exported, particularly to Portugal and to Spain (whose rulers thereby spent much of the gold of the Americas). Many gunners aboard Portuguese and Spanish ships were Germans or Flemings. Though Spain founded arsenals of her own, she often depended on the enemy's manufacture. England, too, though making iron guns in the Ashdown Forest, also bought many from abroad, particularly from the Flemings. Later, the English cast-iron guns, because of the phosphorus in the soil of Sussex, turned out to be more robust than those cast on the Continent. They did not blow up so often at the wrong moment. They remained heavier than bronze guns, but they did not heat so much, and were three of four times less expensive. English guns thus became items for export, particularly to the Dutch in their wars against Spain.

Meanwhile, for the first time since the era of the Vikings, a Scandinavian country began to count in the 'world's game', as Pope Julius II put it. This was Sweden, newly independent from Denmark after her rebellion in 1521 under Gustavus Vasa and rendered Protestant at much the same time. Sweden, with her charcoal forests and ample copper, tin and iron, also began to make guns. At first they were wrought-iron guns, then bronze, then cast-iron, in the English style. In the seventeenth century Swedish cannon were sold all over Europe, numbers enough to 'equip a small fleet' often being exported in a single year. In contrast, the French arms industry, despite the efforts of Colbert, was sluggish, and the armies of Louis XIV bought abroad.

By now artillery was not the only use for gunpowder. There was also the hand-gun. This recalled the blow pipe used for Greek fire but it played a small part till the seventeenth century. The first hand-gun was a weapon fired with a slow match applied to a touch hole in the barrel, in order to light the fire-priming powder on the firing pan. A matchlock followed, with an arm which, when the trigger was pulled, brought the match down on to the priming. That was a faster method, but the match had to be kept alight.

That was difficult to assure in the middle of a battle. Some of these weapons nevertheless were effective: Talbot, Earl of Shrewsbury, was killed with a hand-gun in the last battle of the Hundred Years' War, in 1452. Rifled hand-guns, as devised in Leipzig in 1498, were common in Central Europe during the sixteenth century.* Then, about 1525, the Italians devised a pistol with a wheel lock, which was favoured for a long time for use when mounted. A key was used to wind a spring, whose release turned a rough wheel against pyrites. The sparks so caused touched the priming. But the winding meant that the weapon could not be fired quickly twice. So its use was confined to cavalrymen. They would fire and then charge, sword in hand.

Other hand-guns were soon made: for example, the arquebus (from the German *Hakenbuchse*, or hookgun, from the hooked shape of the butt) and the musket. The first may have been in use in the late fifteenth century. Spanish arquebusiers were in action at Pavia in 1525, originating the modern infantry force. Filippo Strozzi of Milan enabled that weapon to be effective from five hundred paces. Muskets (from the Italian *moschetto*, a sparrow hawk) were heavier and more powerful than the arquebus (they were effective from six hundred paces), firing, to begin with, from a rest stuck into the ground and using a matchlock. It was the arquebus which won much of America for Spain: when Cortes fired a shot at a man's arm he was thought by Indians to have in his hand an object which could produce lightning at will.

The rifle, meantime, was devised about 1475, though it was scarcely used for military purposes till the Thirty Years' War. Until then rifles had been used by rich sportsmen who could afford to pay for accuracy when shooting at birds – a new sport – and did not mind the slow business of filling up the barrel by a ramrod – activities far too time-wasting in war. But about 1630 something like a modern rifle was made possible when a flintlock rifle was invented in France. A flint was pulled back and, when the trigger was released, it was driven by a spring against a metal plate over a firing pan, into which sparks flew. That system was quickly adapted to the musket and, when made lighter, it could be used from the shoulder, without a stand.

The rifle of those days could only expect to be accurate for one hundred yards. It was not a battle-winning weapon. Even so, it

---

* A 'rifled' gun is one with spiral grooves in its barrel. It causes the bullet to spin and, therefore, to be more accurate.

was introduced into the French army by Louis XIV. It was copied by both the English and the new German army of the Great Elector of Prussia, who also invented paper cartridges about 1670. The bayonet, a sword blade devised at Bayonne and fixed on to a musket for use in infantry charges, completed the characteristic equipment of European soldiery of the eighteenth century, though a steel-headed pike on a shaft of wood remained the weapon of foot soldiers till 1700.

These new weapons were all soon used outside Europe and by non-Europeans. Jewish gunsmiths helped the Muslim armies of Suleiman the Magnificent to develop field artillery. Field guns and siege guns were used in India by 1500. Chinese artillery was as good as European in the sixteenth century. But they did not make bronze guns as satisfactorily as was done in the West, and their cast iron was by 1600 less well made than the British or Swedish type.

This failure by the Chinese to exploit their great advantages has been touched on before. It will remain one of the great problems of history. The careful system of supplies, training and tactics in, for example, China during the T'ang dynasty (AD 618–907) would alone have made their forces superior to those of any Western army of that time. But in the seventeenth century, by an odd paradox, the Portuguese tried to prevent the knowledge of modern foundries passing to the East, as the Chinese had tried so often to do with their own best inventions. Eventually the secret was communicated to China, apparently by the Jesuits, who are understood to have offered to pass on what they knew in return for the right to set up missions. Even so, the Chinese continued to make only small iron guns, able to attack castles yet inadequate against the big walls of new fortified cities. Perhaps the Chinese government feared internal bandits as much as foreign invasion. There was, of course, also no internal arms trade in China – unlike Italy, where Francesco Datini, 'the merchant of Prato' in Iris Origo's book of that name, was busy as an arms dealer in the early fifteenth century. In England the ironsmiths who wished to sell guns abroad won their arguments successfully against an initially sceptical Crown. They had no equivalent in China, where the all-powerful rulers controlled every craftsman in their country's arsenal. The low social status of the craftsman was one more reason for the failure of China to take advantage of her advanced technology.

Admittedly, Chinese junks were able to compete against Western sailing ships in mercantile activities, though they never made effective men-of-war. The Korean navy in the sixteenth century put long-range artillery on their ships, an idea taken over by the Japanese. But that era of Japanese expansion was short and ended in the 1630s, when Shogun Tokugawa Iemitsu, who desired to avoid all foreign influences, both banned his countrymen from sailing anywhere, and prohibited the manufacture of ocean-going ships. That decree, short-sighted or sagacious as it may alternately seem, delayed Japanese international action for 250 years. Though the Chinese governments were more open, their society was equally resistant to change. Chinese gunpowder remained curiously second-rate in the late sixteenth century. Their firearms were bad, while their old bamboo pikes, sharpened by fire or with iron tips, like their scimitars of iron or tin cuirasses, were no match for those of the West.

Some non-Europeans did eventually make effective use of European weapons. But in the seventeenth century the only successful opponents to Europe were the Omani Arabs whose Imams formed a fine navy of well-gunned warships which fought the Portuguese in the Indian Ocean between 1650 and 1730.

In the late sixteenth century some seventy per cent of Spanish state revenue was spent on weapons, and two-thirds of the revenue of other European countries probably also went thus. Yet, by the standards of both antiquity and the modern era, numbers concerned in battles were small: at Lepanto 208 Christian galleys faced 230 Turkish ones. The English fleet at the Armada in 1588 numbered a mere twenty-five galleons along with pinnaces and other small craft. Fairfax had only 26,000 men at Marston Moor: but that was, as Dr Laslett says, 'one of the largest crowds assembled before Napoleonic times in England'. The Spaniards at Rocroy also numbered 26,000. The largest expedition in the seventeenth century despatched from Europe to America was the 12,000 men sent by Spain in 1624 to resist the Dutch attempt to capture Brazil. They were carried by seventy ships. The Dutch believed that they were making a major commitment when in that year they sent 3,300 men in twenty-six ships against Bahia.

That did not mean that wars were modest affairs. The Thirty Years' War cost Mecklenburg eighty per cent of its population and other parts of Germany not much less. The murders, the loss of harvests, the thefts, the epidemics, the 'sackings' of towns reproduced for Germany, on a worse scale, the troubles experienced during the Hundred Years' War in France. In Bohemia only 6,000 villages out of 35,000 were habitable after the Thirty Years' War, and the population there is said to have fallen from two million to 700,000.

A great effort was made in the sixteenth century to revive the fortress against the threat of artillery. Cities in zones of war went to much trouble to create new systems of defence, such as Perugia's projecting towers 'spread out like a man's hand' – thereby putting the heart of the city beyond the reach of enemy guns. These elaborate fortifications, the *traces italiennes* as they were known, designed by engineers, mathematicians and artists (Michelangelo helped to plan Florence's fortifications in 1527), took over from simple walls of masonry, placing a burden of expense on the local municipality and rendering more difficult the survival of small states and cities which did not have powerful friends. Because of them the siege and not the pitched battle, nor the war of manoeuvre, became the characteristic form of European land warfare for nearly a hundred years.

The elaborate grandeur of these fortresses with their low silhouettes, round towers to deflect shot and designed to cover every inch of wall by enfilading fire from bastions, began to be rendered ineffective after the development of the telescope in 1590, which vastly improved the accuracy of artillery. The increased mobility of supplies, on slowly improving canals and roads, and better organised commissariats, gave an impetus to the mobile army such as had not been seen since the early Middle Ages. In reply, military engineers discovered that earth was a better fortification against cannon than brick. Outworks suddenly counted far more than traditional ramparts. Even so, the Spaniards in the New World put faith in fortifications. Cartagena, the 'gateway to South America', was rendered impregnable to the invader by the mid eighteenth century; and equally awe-inspiring fortresses were built elsewhere.

The civil wars of the late sixteenth and seventeenth centuries (the French and English civil wars, the Fronde, the Thirty Years' War, the Eighty Years' War between Spain and the Netherlands) saw in many countries the establishment anew of standing armies. It is true that England, then the most vigorous and most commercially successful country, avoided such a development. But most other strong countries set up such armies, and thereby simplified the art of government. Military barracks had the same place in baroque Europe as monasteries had in mediaeval Europe.

Champs de Mars, arsenals and large squares designed for review
became the characteristic of the new fixed capitals, while turning,
drilling, parading, blaring of the bugle and beating the tattoo
were, as Lewis Mumford suggests, the new ceremonial in an age
when the Church was beginning to lose its appeal[5].

Many of the early conflicts between 'gunpowder monarchies'
occurred in America or India: for example, the 'Sugar War' between the Dutch and the Portuguese in the early seventeenth
century to control Brazil – a war in which the native Indians had
little part. This war was the first real world war since battles were
also joined in the hinterland of Angola, the island of Timor and
the coast of India. (The prizes included the cloves and nutmegs
of the Moluccas, the cinnamon of Ceylon and the pepper of
Malabar as well as gold from Guinea, silver from Japan and slaves
from Africa). It was won by the Dutch in the East – giving the
Spice Islands to the Dutch East India Company – but it left the
Portuguese in control of the Angolan and Mozambique coasts of
Africa, as of Brazil and Goa.*

The big guns of the new artillery also meant that force was
concentrated in fewer hands. The artillery-powered empires
needed, in return, heavy and regular taxation. Perhaps that was
less destructive than chaos. Burckhardt regarded the introduction
of firearms as doing 'its part in making war a democratic pursuit'
because, henceforth, the skills of humbly born technicians, such
as engineers, were as important as those of noblemen[6].

In old books of history the role of war was often exaggerated,
and even those who wrote of war often neglected the ordnance
and the economic strength needed. But war determined the frontiers of states and decisively affected the character of governments
which, in the age of enlightenment as in that of agriculture, remained primarily organisations for managing armies, though not
necessarily for the waging of war. It also benefited the revival of
capitalism. Firms such as De Geer and Trip of Amsterdam established themselves as munitions merchants of the Thirty Years'
War, supplying not only Sweden and the States General in Holland but also sometimes their Spanish opponents. In the English

---

* The reasons for the outcome of this war in the East were superior Dutch
economic resources and superior sea power. The Portuguese won their decisive
battles in Brazil at Guararapes in 1648 and 1649 with men more inured to the
tropics and better equipped for bush war. Even where the Dutch won, they won
few souls for Calvinism, and the Portuguese language survived.

Civil War, the same Dutch firm supplied both the King and the Covenanters, and later supplied the Tsar of Russia.

Critics of military investments by governments sometimes forget that the era before standing armies was one of private armies, often creating a most savage series of conditions even in years of formal peace. Standing armies from the seventeenth century onwards helped to humanise war, since they were disciplined and accepted rules. They emphasised a distinction between civilian and military targets. They were paid better and more regularly than the marauding and prize-seeking hordes of the past, though the European armies which reduced the world were still extraordinarily undisciplined.

Everywhere where big guns were established, the effect was to concentrate force in fewer hands and, despite the bloodshed when one cannon-owning state quarrelled with another one, more responsible ones. In the eighteenth century 'gunpowder empires' led to a superior level of peace, by assisting the growth of the idea that 'all damage done to the enemy unnecessarily . . . is a licentiousness condemned by the law of nature'[7]. Thus though war was ceasing to be chivalrous, it could not be said to have returned to barbarism.

28

Medicine, Food and People

One wrong word may now kill thousands of men.

> Rabelais, in the course of collating texts by
> Hippocrates and Galen for the scholar-printer Gryphius, who
> was eager to get editions out for the book fair at Lyons in 1532

1

In the sixteenth century the world was enabled by the wide circulation of medical tracts – another consequence of printing – to shake off at last the effects of over a thousand years of the influence of Galen. As a result Paracelsus, a Swiss of wide culture, to whom humanity is indebted for the word 'alcohol', sensibly wrote, 'It is nature's balsam, not the surgeon's interference, that heals wounds.' Girolamo Fracastoro worked out in Verona a rational theory of infection, which he rightly regarded as being caused by the passage of minute bodies to the affected person. (Fracastoro also wrote a poem, 'Syphilis sive Morbus Gallicus', a fantasy about the shepherd Syphilus, who insulted Apollo and received a vile disease. Hence the name of the venereal disease then beginning, as a result of the discovery of America, to make its mark on Europe.) At the same time Miguel Serveto (Servetus), a brilliant Navarrese (born in Tudela), discovered that blood was pumped to the lungs by the arteries. Vesalius of Brussels, professor at Padua, then revived the study of anatomy. That had an immediate effect on surgery. Above all he influenced military surgery, that being the sphere where most surgeons gained their experience – so much so that all surgery seemed for a long time to be military; otherwise, only a few barbers pretended to 'chirurgeonly' expertise.

That military bias became even more the case after the French wars in Italy confirmed the importance of gunpowder – an innovation with effects so alarming that it was supposed that wounds caused by it might be poisoned. Ambrose Paré, a French military surgeon who served King François I, was the first to appreciate the importance of an understanding of anatomy for effective surgery. He realised that wounds heal better if they are not cauterised with burning oil or otherwise treated with fire, as had happened ever since the remotest days, and saw that dead tissue in the wound was itself a danger. Paré's realisation of such simple but unrecognised truths, as well as his unerring skill in finding where a bullet lay in the body, made him a genuine pioneer. His contemporary, Alfonso Ferri, proved that all foreign bodies in a wound had to be removed for an effective cure to be possible. Painters of the Renaissance, meantime, concerned themselves with the anatomy as much as the doctors did. It was Leonardo who realised that Galen was wrong about the interconnection of heart and lungs[1].

The medical advances of the sixteenth century were the work of southern Europeans. But Italian intellectual life declined after the Spanish conquests. Spanish life became stagnant – even if Don Quixote was wise enough to realise that 'a tooth is more important than a diamond'. The innovators of the next generation were Protestants, from England and Holland. Thus Zacharias Janssen, a spectacle-maker, of Middleburg in Holland, discovered the microscope and William Harvey, an ex-student at Padua, built on Serveto's ground-work to show that the arteries pump the blood away from the heart while the veins carry it back. Thus the movement of blood was shown to be continuous and in the same direction. It was an Englishman too, Thomas Sydenham, a Dorsetshire physician and a protégé of Cromwell, who wrote that 'disease . . . however prejudicial soever it may be to the body is no more than a vigorous effort of Nature to destroy the mortific matter and thus recover the patient'.

During the following century a Dutch Protestant scientist, Leeuwenhoek, using a magnifying glass, picked out bacteria, and showed that muscles are made up of fibres of their own. His German colleague, Kepler, explained that short- and long-sightedness derive from the crystalline lens of the eye bringing rays of light to a focus which is not in the retina. Robert Hooke found the cells, Jan Swammerdam found the red corpuscle. Boerhaave established a great medical school at Leyden. The reign of the surgeon who was more barber than scientist came to an end. Since then surgeons have had to have training for their work. Next, John Hunter, a British army surgeon, described the nature of shock and of inflammation. Pierre Fauchard wrote the first serious book on the care of teeth. Other Frenchmen gained great if often undeserved reputations for their operations to extract stones in the bladder, a characteristic complaint of the seventeenth century, mostly caused by a bad diet. Surgery was still confined to that, along with trepanning, amputation, incision of abscesses and cataracts. Operations for these were performed better in the eighteenth century than ever before. But they had little effect on the death rate.

The same was true of all medicine. Even in Florence, the great city of the Renaissance, the ignorance was still such that in the eighteenth century the population believed that the two last representatives of the house of Medici, Grand Duke Gian Gastone and his sister, the Electress Anna Maria Luisa, were carried off in a 'hurricane of wind': 'The Devil came for them in a *temporale*,' wrote the English consul ironically. Casanova thought that in his day more people perished 'at the hands of doctors than are purged by them'[2]. Cellini's doctor, Maestro Francesco, two centuries before, seeing his patient improve, without much effort by him, said wisely, 'O powers of nature! She knows her own needs; the doctors know nothing'[3]. Maestro Francesco was unusual only in his recognition of his ignorance. In the eighteenth century a few drugs were used but probably less effectively than in old Babylon or Egypt. Nothing was known for use against typhus or puerperal fever. Charms were still widely believed in, even in Europe. King Charles II purported to cure thousands by the ancient technique of touching. The bleeding and purges proffered by many doctors were worse than useless for most patients. True, there was a marked increase in the number of hospitals in the eighteenth century. England, for example, had only five in 1700, of which two were in London, and in 1800 fifty. But those frightful institutions were, to begin with, worse than useless. No one knew at that time the importance of isolation nor of hygiene. As late as 1854 cholera patients were admitted to a general ward in London. Any patient admitted to hospital then ran a severe risk of contracting a mortal infection. The risk of death in the early lying-in hospitals was greater than at home. The beginning of the use of forceps, in the eighteenth century, and other artificial means for assisting the delivery of babies, also had a bad effect for the same reason.

Then, though some diseases seemed in retreat, others (smallpox, syphilis) seemed on the advance. Syphilis, for example, was apparently unknown in Europe before 1492, when it was brought back from Cuba by Columbus, along with tobacco. (The first syphilitics of Europe were the Indian slaves exhibited by Columbus in 1492, in Barcelona.) The first epidemie was in Naples the next year, and was taken there by a Spanish ship from Barcelona.

Charles VIII's army was devastated by it when he reached Naples. So this American illness was, for a time, known as the 'French disease'. By 1498 syphilis had reached India, and China by 1505. Mercury was used in the sixteenth century against it, without decisive effect. It only began to be used again beneficially in the eighteenth century. Many peoples were seriously affected. Freyre even speaks of the 'syphilisation of Brazil', suggesting that by the eighteenth century Brazil had become the land of syphilis *par excellence*[4].

2

The fall in the death rate which did occur in Europe and then elsewhere in the eighteenth century was due less to medicine than to 'improvements in the environment' as modern scholars put it, and to better food. Obviously the questions of death rates and birth rates are interrelated, for any increase in the birth rate is rendered ineffective by high mortality among infants. As a rule a decline in the birth rate follows, in most societies, a decline of the death rate, by several generations. During the generations when the rates differ, the population goes up. The least prolific of couples can double their number in twenty years. If that were to happen always, increases in population would occur everywhere. But that expansion in the past met resistance from the environment: wild species multiply up to a point where mortality and fertility are equal. That balance was achieved in human history too. It was disturbed in the eighteenth century by, as is now largely accepted, an increase in the birth rate.

Why should that have occurred? It cannot have been the consequence of an increased demand for labour. On the contrary, the rise led to rural poverty in England and occurred everywhere in Europe. In England the population's increase expanded the labour available at a rate faster than agriculture could absorb it and produced the landless, often unemployable, labourers observable in all sorts of villages, both enclosed and open. Actually, industrialisation in the eighteenth century saved Europe from the effects of overpopulation, as emigration to the Americas would do in the nineteenth.

The rise in population in the eighteenth century was comparable to that of the thirteenth, of which it was, to a great extent, a continuation, after an interruption. It was assisted by a decline in great epidemics, such as plague, and by the optimism which the disappearance of plague itself inspired. It may have been affected by the improvement in diet following the discovery of America – the potato and the Jerusalem artichoke, for example, being available – and must have been assisted by the improvements in European agriculture, though the increase in population was as great, indeed greater, in the eighteenth century in Russia, where the improvements in diet and agriculture were scarcely noticeable. Perhaps the creation of strong states and an end of private wars were as important as anything. (Yet the strongest state in the eighteenth century was France, which grew in population less than any other country.) Asia, and particularly China, was better administered in the eighteenth century than before. The population of the Americas was increased by interior immigration and continual movement, though not yet keeping up with the ravages of plague and other diseases introduced by the Europeans. At that time only in Japan were there any official restrictions on birth, such as encouragements by the state to celibacy, late marriage and even abortion. But, in the East in general, newborn children were often abandoned, and some tribes still practised infanticide.

The country which increased its population least in the eighteenth century was France; that which grew most as a result of natural increase, rather than immigration, was Russia. Did France's population fail to grow in order that holdings might not be subdivided? Did Russia's grow because of the realisation that there was land available in the east and south, newly conquered? Neither country anyway made substantial contributions to the coming of industrialisation, though France did more than Russia.

Europe by the early eighteenth century was the focus of the world's vital forces. Its population was, however, still modest in comparison with modern times. France and the Empire each had about twenty million people, Italy fifteen million, Russia fourteen million, while Britain and Spain had about seven million each. The biggest states in Germany, Prussia and Bavaria, numbered two million and one and a half million respectively. As for cities, by 1750 London and Paris each numbered about 600,000 to 700,000. Lyons was the only other French city over 100,000 (it was about 110,000). No other English city was larger than 100,000. Naples was in 1750 the only Italian city over 150,000, and Rome was a little less than that. Venice had dropped to 140,000, Milan to 100,000, Florence, Genoa and Turin had above 70,000 each. Only three Central European cities had populations over 100,000 – Vienna (225,000), Hamburg (150,000) and Berlin (140,000). India's population was over 100 million and China's, thanks to a long period of peace under the early Manchus, perhaps 300 million by 1800. Total population of 450 million for Asia might be a correct estimate⁵.

Africa's population in 1750 is hard to guess: 100 million? It could not have been much more. Australia, unknown to the West till the 1770s, was negligible. The Americas were the emptiest of the big continents, in 1750 perhaps numbering two million in the North, fifteen million in the South. Half the population of the North were white, but only a fifth were so in the South. The rest were Indian, Negro or mixed in one way or another.

There are some special points to be made about population between the sixteenth and the eighteenth centuries particularly in respect of Europe (and the US) which, as in so many other things, begin to be different from the rest of the world. First, in most of the world and probably in mediaeval Europe, people married young, and the majority married. Very few remained single: perhaps two per cent at most. But in Western Europe about 1600, and certainly by 1750, people married late, and the number of bachelors and spinsters in their late forties approached seventeen per cent. This pattern was reversed for the first time after 1945,* so that Dr Laslett can tell us authoritatively that 'despite Romeo and Juliet, all records declare that in Elizabethan England, marriage was rare at fourteen and not as common in the late teens as it is now'⁶.

The first question which occurs is, how was it possible in primitive societies and in nearly every society except Western Europe between 1500 and 1945 to arrange that nearly every woman married? That seems difficult to imagine since most people lived in small communities of a few hundred and the number of possible partners, small at the beginning, was reduced by conventions and castes. Was the professional marriage broker responsible? Or polygamy? Or the fact that in primitive societies remarriage was universal – as it was in mediaeval Europe, despite the Church's disapproval? This question is not easy to answer unless it is appreciated that one of the main preoccupations of primitive society was to arrange marriages, while much attention was paid to marriage rituals which played, and play, a critical part in the entertainment of the population, partly because bridesmaids and pages appeared as the potential bridal pairs of the future. A marriage

---

* Perhaps because of the fall in the age of sexual maturity of women during the last few generations, which has been widely noticed, never explained.

feast was an occasion to show off the potentialities of other daughters, as well as to celebrate the wedding.

The second question is, why did this change in patterns of marriage occur only in Western Europe? Now Professor Hajnal of Oslo has an answer. He attributes it to a change in landholding. The collapse of feudalism created smallholdings with single heirs who often waited for their fathers to die and leave them the farm. Large estates, such as still existed in Eastern Europe, could absorb the youngest married couple more easily[7]. This may be part of the explanation. But there is another: the cult of romantic love in the Western world since the Renaissance.

Dr Johnson dismissed love as an artificial emotion invented by novelists and adopted, by both men and women, as a cover for sexual desire. The cult was invented in Europe by the Provençal troubadours (perhaps deriving from the Arabs), stimulated by chivalry, and was one more idea which began to be diffused (despite Dante's passionate views on the matter), it would seem, to a wide audience only after the invention of the printing press. *Amadis de Gaul*, the first romance of chivalry, published in 1508, describes the adventures and constancy of an attractive hero and a beautiful heroine in a way which still has its copies in popular magazines. Love was an idea embellished, as Johnson implied, in the seventeenth and eighteenth centuries, and made into a mass cult by popular novelists, mass circulation magazines and films in the twentieth century. Certainly, the concept of romantic love made old-fashioned ideas of arranged marriage more and more unacceptable, and that began earlier than is generally supposed: Benvenuto Cellini's father married for love in the late fifteenth century.

At all earlier times, and in most primitive societies, marriages have been arranged or even settled by lot, as was the case with the Moravians in the US in the eighteenth century, about whom Benjamin Franklin complained. (Franklin said, 'If the matches are not made by the mutual choice of the parties, some of them may chance to be very unhappy.' 'And so they may,' answered his interlocutor, 'if you let the parties choose for themselves.' 'Which indeed, I could not deny'[8].) Laurence Stone points out that before the Renaissance marriage was not an intimate association based upon choice, but a means of tying together two families[9]. He also argues that this concept of a marriage, as an alliance between two families, was itself a development of the later Middle Ages since, earlier, marriage seemed a very informal affair in

Europe with much casual polygamy and even polyandry, many bastards and relatively easy divorce (at least till the Hildebrandine reforms).*

Professor Hajnal suggests that we should see, in these European 'marriage patterns' of the Renaissance and afterwards, the roots of modern capitalism. For, he says, these habits gave many people a period during which savings would be easier since they had no responsibility for children. Those who did not save demanded goods other than what might be needed for survival. From the Renaissance onwards the culture of Europe, particularly Protestant Europe, stimulated the growth of an attitude in which people were persuaded not to marry until they were able to support a family. No doubt Professor Hajnal is correct to mention this as one cause, as important as Protestantism or coal, of the birth of the new capitalist spirit. But Confucius also believed marriage should be delayed till thirty for men, and twenty for women; Aristotle thought men should marry at thirty-nine.

Furthermore, a state of affairs comparable to that which prevailed in the Renaissance prevailed in Rome too. In the time of Hadrian, Professor Carcopino assures us, a father did not dream of forcing his daughter to marry against her will[10]. In Rome between about 100 BC and AD 100 the concept of romantic love had an early demonstration, as the poems of Catullus suggest. Love poems were similarly written in ancient Egypt.

3

The most likely single explanation for the swift increase in the world's population in the eighteenth century was the improvement of food almost everywhere. That was partly a result of more enlightened agriculture, as will be discussed later. However, a more striking agricultural change than anything else in the sixteenth century was the transformation caused by the export of certain plants to America and the import of some American crops to the Old World, Asia and Africa included. Like most events of the Renaissance, this history has its origins in the Middle Ages.

Rice, for example, had been carried to Europe by the Arabs from China. In the early Middle Ages it was being sold at the fairs of Champagne. Though grown in several Mediterranean countries and, therefore, well established in Italy by the time of the Re-

---

* For example, the daughters of the Cid were divorced, the daughter of the first count of Castile was married three times, etc.

naissance, it was regarded as a supplement to corn in an emergency, never greatly tempting those (the rich) who decided the fashions and owned the land. Rice was thus grown in Mediterranean countries only sporadically.

The discoveries and conquests in America had a far greater effect. They brought to Europe maize, tomatoes, potatoes, turkeys, Jerusalem artichokes and chocolate. The discoveries also led to the cultivation in America, on a large scale, of sugar and coffee, plants indigenous to the South Seas and Ethiopia respectively. The regular journeys eastwards stimulated a trade in tea from China and later stimulated the cultivation of tea elsewhere in the East. Both were encouraged by imports of sugar from the West Indies, San Thomé (in the Gulf of Guinea), Madeira, the Azores and Brazil. From being a luxury comparable in rarity to cinnamon or cloves, sugar became a drug endowed with medicinal properties and then an indispensable condiment.

Sugar cane is one of the most interesting of crops. It is part of a large family of canes, bamboos and grasses which have often been used for fibre or for thatch. Carried very easily to South-East Asia and to India, it was crushed, in one way or another, to provide juice. The boiling of the juice to make solid sugar was probably begun in India or Persia about AD 600. Cane was taken to the Mediterranean from India and flourished in the late Roman world in Egypt, Sicily and Andalusia. The prophet Isaiah includes a reference to sweet cane. Both Ezekiel and Jeremiah speak of it too, but presumably no sugar in our modern sense was then made from it. In the region near Canton in China, cane was known by the third century AD, but again that does not seem to have been turned into sugar proper. There, as in the European Middle Ages, honey provided the best sweetening available: there was also some in wine. Cane was unpopular among early farmers, since it prevents the growing of other crops by rotation (a cane plant lasts seven years). It cannot be grown north of the line where frost is a possibility. But it figured in the pharmacopoeia of the School of Salerno in the tenth century. Islam carried it anew to Spain at that time, and with it the waterwheel, the *nora*, associated with the pleasant poetry of the mediaeval countryside, with its ropes, canals and pullies. The Crusaders grew cane seriously on Cyprus, and made loaves of sugar from it almost in conditions of a plantation. In mediaeval England, loaf sugar was imported via Venice or Germany to make marzipans or sweetmeats, costing 1s to 2s a pound in the thirteenth and fourteenth centuries, dropping to 10d in the fifteenth century because of the successful exploitation of the Canaries and later of Madeira, the Azores and the Cape Verde Islands – all in conditions of plantation.

From the Renaissance onwards, sugar has been grown continuously in, first, the West Indies, and then on the South American mainland. Cane was carried to the Americas by Columbus on his second voyage. The first sugar mill in the New World was established in 1508 in Santo Domingo. The main crop of Cortes' estate in Oaxaca was sugar cane. Fiscal advantages were given in the Spanish Empire to those who founded sugar mills, Already by 1520 cattle were exported from Spain and slaves from Africa, to the Indies, specially in order to power the mills and to cut cane. Cane, unknown to the Americas before Columbus, was firmly established. The north-east coast of Brazil between Recife and Bahia became the centre of sugar plantations which were for a time in the seventeenth century most important in the world's carrying trade – perhaps the most important after the Dutch trade in corn from the Baltic.

For well over a hundred years at the most critical era of the world's commercial history, sugar was the most important item of commerce. To an Old World used to the sparing use of sucrose provided by honey, West Indian sugar transformed diets. The merchants responsible for both sugar and slaves accumulated fortunes – in Bristol, Liverpool, Nantes, Cadiz, Lisbon – and that helped to finance some part of the great capital enterprises of the Industrial Revolution, though analysis might show that the greatest fortunes of the eighteenth century were made by men who equipped armies, not sugar plantations.

Sugar stimulated the use of coffee, tea and chocolate, above all the first two. Coffee, native to Ethiopia and not exported for drinking before 1500, was known in Constantinople by 1600 and sold in a Paris café in 1672. Coffee houses were open in London by 1652. Most of this early coffee came from Mocha (Arabia). The plant was soon established by the Dutch in Java and it followed sugar cane to the Americas. It was known in Cayenne in 1722, Martinique in 1723 and Jamaica in 1730. Curiously enough, however, the demand for coffee only grew fast when the general availability of sugar began to make it less bitter to an increasingly self-indulgent public. In 1724 Dominie François Valentyn complained that the use of coffee had become so common in Paris 'that unless the maids and seamstresses have their coffee every morning, the thread will not go through the eye of the needle'.

From the eighteenth century, coffee was accessible, at least in Britain, France, Holland and, to a lesser extent, in Spain and Italy. Each Caribbean island grew some but, in the end, the largest producer was Brazil after the 1880s. The major coffee plantations in Ceylon had been destroyed by a terrible blight and Brazil seized the opportunity offered. Coffee had been introduced into Brazil in 1727, at first in Pará, then in Maranhão in 1732 and in Rio de Janeiro in 1762. The first cultivators were the Franciscan friars of the convent of St Anthony. From Rio the cultivation of coffee spread to São Paolo and Minas Gerais and by the late nineteenth century it had displaced sugar as the chief product of Brazil.

Tea, meantime, had been used for many generations in China. First of all, the Chinese merely chewed the leaf, which grows wild in northern China. It was being cultivated there by about 2000 BC. The leaves were later allowed to dry either by artificial heat ('green' tea) or by the sun (the tea leaves would then be fermented and become 'black' tea). Both types of leaf were rolled by hand. By the time that trade with Europe had opened up again, tea was being shipped in lead chests to the buyers. It was not taken to India before the Europeans reached the Far East.

In 1609 the newly founded Dutch East India Company brought back several cargoes of tea from China to Europe. The British obtained some from the same source a few years later. A trade in tea leaves began. The crop itself was unable to bear European winters (it will not stand frost and suffers from drought). An increase in the consumption of sugar coincided with the subsequent boom in tea, which affected all the European countries save for France, since she remained mistress of the coffee and chocolate islands in the West Indies.

Tea and coffee entered the European markets only in the seventeenth century, and only in the eighteenth did they become of great importance. But then they did become great trading commodities. On a smaller scale, chocolate did too. It had begun to be drunk in Mexico about 1450. It was introduced to Europeans as a drink and, though 'slabs' of chocolate were known in Spain in the sixteenth century, it took the mass manufacturers of the nineteenth century to make solid chocolate popular and cheap.

Still, these comments about a few commodities dear to the hearts of eighteenth-century Europeans do not do justice to the immense interchange of crops, fruits and domestic animals made possible by the conquests and discoveries of the sixteenth century.

The benefit was not Europe's alone. Indeed, if such new foods in Europe are considered against those made available to Africa and America as a result of the discoveries, the gain might seem to accrue to the latter. American crops such as papaya, sweet potatoes, pineapples and potatoes, not to speak of maize, manioc (cassava) and groundnuts, were taken to Africa, while wheat, chickpeas, sugar cane, beans, bananas, rice, citrus fruits, yams, coffee, breadfruit and coconuts, as well as sheep, horses, chickens and cattle, went to the Americas and eventually to Australasia. The contributions of Africa to Brazil, for example, are described by Gilberto Freyre as the dende palm and the malagueta pepper; the quiabo or okra plant; and a great deal of African culinary techniques including spices and condiments. It is worthwhile noticing too – though this is to anticipate – that it was Europeans who in the end took tea from China to India. Fray Tomás de Berlanga, a Dominican priest, brought the banana to America in 1516 and is deservedly remembered for that in every 'banana republic' – a zone where he served as Bishop (of Panama). The mango reached America from India: a good exchange for the pineapple.

The chronicler Bernal Díaz took oranges to Mexico, while a Negro with Cortes planted the first wheat field in Mexico. Chile eventually became a vineyard, the first vine being planted there years after the conquest. Willow trees and eucalyptus trees followed – though the eucalyptus had to wait till Australia was discovered. Other benefits of discovery for the Americas included the coconut, taken to Mexico from the Philippines in 1569 by Alvaro de Mendaña. The staple crops of the Guinea and Congo forests are today maize and manioc, for instance.

The changes were, ironically, the result of journeys serviced by sailors who themselves lived on dried cod, jerked (*charqui*) beef, salt pork, dried peas and ships' biscuits often alive with weevils. Much of the food of those who made possible the world's greatest dietary revolution was probably damp, too. Wood absorbs water when it floats. Thus it was hard to keep anything dry in old ships. Ships' biscuits, dried to hardness so that they were impossible to break by hand, were edible for fifty years if mixed with water, but fresh water was rarely in lavish supply. Then it was realised by physicians in 1600 that citrus fruits were effective against scurvy. But it was not till the eighteenth century that there was official recognition of this. Ships thereafter issued a daily ration of lemon juice after the fifth or sixth week out.*

The immediate effect of this revolution in diet should not be exaggerated. Bread, cheese, meat and beer continued to be the regular foods of the poor in eighteenth-century England. Gruel or soup, bread, cider and bad wine, fish and meat, dominated French food till the Revolution. Only in the eighteenth century did sugar and potatoes begin to have a serious effect in a few countries. Tomatoes, though domesticated in Mexico before 1492 and taken to Europe before 1550, were unpopular for several centuries, for they were looked on as poisonous because of their connection with the nightshade family. But the effect on the Americas of the Spanish import of horses and cattle was immediate. Nor were American Indians slow to appreciate the chicken. The horse even changed the North American Indian from being a farmer to becoming a nomad once again.

4

The Reformation and Renaissance in northern Europe also had some interesting effects on habits of drinking. To begin modestly: the use of hops began in Holland for brewing as a development of its other market gardening activities. It was said that: 'Hops, Reformation, bays and beer, Came into England all in one year.' This enabled beer to be kept longer and, after initial suspicion, it began to be popular in northern Europe from the Renaissance onwards (the ale of the past could not be kept more than a few days unless brewed strong). From that time a great variety of beers became available, from 'stout' to 'small beer' – a table drink for children (an allowance at Christ's Hospital School in London in the seventeenth century allocated each boy about 2½ gallons a week). Though home-brewing declined, a great deal of it continued.

Britain was the first country to decide that the sale of alcohol

---

* The diets of the seamen who made this great change possible were scarcely impressive but even so totalled 3,385 to 3,889 calories. Admittedly, the captains and officers often ate and drank very well while the sailors suffered. In 1560 the diet for a Spanish crew was: daily rations – 24 ounces of bread, 3·8 ounces of beans or chickpeas, a quart of wine, a little olive oil, and vinegar. On Sunday, Tuesday and Thursday there would be 8 ounces of salt beef; on Wednesday and Monday, 6 ounces of cheese; on Fridays and Saturdays, 8 ounces of salt cod. There would be frequent but unmeasured disbursement of olives, hazelnuts, dried dates, figs, quince marmalade, cinnamon, cloves, mustard, parsley, pepper, onions and garlic, and saffron. This would be served on wooden plates – with knives but no forks[11].

was a different matter from the sale of other foods and drinks, and Acts regulating the sale of beer characterise the English statute books, from the fifteenth century onwards. (Edward VI also devised a law whereby drink could be sold only at licensed places.) Towards the end of the age of agriculture in the 1720s, Benjamin Franklin recalled a typical occurrence in London: 'We had an alehouse boy who attended always in the house to supply the workmen. My companion in the press drank every day a pint before breakfast, a pint at breakfast . . . a pint between breakfast and dinner; a pint at dinner; a pint in the afternoon, about 6, and another when he had done his work.' He did this because he thought it made him strong. Franklin said that it couldn't be so, but he was unpersuadable 'and spent four to five shillings out of his wages every Saturday night'[12]. By that time, however, beer, even in England, was being challenged by a new form of drink: spirits.

Spirits were not known to the Romans. Their origin is obscure. Alchemists knew of the principle of distillation in the first century AD. A good claim to have invented brandy is that of Arnau de Vilanova, a Catalan physician who distilled alcohol from wine in the late eleventh century, in order to treat wounds. He also discovered that, if mixed with aromatic plants, the spirit would become palatable. The Chinese, on the other hand, are believed to have invented a still even earlier. At all events, stills in Europe are not known to have existed before the early Middle Ages. Arnau de Vilanova gave his drink when made from grape juice or wine the name of *aqua vitae* since, he said, it 'preserved youth, revived the heart, cured colic, dropsy and paralysis, calmed toothache and gave protection against plague'[13]. (The Germans called this *brant Win* – burnt wine – hence brandy in English.) The appeal of these 'spirits' was slow to spread. A few monastery gardens began to experiment with mixing exotic herbs with spirits, and began the tradition of monastic liqueurs. Spirits were given a stimulus by the Black Death. Physicians prescribed brandy for psychological as well as therapeutic reasons. But little was being drunk for pleasure. It was left for the countries of the reformed Christian Church to bring in the diversity of alcoholic spirits which have altered the drinking habits of the modern world so strikingly.

The pioneers were the Dutch. It was they who, in their commercial activities, helped to make available a new range of spirits: not only those distilled from wine such as cognac, armagnac, marc, but also calvados, from apple juice or cider, kirsch from cherries, gin from juniper berries (*ginevra*), vodka from grain (the Russians learned little from Europe in the sixteenth century, but they did learn the art of distilling), *aguardiente* from the juice of sugar cane and, finally, whisky, an Irish and Scottish spirit, which began to be regularly distilled from malt barley or rye in the sixteenth century. Everywhere in that century, it is evident, drunkenness increased, encouraged by the Dutch. Several old drinks such as mead (previously drunk a good deal in both England and Russia) disappeared after distilling had become well known.

Thus in the last part of the age of agriculture a new world opened to lovers of alcohol. Peasants such as those in Russia could 'pass', says Richard Pipes, 'quickly from abstinence to stupor'[14]. In the Americas, brandy, rum and *aguardiente* as well as a brandy (*mezcal*) distilled from the Mexicans' own drink of *pulque* (the juice from the heart of the maguey cactus) rivalled smallpox as Europe's 'poisoned gifts' to the New World. European stills were carried to China at the same time. Rum, another, lighter product of sugar cane through molasses, was also developed in the seventeenth century. It became the standby of the British Navy.*

Everywhere the Dutch went on the seas the desire for spirits went too. The Dutch wars of the seventeenth century might have been won by the English, but English drinkers were conquered by Dutch gin.

The seventeenth century also saw the emergence of such refinements as champagne, port and other lightly spiced wines, the second being preservable almost indefinitely, like spirits. Thus the drinker in the eighteenth century had a wider choice than at any previous time. Furthermore, corks were used to stop bottles and enable even unspiced wine to be kept for years. The cylindrical bottle of the present-day size was introduced during the eighteenth century. Special vintages began to be sought. Spirits could be sold everywhere without licence and little tax. It was said that, about 1750, every fourth house in St Giles's Circus sold gin. Special 'straw houses' existed where anyone could get drunk for a few pence and where the landlord gave straw to those unable to walk home. Beer drinking suffered a drop. Nor was it only England that sold quantities of spirits: there was so much cheap brandy in

---

* Rum was given out neat in the British Navy till 1740. Then Admiral Vernon issued rations of rum and water which, since he wore a cloak of 'grogram' cloth in bad weather, was known as 'grog'. In the Napoleonic Wars, lemon was added and, later, lime: hence limey.

Catalonia that, for a time, the world price was set by the market at the little town of Reus. Brandy was, with cotton, the basis of a Catalan Renaissance. Rum too had an empire of its own, based on Jamaica, available to all the navies and armies which haunted the Caribbean. Benjamin Franklin recalls that in his expeditionary force to Canada in 1757 it was agreed that the chaplain, a Presbyterian, should give out the rum ration – a gill of rum a day – after morning prayers: 'Never were prayers more generally and more punctually attended'[15].

Drunkenness increased. Most observers thought that it increased particularly in Paris and Madrid, in whose taverns much could be drunk without paying the urban tax levied on wine. C. R. Boxer, the most distinguished English historian of both the Dutch and Portuguese empires, wrote that in the seventeenth and eighteenth centuries 'most of the Dutch and English males who died in the tropics died of drink even making allowance for the heavy toll taken by dysentery'. Later the wine trade became the subject of politically inspired tariffs: for example, the Navigation Acts in England in the seventeenth century excluded much brought from France or Germany in Dutch ships, while Lord Methuen's Act of 1702 in England imposed a tariff on French wines, to inaugurate the era of 'port', the spiced wine from Portugal.

Why did not the Spaniards take the vine to the Americas, except, late, to Chile and California? Whatever the reason, Spanish America preferred to import its wine, like most other things, including flour and olive oil; and native America continued to subsist on maize, flour from manihot roots (in Brazil), manioc and *pulque*. The colonists preferred the importing of wine to its propagation, while the shippers wanted the colonists' custom.

Europe and the Mediterranean became, in the last stages of the age of agriculture, a civilisation based as much on wine as on wheat. Like grain, wine could be, and in many instances had to be, traded. Christianity, with its emphasis on the sacramental part played by wine, emphasised its necessity. In other civilisations, men have been content to drink what has been locally available. No great trade has ever been necessary in pulque or rice wine – nor in the fermented water which served as an alcohol in many parts of India.

The days of the Renaissance also began another 'revolution' in food apart from the growth of spirits, vegetables and the potato. That was the beginning of a change in the physical way that people ate their food.

Most people in the age of agriculture in Europe carried a knife. Forks, on the other hand, with two prongs, like garden forks, had been used for hundreds of years only in kitchens. In Byzantium, it is true, small forks were employed at dinners from the tenth century. But they were not known in Italy till the sixteenth century, then being taken to France, it is said, by Catherine de' Medici on her marriage in 1533. They did not become popular, since they were expensive and difficult to make. Until the eighteenth century most people in Europe went on eating with their fingers and a knife. Then mass-produced forks became possible, like knives and indeed spoons, though those had always been common for serving soup. Men such as Matthew Boulton, whose other contributions to the Industrial Revolution in combination with Watt were so signal, made their original fortune in the manufacture of these small objects which are now taken for granted but which played so little part before 1750. Nor, before the eighteenth century, did many people have their own plates or drinking cups. People usually ate in pairs, one cover being enough to serve two. Poor diners in mediaeval Europe also often had, instead of a plate, a thick slice of stale unleavened bread, the 'trencher' of England's stout 'trenchermen'. It absorbed juice and might afterwards be eaten. By the eighteenth century a wooden plate with a circular depression in the middle became common enough and, by the early nineteenth, mass-produced 'china' followed: a vast benefit.

China, in this as in most things, had early been innovative and then conservative. Chopsticks were used there by at least 400 BC, and they thence spread to Japan. Nothing much changed afterwards. In the Americas people had nothing more than a knife. In Africa the majority did not have even that, before 1750. India had knives but escaped the chopstick, despite her use of rice.

5

The discovery of tobacco completed the New World's contribution to Europeans' sensuous pleasures. South American Indians had cultivated tobacco for many generations before 1492 – sometimes for use as in north-eastern Brazil 'in the form of a beverage and in certain ceremonies', sometimes, as in the Atlantic seaboard of Brazil and in Cuba, by smoking in a pipe. Tobacco existed in both Americas in pre-Columbian times, and in Cuba also, though not in a wild state. The first Europeans to observe the smoking of tobacco were Luis de Torres, a Jew who was an excellent linguist and used by Columbus on his first voyage as a possible interpreter, and a certain Rodrigo de Xerez, from Ayamonte. They made, as Columbus's diary explains, a little journey into Cuba and saw these 'dried plants put into a certain leaf, dried . . . to the shape of a squib made of paper . . . they light it at one end and, at the other, they suck, or chew, or draw in with their breath that smoke with which their flesh is benumbed and, so to speak, it intoxicates them, and in this way, they say they do not know fatigue. These squibs they call . . . *tabacos*.' As the Spaniards and Portuguese conquered more and more of the Americas they encountered more and more different varieties of tobacco; they took the seed home, cultivated it indifferently, smoked it, profanely as the American Indians thought, and in the end christened its best product a *cigarro*: because its shape and colouring resembled the large cricket – *cigarón* – that abounded in Andalucía. The Latin designation Nicotiana (hence nicotine) derives from Jean Nicot, the French ambassador to Portugal, who introduced the leaf to France.*

Tobacco was from the beginning made available in a variety of forms. But *cigarros* were made in Europe till the eighteenth century. The use of tobacco farmed in the New World continued to be in the form of a twist, sometimes sealed by molasses (sometimes molasses and seawater – a bad recipe).

The consequences for the growth of population of some of these developments seem tenuous. New foods, spirits, knives and forks, like the cult of love, may all be interpreted in different ways. One major occurrence of the sixteenth century, though, needs to be noticed because of the shadow that it caused to fall across the future demography of Africa and America and is continuously being reinterpreted. This was the beginning of that extraordinary movement of labour known as the slave trade.

Slavery had almost ceased in Europe by the fifteenth century, but it had done so nowhere else. The idea was revived in Europe, primarily for domestic use, by the Portuguese when they began their travels around the west coast of Africa in the 1440s. Between then and the end of the fifteenth century they established a flourishing trade. They made spectacularly successful use of Negro slaves on the previously uninhabited islands of São Tomé and

* Another explanation is that the early smokers of cigars used to do so after dinner in their orchard (*cigarral*) outside Toledo.

Principe in the Gulf of Guinea, which proved to be propitious for the growing of sugar. Sales to Spain began too. When the Spaniards founded plantations on which to grow sugar in the Canary Islands, they employed black slaves there as well as the unfortunate indigenous inhabitants, many of whom were shipped off elsewhere as slaves. Though some African slaves may have been kidnapped, most were sold by African chiefs, the slaves themselves being, as in antiquity, debtors, or prisoners captured in war, or criminals. The European interest stimulated trade in slaves from Guinea, a territory which was previously a place of subsistent farming and no large undertakings: though a major trans-Saharan slave trade to the Red Sea from West Africa had existed since the tenth century at least, for the benefit of Arabs.

Naturally, in the circumstances, Columbus, who had interests in the Canaries, took African slaves with him to the Americas, and by the end of the sixteenth century the traffic in Negro slaves to the Spanish colonies was a profitable enterprise. Perhaps 275,000 slaves had gone by then to the Americas. The slaves worked above all in the mills founded for the grinding and manufacture of sugar from cane. These horse-, oxen- or water-driven sugar mills were begun by the Spaniards in the first years of their occupation and by the Portuguese in Brazil soon after 1530.

This industrial use of slaves reinvigorated an institution which for some time had been built around domestic employment. Slave traffic, in the vile conditions which characterised all Atlantic crossings till the coming of steam, became more and more important, particularly when the French, British and Dutch colonists established themselves in the West Indies, alongside the Spaniards and Portuguese. About 340,000 slaves were carried to the Americas in the seventeenth century, six million in the eighteenth and two million in the nineteenth[16]. The production of sugar remained the biggest slave enterprise, for sugar demanded in its pre-mechanised days a very large number of slaves. The gold mines of Brazil, the coffee fields of Sainte Domingue, the tobacco plantations of Virginia and later those of cotton in the same place also depended on this labour force, carried at great expense and greater profit from West or South-West Africa, where the trade had become the most important commercial activity by the eighteenth century. Probably the colonists of what became the US played a modest part in these imports: 400,000 slaves in all were probably imported there, for the US black population of the present derives mostly from natural increase.

Black slaves existed for a time in Spanish America alongside indigenous Indian ones who were less manageable, strong and developed. The numbers of these Indian slaves were greater than is often realised. Both the Spaniards in the West Indies between 1510 and 1520, and the Portuguese in Brazil after 1540, used Indians in great quantities. Indeed, Queen Isabel I's order of 1503 that those designated as Caribs – 'cannibalistic and uncontrollable' – could be captured as slaves opened the way to the extinction of the native population of the Bahamas, Barbados and other small Caribbean islands. In Brazil the Indian slave trade continued for many generations. The *bandeirantes* of the sixteenth century went to great trouble, incurring many hardships, to steal souls from the remote interior on behalf of Portuguese settlers in São Paulo who were too poor to afford African slaves.

This revival of slavery by Europeans in the Americas was unexpected. By the fifteenth century only the Spaniards and Portuguese among Europeans had anything like a slave code still in existence. Some have suggested that slaves received better treatment in Spanish or Portuguese colonies in America than in the Protestant North. That case is hard to sustain: Spanish slave laws, like other laws of that nature and like so much other Spanish legislation, were indications of what might be hoped for, not what was done. Still, the comparatively small size of Spanish operations till the nineteenth century made conditions for slaves better in their colonies for many generations than they were in the huge plantations of the British and French West Indies. Spanish slaves, like Roman ones, could also buy their freedom. Domestic slaves throughout the Americas were in a privileged position and often gained their freedom in the end. In general in the Americas slaves were able to rely on better food than the free poor white, black or mulatto. It was chiefly these latter who, owing to a lack of vigour induced by undernourishment, fell a prey to anaemia, beriberi, worms and buboes.

Revolts of slaves in the West Indies often occurred. The small size of the islands, accompanied by the unmistakable colour of the slaves, prevented any being of consequence until the late eighteenth century. Then, the revolt in Sainte Domingue was successful. It ruined the French colony there. Out of the richest colony in the world, the rebels created the poorest republic. The result was to put the slave owners of the rest of the Americas on their watch. Revolts of slaves in North America were fewer. The consequence was ultimately to make the issue of the extension of slavery one of the causes of the worst war which the Americas have yet experienced; though the origins of the American Civil War were at the time not so clear as they subsequently have seemed. In Brazil, a successful slave revolt established something like a socialist community at the stockaded town of Palmares near Pernambuco which lasted seventy years before being crushed in 1697. In the Dutch East Indies where slavery also prospered slave revolts were endemic – above all in the plantations of Surinam, but in most other islands too.

The iniquity of the business of dealing in slaves has most impressed later historians. Iniquitous it was, and a contrast with standards of behaviour which had come to be accepted. It can hardly fail to cast a lurid light over the history of European business in the West Indies and over African monarchs who connived at it for so long.

Even so, however, the slave society of the Americas, including that of sugar plantations, did produce what Gilberto Freyre, the greatest student of 'tropical feudalism', spoke of as a 'union of cultures' in Brazil, even 'one of the most harmonious unions of culture with nature and of one culture with another than the lands of this hemisphere have ever known'[17]. The creation of modern Brazil was a great achievement. How was that carried through? Gilberto Freyre faced the question in *Casa Grande e Senzala* with conspicuous honesty: 'Only a method of colonisation based upon large scale property and upon slavery would have been capable of surmounting the enormous obstacles in the way of the European colonisation of Brazil'[18].

The effects of the slave trade on Africa need to be measured too. During the early years the African monarchs profited from the trade, and the weapons, cloth, metal and spirits which they obtained in exchange had the effect of increasing the wealth of the peoples concerned. Harsh and insensitive comment though it may seem, the loss of population – which might have been about 40,000 persons a year at most – was economically acceptable. The loss, if loss it was in an economic sense, was more than compensated for by the wealth that accrued to the Gulf of Guinea as a result of trade with Europe. Angola and East Africa did suffer as a result of their losses of population, since they were less populous. Guinea also suffered political consequences. Large kingdoms came to be established just inland from the coast – such as Ashanti and Dahomey – in the creation of which firearms played a critical part but which were as much the creations of the slave trade as were Jamaica or Barbados. Arab slave traders, meantime, continued to ply their commerce generations after the British abandoned it; indeed, there seems every reason to believe that the trade flourishes still.

Book Four

Our Times I:
Industrial Triumphs

From all these valuable presents which she had received from the gods, the woman was called Pandora, which intimates that she had received *every* necessary gift . . . Jupiter after this gave her a beautiful box which she was ordered to present to the man who married her . . . Epimetheus opened the box . . . there issued from it a multitude of evils and distempers which dispersed themselves all over the world and which, from that fatal moment, have never ceased to afflict the human race. Hope was the only one who remained at the bottom of the box. . .

Lemprière, *Classical Dictionary*

Since 1750, the world has been transformed by machines. Agriculture has benefited as much as manufacture. It requires an effort of imagination to realise that, in the lifetimes of the grandfathers of our grandfathers, the overwhelming majority of the world's population lived in the country. In the course of these two hundred years, new empires and new creeds have risen and fallen fast. Final solutions have everywhere turned out to be provisional. Words have taken on new meanings and then lost them. The complexity of problems has given support to absurd simplifications.

The age of industry began at the same time as Romanticism: Goethe's Romantic writings and Byron's life coincided with the start of the factory system, and the beginnings of 'mass culture' were not far behind. Yet, alongside the industrial achievement, the anonymous work of thousands of engineers and millions of labourers, we have known a cult of the individual, and of the individual achievement. Biography as a work of art has in modern industrial society overtaken fiction in popularity. Respect for the individual conscience as directed by God without the need for an intermediary in the form of a Church was an element in Puritanism which survived in modern Europe, via Holland and England. The great inventions of the eighteenth and nineteenth centuries were private masterpieces in many instances: but there were many ambiguities. Was individualism even in the nineteenth century too stern and too lonely a creed? Matthew Arnold believed that it had been so in the days of ancient Greece. The hellenic conception of human nature (spontaneity of conscience), he argued, in Culture and Anarchy, *was premature at that moment of man's development: 'the indispensable basis of conduct and self-control, the platform upon which alone the perfection aimed at by Greece can come to bloom was not to be achieved by our race so easily; centuries of probation and discipline were needed'. That is pessimistic; Keynes posed the problem thus: 'I think that capitalism wisely managed can probably be made more efficient for attaining economic ends than any alternative system yet in sight, but that in itself is in many ways extremely objectionable. Our problem is to work out a social organisation which shall be as efficient as possible without offending our notions of a satisfactory way of life.' Capitalism, since Keynes, has developed vigorously and humanely but it is still often its own worst enemy, it lacks morale and is outmanoeuvred in debate – which, in an age more conscious than ever of presentation, affects its morale.*

Most of the labour of the industrial countries admittedly remained, for many years after the coming of industrialisation, outside the factories. More people worked in trade, manufacturing and handicrafts in England than in agriculture in 1811 but that did not become true of Germany till about 1895, of the US about the same time, and of France and other European nations till after 1945. By that time, every year an increasing proportion of the labour force in rich countries was already working in service undertakings of one sort or another. The factory was the symbol of the new era. But it never employed more than a modest proportion of those who lived through it.

29

Cotton as King

The machine is a mission of redemption: to enable man to produce at a maximum with a minimum of effort . . . the only really new element in Western civilisation.

Artur Coelho, of Manaus (1880)

1

The essential characteristic of our times (the years since 1750) is the manufacture of goods for sale outside the neighbourhood concerned, in a factory, and by a machine. This development began in England in the eighteenth century. It was the equivalent of those agricultural innovations in the Near East of about 8000 BC. The critical innovation in the early history of agriculture was the realisation that crops could be made to grow again and again. The decisive innovation in the eighteenth century was a combination of four things: first, the mechanisation of the textile industry, causing a change in the clothing habits of the world, subsequently spreading to other industries; second, a series of organisational innovations, in particular the factory system; third, a series of inventions in power; and fourth, new commercial opportunities, relating both to the purchase of raw materials and to sales.

The technical changes in the textile industry were associated with cotton, rather than wool. Before the eighteenth century, cotton had nowhere been an important textile.

The substitution of machinery for individual manufacture was the fundamental change. Everything else which seems to characterise the industrial age had existed in the agricultural past: capitalism and long-distance commerce; the widespread use of money; the concentration of large numbers in a single place;* but the use of machinery meant mass production.

Mass production, in its turn, meant a new method of organisation of labour: the factory, the initiator of all modern things. It

* Elie Halévy's definition of the Industrial Revolution was 'the establishment of large factories in which all the motive power was supplied by a single mechanism installed in the centre of the factory and looked after by a large number of hands working under the supervision of one man''.

implied innovations in the use of energy, with steam taking the place of animal, wind or water power; and it resulted in innovations in transport, though, to begin with, those were confined to the construction of canals and the improvement of roads.

The least confusing way of explaining industrialisation is to indicate what occurred in respect of the English cotton industry.

In the seventeenth century the British and the Dutch East India companies began to import cotton calicoes and muslins from India on a scale sufficient to disturb wool merchants. Some Indian-manufactured cotton cloth had been imported into Europe since time immemorial, and there had been feeble attempts to copy it. In the sixteenth century the Venetians were selling raw cotton to Antwerp, and some Dutch cotton manufactures went to England. Still in 1700 nearly all the cotton goods sold in Europe came from India or elsewhere in the East: Manchester produced a poor imitation. The Dutch East India Company was still the largest importer and both it and its British competitor re-exported largely to Europe and the Americas. When, in 1721, Indian cotton goods were banned, on the insistence of the wool merchants disturbed by the 'Indian craze', an opportunity opened up in England, particularly when Liverpool, a developing port, growing rich on the slave trade, began to import raw cotton from the West Indies and Brazil.

The spinning of cotton needs a damp but stable climate. Lancashire could offer that. Manchester, forty miles inland, began to produce fustian (the old mixture of linen and cotton) and imitation Indian patterns using engraved plates. This industry began as a subsidiary of agriculture comparable to that of wool. Then the fustian masters began to buy raw cotton in bulk (the linen being in thread) and to 'put it out'. As a rule, these merchants were self-made men, with a weak system of guilds. The industry which they formed was more free of restrictions than was the wool one. It was, therefore, ready to take advantage of a number of changes in technology offered by several inspired, though in the main personally unfortunate, inventors.

It would have seemed improbable to the men and women of the eighteenth century in Europe, with their high powdered head-dressings and wigs, their hooped skirts, knee breeches and silk stockings, their coat tails and their négligés, that the transformation of society would be caused by a revolution in the manufacture of clothes; but so it was.

For centuries, water-driven or horse-drawn fulling stocks had thudded down on to wet cloth of all sorts, beating and thickening it. The 'finishing' stages of the preparation of the cloth had thus been 'mechanised' for a long time. But now the more complicated earlier stages were mechanised too.

Until the 1730s weaving had been done by throwing the shutttle through the alternate threads of the cotton. The weaver did that with one of his hands, and caught the shuttle with the other hand. In weaving broad pieces of cloth, two men were needed. They threw the shuttle back and forth to each other. The cross stitch (the 'weft', as opposed to the 'warp') was closed after each throw of the shuttle by a layer of wood extending across the piece of cloth being woven. In the early 1730s John Kay, the son of a wool merchant from Bury in Lancashire, added to this layer a grooved guiding board in which the shuttle could be thrown from side to side by a mechanical shuttle driver. This 'flying shuttle' needed only one hand, the other being available for closing the weft. The output of a single weaver was thereby doubled and the quality of the cloth improved. This enlightened device was rejected by the wool merchants. Kay was menaced by mobs who broke up his house and all within it, and he apparently died in poverty, unknown and unhonoured, in France. But his weaving machine began to be used by cotton manufacturers.

Spinning machines began also to be made. The first of them was patented in 1738 by John Wyatt and Lewis Paul, and built in London by Edward Cave, a printer from Rugby, using the power of the Turnmill Brook which flowed into the river Fleet. This machine seems not to have been used. The 'spinning jenny',* devised by James Hargreaves and patented in 1770, was the first mechanical spinner. This was a rectangular frame on four legs. At each end there was a row of vertical spindles. Between them the 'carded' cotton would be passed backwards and forwards. The thread could be drawn and twisted at the same time. A single workman could thus spin several threads. His productive power was multiplied by eight. The jenny was denounced by those who believed that such machines would cause unemployment. But, since the jenny needed no motor power, it seemed to be likely to revive, rather than bring an end to, cottage industry. Hargreaves, the inventor, was a carpenter and hand-loom worker from Standhill, near Blackburn in Lancashire. As with Kay, the inventor's house was sacked. The first jenny was burned and Hargreaves fled to Nottingham.

* The reason for the name is not known.

The decisive innovator in the cotton industry was Richard Arkwright, an organiser rather than an original inventor. First, he built a machine like Wyatt's and Paul's. Then, fleeing temporarily from the hostility shown to him and his machines by the workmen in Lancashire, he put several of them in a single workshop at Nottingham. He went next to Cromford near Derby. There he used water power to work the machines in another factory. This 'water frame', a machine in a stricter sense than the 'jenny', produced stronger thread than the most skilled spinner made. He could thus make pure cotton goods more easily, instead of the fustian mixture of his predecessors – the earliest spinning machines produced a thread which broke unless it were mixed with linen. Arkwright was later shown to be a pirate. 'His' spinning machine had apparently been devised by Thomas Highs, a mad inventor with no business capacity. But Arkwright only lost his patent. He still had his factories. He continued to build these in numerous places, sometimes in collaboration with others (for example, Strutt of Belper, or Peel of Bury) or a group of shareholders. He was also quick to use the steam engine after Watt's invention of it.

Arkwright's achievement was the factory, a social device which has dominated history ever since. For the complicated, delicate, expensive, largely wooden, hand-made and high-powered machinery which made the best, and most sought after, cloths could not be managed in cottages. So factories were built to employ first tens, then hundreds, of people, as often as not in hamlets or on hills outside old towns, leading to the establishment of new communities without previous history, which gradually themselves turned into great cities. Manchester between 1790 and 1800 seems, in the memoirs of Robert Owen, to be like a new colony into which a stream of adventurous, enterprising immigrants were pouring. There was, for a long time, an immense variety of systems working side by side. A fustian master might gather numerous hand-machines in his workshop; sometimes the plant and the raw material might be owned by different people, sometimes small spinning mills might receive cotton raw and send it back as yarn. Factories for a time competed with cottagers. Often, when a factory was built, it was in danger of being burnt or looted on the first industrial crisis, the manager having to withstand a siege and even spend days and nights under arms. Meantime, the import of printed cottons remained forbidden, hence giving protection (even if muslin, yarn, and undyed material continued to be brought in), while a bounty was given to all calicoes or muslins *exported* from England.

The concentration of labour in one place in a factory had occurred before: even in England in the sixteenth century Jack of Newbury employed 260 men, 100 women, 150 boys and girls together with fullers and dyers in Berkshire. In the early eighteenth century, something like the factory system was invented by pioneers of the English silk industry. About 1715 the son of a Norwich weaver, Sir Thomas Lombe, sent his brother John to learn how to throw silk at Livorno in Tuscany and, on his return, the two brothers set up silk-throwing machines on the Italian pattern on an island in the river Derwent, in a large building 500 feet long, five to six storeys high with nearly 500 windows. The machines were worked by a waterwheel from the Derwent. Their task was to give the threads a twist by a rapid rotary movement. The 300 workers had to reknot the threads. Later, there were larger silk factories in England. But the industry never did well, for the raw material was expensive, particularly after the King of Sardinia forbade the export of silk because of the competition of the then thriving Spanish, French and Italian silk industries.*

Concentration of labour on factory lines was also normal among slaves in the sugar plantations of the West Indies: indeed, the word 'factory' had, previous to the late eighteenth century, been used in English for an establishment for trade abroad such as that which traded slaves in West Africa. In the English dominions in 1750, slave-powered plantations were the largest units. Very often governments had, as in Rome, established arsenals, to make arms and armour, linen, wool, dye and even silk. Perhaps Rome was on the brink of achieving a modern factory system. Then, in seventeenth-century France, Colbert established several state factories. Some were run directly by the state. Others were undertaken by private people with state subsidies. Under Louis XIV these foretastes of twentieth-century practice produced two-thirds of the cloth of France. They were copied in Spain. At Guadalajara, a state factory for wool was set up; and there was one for tapestries at Madrid. The difference between those factories and those founded by Arkwright was that the former lived by subsidy,

---

* The best silk in Europe was then grown at Valencia, the Spanish government encouraging domestic producers by banning the import of raw silk and the business being organised on a 'putting out' basis. There were 5,000 looms in Valencia in 1787.

and bureaucratic direction. The same was the case with the textile plants set up in Italy in the eighteenth century. In all those places, at those times, the genuine merchant, who did not have a subsidy, operated by 'putting out' the material, which in turn was worked for a wage by an artisan.

The factory's main feature is that all the processes of manufacture are concentrated in a single plant. The larger the factory, the more economic the enterprise and the larger the machine. The machines are specialised and driven by non-human power. The workers are supervised by skilled management, for stipulated wages and fixed hours (not piece work), and the production is for the general market.

The size of the early factories seemed at the time the largest innovation in comparison with past practice. Thus Matthew Boulton (whom Boswell named an 'Iron Captain in the middle of his troops') in the 1770s employed about 700 to 800 workers in his factory at Soho for the manufacture of everything metallic from steam engines to nails and screws. Josiah Wedgwood had several hundreds, making 'china', at his splendid works, 'Etruria', near Hanley in Staffordshire. This compared with, say, 500 employed on the largest sugar plantation in the West Indies, in about 1770 (in the French colony of Sainte Domingue). But there was no immediate growth in the size of factories. In the 1830s English flax mills employed an average of nine persons per plant; silk mills, twenty-five; wool factories, forty-five; and even cotton mills, only 175. The average coal mine in Britain then employed about fifty people above and below ground. The exceptions to this modest scale of operation were principally ironworks, of which the biggest, Richard Crawshay's ironworks at Cyfarthfa, outside Merthyr in Wales, employed 2,000 during the Napoleonic Wars. Shipbuilders also employed many people. The average shipbuilding yard occupied 570 men, more than any other enterprise. But of 8,500 factories using steam or other types of new power in London in 1898, the average number of workers was still only forty-one. The average size even of US factories was only forty-two in 1929. In Germany, proportions were even smaller – twelve per manufacturing business in 1910, while in 1848 most French workers worked in firms of only five people.

The earliest factories have become known as 'dark satanic mills' because of William Blake's eloquent hostility to them. Unpleasant though some were, beneficial changes were introduced from the beginning. Lighting, ventilation, schemes for the absorption of shocks, improved places for eating or resting, medical advice and increased safety were started by a few high-minded employers and their example was insisted upon by inspectors. The subsequent substitution of electricity for steam in so many undertakings later also caused beneficial changes. Many laws began to protect employees against processes likely to be a danger to health. Reading aloud and, latterly, music (and in some countries, patriotic exhortations) varied the monotony.* But the enforcement of such rules was imperfect. Work in factories also became less interesting. In the 1870s factories began to be equipped with overhead conveyor belts. The meat-packing houses of Chicago showed the way. The mass assembly line designed for the Chicago mail order plant of Sears Roebuck in the 1880s was another step towards full mechanisation. The process was then brought to a logical conclusion in 1910 by Henry Ford (who studied Sears Roebuck's innovation) when he set up a plant at Highland Park, near Detroit, for the manufacture of the Model T car, the first motorcar within the financial reach of ordinary workers. Finally, there came in the 1920s the fully automatic assembly line whereby the worker, no longer condemned to repeat his movements endlessly, supervised an intricate process which functioned, and had to function, like a watch, accurate to the split second.

A second development in the history of the factory has been the increasing scale and scope of the company which operates it. This has had three dimensions: economics of scale; stability made possible thereby in prices; and a means of standardising different items. Industrial enterprises operating over a wide market – and, since 1945, over several nations – began to spread. This process was started on a major scale by J. D. Rockefeller's Standard Oil Company (1870). Legislation began to benefit large firms in most industrial states. There soon came not only 'horizontal' but 'vertical' combinations, which drew successive stages of an industry into a single organisation. The US Steel Corporation, for example, brought under one management the sources of ore, mines, furnaces and ships for the carriage of ore.

The personal consequences of these changes were summed up in 1863 by a man working in Chubb's factory for locks in London: 'I was a master locksmith for twenty-two years . . . but we all work in large shops now.' Men who had been master craftsmen in minor trades became, as a result of factories, overseers in large

* After the 1920s, the radio.

establishments. Factories also took away the rural base from the worker, who was cut off, therefore, from an auxiliary source of food and the sense of independence which comes from even the smallest holding[2]. Further, the earliest factories had the effect of dividing workers into two classes: the skilled men who needed to understand the machinery; and those who performed the purely 'mechanical' tasks which could be carried out by the unskilled, whether male, female or child.

Specialisation, with its benefits and miseries, is not however a new problem: Xenophon in the fourth century BC wrote: 'In small towns, the same man makes couches, doors, ploughs, tables, and often he even builds houses . . . In large cities, one man makes shoes for men, another for women, there are even places where one man earns a living by just mending shoes, another by cutting them out[3].

Most inventions were obstructed at the beginning by protests over unemployment. The uproar caused by the work of Kay and Hargreaves has been observed. There are other instances, and earlier ones. Thus the practice of knitting had been known among the Arabs for hundreds of years and was undertaken as a domestic art in Europe during the Middle Ages, as it is now. In 1589, William Lee, curate of Calverton, Nottinghamshire, invented a machine for knitting socks and stockings.* He was discouraged from pursuing that by the Crown and poor Lee (like Kay later) had to take refuge in Paris (where he died of grief) for fear of armed rioters outside his house. Similarly, a ribbon loom, devised in Danzig in the sixteenth century, reached London by 1616. But its use was also delayed by rioters. The stocking frame was, nevertheless, beginning to displace knitting by hand by the late seventeenth century. Knitting was already an 'industry', the frame being as a rule 'rented' by the worker who used it at home, the 'rent' being deducted from his wages. The clash between innovators and suspicious labour continued.

In 1811 Nottingham was near to insurrection because of the organisation of well-disciplined breakers of stocking frames.[4] Byron made his maiden speech in the House of Lords in support of the frame-breakers near his estate in February 1812. That year, Yorkshire was said to have been reduced to an 'insurrectional state' by rioters 'the chief of whom, be he whomsoever he may,

---

* It is said that he devised the frame because a girl to whom he was paying court devoted more attention to her knitting than to him.

is styled General Ludd' whose mission was to break looms. One manufacturer, a certain Horsfall, was actually murdered at Huddersfield by rioters that year. About 12,000 troops were posted in the 'disturbed counties'.

Doubtless if the governments of the early industrial age had wished, or been forced, to please the workers, the factory movement and the Industrial Revolution would have been brought to an end. Even an enlightened despot would have agreed with Diocletian: when an engineer offered to design a machine to raise the columns of a temple, the Emperor refused, saying, 'Let me rather feed the common folk'[5]. The Emperor could not conceive that the population might be better fed than through back-breaking work. Equally, even Montesquieu, one of the cleverest men in the eighteenth century, went so far as to criticise watermills for 'depriving labourers of their work'. When Jacquard invented a power loom in France in 1803, Napoleon sent for him from Paris. He was in doubt as to whether he was going to be rewarded, or arrested[6]. Adam Smith, however, argued that mechanisation spelled no danger and that those displaced would find other jobs. That has proved to be true. By and large, and making every allowance for short-term and local unhappiness, as well as the fact that the history of unemployment is ill chronicled, the active or employed population of rich countries such as those in Europe, though not always fully employed, is far larger than it was in the days of those who rioted against Robert Peel's cotton printing factory in the 1770s.

Employed Population of Europe
(1980 frontiers)

	1770s	1980s
France	13,000,000	20,904,000 (1979)
West Germany	8,700,000	25,848,000 (1978)
Britain	5,500,000	21,906,000 (June 1980)
Italy	8,700,000	20,515,000 (April 1980)

To carry through these changes, men of the determination of Arkwright were needed. The founders of factories were almost always men of humble origin since, Halévy wrote, 'a man who was not of the common people would not have had the energy – brutality if you prefer it – to triumph over the local population to the execution of his designs'[7].

A few more technical innovations completed the picture as it was left by Arkwright: first, a combination of the spinning jenny and Arkwright's water frame, the 'mule' devised about 1779 by Samuel Crompton, a violinist at the Bolton Theatre. It gave a thread as tough as Arkwright's but as fine as that of the jenny. Crompton, an independent and philanthropic man of courage, prospered no better than most other inventors, though his machine was soon used in hundreds of English factories. There were thereafter few major developments in spinning. Weaving, however, was a different matter. A great change there was brought about by Edmund Cartwright's power loom, a device distantly related to the old ribbon looms of France and of Danzig. Cartwright, a country vicar and scholar, placed a bet that he could produce a weaving machine to make rapid use of the new quantity of thread now available as a result of the spinning machines. He was successful and set up a factory at Doncaster with a steam engine in 1789. Though he was a bad manager, his invention was successful. It was soon realised that two steam-powered looms tended by an unskilled man were three times as productive as one old one looked after by a skilled man.

Other improvements in the textile industry included a copper cylinder with a revolving press, which would make a pattern automatically (1783); and Claude Berthollet's discovery in France in 1784 of the bleaching capacity of chlorine – a device taken up at the St Rollox factory founded by Charles Tennant, a bleacher of Glasgow. The ancient sight of great quantities of stuffs spread out in the open air to be bleached by the sun, which had previously marked weaving villages, vanished.

By the end of the Napoleonic Wars, all stages of the manufacture of textiles could be carried out by machine – shearing the nap off cloth with revolving knives, printing the calico with revolving rollers, pressing and even packing. Watermills were beginning to give way to steam engines. The first steam-powered loom in Manchester dated from 1806. Horse-driven machinery in the cotton industry had vanished by 1830. Hand spinning was dead in England by then, though the steam-powered looms for weaving employed only about 20,000 to 30,000 people. Looms were still worked by hand by half a million outworkers in the 1820s, who often clung to poor conditions with determination. Meantime, both spinners and weavers in England became used to 'striking' for higher wages and were drawn into the political turbulence of the years immediately after the Napoleonic Wars.

Long before then the world's cotton economy had itself been transformed. Until the late eighteenth century most raw cotton came to Europe from the West Indies or the Levant. In 1786, Sea Island or long staple cotton was introduced to the US, but it could only be grown well near the sea[8]. In 1793, Eli Whitney, a farmer's son from Massachusetts, invented the cotton gin in Georgia: a fan and brush, which shook the seeds from the cotton boll so successfully that even short staple cotton (the old Eastern type, which could be grown inland in the USA) repaid cultivation. This transformed the economy of the US South. Slavery had been in decline there, as elsewhere in the US. Now the number of slaves fell short of demand. Cotton became the South's main export. A single cotton gin could clean 300 pounds of cotton a day, instead of the one pound (of short staple cotton) which had been done by a man by hand. The demand for raw cotton (soon in US cotton mills as well as in Europe) was soon great. Eli Whitney enabled it to be satisfied. By 1860, cotton produced in the US had risen from 1½ million pounds a year in 1790 to 2,300 million pounds. The US plantations were producing five-sixths of the world's cotton, of which Britain was using 1,000 million pounds, the European continent 700 million and the US 350 million. The cost of a slave in the prime of life (a prime field hand) had risen from $250 in 1815 to nearly $2,000 in 1860, while in 1860 there were four million slaves in the US in place of 700,000 in 1790. Nor was production of cotton confined to the New World: one event indicating a reawakening of Islam was the revival of the cultivation of cotton in Egypt under Muhammad Ali.

The availability of this easily worked and cheap raw material completed the transformation of clothing. The West Indies had played, by the production of sugar and coffee, a considerable part in the economy of the eighteenth century. Sugar (and slaves) had assisted the accumulation of capital. But cotton provided the first occasion when a pastoral country made, at the same time, a substantial contribution to Europe's industries and also began to transform its own economy thereby.

In those days, cotton manufacturers represented half of Britain's exports – the largest such export from 1814 till 1938. In the mid nineteenth century English cotton mills employed between 200,000 and 250,000 people, while a force of the same number was employed at hand looms. Probably a majority of the total was made up by women and girls. Most mills were still small, employing 150 to 200. Most English cotton workers, hand or factory workers, lived in Lancashire (312,000 out of 527,000 in 1851). US manufacturing was never far behind Britain's. In 1800 there were eight US cotton mills; in 1810, 269; in 1860, 1,091, employing 122,028. But a sense of proportion is needed. In this critical trade of the nineteenth century there were still, in 1830, some fifty per cent fewer people engaged than there were as servants.

The raw material for this industry continued to be grown (as opposed to being cleaned) by primitive methods. The cultivators of the US South used few fertilisers, had little idea of rotation of crops and employed slaves (who were employed all the year). This system needed unlimited quantities of land: hence the steady movement westwards of cotton culture. The numbers of slaves grew: from 700,000 in 1790, the US had nearly four million in 1860, mostly by natural increase, with perhaps some stimulated breeding, and a few imports, mostly from Cuba.

The manufacture of cotton goods by machine was no longer an Anglo-Saxon preserve. Alsace, and Mulhouse in particular, had become as important to France as Lancashire was to England. The first steam engine was established in France for spinning cotton in 1812. By 1860 the hand loom had vanished more completely in Mulhouse than it had in Lancashire (though other parts of France retained it for many years, especially Rouen and Lille). A cotton industry also began in Catalonia. There, there was the advantage both of raw cotton imported from the West Indies and of the South American market. There, as in England, cotton merchants were not organised in guilds. There, too, there had been a helpful ban on the import of Asian cloths (1718). The government also encouraged cotton manufacture through tax concessions. By the 1790s there were in Catalonia over 100 cotton factories, employing 80,000 workers (mostly women, as usual), with 3,000 looms. At least fourteen spinning machines had been imported, from England. No French city had a comparable cotton industry. Equally, there was no comparable industry to that of the cotton one of Catalonia in Spain. It was in this industry that, after years of ruin, brought about by the Napoleonic Wars (and the failure to re-equip afterwards), labour unrest first occurred in Spain; but the Catalan textile mills continued to provide till the twentieth century the biggest industry in Spain.

Wool (much less linen) did not share in all these changes. Till the late eighteenth century, wool was in England a local industry, concentrated in Yorkshire. There was a long fight by the half-organised labour movements of the day against factories. In 1803 only one-sixth of the cloth woven in the West Riding was produced in large factories such as that run by Benjamin Gott, a Yorkshire spinner, who sought to introduce into the worsted wool trade the mechanical changes which had transformed the cotton industry. But with woollen cloths other than worsted, the thread was, for a long time, too fragile to allow a shuttle to move faster than it could in a hand loom. It was only when the power loom was at a more advanced stage that it was widely used. That coincided with a great increase in the world's wool production – above all, after 1830, in Australia whose inland plains were scarcely fit for anything other than sheep at that time. Among silk weavers, on the other hand, power was even used in cottage industries; for example, in Coventry.

The first stage of the Industrial Revolution, characterised by cotton and other articles of clothing, was completed by events in the US. At the Great Exhibition in London in 1851 much attention was paid to the new US mechanical reaper, made by McCormick,* a tardy reminder that mechanisation could affect agriculture as much as anything else. But the sewing machine was also shown in 1851, having been devised the previous year by Isaac Singer, an inventor from New York, ready to become both the pioneer of hire purchase and 'the real hero of the American Civil War', when the demand for uniforms and boots would give a great opportunity to machine-stitching. Machinery had also begun to affect shoe-making. Factory-made shoes – an English factory, Clark's – began to be used in the 1820s in Brazil. Though a machine for sewing soles was only introduced into America in the last year of the Civil War, 1864, the mechanisation of leather-made shoes was soon driving out wooden clogs and bare feet from the floors of the richer world. Modern man could, in the 1870s, first in the USA, then in Europe and then slowly in Latin America, dress himself from head to toe in cheap, manufactured goods. Could people have lived in the modern city without the machine-made shoe? It is hard to believe. Thus, just when the Russian nihilist Pisarev was telling his readers that a pair of boots was more important than the plays of Shakespeare, their price began to fall. Within a few years, machine-made footwear came within the reach

---

* See below, page 420.

even of Russians; and boots play a great part in the books of later Russian novelists.

The wars of 1861–64 in the US and of 1864, 1866 and 1870–71 in Europe spelled the end of the age of cotton. The first of those wars was inspired by the spread of slavery on the cotton fields. The last of them ruined the French cotton industry, for the time being at least, since the country lost Alsace, including Mulhouse. During the war of 1864 in Holstein, Britain's inaction in the face of German determination had convinced Bismarck that Britain was irremediably pacific and would pose no difficulties. Cotton admittedly continued to be of importance. The US recovered her cotton industry, developed new steam gins and used cotton seeds for oil and fertilisers, while a new loom caused the machine to stop automatically should the thread break (a single weaver could now attend eighty-four looms in place of eight). Until 1945 cotton was still the largest item of US merchandise. But capital invested in cotton in the US after the Civil War was always less than it was in iron and steel and, particularly, food products. Similarly in France, though cotton recovered after the loss of Alsace (many cotton families moving away from there), those who controlled the cotton trade came, in Theodore Zeldin's words, 'to be the archetype of the conservative family business'[9], with their sung graces before Sunday lunch, secrecy, prudent economy, hard work and self-reliance.

As for England, the cotton trade declined slowly after 1880, rapidly after 1918, leaving Lancashire a shadow of its past splendour. British firms were still building new factories with old mule spinners in 1913, but Germany and even Austria had introduced ring spinning. After 1945 the number of cotton spindles and the output of cotton yarn produced in England fell below that of most large continental European countries. Russia, which in the 1930s produced less cotton goods than Britain, produced ten times Britain's output in the 1970s, and produced more raw cotton even than the US. In the 1980s cotton no longer seems to play such a decisive part. Though some cotton goods have had revivals, for example jeans,* much of the increased population of the world dresses itself in artificial textiles made from oil or pine trees. 'King Cotton' has gone the way of most other European monarchies.

---

* The word derives from Gênes, the French for Genoa, where twilled cotton of this sort was traded.

30
How Long Did They Work?

'It's fine talking about having supper when there's a coffin promised
to be ready at Brox'on by seven o'clock tomorrow morning and
ought to ha'been there now and not a nail struck yet. . .'

George Eliot, *Adam Bede*

Factories and mechanisation from the beginning cut the hours of
work of most people. In the age of agriculture, most people
worked as hard as they could, from dawn to dusk and from
childhood to old age. That is the same with most agricultural
enterprises of the twentieth century. Whether a rural wage earner
of 1914, or even 1980, did less work than those who worked on
the land before 1750 is difficult to say. Mechanisation has lightened work in agriculture,* but many agricultural workers work
alone. So the work may be heavier and more boring than it used
to be. A day's management of a combine harvester can scarcely
be lighter work than a day's harvesting was on the same estate in
1750.

Still, in 1750 there were few prescribed hours of work anywhere,
in any profession. In cottage industries, many women and children
in summer worked a twelve-hour day. In winter, they may have
worked eight. Many children began to work at the age of five. In
Venice a ban on child labour in dangerous trades was introduced
in the Middle Ages, and in England a statute of 1563 provided
that all craftsmen and labourers should, if hired by the day, between March and September, be at work by five a.m. and go on
till eight p.m. save for half an hour's 'dinner', sleep of one hour
and drinking of half an hour. This twelve-and-a-half-hour day was
to be five days a week. Such statutes were introduced as much to
exhort the workers to work as to prevent their exploitation. The
over-use of child labour was denounced in 1579 at Amsterdam; it
was alleged that some employers 'often took in two, four, six or
more working class children on the pretext of charitably providing
for them . . . whereas they treated them more like slaves than
apprentices'. Thus when the era of the factory began, no one

* Mechanisation of agriculture is discussed in Chapter 38, below.

thought that anyone's hours would be altered: whether the factories increased any hours or lowered the age when children began to work is doubtful[1].* 'To request my people may be at work as soon as it is light, work till it is dark, and be diligent while they are at it can hardly be necessary,' reflected George Washington, in, of course, a rural setting, adding 'the presumption is that every labourer does as much in 24 hours as his health . . . will allow'[3].

This applied at first to the men, women and children who went into factories – willingly since they might have starved, as they had done in the remote past. The new industries were a godsend to overseers of parishes who increasingly had had their work cut out to find work for children made destitute by the rise in population. In innumerable English cotton factories, boys were taken in return for their keep, though after 1784 magistrates forbade parishes to place children in factories where there was work at night, and philanthropic manufacturers such as David Dale built good housing for their workers (such as the famous model village of New Lanark of which Robert Owen, Dale's son-in-law, became manager in 1797). The work of women and children, meantime, was specially sought in the Industrial Revolution because they could now do work which in the past was performed by men; spinning is easily learned and no strength is needed. Indeed, children were prized because their touch was delicate.

The invention of gas by William Murdock, Matthew Boulton's foreman at Soho, at the end of the eighteenth century altered the complexion of things. It meant that the factories could be lit at night. Workers could be made to work long hours even in winter. The consequence was immediately to bring limitations of hours and conditions of work. As a result of the activity of Mancunian philanthropists, in 1802 Sir Robert Peel, a rich cotton millowner of Bury and associate of Arkwright's who was also a member of Parliament, introduced a Bill which insisted on new standards for those children in factories for which the state had accepted responsibility. Working hours for children under fourteen years were not to exceed twelve. Sexes were to be separated. One free suit was to be provided yearly by the state in maintained factories. Every such factory was to be whitewashed twice a year. There were only to be two children to a bed. Education, the learning of the three Rs, and religious education once a week, was made

---

* John Locke, writing in 1697, said that children of the poor should work for some part of the day when they got to the age of three[2].

obligatory. This law established also the principle of the inspection of factories.

On the whole, since Britain lived under a state of law, those modest rules slowly began to be carried out. But clearly magistrates did often neglect their duty to guarantee the law; annually elected overseers sometimes had neither desire nor capacity to carry it out. Further, to begin with, the large mills of Manchester did not use labour provided for by the workhouses: ordinary child labour was available. Later modifications followed.

Thus an Act of 1819 banned all children under nine from working at a cotton mill. In 1849, in a typical factory in Britain or America, work averaged twelve hours fifteen minutes a day for six days a week -- that is, a working week of 73½ hours. The following year a new Factory Act in Britain limited the working week to 60 hours for women. From then on a half holiday on Saturday was normal (though Lloyd's underwriters would remain open on Saturday afternoons till 1854). In the meantime, a campaign for a ten-hour day began in the US. A limit to that level for workers in all state establishments had been imposed by President van Buren in 1840. A ten-hour day was considered a maximum for all women by a law of 1869, and for everyone under the age of eighteen. In the 1860s most workers in the US were working about 63 hours a week, or slightly over ten hours for six days a week. That figure had fallen to nine by 1915. In the USA eighteen per cent of all children in the country were still employed between 1890 and 1910 -- unlike even Russia, where the employment of children under twelve had been formally banned from factories in 1882. French and German workers were then working ten hours a day as a rule. In Russia a legal maximum day of 11½ hours for all, regardless of age or sex, was introduced in 1897. Ten hours for nightwork was also the Russian limit. In England the working week had been cut to 56½ hours for textile workers in 1874, and in 1900 the country probably averaged a little over 54 hours. Under pressure from unions, an eight-hour day was agreed for Britain's miners in 1909: the first legal restriction on the working day which applied to all workers rather than specifically to women and children. But shops in England were then open seventy-four or even eighty hours a week -- a source of drudgery for children (as was both domestic service and the use of errand boys). By 1914 children under fourteen in most industrial countries had been withdrawn from the factory in order to go to school, though children over twelve were still found 'half time' in English factories till 1914, that is, thirty-three hours a week: the rest of the time they went to school.

After the First World War the industrialised countries moved towards a day of eight hours work or a week of forty hours (achieved in the US by 1938, with half days on Saturdays) and also towards a world in which children under fourteen were never really employed. Agricultural workers began to demand such conditions also. The only people who stood out were the resilient merchants, along with scholars, soldiers, doctors and politicians – though such a comment ignores the great army of those who, in all industrial countries, now work many hours for payments in cash after official hours in order to avoid income tax, a menace which only began to affect ordinary people after 1945. Whether those secret hours of 'moonlighting' point the way to a new pattern of employment seems uncertain. It is possible. But at all events, less work is done in the twentieth century in rich countries than ever before. (Both entertainment and education have, as a result, given rise to large industries of their own.) In the nineteenth century most people worked at least 3,500 hours a year (the German figure for 1877 was 3,300). In the 1970s, most people in the industrialised countries had (including the Soviet Union) an official working year of about 1,800 hours. The majority of people in the US or Western Europe thus do less work now in their seventy years of life than their ancestors did in their forty or fifty years. In a single week nowadays the average worker has nearly twice as many hours of 'leisure' (seventy-two hours) as he has of work (forty hours) not to speak of fifty-six hours' sleep. These relaxed hours have not, however, yet arrived in dictatorships; in early 1981 the Polish trade union movement Solidarity were still demanding a week of forty hours and risking even a world crisis thereby.

Most advanced countries would profit by having longer working hours. The proof of this lies in what happened in France between 1936 and 1939. In 1936 a forty-hour week was introduced. Industrial output fell, unemployment and inflation increased and purchasing power was cut. In 1938 the hours of the working week were increased by the abandonment of regulations curtailing them. The number of unemployed dropped. Production rose fifteen per cent, exports seventeen per cent and the increase in prices slowed down. The lesson implicit, wrote the French sociologist Alfred Sauvy, should be taught to students of political economy as the battles of Austerlitz and Tannenberg are taught at military academies[4]. It never has been.

The preceding chapter may read as if it is being suggested that the 'dark satanic mills' of the industrial age were oases of 'sweetness and light'. That is *not* its point. But it is suggested that the evil conditions castigated by, for example, Mrs Gaskell, in her novels or by Dickens in his, affected only a minority of the employed population. It is wrong to found any general theory of human behaviour on the basis of evidence collected in Manchester in the 1840s. Furthermore, in deploring the conditions in which cotton workers lived, we should not forget the cloth which they produced and which served to keep millions clean and warm.

31

The Power of Steam

Pasha: '. . . whirr! whirr! all by wheels! – whiz! whiz! all by steam!'
Traveller (to the Dragoman): 'What does the Pasha mean by whizz-
ing? He does not mean to say, does he, that our government will
ever abandon their pledges to the Sultan?'
Dragoman: 'No, your excellency, but he says the English talk by
wheels and steam.'

Kinglake, *Eothen* (1844)

1

The machine age has depended on an intensified use of irreplaceable energy (coal, lignite, gas, oil) instead of (as until then) inexhaustible replaceable sources (wind, water, wood, animal or man
power).

Industrialisation began with old sources of energy. The first
factories of England, including Arkwright's mills at Cromford,
Wedgwood's factory at Etruria, Lombe's silk factory on the Derwent, all used water power. As late as 1848, France had 22,500
watermills in use (17,300 for corn) and only 5,200 steam engines.
The first US factories were also powered by water. Seventeenth-
century Holland, then the most industrially advanced region, was
run by wind. In addition, an increase in the numbers of horses
and oxen (Europe had 14 million horses and 24 million oxen about
1789) had also recently improved Europe's resources of animal
energy[1].

Still, the use of steam soon gave the factory a new dimension.
Anaxagoras (a mentor of Socrates and Pericles) who died in
428 BC had shown that water can only enter a vessel when the air
goes out of it. Hero's *Pneumatica* showed that the expansive force
of steam was known in the first century BC. But nothing was done
to make use of it for 2,000 years. Did the brilliant Gerbert (later
Pope Sylvester II) build a steam organ in AD 1000, as suggested
by William of Malmesbury? Probably not. Still, some steam-powered sprayers existed in the thirteenth century. Leonardo sketched
steam-powered bellows and cannon. In his day some experiments
were also carried out to try to turn a spit by steam.

The power of atmospheric pressure was only fully realised during the seventeenth century, when Denis Papin, in Holland, was

320

able to write, about 1690: 'Since it is a property of water that a small quantity of it turned into vapour by air has an elastic force like that of air . . . I concluded that machines could be constructed wherein water, by the help of no very intense heat, and at little cost, could produce that perfect vacuum.' Not long after, Captain Thomas Savery of Devonshire, an army officer, devised a pump powered by atmospheric pressure to get rid of water which had flooded copper mines. A blacksmith of Dartmouth, Thomas Newcomen, had the same idea for a more developed 'atmospheric machine' first used in 1712 at a colliery at Dudley Castle. It lifted ten gallons of water 153 feet in a minute. It was much sought after, and two such machines were built per year for two-thirds of a century, many being exported. One Newcomen machine worked continuously from 1750 to 1900 at Bristol.

The efficiency of these and other comparable mechanisms was limited by the impossibility of boring accurate cylinders, such as were needed for good pumps. Thus the growth of precision proved to be as great a development as any other of the late eighteenth century.

James Watt, the son of the borough treasurer of the Glaswegian suburb of Greenock, was the father of the most famous device of the early Industrial Revolution, the steam engine proper. He first learned French, German and Italian, in order to be aware of all the contemporary developments in his subject. Watt reached the conclusion that the reason for the weaknesses of the Newcomen engine was that the cylinder was allowed to cool between each stroke. About 1765 he suggested two improvements; the chamber in which the steam was condensed should become a separate vessel different from the cylinder; and the steam should act on a piston, not by atmospheric pressure. This last idea came to him suddenly, as if by intuition, on Glasgow Green, during a Sunday walk; since steam was an elastic body, it would rush into a vacuum and, 'if a communication were made between the cylinder and an exhausted vessel, it would rush into it and might there be condensed without cooling the cylinder'[2].

During the next few years Watt was busy completing a machine embodying this idea. His difficulties were both technological and financial: first, he had to bore an accurate cylinder to avoid any escape at all between its wall and the piston. Only millwrights were skilled engineers at that time. Watt consulted the prince of those, John Wilkinson, whose new boring mill (designed for cannon) could serve his purpose. Watt's financial problems, on the

other hand, were first helped by John Roebuck, who wanted
pumps for his coal mines. Roebuck thus set up the steam engine
at Kinneil House, Edinburgh. Unfortunately, Roebuck went
bankrupt. Matthew Boulton, the pioneer of accurate workman-
ship, of Soho, Birmingham, was willing to take Roebuck's place.
Boulton, who already employed 600 workmen, was renowned as
a manufacturer of buttons, knives, watch chains and shoe buckles.

By 1775 Wilkinson had ordered one of Watt's machines to blow
his furnaces. In 1777 Périer Frères ordered one for the water
supply in Paris. In the 1780s Watt's machines had begun to be
commercially profitable. Many ironmasters began to use them.
Brewers followed, and then manufacturers of china. A steam
engine was used experimentally in Cuba for sugar manufacture in
1797. The steam-powered Albion flour mills in London became
a great sight from 1785, and the same year a steam-powered
cotton spinning mill was set up at Papplewick. The German statesman Stein went to England in 1787 to take back a steam engine
to Prussia, and Catalonia had one by 1790.

Boulton and Watt built 496 machines, of which 164 supplemented the work of Newcomen engines as pumps in coal mines,
24 were used as blast furnaces and 308 were used as machines.
Steam was by then on its way to freeing industry from the shackles
of geography. Unlike water power, it did not depend specifically
on valleys.

The Napoleonic Wars for a time interrupted all commerce. In
1815, even in England, the steam engine was confined to the wool
and cotton industries and a few blast furnaces. But, afterwards,
trade in these machines revived. Watt's patent had run out in 1800
and the technical difficulties of making accurate and, therefore,
safe machines were beginning to be overcome. Watt thought that
a further refinement, the high-pressure steam engine, would prove
too dangerous. But that was patented in 1802 simultaneously by
Richard Trevithick in Coalbrookdale (Shropshire) and Oliver
Evans, in Delaware in the US. This engine, with a cast-iron boiler
1½ inches thick, developed steam pressure of 145 pounds per
square inch (ten times the pressure of the atmosphere). It allowed
Trevithick in 1804 to build the first steam locomotive. Oliver
Evans drove an amphibious steam boat in 1804. Regular trips
were possible by steam along inland waterways in the US from
1807 onwards.

After Waterloo steam began to affect all forms of machinery.
The first packet boat from Dover to Calais ran regularly from

1821; the railway engine after 1829; the ocean-going steamboat after 1850 (the delay there was caused by inadequate knowledge of how to carry sufficient coal); and there was also soon the steam reaper.* *The Times* in London was printed by steam from 1814. Cuba had fifty-five steam engines by 1860, making it the largest exporter of sugar and the richest colony that the world had seen, though it was still attached to a then rather poor metropolis. A 'milling machine to grind cane' was imported by Englishmen to Brazil in 1819. Both there and in Cuba the new machines transformed the need for slaves.

There were no further major innovations in the world of steam till the turbine (a kind of steam windmill) was created to drive a dynamo at a speed which the by then old steam engine could not attain. Charles Parsons, one of the few engineers to be the son of a nobleman, took out a patent for that in 1884. The same year the turbo-generator came into being. It became established as the main motor for the growing electrical industry, and after 1894 for large ships. By 1910 both British passenger liners and ships of the navy were using these elaborations.

2

An important contribution to industrialisation was made by the then old profession, already noticed in passing, of clockmakers and scientific instrument makers. They used accurate screw-cutters, dividing machines and lathes. Such machinery was, of course, made by hand until the nineteenth century, as were the essential parts of steam engines. In 1764 John Harrison made a watch-sized timepiece which determined longitude to an accuracy of half a degree and enabled more accurate sailing – of great benefit to explorers. That stimulated the craft of watchmaking in England. The fifty cylinders made in 1776 by John Wilkinson at his works in Denbigh for Matthew Boulton, to use in his steam engines, did 'not err the thickness of an old shilling' in any part[3]. That accuracy was an essential contribution to the success of steam engines and of subsequent machines.

3

These changes took time to make an effect. In 1824 an English parliamentary committee of enquiry on monopoly asked: 'A great many manufacturers make their own machinery?' 'They do,' was

* See below, page 420.

the reply from a Lancashire manufacturer[4]. Most machinery was still wooden, fitted with metal tips like the iron parts of a plough. The spinning jenny and flying shuttle were made by craftsmen living at home. But soon machines began to be made by manufacturers and put up for sale. Once precision was achieved, individual parts could be made separately. By 1856 Sir Joseph Whitworth had, in his workshop at Manchester, machines capable of measuring one millionth part of an inch, enabling the standardisation of screw threads. Soon, beginning in the US, interchangeable parts of machines were produced: an improvement originally associated with spare parts for muskets. (Printing had, in effect, anticipated this in the fifteenth century.)

One benefit was the effect on coinage. That was an idea of Matthew Boulton to defeat forgers. Boulton built a coining press powered by steam in which the coins, held in place by steel clamps, were stamped automatically, with an accuracy never previously achieved. Each press could stamp 50 to 100 coins a minute. This was a great success, and Boulton received orders from all over the world, including revolutionary France, Russia and finally, in 1797, from his own government.

Although cotton was the raw material *par excellence* of the early days of industrialisation, the history of pottery has its lesson also.

4

During the sixteenth century an unprecedented quantity of Chinese ceramics began to be brought back, first by the Portuguese, then by the Dutch – blue and white porcelain, transparent enamels – to be admired in every fashionable city of Europe. Indeed, the Dutch finished what the Portuguese had begun. As early as 1614 the Dutch began to imitate the blue and white Ming ceramics, above all at Delft. The Dutch were (unsurprisingly) unable to export these successfully to the East, but the Japanese did copy some original Dutch patterns. A chemist to Augustus the Strong, King of Saxony, Johann Friedrich Bottger,* copied these Chinese treasures for the first time exactly, at Meissen in 1709. A French state factory at Sèvres in 1768 began to use the Chinese method too. Copies began also in England, in the Staffordshire potteries, where John Astbury's translucent stoneware began to make the fortune of that region by bringing the chance

---

* He believed that he could turn base metals into gold and was accordingly kept a prisoner.

of obtaining 'china' to a mass market. By 1750 double firing began to produce the characteristic earthenware of Staffordshire. Then, in 1759, Josiah Wedgwood, a connection of Astbury's, founded his business at Burslem, and ten years later he established his factory, 'Etruria', not far away, as has been seen, bringing the clay from Cornwall and elsewhere by means of the great Trunk Canal which he helped to finance. (He was inspired by the recent discoveries at Pompeii.) Steam engines soon began to be used for mixing clay and grinding flint. Josiah Spode began in 1797 to add bone ash in his factory at Stoke-on-Trent. These large factories, and others founded like them on the Continent and in the US, transformed the eating habits of the world, since china and pottery were much easier to clean than wood and pewter.

The result was that by 1850 the latter had vanished in all but the most impoverished homes. Cheap china, usually earthenware, had taken their place, an immense sanitary achievement which benefited millions even though the English master potters employed child labour for many years later than other enterprises. The final shaping of pots continued to be performed by hand till the 1840s, while steam was not applied to the potter's wheel before the 1870s.

5

The steam engine could perhaps have been introduced with fuel other than coal. But coal was the main source of power everywhere during the first half of the Industrial Revolution and, indeed, is still a major contributor to power in most nations. Production of coal in the 1970s was well over 2,000 million tons a year, is increasing annually again as a result of the crisis in oil production, and contributes a third of the world's production of energy. Manufacture thus still has its roots deep in the soil[5].

Coal had been used for heating houses in China on a modest scale for 3,000 years, and in blast furnaces too. In the Middle Ages in Europe, coal was used in limekilns, to heat houses sometimes and also in some ironworks, though never on a scale to rival charcoal. Liège had started to use coal in the fifteenth century for its metallurgical works. Similarly in the sixteenth century Newcastle began to use the coal mines of Durham to fire its salt industry (made from seawater), afterwards for other local industries and, finally, in bakers' ovens. Then, carried by sea to London, coal was used for heating in houses when the shortage of wood began to be acute in the days of Elizabeth I. By 1660

Britain was producing half a million tons of coal a year, probably then five times the entire produce of the rest of the world. The river Tyne was always full of colliers ready to leave for London, where windows of glass were being built in most new houses to keep in the heat of the new coal-burning fireplaces. Mortar from coal-burned limestone helped to keep together the houses themselves, which were increasingly built of brick and stone.

The coal of that time was not much used for manufacture, though a little smelting of lead, tin and copper was done. Coal was held to impair the quality of iron when employed for smelting, and to have a bad effect on malt when employed in breweries.

In Derbyshire in the late seventeenth century the brewers started to char their coal in order to make coke and then to use coke to dry their malt. This experiment worked. Abraham Darby, son of a farmer near Dudley, a town in Worcestershire known for its seams of coal, was serving an apprenticeship to a malt mill manufacturer. In 1709 he began to use coke in a blast furnace at Coalbrookdale, on the Severn in Shropshire. His son, of the same name, later studied how to make cast iron acceptable to forges. He found that there was little phosphorus in the ore of coal. The coke which he made began to be used for the smelting of iron, a turning-point in the history of that and all metals.

Canals enabled this raw material to be carried to inland cities. In England there had until recently been no interest in those artificial rivers, unlike the state of affairs in France, where for example the Languedoc canal, linking the Atlantic with the Mediterranean, had been constructed between 1666 and 1681.

Both seas and rivers had, from an early time, of course, been supplemented by canals, which criss-crossed ancient Egypt, Iraq and the Yangtze valley as if they were cobwebs. Of those, the best known were the Pharaoh Necos' attempt to link the Red Sea with the Nile, upon which project 120,000 Egyptians are said to have died between 609 and 623 BC, and Sennacherib's stone canal, which brought water to Nineveh from fifty miles away with a fall of one in eighty. Wide valleys were crossed by aqueducts. Roman aqueducts were famous. But they were used only for the supply of water to their great cities, not for the shipment of goods. In the Middle Ages northern Italy was converted into a criss-cross of irrigation canals, which compensated Milan for being surrounded by land. They could ship all manner of goods to the Po and to Ferrara.

In England in the early eighteenth century both the river Doug-

las and the Sankey river were deepened, in order to carry coal
from Lancashire to the sea more easily. An inspired engineer,
James Brindley, suggested to Francis, Duke of Bridgewater, that
instead of carrying coal the seven miles to Manchester from his
colliery at Worsley, at nine shillings a ton, a canal might be
created. That was done. The water was kept at one level by
aqueducts (one over a river, the Irwell) and tunnels, and the coal
was carried by barges. The price of coal fell by half. The Duke
went on to finance and build a canal from Manchester to Liverpool
and then one from the Trent to the Mersey. The latter linked the
North Sea to the Irish Sea. Brindley is thought later to have
sketched a network for an English canal system. Though that was
not carried out, England in the next generation was transformed
by the growth of canals. 4,250 miles of inland waterways were
built. The work was all done either by private persons or joint
stock companies. The government limited itself to enquiries and
granting permissions.

6

The creation of canals meant that new sources of coal could be
exploited: in Lancashire, South Wales, Staffordshire, Yorkshire
and Scotland. Coal output increased from 6 million tons in 1770
in England to 66 million in 1856 (ultimately to a maximum of 287
million in 1913).

The increase in English production of coal was made possible
by cheap labour (including many Irish immigrants) and because
of the availability of steam engines to pump deep mines free of
water, universal long before the end of the eighteenth century.
Subsequently, steam engines were also used to hoist both coal
and miners. In the early nineteenth century, though, women were
still being used to carry coal up (as much as a hundred feet) on
ladders while their husbands were cutting at the mine's face.
Children opened the gates to let the horses pass to fill the trucks
and women led the horses. Sometimes the managers of mines left
the miners themselves to pay the women and children. Probably
a majority of miners in England lived, says Halévy, like 'savages
utterly cut off not merely from the middle class but also from
other workers'. Conditions in Scotland were specially bad.
Workers in coal mines and in salt pits were still legally serfs,
bound to the mines for life. They could be sold with them, and
even wore the visible sign of slavery in the shape of a collar.

In the early days new seams of coal were opened up by haphazard blasting, by use of black powder. The miner worked with handpick and crowbar and put his coal on to a sledge to be pulled by women, children or ponies, Thomas Wilson of Tyneside introduced iron rails in the 1780s to alleviate the work of the haulier. Rails had been used above ground for many years. The rails were placed on a slope if possible so that the heavy trucks of coal might run of themselves – and every full truck could thus pull up an empty one. Even so, every large mine had miles of paths, at increasingly great depths, down to 1,000 feet by 1825, 2,000 in the 1830s. These depths were achieved by outstanding engineers, who devised winding machines to raise the coal on hemp cord and then wire rope (an innovation first used in Germany in 1834). But these early mines were ill lit by dangerous lanterns, which caused disasters. In 1816 the lamp invented by Sir Humphry Davy enabled a naked flame to be kept alight safely under ground, even in damp and gassy mines. A safety shaft was also introduced by the middle of the nineteenth century. But the diseases caused by coal dust were not appreciated for many years while safety precautions were ignored, until terrible disasters had given gruesome warnings.

By 1880 most coal was being raised from the pits by machine, not by women, but the hewing remained a handicraft. Coal-cutting machines took a long time to be introduced. No effective conveyor to take the coal from the face to the surface was introduced before 1912.

By then the coal miners were among the most formidable of labour forces, proud of a long tradition of dangerous work, conscious of their importance in the economy, united in their organisation and numerous: in 1911 there were 1·2 million miners in Britain, in comparison with 20,000 in 1829, more than in any other single trade except the workers in agriculture and metallurgical trades. Almost everywhere in Europe miners lived in homogeneous settlements which were really 'veritable republics of their own, which soon discovered their power – including power to send representatives of their own class to parliament'[6]. Kaiser Wilhelm II in Germany conceded the importance of the coal industry by siding with the miners against the coal owners in a great strike in 1889, to Bismarck's disgust.

Coal miners were everywhere powerful. In 1789 Belgium had mines 600 feet deep at Mons. Belgium's membership of the French Empire under Napoleon gave her coal the run of the French market. In 1830 Belgium had about 300 collieries, each employing

100 men. France was not competitive in respect of coal. Her coal was hard to work, the seams were thin, the prices high and the coal itself inferior to that of England. Though French coal production increased, it only attained forty-one million tons by 1913 and a maximum of sixty million tons in 1958. France imported during the twentieth century twice as much as she raised. France's relative industrial backwardness in the nineteenth century cannot be entirely explained by her shortage of coal, but that was a disadvantage to her at that stage of the age of manufacturing.

Equally the early success of Germany can be explained by her possession of great hoards of coal, partly in the Ruhr and Roer (at the eastern end of the Belgian fields) and also in Silesia, the territory won for Prussia by Frederick the Great – and later lost, to Poland, by Hitler. Railways gave particular importance to this German coal. Having never made use of the commodity before the age of industry, and being uninterested in canals, German production of coal was only at the French level in the 1830s (about three million tons). But after the coming of railways, production moved ahead fast. (She was just behind Britain in 1913 and overtook Britain in 1921.) During the Nazi era Germany was producing 380 million tons in 1938 to Britain's 230 million, a superiority she maintained after 1945, even during the high days of the era of oil. Indeed, in the 1970s East Germany alone was producing more than Britain. US production of bituminous coal exceeded that of Britain in 1902, was twice British production in 1913 (478 million tons) and has never fallen below that since.

The importance of coal in the first stages of industrial development can be seen from the history of the coal-less countries. Their mechanisation was delayed. They had to import coal at expense, just as countries have to import oil in the twentieth century. The need to import coal limited the external politics of the countries concerned. In 1920 the Italian Communists believed that they could carry through the same type of revolution which Lenin had managed in Russia in 1917. 'Do you take into account that Italy has neither wheat nor coal?' Lenin asked, and advised against revolution. Italy under fascism, up to the 1930s, imported sixty per cent of her coal from Britain. In 1936, as a result of sanctions under the League of Nations, coal imported from Britain fell to one per cent of Italy's needs. Thereafter, though Russia sold her a certain amount, the bulk of Italian imports came from Germany: 'As soon as the Italians adapted their factories to . . .

German coal,' wrote Denis Mack Smith, 'they found that the change was, for technological reasons, as well as political, almost irreversible'[7].

Long before the days for which these last statistics have been given, coal had surrendered to oil as the main power behind mechanisation. A symbolic alteration was the action of Winston Churchill as First Lord of the Admiralty in changing the fuel of the British navy to oil in 1911. Even so, coal continued to have much significance in all industrial countries. In the 1970s the use of coal in electricity power stations gave coal miners power to shake governments.

The world by the 1970s was said to be using more coal in one year than had been generated in a hundred years through carbonisation; so that some were saying, as early as 1940, that the 'use of fossil fuel' could only be 'an episode'. This anxiety was not new: in 1805 men were 'wondering how many centuries it would take to exhaust the mines'[8]. Those hundreds of years of carbonisation were a long time ago and the 'episode' seems like continuing, for large reserves still exist, while the future of oil seems unpredictable. A recent study of world coal production suggested that the US might, by the year 2000, have to consider mining three times more coal than it did in the late 1970s; and that while the world's annual coal production was 3,400 million tons, reserves were no less than 11,500 billion tons though only 740 billion are held to be recoverable. But even that is five or six times the current estimates of proved reserves of oil. The 'energy crisis' seems from the point of view of a coal miner short-term and manageable in the sense in which the word is usually employed. Of course, the increase in the burning of coal could pollute the atmosphere. The recovery of coal from many beds under the oceans will be difficult. The demand for coal will outrun the production of many nations, resulting in the necessity for an elaborate commerce. Coalfields will continue to be dangerous places. The despoliation of beautiful or agricultural land is disagreeable. Nevertheless, these things can all be overcome. One unfortunate paradox, however, is that the economically recoverable resources of coal are mostly in those countries which are already stable: the US, China, Russia and Western Europe. All the same, coal is certain to remain abundant at low cost for a long time and new methods of recovering it – machines at the coal face – will surely remove its ugly legend.

32
Iron and Steel

Many men in steel preferred the seven-day week and the twelve-hour day to the six-day week and the eight-hour day at lower wages not because the lower wages would have meant actual hardship but because they would have meant less opportunity . . . to rise.

Bertrand Russell, *Freedom and Organisation 1814–1914*

1

Steam and coal were the characteristic sources of energy and fuel of the industrial age in its first stages. The raw material concerned was, primarily, iron.

Iron has been used continuously from its discovery in Asia Minor before 2500 BC. It is a harder metal to work than is copper: pure iron melts at 1,535° centigrade, while copper does so at 1,083° centigrade. Thus, until the development of the blast furnace (in China before Christ, but in the West not until the fourteenth century AD), molten iron could not be produced for casting. Iron could be made red-hot by a great fire. The heat could be increased by bellows. But repeated hammerings were needed to create wrought iron from the crude iron. The consequent produce could be neither sharp nor pure. Hence, to begin with, iron was used primarily for ornaments, and only later for swords, axes, helmets and daggers. Those refinements were made easier by hinged tongs which assisted the smith's work. They were developed in the same biblical times as the hand tools which have remained the same in shape ever since: such as small saws, files and anvils (for making nails).

As has been seen, ironworking was a secret of the Hittites. Other contemporaneous civilisations, such as that of Mycenae, knew of iron, but it was rare and was mentioned by Homer still only as an ornament.

The Hittite Empire collapsed in 1200 BC. The ironsmiths were scattered. Iron began to be mined and worked in many parts of the Mediterranean. 'Heaven-sent' iron from meteorites, in particular, was used for tools in the ancient Mediterranean, just as was iron from one which fell in Greenland in the nineteenth century. Though Asia Minor remained the main source of the metal in the Old World, iron from the eastern Alps was worked

331

by Celtic tribes very early on. The Assyrian Empire was based on iron weapons, such as the iron-capped battering ram. The Etruscans were preoccupied by iron, having discovered large deposits at Piombino-Populonia (a mountain range full of other useful metals such as lead, copper and tin). Their smelting was done in furnaces of clay or stone, stoked with wood. They exchanged iron products in Greece and elsewhere in Italy for gold.

Iron also began to be used by the Carthaginians about 800 BC, and the art of making it was taken south into Africa. Iron was smelted in the Nok kingdom in Nigeria by 300 BC, in the Congo earlier, in Kenya by AD 100 and in Rhodesia by AD 300. Iron was of special use for clearing the ground for Africa's early agriculture. The gardens created for yams and bananas were made possible by iron tools. Much later, Central Africa enjoyed a 'great burst of iron engineering' after AD 500, leading to the organisation of kingdoms whose weapons were iron spears. The Iron Age in the Congo may even have preceded agriculture there. The acquisition of iron weapons and agricultural tools by West African Negroes between 250 BC and AD 1 led to the thrust by that people east and south which in turn created the Bantu world of South and Central Africa.

Iron smelting also began in India not later than 516 BC when Darius the Persian made north India his twentieth satrapy. Some believe that iron reached there as early as 800 BC. Then, in the Mediterranean, iron weapons and armour equipped the armies of both Greeks and Romans. Roman agriculture had iron parts for ploughs, spades, sickles, axes, hatchets, chisels, mallets, hammers and lathes. Vast numbers of these iron implements were passed down from the Roman to the mediaeval world, and were in use at the time of the Renaissance.

All this time China was casting iron freely, though she did not start forging before the third century AD. Why should she? Cast iron is more useful than wrought iron. The Chinese success in casting iron so early was because they could heat their blast furnaces at a higher temperature than anyone did in the West till the fourteenth century AD. That was because the ores of China had a high phosphorus content. Chinese blast furnaces were heated by bellows, with pistons worked by paddle-wheels. The West still could not melt iron fully, though certain Catalan furnaces managed in Roman days to produce malleable iron by using large bellows to maintain a constant blast.

The decline of Rome and of the Roman civilisation was marked as much as anything else by the decline of metallurgy. The recovery of the art of smelting in Carolingian Europe coincided with the opening of new mines along the Rhine and Meuse in the Ardennes; and also in England. The mediaeval peasantry in Europe used iron on a scale 'inconceivable in any earlier age'[1]. The tools which were made by blacksmiths were the indispensable supports of mediaeval agriculture. In particular, there was the heavy iron axe for felling trees which accounted for the great extension of arable land in the tenth century. The symbolic figure of the early Middle Ages was the knight in iron armour, equipped with iron weapons and supported on his horse by iron stirrups. His efficiency was secured by a vast number of little ovens for iron dotted around Europe (for there was iron in innumerable European hillsides), to which the broken-up iron would be taken to be smelted, and afterwards removed to forges, to be beaten on the anvil[2].

Blast furnaces, in which iron could be rendered liquid, were first set up in Europe in Germany during the fourteenth century. A direct connection with China is hard to find. Doubtless it will be. At all events, and as a result of war, the blast furnaces transformed Europe's technology.

In the course of the Renaissance the frequency of war increased the demand for iron. The demand for new agricultural tools, cooking pots, forks, knives, fire-backs, fire-irons (for the new chimneys) and anchors for ships (a demand specialised in by the Basque country) was also considerable. At the same time charcoal was short, thus causing a further geographical shift of iron industries. Blast furnaces spread, to Sweden, as to Spain. The ironworks established during the seventeenth century in Santander and Vizcaya (in the Basque country) were, to the Catalan historian Vicens Vives, 'one of the few encouragements of that moribund century'[3]. In the eighteenth century 'almost every village in the Basque country seemed to have a forge', comments Richard Herr[4]. Despite the increase in demand for iron, production in Europe was no more than 150,000 tons a year in 1600, a figure exceeded by England alone about 1800. Don Quixote thought that, in the seventeenth century, he lived in an iron age already. Even in 1800 the world's production of iron was a mere two million tons.

Sixteenth-century England was running out of wood for fires.

So, as has been seen earlier, coal began to be used instead.* But English coal was unsuitable for smelting iron, since it had a bad chemical effect on the ore. About 1700 England was still importing iron and, though a rising power, was less important as a producer of that mineral than Sweden, Germany or even Russia. English ironworks were scattered and specialist, chiefly employing shoe bucklers, sword cutlers and nail makers. Abraham Darby† transformed this state of affairs. He had noticed that Dutch smelters used sulphur. He experimented in Coalbrookdale, his Shropshire valley which was full of iron. By making the right mixture of sulphur with coal, he invented coke. Using carefully selected ores, he cast, in his blast furnaces, an iron more liquid than any previously achieved outside China. With this he made cast-iron pots. His son, Abraham Darby II, improved on his father's process, and was making iron bars by the 1730s. By 1760 there were numerous coke furnaces, all emphasising the dependence of iron on coal. This iron came soon to be produced in oblong 'pigs', ready for use in wheels, hammer heads or anything else.‡

The process known as 'coking' devised by Darby made England overnight the major iron manufacturer. Her manufacturers established a dominance over this trade that few merchants had ever had before. Coking freed the manufacturers of iron from reliance on charcoal. The two wars of 1756–63 and 1774–83 stimulated the English demand for iron, and made fortunes for a new breed of English ironmasters. The innovations in making iron in England were continued. The first hydraulic cylinders, in 1761, gave to John Roebuck's ironworks at Carron (near the Forth) an unprecedentedly strong blast of air. Rolling mills for flattening the iron instead of hammering it were built at Henry Cort's mills at Gosport in 1781. A twenty-pound steam hammer, built by James Watt in 1783 at John Wilkinson's Broseley ironworks in Coalbrookdale, could strike 150 blows a minute. Machines for cutting and drilling iron, turning screws and metal-boring lathes were built by Henry Maudslay of London. Machines for forging nails were the achievement in 1790 of Thomas Clifford.

These inventions not only expedited work and saved labour, but helped to give that uniformity of shape to products which, always desirable, was becoming essential. Probably the most im-

---

* See above, p. 325.
† See above, p. 326.
‡ The phrase in English is meant to refer to the little pigs suckled by their mother.

portant of these inventions subsequent to that of Darby was the discovery in 1784 by Henry Cort, an ironmaster who was the son of a mason from Lancashire and who had a mill at Fontley near Fareham (Hampshire), of the process known as 'puddling'. That meant a stirring and raking of the molten iron in the furnace, giving it air and producing a far purer iron. This permitted Richard Crawshay, the 'iron king' of Cyfarthfa, to increase his production of bar iron from 10 tons to 200 tons a week. Coal, instead of charcoal, began to be used for the manufacture of wrought iron, the market for which survived for architectural and artistic reasons. Indeed, wrought iron made in coal furnaces provided the roof trusses for innumerable railway stations (for example, Euston, in 1839); for the incomparable Reading Room of the British Museum, finished in 1857; for the Menier chocolate works at Noisiel-sur-Marne, finished in 1872; and, some years later, for the Eiffel Tower, to mark the centenary of the French Revolution of 1789, constructed from 12,000 prefabricated parts. Wrought iron was thus the material for many of the noblest buildings of the Victorian age.

Iron Ore Production (million metric tons)

Country	1880	1913	1938	1977
Britain	18*	16	12	1
France	3	22	33	11
Germany	5	29	11	1
Russia		9	27	200
USA	7	62	72	35

*Note: 1880 was the year of the highest production of iron ore in Britain.

The greatest figure of the first generation of British ironmasters was John Wilkinson, son of an enterprising Cumberland labourer, who, to begin with, used a blast furnace for wrought iron. Wilkinson built five or six blast furnaces at Broseley, obtained coal from mines which he himself owned, bought tin mines in Cornwall and constructed landing stages on the Thames, while his brother William established an ironworks at Indret, near Nantes, and subsequently built modernised furnaces for the French iron town of Le Creusot. John Wilkinson made iron chairs, pipes, vats for brewers and bridges at Coalbrookdale (in 1770), Sunderland (in 1796) and across the Severn (in 1779). His London Bridge of 700 feet, built in 1801, was deemed by Canova to be worth a journey to England from Italy to see. Wilkinson launched an iron barge on the Severn in 1787 and even forty miles of cast-iron pipes for the waterworks in Paris. His machine for boring metal (originally for military purposes) made possible the cylinders in Watt's first steam engine. He made a steam threshing machine on his own farm, devised the first coal-cutting machine and issued his own currency, which had a wide circulation in Staffordshire and Shropshire. Much of the artillery used to win the Napoleonic Wars was cast in one or other of Wilkinson's furnaces. When he died, he was buried in an iron coffin.

Wilkinson was only the most protean example of an astonishing generation of Englishmen. Superior to him, in wealth, though not in invention, was Anthony Bacon, who realised as early as 1765 the critical importance of an interconnection between iron, coal and the vicinity of streams to supply power. All knew that South Wales had iron, but the bad roads had hitherto rendered it valueless. In 1765 Bacon, withdrawing from a lucrative career as chief supplier of food and equipment to the forces[5] – a commission more valuable than any other at that time – gained, for £100 a year, a concession from the landowner Lord Talbot to exploit the mines within forty miles of Merthyr. The subsequent building of the Glamorgan Canal made Bacon's fortune. He created Merthyr as the greatest centre of iron in the world out of a pastoral land. In the war of American Revolution, Bacon provided the government with artillery. In 1782 he sold off his works to a variety of entrepreneurs, whose names were all pioneers in ironmaking for several generations.

Other great iron kings made their fortunes in the lowlands of Scotland, Sheffield, Newcastle and Rotherham. These men were the first real 'captains of industry', revolutionaries in the proper sense of the word, wrote Halévy[6], who would seem later, to prejudiced eyes, the tyrants of a new age. In their own time they seemed innovators, philanthropists, winners of wars, men of vision and the creators of work for a growing population. During the early nineteenth century these ironmasters and their successors became the essential providers for English industry: in particular serving the railways with iron rails and parts of engines. A vast export (over a quarter of output in 1848) was also possible, since both the USA and France laid down British rails on their first railways.

Countries other than Britain had entered the new iron age before the mid nineteenth century. In France the royal foundry at Le Creusot, near Chalon-sur-Saône (founded in 1782 with the help of William Wilkinson and converted for the production of munitions by Napoleon), began using coke in 1810. It was anglicised (modernised) after Waterloo by English technicians, before passing to the family of Schneider, under whom it became great. But until 1850 three-fifths of French pig iron was still coming from charcoal furnaces. The transition to modern furnaces began during the Second Empire. The crisis of 1870–71 delayed growth, as well as cutting off the country from Lorraine's iron deposits, whose size was not then known. But from the 1890s onwards France was beginning to compete with Britain and Germany. The ore came from Meurthe-et-Moselle, particularly the Briey-Longwy corner, later disputed by Germany. By 1914 France was producing twenty-two million tons of iron ore, to Britain's sixteen million and Germany's twenty-nine million.

Germany had abundant metallurgical knowledge. Excellent ores had been mined for generations in the valley of the Sieg. But little was done before 1860. In 1846, the furnaces of Germany were still worked by water power and on a small scale. Iron-mining was a 'peasant bye-industry'. (An exception was the iron industry in Silesia; a symbol of which was the iron bridge in its capital, Breslau, built in 1800.) In the 1860s, however, Germany began to industrialise. After faltering again in the 1870s, due to the discovery of, and conversion of Britain and the US to, the Bessemer steel process, Germany gained the lead in European ironmaking, overtaking Britain in 1906 (as she had done in the case of steel in 1893). The great mines of Luxembourg and newly acquired Lorraine were the springs of that. In the development of German iron, as in many other things, the Prussian state (through its educational enterprise) played an important part; Borsig, the first great German iron manufacturer, for example, was a prize pupil of the Gewerbe Institut of Berlin. The German ironmasters also constituted themselves in the 1870s a powerful pressure group against free trade.

Very different was the history of iron in the US. There, while pig iron was smelted with charcoal, the American colonies, as they then were, were well placed. They exported (especially from Maryland) pig iron to England. Thereafter, however, the coming of coke, the invention of better machinery and much reduced costs made iron more expensive in the US than in England till the 1840s. The US was not particularly quick to take up new ideas in ironmaking. Puddling, for example, was not done in the US till 1817. The first US railways were built with rails imported from England. Then the use of anthracite, used by blacksmiths in the

Wyoming valley since about 1760, and a new hot air blast system of heating furnaces transformed the position. Coke began to be widely employed in the US about 1850. Thereafter rails were made there too. Cast iron was substituted for the wooden parts of steam engines, as in the case of other heavy machinery. Sewing machines, stoves and other domestic tools were soon being constructed from that metal. The American Civil War, like all wars, ancient and modern, impelled a new demand for iron. The subsequent peace was even more demanding. In the 1880s the completion of the American railway system took US production of iron beyond Britain's by 1890.

2

Where iron played a great role in the first part of the Industrial Revolution, the second part of that upheaval has been characterised more by steel than by anything else.

Ordinary iron cannot give a sharp edge to an object. Steel can. It began to be made by the Chalybes of Asia Minor, a sub-tribe of the Hittites, about 1400 BC. Iron bars were hammered when in direct contact with heat and charcoal, and then thrown hot into water (hot iron becomes tougher when so tempered, unlike copper and bronze, which become weaker). Throughout the ancient world and the Middle Ages, this early 'wrought' steel continued to be made in small forges. Makers of steel were, for a long time, a special subdivision of ironmasters. They concentrated on the manufacture of knives and swords. Almost every country had its centres where such objects were made best: Sheffield or Toledo. Steel was used as a metaphor for hardness: 'The friends thou hast,' Polonius said to Laertes, 'Grapple them to thy soul with hoops of steel.' Steel seemed almost a precious stone, man-made though it was. Then, about 1740–50, a Quaker clockmaker of Doncaster, Benjamin Huntsman, smelted cast steel for the first time. He used a very high temperature, because he was dissatisfied with the quality of his steel instruments. He set up a factory at Attercliffe (a village near Sheffield). He began to be prosperous about 1770, making edged tools and parts for clocks.

The cutlers of Sheffield were hostile to Huntsman's process. They thought his steel *too* hard. But Huntsman's trademark became famous. Though the inventor tried to keep his process secret, it was betrayed. Even so, steel remained a minor side of the Industrial Revolution for a hundred years after this first smelting. The steel of those days was not faultless. Even in 1849, when

Krupps' were testing their first steel gun, they found that the steel could not stand the pressure of the explosion. About that time, however, William Kelly of Kentucky, a manufacturer of sugar kettles in a small way in Louisiana, observed that an air blast on molten pig iron caused more heat than ever when the iron was not covered with charcoal. That led him to the conclusion that the carbon in pig iron could be blown out by air. The carbon itself would act as a fuel. Kelly tried to develop this idea, but went bankrupt. He made over his claims to an English genius of Huguenot origin, Sir Henry Bessemer.

Bessemer had already invented a perforated die stamp, a method of making imitation Utrecht velvet and a machine for setting type. Inspired by the need to create a stronger steel than that used in the guns of the Crimean War, Bessemer read a paper on the subject of 'how to make steel without fuel' at a meeting at Cheltenham of the British Association in 1856. After a few years of experiment, the 'Bessemer process' was in use – above all at Sheffield in the inventor's own factory, using steel without phosphorus, though he was too late for the American Civil War. Subsequently Friedrich Siemens, one of three brilliant scientific brothers from Hanover, with help from Sidney Thomas of Canonbury and his cousin Percy Gilchrist, developed the 'open hearth method' which enabled steel to be made straight from the ore; particularly the highly phosphoric ore of Germany. These two systems transformed the manufacture of steel in the industrialised countries.

Britain, the old leader of the Industrial Revolution in its iron and cotton days, was slow to see the benefits of steel. They even delayed twenty years till they introduced steel into guns. Only in 1877 did the British Board of Trade permit the use of steel in bridge-building (John Wilkinson had not *needed* such permission for his iron bridge a century before). Though the Forth Bridge was built of steel (1882–89), the USA took the lead in steel manufacture. All the later railways of the US were built from steel, and the age of steel there begat a new generation of financiers and captains of industry (such as Carnegie and Frick) who caused their European contemporaries to seem men of modest stature. Steel was used by 1900 for buildings (above all, skyscrapers in New York and Chicago, where sites were so expensive that it was economic to build upwards), for bridges, for wire and for offices – then, after 1909, for cars. In 1909 there were 654 iron- and steelworks in the US employing 278,000 people, already worth $1,500 million. They produced twenty-one million tons of steel. In comparison Britain was producing eight million tons, Germany thirteen, France three – and Russia already three.

Russia through her steel production was becoming a major industrial power for the first time. Her output two years later of five million tons was already greater than France's. Her increase in production since 1870 was 500 times faster than that of any other country. It was also faster than it was under communism after 1917[7]. Meantime, by the First World War, Thomas's and Gilchrist's 'open hearth' method of steelmaking had largely taken over from the Bessemer one (twenty million tons of steel were made in the US by the 'open hearth' method in 1913 against ten by the Bessemer one). That became the normal method.

After 1918 US pre-eminence in steel manufacture was more pronounced than ever, being led by the boom of the 1920s in which Europe did not greatly share. In 1929 the USA was producing half the world's steel (56 million tons out of 128). It served new rolling mills for the automobile industry, and made use for the first time of new ferrous alloys by which tough but light springy steel could be produced. Even when, during the depression of 1929–33, US steel production fell to thirteen miilion tons (below her production of any year since 1901), she was producing more than France and Germany combined. Subsequently, the US revived, being back to the level of 1929 by the 1940s. She had doubled that level of production in the 1960s. After that date, steel ceased to be the dominant manufacture in the US that it had been since 1900. Steelworks were running down, seeming overmanned and too large. The world since 1960 has apparently been one of plastics, concrete and glass. By the end of the 1970s the US had been overtaken as a manufacturer of steel by Russia (114 million tons to 146) and was being approached by Japan, a new contender.

Even so, it was only the old great producers which were running down their industries. World-wide, the steel industry was still expanding in the 1970s. Newly modernising countries in South-East Asia were building new and more efficient plants. Between 1960 and 1978 the Europeans were spending a great deal of money expanding their capacity to export steel: but to a world which wanted to make its own. Therein lies the tragedy of many old industrial countries.

33
Revolution by Railway

Lines of carts stretched along the roads; they lumbered aside at the level crossing and, from the furiously speeding train, it seemed as if the carts stood still and the horses were marking time.

Boris Pasternak, *Doctor Zhivago*

One is told that Stalin himself sometimes came down to the Moscow goods siding.

Julian Huxley recalls a visit to Moscow, 1934

1

The first consequence of the development of steam, coal and iron was 'the railway age', which itself had consequences of the first importance. For coal not only powered the early railways. The railways carried coal to innumerable destinations for further development.

The railway, as opposed to the railway engine, was born long before the nineteenth century. Sometime, among the German mines of the sixteenth century, perhaps about 1550, wooden rails were introduced to haul heavy trucks. These had flanged wheels before 1600, and were known also in English coal mines before that date. By the eighteenth century the edges of these wooden rails, running from the pithead to the point where the coal could be embarked, were protected, as ploughshares had been for generations, by iron. A cast-iron edged rail, on which the wheels of wagons were kept steady by flanges as in modern lines, was to be seen at Loughborough in the eighteenth century. Thus railways were, to begin with, an accessory to coal. They began by being established in all industrial areas for that purpose. The use of canals enhanced these usages. Cast-iron rails were being made by Abraham Darby II at Coalbrookdale by 1767.

The locomotive has a less ancient history than the rail. Even so, the French engineer Nicolas Joseph Cugnot constructed a steam carriage in 1769. William Murdock, the foreman at Boulton's works at Soho, built a model locomotive which travelled at eight m.p.h. in 1785. In 1801 Richard Trevithick, son of the manager of a Cornish mine, designed a steam carriage for use in

341

collieries (he was influenced by Murdock, then living at Redruth). Trevithick's carriage was a success. In 1803 he drove another such vehicle four miles in London, from Holborn to Paddington. In 1804 he devised an engine to pull seventy men and ten tons (of iron) at the Pen-y-Darran ironworks near Merthyr.* Then in 1813, George Stephenson, an engine-wright at the Killingworth colliery in Durham, built a travelling engine between his colliery and the pithead. The cost of fodder for the horses which had drawn the carts full of coal was rising. Stephenson had seen one of Trevithick's engines at work near by at the Wylam colliery, eight miles from Newcastle, where his father had been a fireman. Stephenson's *Blucher* (an appropriate name for an engine of that year) ran in 1814 from Killingworth to Tyneside. It was a success. Ten years afterwards Stephenson built an engine for commercial use on a line which had been built between Stockton and Darlington, by a Quaker, Edward Pease, the son of a woollen manufacturer.

The success of that first railway journey (in 1825) caused a competition for an engine for the route between Manchester and Liverpool. Stephenson's *Rocket* won the competition. The line was opened in 1830. The permanent way between those two cities was finished before the question of the traction had been decided. Some thought that horses or cables, with a stationary engine, would be best. As much concern was spent on the character of the permanent way as on the engine, for the crossing of the bog known as Chat Moss necessitated the sinking of faggots of wood onto which large loads of stone and earth had to be tipped. The early railway lines thus required as much care as the building of Venice. Subsequently cuttings and embankments were dug, as well as special drainage works. A phenomenal amount of work had to be done by pick, shovel and wheelbarrow. Tunnelling meant hard work in disagreeable circumstances. Still, even when the back-breaking labour is recognised, the drive, local patriotism and conviction of engineers and local businessmen interested in the construction and the service which it would give to the community should also be recalled. Even many workers creating the railways were brought to 'love the locomotives', as the Spanish anarchist Angel Pestaña admitted[1].

Once these early problems had been resolved, country after

---

* Trevithick went in 1816 to Peru in order to make his fortune by running the silver mines at Cerro de Pasco. He lost everything, returned and died in poverty, his funeral being paid for by the workmen at John Hall's factory at Dartford (1833).

country began to be criss-crossed by a network of railways, most undertaken by private enterprise, with nearly every nation transformed in the process.

By 1850 Britain had 16,200 miles of railways. The problems of monopoly, rights of passage and where the trains should stop had become major questions of political business. The railways were carrying sixty million tons of freight and over 100 million passengers. An elaborate system of signals, based on the semaphore devised in 1792 by Claude Chappe (to help the French Revolution), had been introduced to serve this upheaval. In the 1850s an electric telegraph* began to be used along most lines. Trains travelling at sixty miles an hour were by then common. These engines burned mostly coke but, later, coal. On the Continent wood was more common. For the generation after 1830, British engines, British engineers, British (and Irish) railway workers and British rails were carried all over the world, taking the message of Stockton and Darlington not only to the Continent but to Brazil, India and Australia.

Belgium, Britain's nearest and best client, was even more vigorous than her political protector (as Britain became, after Belgian independence in 1830) in organising a railway network. The government there, in the first flush of its independence, decided on a national, planned network. By 1844 a system linking the main Belgian cities had been made, owned by the state. In France a long discussion ensued as to whether the railway should be public or private. There were compromises. Thus, though private companies did the work, the state assisted by buying shares. The government also insisted on laying down, in 1842, a national programme for railways, with lines radiating outwards from Paris. The government would provide the land. Local authorities would be asked to finance the infrastructure (including bridges, tunnels and permanent way) while private enterprise would finance the superstructure (rails, rolling stock and running costs). In the event the local authorities dropped out of this finely conceived plan. Private companies were responsible for all the building.

The French network was finished during the Second Empire. Six large companies managed the great trunk lines[2]. Napoleon III made use of railways in 1849 during his intervention in Italy, and thereafter rail, to supply and make possible a new epoch of armies a million strong, became the dominant factor in strategy.

* Discussed on page 388.

Germany was ahead of France in realising the possibilities of the railway. An 'English coal road' had been in use in the Ruhr by 1800. An experimental freight line was laid in Elberfeld in 1826. A passenger line between Nuremberg and Fürth was opened in 1836. The economist List soon proposed a national network of railways (he was aware of their military potential). Though the governments of Germany were well disposed to railways (and bought shares), private companies did the work. By 1848, 2,500 miles of rail were open in Germany. The German railways were dominated by the Prussian companies, and von Moltke in 1866 made the fullest use of the five railways at his disposal in taking troops to the front during the Austro-Prussian War. The railway had, in Germany as in many other countries, by then compensated for the poor roads, which in the past had hindered both commerce and war.

The railway helped to unite Germany. It played little part in the achievement of Italian unity. The Italian railways in 1859 were still organised within local frontiers, save for the line from Turin to Genoa of 1854 (one of Cavour's favourite projects, reducing the journey between the two cities to a day) and ensuring that Genoa would remain firmly tied to Turin. The role of railways, on the other hand, in creating a nation out of both the USA and Russia was fundamental.

The first railway in the US was built in 1830 in Baltimore, though horse-power and land sails were used as the source of power. Only in 1832 was steam decided upon as being better. In the 1830s US lines were radiating out from the few big towns. Wooden rails were made locally, while English engines were imported. Difficulties derived from the vested interests of canal and turnpike companies. In New York the Erie Canal had become a state enterprise. Competition was not desired by the legislators. Until 1851 New York State as a result even forbade the carriage of freight on railways. In addition, railways were considered by many to be undemocratic. They seemed monopolistic by implication. The 'open road' seemed the best transport for a nation of free men.

Railways had one obvious contribution to make to America. Roads and canals followed the natural line of the country. That meant that travel was usually from north to south. But many Americans, particularly pioneers, wanted to move from east to west. Railways enabled them to do so. By rail they could soon also travel more cheaply. That enabled the colonisation of the empty West of North America. The US by 1870 had a network of 53,000 miles of rail compared with 50,000 in all continental Europe. A great part in this development was played by the individual states. From 1835 onwards the states gave help by subscriptions to stock, loans, guarantees of railroad securities and so on. Federal aid enabled the completion of the railroad to the Pacific in 1869. Faced by a choice of what appeared to be the three evils of private monopoly, public monopoly or public regulation, the US chose private monopoly, thereby enabling alternative forms of transport to make a competitive challenge earlier than anywhere else[3]. In return the states gave grants of land to the railway companies of a size only equalled perhaps in the history of landholding by the grants made by Portuguese monarchs to their first noble colonists in Brazil; for instance, the Northern Pacific Company received no less than thirty-nine million acres.

Russia was a generation behind the US in opening railways. She had only 125 miles open in 1860. In 1913 she had 40,000 miles, a system of communications which, single track though the trans-Siberian railway was, had enabled the Tsarist authoritarian state to be consolidated, east to the Pacific and south to the mountains of inner Asia, laying a foundation for the totalitarian tyranny that was to follow. Gorki has a novel, *The Life of a Useless Man*, in which the anti-hero is crushed by the unstoppable advance of a train, symbolising 'the Revolution', as he flees. How many train journeys occur in late nineteenth-century Russian novels! The most famous heroine in Russian literature, Anna Karenina, threw herself before a train which was to take her lover, Vronsky, to the war in the Balkans in 1878. Anna's creator, Tolstoy, also, fittingly, died at a railway station. How appropriate that the last of the Tsars, Nicholas II, should have ended his days as autocrat of the Russians shuffling from station to station in the royal train, seeking a place to come to a weary halt before his abdication!

The railways of the nineteenth century were not confined to Europe and to South America. The Sultan Abdul Hamid's attempts at centralisation of the Ottoman Empire were greatly helped by the invention of the railway and the telegraph. India began to create a railway system, following the recommendation of the then Governor-General, Lord Dalhousie, in 1853: one of the great achievements of British India. Karl Marx's remarks about it are well known.* Cuba, the last and richest colony of Spain, began to build private railways for the sugar industry in 1837; the network was completed for the whole island after 1900. Latin American railways proper began in the late 1840s, with British investors prominent. Brazil built her railways between 1852 and 1868, and the line between São Paulo the great centre of coffee and the port of Santos confirmed the grand role of Brazil as the supplier of two-thirds of the world's coffee. Mexico's first railway linked the capital with Vera Cruz and was complete in 1873. It, too, was English built. A line between Cairo and Alexandria was opened in 1856, and one from Cairo to Suez in 1857. Australia opened her first railway in 1854 at Melbourne.

2

The first railway age was built, of course, on iron; the second was constructed on steel, after 1870. Steel rails turned out to be fifteen times more durable than iron ones. Steel bridges were tougher than iron ones. The compound engines of the late nineteenth century were more powerful than their predecessors. That meant further investment in lines and cuts in costs. In 1868 wheat per bushel carried in the US cost 42·6 cents. In 1910 it cost 9·6 cents. The US added 70,000 new miles of rail between 1880 and 1890 alone. Britain doubled its length of rail between 1860 and 1913. France quadrupled hers, Germany increased hers six times. Italy trebled her mileage between her unification in 1870 and 1913, and linked herself internationally to France and Switzerland by the Fréjus and St Gotthard tunnels, opened respectively in 1871 and 1882. Spain, late into the railway age, had a mere 625 miles of line open in 1860, but had over 9,000 in 1913. Even in serene London large zones of the city were emptied of people to make way for marshalling yards. Basle, the quiet Swiss university town, the city of Aeneas Sylvius, Erasmus and the young Holbein, was dominated by a great railway station.

Many of the political visionaries of the second half of the century were, like Cecil Rhodes, 'fanatical believers' in the virtues of railways. After the building of lines in South Africa in the 1880s, railways were extended into Central Africa where they were, in

* 'The railway system will, therefore, become in India today the forerunner of modern industry. . . Modern industry, resulting from the railway system will dissolve the hereditary divisions of labour upon which rest the Indian castes' (*New York Daily Tribune*, 8 August 1953).

the words of the historian of Rhodesia Robert Blake, 'the greatest single cause of a social and economic change'[4]. Kitchener used railways to defeat the Mahdi at Omdurman in 1894. But Britain failed to carry through the railway from the 'Cape [of Good Hope] to Cairo', which both Cecil Rhodes and Joseph Chamberlain believed would be the spine of a new great African empire.

The Russo-Japanese War of 1904 was a war *against* the railway. For the Japanese attacked when they did because they thought that they had to act before the trans-Siberian rail was completed. While there was a gap in the line at Lake Baikal, they believed that the reinforcements of Russian troops would be slow.

Electric railways began in the US in the 1880s, with elevated services inside New York and Chicago. After an overhead trolley railway was tried out in Kansas City (1895), inter-urban electric railways began in the US as a competitor to steam. The lack of a steam locomotive cut costs, and the absence of steam made less dirt, while frequent stops were easier. Another innovation was the underground railway begun in 1863, with the Metropolitan line in London which passed through central London in built-over cuttings, just under street level. The first 'tube' train was the City and South London line under the Thames of 1890. Subways with traction were also tried out in Glasgow, but not pursued. By 1900 most modern capitals had underground railways. But Moscow did not have one till the 1930s. Another change assisting the ease of long-distance travel was the introduction of the dining car and sleeping car on the train, which began after the Civil War in the US where distances were so great. They were soon copied in Europe, particularly in Russia, where the train which crossed Siberia had a chapel as well. Electric lighting in trains, by dynamo under the carriage, was introduced during the 1890s.

The train symbolises the golden age of bourgeois Europe. In France, Theodore Zeldin says, the century from 1840 to 1940 'could be written round the railway', life centring on the station more than on the church or town hall, cheap fares keeping families divided by industrialisation together. Proust's *petit train* to Cabourg was characteristic of a part of French life so complete that no one could remember what had happened before; and for Proust even Time had 'des trains express et spéciaux'[5].

The early railways were distinguished by magnificent station terminals, vast arched roofs of iron of a spaciousness unknown among buildings since the cathedrals or, as some said, the pyramids, allowing the separation of passengers from freight. The most grandiose of those such as St Pancras in London or Milan were among the largest of buildings of the age.

Two other great achievements of the railway builders were the construction of tunnels and bridges. There were few tunnels before the nineteenth century, except those built in the previous fifty years for canals. Those had been carried through rocks by old-fashioned mining methods. From 1830 the railway builders began a new generation of constructions. There was the Liverpool tunnel of 1830, the Rotherhithe tunnel of 1843 and there were the great Alpine tunnels: the Mont Cenis (eight miles, opened in 1870); St Gotthard (nine miles, opened in 1882); and, finally, the Simplon tunnel (twelve miles, opened in 1906). Though plans for a tunnel beneath the English Channel were never carried through, comparable tunnels were soon constructed in the US. All were built by the use of iron shields, pushed forward and pre-constructed, on the inspiration of Marc Kingdom Brunel,* a Norman émigré who fled from France during the Revolution.

The bridges of the railway age were equally spectacular. The decisive innovation was the suspension bridge. Now this was one of the many ideas first put into use by the Chinese – in this respect as early as the sixth century AD. The Chinese origin was apparently not known by its Western initiator, James Finley in Pennsylvania, in 1800. Suspension bridges could be made off the site which they were to serve. They enabled engineers to dispense with pillars of masonry in rough rivers, or even seas (for example, over the Menai Straits). There were several fine bridges of this sort built in the 1830s and 1840s. The climax came with Isambard Kingdom Brunel's bridge at Clifton, opened in 1862; the grand Trunk bridge, at Niagara, of 1858; the Brooklyn bridge, of 1883; and the Forth railway bridge, of 1890. All these transformed local communications and showed how technology could alter the old presuppositions of geography.

This second great railway age created fortunes everywhere. In France the railway companies became gilt-edged investments, but also bogey-men for the socialist opposition. Rails made riches, above all, in the US. Combined with the increase in the size of ships, the railway also made possible the vast emigratiions of the nineteenth century from Europe to the Americas.

In the end this chief production of nineteenth-century civilisa-

---

* Father of Isambard Kingdom Brunel.

tion became, as Norman Stone put it, 'the chief agent in its destruction'[6].

To some the railway engine had for a long time symbolised a continent out of control: in 1908 the German Impressionist poet Detlev von Liliencron wrote 'Der Blitzzug' about a train which raced across Europe to end in a disaster. 'Is it going to arrive late in heaven's station?' asked the poet and, like Pilate, he did not stay for an answer. In 1914 trains provided the warring nations with essential logistical support. For Germany all depended on the country's capacity to use the rail service to carry its army to victory 'by timetable' in three weeks, as A. J. P. Taylor put it[7]. In Russia industry failed to organise adequate supplies for the front because the main trans-Siberian railway could only take 280 wagons, of which 100 were reserved for railway material and 140 for government stores. The historian of the Russian front adds: 'It was not trains but timetables which offered problems. Trains chased grain, not the other way about . . . The government watched grain, train and fuel competing, and each falling into chaos'[8]. The trouble was that the horses at the front (essential to overcome the problem of local transport) needed a daily supply of fodder. For his Bessarabian offensive General Ivanov needed 667 wagons for men and 1,385 for horses (over half the grain harvest of Russia was needed for horses at the front).

In both Britain and France governmental control of the railways during the First World War offered a foretaste of nationalisation, providing a good example of that cold, ideology-less, but in the end stifling, socialism which war in the industrial age brought even to capitalist countries. During the war Victoria Station and the Gare de l'Est, in London and Paris (which Guillaume Apollinaire described as having 'mangé nos fils'), seemed to be gateways to death as they carried hundreds of thousands to the front. Further, when the Great War came to an end, the 130 railway companies in England of 1913 had been reduced to four, and French railways were already a public service.

At the end of the war the chaos in Russia gave authority to the railway union, remarked Adam Ulam, 'perhaps greater than that held by the army or the state itself'[9]. Russia before the war had seemed a nation built on railways. In 1918 the Bolsheviks might not have won the civil war if they had not controlled the railways.*

* 'Though a minority,' said an eyewitness, M. Philips Price, 'they [the committee of the poorer peasants supported by the Bolsheviks] possessed a central apparatus and controlled the railway system.'

Trotsky controlled the Red Army from an armoured train which exerted a powerful (if misleading) effect over the imagination of revolutionaries for a generation.*

In the West, meantime, the Armistice which ended the war was, appropriately, signed in a stationary train – of such symbolic importance that Hitler in 1940 insisted on sealing the surrender of France in the same carriage.

The First World War, however, brought the age of railways to an end, even though the mileage of railways continued to grow in the US till 1924, in France till 1935 and in Russia to the 1960s, and even though Reza Shah made a serious attempt to unite Iran around his trans-Iranian railways of the 1920s. With the coming of the car the railways ceased, even in the USA, to be primarily private enterprises. The combination of automobile and aeroplane reduced the railway mileage in the US after 1939, so that except on the east coast the train became a memory: a disappearance which Americans may regret in the 1980s. The American pattern was nowhere followed so extensively but, all the same, the decline was absolute.

The Second World War was a conflict primarily of air and road traffic. But the railways which led to, and stopped, at Auschwitz (built by the Austrians when that town was a part of the Austro-Hungarian Empire) carried more millions to their death than did even the southern line in Britain, or the eastern one in France, during the First World War. Before and afterwards, the trains of Russia have also formed the 'slave caravans' of the 'Gulag archipelago', in the phrase of Solzhenitsyn. In red cattle-cars along Russian railways, millions of peasants were transported to cities of the north in 1929–31. That is also how the Volga German Republic was physically removed to Kazakhstan in 1941, and how millions of Russians were sent back in 1945 from the free countries of the West.

Railways produced forceful unions. Here, as in other ways, their history in France is characteristic. The French railway union numbered 44,000 in 1854, and 310,000 by 1914. They had ensured by then a twelve-hour day for drivers, though only a fifth of railwaymen were members of the union. To begin with they had been organised in order to expel English train drivers. Later they became bourgeois in outlook, despite occasional strikes. Later

---

* The armoured train had apparently been invented by Lord Fisher as a captain 'after the occupation of Egypt in 1882'.

still, the French railway union became dominated by Communists. They used their power conservatively, keeping down fares, the railway staff living like civil servants, proud of the skilled organisation which enabled so many special trains to travel so punctually at the beginning of the annual holidays. Now that the trains run by computer it is scarcely possible to recapture the delight and the skill required to maintain in the railway age the punctuality and accuracy of thousands of trains.

The railway was for several generations the decisive unit of modernised transport. Along the tracks came the food and the coal which enabled the modern city to survive, even to be constructed. Though railway traffic did not grow fast in the 1970s, it seems that if coal becomes again the major source of energy, as is possible, the railway will be revived in many countries, at least as a carrier of freight. It should be realised too that railway traffic in general, measured in terms of net ton kilometres, trebled between 1950 and the late 1970s and increased, even in the 1960s and 1970s, on a world basis as fast as it ever had. This was particularly true in respect of Russia which now accounts for over half the world's freight traffic.

World Rail Traffic (freight ton kilometres)

	World	Africa	North America*	South	Asia	Europe	Australasia	USSR
1950	1,995	35·5	955	27·0	115	248	12·0	602
1960	3,338	56·5	947	31·9	386	397	15·1	1,504
1977	6,209	118·6	1,446	77·3	595	606	35·8	3,331

* Including Central America and the Caribbean

34

A New World of Energy

Take Standard Oil stock and your family will never know want.

J. D. Rockefeller I

1

The sources of the world's energy had meantime been transformed. Coal was not the only means of powering enterprises in 1900. Gas was discovered by William Murdock, son of a millwright of Ayr. Murdock gained employment in Boulton's factory in Soho, Birmingham, in 1777. It was said that he was offered his job because he went to see Boulton wearing a wooden hat which he had turned on a lathe of his own making. He was sent to Cornwall to supervise the steam pumps being used in mines there which had been provided by Boulton. About 1792 Murdock began making experiments in the illuminating properties of gases emanating from coal and wood and, a few years later, was using gas to light his house in Redruth. On his return to Birmingham in 1800 he continued to experiment. He ensured that the Peace of Amiens of 1802 could be celebrated in Birmingham by extensive gas illuminations. In 1803 the foundry at Soho began to be lit by gas. In 1804 the firm of Phillips and Lee, cotton spinners of Manchester, decided to light their mill with gas. From then on, gas light became generally popular. Work similar to Murdock's had been done in Paris by Philippe Le Bon and the idea caught on there even faster than it did in England. That essential assistance to hard work in modern times, artificial light, spread soon thereafter, through factories, hospitals, barracks and, later, streets and houses. Large gas tanks were distributed at random, often causing 'gas house districts' polluting the air foully, symbolising very well, as Lewis Mumford put it, the 'ambiguous face' that progress has sometimes seemed to give to the world[1].

Gas companies, often under British control, spread throughout the world, though it was not till 1834 that gas was introduced in the US and not till 1844 that a coal gas plant was introduced into Latin America – in Havana, to be precise, where the streets were lit by gas in 1848. Thereafter most streets of Latin America were so lit during the 1850s and 1860s – chiefly as a result of investment by British firms, to begin with. The new illumination in cities made reading infinitely easier. It was probably as responsible for the growth of literacy as was education. It led in the end too to gas fires, gas heating and to gas cooking. It also successfully challenged the candle of whale sperm and the oil lamp from whale oil which had made whaling so dramatic a part of the West's commerce in the days of Melville.

2

Even so, a more effective new challenge as a means of securing energy was electricity. In 1881 the President of the British Institute of Mechanical Engineers said, 'It is possible and even probable that one of the great uses to which electric power will be applied *eventually* will be the simple conveyance of power by . . . large wires.' During the next ten years, that prophecy was fulfilled.

The history of electricity is long. The first philosopher, Thales of Miletus, discovered that amber, when rubbed, attracted light substances such as cork, pith or parchment. It is from the Greek word for amber (*elektron*) that this energy derives its internationally used name. (Electra, the 'bright one', was a daughter of Agamemnon, whom she avenged, with the help of her brother Orestes.) Between Thales in 580 BC and William Gilbert in the seventeenth century AD in England progress, as in many things, was modest, though the prince of early naturalists, Theophrastus, discovered that some minerals become electrified when heated. He also knew that some fish give out numbing powers, and that the glow-worm and fire-fly have extraordinary qualities.* William Gilbert, a scientist from an old Suffolk family, in his study of magnetism, *De Magnete*, first used the word 'electrica' for these reactions. A hundred years later Robert Boyle showed that the attraction between the body and the object which it attracts is mutual. Otto von Guericke, in Magdeburg, then built an electrical machine, with a revolving ball of sulphur, while Isaac Newton, in Cambridge, substituted glass for sulphur in his version of the same machine.

Many others noticed that electricity could be made by subjecting silk, hair or wool to movement. Charles François de Fay in France established that electricity is of two kinds, repelling and attracting, negative and positive. In 1745 E. G. von Kleist and Musschen-broek in Pomerania and Holland independently discovered the

---

* Theophrastus died in 288 BC, aged 106, regretting that life is short.

'Leyden jar'. That object was less elegant than it sounds, but it was a work of art all the same, like most early inventions. A thin flask was partly filled with water and corked up. A metallic nail was pushed through the cork until it touched the water. With the bottle held in the hand, the nail was presented to an electric machine. A release of energy followed. Then a scientist from London, Sir William Watson (who also discovered that 'holly was polygamous'), found that a chain and iron or mercury could be substituted for the hand and the water respectively. Subsequently Benjamin Franklin, the first great scientist to be born in the US, made his famous identification of lightning with electricity by sending a silk kite into the sky during a thunderstorm. He argued that electricity was not created by friction, but merely collected from its diffused state through other matter, by which it was attracted. A glass globe, he said, when rubbed, attracted electricity from the person who rubbed. The same globe was able to give out electricity to anything or any person which had less of it. Franklin also proved that in electrical undertakings as much electricity is added on one side as is subtracted on the other. A little later, Alessandro Volta, professor of physics at Pavia, discovered that when a pile of copper or silver discs is divided from zinc discs by a wet cloth they cause electricity, provided the least large one of each group is connected to a conductor. He thus invented the new word 'volt' and, in effect, produced the first electrical battery. Volta also realised that all metals could be placed in a series so that each one could become positive when coming into contact with the one next below it in the series.

In 1807 Sir Humphry Davy, a genius from Cornwall and a Methodist like many early innovators, announced his discovery of the electrical decomposition of the alkalis, potash and soda, so obtaining two new metals, potassium and sodium. The Royal Society in London gave him 2,000 pairs of electric plates with which he produced the first electric arc light – the first practical use of electricity. Next, Hans Christian Oersted, a professor of chemistry in Copenhagen, established in 1819 that when a wire joining the last plates of one of Volta's piles is held near a pivoted magnet, or the needle of a compass, the latter is deflected to stand transversely to the wire. That indicated a magnetic field around the conductor. A year later François Arago, from French Catalonia, and Humphry Davy both independently discovered the power of an electric current to magnetise iron or steel. Another

Frenchman, André-Marie Ampère, professor of mathematics in Paris, who came from the neighbourhood of Lyons and whose father was executed in the Revolution for standing out against revolutionary excesses, in 1820 told the French Academy of Sciences of his discovery of the dynamic interaction between conductors conveying electrical currents.

The early discovery of electricity was thus an international enterprise. Governments played little part. Both characteristics continued throughout the nineteenth century. Among numerous great men of electricity Michael Faraday is outstanding. He was the son of a blacksmith in Surrey. Apprenticed to a bookbinder, Faraday went in 1812 to lectures by Davy, to whom he became assistant. In 1822 Faraday caused a wire carrying an electric current to rotate round a magnetic pole. In 1831 he established that electricity could be generated by rotating a copper disc between the poles of a magnet. He also caused a wire carrying an electric current to circle a fixed magnet.

These discoveries led to the creation of a whole new industry. They are a good example (rare in the early years of the Industrial Revolution) of science influencing technology, rather than the other way round. As a rule, theorists worked out the principles of an invention after the inventor had finished his work. Faraday's rotating copper disc, meantime, became the parent of innumerable machines. Two years later at Göttingen, Karl Friedrich Gauss, director of the observatory, with Wilhelm Weber, his assistant, sent electric signals to the house next door by means of a wire placed on the Johannes Kirke in the city. The development in the 1840s of the telegraph* was the first major practical use of this power.

Between 1832 and 1870 the sciences dependent on Faraday's discoveries began to take shape: William Thomson (later Lord Kelvin) was working from 1842 on electromagnetics, Werner von Siemens on the dynamo and James Clerk Maxwell on experimental physics. In 1870 the dynamo had been achieved by the Belgian, Zénobe T. Gramme.

These developments enabled the introduction of machinery powered by electricity. The application of electricity to the manufacture of machine tools was demonstrated at the Vienna Exhibition of 1873. Electricity began to replace steam for driving the

* See below, page 388.

overhead belts which were then common in large factories. The earliest practical uses of electricity were for lighting. In 1858 the lighthouse at Dungeness on the south coast of England used electricity for its lamps (created by Faraday, with an assistant, Holmes). Other filaments were tried out during the 1860s. The Gare du Nord in Paris and the Menier chocolate factory (ever in the van of technology) at Nosiel-sur-Marne were lit by electricity in 1875. In 1878 Joseph Swan, a chemist from Sunderland, made the first satisfactory filament lamp, but Thomas Edison, son of a Canadian-born shingle merchant on the south shores of Lake Huron but who had begun life as a newsboy on the Grand Trunk Railway, developed another type, which he propagated with determination. Swan and Edison merged their undertakings in 1883. The lighting by electricity of Boston and of other US cities followed fast. Edison had already established a station for the supply of electricity in New York in 1881. He went on to become one of the great entrepreneurs of industrial society. The same year a similar electricity station was built in Milan. Debates in the House of Commons in England were lit by electricity in 1881 too. House-to-house installation followed. By 1900 the supremacy of incandescent electric light over gas and all rivals was established. Safer and more reliable than gas, it was also cleaner.

These inventions had vast commercial consequences. Thus in Germany an engineer, Emile Rathenau, bought the German rights of Edison's invention, and between 1883 and 1903 his AEG (Allgemeine Elektrizitäts-Gesellschaft) transformed Germany, filling the country with more electrical appliances than any other in Europe so far. The distributors and manufacturers of electricity organised themselves into a formidable cartel or vertical collaboration between the different elements within the enterprise.

The use of electricity for industry came more slowly than for light, since generators could only supply the maximum capacity of electricity for a short period during each day. Large-scale use, therefore, seemed too difficult. But those problems involved were resolved by the 1890s. Electricity was particularly important in new industries: electrochemical firms were established producing aluminium and calcium soda. Even in Italy, installation of electricity for industry was beginning in 1892[2]. Here, England was somewhat laggardly, behind the US and Germany, for it was only between 1903 and 1905 that large power stations began to provide energy in bulk rather than in each locality. A decline in the comparative rate of adoption of new technology in Britain was thereafter evident.

The use of electricity for industry was assisted by the growth of hydroelectricity after 1890. Ever since 1829 it had been known that waterwheels could be fitted with a turbine (a discovery of Benoit Fourneyron). One of the earliest machines so developed operated at 2,300 volts per minute, under a 350-foot waterfall. But there are not very many such waterfalls in Europe. The first successful hydroelectric installation was not set up till the one at Niagara in 1886. Subsequently the water resources of the Appalachians were used in the US, while Barcelona's electricity came from the hydroelectric plants in the Pyrenees. The use of turbines began soon after, though the greatest achievement in that method of producing energy was in the steam versions which were introduced into ships by Charles Parsons after 1884 and came to be employed in the technically advanced British Navy after 1897. The swiftness of the Dreadnought battleship after 1905 was the consequence of the turbine.

By then, too, electricity had come to be used in a number of other undertakings. First in importance after the telegraph, no doubt, was the telephone devised in 1876, but there was also the microphone, invented about the same time.* From 1902 electric railways, in deep tunnels, were introduced into many cities. From 1904 mainline railways began to try out electricity in place of steam. In the course of the next generation electricity came to be the main method of providing energy in numerous other ways. Lighting, cooking and heating by electricity all caused the average inhabitant of rich countries to depend upon centralised springs of power in a wholly new way. Subsequently new sources of diversion and education such as radio and television also depended on electricity. Similarly, the consumption of electric power gives as good an indication of the relative wealth of nations as anything else.

Unions running electricity works were early aware of their power: Pataud, the leader of the French electricians during *la belle époque*, plunged Paris into darkness by a strike in 1908 and, on another occasion, secured a strike at the Opéra, during a royal visit. The increase of wages demanded came within minutes of negotiation. Electricity workers have never forgotten the lesson implicit. Nor have politicians.

---

* For these benefits see below, page 392.

Installed Electricity 1977

		million kilowatts
1	US	576,206
2	Russia	237,805
3	Japan	122,349
4	W. Germany	79,131
5	Britain	72,671
6	Canada	52,451
7	France	25,063
8	India	17,218
9	Haiti (for comparison)	102

Electricity has brought ease to the majority of those who have been able to use it. But the contributions made have not been entirely beneficial, since the use of electricity for war, and even for torture, have in the twentieth century given a new dimension to brutality. Lenin said that 'socialism is the dictatorship of the proletariat plus the widest introduction of the most modern electrical machinery'. General Franco might have paid the same tribute to the electric filament which he installed in the smallest villages when justifying his own system.

Long before 1900, too, there was not only a new method, electricity, of using energy to take the place of steam so as to power the Industrial Revolution, but a new source of energy to obtain steam and electricity: namely oil.

3

The use of petroleum for energy antedated gas and coal. There are innumerable places between the Nile and the Indus where oil appears on the surface of the earth, mostly in Iraq. There, mysterious 'naphtha', as it was called, came out of the rocks to perplex the Babylonians. Mixtures of bitumen were used to caulk ships and to waterproof floors in the ancient world. It was continuously an object of commerce after 3000 BC, and was used in the Middle Ages for 'Greek fire'. Oil was used again in the Renaissance on ships, while the Aztecs used bitumen as a chewing gum. The lake of asphalt, a form of bitumen, in Trinidad was prized from the sixteenth century onwards for many purposes. All this oil was on, or very near, the surface and had to be little more than scooped up.

In 1848 James Young, a chemist from Glasgow of humble origins (like the majority of innovating geniuses), used a spring of oil which reached the surface at Alfreton, in Derbyshire, as a means of lubrication. Subsequently, by dry distillation of coal he made paraffin. This he sold as 'paraffin lubricating oil' and made a fortune which he employed partly to finance David Livingstone's missionary journeys. A variety of this paraffin, made from asphalt, was marketed in the US as 'kerosene'. A good deal of sporadic drilling in the deserts of the world was going on at that time. The search was for water or salt. This method of drilling deep bore-holes was Chinese in origin: there were instances of it in Szechwan dating back to the first century BC. Some of these drills met oil instead. George Bissell, of New Hampshire in the US, wondered whether to embark on drilling for oil alone. He consulted Professor Sillman of Yale, who advised him to do so. Bissell, thereupon, sought oil in 1857 in Pennsylvania. He found it seventy feet down. Within fifteen years, Pennsylvania was producing ten million barrels of oil, each holding 360 pounds. The US soon began to make lamps for kerosene, as well as kerosene itself in large quantities. Much was exported. Then an engine based on the use of oil was made in Vienna in 1870. Another such machine was made in New York in 1873.

There was soon much drilling for oil elsewhere. Wells in Galicia (Poland) had been opened in 1863, others in Romania in 1857 and in Russia, near the Caspian Sea, in 1860, the last of these being the work of Ludwig and Robert Nobel, two great Swedish entrepreneurs and founders of the Nobel Prize. By 1900 Russia was producing ten million tons of oil a year, or about half the oil in the world. Baku, previously the fortress city of a minor Turkish khan, was incorporated into the Russian Empire in 1806. It had 46,000 inhabitants in 1886, and 108,000 in 1896 – a focus for German conquest both in 1918 and 1942 since it was the main source of Russian oil. Huge reserves of oil were also discovered in 1870 in Venezuela and in 1901 in Texas. Most of this oil was found in small places in porous rock, usually under some form of pressure which was (and is) released by the well.*

All these adventures needed a large infrastructure of commerce: oil was first carried in wooden barrels, then in tin cans, then in iron or steel drums and finally in steam tankers (earliest in use on the Caspian in 1879). Long pipelines of steel were built in both Russia and the USA in the 1870s and subsequently elsewhere.

The paraffin or kerosene lamp had a long history and it survives. Kerosene was burned in lamps which had until then burned whale

---

* Subsequently a good deal of oil has been recovered by artificially increasing the pressure on the deposit of oil by pumping water or gas into the reservoir.

oil. But the most striking development based on oil was, of course, the motorcar, the private means of travel which, with the truck,* in the twentieth century dethroned the railway from its dominant position. Various experiments in the 1880s ensured the success of an engine based on internal combustion and a continuing market for oil. Unlike the shipment of coal, that of oil needed, from the start, a business with great capital. From the 1880s onwards good profits would be gained by those who could control the distribution of oil. John D. Rockefeller was the first to realise that idea, with his Standard Oil Company. Others followed.

In the course of the twentieth century the oil companies of the world became among the largest private enterprises, if not the biggest of all, in the main industrial democracies. Some of those companies had budgets more substantial than those of independent states. The world of oil came soon to be dominated by these companies, each of which formed fleets which were also grander than those of most states. Some of them signed treaties (such as that of 1902 between Shell, Royal Dutch and Caucasian interests) of greater importance than many formal international pacts. This was not a new occurrence: Italian bankers in the Renaissance and the East India companies in the seventeenth century were forerunners. There was sometimes state intervention. Thus, the Anglo-Persian oil company was set up in 1909 to exploit a concession granted to a prospector from New Zealand, William d'Arcy (oil had been discovered in quantity in Persia in 1908; it began to be exported in 1912). The British government became a majority shareholder of that company in 1914, after Winston Churchill, an ebullient First Lord of the Admiralty in Britain, had taken the decision in 1913 to fuel the British fleet with oil.

Thereafter oil played an increasingly important part in international politics. Britain and other countries sought to gain strategic control over their oil supplies. World production of petroleum, about 20 million tons in 1900, rose to 34 million by 1910 and doubled between 1910 and 1920 (to 100 million). It doubled yet again between 1920 and 1930. Even the years of the depression between 1930 and 1940 saw an increase in oil production by another fifty per cent. During and after the Second World War the further increase was enormous, the production reaching

---

* Known in England as the 'lorry', a curious word and one of the few instances of an English original being *worse* than the American innovation. It is not an old word, despite the *Daily News* of 2 September 1881 speaking of 'the time honoured lorry, indigenous to Liverpool'.

about 3,000 million tons by 1980.

The political significance of this convenient form of energy scarcely recognised as such a hundred years ago has been considerable. Ludendorff attributed the defeat of Germany in 1918 to a shortage of oil and Lord Curzon, agreeing, put it more ceremoniously when he said, 'Victory came to us floating on waves of petrol.' The US tanks, which in 1918 determined the outcome of the First World War, on the western front, were of course oil-powered.

After 1918 ships, aeroplanes, motorcars and lorries all began to use oil on a huge scale. Oil caused from the beginning political opportunities, problems and delusions. Thus oil poured out of Persia, most of it through the barrels and the pipes of the Anglo-Iranian Oil Company, which till 1950 was a most successful economic enterprise, paying a dividend of seventeen per cent to its shareholders between 1920 and 1950. After 1927 the Turkish Petroleum Company, then owned by Britain, produced oil in Iraq, and after 1933 the ARAMCO, an American company, did the same on an ever increased scale in Saudi Arabia. After 1945 the other principalities of the Persian Gulf sought oil and found it, most of them on a scale to make them rich beyond the dreams of Croesus.

From the 1930s onwards oil became again the determining source of energy in war. The help of the Texas Oil Company was very welcome to General Franco in the Spanish Civil War. Much of the Second World War can be explained as a battle for oil, one of the raw materials in which Germany had not made herself self-sufficient. Hence the necessity for Germany to capture Romania's ample oil wells. Hence too her unsuccessful drives towards the Middle East fields and to Baku, the main oil port of Russia's huge oil industry. War in the Far East began in 1941 when the US sought to restrain Japan from building a mainland empire on the (apparent) ruins of the Chinese one by cutting her off from oil in Java. The inadequate supplies of oil of the countries of the Axis was their main weakness. The decisive weapons of the 1940s, aircraft and tanks, depended absolutely on petroleum, as did the car and the half-track vehicle. In the end, Germany's use of oil from Romania and Japan's use of oil from Java continued till late in 1944. On the other hand, the oil resources in both the US and in Russia (as well as the former's access to the wells of Mexico and of Venezuela) were of critical importance in the long war which the Germans succeeded in imposing on the world.

Since 1945 the two most powerful countries in the world have been those which were over the length of the whole era the largest oil producers, the USA and Russia – and the diplomacy of oil has been infinitely complicated. The Suez crisis derived from European anxiety over a safe supply of oil, and the turning-point in the history of the breach between the USA and Cuba occurred in 1960, when the major US oil companies refused to refine, in their Cuban installations, oil imported from Russia.

From 1950 onwards, and more particularly after 1970, the oil-producing countries fought a continuous battle against the consumers, often to their own long-term disadvantage perhaps but in the short-term with vast political success. The Middle East governments who produced oil first insisted on receiving from oil companies a half-share of profits. That was agreed, and the US government agreed to compensate US oil companies for any loss in their revenue. This undertaking, equitable though it seemed, from the beginning gave a substantial boost to the idea of the governments' role in the economics in the producing countries. This was bad, generally, for trade, and bad for the economies of the countries concerned. Then an organisation was formed of countries which exported oil. This was the Organisation of Petroleum Exporting Countries (OPEC), devised in 1960 by the brilliant Venezuelan Minister of Mines, Juan Pablo Pérez Alfonso. It failed to reach any agreement within itself till 1971. Then the Shah of Persia insisted on a rise in prices following the war between Israel and the Arabs in 1973; the Arabs forced another rise in prices with the intention of persuading the democratic industrial countries to require Israel to withdraw from territories which she had occupied after the war of 1967. Subsequently the Arabs brought equal influence to bear on all the industrial countries, which had taken cheap oil for granted.

The world has since seemed to be suffering from a crisis in energy. Certainly, the need to import oil from a remote source has made the industrial nations nervous. After 1972 the US became for the first time a major importer of oil and, by 1980, oil imports reached sixty per cent of her needs – most of it coming from Saudi Arabia. Still, a sense of proportion is needed. There is a great deal of coal in the world and there are new oil fields – such as those discovered in the 1970s in the North Sea and the Gulf of Mexico. There are new sources of energy such as nuclear power, tidal power and solar energy. Some natural growth (such as sugar, starches and celluloses) are already playing a part.* There is hydrogen. The planets apparently have oil, and large reserves of natural gas may lurk in the deep interior of the earth. Thus, the 'energy crisis' is due to a rise in prices of oil at a time before alternative sources of energy have been adequately prepared. Even so, the dependence on oil from the Middle East by the industrial democracies and the possibility that Russia may become an oil-importing country make the danger of international conflict over the sources of Middle East oil quite severe. Sixty per cent of all the non-Communist world's oil, after all, came in 1980 from parts of the Persian Gulf. Further, the income from oil in the countries of the Persian Gulf has transformed the politics of that explosive region with its tyrannical or feudal governments. Western governments and oil companies alike have become unhappy clients of despots.

The 'oil war' of the 1970s, particularly 1973, has occupied the minds of men continuously, often ignoring the farce of a state of affairs in which a product which costs ten cents a barrel to produce (the cost of oil in 1980 in Kuwait to the producer) can be sold at $19·50 (the posted price of oil there) – or a profit of 19,500 per cent. The governments of the states which produce oil without contributing effort, capital or skill of their own have acquired large fortunes which they do not know how to use. In 1960 the Middle East oil states received $1,720 million in revenue, the companies the same. In 1974 the oil states received $76,500 million, the companies $1,516 million. Later figures show an even more bizarre imbalance. For example, Saudi Arabia received $1·2 billion in 1970, $29 billion in 1974 and $70 billion in 1979 from oil. Governments which received $0·99 a barrel in 1970 received over $30 in 1980. The Middle East oil states apparently had reserves of $145,000 million at the end of 1977. The enrichment of these states is achieved by the gradual deterioration of the trading position of all but the economically strongest countries – a deterioration which has been only staved off by loans from the rich countries[3]. The explanation of this is the simple one that governments have established a cartel to elevate oil prices to a level which must be twenty times what it would reach in a free market. These developments have been of immense psychological importance for all Muslims. But the gold obtained looks like being fairy gold in the end.

* 150,000 cars in Brazil were produced to run on alcohol in 1979; some two million such cars are expected to be produced by 1985. France is also experimenting successfully with energy from the Jerusalem artichoke.

4

During the first half of the twentieth century the essential chemical elements in the world were revealed as numbering about one hundred. Could any of these be broken down? And with what consequences? In January 1939 Otto Hahn and Lise Meitner, two German physicists, after many years of research by Rutherford in Cambridge and others, showed that the atom could indeed be split, causing a formidable release of energy. Subsequently, a group of Central European émigré scientists in the US, afraid that the Germans would put this discovery to destructive purposes, devised the first use of nuclear energy, the atom bomb. It was tested in July 1945 and dropped on Hiroshima in Japan in August 1945. Another such bomb was dropped on Nagasaki. The two bombs helped to bring the Second World War to a swift end. Since then this energy has given rise to a range of weapons which have altered international relations.*

Nuclear energy was the first example of a major source of power being first put to effect for the purpose of war: water power, wind power, coal and oil had all been used first for peace. It was also the first major scientific development which owed its character wholly to state-sponsored research. Since 1955 nuclear energy for peaceful purposes has also become possible. In 1975 it was responsible for about five per cent of the world's sources of energy, nine per cent in the US; by the end of the 1980s it is expected to be approaching thirty per cent. In France nuclear energy was already the main base for electricity in 1980.

Nuclear energy will be an important source of power in the future. But the dangers of loss, or misuse, of the raw material are considerable. Bombs could easily be made out of stolen uranium or plutonium (the man-made element which powers hydrogen bombs). Even a small loss of the material could be fatal to anyone who came into contact with it. Accidents already have occurred of unparalleled destructiveness in the closed community of Russia. The problem of what to do with nuclear material which has once been used is also formidable, and as yet unsatisfactorily resolved. But there is hope that this difficulty will be disentangled by storing such material in deep geological formations. Nuclear power is so baffling to the layman that he has ceased to reflect on it. Even so, it seems that much of the energy needed by man in the next century will be the consequence of it.

* These are discussed a little later, in the chapters on the Cold War.

35

Faster and Faster Journeys

Have the elder nations halted?
Do they drop and end their lesson,
    wearied over there beyond the seas?
We take up the task eternal, and the burden and the lesson
    Pioneers, O pioneers!

Walt Whitman

1

The nineteenth century may have seemed the age of railways but the railways themselves made possible a growth in the quantity of shipping, and a change in its character. Between 1750 and 1900 the changes in the character of ships were so great as to suggest that they constituted a new method of transport. 'No man will be a sailor who has contrivance enough to get himself into a jail,' said Dr Johnson about 1770, 'for being in a ship is being in jail, with the chance of getting drowned'[1]. Those who reclined in the staterooms of the Cunard or Pacific & Orient lines a hundred years later would have smiled condescendingly at that comment. The development of shipping can best be observed, first, in the quantity of British shipping which totalled a million tons (about 12,500 ships) in 1788; five million tons (27,000 ships) in 1861; and twelve million tons in 1913 (18,570 ships). British figures here as elsewhere give a good general impression, since in the late nineteenth century Britain was responsible for sixty per cent of the world steam tonnage. Sir William Petty thought that there were two million tons of ships in the world in 1666. There may have been four million in 1800, twenty million in 1900, but there are over 400 million in 1980: statistics which should caution those who believe that the ship has had its day.

Behind these statistics, however, lies an irregular story. In the eighteenth century the sailing ship then seemed incapable of further development. The only recent innovation had been the introduction, during the American Revolution, of copper bottoms, which were able to resist the destructive ship-worm found in tropical harbours. One further change of the 1760s was the 'chronometer', a really accurate watch which kept precise time during a long passage at sea – an essential possession when an inaccuracy

365

of only a few seconds was enough to produce a major error of longitude. Captain James Cook used one to make more accurate charts than anyone had made before.

Almost before Watt's steam engine was on the market, however, attempts were made to power ships by steam. In 1775 a boat powered by an eight-inch steam cylinder was tried out unsuccessfully on the Seine. In 1783 Jouffroy d'Abbans made his way up the Saône near Lyons in an 183-paddle-wheel steamer, the *Pyroscaphe*. The same year Oliver Evans, who had been apprenticed to a wheelwright and had become a miller at Newport in the US, began experiments on steamboats. Others tried to power ships by drawing in water at the bows and driving it out by steam at the stern: an early example of jet propulsion. In 1801 Lord Melville employed a small steamboat for touring a Scottish canal. In 1807 Robert Fulton, a Pennsylvania engineer of poor Irish ancestry – he had been apprenticed to a jeweller – returned to the US after years in Europe. In England he had met James Watt and the Duke of Bridgewater and worked for a time on improving the locks on canals. In France he constructed a submarine and a torpedo, but failed to interest the artillery-conscious Napoleon I. Fulton experimented with steam power and built a boat in Paris based on that use of energy. He first employed it satisfactorily when he despatched a steamboat, the *Clermont*, between New York and Albany, on the Hudson River.

Thereafter many such vessels were promoted on US internal waterways, particularly on the Great Lakes and, after 1817, on the Mississippi. The great days of the Mississippi steamboat were marvellously depicted by Mark Twain. That was a momentous development making possible viable settlements to the west of that river. Meantime, in Europe, the Clyde had a steamboat in 1812, as did the Seine in 1822. In 1825 there was a service on the Rhine, and also one on the Swiss lakes. A service by steam packet boat across the English Channel opened in 1821. Another service was soon arranged between St Petersburg and Stockholm. These ships made Europe more one continent than it had ever been.

Nevertheless, the use of these steamers on the ocean was delayed. When Flaubert caused his hero in *L'Education Sentimentale* to reflect on the 'mélancolie des paquebots', they were still short-distance or river boats. Naval architects were convinced of the superiority of sailing ships for war. In England the Board of Admiralty found it 'their bounden duty to discourage, to the best of their ability, the employment of steam vessels as they con-

sidered that the introduction of steam was calculated to strike a
fatal blow at the naval supremacy of the Empire'. So the mercantile marine continued to be dominated by the sailing clipper, which
derived from the eighteenth-century American two-masted
schooner.

Clippers specifically designed to carry European emigrants to
the USA in the nineteenth century were built for driving through
the worst seas, crossing the Atlantic in twelve to fourteen days
and even achieving 400 miles a day. The smaller clippers which
raced to bring back the much-prized new tea crop from China
could get to London in ninety days. The finest of these clippers,
the consummation, it might be said, of centuries of shipbuilding,
were built by Americans for British owners, as were the best ships
in the trade with Australia – to which other emigrants were also
making their way by much longer journeys (140 to 150 days in
1816–20, 120 days by 1850).

The delay in turning over to steam for ocean-going ships was
primarily caused by the difficulty of arranging for sufficient fuel.
Early attempts at steam-powered ships (for example, Brunel's
Great Western) underestimated the amount of coal needed. In the
end, this difficulty was resolved by the establishment of regular
coaling stations. Thereafter the arrangements for 'bunkering' coal
on board became adequate. The invention of the screw propeller
made of iron to take the place of the wooden paddle also saved
fuel, as well as giving the ship more thrust and being more efficient
in other ways. Steam began steadily to take over from sail, though
until the early 1900s more tonnage was registered under sail than
steam, even in Britain. Steamships were often slower than sailing
ships. The sailing ships had the advantage of paying nothing for
the power that worked them. It was not until 1904 that Britain
launched more steam- than sailing ships.

A second development of the mid nineteenth century was the
shift from wood, first to iron, then to steel, as the basic material
of shipping. Iron barges and canal boats led the way. Wilkinson's
iron barge has been noticed. Aaron Manby launched the first iron
steamer in 1822 on the Seine. But in 1850 iron ships were still
rare. In 1858 the French, having learned several lessons from the
early months of the Crimean War, began to encase their frigates
in iron. The British followed. The idea then caught on generally
for sailing ships. But the age of the 'ironclad' was short. Steel
ships were being constructed by the South in the American Civil
War, and in 1877 the British navy began to go over to steel –

which saved them one-fifth in the thickness of metal. By the end of the century new battleships were all steel, as were many other ships, from the Cunard passenger liners to oil tankers, which in the 1870s began to exercise the domination over big shipping which has grown ever since.

Alongside these nautical alterations came improvements in lighthouses and large new harbours, including some entirely artificial, such as that begun by the French at Cherbourg in 1780. New docks, such as the West India Dock, transformed commerce. Floating docks were devised, able to be towed to wherever a dry dock was needed, in whatever part of the world.

One aspect of the world's shipping was transformed by a single industry. The invention of refrigerated ships in the 1860s made it possible to carry raw meat long distances as a major item in commerce (so much so, indeed, that after 1895 the value of imports of meat into England exceeded that of raw cotton and, between 1919 and 1939, became Britain's most costly import). Even before the coming of these iced meat ships, refrigerated fishing fleets enabled trawling to take over fishing, following Sam Hewett's use of ice in his Yarmouth fleet about 1855. Thus were foreshadowed the Atlantic fishing fleets of the 1970s, with their 'mother' storage vessels, their colossal fish catches and their unprecedented reach.

Britain's dominance in shipping was still obvious in the late nineteenth century, when the merchant fleets of her commercial rivals were tiny. The US was more than ever reliant on Britain's merchant vessels (as on the protection of her fleet) during the years when she was in other ways overtaking Britain's economic prowess. Germany made headway in the Wilhelmine era, starting from an initially small tonnage. In 1880 German steam tonnage stood at 216,000 tons, less than that of Spain, but it had risen to two million by 1914. Similar headway was made by Italy, as a result of subsidies by the state to certain companies.

During the nineteenth and twentieth centuries this European thalassocracy was completed by substantial investment in fleets for war. The wooden walls which gave Britain her victories in the Napoleonic Wars were worthless after the development of the shell gun in 1832 – a fact made evident after the battle of Sinope in 1853, when a squadron of wooden Turkish frigates was blown to bits by Russian shells. Hence Napoleon III's invention of the ironclad, hence, subsequently, the steel fleets and the Dreadnoughts. In 1914 Winston Churchill looked on the British fleet which he as First Lord of the Admiralty had mobilised as the living symbol of imperial might: 'We may now picture this great fleet, with its flotillas and cruisers, steaming slowly out of Portland Harbour, squadron by squadron, scores of gigantic castles of steel winding their way across the misty shining sea, like giants bowed in anxious thought'[2].

'Giants' certainly, but clumsy giants, for those great fleets of 1914 on which so much time, energy and money had been spent, and rivalry between which had undoubtedly exacerbated international competition, played a modest part in the combats of the twentieth century. The great Lord Salisbury, British prime minister in the 1890s, observing the troubles ahead in the world after the death of Bismarck, used an appropriately maritime metaphor: 'This is the crossing of the bar: I can see the sea covered with white horses.' But the only way in which fleets played a decisive part in the First World War was in providing convoys for food ships. Submarines, on the other hand, nearly won both world wars for Germany. The age of great ships and naval battles was over. But, even so, during the twentieth century the US, previously unimportant as a mercantile power, twice saved Europe from German conquest (and from starvation) by a vast shipping programme. In 1914–20 the US launched ships totalling three million tons and, in 1943, ten million tons, creating a 'bridge of ships' to supply US forces abroad or allies with material and also to carry troops. In 1945 the USA had a merchant fleet of thirty million tons, in comparison with twelve million in 1939, while the once proud rulers of the waves, the British, had a mere ten million.*

Tankers for oil accounted in the 1970s for about two-fifths of tonnage in the world (175 million tons against 406 million tons in 1978). Indeed, oil tankers alone exceeded the tonnage in the world's maritime commercial fleets of 1913. In 1975 registered tons of new ships in the world reached thirty-five million and still employed 980,000 people. Even so, the increase in carriage of goods, as well as of passengers, by air, has grown faster than the increase in shipping, and the twentieth century has seen few innovations of importance in the nature of shipping comparable to the extraordinary occurrences on land and in the air; while gross output in 1978 had fallen to ten million tons and employed 825,000 – Europe being the loser: above all to Japan, South Korea, Taiwan

---

* Direct comparison of tonnage in the 1970s is misleading because of the artificially high figures for Panama, Greece, Liberia, etc.

and Brazil – a foretaste of a 'different' future than that anticipated
fifty years ago.

2

Industrialisation was also marked by a continuation of that improvement in roads which had already begun in France at least.
Napoleon desired to establish fourteen highways radiating from
Paris to assist his movement of troops. This affected all countries
adjacent to France, in particular that region of West Germany
which was a part of Napoleon's empire. Those roads were of help
to Prussia in the days after 1815, since they remained the best
roads in Germany, a country which had not benefited from the
network of Roman carriageways.

Equally, in the USA, the era of 1790 to 1820 was a time of
constant improvements. Numerous 'turnpike' companies were
formed. The cost of roads was met by the tolls levied on those
who used them. States and the federal government, however,
gave assistance from the beginning. The federal government was
responsible for the 'Cumberland road' built between Maryland
and St Louis and finished in 1836. In England at much the same
time John Macadam, a Scotsman who had been brought up in
America and made a fortune there as 'agent for the sale of prizes',
introduced, after 1827, his well-known method of surfacing roads
with granite lumps on top of a well-drained soil surface.

But these changes did not alter the costs of carrying goods. It
was still in 1830 more expensive to transport merchandise on land
than on water in almost every country under the sun. It cost $10
a ton, for example, to take grain from Philadelphia to Europe but
$100 a ton from Philadelphia to Pittsburg. The sedan chair and
the litter still seemed the best way to travel in many cities in the
Americas as in the East.

Railways brought, to begin with, a decline to both roads and
canals. Turnpike trusts in all rich countries were hard hit. Even
so, innovations on the roads themselves were continuous following
Macadam. Most European cities, for example, began to be paved.
Paved raised footpaths ('pavements'), first seen in London in
1765, came into general use. Asphalt began to be used in France
after 1835. 'Tarmac' was first seen in Nottingham in the 1830s. A
steamroller to crush this mixture was invented in France in 1859.
The first machine for crushing stones was introduced in Central
Park in New York after 1858. That was needed more in the US
(where labour was always expensive) than in Europe, where the

breaking of stones by hand continued until, in some places (Spain for example), the 1970s. Indian roads were not paved before 1900, and few streets in Indian cities were paved before 1914. That went for the rest of the world also.

The railway, though it chiefly affected long-distance travel, also increased the number of short journeys within cities: a factor shown by the growth of an army of taxis in most centres of the industrial world – 15,000 horsecabs plied their fares in London in 1881 – and by the creation in Paris in the 1820s of the omnibus, an idea and a word carried to London in 1829 by George Shïlli-beer, a retired midshipman who began his career in Paris. It was not, however, till the 1850s that 'buses' became a prominent method of travel inside English cities. They were challenged by short-distance city trams devised in New York in 1832. A tramway car with thirty seats ran that year in the Bowery in New York, along four flanged wheels. It was unsuccessful, but was revived in the same city in 1852, by a French engineer, Loubat. A better system was introduced into Philadelphia in the 1860s and was widely copied, from Europe to Brazil. All these new forms of travel within cities, including trams, were drawn by horses to begin with, but they never went faster than six or seven miles an hour. Steam cars soon began to be used in France, dirty and noisy though they were. The first cable tramway was built, at San Francisco, in 1873. The tram came into its own with the introduction of electricity after 1884, and the beginning of the overhead trolley car system.

The decline of roads, therefore, during the railway age was relative. The decline in the use of canals and rivers was in some countries (the US, Britain) absolute, even on the continent of Western Europe, where waterways continued to be used for commerce. Throughout the US and Britain, nevertheless, a nation-wide canal system had been completed by the 1820s. The quantity of coal carried along those canals (and improved rivers) was enormous. A good example of a waterway which transformed the economy of a country was the Erie Canal. It was opened in 1825 and not only brought grain from the Great Lakes down to New York City (which was then growing fast), but also confirmed that city as the commercial metropolis of the nation. Much work too was done in the nineteenth century on the improvement of rivers such as the Danube, Rhine, Guadalquivir, Mississippi and St Lawrence. Those works coincided with much legal discussion about the status of international waterways such as the Rhine; for in the early nineteenth century a cargo boat paid toll fourteen times on the Elbe between Hamburg and Magdeburg. Finally, at the end of the age of canals, three most striking examples were constructed: the Suez, Kiel and Panama canals, opened in 1869, 1895 and 1914 respectively. The first of these confirmed the critical position of Egypt on the way between Europe and the East, indeed restoring Egypt to the importance in the world's communications that she had lost when the Portuguese circumnavigated Africa. Both the second and third of these canals had strategic significance from the beginning; both transformed the commerce of the Pacific and the Baltic also. Further large canals were constructed by forced labour in Russia under Stalin: for example, the canal linking the White Sea with the Baltic which probably cost more lives than the digging of the Suez Canal or the Pharaoh Necos's canal put together.

Still, the new age of communication was in the end dominated by new methods of transport. The two developments were the car on the ground and the aeroplane in the air. They were preceded by the bicycle.

There were some ideas for bicycles in the early nineteenth century. Thus Baron Drais von Sauerbronn, director-general of rivers and forests at Baden, devised his two-wheel 'draisine' in 1818. He took it to Brazil where it created a great sensation. But it was almost more a piece of gymnastic equipment than a means of locomotion. Then Gavin Dalzell, of Lesmahagow, put cranks on to a hobby horse in 1836. The idea of treadles and a brake were thought of in the 1840s, while Pierre Michaux placed pedals on to the front wheel and formed a company in France to sell 'velocipedes' in 1861. By 1865 he and his brother Ernest were making 400 'velos' a year.

The idea was taken up in Coventry in England and in the US, whither one of the Michaux's mechanics emigrated. By 1885, 3,000 men were making bicycles at Coventry. There were soon innumerable varieties on the English market, including a tricycle. Most were penny-farthings to begin with, though the modern 'safety bicycle' with two wheels was created in 1885. In 1881 John Boyd Dunlop, a Scottish vet living in Belfast, patented the pneumatic rubber tyre. The 'bicycle craze' then began. 'Every morning,' wrote a participant, Amy Strachey, 'from eleven to lunch time, everyone who was idle enough to take two hours off and rich enough . . . went to Battersea Park . . . on Sundays, we went further afield . . . I have a little picture [in my mind] of Mrs

[Beatrice] Webb, who rode extremely well, scudding before us down Lupus Street with both hands behind her back, steering by her pedals. She was a graceful and intrepid rider'[3].

Though this sporting craze faded with the advent of cars, the numbers of bicycles in use steadily rose in, for example, France (981,000 in 1900, 8·7 million in 1938). Only the coming of the cheap car after 1945 in Europe led to a decline of the bicycle but in the 'energy crisis' of the 1970s it experienced a revival. In Holland there are twice as many bicycles as there are cars: seven million bicycles to fourteen million people. Bicycling remains a popular sport. In France, in particular, bicycle manufacturers worked hard in order to ensure that. The press have helped to turn bicycling champions there into public heroes.

The bicycle was followed by the motor bicycle, a high-speed petrol engine devised by Gottlieb Daimler, an engineer from Württemberg. Werner Frères of Paris marketed a machine of this type for the first time. But the motor bicycle did not become popular till the First World War, in which it played a considerable part, usually serving despatch riders – of particular value since it could travel along worse tracks than cars could and, of course, it travelled faster than any horse. Motor bicycles subsequently have served a small but fairly consistent public; there were 50,000 in France in 1920 and over half a million in 1935.

This new means of communication would have been very different had it not been for the essential contribution of rubber. The plant from which this essential source of pneumatic tyres came was indigenous to Brazil. The French scientist Charles de la Condamine went down the Amazon in 1743 and was much impressed by a waterproof and elastic product used by the Omagua tribe in Pará province. They used it to make unbreakable bottles, boots and hollow bouncing balls, and called it *cahout-chou*. The Portuguese used this India rubber, as they called it, to erase pencil marks from paper. The Brazilians tried to keep the seed of the rubber plant to themselves. But 70,000 were smuggled out by H. Wickham in 1870, taken to Kew Gardens and subsequently sown in the East.

The European demand for rubber from the 1880s onwards (first for bicycles and motor bicycles, then for cars) gave rise to a great boom for rubber on the Amazon in the late nineteenth century, and thereafter Ceylon and Malaya were converted by the English into great producers. Still the Opera House at Manaus on the Negro stands as the great monument to European demand for rubber. Afterwards Brazil was undercut by the large rubber companies of Malaya of whom some (Batu, Caves Rubber, Linggi Plantations, Bukit Rajah Rubber) returned some of the world's largest profits ever made by any company between, in particular, 1910 and 1914.

The motorcar, meantime, had arrived on the roads of Europe and North America. The preparation for this was long drawn out. Thus Trevithick, the inventor of the locomotive, in 1800 built a steam road carriage which would carry several people. Oliver Evans, the pioneer of steamboats, did the same in Philadelphia in 1804. Sir Goldsworthy Gurney, a Cornish surgeon, devised a steam carriage which travelled from Bath to London in 1829. It ran for hire for three months regularly between Gloucester and Cheltenham, at about nine miles an hour. But Gurney was prevented from continuing his work by a legal ban on steam vehicles on the road. In the mid nineteenth century there were other attempts to use steam for road travel, but apart from the steamroller of 1857 and steam plough of 1850, and a few unsuccessful creations by an Austrian, Siegfried Markus, in Vienna in the 1860s, nothing was done till the 1870s.

In 1876 Dr Nikolaus August Otto, a German engineer, made a stationary gas-powered engine, of which 50,000 were sold for various purposes. But it became clear that oil-powered engines had a greater future, at least for undertakings which would try to ensure movement, for oil is easily transported and stored. It also yields more heat per unit of weight than coal. From the 1870s petrol was available to meet a demand for this type of fuel. In 1885 Gottlieb Daimler, who had previously worked with Otto, applied a single cylinder and an air-cooled vertical machine to a carriage. These engines then began to be used not only for carriages but also for boats and stationary machines. In 1887 Daimler created his first 'four-wheeled, wooden-built light wagonette' powered by petrol. The same year René Panhard and Emile Levassor gained French patents for road carriages. Karl Benz of Mannheim then built an engine specifically intended for motorcars, leading to the four-wheelers of 1893, and Levassor invented the gear box.

In 1894 *Le Petit Journal* in France gave impetus to the new invention by organising a trial run of motorcars from Paris to Rouen. In 1895 a race was organised, from Paris to Bordeaux. The winner averaged fifteen miles an hour. During the 1890s the French led the world in production of cars. In 1896 cars took part in French army manoeuvres and, in England, they were allowed to travel on roads at fourteen miles an hour. Henry Ford in the US began making cars in 1896, particularly his twin-cylinder water-cooled engine, which travelled at twenty-five miles an hour. In 1899 the first tactical motor vehicle, a four-wheeled bicycle with a Maxim gun* on top, was exhibited in England, and the following year the politician Arthur Balfour predicted in the House of Commons that the future might well see 'great highways for rapid motor traffic'. By that year, all the fundamental technical problems of the automobile had been solved, and though until then all cars were 'custom' built to order, the market was ready for mass production.

In 1908 Henry Ford, a farmer's boy from Michigan with little education, after careful examination of the Sears Roebuck factory, began mass production of his Model T car, which sold in the next twenty years to fifteen million people. The benefit of this mass-produced machine was that it was cheap. The consequence was that in 1913 there were already a million motorcars on the US roads as opposed to 200,000 in Britain, 90,000 in France and a mere 70,000 in Germany. France, leading the world in the early days of automobile manufacture, was still concentrating on hand-made vehicles.

So began the age of the car and the lorry. In all cities of Europe and North America provisioning and travel still generally depended on the horse till 1914. Indeed, it is often forgotten that despite canals, railways and steamships, the long century of peace 1815–1914 marked the apotheosis of the horse – whether it was typified by the horse-drawn coach or the single steed. The horse population of the world was certainly at its height in 1914. When the rich countries made peace again the horse belonged to the past. The stables, blacksmiths, provenders of barley, hay and straw, gave way to the garages and petrol stations which symbolise our times almost more than anything else. Ford's company produced a million cars in the single year 1920. Paradoxically, the innovator of this new era, Ford himself, detested modernity, hated cities and thought that the only Americans worthy of the name were those on farms in the Midwest. He had no understanding of history, politics or literature, and though he was a pacifist he believed in the truth of the Jewish conspiracy to capture the world known as the 'Protocols of the Elders of Zion'.

Meantime, the lorry or truck began to take over from the ox-

* See below, page 641.

wagon, the bullock-cart, the horse and cart and, in the end, the railway as a means of carrying merchandise. No greater change in history has occurred.

The automobile industry has now become the largest enterprise in all the richer countries. Cars were not mentioned in the census of US business in 1900, but by 1929 their makers were at the top of the list. They have remained there. The industry has become the centre of a host of connected industries which even by 1939 were consuming, in one way or another, 90 per cent of the oil products of the US, 80 per cent of the rubber, 75 per cent of the plate glass, 68 per cent of the leather and even 51 per cent of the malleable iron. Motor manufacturers employ in 1980 four million people throughout the world, support another six million who make the components and give employment to another twenty-five million people who depend in some way on the industry.

Already by 1939 the manufacture of cars in the US was concentrated, in three companies: Ford, General Motors and Chrysler, which were together responsible for ninety per cent of production. Of these, Ford's was still owned by one family and directed by it. That family owned everything from the iron mines, which made the ore, which made the steel (which was used to make the chassis), to selling agencies. Ford's had long before that carried standardisation to the limit. General Motors was more decentralised. In 1978 it was the world's largest corporation, with a budget which exceeded that of all but twenty-two sovereign states. In the 1980s robots probably will make such motorcar firms as survive into greater producers than ever – with smaller cars.

The demand for cars led to improvement in the standard, and number, of paved roads. In 1916 the federal government in the US revived grants of aid for building roads, which they had abandoned for two generations. There were then 250,000 miles of surfaced roads in the US. By 1940 there were over a million and a half. In Nazi Germany new roads became an economic achievement, a metaphor and a symbol: 'the new road of Adolf Hitler, the autobahn, is in keeping with the essence of national socialism . . . we wish to fix our goal far ahead of us . . . we create for ourselves a road that leads only forward'[4]. Though Nazi Germany was defeated, most other countries have since copied, with 'motorways', the autobahns which were the Nazis' proudest achievement.

The swiftness of cars, and the recklessness with which they were driven, gave rise to a new major source of death. In a rich country such as the US, 40,000 deaths a year in the 1970s were attributed to accidents on the road, with thousands of injuries on top of that. Restrictions on speed and other measures have, however, maintained these numbers steady since the 1930s when there were far fewer cars. Cars also encouraged sedentary habits which, from the 1920s onwards in the US and from the 1950s onwards in Europe and other industrial democracies, created obesity and heart disease.

In the 1970s too, the 125 million cars and trucks on the roads of the US used up sixteen per cent of the energy consumed by the US and a third of the liquid fuel used. But in the future less petrol per mile will be used, though it may be some time before the car using one gallon for 1,000 miles is on the market: a machine which performed that feat won a prize in the US in 1976. Hydrogen may also one day be used as a fuel for motor vehicles. Otherwise, the evolution of the car has continued by a series of predictable, gradual steps. In the 1970s about a fifth of the world's vehicles were used for commercial services (57 out of 270 million).

In the USA the automobile came within reach of the average wage earner in the 1920s. It did not do so in Europe till the 1950s. Thereafter the ownership of cars seemed for a time almost an index of development, thus:

Motor Vehicles

	France	Britain	USA
1923	91,000	209,000	1,253,000
1929	930,000	1,409,000	26,704,825
1938	1,818,000	2,527,000	49,161,000
1979	19,340,000	16,092,000	135,155,000

Public opinion from then on swung in favour of machinery everywhere and in every craft. The eclipse of the horse and blacksmith was soon followed by that of the servant.

The differences between rich and poor countries are shown in the contrasts in numbers of motor vehicles in the different continents. Of about 285 million motor vehicles in use in 1977, Africa had about 7½ million, South America 15 million, while Asia had 40 million. North America (including Central America and the Caribbean) had 160 million, Europe 116 million and Australasia and the Pacific had 8½ million.

The increase of prices for oil, meantime, led to panic and nervousness in North America after 1973. The extent of American society's dependence on the internal combustion engine became more evident than before.

Most innovations in transport or mechanisation have, like railways and aviation, steam and oil, had decisive effects on war. But, apart from taking soldiers to war, officers to conferences, and infantry to blitz attacks, the motor vehicle has had a modest role in military affairs. Its troubles have been those of peaceable people. Many have died because of it; few in battle. Russia, the country which in the late twentieth century devotes more of its research to war than any other, has little to spare for the private car.

3

The history of motorcars has been mainly the history of a private possession. That of aircraft has been one of public considerations.

Human beings began to dream of flight as soon as they began to watch birds. The Greek legend of Daedalus who invented wings with which to escape from the labyrinth in Crete has echoes in other civilisations. The ancient Chinese flew kites and enabled men to be lifted by them. The Greeks and the Romans speculated on the matter. Leonardo did the same. In 1716 Emmanuel Swedenborg, a Swedish philosopher of innumerable interests, drew a detailed plan for a flying machine; he added: 'There are sufficient proofs and examples from nature that such flights can take place without danger.' Still, no successful ascents into the air were made within sixty years of that remark. When they were, they were made in balloons, mostly in France. The first such was made by the brothers Montgolfier in a paper balloon in 1783, lifted by hot air. In 1785 Jean-Pierre Blanchard and John Jeffries, an American physician who had sided with the British in the War of Independence, crossed the English Channel in a balloon. A balloon was used for observation by the French at the battle of Fleurus in 1794. After that, for a hundred years, balloons were mostly to be seen at fairs and carnivals, though some were employed in the American Civil War in the 1860s and in the siege of Paris of 1871. It was, after all, still widely thought that if God had meant us to fly he would have given us wings.

Then in 1884 a balloon was fitted with an electric engine by Renard and Krebs at the French Military Aeronautical Department. It was driven five miles, at fourteen miles an hour. One of these new balloons was used by the US in 1898 in their war against Spain, for reconnaissance at San Juan hill. In the 1890s both the French and Germans experimented with airships which worked by pressure. In 1900 General Count Ferdinand von Zeppelin, an aristocrat from Baden who had fought in the American and German wars of the 1860s, launched the first of his military airships. It stayed in the air for twenty minutes, but was wrecked when it landed. But, hoping for war, he persevered.

The first mechanised flight was in 1903, when after years of experimenting with gliders two American makers of bicycles from Dayton, Ohio, Orville and his brother Wilbur Wright, sons of a bishop of the United Brethren in Christ, flew a home-built, petrol-engined, heavier-than-air machine equal to twelve horse-power on sand dunes at Kitty Hawk in North Carolina. For a few years the idea was neglected. Then once again the French, so adventurous both in early ballooning and motoring, began to appreciate the possibilities of such machines. In 1906 a Brazilian, Alberto Santos Dumont, made a flight in a byplane in Paris – thereby causing his countrymen to believe that they could conquer space earlier than others; he became the hero of Edwardian Brazil. Two years later Wilbur Wright flew fifty-six miles across France. In 1909 Louis Blériot flew from Etampes to Orléans and then from Calais to Dover, across the English Channel. The Comte de Lambert next flew from Juvisy round the Eiffel Tower and back: the first flight over a town. In 1910 Chavez flew over the Alps and, in 1911, the aeroplane was first tried out in war: Hamilton, an American pilot, carried out a flight over Ciudad Juárez in the early days of the Mexican revolution. The Italians also used aircraft for reconnaissance in the Italo-Turkish war, which ensured them the colony of Libya, while the Spaniards were soon dropping explosive devices, the forerunners of bombs, from aircraft against the Riffs in Morocco. By 1912 both the British and French governments were convinced of the promising possibilities of aeroplanes for war. Until 1914, however, aviation was a brilliant sport for the daring, a stunt with some military possibilities. It played almost no part in commerce or transport. An aeroplane carried the post from Melbourne to Sydney in July 1914 but bad weather and technical delays caused the pilot to spend three days *en route* – longer than the train.

The First World War transformed this state of affairs. To begin with, aeroplanes were used, as balloons had been used at Fleurus, for reconnaissance. Fighters were needed to protect such 'spotter' aircraft. Both functions were filled by two-seater aeroplanes, with engines of 150 horsepower, which flew at most at eighty miles an hour. Anti-aircraft guns forced these aeroplanes to fly high, up to 15,000 feet, while night flying began regularly. Bombing, photo reconnaissance patrols in formation, signals by coloured lights, the escorting of slow planes by faster ones and sensational air combats between individuals were among the early innovations of the Great War. Large, twin-engined flying boats were used against submarines. Aircraft had 400 horsepower, and the height at which they could fly came to be limited more by the endurance of the pilot with oxygen than by the ceiling of the new machine. During its course, a phenomenal number of aircraft were built. In 1914 Britain had 272 aircraft; in 1918 over 22,000. In the US in 1913 only 43 aeroplanes were produced. In 1918 there were 14,000, nearly all military.

Innovatory though it was, and important though the war was for its future, aviation did not play a decisive part in the battles of 1918. Bombing was then a minor activity. Tanks, gas, and propaganda were more important. But the First World War prepared aeroplanes for a new role in transport. There were also soon new achievements. In 1919 John Alcock, son of a Manchester horse-dealer, and Lieutenant Arthur Brown, a young Glaswegian electrical engineer before 1914, flew across the Atlantic in a Vickers Vimy bomber. Passenger services soon began, though many commercial airways started their careers with a grant from their governments and with directors appointed by the government: a contrast from the independence and financial success of railways at their beginning. Among countries which early interested themselves in commercial flying, only the companies in the US made profits; and there those who travelled did so more cheaply. But even in the US there were still only 358 aircraft in service by 1940. It was only after governments in the Second World War gave the manufacture of aircraft such priority that civil aviation came to be commercially viable throughout the world – even though most of the world's airlines have continued to receive state subsidies, hidden or explicit; for modern states regard airlines as a source of prestige and nearly every one of them regards aviation as an essential state service.

The innovations of the next generation of aircraft were primarily connected with war. In the 1930s a doctrine that the 'bomber will always get through' (Baldwin's words, which reflected the thoughts of the Italian general, Douhet) inspired widespread fear. Much bombing of civilians (in the Italian war in Abyssinia; in the Spanish Civil War; in the Sino-Japanese War, which Russia joined; in Britain, Germany, Japan and, later, Vietnam) has always failed to break morale. In London in 1941 'after four months of almost ceaseless bombing, morale was "far better" than a year before, when the war was stagnant', Orwell noted. In the first of the fire-storm raids by the British and Americans on Hamburg in 1943 243,000 people were apparently killed or injured out of a population of 1·5 million. Even so, thanks to a well organised civil defence the services in that city were functioning normally soon afterwards, and historians of the Second World War doubt whether the bombing weakened the German will to resist any more than similar campaigns did over Vietnam in the 1960s. The bombing of Hiroshima and Nagasaki by nuclear weapons in 1945 did help to cause the end of the war in the Far East, but that was, as it were, a *coup de grâce*, following innumerable other raids which had destroyed Japan's capacity to feed herself by eliminating her merchant fleet.

Some precision bombing in the course of the Second World War, such as the American and British raids on Germany's installations for oil in Romania, was also effective, but only at the end of that conflict. In 1944 German production for war had not been seriously damaged. Characteristic of military attitudes by then was the approach of most governments to innovations. Frank Whittle, then a test pilot, applied for his first patent for a 'jet' engine in 1930 and submitted the idea to the British Air Ministry (who thought the 'practical difficulties' were too great). He only flew a jet-propelled engine for the first time in 1941.

More important than bombing in most wars since the development of aviation has been the use of aircraft as a means of substituting for artillery. An air force able to destroy an enemy's force on the ground (as Israel did with the Egyptians in 1967) is able to establish an air of superiority over the battle which allows him to use his aircraft as firepower, attacking men, tanks, lorries, lines of communication and other land-based weapons with impunity. The Yak fighters which Russia was able to throw into the battle were the decisive element in the Second World War between 1943 and 1945.

After 1945 types of fighters and bombers continue, indeed, to succeed one another, sometimes without ever having been tested in a major battle. Innumerable fighters in several countries travel faster than the speed of sound. Since 1957 aircraft have come to be supplemented by rockets and even substituted by them. Some of them are fired from aircraft. But mostly they come from the ground or from submarines. Thus the age of military aircraft seems, at one level, to be near its end. Yet there are many small wars in which conventional aircraft continue to play a part, carrying troops, destroying communications on the ground, attacking infantry from heights and photographing land more effectively than spies could ever 'sketch' it. Those small wars will presumably continue indefinitely.

Civil aircraft also play a determining role in international and, in the case of an increasing number of countries, internal, travel. The decisive change here was the development of Whittle's jet aircraft for civil purposes, after the middle of the 1950s. In the early 1970s aircraft trebled in size while, from 1975, a commercial aeroplane, the Concorde, faster than sound, was flown on a few routes. By the late 1970s over 3,000 million kilometres a year were being flown by regular airlines and some 128 million passengers were being carried each year.

People can now travel round the world in the same time (say forty-eight hours) it once took to get by rail and boat from London to Berlin. Before the age of railways it would have been difficult to have travelled further in forty-eight hours from London than to York. Vast numbers of people, therefore, now travel fast to remote places on business or for pleasure. But the shortness of the journey makes it impossible for them to inform themselves fully on the significance of the country to which they are travelling. Also the ease with which distant travel can be accomplished has led to, or at least been accompanied by, an increase in the restrictions enabling entry into countries. The 'jumbo jet' airliner allows emigration from Asia to Europe or America on a scale which would make that of the nineteenth century seem modest. But no advanced countries open their doors to unrestricted immigration. Indeed, easy travel has coincided with a period in which the possibility of removal from one country to another has been rendered more difficult than it has ever been. Vast regions of the world also remain as much out of bounds to the traveller as they were in the last century. All prophecies that aviation would abolish frontiers have been proved false. On the contrary, it is only since aeroplanes have become in constant use that, as Orwell pointed out, frontiers have become impassable[5].

The beauty of flight, to begin with, inspired numerous artists. The Futurists of 1910 looked to 'the pilots of the purple twilight', as Tennyson put it, as a means of purifying mankind. Gabriele d'Annunzio praised the aeroplane in *Forse che si, forse che no* in 1911. The crazed poet Marinetti dedicated his play *Poupées Electriques* to Wilbur Wright, who 'knew how to raise our migrant hearts higher than the captivating mouth of a woman'[6]. Antoine de Saint Exupéry and André Malraux also had fine lines about flight, particularly the former, while the latter in the Spanish Civil War organised a brigade of fliers in order to give himself the raw material for a novel (*L'Espoir*). But since 1939 there has been as little good writing about aeroplanes as about cars. Illustrative films and memoirs there have been without number. Aviation also remains for a few the sport that it first was during the heroic days. But it is hard to make the crowded airliners of the 1970s a fit subject for art, apart from the miracle of flight itself.

4

One further type of physical communication should be mentioned; the series of actions made possible by the development of rockets, which has as yet had no direct commercial benefits.

The idea of a rocket was first worked out as a firework for diversion by the Chinese in the twelfth century AD. Taken to Europe, rockets were sporadically used as entertainments and as missiles in war from then on, usually the former. Elaborate festivals of fireworks were given in European countries from the time of the Renaissance onwards, particularly at ceremonies of triumph or thanksgiving. Indians, however, used rockets in combat against English troops, and English troops subsequently used an artillery rocket both in India and against Napoleon.

All these rockets were propelled by gunpowder. Some were used during the First World War in order to destroy observation balloons, but ineffectively. It then became known that the use of liquid fuel would make possible more impressive performances: Robert Goddard, an American engineer, shot up a rocket with liquid fuel for the first time in 1926 at Auburn, Massachusetts. No one took much notice. Similar work was carried on in Germany. There, such activities were regarded less sceptically. The German army took over the organisation of the Society for Space Travel at Peenemünde, on the Baltic coast. That led, during the Second World War, to the V.1 and the V.2 long-range rockets, and other smaller guided missiles, of which 2,000 crossed the English coast in 1944–45, travelling at 360 miles an hour, each with a ton of explosive. The British and US also began some less ambitious experiments during the Second World War, among them the bazooka or the anti-tank missile. German scientists in 1944 were considering intercontinental missiles which would travel at 800 miles an hour.

After the Second World War, research on these rockets continued, partly concerned with space travel, partly with the idea that
guided missiles might replace manned aircraft for carrying
weapons, including nuclear ones. The first artificial satellite, the
sputnik, was launched by Russia in 1957 with the help of captured
German scientists. Soon after, the US, also with the help of
specialists born in Germany, began to launch such objects. By
1980 there were already 5,000 such artificial satellites circling the
earth, contributing to meteorology, communications of many
sorts, espionage and preparations for war. Space journeys by men
began to be undertaken by both Russia (in April 1961) and the
US (in May 1961). (Actually, two Russian dogs were the first
living creatures lifted into, and then brought back from, space, in
1960.) In 1967 the Russians landed a collection of instruments on
the planet Venus, while in 1970 two Americans, Neil Armstrong
and Edwin Aldrin, landed on the moon. Satellites were subsequently launched into the air by the Chinese and the French.
Curiously, the names of the early heroes of space failed to establish themselves strongly in the public memory. Was it that the
modern public realised that they were merely cogs in a state's
machine?

A more sinister use of rockets also began during the 1950s.
Subsequently, these assumed major importance. These were con-
tinuations of the programme for rockets undertaken by Germany
in the Second World War. Both the USA and Russia had, by
1980, several thousand rockets of various ranges. Many were
equipped with nuclear weapons. Peace between these states and,
hence, in the world seems to depend on the maintenance of the
'balance of terror' established between them. None of these rockets, so far as can be seen, has any future as a method of peaceful
travel, though the satellites have evidently transformed telecom-
munications and meteorology. But perhaps the moon and the
planets will become sources of energy or raw materials, or be
settled permanently: perhaps as prisons.

6

In 1820 an Austrian official, asked by a student who wished to
return home by a different route to that by which he had set out,
angrily retorted: 'Do you think the Empire is a dovecote where
everyone can fly around as he pleases?' Since 1945 the world has
become that dovecote, but the spirit of Austrian officialdom is far
from dead. At the same time, railways, motor vehicles and aircraft

have so shrunk the world that the installations which now girdle the earth now conform in all essentials to universal patterns bearing no more relation to traditional modes of transport than they do to local ecological systems.

36
Another Revolution in Information

Ideas outline the conditions which gave them birth and words outlast ideas.

Sir Lewis Namier, *England in the Age of the American Revolution*

1

Most 'revolutions' are deceptive. Not only are they usually held to have been betrayed by someone but, often, radical political changes often seem to historians to have been introduced to withstand, rather than implement, economic change. The French Revolutionaries, though they sought to create an unbridgeable gulf between themselves and the past, turned out, in the words of de Tocqueville, to be 'almost a natural outcome of the very social order which they made haste to destroy'[1]. But there has been one real revolution in the world and that has been the revolution in communications. In a sense this is the industrial stage of the revolution which began with the invention of printing. This goes far to explain many of the crises of the twentieth century. What this meant was well put by Carmelo Lisón Tolosano, a social historian from Spain: 'In the decades before the advent of the Republic [in Spain, 1931] life in the community [in Aragon] followed its daily rhythm in a monotonous but peaceful way. The cultivation of the land kept the residents occupied. There were no radios to put the people in contact with the outside world, and, normally, no newspapers were received. Life was generally poor and hard, since fields were generally cultivated with the Roman plough, and the use of fertilisers and selection of seed . . . unknown. The community as such enjoyed tranquility, and unity, and order; there were no signs of internal hostility . . . months [only] before the rise of the Republic, one of the men who was to become leader of a political faction in the town organised an excursion in which everyone who wanted to could take part independent of . . . political differences [which], in fact, hardly existed. . . Such a community excursion . . . would have been inconceivable just one year later'[2], when radio, newspapers and political pamphleteering all brought a complete transformation in the town.

The revolution in information has made possible diversity. But it has also made possible an unprecedented control by the state in every sphere of life. Before the twentieth century, states could seek or even claim such control. They could not hope to exercise it. Now they can.

2

The first part of the revolution in communications affected a very old form of contact between people, namely the post.

Some kind of postal service had existed fitfully from the days of the Persian Empire and in China since the Han dynasty. The more stable the empire, the more repressive the empire, the better the system of posts. All early posts were state monopolies, organised for the benefit of the government. In the Caliphate, the postmaster-general was often at the same time chief of intelligence. Private persons, if they wished to communicate with others who lived at a distance, organised their own couriers, or persuaded (or bribed) governmental messengers to do the work. In mediaeval Europe, private merchants such as the Medici family organised their own postal services. As noticed earlier, princely families, such as the Thurn und Taxis family in Germany, later arranged a public service. They opened the letters and read what was in them. Thus they were able to run an espionage service and a news agency at the same time as providing a public service. In most European languages the word for 'post' recalls the Roman postal service along routes designated by posts. The Spaniards with their *correo* are an exception. Their word recalls the use of runners.

The history of posts in France before the age of industry is characteristic of European developments. The University of Paris had an internal post during the Middle Ages. A service for private letters was organised by Louis XI. The right to collect income from it was (as usual in old France) farmed out. Parcel post existed by the time of Richelieu. There was even a French book post in the eighteenth century: the parcels to be left open at both ends. A penny postal service was introduced by the English in the late eighteenth century, and a similar cheap service for Paris also created.

By about 1820 most European countries and many others (for example, in South America) had well-established postal services. Some stretched back, like those in Venice, to the Renaissance. Austria introduced a postcard in 1869, Sardinia a stamped postal paper in 1818, Britain a postage stamp in 1840 (and a new version of the penny post), and the postage stamp was copied by other countries.

The critical change in the history of the post derived from the use of railways, to carry the letters so stamped. The availability and cheapness of paper and the growth of literacy assisted the establishment of good posts. True, the creation of post office savings banks (in England, from 1862), of a money order department (in France from 1627), of postal orders (in England from 1881) and the subsequent unfortunate marriage of post offices with telegraph and telephone services may have stimulated this service. But it was the mail trains which made possible a golden age of letter-writing (say from 1850 till 1939), whose character is, as a result, better documented than any era before – or since, for the letter gave way after 1945 to the telephone as superficially the best means of communication between people in the same country.

3

The telegraph had a shorter life than that of the letter, and its decay as a result of the telephone (and telex, since 1960) seems absolute. But visual signalling is old. Torches, bonfires and smoke signals were used from the days of the black sails which Theseus hoisted and which caused the death of his father. Naval signalling began to be rendered coherent by two English admirals, Richard Kempenfelt, a man of Swedish origin (who sank in 1782 with his flagship, the *Royal George*, in a famous English maritime accident), and by Richard, Earl Howe, a man known to be 'undaunted as a rock and as taciturn', in Horace Walpole's words. In 1792 Claude Chappe devised semaphore by using movable shutters and wooden arms like railway signals, in order to assist communications between Paris and the French revolutionary army. The first signal to be sent that way was despatched in August 1794, during the French invasion of Belgium. A communication so sent could travel at 150 miles an hour. The English copied Chappe's system, speeding it up so that a message could soon go from London to Deal in a minute. Berlin could soon get an answer from Coblenz in four hours and from St Petersburg in fifty. But semaphore depended on good weather and governments reserved the system for themselves. Pigeon post, on the other hand, began to be used by private traders, and it was from that that the decisive modern developments derived. Chappe, meantime, killed himself in 1805 out of melancholia because the originality of his idea had been questioned.

The idea of an electric telegraph had been suggested, soon after the discovery of the Leyden jar, by a surgeon of Greenock, Charles Morrison, who wrote of it in the *Scots Magazine* in 1753. Various other people worked on the same scheme in the eighteenth century. Madrid was linked by wire with the summer palace of Aranjuez as a result of the efforts of a Spanish engineer, Francisco Salvá, in 1795; an indication of the high level of technical achievement in Spain in the eighteenth century. Then in 1833 Karl Friedrich Gauss, with Wilhelm Weber, sent his famous message by electricity from the observatory to the spire of the Johannes Kirke. At the same time in the US, Samuel Morse, the son of a Massachusetts congregational minister, who had begun life as a painter, reflected (on board the packet-boat *Sully*): 'I see no reason why intelligence may not be transmitted by electricity.' In 1837 Morse made a circuit of 1,700 feet of copper wire. He later sent a message on it by means of the code which he had devised. The scheme was soon commercially exploited, though not immediately to Morse's benefit. In 1844 a telegraph line using Morse's plan was laid between Baltimore and Washington. Within four years most of the US east of the Mississippi was linked up. In England, a telegraph line was laid along the railway from Paddington to Slough in 1843, and the company of Cooke and Wheatstone established 4,000 miles of telegraph in Britain within four years. A Prussian state telegraph service followed in 1849. The success of these innovations led to the use of the new system throughout Europe. The telegraph ceased to be confined in its use to railways. Money orders by telegraph could be sent from 1850 in Britain and the laying of a cable between Dover and Calais, the next year, meant that the stock exchanges of the two capitals could compare prices on the same day. A cable was laid successfully across the Atlantic in 1865 and, the same year, one from Europe to India. The era of the submarine telegraph dawned in 1869 in Latin America. In 1873 Australia was in direct cable communication with Europe.

The subsequent story of the telegraph is best told in figures:

Telegraphs Sent

	France		Britain
1870	5,664,000		11,800,000
1913	52,217,000	(1914)	87,100,000
1938	36,444,000		58,000,000
1969	27,332,000		29,000,000
1979	14,800,000		8,400,000

Even so, bare figures do not indicate what a radical change the telegraph brought. How easy it was in the 1860s in Australia, say, to be two months without any news from England! How important it was to communicate news fast of an investment or a sale!

On the continent of Europe, most telegraph services were from the beginning owned by the state. In the US and in other American countries, control remained in the hands of private monopolies. In Britain, well-intentioned public servants demonstrated in endless memorials that only the state could provide an efficient, cheap telegraph service. The private companies were bought by the Post Office in 1869. It looks as if that body may abandon telegraphs altogether in the 1980s.

The early significance of the telegraph is to be seen in the career of Julius Reuter, born into a Jewish commercial family in Germany as Israel Beer Josaphat. A clerk in his uncle's bank at Göttingen, he chanced to meet Professor Gauss at Cassel. In 1840 he began to work for a French agency, headed by Charles Havas, a Portuguese entrepreneur from Oporto. Havas had bought up the *Correspondance Garnier*, an office which translated foreign newspapers into French. Reuter managed to turn Havas into an agency for collecting information by pigeon-post between London, Paris and Brussels. Reuter began on his own just after the general acceptance of the telegram and, for a time, made money by providing a link (again by pigeon) between two telegraph services, the Berlin–Aachen line and the Paris–Brussels one. Reuter moved to London in 1850 when Paris became telegraphically linked to that capital, and began an agency for news by providing English clients with the closing prices of stocks and shares in Paris and vice versa. Then he extended his activities to other capitals. Newspapers, to begin with sceptical, started to take Reuter's despatches after *The Times* had published a speech by Napoleon III sent to them by Reuter's man in Paris in 1855. Offices in New York and Bombay were soon established[3].

Though it was the first news agency, Reuter's was not the only one. Havas in Paris copied their ex-employee and Wolff created a similar enterprise in Germany. The three exchanged news so as to make it possible to share the world's market between them. Associated Press of New York later joined these three, and another American agency, United Press, came on to the scene in 1907. These agencies seemed almost to be departments of government. Havas, in particular, had close relations with the French government from whom it later received a subsidy, in 1938. Associated Press, led by an indefatigable individualist, Kent Cooper, challenged the old agencies and by 1934 had the right to sell news everywhere throughout the world on an equal footing with Reuter's.

For ordinary people, the telegram was for a few generations the most usual means of communicating a victory or a tragedy. The arrival of the 'telegraph boy' filled people of all classes between 1850 and 1950 with a mixture of dread and excitement. A scholarship? A proposal of marriage? Death in action? But the political significance of the telegram was everywhere to increase the authority of central government and to reduce the scope for individual initiative. George Orwell exaggerated only slightly when he claimed that it ruined the British Empire; it also greatly assisted large centralising regimes such as Russia and Turkey. Even so, as late as 1890 a British Consul could declare a protectorate over Nyasaland (Malawi) with no authority whatever. Such a thing could not have occurred twenty years later.

To historians, the world of the telegram has been the world of the diplomatic message, despatched at what taxpayers would regard as inordinate length, but, even so, not always making clear the full meaning of the sender. The telegram sent from Ems by King Wilhelm I of Prussia in 1870 was construed by Bismarck to justify the Franco-Prussian War. The exchanges of telegrams between diplomats and generals representing the European powers in July 1914 put the greatest strain until then experienced on the European telegraphic services. There was confusion, even on such an important matter as to whether Germany did or did not wish her ally, Austria Hungary, to mobilise, despite the ease of communication: 'Ich habe es nicht gewollt,' said Emperor Franz Josef ruefully, after the war had begun[4]. Later, the breaking of the telegraphic cyphers in which military messages were hidden gave the British one of the greatest of their technological triumphs.

4

In the 1980s important exchanges such as those between the German and Austrian chiefs of staff would have been over the telephone, one of the inventions of the nineteenth century which the twentieth is still using increasingly every year. In 1977, for example, the world's 420 million telephones numbered nearly fifty per cent more than there were only five years before. By that time in the USA there were over 74 telephones per 100 inhabitants against a world average of 10·4.

This instrument derives from the telegraph. Several inventors, such as Dr C. G. Page in Massachusetts, Charles Bourseul in Paris and Philipp Reis in Frankfurt, came close to devising a telephone between 1835 and 1865. Alexander Graham Bell, a Scotsman from Edinburgh living in Boston, Massachusetts, was, however, the first person to create, in 1875, an electric current whose strength varied at every instant according to the vibrations caused by the human voice. (Bell was primarily concerned, as a professor of vocal philology, with work for the deaf.)

The first telephoned message was transmitted in 1876. A conversation between Boston and New York was held in 1877. Soon after, Thomas Edison, subsequently the pioneer of electricity, devised another type of telephone on which the first telephone exchange in New York was based. By 1880 the United States had 54,000 receiving telephones in operation, in 1900 nearly two million (more than India had in 1980) and, in 1912, 8·7 million. A line from New York to Chicago was opened in 1892, one from New York to San Francisco in 1915. This swift development was mostly carried out by a private company which, after 1918, established a near-monopoly, the American Telephone and Telegraph Company (subsequently, International T & T). In Europe, Germany led the way, as in most electrical industries, so that she had by 1912 four times as many installations as had France, and her people talked on the telephone four times as often as did the French. Britain was slow to develop the telephone. That was partly due to the argument put forward by the Postmaster General that the telephone was an implement covered by the Acts relating to the telegram, giving him a monopoly. After the idea of municipal management had been abortively tried out, a national telephone company, under state management, was founded within the Post Office, and in the 1890s installation was going ahead fast.

The field telephone played a large part in the First World War. In the Spanish Civil War many critical incidents revolved round the use of the telephone, or the capture of the telephone exchanges, correctly estimated to be as important in modern life as town halls: as early as 1909 a Spanish civil governor, in order to keep the rebels in Barcelona from communicating with Madrid, lighted on the idea of banning long-distance calls. In the 1920s the landlords of Andalusia were critical of the idea of a telephone service, for they feared that it would enable their anarchist enemies to consort too easily. In the 1940s and 1950s the use of the telephone assisted General Franco's government, like many other such military regimes, to pursue its enemies more effectively.

The tapping of the telephone became a recourse of governments (and spies). Mussolini was believed to spend more time reading reports of such tappings than on public business. Mussolini's ministers knew that the quickest way of getting information to their leader was to work it somehow into a telephone call which they knew would be tapped. It is evident that the existence of a telephone line to Hitler's headquarters in 1944 caused the generals' rebellion of 20 July of that year to fail: if only General Fellgiebel had blown up that communication centre as he had promised! His mistake was what J. W. Wheeler Bennet described as a 'major disaster for the conspirators, for unrestricted and undamaged communications were a vital factor in quelling the revolt'[5]. In Russia after 1945, Solzhenitsyn symbolically made the work of certain privileged prisoners that of identifying a voice from an intercepted telephone. That was the main theme of his greatest novel, *The First Circle*. Stalin's conversation with Pasternak on the telephone in 1934 after the arrest of the poet Mandelstam would rank high in the most celebrated telephone conversations of the world.* The telephone has been to centralisation of government what the loudspeaker has been to the mass orator. King Juan Carlos's use of the telephone to rally military support for democracy was probably critical during the attempted *coup d'état* in Madrid in February 1981. Yet one of the most successful statesmen of our time, Charles de Gaulle, is believed never to have used the telephone: wisely, since the recorded telephone dialogues of politicians reveal a naïvety, ignorance and opaqueness rarely encountered in ordinary life. The world was mildly comforted by the establishment of a direct telephone line between the leaders of the US and Russia after the Cuban crisis in 1963. Relations have not, however, subsequently much improved.

---

* The telephone rang one day in Pasternak's flat in Moscow. A voice said, 'Comrade Stalin wishes to speak with you.' Pasternak was quite unprepared for such a conversation. Stalin came on the line and asked, 'Tell me, what are they saying in your literary circles about the arrest of Mandelstam?' Pasternak rambled a bit: 'You know they are not saying anything because . . . There are no literary circles, nobody says anything . . . they are afraid.' There was a lengthy pause at the end of the line and then Stalin said, 'Very well. But now tell me your own opinion of Mandelstam. What's your view of him as a poet?' Pasternak said: 'Of course he's a very great poet but he has no points of contact with us . . .' Stalin listened and then said mockingly: 'I see you just aren't able to stick up for a comrade,' and put down the receiver.

The most serious comment on the history of the telephone was made by Dr Henry Kissinger in his memoirs: 'Before the era of instantaneous communication, instructions to a negotiator had to be conceptual and, therefore, they gave an insight into the thinking of statesmen; in the age of teletype, they are usually tactical or technical and, therefore, are silent about larger purposes and premises'[6]. The trouble is that the absence of a need to declare these larger purposes may mean that they are never considered at all. Still, perhaps these gloomy conclusions will be confounded by the new system of telephone by light wave which the Bell Telephone Company plans to introduce into regular service by 1980.

5

Some notice in a discussion of methods of communication should be paid to the typewriter, which came to be used extensively for the first time in the 1880s. A printer in Marseilles in the 1830s had devised what he called a *machine cryptographique* which, he argued, could write as fast as a pen. It had each character printed on a separate bar. Later, Christopher Sholes, a journalist of Pennsylvania, worked out the idea of the inked ribbon and solved the question of where best to put the letters: letters used often next to one another should be placed apart. Sholes sold his patent to Remington and Co., famous arms manufacturers: Eliphalet Remington received a large armaments contract from the federal government during the Civil War. Remington put a typewriter on the market in 1873. The effect of that in the long run was to increase the number of copies of documents, many of which were unnecessary. The greater level of business correspondence (also much of it unnecessary) began the increase in the number of secretaries and assistants which, in the twentieth century, mark businesses, universities, armies, police forces and government departments alike. The typewriter has also widened the gulf between scholars and writers. Most of the former refuse to type. Most of the latter have to. Nietzsche was apparently the first famous writer to use a typewriter: *absit omen*.

6

Forty years before the typewriter, photography had begun to transform visual memory. The result has been to affect adversely the memory of the mind's eye. The idea behind photography had been thought of often before the nineteenth century. For example, the fact that a pinhole admitting light into a dark room projected an inverted image of objects outside, was known to Euclid (c. 300 BC) as to Alhazen (who died in AD 1038), the best known mediaeval Arabic writer on optics. In the eighteenth century the sun's light was observed to darken silver salts when they were exposed to it, just as it could also cause sunburn. A few interesting experiments were conducted by Humphry Davy and Thomas Wedgwood, a celebrated chemist and son of the potter. Indeed, Wedgwood can dispute with the French pioneers the distinction of having made the first real photograph. At all events, Nicéphore de Niepce, who had retired from the French army because of failing sight, obtained images on a bituminous film and, in 1813, began collaborating with Louis Daguerre, a scene painter at the Opéra who had once been an inland revenue collector. They were successful, and Niepce took a photograph of his home town in Burgundy of Chalon-sur-Saône. The exposure took eight hours. There could be only one copy of the print, and the result was not sharp.

Daguerre soon improved on that achievement. In 1839 he showed his first collection of 'daguerrotypes' at the French Academy of Sciences. 'From today, painting is dead,' exclaimed Paul Delaroche, an artist who had made Romanticism acceptable. Actually, the immediate effect was to make realistic painting fashionable. Meantime W. H. Fox Talbot, an English mathematician and landowner, evolved a form of photography which is more clearly the ancestor of the modern type. His experiments, carried out independently of Daguerre's, make him the co-founder of this art. Wrangles over patents, however, disfigured those early days. The inventor, in 1851, of a glass plate of 'collodion' (a solution of gun-cotton in ether), leading to the first practical application of photography for those other than scientists, was an English sculptor of no great talent, Frederick Scott Archer. Even then it was only in the 1880s, with the invention of the first ready-made dry plate, that photography came within reach of the ordinary amateur.

Mass-produced 'cameras' were soon available. The Kodak box camera was invented in 1888, the celluloid film in 1890, while the first newspaper pictures began to appear in the 1890s; for example, in the *New York Daily Graphic*. The next thirty years were as well commemorated in photographs as they were in letters. The portrait painters of the era, such as Sargent and Whistler, were as careful in depicting features as any cameraman. People desired painters to be as accurate as photographers and many painted portraits from photographs (Manet so painted *The Execution of the Emperor Maximilian*). Ingres, Corot, Meissonier and Degas were also influenced by photography. Subsequently photography became a hobby of millions, with pictures dominating newspapers and, after the second half of the twentieth century, even 'books'. In Paris, already in 1847, half a million photographic plates were sold, and in the 1850s and 1860s the photograph, in the shape of a postcard, brought this invention within reach of all. Colour photography, however, was not developed before the 1930s and was not generally available before the 1960s, save in advertising.

7

The emergence of the popular press and much cheaper printing and distribution costs is the next part of the 'revolution in communications' to which attention should be paid. In England, the *Spectator* in London was selling 2,000 copies a day in 1711, the *Gentleman's Magazine* 10,000 in 1739. Other countries copied these successes. Thus in Germany there was a *Litteratur Zeitung* which was 'read by everyone' (and sold 2,000 copies). Most cities in Europe and North America had some journals of comment, mostly of a polemical kind, by 1750. Freedom to write with no censorship in newspapers began its history in Holland during the seventeenth century. In England, a system of licensing existed, but that was abolished in 1695, because it had by then become impossible to control illegal pamphleteering. Between 1700 and 1760 a hundred and thirty provincial newspapers made at least a temporary appearance. In 1753 seven million newspapers were being sold every year in England, 20,000 a day, a figure far in advance of any other country at that time. Large sums were paid out of public funds to editors who supported governments and, as a rule, newspapers had to pay taxes. Neither they nor periodicals were free from persecution. Yet they were established as a 'fourth estate' before 1789 in England. Newspapers in the US were also well established before the revolution of the 1770s. Indeed, the *Boston Evening Post* contributed to that revolution. In comparison, French periodicals and newspapers before 1789 were feeble. The state controlled all publications and the most celebrated literary works were published abroad. The *Mercure de France* was believed, however, particularly by its contributors, to have played a great part in the coming of the French Revolution. Manuscript newspapers were theoretically forbidden, but they flourished in eighteenth-century Paris. As for Spain, no publisher could print anything there without a licence and no licence was given for a publication until a report had been made by a careful judge.

The French Revolution was the father of hundreds of papers. Almost every political group between 1789 and 1794 had their own. The same was true of Latin America during the wars of independence from Spain: between 1810 and 1821 there were forty in Mexico alone. Printing presses such as that in Chile founded by Jesuits to serve the faith were made to serve the cause of revolution.

All those newspapers and journals were, however, published and printed in much the same way as they would have been in the Renaissance. In the nineteenth century a transformation was caused by technical innovations making possible mass-distributed newspapers.

In 1800 Charles, Earl Stanhope, a radical English peer interested in science and the brother-in-law of William Pitt, employed iron rather than wood to produce wood engravings and heavy type. In 1810 the *Annual Register* and, as noticed earlier, in 1814 *The Times* in London, then with a daily circulation of 5,000, began to use its steam press. Other newspapers copied it, for it worked four times faster than a hand-operated press. Thereafter the intellectual and economic upheavals caused by the Industrial Revolution, which threatened violence after 1815 in many countries, particularly England, were marked by, perhaps really were caused by, the greatest outpouring of books, satires, pamphlets and political poems ever known till then. Working-class papers made their first real appearance. The prints of Gillray, Rowlandson and Cruikshank circulated too. The poems of Scott and of Byron also sold in formidable numbers: Scott's poem *Marmion*, for instance, seized hold of the public 'like a kind of madness; the lines not only clung to the memory but they would not keep off the tongue: people could not help spouting them in solitary places and muttering them as they walked about the streets'. Private and state patronage died out. It became possible for the Prime Minister Canning to say, when asked to patronise a scheme for a Royal Society of Literature, 'I am really of opinion with Dr Johnson that the multifarious personage called The Public is after all, the best patron of literature and learned men.' Publishers in London and Paris became rich, powerful – and competitive. Authors were released from penury. The Romantic Age gave birth to the first international intellectual movement – characterised by the distribution of innumerable translations of Chateaubriand, Hugo, Byron and Goethe throughout Europe and the Americas.

In the 1820s and 1840s railways began to make possible national presses, though newspapers outside the capital remained important. In the 1840s the invention of the telegraph allowed the creation of efficient news agencies, and the commissioning of regular foreign correspondents. Newspaper taxes were removed in Britain in 1855. In the late 1840s Richard Hoe of New York, son of an English-born printer, designed the rotary press, while the web press was invented by William Bullock in 1865. These made possible the modern newspaper. The rotary press could produce 20,000 impressions an hour. From 1865, a continuous roll of paper could be introduced into these machines, instead of having to be fed at different levels by twenty-five people. Meantime, a large new reading public, every day more literate, in almost every country, sought serenity or excitement in the innumerable novels, poems and political works which the nineteenth century – the first mechanised age, but one before mass communication, as that phrase is usually understood – made available.

The increase in books and newspapers, and the number of letters exchanged, stimulated a demand for paper which defeated the old way of making it from cotton, linen and straw scraps. The solution reached (without which the paper revolution of the twentieth century would be unimaginable) was to employ wood pulp. After 1874 a chemical method of using that was devised which enabled the paper manufacturers to meet a huge new demand.

Finally, lino-type machines were devised in the USA in the 1880s. They were introduced into Europe ten years later. The US also led the way in machine-setting of books with the monotype machine in the 1890s, even though most books were set by hand until 1914. No great change occurred thereafter for sixty years, but in the 1960s and 1970s printing underwent another great revolution, this time an electronic one. This led to computerised photocomposition, image-scanning for the reproduction of pictures, offset-printing and photogravure printing. The idea of dispensing with metal type goes back to the nineteenth century but only became possible in the course of this 'second industrialisation' of the 1960s. The five-hundred-year life of the compositor looks to be nearing its end, and within a generation setting from metal type may be restricted to antiquarians and amateurs[7]. Perhaps by then, too, some version of electrostatic or pressureless printing will have been invented.

The first consequence of these developments was an immense increase in the sale of newspapers and books, at least in countries where there was no censorship. A typical development was that in the United States:

US Newspapers

	Number of daily papers	Circulation (daily) (20)
1850	254	758,000
1880	971	3,556,000
1900	2,226	15,102,000
1914	2,580	28,777,000
1956	6,315	78,090,000
1978	1,829	61,990,000

The second consequence was the realisation that, in democracies in which an increasing proportion of adults had the vote, and as expressly stated in the *Rights of Man* of 1791, or as put by Tocqueville in 1835, 'the independence of the press is the chief and . . . constitutive element of liberty. A nation that is determined to remain free is, therefore, right in demanding at any price the exercise of this independence.' The classic toast of English Whig banquets in the early nineteenth century was 'The liberty of the Press – 'tis like the air we breathe – while we have it, we cannot die'[8].

The importance of this was appreciated by tyrants of the old sort as by those of a new: Napoleon I suppressed sixty out of seventy-three newspapers when he conquered Italy and handed over the censorship to the police. He remarked, *à propos* of France: 'People complain we have no literature: it is the fault of the Minister of the Interior'[9]. Napoleon III controlled the press as rigidly as any government had before 1789. After 1815, in Piedmont, everyone who wanted to read a foreign newspaper had to obtain a permit for so doing. Even the British government introduced laws between 1792 and 1815 against the expression of opinion which were on a scale unknown in the eighteenth century.

The problem of censorship became more and more serious as literacy increased in the nineteenth century. Thus there was no official censorship in Russia before 1790, when Catherine the Great banned Radishchev's account of his journey from St Petersburg to Moscow. Before that, few Russians could read and the government or the Church owned all the printing presses. For Russia, the age of censorship began in 1826, after the Decembrists' revolt, with a literate population which perhaps numbered ten per cent of adults. A code was introduced insisting that all publications had to meet the government's approval and to make a positive contribution to public morals. With alternating times of repression and tolerance, and different definitions, that system has continued in Russia.

A third consequence was the heightened importance of newspapers in political life. In the late 1890s the Hungarian-born proprietor Joseph Pulitzer, and the Californian William Hearst in the US, Alfred Harmsworth in Britain and Charles Dupuy in France created mass journalism. Moïsé Millaud in France had sown the seed in the 1860s with *Le Petit Journal*, which sold 582,000 copies in 1880 – four times that of its nearest rival. In every advanced nation the press gave a new dimension to both literature and politics, establishing a new world half-way between entertainment and education. Halévy believed that 'the modern newspaper reduced the dimensions of an entire country to those of an ancient agora'[10]. Alongside the national and provincial daily press, every country began to publish specialised newspapers and journals dealing with medicine, music, sport, children and religion – everything under the sun. France was in the *avant-garde* of this new 'mass culture'. *Le Petit Parisien*, for example, belonging to Charles Dupuy, son of a well-to-do shopkeeper, achieved in 1916 the largest sale hitherto reached in any country – 2,183,000 copies. The illiterate peasant in Andalusia also bought a paper and gave it to his companion to read.

Since the late nineteenth century, politicians have enjoyed, in democracies, close and often unhealthy friendships with the press, sometimes flattering newspapers as essential to liberty, often denouncing them as squalid merchants in intrigue. They have often been both, as have politicians. When, at the end of the First World War, President Woodrow Wilson promised a new era of 'open covenants openly arrived at' in place of secret diplomacy (such as, as he implied, had led to the war) he meant that editors of newspapers should learn of governments' decisions sooner than they had done before 1914. But the events of 1918–19 showed that the voice of 'public opinion' (and, even more, 'international opinion') was no guarantee of serene policy-making. Public opinion wanted to 'hang the Kaiser'. Public men prevented that from happening. Manipulation of the press by governments, and the playing by public men on the emotions of peoples through the medium of the press (often by use of the calculated indiscretion to the carefully selected journalist), has subsequently characterised, sometimes even dominated, public life, and only rarely to the public benefit.

The history of the press has probably been at its most instructive in France. In the nineteenth century, journalists, like Balzac's Lucien de Rubempré, arrived in Paris determined to seek 'the bubble reputation'. Others, like Emile de Girardin, presented themselves as pioneers of mass education and, with such cheap papers as *La Presse* (which he wrote as well as published), inaugurated the popular newspaper. (Successful as a proprietor, Girardin failed, like many others afterwards, to convert that success into the political power which he coveted.) Journalists soon began to make large incomes. Newspapers, on the other hand, began making money from advertisements as early as the 1840s (though in France that was never so great an element in their financing as it became in Britain or the US). They also continued to receive bribes to put over a certain point of view from all sorts of quarters: from novelists, wanting their books well reviewed, or foreign governments. Russia distributed two million francs a year in France to enable her to raise loans after 1905. 'A large number of highly respectable journalists accepted, even solicited, bribes,' wrote Theodore Zeldin, 'as a condition of writing articles in favour of Russia'[11] – among them the secretary of the journalists' union. Some French papers even received bribes from Germany during the First World War.

The golden age of the press was short: from the Franco-Prussian War till the Second World War. In 1871 the telegraph linked Europe with America to enable the telegram to give immediacy to the news. The appetite for knowledge of remote places was great. Foreign correspondents were among the heroes of the day (the young Winston Churchill in South Africa; Hearst in Cuba). But by 1945 the radio had already cast its shadow over newspapers, which were beginning to close in the face of the challenge by government-sponsored news services. Television, a mass medium in the United States from the 1940s and in Europe from the 1950s, transformed the old status of the press. In the 1970s labour troubles also menaced the press's future in most democratic countries in ways which would have seemed extraordinary to those who struggled for a free press in the eighteenth century. There were other threats: 'Today,' remarked Luigi Barzini, 'the Italian press is free in the sense that there is no censorship. But if you read our papers, you at once realise that eight out of ten newspapers have already succumbed to the temptation of pre-emptive capitulation . . . they are trimming their sails to what they think will be the wishes of their next masters, the communist party . . . the "workers' committee" which includes the printers . . . have the final say in what gets printed and what does not. Editors, journalists and writers, realising that these censorships exist, very seldom risk their jobs by challenging the powers that be"[12]. Similar remarks can be made almost as truthfully about other nominally democratic countries.

Still, the circulation of newspapers is huge in comparison with anything which prevailed before the 1870s: 293 per thousand people in the US, 443 per thousand in Britain, 220 in France, even 536 in Sweden. Russia also claims high figures for circulation of its papers but, in a closed, censored and confined society, such boasts mean little.

37

Mass Media

Everything is quiet . . . there will be no war.

Remington (in Havana, 1897, for *The Journal*)

Please remain . . . you furnish the pictures and I'll furnish the war!

Hearst (New York, proprietor of *The Journal*)

1

Three new means of communication have come to dominate the mass democracies of the twentieth century: radio, cinema and television. They affect peoples who live under totalitarian governments, as they do those under democracies or more traditional tyrannies. The origins of these three technical innovations of the twentieth century are easier to indicate than their consequences.

First, consider the radio. Michael Faraday's experiments in electromagnetism began it. The Scottish professor James Clerk Maxwell proved that radio waves existed, in 1879. But he did nothing practical about his discovery. In the 1880s Heinrich Hertz in Berlin established by experiments that light and radio waves were similar. In 1895 Ernest Rutherford, a young New Zealand physicist who had only recently come to Cambridge, carried those ideas further by transmitting messages over three-quarters of a mile. Four years later Guglielmo Marconi, a scientist from near Bologna (with an Irish mother), sent radio waves between two cruisers during British naval manoeuvres and, subsequently, between France and Britain. In 1901 he despatched a similar message from Cornwall to Newfoundland. Sustained by obstinacy, resolution and a private fortune, Marconi carried on to establish wireless telegraphy between the Americas and England. But, until the First World War, wireless radio communication was only used by ships. It was realised how useful radio might be in the pursuit of crime when the murderer Dr Crippen was apprehended, in 1910, after crossing the Atlantic, by means of a radio message sent from London. In America, Marconi formed a company for the commercial transmission of radio. Little progress had been made before 1914. Large firms concerned with electrical communication showed

scant interest in the 'dazzling possibilities' of communication without wires. 'Wireless' was regarded as a new kind of telephone.
No one before 1914 foresaw the value of wireless communication
for the broadcasting of public programmes of music or of speech.
The First World War transformed the world's radio services.
Large transmitters were built which could send messages between
the ground and aircraft on reconnaissance. The companies concerned in the installations were subsequently able to influence
governments to permit peacetime broadcasting. In March 1919 a
wireless telephone transmitter was built by the Marconi Company
in England. Telephonic transmission to the United States followed. The singing on the wireless by the Australian opera singer,
Melba, in 1920 was a turning-point in this art. A broadcasting
corporation sponsored by the government was soon established in
England, in 1922. Similar institutions were established on the
continent of Europe. Little hostility to this state interference was
expressed. That curious monopolistic achievement was the effect
of the First World War, which had accustomed people to an
apparently benevolent state dominating its affairs. The British
Post Office also feared that broadcasting would interfere with
their work unless it was state-controlled[1].

In the US, where the first broadcasting station was opened in
1920, 'radio' remained in private hands, though most wavelengths
were soon controlled by three companies. The US government
established a federal commission to license stations, assign wavelengths and establish standards of conduct. Since radio competed
with the press, newspaper companies began to buy radio stations.
Established in 1920 in Pittsburgh for the first time as a means of
communication (or entertainment), radio in the US grew as an
industry even faster than the manufacture of automobiles in the
succeeding twenty years. By 1938 twenty-six million families had
radio sets in the US, and by the 1970s the US had over 400 million
radios or the extraordinary figure of 1,882 per 1,000 inhabitants.
Though the influence of radio declined after the growth of television, it continues to play a great part in all countries, rich and
poor alike.

Radio was well enough established in Europe for it to be of
political importance by the 1930s. On Britain's three million radio
sets in 1930, the voice of King George could be heard counselling
national unity. The 'fireside chats' of President Roosevelt, the
judicious commentaries of Raymond Gram Swing and the demagoguery of Father Coughlin were all, in the 1930s, brought by

radio to millions of Americans, completing the process of the making of a modern nation which railways had begun. The radio was scarcely used in political campaigning in Germany before 1933, but on the 3½ to 4½ million sets of Germany after 1933, the Germans heard the increasingly irresistible voices of Hitler and his propaganda minister, Josef Goebbels. The Ministry of Propaganda encouraged the production of cheap radio sets, so that all Germans could afford one. By 1936 thirty million people could be reached by radio, not including the public loudspeakers. In 1938 there were nearly ten million German radios. On these, the voices of Goebbels and other propagandists fumed venomously. On the 300,000 radios of Spain during the Civil War, General Queipo de Llano introduced war propaganda, while, on their nine million sets of 1940, the British heard Churchill use his Augustan prose to preach resistance to Nazism. Listening to the BBC was a capital offence in the Nazis' 'new order', but it was a frequent crime, and that radio service did as much for the Allied cause as did many divisions. Still some of the morale that Germany managed to sustain until 1944 was due to the radio, as it was in the other belligerent countries.

The attention paid by the Nazis to the number of sets available has been followed by Communist countries, in this, as in other ways, successors to fascism rather than its opposite. Russia's figure of 480 sets per 1,000 inhabitants in 1975 was one of the few indices of consumer standards which, if true, places that country nearly on a level with the West (compare Britain, 706; France, 330). Whether these radio sets – estimated at 107 million in number throughout the Eastern bloc – have been helpful to the Soviet regime seems most doubtful. The cost of jamming equipment may be very great: there are held to be 3,000 jamming transmitters. Even so, fifty million or so citizens of the Soviet bloc listen daily to Western broadcasts.

Since 1945 the airwaves of the world have been fought over continuously by Radio Moscow, Peking Radio, the BBC, the Voice of America, Radio Free Europe, the Voice of Cairo and other stations. While criticism of the Russian empire is sustained by Radio Free Europe, the ubiquity of transistor radios bringing the 'Voice of Cairo' into every corner of the old kingdoms of Arabia and the East and throughout the Persian Gulf was a major cause of the final British withdrawal from there. The battle for the soul of Africa is still largely being fought on the radio waves, for in that continent the number of radio sets increased from a mere 360,000 in 1956 to over twenty million by 1976. Foreign radio transmissions ruined the attempts by the Polish regime in 1980 to maintain silence about the spread of the strike movement in Gdansk.

2

An essential adjunct to the radio in the twentieth century has been the gramophone. As with radio, an early pioneer (in this case, Leon Scott) developed the theoretical possibilities, without considering practical ones. Scott demonstrated a 'phonautograph' to the British Association in 1859. That showed, for the first time, that sound was a form of energy. In 1877 Thomas Edison, intimately concerned with all the late nineteenth-century developments in relation to electricity, devised in New York a method of cutting a permanent imprint of sound waves so that, by reversing the process, the 'record' thus formed could be 'played back'. Edison cut his 'record' on tinfoil. Later, that was replaced by wax. Then in 1887 Emile Berliner, a German immigrant living in Washington, began to duplicate and to market gramophone records. Vlademar Poulsen of Denmark invented magnetic recording the next year. The age of the 'Gramophone' (originally a trade name, in which the rights were held by the His Master's Voice Company) had begun. More recently, tape recorders have in the 1970s begun to dethrone the gramophone, though gramophone records are with us still. Sometimes they have been used for political purposes too.

The essential contribution of the gramophone was to increase the amount of music available, though, like the radio, it helped to reduce the numbers of those able to practise music. Famous 'artistes' reached an immense audience, while the obscure village pianist or the daughter of the household could not compete. The sale of pianos fell in proportion to the rise in the sale of records. Still, the number of people able to appreciate music has patently increased, even if all discerning people are infuriated by the toneless piped 'Muzak' of the 1970s. Pianos have ceased to be the 'symbols of bourgeois respectability', as Theodore Zeldin thought them[2], while guitars and wind instruments have become infinitely more popular.

3

Finally, there has been the cinema. Who can picture the twentieth century without it? Vast numbers have preferred films to books.

Even intellectuals have delighted in its naïvety: 'I like straightforward films where people kill each other and make love,' remarked Louis Aragon[3].

The film can be given a long history. Ptolemy knew in AD 130 of the illusion known as 'persistence of vision'. The idea of a magic lantern was thought of by Fr. Athanasius Kircher, a German Jesuit, who taught mathematics in the Collégio Romano in Rome in 1645. Still, nothing much transpired between his day and the 1820s. Then in 1826 Dr John Paris, a physician from Cambridge, devised the 'Thaumatrope', a cardboard disc which had on it two separate images. When spun, the first was superimposed upon the other. A Belgian physicist, Joseph-Antoine Plateau, who had gone blind looking at the sun too long, in 1833 carried this idea further and made a 'Phenakisto-scope', which produced a moving image. In 1834 William George Horner, a schoolmaster of Bath, produced the 'Zoetrope', or 'wheel of life', a hollow cylinder with vertical slots round the sides at regular intervals. Pictures on strips were put inside, spun round and viewed through the slits. Then in 1877 Reynaud produced his 'Praxinoscope' which adapted this scheme to drawn images.

The development of the photograph transformed the situation; for, in 1872 Eadweard Muybridge, a British-born photographer living in California (born Edward Muggeridge, and son of a corn chandler), proved by gathering a battery of cameras together that there are moments when all four legs of a horse are off the ground when it gallops: a fact never previously known for sure by painters or sculptors. Muybridge put his images of horses and other animals on a 'Zoopraxiscope', first used to show horse races. Next, in 1880 George Eastman of New York began to sell celluloid film for use in his Kodak cameras. That gave experimenters in the cinema an essential raw material which they had previously not had. In 1890 Etienne-Jules Marey, professor of physiology in Paris, achieved his first filmed series of photographs. Thomas Edison perfected his 'Kineoscope' which resembled a modern cinema in every respect save that it could be seen by only one person at a time.

All over Europe and the US great efforts were then made to be the first to put a moving picture on to a screen. The competition was won by Louis Lumière and his brother Auguste, two French photographers who showed two two-minute newsreels at the Grand Café in the Boulevard des Capucines, Paris, at the end of 1895. They exhibited their 'cinématographe' at the Empire Theatre, London, in early 1896. Edison then devised a 35-millimetre film; and in 1898 a film cameraman accompanied General Kitchener to the battle of Omdurman. In 1900 'moving pictures' were a side show at all places of entertainment.

The commercial cinema then got under way, a little slowly, for it took ten years for serious actors or actresses to agree to appear in films. Early films ('shakies') were too spasmodic in movement, as well as being silent, to tempt great performers. Still, Réjane appeared in *Madame sans gêne* in 1911, and Sarah Bernhardt in *Queen Elizabeth* in 1912. By then, 'stars' were consciously created by US film companies, seeking publicity in a commercial war. The first of those was Mary Pickford, 'America's sweetheart' and D. W. Griffith's best money-maker. Religious films were popular till the Pope banned them. Detective tales and idiotic comedies followed, particularly the Keystone comedies, in which Charlie Chaplin first appeared, copying the behaviour of the French professional fool Max Linder. Cinema receipts in France in 1914 reached sixteen million francs a year and films were already a large commodity in international trade.

The war of 1914 confirmed both the promise of films and the US lead in their making. US producers shot their films out of doors. They built cinemas faster than Europeans did. While Europeans found it hard to sell films in the US, US films were immediately saleable in Europe. During the war, too, resources in Europe had to be directed away from films, while that was the time when Chaplin made his name as 'king of the silver screen'.

After 1918 the film industry, like the radio one, grew fast in all the rich countries. Film stars achieved unprecedented fame, setting fashions and commanding large fees. Films of epic dimension were built in enormous studios. The Communists in Russia were quick to see the value of the cinema for propaganda, and that aspect of the matter was at the back of the minds of even the greatest of Russian film makers, such as Pudovkin or Eisenstein. The 'sound track', introduced in 1927 (earlier there had only been the 'cinema organ'), afterwards transformed the industry. Many of the earliest 'stars' gave way to a new generation who mostly came from the stage. Film versions of nineteenth-century novels enjoyed a long vogue. By the end of the 1930s the 'motion picture business' was the fourteenth most important one in the US, while some seventy-five million persons there (fifty-eight per cent of the population) visited the 'movies' every week. Large cinemas were built all over the US and Europe. Their auditoria were also used for the colossal public political meetings which had a heyday in the 1920s and 1930s. The Spanish Fascist party, the Falange, was launched in the Cinema Monumental in Madrid, for example, and many theatres of the past were transformed into cinemas. The cinema queue, curling away into the distance, seemed the most characteristic sight in rich countries of the 1930s and 1940s.

The dominance of the US was shown in the 1920s for the first time by this new medium. It was a foretaste of the hold that the US had over intellectual life in all the West after 1945. No matter that the US refused to join the League of Nations and to take part in any organised reaction, to begin with, to communism or to fascism. The cinema gave to the US a taste of world power. The early hopes for a new great British industry faded. Americans bought up European cinemas. The leaders of the industry, even in France, thought that there was more money to be made distributing American films than making French ones. A few brave people, however, pre-eminently Germans, continued to regard the cinema as potentially an art. Inexpensive films with aesthetic aims were shown in small cinemas, particularly in Paris: 'Studio Vingt-Huit – high up a winding street of Montmartre in the full blasphemy of a freezing Sunday; taxis arriving, friends greeting each other, an excitable afternoon audience. In the hall stands a surrealist bookstall . . . a gramophone plays disturbing sardanas'[4]: so the critic Cyril Connolly recalled going to the cinema in the 1920s.

Once Hitler was in power, the German cinema was used for propaganda as much as it had been in Russia. A Reich 'chamber of films' was set up by Goebbels to control every phase of the making of films and their distribution. Films were made of Hitler's rise to power, to illustrate the Nazi view of history and even to record the Nazis' own behaviour for immediate, and posthumous, observation. The annual rallies of the Nazi party at Nuremberg were filmed for domestic and international propaganda. Hitler himself, it seems, saw a film a day when in power. The rallies of the Nuremberg conference of 1934 were designed so that Leni Riefensthal could make her film *Triumph of the Will*. In the Second World War, films cheered spirits on all sides, as well as making good propaganda. Churchill saw films as often as Hitler did. Afterwards the industry experienced a decline because of the arrival of television. By the 1970s films had ceased to be a major method of influencing opinion. Cinemas were concerned either to show works of art, pornography or spectacular films deliberately created for a world-wide audience. In 1959 the average Englishman went to the cinema nearly every week; in 1978 twice a year. At what seemed to most the end of the great era of the cinema, Ronald Reagan, a successful actor who had helped to defeat the Communist subversion of Hollywood in the 1940s, became, appropriately, President of the United States. In a country where politicians had become very often showmen, a professional showman seemed to most Americans a better gamble than an amateur one.

4

Television had made its bow in the 1920s, a direct if initially impoverished offspring of radio and of photography. There had been continuous experiment between the 1880s and 1920s as to how to transmit a picture, and among the forefathers of the genre must rank Paul von Nipkow, a German who in 1886 devised a rotating disc; Ferdinand Braun, who produced a cathode ray in 1897; and Alan Campbell Swinton, an inspired inventor of innumerable mechanisms, who wished in 1911 to use Braun's invention to scan an image. But the first transmission of a pictorial image was that affected by John Logie Baird in 1924.

Baird was the fourth son of a Scottish clergyman. He suffered in early life from continuous bad health. He retired to Hastings in 1922 and, in an attic there, brought together a makeshift television apparatus on a washstand. The elements of his invention were: a tea-chest, a biscuit tin to house the projection lamp, scanning discs cut from cardboard, four cycle lenses (held together by scrapwood), darning needles and sealing wax. By this means, he despatched the dim image of a Maltese cross across the dingy room. Eighteen months later he gave an exhibition of television in an upper room in Soho in London to fifty people. In 1927 Baird sent an image from London to Glasgow. He then formed a company and in 1928 sent a picture across the Atlantic to New York, giving demonstrations of television in colour and stereoscopic television. Baird demonstrated television on a big screen in 1930 and televised the Derby in 1931. The next year the British Broadcasting Corporation, previously concerned only with radio, felt driven by the collectivist spirit of the time to interest itself in television as well as sound broadcasting, and bought Baird's company. In the US, meantime, a Russian émigré, Vladimir Zworykin, invented the iconoscope in 1928 which sent pictures by television more quickly.

This new idea, however, took a little time to become established. Most people had bought their radios in the 1920s and had become accustomed to go regularly to the cinema. In the 1930s, because of the economic crisis, there was little money available for new purchases of luxuries. Regular broadcasting of television only began in England in 1936. It did not do so in the US till 1941. There was no television elsewhere before the Second World War, in which the new medium, unlike radio, played no part. After 1945, however, first the US, then Europe, and then the rest of the world developed television for the mass market, so that by the 1970s the world's television services (many of them in colour) looked something like this:

Television Receivers (1975)

	Number of receivers	Number per 1,000 inhabitants
US	121 million	571
Britain	18 million	317
France	14·5 million	274
Japan	26·5 million	239
Russia	5·5 million	217
Haiti	14 thousand	0·3
India	280 thousand	0·5

Television began to be politically important in the US elections of 1952. Senator Joseph McCarthy, about that time, was the first demagogue to create a national reputation on television. In Europe, television hardly reached mass audiences enough to tip the balance in the politics of any country till the 1960s. The first impact of television on international affairs was in 1950 when the US were helped to resist the Communist invasion of South Korea because of the televised showing of debates in the UN. In 1960 Cuba had more sets of television per head than some European countries such as Belgium or Holland, and these were used to devastating effect by Fidel Castro: capitalism in Cuba was defeated by one of capitalism's own most successful creations.

Subsequently television has played a considerable if ambiguous part in democratic politics. The constant illustration of the war in Vietnam on television caused a revulsion in the US against that conflict, though it is not evident that the people of the US were made much the wiser as to what the war was about. In the 1970s television seemed in most countries to be more a substitute for the circus of the later Roman Empire. It satisfied a craving in human nature to supplement with fantasy the mundane activities of ordinary life – a desire which, in the past, had been satisfied by popular opera, church music and the Sunday afternoon band in the rose garden. It also offered most central governments the temptation of increased power and, even in democracies, statesmen (such as Charles de Gaulle) have not scrupled to manipulate it for their own purposes. Though a 'medium' as influential as newspapers, it is more difficult for private persons to approach than the press. It creates a caste of managers whose professional ethics hover uneasily between their desires to preach, to educate and to entertain. In tyrannies of the future it will clearly play a decisive part in ensuring the subservience of masses. It is already decisively affecting education: in the US, it is said, most children spend, before they are eighteen years old, between 10,000 and 15,000 hours watching television (between fourteen and twenty-two months in all).

Television also offers to mass man a standardised and conformist leisure life: destructive of variety but informative, no doubt.

5

The two critical implements in modern politics are the loudspeaker and the television screen. The first has transformed electioneering and all large meetings. It has destroyed the constructive heckler. Today only a few old men, the last survivors of their generation, can remember what it was like to wear out their voices by speaking night after night in crowded halls, during elections. The television screen is not a medium for rhetoric. But it also poses great attractions to the artful despot.

The impact of the 'media' on politics and society is much discussed, but usually as if it were something which affects only the present and the future rather than the past. But the subject already has a history, for in the years since the 1890s, first the popular press, then the cinema, then, after 1919, the radio and television and more recently the transistor and the cassette have already exerted decisive influences in many societies, not only transforming taste but, on occasion, opening the way to demagoguery and the distortion of society into new ways. The Fascist and the Nazi capture of power in the 1920s and 1930s owed a good deal to the way that those movements used the press; Castro's revolution owed much, as earlier said, to television. It is said that the overthrow of the Shah of Iran in 1979 was due to the clever manipulation of crowds by exhortations contained on cassettes. The growth of nationalism since 1945 owed a great deal to the radios which can effectively be placed in public places – an equivalent to the circulation of millions of pamphlets before 1914. Radio can influence the illiterate and both radio and television can dispense with rational argument if the manipulators concerned so desire. Of course, as Raymond Aron put it when discussing the French students' 'revolution' of 1968, 'the fire would not have spread if it had not reached inflammable material'[5].

Even so, the 'inflammable material' does not as a rule represent the best in a community. The inflammable might be the most brittle. The point is important since the history of modern nationalism is inextricably implicated in the history of communications. The European empires in the nineteenth century were often beset by guerrilla war, political assassination and violence generally. No one took much notice because the coverage by the press was either non-existent or serene. Meantime, radio and television have turned out, as George Orwell foresaw, 'a means of insulating one nation from another'[6]. During the course of the last two centuries, people of diverse ethnic origins developed an increasingly intense devotion not only to their locality, their region, their family or their ethnic group, but to a tract of territory which they began to think of as *the nation*. This has been greatly increased further by the chief consequence of the 'revolution in communications' since the nineteenth century. Songs, dances, poems and religion fanned the flames. Wars were not only caused by but stimulated the process further. So, in the end, did sport and mass media. A process which began with a stirring speech was continued with schools of historical philosophy and school textbooks used in mass education.

38

A New Agriculture

A great part of the Downs comes by a new method of Husbandry,
to be not only made Arable which they never were in former days
but to bear excellent wheat and great crops too . . . and never
known to our Ancestors to be capable of any such thing.

Daniel Defoe, *A Tour of Great Britain 1724–1727*

1

The world of agriculture was more than anything else transformed
by a series of changes in agriculture itself. New technology and
methods were brought to bear on old techniques, tools and crops.
The old kingdoms of wheat and rice, maize and potatoes were
cast thereby into other moulds.

Some of the changes were really improvements or refinements
on what had been long practised in imaginative societies. Thus,
in many of the old European open fields, beans, peas, barley,
oats, vetches, hemp and clover had been grown in the spring corn
field, sometimes to provide the winter feeding for livestock. There
was also barley, for beer. The old three-course rotation of European crops (winter corn, spring corn, fallow) had been challenged
even in the early Middle Ages. Holland, in the fifteenth century,
for example, had a complicated cycle of nine years, the soil increasingly invigorated by fertilisers (lime, pigeons' dung, ox blood,
soot and bones). The Dutch preferred to import their corn, and
sell, in exchange, vegetables, fruit, bulbs, hops and, in the seventeenth century, tobacco. Their agriculture depended on the
careful husbandry of a small portion of the soil. It included ideas
for the reclamation of land from the sea by the use of dykes and
of mills for drainage, driven by the wind. By 1650 the Netherlands'
experiments had been so successful as to enable them, for the first
time in Western agriculture, to abandon the year's fallow – an
achievement from which much flowed.

The use too of clover (brought from Italy) both improved the
supplies of winter fodder and attracted atmospheric nitrogen. That
restored the fertility of the soil miraculously[1]. Sainfoin, lucerne
and turnips played their part too. A merit of the last-named was

the indirect one that it necessitated hoeing. The arable land was cleansed, as if it had become a branch of horticulture. Garden methods took over from tillage. Digging became easier after the three-pronged iron fork was invented in the fifteenth century. Netherlands farmers also started laying down their arable fields from time to time for pasture, instead of fallow: another source of invigoration. Stockbreeding improved because of better food.

These excellent Dutch ideas spread to England, where the Flanders 'seven course' became the 'Norfolk four course' (wheat, turnips, barley, clover), to Prussia and to the Plain of Lombardy. Flanders itself soon had something like an eleven-course rotation: wheat and, after it, turnips, oats, clover, wheat, hemp, wheat flax, coleseed, wheat, beans and wheat. Thus there was a European revolution in agriculture, Flemish in origin, but put into practice on a large scale in England, whose landowners in the eighteenth century, interested in ideas, free from feudal restrictions and able to rely on contract labour rather than labour provided by custom or status, became preoccupied by innovation. The nub of this revolution was the spread of flexible ideas of crop rotation, so improving fodder, which enabled the land to bear more stock, which in turn could enrich the land by more manure. These ideas did not spread fast to nations where the ghosts of feudalism were still at large such as France: many agricultural methods there of the mid nineteenth century would have seemed orthodox to a visitor from the thirteenth – though it is fair to add that the system practised at that same time in the American Midwest would have appeared barbaric even to a mediaeval European: a one-crop system (wheat) without fertilisation or rotation of crops.

In addition to improvements in methods of growing crops, there were several innovations in technology. The most important was Jethro Tull's horse-drawn drill to plant seed in rows, devised about 1730. That was superior both to the old method of broadcasting seed indiscriminately and to that of dropping seeds into holes prepared, one by one, by a dibble. Tull, a lawyer from Berkshire, who farmed land which he had inherited, arranged that the horse which pulled his drill should drag a bush harrow to cover the seed behind, though, for a time, this mechanised sowing excluded corn and only affected beans, peas and turnips. About the same time, a light swing plough was devised in Holland, with a curved iron mouldboard, needing few animals. Some forty years on, Robert Ransome, a brassfounder from Norwich of Quaker ancestry, developed his self-sharpening, cast-iron ploughshares* and, in 1789, the first all-iron plough. A threshing machine had also been devised in the 1750s and was in use by 1815 in England and by 1830 in France on all good farms, while a machine flail to separate grain from straw was invented in 1784 by Andrew Meikle, an elderly millwright from Dunbar – the farms of Lothian being at that time probably the best managed in the world. After Watt's invention of the steam engine the Duke of Bedford ordered a steam engine to thresh and grind corn at Woburn. These and other innovations depended on inventions in other commodities. For example, mass-produced farm forks and spades had as big an influence as any, just as mass-produced kitchen knives and forks had. All depended upon cheap, more easily smelted iron.

2

There were, however, also critical changes in landholding. In England, the country which was the first in the field in industry, these changes were associated particularly with the word 'enclosure'. To this subject Karl Marx devoted some of his most affecting paragraphs (in Chapter XXVII of Volume I of *Das Kapital*) but they were prejudiced.

The movement called 'enclosure' meant the final end to collective farming based on tradition and mutual obligations, and the establishment of an individualist system. It also meant the end of, and the distribution of, common or open fields, meadows, pastures and wastelands as it did of the old village. Many of these changes occurred by common agreement.

In the early eighteenth century, when only about half the arable land in England remained in open fields (concentrated in the Midlands and the central south of the country), enclosures became more frequent. Many landowners had recourse to private Acts of Parliament to confirm what they wanted, since, though expensive, they provided legal certainty. They enabled the rest of the English common and wasteland to be divided up. Enclosure was popular among landowners, for it allowed the conversion of land for new and more profitable uses. It expanded the area under arable. It improved the health of cattle.

* The underside of the ploughshare was chilled by casting it on an iron mould, the upper part of the mould being of sand. The underside of the share was thereby made harder than steel while the upper part remained tough and soft. The upper part wore away faster than the lower and thereby sharpened itself.

Now it was once argued that the commissioners appointed to carry out the reallocation of land acted only in the interests of the great, and indeed might be nominated by them. That was Karl Marx's view, it was the view of the great French historian of the Industrial Revolution Paul Mantoux and it was the view of the eloquent economic historians the Hammonds. Enclosure entailed 'massive violence exercised by the upper classes against the lower', wrote Barrington Moore Junior as late as the 1960s. But the same writer conceded that enclosure meant that 'modernisation could proceed in England without the huge reservoir of reactionary forces that existed . . . in Germany and Japan, and removed the possibilities of peasant revolts'.

That qualification points the way to a realistic interpretation of what happened. Many modern historians have been impressed by the fairness of the commissioners in what was usually a complex affair. The occasions when acts of enclosure were deliberately framed against small farmers appear to have been few. Not all poor farmers were against enclosure, nor were all rich landlords in favour. Many farmers with few acres found that the concentration of their land in homogeneous parcels made it worth more after enclosure than before. Owners of small plots in England are found to have been increasing in numbers precisely in the years 1760–80 and 1793–1815 when enclosure was at its height. The end of various types of mediaeval lease was also an encouragement to many small farmers. The farms of England were increasing in size for reasons other than enclosure. New hedgerows created shade, birdsong, and shelter for animals. The health of herds improved and there was a drop in those diseases of cattle which can be transferred to men. Finally, though poverty probably did increase in the English countryside in the early nineteenth century, it was no more marked in places where enclosure was new than where there had been enclosure for a long time.

The reason for the increase in poverty was primarily the rise in population which was also the fundamental cause of the greater availability of labour. Agricultural employment seems to have been improved, not damaged, as a result of enclosure. There were more families employed on the land in England in 1831 than there were in 1801 (761,348 to 697,353). It would appear certain, commented Halévy, that the years following the execution of an Enclosure Act 'always witnessed an increase of the population at the place where the enclosure was made'[2]. Cobbett, on his rides through the south of England, painted a picture of silent and deserted villages. But the reason was not that agriculture had failed, but that the small woollen manufacturers, small iron mines and smelting works had been transformed.

This process of enclosure occurred elsewhere in Europe but only in Denmark, southern Sweden and some parts of Germany was it possible, as it were, for a radically liberal state to encourage the idea. Marat toyed with it in France. But, though the revolutionaries in theory disliked feudal survivals, they did not do more than condemn compulsory rotation and proclaim liberty of enclosure. The Third Republic eventually adopted a compromise whereby all feudal obligations were abolished in principle but each municipality had the right to ask for their continuance. Some parts of France had enclosure from the sixteenth century 'at an almost English pace' (for example, in Normandy). Elsewhere, the old system was dented; for example, lords began to try to secure some means of exempting the meadows from collective grazing or of postponing the entry of the common herd until the second crop of hay (aftermath) had been cut. Gradually, forage crops (clover, sainfoin, lucerne, turnips) began to make for that victory of horticulture over tillage which potatoes and sugar beet completed in the fields of northern France.*

Of course, there were some evils in enclosure in England, as elsewhere. The abolition of waste and of collective grazing had disadvantages for small farmers, though the poorest gained something from the division of common land. Squatters suffered. Those with access to the common by custom, not right, were not always recognised by the commissioners. But the common rights in the past had never belonged to all. They had belonged to those who had holdings on the common field. Sometimes widows too lost the rights which they had held under the old system to their husband's plot: hence, according to some, the increase in 'witches' in England after the sixteenth century.†

As important in transforming agriculture as enclosing was an increase in the yield, or the number of times that a seed takes to

---

* Subsequently, in the nineteenth century, French peasants did much exchanging and rounding off of their holdings. But never was there any governmental policy of consolidation. In Germany, the end of open fields was promoted by governments, but modestly. A Prussian law of 1872 provided that an open field or part of it could be re-arranged, provided a majority of owners desired it. But manorial courts continued in Prussia till 1892.

† 'Witches are usually such as one destitute of friends, bowed down with years, laden with infirmities,' wrote a contemporary.

reproduce itself. Typical yields throughout the agricultural era were 1 to 3: an annual doubling of the sown seed since every year one grain of every one harvested had to be set aside for seed. Sometimes 1 to 4 might be gained. Much higher yields were gained in exceptional circumstances. Many parts of the world do no better than 1 to 3 in the twentieth century. Most did no better in the nineteenth. Russian yields averaged 1 to 3 between the fifteenth and twentieth centuries. Such a ratio is enough to support life but little more. In Europe, agricultural yields reached 1 to 5 in the thirteenth century and 1 to 6 or 1 to 7 in the sixteenth and eighteenth[3]. That meant a surplus growing at a geometric rate. It permitted urban and commercial life. Below a yield of 1 to 5, the farmer has no surplus. He and his colleagues cannot support a population with interests other than farming.

The changes in agriculture between the Renaissance and the eighteenth century were thus numerous. But its social and political character remained unaltered. In every country, even in England, in 1750 it employed the vast majority. Those people too mostly used the same methods that they had used since the dawn of time. The sickle or the machete, the ox, the horse and the earthen threshing place were the dominant instruments. Indeed, they would thus remain for another hundred years or so, even in advanced nations. On Brazilian sugar plantations, the ox-cart seemed in 1850 still the great motor of profit and civilised commerce. But everywhere in the Old World agriculture felt the pressure of population in the eighteenth century. The pressure caused particular social unrest in places where there were minifundia, handkerchief-sized plots, next to latifundia. One consequence was the birth of legends about the old rural past. The Chartist rebels in the 1840s in England said that they wished to 'live to see the restoration of old English times, old English fare, old English holidays and old English justice, and every man live by the sweat of his brow . . . when the weaver worked at his own loom and stretched his limbs in his own field'. As E. P. Thompson puts it, 'the myth of the lost paternalist community became a force in its own right – perhaps as powerful a force as the utopian projections of Owen and the Socialists'[4].

The countries which prospered in the early generations of enlightenment were those which succeeded, by hook or by crook, in resolving such mediaeval or feudal patterns of landholding.

Mechanisation began to have an effect on agriculture only in the second third of the nineteenth century. That began to occur in, above all, the US, a country where labour was short and where, therefore, inventions were always popular. The US was also in the fortunate position of having no traditional landowning habits to destroy and (apart from slaves and Indians), no entrenched or backward classes; and agriculture remained there the main source of wealth till the 1880s.

The decisive years were those between 1830 and 1860. Until 1830 US agriculture was traditional. All work on farms was done by hand, save for ploughing and drawing loads, accomplished by oxen or by horses, though Jethro Tull's seeding methods with a drill were in use. Then, first and foremost, came the iron plough. It had been suggested by Charles Newbould in New Jersey in 1797, but Jethro Wood made one in 1814 out of several castings, and tried it out on his farm at Poplar Creek in Cayuga county, New York State. That plough began to be used generally in the east of the US after 1830. Improvements were suggested. John Lane in Chicago introduced a steel mouldboard to which soil did not stick. Even before that, a 'cradle scythe' had been invented which replaced the sickle, and ended the stooping imposed by the traditional method of reaping. The cradle acted as a gathering rake too, for every swing laid the cut corn in even piles, easily gathered up. Then in the mid 1830s Obed Hussey in Cincinnati and Cyrus McCormick in West Virginia separately invented a mechanised reaper. Though Hussey was the first to register a patent, McCormick began manufacture of this device which, to begin with, cut hay as well as corn. McCormick also founded a factory in Chicago in 1847 and introduced the reaper to an admiring world at the Great Exhibition in England – a country which had just seen the success of a very effective lobby on food matters, 'the most effective political machine the country had known – the Anti Corn Law League'[5]. By then threshing, which had traditionally been done in the US, as everywhere else, by a wooden flail on an earthen floor, had also been transformed by a new and much more effective machine devised in 1837 by Hiram Pitts of Maine. He too moved to Chicago and built a factory to market his invention, which made its first appearance internationally at the Paris Exhibition of 1855 and threshed 740 litres of wheat in one hour, instead of the 36 which six men could do in the same time[6].

Other inventions followed: a cable plough in 1850, and a steam one devised by John Fowler in 1858; a horse-drawn rake and a revolving hay rake; hand-binding harvesters, wire binders and twine binders were all put on the market by McCormick (who was among the businessmen to use field trials, guarantees, benefits for cash and deferred payments).

There was no practical limit to production through an inability to harvest crops. The most important farmers' difficulties were thus removed – or removable. A crop could be harvested immediately it was ripe (unless the reaper went wrong) and the losses would not be great. Cheap, swift transport by railway or good roads reduced the importance of distance, enabling meat, in particular, to be carried much farther. The telegraph carried news of the markets. William Seward, secretary of state in Lincoln's cabinet, praised McCormick's invention as something which enabled 'the line of civilisation to move westward thirty miles a year'.*
In the 1840s machines were introduced to make clay pipes, so rendering drainage easier. Naturally, these developments favoured the creation of large farms. On smaller ones, farmers continued old methods or, perhaps, agreed to hire a machine for a few days – never a satisfactory alternative, since the days arranged might coincide with bad weather.

Early reapers had merely cut grain. People were still needed to rake it into sheaves, others still to gather and bind it. After 1860 there were experiments with a 'self-raking reaper' and a 'self-binder', a twine binder and, in 1885, the combined harvester-thresher, made possible by the substitution of oil for steam and horsepower. In use by 1900 too were agricultural elevators, for transferring and storing grain. 'Cakes' made from cotton seeds or linseeds for winter feeding made it easier to keep cattle alive during the winter. Finally, cheap wire after 1860, and then barbed wire, were far from being the least of inventions; to fence forty acres with wooden rails in 1839 cost between $200 and $300. Stone was expensive in the US plains, while hedges took too long to grow in a country where it was essential to define ownership. All such demarcations were too expensive till the coming of cheap wire.

* Seward was the secretary of state who wisely bought Alaska from Russia for $7·2 million against the wishes of public opinion, which dubbed the new territory Seward's 'ice box'.

4

Equally important for agriculture was the work of Julius von Liebig, professor of chemistry at the small town of Giessen, son of a dry-salter and dealer in dyes from Darmstadt, who laid the foundation for the chemical study of soils and manures. In 1840 von Liebig proved that plants did not derive their organic sustenance from the soil, but from the inexhaustible supply of carbon dioxide in the atmosphere. Von Liebig confirmed the importance of lime in regulating the acidity of the soils. His ideas were put into practice by an English landowner, John Lawes of Rothamsted, who had been working on similar schemes on his own. (Maintaining Rothamsted as the first real agricultural research station, Lawes ran a commercial factory for making superphosphates at Deptford.) Another consequence of von Liebig's discoveries was the increase in the quantity of guano traded as manure: Britain imported 2,000 tons in 1841, 300,000 in 1847. Sodium nitrates, similarly beneficial for agriculture, were imported on a large scale from Chile by all agriculturally adventurous countries. Large-scale foreign, principally British, investments in Chilean nitrates followed in the 1880s. 'Nitrate kings' such as John Thomas North exercised a brief sway[7]. The discovery of microorganisms by the great French chemist Louis Pasteur* further transformed agricultural research. It was hard to look at soil in the same way as before when it was realised that a saltspoonful of dry garden soil contained twice as many bacteria as there are people on earth[8]. The age of fertiliser began; the age of slavery ended! The custom of abandoning land when it was exhausted which had characterised many colonial territories came to an end. Still, chemical fertiliser is not everywhere desired or available: in 1967 in a survey of north-eastern Brazil, over half the farmers interviewed said that they had never heard of chemical fertilisers[9].

The mechanisation of agriculture spread. Thus France, which long retained its ancient rural characteristics, became decisively mechanised between 1890 and 1910. French governments considered their most important task to be to keep France self-sufficient in bread. The country was already using much chemical manure after her conquest of Tunis, with its sources of phosphates, in 1880. Some indication of what happened after 1890 can be seen in figures from the Haute Garonne, a department full neither of large holdings nor of specialist products. In 1892 there were, in the province, 450 mechanical ¡nowers of hay, 180 reapers and 60 reaper binders. In 1908 those figures read 15,000, 25,000 and 1,200 respectively. That meant the end of subsistence agriculture, and of a self-contained way of life. The agricultural way of life survived a generation or so longer in France, until the 1950s, and longer in some parts of Spain. But already by 1910 signs of change were everywhere visible.

The use of fertilisers completed the liberation of farmers from fallow. They no longer relied on cattle to provide manure, thereby breaking the age-old association between corn and cattle. That, in turn, freed farmers from their concern with forage, the cultivation of which had been essential since the beginning of agriculture.

Still in Spain, the Old World survived. Even in the 1950s a calendar like this, as recorded by Gerald Brenan, could be found: The year begins with olive picking, by women, then vine and fruit pruning, then the planting of garlic and onions, two cash crops and the hoeing of cornfields. In early May the harvest might begin on the coast, first barley, then wheat. The harvest would spread up the mountainside, 300 feet making a difference of four days, and the high mountain farms not being ready till September. The crop would be cut by the old short sickle and would be done at night as well as day if there were a moon. The corn would be spread about on the threshing floors, two mules would haul the primitive, iron-teethed threshing machine, the region's only concession to mechanisation, which had taken over at last from the flail. At night, there would be winnowing, or tossing of the ears of corn with forks of ash[10].

5

Agriculture soon also began to be international as well as mechanised. This development was assisted by artificial ice, first devised by Sir John Leslie, professor of mathematics at Edinburgh, a friend and admirer of David Hume, in a laboratory in 1810. But, though Sir Robert Peel in the 1840s was known to his critics as 'the refrigerator', and though fish was taken to London in ice by George Dempster in 1830, artificial ice was only available from 1850. In that year James Harrison in Australia designed an ice-making machine, based on the idea of the evaporation of ether which produces a fall in the temperature, the liquid being regenerated by compression. Carré, a French engineer, found a better method, by using ammonia gas. A plant capable of holding 8,000 pounds of ice at one time was shortly built in Sydney. By 1869 refrigerator cars were being built for US railways. A great impetus was thus given to the meat-packing and the slaughtering industries. By 1914, from accounting in the US for a mere $29 million in 1860, those two trades had grown to $34 million, and become the nation's largest.

Long before then, both Australia and Argentina had begun sending meat to Europe by ice ship. The first successful transoceanic refrigerated ship was the French engineer Charles Jellier's *SS Frigorifique*, which sailed from Buenos Aires to Rouen in 1877[11], with stocks of Argentina's much prized beef on board. Australia followed, in 1879. Ice-making machines on steam trawlers enabled new banks to be swept for fish. Railways enabled quantities of fish to be carried inland. That permitted a decline of salted and pickled herrings, which for so long had been the only fish known away from the coast. The salted herring had made the merchants of the Hanse rich in the fourteenth century. Ice made those of Norway and Hull rich in the nineteenth. Fresh fish had never before been a big business except for a few carp, tench or trout, caught in rivers or artificial ponds. Ice too became a commodity to be exported and carried immense distances. In New York in the 1870s jugs of iced water began to appear on dining tables as a matter of course.

At the same time among the exotic crops about to become normal at the European or American breakfast table, tea (from India and Ceylon as well as China), coffee (from the East Indies or Brazil) and chocolate (taken from the Americas to Ghana and Nigeria) were added to sugar (still coming from the West Indies, though European beet was by then a serious competitor). Grain from Russia came in on the new great railways from the East.

These exchanges greatly benefited the Western city. The transoceanic suppliers enabled Britain to feed her own population far better than was possible from British farms alone. Many farmers in the US, Russia, Australia and Argentina made fortunes. But the farmers of Europe did not prosper. Despite the fertilisers, machinery, new seeds and livestock breeding, European farming in the late nineteenth century went into a decline.

Mechanisation, after all, had no powers against bad weather, nor against the liver rot in sheep and foot and mouth disease among cattle, which marked European farming in those days. The cheapness of imported wheat caused the crop area of Europe to drop. Only dairy farmers did well.

6

The twentieth century saw the completion of the mechanisation of agriculture through the development of the tractor. This idea, which followed in the wake of the car, began in the 1880s, when British engineers designed steam engines for heavy work on farms. In the US, the idea was launched of a mechanised plough powered by internal combustion. The Burger oil-powered tractor appeared in the Midwest in 1889. Though heavy, it, or versions of it, soon replaced the steam tractors used previously. By 1913 there were already 8,000 tractors in the US.

The demand for food in the middle of the First World War increased the attention paid to this new machine, and the British government instructed its Ministry of Munitions to develop a utility 'tank'. As a lightweight tractor, that was copied in the US. In 1919 the US had over 160,000 tractors. In 1939 they had a million and a half; and 4½ million in the 1970s. That meant the end of the long-established part played in agriculture by the horse and the ox. It also meant substantial drops in the agricultural labour force of countries equipped with tractors, and huge increases in output.

Other innovations followed, with equally important consequences. For example, a mechanised cane cutter was used in sugar harvesting in Australia from the beginning of the twentieth century, though, because of the character of the crop or opposition by labour, it took a long time to be generally introduced among other cane growing countries. (The Cuban revolutionary government of 1959, after it had destroyed the free unions, began to use cane cutters in the late 1960s). A machine to pick cotton was developed in 1889. The insecticide DDT began to be used in 1939 against destructive insects. Artificial insemination to improve livestock was introduced about the same time. After 1950 production of chickens and turkeys in concentration camps began. In the 1960s, too, a new method of growing wheat began to be tried out first in Mexico and then elsewhere in tropical zones. This requires some attention.

For a long time it had been noticed that when plants are heavily fertilised in the tropics they shoot up excessively, and then collapse. If grown closely enough to one another to avoid that, one plant shields another. In Mexico, a thickly sown, short-stemmed grain planted on well-irrigated and fertilised soil was found to give high yields[12]. That gave rise to a new 'green revolution' affecting many plants, not simply wheat. 'Miracle strains' of the main food crops were devised. The use of large quantities of fertiliser was found to give disproportionately impressive results. It was for a time believed that all the world's fears of future food shortages with a high population were needless. Thus a huge rise began in the quantity of tomatoes produced, combined with a decline of land planted. That was possible because of an increase of yield per acre from, say, 13·5 tons an acre to 51·5 tons in California[13].

The most obvious effect of these changes in technology and science directed to agriculture was to bring a greater amount of land under the plough than ever before and to increase greatly the food available. By 1970 about 88 per cent of the total cultivable land in Europe was being worked, 83 per cent of the cultivable land in Asia (excluding Russia) and 64 per cent of the cultivable land in Russia. Even in some of the less well-populated continents, there had been increases. The figures for North America (including Mexico and Central America), Africa, South America and Australia are 51 per cent, 22 per cent, 11 per cent and 10 per cent. Much land remains, it is true, to be cultivated. The total land which could be cultivated is said to be about 4,100 million hectares, of which less than half is now given over to crops in any single year (these figures count more than once areas where multiple crops are grown). Even so, the greatest potential increase in food production lies in the more intensive cultivation of the areas currently devoted to crops.

The transformation achieved by the tractor, the combine harvester, pesticides and fertilisers has been the most remarkable development in the history of agriculture. An idea of the changes caused can be seen in the increase of the production of grain in the US, which rose a few thousand times from 378 million bushels in 1839, before the impact of McCormick's invention had begun to be seen, to 3,422,000 million bushels in 1957. Yield of wheat is now in the order of a ratio of 1 to 20 instead of 1 to 4 or 5 in the seventeenth century.

The kind of agricultural revolution caused by the 'green revolution' can best be described by some simple figures: thus after 1948 until the mid 1970s India had often to import huge quantities of food. In normal years since then it has fed itself: Indian wheat production rose from 12·3 million tons in 1965 to 35 million in 1980, rice production from 46 million tons in 1965 to 74 million in 1977. Indonesia increased its production of rice by 37 per cent in the 1970s, the Philippines by 40 per cent.

Yet the increase in agricultural efficiency has not by any means solved all the problems of the world's food. First, the benefits of the 1960s and 1970s are being followed by disappointments. For example, after a certain level of miraculous growth, arable yields cease to rise in proportion to fertiliser per acre. By concentrating certain strains of crop with high yields, there is a genetic danger. It is dangerous to depend too much on a single strain. That may be attacked by a disease which destroys it. Weedless fields are easier prey to infections which, in the past, might have been stayed by diversity of strain. Reliance on fertilisers from chemicals also increases dependence on international trade.

In addition, prehistoric men and women enjoyed a more varied diet than people do now, since they ate species of plant and several hundred thousand types of living creature. But only a tiny percentage of these were ever domesticated. Modern shops have accelerated a trend towards specialisation which began in the earliest days of agriculture. The food of the rich countries has become cheaper relative to wages. It is speedily distributed in supermarkets. But the choice annually becomes less and less great. Even individual foods themselves become more standardised. We live in the world of the carrot specially blunted in order to avoid making a hole in a bag, and the tomato grown to meet a demand for a standard weight of eighteen tomatoes to a kilo. Siri von Reis Altschul asks: 'Only the three major cereals and perhaps ten other widely cultivated species stand between famine and survival for the world's human population and a handful of drug plants has served Western civilisation for several thousand years. A rather obvious question arises: are we missing something?'[14]. After all, there are 800,000 species of plant on earth.

But there have also been more difficult developments in modern agriculture, partly related to technological change but also partly related to illusions about the management of land.

The increase in the amount of food available in the nineteenth and twentieth centuries has occurred in places where the number of farmers has been reduced. The success of modern agriculture has been related not only to its mechanisation but to the concurrent decline in the numbers of those working in it. Thus, in Britain, a little over a quarter of grown men were linked with agriculture in 1850, but in 1911 the number was down to less than one in twenty. In 1961 the agricultural labour force in Britain was 874,000, less than those engaged in manufacturing, building, commerce, transport and a whole range of services. Comparable figures would soon be so, in most other European countries. This major social change, from which so much else flows, was first marked in Britain, and later in the US (there were more non-agricultural workers than farmers there in the 1870s) and Germany (in the 1880s). By 1970 agriculture, in almost all European countries, was less important as an employer than manufacturing services or transport. It is true, too, of many nations of South America. The paradox is that the food supplies of Asia and Africa will only be assured when the same is able to be said of those continents.

There are several other paradoxes in the history of modern agriculture. The first is that the increase of the food available has helped – more than medical advances – to increase the world's population. That, in turn, has increased the pressure of population on food supplies.

This has led to the second paradox. Traditional agriculture assumed that a district's food would be supplied by its neighbourhood. In the Mediterranean world, that system was beginning to be overthrown by 500 BC. The Athenians bought their grain from the Ukraine, the Romans bought theirs from Africa. Such commerce broke down in the Dark Ages, to be successfully revived, with other classical habits, during the Crusades. Then, and during antiquity, however, only rich coastal towns or towns on navigable rivers were able to resort to these imports.

During the nineteenth century, as has been seen, railways and improvements in shipping made possible the beginning of a new international commerce in food. Some of these developments have been noticed in consideration of railways and of shipping. By 1913 most regions in the world expected to grow grain and certain other foods. Europe alone imported such staffs of life. That equilibrium continued till 1939. But now, with the increase of consumption of food in the poorer parts of the world as a result of increased population, and the relative failure of political experiments such as communism (in agriculture particularly), the three large English-speaking nations of the USA, Australia and Canada supply most of the grain which is exported. 'It seems as if the less developed regions of the world are losing the capacity to feed themselves,' wrote Dr Lester Brown[15]. The alteration since 1939 is expressed best in the accompanying table.

7

Of course, the problems of food have been observed by governments. Many of them have sought to alleviate them. Two policies

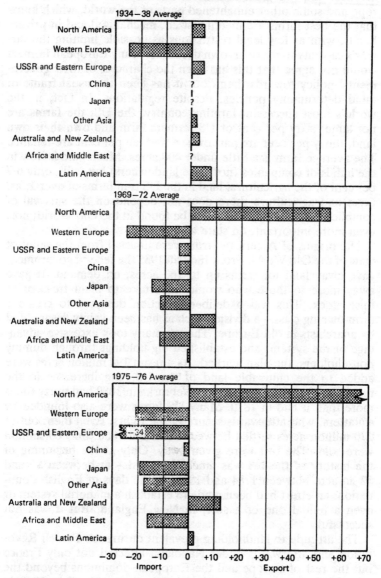

THE WORLD GRAIN TRADE
Net Grain Trade (Millions of Metric Tons)

Source: Scientific American September 1975

can be distinguished. The first is that which, roughly, has char-acterised the two great nations of North America, Western Europe and some other enlightened parts of the world, which know that the best farms are medium-sized, mechanised and in private hands, with as few legal restrictions as possible limiting the far-mer's capacity to make his own decisions. Many European farmers would not agree that this has been the character of their govern-ments' policy towards them, but it has been the usual frame of mind determining policies, despite regulations. In fact, in the world's most successful farming country, the US, the farms are not large: sixty per cent of US farmers farm and own their own land, thirty per cent are part owners and ten per cent are tenants. The average farm is a little under 400 acres. Much land is now in the hands of companies (not large landowners) but, still, only 6·7 per cent of the agricultural land in the US is in farms of over 1,000 acres and agriculture there does not depend on the survival of complicated leases such as are to be found in the Old World; nor, even more important, on state enterprises.

The origins of American farms were unusual from the point of view of the Old World. From 1860 till 1935 the federal government gave away land for farms up to 160 acres, on demand. It gave away more to those who would undertake to plant trees or to raise stock. This was a deliberate action designed to create a farm-owning class – a division such as has been vainly dreamed of by anarchists in old Europe. Though many took excessive advan-tage of the system, and established big holdings through dummy householders, the plan worked. As a result 190 million acres were added to the cultivable land of the US. Big increases in the numbers of cattle occurred too: Nebraska in 1880 had thirty times more than it had in 1870. Many US farms were also founded by squatters, who afterwards secured legal rights. Even then, out of 270 million acres settled between 1841 and 1860, only 69 million were sold. The rest were given away. Only at the beginning of the history of the US was much land sold – at between $1 and $2 an acre between 1784 and 1820. In the days of English domi-nation, an effort had been made to establish a manorial system or even a feudal one of a sort, in New England. But it was not successful.

The attitude to landholding prevalent during the French Revo-lution and afterwards under Napoleon affected not only France but the rest of Europe and the European dominions beyond the sea. Clerical land and 'national land' were sold off in 1790 in conditions which placed poorer peasants at a disadvantage and which emphasised the essentially 'bourgeois social character' of the Revolution in a way more striking than any other. The Revolution destroyed the feudal legal structure of France, Albert Soboul pointed out, it damaged the aristocracy but it assisted the landowning peasantry and middle class[16]. Much the same happened in Spain in the course of the nineteenth century. The Conde de Campomanes, the liberal reformer of Spain, had argued in the 1780s that he would like to see every Spanish peasant owning a house and garden, a yoke of mules and fifty acres. But how could that be arranged by the state? The liberal Cortes of Cadiz in 1812 began to sell common lands in order to pay the national debt. Spanish liberals in the 1830s resumed the practice. A few years later, Church property began to be sold. But the consequence of these and other state-inspired sales was not encouraging. The peasantry hated being deprived of grazing and gleaning rights. An increasing population on the land found itself at the mercy of a new class of legally minded, doctrinaire liberals who were only interested in producing food for the market. Hence the formulation of a series of illusions about the desirability of a different agrarian reform which, unlike that inspired by the French Revolution, would in the minds of the reformers benefit the population as a whole. Such ideas failed to take into account the fact that in old nations such as those found in Europe or Asia there is really only one method of agrarian reform which increases production: that is, that which occurred in the Mediterranean countries after 1945, inspired by the desire of the peasants themselves to leave the land for the city, where they would themselves help to make, among other things, the machines which would modernise the farming in the fields which they had abandoned.

The agrarian reforms introduced by Communist countries have been various. First, there was the Russian reform. In 1913 most of Russia's twenty million peasant families lived in communes from which they gained, for a specific number of years, a certain number of strips of land. When their children grew up, they too would demand a strip. The Russian peasant of the days before 1914 was thus in practice more a self-employed individual than a cooperativist. Only a tenth of the land sown in Russia in 1914, it should be realised, belonged to great estates.

To begin with, the Communist government after 1921 treated its agricultural problems with some subtlety. In the course of the civil war, the leaders had observed the ineffectiveness of idealistic

programmes for agriculture designed to benefit the whole community. So they formed cooperatives on the large estates of Russia
and other confiscated land and, on the rest of the territory – at
least three-quarters of Russian farms – permitted private farmers
to survive much as they had done before 1914. But this compromise did not work. On the cooperatives, the land was state-owned,
but the farmers were regarded as owners of the livestock, buildings
and tools. All received a payment in cash and an allocation of the
produce, after charges for state seed and other services had been
deducted. The centres of these farms were, however, the Machine
and Tractor Stations (MTS) managed by politically appointed
agents. (Russia made a big investment in tractors, and had 280,000
in 1934 compared to the USA's one million in that year.) Each
peasant was also allowed a plot of ground varying from half an
acre to two acres, on which he could hold a few cows and sheep
and an unlimited number of chickens and rabbits. These private
plots created many problems. The certainty of making a profit out
of them caused peasants to put their heart into them, rather than
into the collective farms[17].

At the same time the peasants on the rest of the land were
recalcitrant. Perhaps because the Russian government, particularly after Lenin's death, was managed by men who had been
peasants or the sons of peasants, it used its political power with
a bluntness which made the rule of the Tsar seem in retrospect a
Utopia. The peasants were only legally allowed to sell their crop
to state boards on which the bureaucracy of the old Russia merged
with the brutality of the new commissar. In most villages, too, the
'elders' were an obvious focus of opposition to the Communist
party, in whom the government placed trust. Thus the food production of Russia was in unsure hands and many peasants, without
the chance of making money in the old way, simply refused to
sell grain. In all items of production, Russian agriculture in 1928
was well below the level obtained in 1913, even taking into account
the loss of territory caused by the substantial defeat in 1918.
Meantime, the Russian government was anxious to press on with
a programme of further industrialisation linked, like that of Peter
the Great, to preparations for war.

The consequence was the brutal agricultural revolution of 1929–
33, whose aim was to force the bulk of the Russian rural population into the towns and to establish state direction on the land.
This was, in effect, the real Russian revolution, more important
and more destructive than the events of 1917–21. It was a subju-

gation ruthless, chaotic and swift. Communists came out from the
towns accompanied by the secret police and, often fortified by
brandy, forcibly took over land, grain and stock, and expelled or
killed the peasants. A 'saturnalia of arrests', as Roy Medvedev
put it[18], followed. Tens of thousands died of starvation, and millions were deported or fled to the cities. Thousands were shot for
burying or even consuming grain which they had grown themselves. 'Dizzy with success', Stalin described himself in 1930; but
he later implied, in conversation with Winston Churchill, that ten
million people had died during this time which was, in effect, a
civil war fought against the whole peasantry.

This revolution has been explained away as enabling Russia 'to
skip the capitalist stage of development altogether'. Actually, it
established a kind of state feudalism in which workers were bonds-
men more than they had ever been. Although attention was given
later to modifications of the cooperative, most Russian farms have
become state farms, where the workers are day labourers on a
large estate – the average size of 'state' farms is 40,000 acres and
'collective' farms 13,000 – in which they are just as 'alienated' or
remote from their masters (or more so) than those on a great
estate of the past. This lack of concern with agriculture derives
from Marx's sense of the 'idiocy of life', a notion which doubtless
could have been justified in nineteenth-century Russia, had he
ever visited it.   *WHAT HAS HAPPENED TO THE*
                                          ARAL
Communist agriculture has admittedly had some successes. Rus-   *SEA ?*
sian cotton is a successful product. Then, the area under wheat in
Russia seems to have more than doubled, from about 80 million
acres to about 170 million, between 1913 and the 1970s. But then
the Russian population has nearly doubled too.* Russia is now
also the largest sugar producer in the world (if pressed hard by
Brazil). Russian livestock has apparently trebled since 1913 (32
million to 112 million in 1978). Russia produces infinitely more
potatoes than any other nation. Russia seems since 1917 to have
used a large female labour force in agriculture – in 1959, half as
many again as men. Output of wheat has gone up three and a half
times (in aggregate, not per head) from 28 million metric tons in
1913 to an average of about 100 million tons in the 1970s.† But

---

* The Russian population increased since 1913 from about 150 million to 260
  million in 1977.
† The following figures should all be regarded as uncertain since Russian statistics
  are often published with a political, rather than a true, purpose. Black marke-
  teering may account for an error of underestimation of twenty per cent.

still, Russian harvests continue to be most unreliable. Instead of being a major exporter of wheat, as she was during the generation between 1870 and the First World War, modern Russia stoops to importing grain from the capitalist USA. Communism has thus had the effect of diminishing the grain available for the rest of the world. Furthermore, such statistics as are available suggest that the ruins of private farming continue to be more productive than state farming. In 1980 the fifty million or so tiny plots which are farmed as small private allotments by persons who otherwise work on collective farms take up three per cent of the total cultivated land; but they produce nearly a third of all meat and milk produced in Russia, a third of the vegetables, over a third of the eggs and almost a fifth of the wool. The old failures of harvest also continue to dog modern Russia. Communist or no, Russia is a formidable agricultural nation, and the government has absorbed many lessons from Western practice. But, even so, both there and in Eastern Europe, agriculture has been a discouraging aspect of the Communist regimes measured in terms of production and of social integration.

The second major Communist experiment on the land was in China where, in 1949, a Communist party at that time much influenced by Russia gained control. The Communists were led by the son of a peasant, Mao Tse-tung, who had himself worked on the land between the ages of thirteen and eighteen. In his early life as a founding member of the Communist party in China, Mao was a specialist in peasants' affairs. In 1927 he was chairman of the All China Peasants' Union. When he and his friends came to power in 1949 their first measure was to make freeholders of all peasants who previously had rented land. That move endeared the regime, to begin with, to peasants who were not well informed of what had happened earlier in Russia. After about six or seven years, the Communists embarked on a programme of inducing all farmers to pool their undertakings in a cooperative. This idea was offered both to new owners and to old freeholders. Boundaries between plots were eliminated. The whole village worked the land as a large farm under the direction of the committee elected by the cooperative: 'The great power of the propaganda machine,' wrote Professor C. P. Fitzgerald, 'the constant exhortation of party cadres at meetings, an incessant campaign to convince the peasants that all these measures would secure them against the risk of famine . . . all combined to persuade the peasant, no doubt with some misgivings, that the "Higher Stage of Co-operation" was a blessing . . . and it did, indeed, bring much land into cultivation and make possible the rationalisation of irrigation and water conservancy'[19]. Perhaps that description fails to evoke the reality of events in China in the country in those years. It is impossible as yet to know how that 'stage' of the agrarian revolution happened. It may have been as severe as the comparable one in Russia.

The era of the cooperative, however, did not mark the end of the agrarian changes in China. In 1958 the government in Peking decided to merge the cooperatives into larger units, to be known as 'communes'. The same historian, C. P. Fitzgerald, calls that decision 'rash, unwarranted and disastrous'[20]. Severe droughts adversely affected the experiment in the early days. So did ideas of 'scientific agriculture'. The pressure of population on the land was exacerbated by a unique period of political stability. All that can be said of the Chinese agricultural experiment is that, though rationing has been continuous, famine seems to have been usually averted, even if there were apparently no increase in food *per capita* and even if the five per cent of farmland in private hands produced twenty per cent of the food. Even so, by concentrating on ensuring an adequate, if modest, supply of food, and avoiding prestige projects and latterly seeking a control of population, China has apparently cut her coat according to her cloth. The government has successfully established hoards of rice and grain adequate to feed even overgrown cities such as Shanghai. It seems that China, which has remained self-sufficient, has managed in agriculture to devise a system which was an improvement on the chaotic past during the age of 'warlords'. But that, of course, was an era of civil war. Meantime the water buffalo, the rice and the irrigation works continue remarkably unchanged.

Since the death of Mao, the commune has begun to follow the cooperative into disgrace, and perhaps the private peasant will reappear as a symbol of the age of Deng.

The history of agriculture in this century in Russia and China, which comprise a quarter of the world's population, illustrates two points: first, the capacity for destroying settled ways of producing crops now possessed by powerful governments; and, second, the ease with which such governments can conceal absolutely, for many years, the magnitude of colossal disasters in their territories.

The Expanding Stomach

Une cuisine et une politesse! Oui, les deux signes de vieille civilisation.

(Old French Book)

1

The four fundamental changes in the world's diet since 1750 have been scientific, technical, practical and political.

The first of these is the most important. Before the nineteenth century little was known of what food men needed in order to live. Then François Magendie in France, Lyon Playfair and Sir Astley Cooper in Britain (surgeon to King George IV) and Gerard Mulder and, above all, Julius von Liebig in Germany embarked on a scientific study of food. Magendie demonstrated the passive role of the stomach in vomiting while Mulder in Utrecht, in 1838, suggested that there was one nitrogen component of all living matter, plant or animal, which he named 'protein', after the Greek for '1'. Von Liebig taught that all herbivorous animals built up tissues from the proteins of plant foods which were converted into those of muscles and other organs. Then, a generation later, Frederick Hopkins, working in Cambridge in a country (Britain) which, despite the fact that seventy per cent of working-class and forty-five per cent of middle-class budgets went on food and drink, had in the preceding generations experienced a serious reversal in nutrition, showed that all animals, including humans, decline in health when they lack certain factors of diet, even when they have enough protein. Dr Casimir Funk called this factor a 'vitamine' (the final 'e' being later abandoned on the advice of Sir Jack Drummond). These developments are an indication that, even in respect of food, ideas can rule the world.

The second, technical, change in the recent history of food was the invention of the tin can. For centuries, food had been preserved by drying, salting or, in the Andes and among the Eskimoes, freezing. In 1807 an English scientist, Plowden, took out a patent for preserving meat by enveloping it in gravy. A little earlier, there had been a plan for evaporating soups, for use in ships. Then came the development of canning, of which the

French scientist François Appert was the pioneer. About 1810 he worked out a method of bottling fruits and vegetables by subjecting the bottle to heat. This began to be used by the French navy under Napoleon for a variety of goods. Then in England in 1812 Bryan Donkin, a Northumberland-born engineer at the Dartford Ironworks, thought of using metal containers for Appert's method. Between then and about 1820 this idea was established for 'naval or explorers' ' stores. One tin can closed in 1818 was not opened till 1938. The roast veal and vegetables inside were found still to be good, save for a portion affected by part of the tin which had dissolved.

Canning factories were then built, but scandals affecting the purity of the cans' contents prevented this method from becoming of importance till the 1850s. Thereafter the tin can has become reliable, cheap and easy. The use of cans, combined with that of refrigerator vans on railways, and refrigerated ships, for fish and meat, transformed, if it did not enrich, diets. Farewell to the days when the markets of capitals might be crammed with thousands of oxen and even 30,000 live sheep, waiting for slaughter! Cattle need no longer be taken to Smithfield 'on the hoof', as they had been from time immemorial. The demand for tin soon exceeded that for silver. The tin can is almost more a typical object of the twentieth century than anything else, enabling armies, in particular, to live better than ever before. Tinned condensed milk was already one of the successes of the American Civil War. Plastic, a derivation of petroleum, began to play the same preservatory role after 1950.

Also in the 1860s came what for most cooks has been the third, decisive change: the kitchen stove. Until the nineteenth century most cooking was done over an open fire or in a brick oven, heated with coals. In 1795 the eccentric Count Rumford, an Anglo-American-born count of the Holy Roman Empire from Massachusetts, who went to Bavaria after siding with England in the American War of Independence, fed the poor of Munich by means of a stove which economised on fuel. He later developed a range with a closed top which possessed all the heat of a small fire and could be adjusted. That heralded a transformation in cooking. Until then the finer sorts of cuisine could be carried out only by an army of chefs, whereas sautés, soufflés and sauces could thereafter all be done on small stoves and by one person. 'Go, sirrah, find me twenty cunning cooks,' said Capulet in *Romeo and Juliet*: an injunction unnecessary after Rumford.

For about fifty years, iron ranges such as Rumford had in mind were unusual. They only came into general use in northern Europe and the US in the 1860s. The iron stoves at first used solid fuel. They provided the essential foundation for the great meals of the late Victorian era. No more would a Vatel have to contemplate suicide if he were unable to face the humiliation of not having two roast courses ready for a banquet! Even more precise adjustments of heat became possible with the gas stoves of the 1870s. Later, after 1890, electricity gave a clean alternative to gas, though it was not so popular as gas till about 1920, since it gives too slow a heat. All sorts of other innovations followed in the kitchens in rich countries. These included the mechanised domestic refrigerator, whose earliest version was that exhibited by Ferdinand Carré at the London Exhibition of 1860; the 'dishwasher' (1946); the sink, with the built-in 'garbage disposer' (1935); and the planned modern kitchen with smaller mechanised tools, such as eggbeaters and potato cleaners – the culinary equivalent to such striking innovations in the rest of modern households as the carpet sweeper (1859), the machine for washing clothes (1869) and the electric 'iron' (1906), which succeeded the gas-heated one of 1850. The interesting aspect of these inventions is the slow pace with which they came to be accepted or even sought after, in Europe. In the US, the kitchen was scientifically re-arranged by 1939. In Europe, many kitchens are still not so. The explanation that the 'servantless household' came quicker to the US is bad. French households are old-fashioned, whether there are servants or not.

The technology of eating was also transformed. Although in 1914 one could still find, in the Morvan in France, tables conveniently scooped out with regular hollows into which soup was poured, plates, cups, glasses, knives, forks and spoons were by the mid nineteenth century general. The generalisation of the use of individual knives and forks, wrote the historian of Brazil, Gilberto Freyre, marks one of the decisive victories of West and East[1].

Equally important, railways made it possible to bring many interesting items of food up to the capital on a regular basis. Milk became far more easily available. Then Pasteur showed that micro-organisms which cause disease, as well as fermentation, are destroyed when fluids are heated to 145° Fahrenheit. This 'pasteurisation' began in the 1890s to prolong the life of milk. By 1900 such familiar sights as the large steel-plate milk churn for use on railways and the milk bottle had been introduced, while dried milk had been invented in 1855.* But it was not till 1922–25 that Dr Corry Mann argued that milk had some special value in the diet of children which could not be measured by estimating fats, proteins and calories.

The history of milk was also affected by several changes in the way that infants are fed. Breastfeeding declined in the nineteenth century. Women working in factories had too hard a life to feed babies. Both poor and rich alike used bottles instead. The wet nurse became a memory. But, at that time, the substitute for mother's milk was cows' milk and water. It later became skimmed milk, perhaps diluted with barley water, and later still, the sickly-sweet condensed (canned) milk. That was enough to inaugurate life inauspiciously. Even worse, nothing was known of sterilisation[2]. Meantime, gin was still often given to keep children quiet. Thus the interconnection between health and food can be said to begin at the mother's knee.

Finally, in the modern history of food, the fourth innovation was the system of rationing introduced in the First World War, designed to operate throughout the industrial countries and subsequently practised during all times of conflict. Of course, in large cities, during sieges or famines, grain and other food available has always been restricted. But the shift of population to the towns in the nineteenth century, as well as their reliance on food from abroad, either as a raw material or in a form ready to eat, changed the position. In modern wars, whole nations can be besieged. This was a practice begun by Britain in her blockade of Napoleon in the early nineteenth century. All the nations at war between 1914 and 1918 embarked on rationing, though Britain only did so, with misgiving, in early 1918. Attempts were made by governments to draw up the precise amounts of proteins and calories needed by the population. By the summer of 1918 governments at war had taken over the shipments of food from private merchants, and made themselves responsible for its distribution. The same happened, even more effectively, during the Second World War. Many countries have been forced to live with rationing during years of nominal peace, and Communist ones have had rationing as a matter of course for many years: a failure in distribution as well as in agriculture.

* Other dehydrated foods have followed.

Two remarkable changes in the history of diet in our times remain to be noted: the decline in the quantity of alcohol consumed and the change in the character of bread in rich countries.

Western civilisation seems often to be built upon the use of alcohol more than anything else. Yet, in nearly every rich country, the quantity of drink consumed per head has fallen. In the US during the 1830s most Americans drank seven gallons of alcohol a head a year. In the 1970s they drank three gallons. The use of spirits in the US is a third of what it was in 1840. This was the result of a powerful and well-organised temperance movement in both the US and Britain, persuading governments to make use of taxes to effect the change which they desired. Even in France, consumption of wine per head has gone down. What needs to be noticed to place this alteration in perspective is that the early nineteenth century, because of mechanisation, was an era of increase in the production of alcohol, as of everything else. Railways ensured that cheap liquor could be carried far and turned into an industrial product. In the early eighteenth century, wine was a luxury in France. In the mid twentieth century the average Frenchman – admittedly a difficult concept for the average non-Frenchman – drank forty-four gallons of wine a year, and nearly a gallon of spirits.

The history of bread has other morals.

In the eighteenth century, white bread, made from wheat which had had most of its bran removed, was looked upon as a token of privilege. Utterly ignorant of the scientific basis of such matters, the population of all Europe considered the brown loaf as 'coarse and coloured'. By 1800 the white loaf was everywhere available and regarded as a symbol of egalitarianism, even if it was really one of the shrinking area of choice. Napoleon's armies took white bread with them wherever they went in Europe as a banner of liberation from old dull bran or rye breads. The proof that it was not a legacy of *la gloire* alone is shown by the fact that it conquered England.

This 'universal taste' for white bread antedated the mechanisation of grinding by almost a century. All over Europe and North America in the early nineteenth century, bread continued to be ground in small watermills or windmills. Finer flours were made by adjusting the grinding stones. Even in the purest breads of that era, however, dirt, sweat and oil got into the bread. For that and other reasons, this new bread did not taste as fresh, nor remain as edible, as long as the previous ones. There were other difficulties. The demand for wheat was greater than ever, not only because of the manufacture of bread: hair powder, so popular about 1800, came from wheat, so did starch, to stiffen the spotless white shirts of Europe in the age of Victoria. Efforts were therefore made in almost every European country to persuade the poor to return to bread made from barley and rye. But even the poorest claimed that they had 'lost their rye teeth'. Other attempts were made to encourage the eating of rice. They failed. Panicky crises over shortage of wheat characterised the early nineteenth century everywhere, particularly in Britain where grain had already begun to be regularly imported from 1755 even if never on a large scale. Only in the late nineteenth century did this anxiety disappear when the fall in the cost of long-distance transport, by ship and rail, made possible shipments of wheat to Europe from the US and Russia. Those two political giants of the twentieth century were already the granaries of nineteenth-century Europe.

By that time, the introduction of metal rollers for grinding grain had begun in Austria-Hungary in the 1840s. It was almost the only major technological innovation of the Habsburg Empire, but it is not one of which the Habsburgs can be proud. These iron rollers (later steel) gave a constant quality to flour. They produced flour fast. The upkeep of steel rollers was easy. The white bread so made was even whiter than it had been before, since the hot steel roller drove the endosperm out of its coating. That left the germ as a minute flake, to be sieved off with the bran. Even the brown bread made by machine kept better since its germ too was killed. For several generations, therefore, this flour was popular with bakers and customers. Manufacturers of biscuits also preferred a standard product.

But the killing of the wheat germ destroyed the real nutrient of grain. As the iron and steel mills spread from Central Europe, superseding the age-old process of stone grinding, the diets of the population of Europe fell in quality. Those who depended most on bread, the poor, suffered most.*

---

* Major elements in stone-ground and roller-ground bread according to Sir Jack Drummond (milligrams):

	Stone	Steel	Needed per day
Iron	13·0	7·0	11
Vitamin A	425·0	0·0	1,500
Vitamin B	1·0	0·3	0·8
Nicotinic acid	5·4	3·8	8·0
Vitamin D	8·0	0·0	Not known

Ultimately, in the late twentieth century, a reaction has begun against these damaging artificial breads. But, even so, most modern types of bran meal bread are not, as a rule, the same as wholemeal bread of the past. Much European brown bread is made from ordinary white flour into which bran has been mixed (or even molasses) added for colour! The chief consequence has been the collapse of bread as a 'staff of life' in most rich countries. Cereal use in the US, for example, has dropped from 300 pounds a person a year to about 130. Modern men seek sweeter and fatter foods. Sugary drinks, fats, oils, an increase in meat-eating and extraordinary manufactured beverages such as the mysterious Coca-Cola have begun to ruin the digestions of both rich peoples and poor, a change only mildly mitigated by the growth of the succulent tomato, which is today the most popular of US vegetables; whereas in 1900 it was rarely eaten, being still regarded as too close a relation to the deadly nightshade.

These fashions were not confined to the self-indulgent West. In the late nineteenth century, white rice became as alluring to the East as white bread did to the West. To polish rice in order to remove its brown outer sheath became the obsession of the Orient. In the process, the rice germ went the way of the wheat germ. The effect on health can be explicitly seen in the rise in the incidence of beriberi.

Some of these criticisms can be levied at those efforts of the 1960s to produce a rice which would grow more prolifically. A new cross-bred rice was grown on millions of acres with a yield three times the traditional one. That great success of the International Rice Research Institute, in the Philippines, however, had disadvantages: it needed a vast amount of water, it attracted the voracious stern-borer insect, and it demanded a great deal of fertiliser. It was also thought to be sticky and lumpy, and so could not easily be eaten with one's fingers. Have the 'miracle strains' of the 1970s avoided these difficulties and, if so, have they created new ones?

Meantime, those who are pleased by continuity should be satisfied by the knowledge that the traditional connection survives in the twentieth century between revolution and grain failures. The failure to deliver the requisite number of poods of grain to Petrograd in early 1917 was the spark firing the Russian Revolution. In the next few months, peasants preferred to use grain for their own consumption. The consequences for them, as for the cities of Russia, were disastrous. The grain failures of Ethiopia in the early

1970s led to the overthrow of the traditional regime there, too, in 1974.

3

Finally, the recent history of a few crops needs to be registered. As indicated earlier, the Renaissance led to the discovery of sugar, tea, coffee and chocolate on the grand scale in richer countries and poor alike. The great American crops continued to be exchanged with European, African and Asian ones – and vice versa. The industrialised countries divided between the great tea-drinking nations (such as Britain, above all, Ireland, Turkey even more, Australia, New Zealand and Japan) and the coffee nations such as France, the United States, Germany and Italy.

In the last century it seemed as if strong tea might become the sole food of poor people in manufacturing England. Tea became a replacement of beer, when taxes and temperance men insisted on taxes on malt. Many, including William Cobbett, regarded this change as a disastrous deterioration in diet. Such doubts did not prevent the English from taking tea for propagation to India (from 1860) and to their crown colony in Ceylon (from 1877) where the existing plantations were converted from coffee to tea. The inability of the urban Englishman to brew beer in the new urban conglomerations was probably, for good or bad, the beginning of a change in the national character.*

Russians, meantime, had liked tea from about 1620 when a Khan of Mongolia had presented a case of it to an ambassador of the Tsar. But it was not much drunk till the nineteenth century, when Chinese ports were opened to Russia. Then, too, came more effective means of communication through the Suez Canal and later the trans-Siberian railway line. Those changes made tea cheap enough to become the popular Russian drink in all classes which it seems to have been in the great days of Russian literature. But today the consumption of tea in Russia is relatively modest, at apparently 519 grams a year *per capita*.

Sugar continued its dominance of the world's export markets until well into the nineteenth century. By then it was being used

* In 1975–77 Britain consumed 3,457 grams of tea per inhabitant, Ireland 3,993, Turkey 1,791, New Zealand 2,518, Australia 1,844 and Japan 1,021. The figures for France, the US, West Germany and Italy were 113, 171, 114 and 58. The coffee figures give Denmark and Finland over 10 kilograms per head, France 5·01, the US 4·33, Sweden 8·6, Italy 3·26 – and Britain 1·74, Australia 1·70 and Ireland 0·71.

for purposes other than simply to sweeten drinks. The pudding, for example, was inspired by the fall in sugar prices in the late seventeenth century. After the 1880s, manufactured jam appeared (it was immediately popular, though many jams contained little of the fruit from which they theoretically came, since they were often concoctions of the cheapest fruits or even vegetables available and coloured or sweetened according to taste).

The import of sugar, the most valuable import into a rich country such as England every year without exception from 1703 till 1814, was, however, an index of general prosperity. The wealth made in the West Indies by Dutch, English, French and finally Spaniards and North Americans (after 1870) contributed to some of the largest fortunes of those days. All the islands of the West Indies underwent a generation or two of prosperity, though since the sugar was all taken back to Europe, and few European families settled in the Indies, the money concerned seemed even more like fairy gold than most swiftly made and swiftly lost fortunes in days of expansion. The exception to this was for a long time Cuba. That island remained the largest producer, and far the largest exporter of sugar, from the 1830s until the 1960s. From the late eighteenth century till 1930 every industrial innovation, from the steam engine to the railway, which could benefit the sugar trade was introduced early into Cuba. In the nineteenth century Cuba thus became the richest colony on earth. Both it and Brazil were societies run by what a Cuban historian, Manuel Moreno Fraginals, has described as a *sacarocracia* – a sugar oligarchy – for generations. In the early twentieth century Cuba was the richest country in the tropics. The unreliability of the world sugar prices, however, made the economy of any country which relied on that commodity seem like a lottery: 'diversification of agriculture', a World Bank report on Cuba argued in 1950, was 'almost beyond capitalist laws'. It turned out to be beyond socialist ones too, though the frustration caused resulted in the nationalist revolution of 1959, which became a Communist one within a year.

Similar difficulties existed in most countries where cane was being grown. Almost everywhere, too, sugar has inspired political disturbances. The sugar workers of the Mexican state of Morelos were the leaders of those who supported Zapata in the revolution of 1912[3]. On the other side of the political battle, the sugar beet companies of Ferrara in 1921 gave heavy financial assistance to the fascist movement[4].

A new dimension had by then been given to the history of sugar by the realisation that a beetroot indigenous to Europe (which before then had been used as fodder) could, just as well as cane, be treated to produce sugar. This realisation came in 1747 to the son, later assistant, of the chief apothecary of the court of Prussia, Andreas Marggraf. Young Marggraf proved his point by showing that there were sugar crystals in the roots of beet. But nothing was done about that until Franz Karl Achard, another Prussian chemist, began after 1789 to produce loaf sugar from beet on an estate in Silesia belonging to the King of Prussia. Napoleon became interested in the idea of sugar beet since he thought that it would help France to beat the British blockade. Like many ideas of Napoleon, the pursuit of sugar beet became popular after his defeat. All northern European countries took up this method of making sugar. By the 1880s more sugar was being made from beet than from cane. Germany became, for a time, a larger producer of sugar than was Cuba. This European lead vanished when the beet farmers went to war in 1914. In the 1970s only forty per cent of the world's sugar came from Marggraf's discovery, Russia being pre-eminent in production.

Beet was a typical development of the industrial age. It could not have been cultivated before the nineteenth century, for it requires deep ploughing and the seed has to be drilled if the crop is to be successful. It is a crop which thus needs the best tools and it is several times more expensive to gain sugar from beet.

World Sugar Production

	World Total
1843	1 million tons
1864	2 million tons
1873	3 million tons
1890	6 million tons
1927	27 million tons
1960	52 million tons
1977	92 million tons

These figures make plain that, however else the modern world is judged, we live in sweeter times than ever before. The consequences have not been beneficial. Decay of teeth has been stimulated by sugar since the early nineteenth century. Over-sugary diets lead to fat in the blood and hence to disease of the heart.

4

Though a major international crop, sugar in no way competes with the old great crops producing grain or rice upon which civilisation was built. Such a role has, however, been played by the potato, now with maize third equal among the important crops in the world.*

The potato is an American contribution to the world's food, indeed a South American one, for it was only taken even to Mexico by the Spaniards. Before 1500 the potato was grown in the Andes. There neither manioc nor maize could be raised successfully. The first Indian immigrants found the wild 'potato' their best chance of a stable food. They already knew potatoes in South America as *papas*, which is still the Spanish word for them. The potato was represented on Peruvian pottery as early as AD 200. It can be stored as well as dried, but loses a third of its strength after three months.

The Spaniards reached Cuzco in 1533. Three years later the first reference was made to a European eating potatoes: Gonzalo Jiménez de Quesada and his men entered the houses of certain tribesmen who fled at their approach and found, as they supposed them to be, truffles, in the village of Socotra, not far from Vélez, high in the Colombian mountains[5]. Soon the potato was taken to Spain. The first reference to it being eaten in Europe, however, was in the Sangre hospital in Seville in 1573. A potato was found in Gerard's well-documented garden in Holborn by 1596. Shakespeare refers to the potato, twice, both times apparently as if it were considered an aphrodisiac. Thus Falstaff: 'Let the sky rain potatoes . . . hail kissing-comfits.'

Potatoes took a long time to become popular outside the Andes. No edible plant in the Old World had been grown from tubers rather than from seed. No other plant previously had such mysterious, white, or flesh-coloured, nodules. The tubers seemed to people, at first, to be deformed, like the feet of lepers. Many, indeed, thought that the potato caused leprosy. When that disease vanished, scrofula was attributed to it. The coincidence of the coming of the potato to Russia with the major cholera epidemic of the 1830s set back cultivation there a generation. 'The things have neither smell nor taste. Not even the dogs will eat them, so what use are they to us?' said the men of Kolberg in Prussia, to Frederick the Great in 1774, when that monarch was trying to

---

* After wheat and rice.

WORLD CROPS 1976 (in million tons)

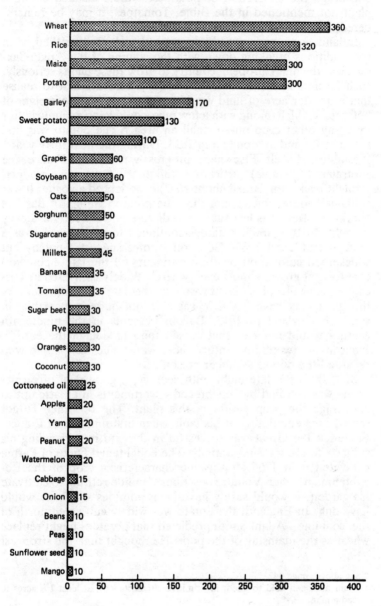

Wheat	360
Rice	320
Maize	300
Potato	300
Barley	170
Sweet potato	130
Cassava	100
Grapes	60
Soybean	60
Oats	50
Sorghum	50
Sugarcane	50
Millets	45
Banana	35
Tomato	35
Sugar beet	30
Rye	30
Oranges	30
Coconut	30
Cottonseed oil	25
Apples	20
Yam	20
Peanut	20
Watermelon	20
Cabbage	15
Onion	15
Beans	10
Peas	10
Sunflower seed	10
Mango	10

encourage the cultivation of potatoes. Others disliked eating a plant not mentioned in the Bible. Tomatoes, it may be remembered, had similar problems to begin with.*

Ireland, a country already devastated and impoverished, with old traditions breaking down with the coming of the Anglo-Saxons, was the first European country to grow these plants seriously. Irish farmers in the seventeenth century were the first to realise that a quarter acre of land would yield twenty hundredweight of potatoes – which, along with a few pigs, could keep a family better than any other crop on so small an area.† The potato was first noted in Ireland at Youghal in 1623. During the next forty years, it established itself. Elsewhere, progress was slow. In France, the Jerusalem (*girasole*) artichoke (another American product, brought back from Brazil about 1607) experienced a vogue. It was cultivated more, for a time, than the potato. Though it has less energy to offer, it is less subject to disease and is nearly as heavy in yield. In Burgundy, potatoes continued to be thought of as a kind of truffle till 1789. Occasional notes suggest a patchy but widespread cultivation on the Continent, till the late eighteenth century, yet grown almost everywhere. 'Widely cultivated in Tuscany, especially at Vallombrosa', in the late sixteenth century though it may have been, it was still 'not quite respectable' in southern England in 1815. Balkan peasants in the nineteenth century would not eat 'that cursed food hidden in the earth'[6]. Even in the twentieth century there were educated people who regarded the potato as 'sheer poison'.

Still, from the late eighteenth century, a good deal of propaganda was lavished by enlightened governments in an attempt to encourage the propagation of this plant. The reformer Turgot served it ostentatiously at his table when first minister of France. Frederick the Great was successful in the end in persuading his subjects to grow it substantially. The enlightened Duke of Parma cultivated it in 1765. It was the characteristic crop of the Enlightenment: when Voltaire describes Candide retiring to cultivate his garden, it would surely have been potatoes which he would have dug. In England, the potato was widely cultivated north of the 'coal line'. Adam Smith predicted that potatoes might replace wheat as the mainstay of the poor. He thought that 'the strongest

---

* See above, page 442.
† Grain has been held to need, in primitive circumstances, at least 1$\frac{1}{3}$ acres to feed a man.

men and the most beautiful women' of Britain (that is, the Irish) all lived on that root[7]. It is indeed possible, as the historian of the plant Professor Redcliffe Salaman once argued, that the subsequent widespread cultivation of the plant 'saved mankind from starvation' in the late eighteenth century. Peasants were impressed since it thrived when the wheat harvest failed. Potatoes also contributed a good deal both to cattle and to industrial alcohol during the nineteenth century. Gradually, prejudice was overcome.

Still, there were setbacks: first, there was the destructive blight which affected the potatoes of all Europe in 1845. Several times before, the potato harvest had failed. The blight of the 1840s, however, attacked plants without warning. It destroyed tubers as well as leaves. It originally came from America. Repeated in 1846, the loss of the harvest led to starvation, scurvy, dysentery, cholera and typhus. It struck particularly hard in Ireland, where the potato had been grown longer than anywhere else, and where the country lived, as it were, around the potato.

The effect was harsh. The Irish population, too poor to buy wheat from England, dropped sharply. Anyone who could afford to do so left for America. (Three and a half million Irish people left Ireland for America between 1851 and 1946.) The Irish saw that their old notion of a small potato plot being able to support a family was not really valid. The area under potatoes fell. Cattle increased. Fragmentation of holdings (which had gone on for generations) went no further. Irishmen became used to marrying late if at all (33·5 per cent of the Irish male population are still unmarried between forty-five and fifty-four years). The Irish population is the only one in Europe to be smaller, much smaller in 1980 (4,367,000) than it was in 1840 (8,175,000).*

The second setback to the potato was caused by the Colorado beetle. It was observed in the Wild West about 1824 happily feeding on deadly nightshade. But Colorado remained almost uninhabited till 1858. Then the gold rush brought the potato there as well as 'pioneers'. The beetles soon found that this new member of the *solanum* family (the potato is related to nightshade) was a most succulent plant. The beetles went east, crossing the Mississippi by 1865, reaching Ohio by 1869, but were held back there by arsenic sprays. There was alarm in Europe. American potatoes were banned. Nevertheless, in 1901 the beetle was found in Tilbury, and on the Elbe. In the course of the First World War, US

* Both figures include Northern Ireland.

troops brought it to France. Within a few months the beetle had spread all over Western Europe. In England, it was held off. Then one beetle was brought back from France in the Second World War, perhaps in one of the Lysander aircraft used for carrying secret agents to work against the Nazis. But chemical sprays defeated it, at least for a time. At the moment it seems a dormant threat. But the experience, both of it and of the blight, in the nineteenth century (as of the phylloxera which hit vines in the 1870s and the elm disease which hit Europe in the 1970s) is a reminder that if great killer diseases are a thing of the past for human beings, they may not be so for plants.

Despite its heavy protein, the potato is the main food able to ensure that the northern hemisphere has something in reserve if a grain crop were to fail.

The histories of sugar and potatoes could scarcely be more contrasting for the one is primarily a matter of commerce, and the other is largely grown for the home market. The first is a manufactured product. The second is eaten untouched. The first has inspired innumerable wars; the eighteenth-century wars in the West Indies were primarily wars for the supply of sugar. The second has merely, on occasion, provided battlefields.

The adaptation of these crops to the modern world has made the greatest change to diets since the age of industry. Nor should we forget the coming of the turkey and of the tomato (other American products) and the conversion of whale oil and other fats into margarine (by Mège-Mouriès, a French technologist working with the navy). The transformation of a nation, such as Italy, from being one where working men might live on bread, ricotta and water into one where nearly everyone is able to echo Johnson's remark that 'he who does not mind his belly will hardly mind anything else', reflects a decisive change.

Every generation has seemed to imagine that food changes for the worse: 'Du temps de mon père on avait tous les jours la viande . . . on égouttait le vin comme si c'était de l'eau.' Thus the Sieur de Goubernville in the sixteenth century, quoted by Fernand Braudel. One hears much the same in the late twentieth century. It would be easy to point to the lack of diversity in the food of our time, or to the artificial colourings or the dangerous preservatives as its chief characteristic. But more extraordinary still is the commercial significance of the humblest diet or the immensely complicated history behind the dullest breakfast. Here is a cup of tea, apparently an unexciting commodity. But the history of the 'china' cup necessitates an excursion into the Industrial Revolution, and to mediaeval contact between old China and feudal Europe. The size and the capacity of the cup is a reminder of countless quaint measures in history, many of which are still fighting a stout rearguard battle against decimalisation and metrification. The tea leaf has an equally diverse genealogy. If coffee is being drunk, the roots of our breakfast return, via the West Indies, to the Ottoman Empire and the plant indigenous in Abyssinia, whose beans were first exported at the time of the Renaissance. The salt on the table commemorates one of the world's oldest trades, and the pepper is a reminder that it was in order to find another route to the spice islands that Columbus set off for America.* The history of bread, of milk, of eggs in modern industrial cities should not be too cursorily dismissed: was it only a hundred years ago that the dairies of London still had their cows on the premises, and no more than that since Pasteur discovered the roots of hygiene, and fermentation? In the history of such apparent banalities there is indeed, in microcosm, a universal history. Even the hours at which meals are eaten have their long chronicles, and the milk bottle has its *histoire morale*: for, as Winston Churchill is believed to have said, 'Democracy means that if the door bell rings in the early hours, it is likely to be the milkman.'

---

* He himself was financed in part by salt merchants from Valencia.

40

Industrialisation and Modernisation

But whither are we going?

Lord Salisbury, 1870

By the time of the American Civil War in the 1860s, and the Italian and German wars of unification, which extended from 1859 till 1871, a new stage of industrialisation was beginning. At first sight, this seemed merely a change in the relative importance of the producing countries. Many countries other than England had begun to mechanise their industries and had done so both more cheaply and more quickly than had Britain. In 1800 the United States had seemed to be a group of agricultural republics which chanced to be able to produce cotton, a sought-after raw material. But the US had become a unified state – because the merchants needed a central government to protect their interests. In 1860 the US was also the nation most concerned to introduce important innovations. An American seemed already more likely than an Englishman to ensure that tiresome and expensive manufacturing was done by machinery. Richard Cobden wrote, in the *Economist*, in 1851: 'The superiority of the United States to England is ultimately as certain as the next eclipse.' Tocqueville had said much the same in the 1830s, coupling the US, with even greater prescience, with Russia.* The sewing machine and the mechanised reaper of 1850 symbolised a new era in which US inventiveness would be greater than that of the Old World. Americans had already by 1860 been forerunners in the use of chloroform for anaesthetics and had first made use both of the Scottish engineer James Nasmyth's steam hammer patented in 1842 and the cylinder printing-press patented in 1847. In the beginning, capital to market such inventions had been hard to come by in the US. Foreign investments were not much found there before 1830. The capital which launched the age of industry in the US mostly derived from savings, helped by local savings banks and insurance companies, rising steadily and, in comparison with all European countries, except for England, fast. From a total of $50 million invested in

* The prophecy is cited on page 692.

the US manufacturing industry in 1820, the figure had reached $1,000 million in 1860. By 1870 foreign investment in the US had also probably risen, to £300 million, most of it British.

Once industrialisation had begun in the US, the advantages of working in a new country seemed great. There were few vested interests, either of landowning capital or of labour, to resist innovators, no frame-breaking rioters, as there had been in Arkwright's mills. Instead, planters stole Whitney's cotton gin in order to use it more quickly. There was always, as has been pointed out, a shortage of labour. The availability of land kept wages high since, had they been low, wage earners would have left and gone west. The early operatives of US cotton mills usually stayed, indeed, for a short time. Yet only during the age of mass immigration, after 1845, were conditions in the US cotton plants comparable to those in the English 'dark satanic mills'. By the 1840s US factories were using power-driven machines, so that, by the time of the Civil War, that system dominated many industries, including firearms, agricultural tools, watches, sewing machines and interchangeable parts of machines. The economies achieved by the latter substitution were sometimes as great as fifty to one. Thus the US was already in 1850 on the way to becoming the greatest industrial power in the world. True, in the 1880s agriculture was still the main source of wealth; but by 1900 the US was predominantly industrial. In 1894 she outstripped Britain in volume of manufactured goods. By 1914 she produced as much as Britain, Germany and France combined.

What were the reasons? After all, not every rich pastoral country has made wise use of resources. Was it due to new methods of salesmanship and advertising? Greater demand from a greater population? The availability of capital? The special genius of the US in devising a system of interchangeable parts? The tariff? The patent law? The cheap transport? Or, perhaps, the free constitution, its enthusiastic acceptance by the waves of emigrants from tyrannies and the free life that it made possible? Surely it was the last factor that really counted.

Looking ahead still further, the inventiveness, willingness to take every opportunity, confidence in the 'system', and ruthlessness enabled the US to continue to dominate the world technically throughout most of the twentieth century. Only in the 1970s, after a brief experience of world power had brought excessive intervention by the central authority in the economy, would the technological and commercial lead of the US falter.

On the continent of Europe, too, the British example had been followed. Indeed, industry often developed under British guidance. The role of British commerce has been noticed. But that of British workmen and entrepreneurs was also important. Many British skilled workers were to be found, in the early nineteenth century, near Calais, in the lace trade in Vienna, in cotton mills in Rouen, and in Alsace. Even Napoleon set up a model weaving shed at Passy in the 1800s to teach weavers from the south how to work a flying shuttle, under the supervision of a Scots wool merchant named Douglas.

German industrialisation was faster than that of any other country in the nineteenth century. Her unification was assisted by the fact that the settlement of 1815 enabled Prussia to dominate the commerce of other German states. Hence the Zollverein which, by 1834, embraced three-quarters of Germany. In one generation, between 1840 and 1875, the Germans passed from the Middle Ages to modern times. Some individuals (the bootmakers of the Palatinate were an example) even experienced three stages of industrial life – industrial handicraft, outwork, and the factory system. A most amazing spectacle is presented by the men through whom a whole people suddenly passes from one stage of culture to another, for instance from nomadism to world conquest, like the Mongols under Genghis Khan: Burckhardt's comment might apply to the Germans in his day[1].

Railways, the end of restrictions on the mobility of labour, a modern financial system and the customs union all occurred in Germany in a single lifetime, accompanied by a swift growth of population. Then, in the next generation, came the great steel innovations, electricity, political expansion, national union and what Fritz Fischer would call the 'grab for world power'.[*] Still, for Germany the critical years were the 1840s, the years when the machine-makers were gathering in Borsig's works in Berlin or the Ruhrort engineering works, forerunners of Krupp's cast-steel works at Essen: the first large private economic enterprises in a country accustomed to the operations of the state. But always the state played a bigger part in German industrialisation than in Britain, France, or the US: the Gewerbe Institut, founded in Berlin in 1821 to spread knowledge of new industry, had no precedent elsewhere. German science was not only financed by

---

[*] Fritz Fischer's *Griff nach der Weltmacht* (1961) was inexplicably translated into English as *Germany's Aims in the First World War*.

the state but it anticipated enterprise: whereas in England, the first industrial research laboratory was established only in the 1870s, when the greatest age of industrial advance was past there. It is not possible to neglect Russia in this discussion. Russia was already by 1914 among the great industrial countries, even if industry there began even more under the shadow of government than was the case in Germany. Old Russia had had a few simple domestic industries, such as iron, salt and coarse cloth. Under the Viking lords who, long before, established the Slav kingdoms and principates, Russia had had a mercantile past. The first grand duchy of Kiev resembled the East India or the South Africa companies.

All that was long ago forgotten. Russia was gradually united around the leadership of the Sultanate of Moscow, a state which grew up as the tax farmer for the Khans of the Golden Horde. Moscow's commercial ties were with the East, not the West, and till the eighteenth century Moscow's trade was primarily Oriental. Many Russian words concerning money are Mongolian. The Khans insisted on being paid tribute in silver: hence perhaps the Muscovites' Oriental business ethics. There was no sense of property, industry or individual enterprise.

Later, when the Golden Horde had been driven off, Russian attitudes to commerce remained Oriental. Only foreigners, controlled and unable to play any part in politics, could be merchants on a grand scale. Still, Dutch and German businessmen set up foundries, Swedes produced paper and the Dutch established wool mills. Subsequently a few Russian merchants were permitted to establish industrial monopolies on the understanding that they would give the Tsar a share. Then came the age of Peter the Great, architect, anatomist, surgeon, expert soldier and consummate economist, as Frederick the Great described him in a letter to Voltaire[2]. Peter sought to create a big standing army. He needed weapons and uniforms exceeding Russia's manufacturing capacity. Those things could not be imported, since the Tsar had no money which would be accepted internationally. Nor did Peter wish to rely on foreigners. Hence, industry was created, under the Tsar's orders and specifically for war. Mines and cotton mills, foundries and fortresses were founded on the basis of slave, or 'temporarily exiled', labour. Whole villages of state peasants were shipped to do the manual work.

This state-directed system continued mostly unchanged till the nineteenth century though Catherine the Great tried to hand over many mines in the Urals, and several metallurgical industries, under the control of rich landed families able to direct labour of their own. In the late eighteenth century the abolition of internal tolls and tariffs, the opening of some state monopolies to general commerce and the permission to peasants to enter the grain market (by the revocation of the decree by which merchants could buy serfs as labourers) did create the beginnings of a commercial economy. But the state continued to dominate most manufacturing. A great German merchant, Ludwig Knoop, was permitted in 1839 to found cotton mills. When he died in 1894 Knoop had become the richest private man in Russia, but neither he nor his fellow foreigners were able to establish themselves as public persons in Russia as Huguenot or German citizens did in other nations. The Russian railways were promoted by Germans, the chemical, oil and later electrical industries were developed by Belgians, Swedes and Germans. The only specifically Russian enterprise was the agglomeration of textile mills, served by serf entrepreneurs (thus ensuring that industrialism could be combined with serfdom and bondage).

Although, in the nineteenth century, the character of Russian industrialisation seemed barbarous, and certain to be less successful than that undertaken in freer countries, the Tsarist pattern of state direction has been carried on under the ideology of communism in the twentieth century. It has also been emulated by other nations incapable of ensuring enterprise in freedom. In Russia, three national plans (1928–32, 1933–37 and 1938–41 – interrupted by war) were devised, which sought to carry forwards the industrialisation begun under the Tsars at a breakneck pace, with an eye, as always in Russia, on military considerations. The methods used were, as well as state direction, a compulsory and brutal agricultural revolution; and propaganda appeals about, and publicity given to, those who like the 'heroic' Stakhanov allegedly cut in one day 100 tons of coal (the average was six). Rewards and comforts were graded in relation to contribution made, 'outstanding' workers being benefited to the detriment of the average. Not surprisingly there were instances, Leonard Schapiro tells us, of Stakhanovites murdered by their fellow workers[3]. Similar things may have happened under Peter the Great. At all events, Russian industrial modernisation occurred in a way that anyone who knows anything of Russian history might have expected; fast, violently, closely connected with military preconceptions, wrapped up in extraordinary rumours and in the tradition of Oriental despotism.

To return, however, to our general survey of the world observed from about 1860. The characteristic of the time was not simply an alteration in the relative position, industrially, of one country or another which indicated the change in the character of the Industrial Revolution after 1860. It was change in what was being produced. Thus the age of cotton was giving way already to that of iron and steel before 1860. Whereas cotton primarily caused a change in dress, iron and steel caused changes in a great variety of other things, from war to means of communication. The age of iron and steel saw the beginnings of the age of electricity as a substitute for steam and of oil as an alternative to coal; and, as factories grew ever larger in size, organised labour began to play as big a part in politics as in economics.

But doubtless a simpler question will be lurking in the minds of some readers: were 'things really getting better'?

Hitherto this book has not much discussed the question of prices and incomes which doubtless, to the modern mind, is the determining one in this matter. There are excellent reasons for that neglect. First, statistics may have been respected in Babylon and in Rome for fiscal purposes, but no serious figures were collected before the Renaissance. Second, and more important, the standards of living of most people could not be expressed in the age of agriculture in terms of the prices available for goods in the remote and unrepresentative capitals. Services, food and labour were not susceptible of being priced. Of course, artisans were paid. Statistics of payment make amusing but, as a rule, meaningless paragraphs in the biographies of great artists. Cardinal Mazarin, we are told, offered Bernini 12,000 crowns a year to go to Paris. Brunelleschi received 100 florins down and 100 florins a year for his work on the Duomo in Florence, but Michelangelo declined fees for St Peter's. But all these grand enterprises were naturally uncharacteristic. Further, the impossibility of making accurate conversions into either contemporary foreign, or modern, money presents an impossible barrier to understanding. How can we even reckon the approximate meaning of Piedmontese *scudi*, Neapolitan ducats, Papal *pasti* and *bajocchi* and Florentine sequins which were used as cash in Italy during the eighteenth century, much less say what they were worth in comparison with the equally bewildering differences of exchange in contemporary Germany? Finally, mass production has altered everything: a spoon in 1700 was as rare as a calculating machine in 1960; in 1800 it was an essential adjunct to a European's daily life. Sugar was a luxury in 1650, and easily available by 1750.

Several general points can, however, be made.

The first is that, during the age of agriculture, the rich communities of the time had experience of inflation. The reason was usually the same as that of inflation today. The wars and building activities of Nebuchadrezzar, for example, meant that prices rose by fifty per cent between 560 BC and 550 BC. Rome experienced a fierce inflation (deriving from debasement of money) in the second century AD and Diocletian even inflicted a death penalty for any infringement of the fixed prices which he introduced in AD 302[4]. A serious inflation of the Middle Ages caused China to desist from using paper money. European prices in the seventeenth century were four times what they were between 1525 and 1550. That first great inflation of the modern world affected every country. The prices of food in France, as accounted by P. Coupère, suggest that another rise of one hundred per cent occurred in the seventeenth century. However, despite these experiences, it does not seem as if any country ever suffered before the 1920s the fate of Germany where the currency, stable in 1920–21 at fourteen times the level of 1914, was 1,475 times that in late 1922 and, in November 1923, no less than 1,422,900,000,000 times the level of 1914. Austria suffered almost as badly. Nor, previously, had countries experienced the prolonged high inflation which characterised South America in the 1950s and 1960s, and Europe in the 1970s. These experiences are partly the consequence of a money economy, of interaction of one economy on another and of the appearance on the political scene, in that money economy, of spendthrift governments. Still, these experiences are not wholly new ones: 'Today,' complained a Spanish aristocrat in 1513, 'a pound of mutton costs as much as a whole sheep used to, a loaf as much as a *fanega* of wheat.'

A more important point is that, despite occasional scandals and panics, prices were remarkably steady for those commodities which can be measured at all during the early years of the Industrial Revolution. Wars increased prices, prices fluctuated often but at a steady level. Between 1661 and 1913 prices in Britain declined by ten per cent overall. True, the growth of population after 1750 in most European countries led to a rise of agricultural prices because of the increased demands of an itself increasing non-agricultural population. But the overall price index scarcely reflected that, since there was such a fall in the prices of manufactured goods, of potatoes* and of imported commodities (particularly sugar, tea, coffee and afterwards meat). Still, the rises in agricultural prices were enough to cause riots everywhere in the late eighteenth century. Even in England, rioters often took over town markets and sold off goods cheap. But those changes did not occur in the nineteenth century. Prices may have fallen a trifle, Sir John Clapham tells us, between 1850 and 1887 and, between 1896 and 1913, have risen very gently, perhaps by three per cent[5].

Given a stability in prices, it seems as if, therefore, the increase in wages in the nineteenth century must have represented an increase in standards of living for the European working people as a whole. Sir John Clapham believed that a man's real wage in England in 1900 was about fifty per cent better than that of someone doing the same job in 1850. In the US, wages in 1900 were probably twice as high as they were in England but they too had gone up by the same percentage. These figures do not take into account that hours of work were constantly falling in the nineteenth century, nor that the population was rising. Thus, by any standard accepted in the twentieth century as giving appropriate indices of levels of income, the workers in the countries becoming industrialised were regularly and, except in the first twenty or thirty years, steadily becoming better off. Marx's theories of 'immiseration', therefore, seem as misleading for his own day as for now.

There are, however, three qualifications to this judgement. The first is that, in the last years of the age of agriculture, a vast number of people gained what was, in effect, extra income – on top of the average of 7/6d a week in England in the mid eighteenth century – by, for example, growing their own vegetables, poaching, shooting, occasional pilfering, as well as spinning. Those unmeasurable benefits disappeared if a man moved to a slum in Manchester, even if he earned more wages, as he usually did.†

Secondly, the uprooting of an old rural family to what was a primitive urban society without traditions and, for some generations, lacking a real culture of its own, created a definite spiritual

---

* The price of potatoes was 10d a pound in 1607 and 2d a pound in 1701.

† Day labourers in the 1770s earned 5s to 6s a week in winter, 7s to 9s in summer and 12s in harvest time. Cotton weavers in factories earned 7s to 10s a week all the year round, cloth weavers 8s, Wilton carpet makers 11s. By 1800 agricultural wages were the same as in 1770, industrial wages up to 16s.

impoverishment. In the end, socialism, nationalism, communism, and, finally, 'humane capitalism', with the car and the television set, posed solutions to these difficulties.

By the late twentieth century, in most rich countries, the new hazard of taxation for the factory worker had appeared and is being met, to a great extent, by innumerable varieties of 'informal, unofficial, illicit sources of reward'* comparable to the benefits obtained by gleaning or poaching in the past.

Thirdly, all tests of income ignore the unemployed worker, the underemployed worker and the need of innumerable people to support unemployed relations or friends.

Yet even so, when every qualification is made, it should be evident that, measured by the simple, practical and generally recognised criterion of purchasing power, the opportunities of most working people in most industrial countries grew steadily during the Industrial Revolution. French figures are perhaps even more conclusive than English or American: Alfred Sauvy, the historian of population, has calculated that between 1810 and 1900 the purchasing power of the average worker increased by 82 per cent, that by 1939 it had increased 255 per cent over 1810 and, by 1965, 338 per cent (these last two figures not taking into account the social security available in France since 1919). The reckoning which enabled Monsieur Sauvy to construct this table was based on primary goods, so that, if bicycles, railways and so on are taken into account, the rise would have been faster still[6]. Nor does his table take into account such matters as shorter hours, nor the provision of holidays with pay. These figures decisively rebut the argument that industrialisation under capitalism brought to most peoples pain and misery.

* In the formulation of the Outer Circle Policy Unit, of London.

41
Capitalism in the Nineteenth Century

> When the leading manufacturers acted in concert, it was not to demand measures of protection but, on the contrary, the removal of all legal restraints upon their absolute freedom to contest among themselves the markets of the world.
>
> Elie Halévy, *History of England in the Nineteenth Century*

The early industrial changes in the eighteenth century were carried out by individuals, families, or groups of friends for whom the mediaeval name of company or *compagne* was appropriate, for the associations formed by Watt and Boulton, Whitney and Wedgwood, would be hardly recognisable by the modern name of a corporation. These associations might be consolidated by common law, but the association brought unlimited liability for all partners, whatever the assets of their associates. The 'companies' of late eighteenth-century England were less sophisticated enterprises than those of mediaeval Florence (they were as a rule less international, for a start). Individualism was the rule. Each manufacturer founded his own fortune and desired to remain sole master thereof[1].

True, internationally competitive merchants, such as the slave dealers of Liverpool, might spread their risk among a group (as a form of insurance) but most such individuals were both shareholders and company directors at the same time. Only a few large mercantile companies, such as the Dutch and British East India companies (the latter with 115 ships and 10,000 sailors in 1815)* and the Hudson Bay Company (which were not pre-eminent in innovating), had a large body of investors and myriad activities in the way that we now conceive of as being typical of 'companies'. Those two English companies had some continental European equivalents, along with a few enterprises favoured by the state. The idea of a shareholder with no concern for the company other than what profit he might make from it was uncommon. Through-

---

* The East India Company was exceptional in that it governed a population of sixty million, held 380 square miles and maintained an army of 150,000 men. It was considered in 1812 to represent a total capital of £21 million and 2,000 shareholders. Its monopoly of British trade with India was abolished in 1813.

461

out Western Europe (indeed, in America too), the memory of the failure of the South Sea Company in England and of the Mississippi Company in France (in the 1720s) was persistent. (Those companies had offered to make fortunes for small savers but, instead, had ruined them.) Thus, until at least 1800, most savers thought that land, or a strong box, were the best means of saving. Prices were, after all, stable in England in the eighteenth century, at least until 1789: a remarkable fact at a time of unprecedented economic growth.

Price Index, England 1700–1789

	All consumer goods	Consumer goods other than cereals	Producer goods
1701	100	100	100
1750	95	91	88
1780	117	108	107

Subsequently there were four developments. First, limited liability, by which stockholders invested in a corporation with an artificial personality. When that personality's money ran out, its creditors could not claim what they thought they were owed by it from stockholders. This idea, in the end, stimulated commercial enterprise, but in the short run limited companies were mostly used for banking, canals and railways rather than for industry. Only after 1859 were they anywhere of much importance in industry.

Second, during the nineteenth century, companies became concerned with many different types of production. The most extreme example of this was to be seen in shipping, but, to a lesser extent, the same happened in every industry and at every level. In shipping, in particular, there was a realisation that 'either there must be an elaborate fitting together of the products of many specialised firms or single, many-sided firms must do most of the essential work themselves, as government dockyards had always done'. Indeed, government dockyards were the ancestors of these new undertakings in more ways than one. A firm which supplied plate had to know all about steel. Its managers should know all about marketing. 'Integration' was the word spoken of in the US: a concept carried through with immense verve and success by the steel and oil kings of the late nineteenth century. Andrew Carnegie was the supreme exponent: 'Mr Morgan,' he once said, 'buys his partners. I grow my own.'

A good example of what happened to large firms can be seen

in the history of the British engineering firm of Armstrong which, to begin with, was renowned for its innovation in the use of hydraulic blast furnaces. William Armstrong, who was born in 1810, was an inspired industrialist who was also an inventor. The inventor of the first hydraulic crane, the submarine mine (for use alongside Bessemer's guns in the Crimean War) and the three-pounder gun, he also founded the engineering works at Elswick, Newcastle (1847), and conceived the idea of using solar energy. He began to make ships in 1868 and bought a shipyard in 1882, in which year his firm launched the first iron-protected cruiser (the *Esmeralda*, for Chile). In 1885 Armstrong opened a branch in Naples to make guns for Italy. Twelve years later he bought Sir Joseph Whitworth's famous gun-making firm and, in 1900, set up armoured-plate shops. Meanwhile, a Sheffield steel manufacturer, Vickers, a joint stock company of the 1860s, began making steel for almost every use, including armaments. In 1897 Vickers bought the Naval Construction and Armaments Company at Barrow and the Maxim-Nordenfelt Machine Gun Company at Erith. In 1902 they absorbed Robert Napier's famous shipbuilding firm at Govan (it had built the first ironclads) and bought themselves a share of William Beardmore's shipbuilding firm at Glasgow in 1902. In the ten years before the First World War, Armstrong-Whitworth and Company with a capital of £9½ million and Vickers with £8 million were two of Britain's largest firms, alternately patronised by the Admiralty with their huge orders, dominating Newcastle, a third of whose population they employed. The two were so close that without the avowed formation of a cartel they were virtually partners. Vickers had on the Clyde the largest shipyards that Britain had known.

In 1924, after the First World War, when both firms had become financially shaky, Armstrong-Whitworth was absorbed by Vickers, to form a firm which survived, with government subsidies even in 1924, in a much changed shape, into the 1970s. This history of what became one of Britain's largest firms is characteristic of modern enterprise generally: an inspired founder, mergers, growth – and, in the end, a government subsidy when the firm has become so big as to be of national importance.

Companies grew bigger, but their structure, when big, seemed increasingly disciplined, modelled almost on the armed forces. The enterprise might be run by managers of different grades, of different social rank from most of the others and who (in England and America, anyway) often had been educated in the classics at remote schools for administrators. The workers could only rarely hope to rise to become managers.

In the United States, a steady increase in the development of the corporate form of organisation continued, particularly in the twentieth century. While 24 per cent of business done was by corporations in 1900, the figure had risen to 52 per cent in 1939. 94 per cent of manufacturing was already being done by corporations by 1939, against 74 per cent in 1904. The size of corporations increased too: in the 1930s, 600 or so corporations each owning assets of $50 million owned over half the corporate wealth.

Each country has a different history for its commercial structure. Thus Japan, for example, modernised quickly in the late nineteenth century. The two greatest firms in Japan were Mitsui and Mitsubishi, both of which were founded by rice merchants whose fortunes in the era before modernisation had already begun and who sold the rice grown by feudal landlords.

Another consequence was the improved development of the 'market', the heart of modern capitalism, a system illogical to those outside it, but really a spontaneous system which happens as a natural consequence when men barter and trade together; to those within it the market is 'a delicate, experimental and easily abused credit mechanism . . . constructed without design . . . modified from year to year . . . without supervision save that of the unseen hand of self interest'.

Corn exchanges and wool exchanges had been first founded and led to stock exchanges. In 1730 stockbrokers were considered barely respectable in England. An Act was passed in 1733 to declare void all wagers relating to the present and future prices of stocks and securities. By 1760 even government stock could be dealt in by brokers. In 1762, towards the end of the most successful war ever fought by England, London's main dealers in stocks formed a 'stock exchange' in a coffee house. It survived the Napoleonic Wars, and in 1815 French and other governmental loans were floated there. From 1804 stockbrokers in London met in a specially built Stock Exchange, close to the Bank of England. By then, dealings in 'futures' were tacitly allowed. Cloth, coal and corn exchanges were similarly built, and chambers of commerce were established. All these developments were privately set up, without the help of the government, and usually against the government's first inclination. All were copied in other capitals of the West.

The foundation of such permanent marketing centres for investment transformed commerce and, with one or two setbacks, financed most of the industrial enterprise of the next hundred years. Money had always been pursued: what characterised capitalism in its new phase was that it was not a series of individual enterprises but a complicated *system* based on calculation of profit and free labour.

Parallel to the creation of the stock-market was the organisation of banking on a new international level. In 1789 the fabric of internationl banking was less intelligently organised than it had been during the Renaissance. But after 1815 much English capital was available, in comparison with the years before the wars. A good deal of it found an outlet in the loans to foreign states organised by such London-based banks as Baring's or Rothschild's. Nathan Rothschild, a Jewish banker who had lived till 1784 in Frankfurt, arranged the subsidies which the British government gave to their continental allies during the Napoleonic Wars. He insisted that the recipients paid their interest in pounds sterling. Later the Dutch (who had led high finance in the seventeenth century but then been damaged by the wars), the Flemings and the French began to invest money abroad in a similar manner. France also finished the Napoleonic Wars with her economy in good shape, since Napoleon had financed his wars by living off tribute from foreign countries. During the wars, also, the continent of Europe had benefited from being for a time one economic unit. Britain's opposition (and Napoleon's ambitions) prevented that state of affairs from leading to anything of any political significance. But in the years afterwards British collaboration and investment again foreshadowed economic union, both Britain and the Continent needing US cotton, and both were affected by the same economic diseases.

This European economy became, however, in the nineteenth century a world economy, a world *maritime* economy, of which Europe (particularly Britain) was the centre. The inhabitants of Britain indulged in a great speculation spree in the 1820s, investing large sums in foreign bonds and hundreds of stock companies abroad. Latin America was a particular centre of attraction. In 1914 Britain, France and Germany supplied over 60 per cent of the world's exports. Britain then had 45 per cent of all foreign investments, France 25 per cent, Germany 13 per cent and the US only 5 per cent. A quarter of Britain's wealth was invested abroad. London was the world's uncontested financial centre, the pound sterling the nearest ever achieved to a world currency. In

London or Paris, experts for all economic undertakings everywhere could be found. Most of the rest of the world save Japan and the US were subject to European states through a mixture of financial or direct military ties. If China and the Ottoman Empire remained unconquered, it was because the European states could not agree how to divide them. Joseph Conrad's wonderful novels, written between 1894 and 1924, well commemorate that open, expanding, increasingly unprejudiced and cosmopolitan world.

Great profits were, of course, made by large companies operating at an international level – particularly between 1880 and 1913, but also until 1929. British companies such as those which ran the São Paulo to Santos railway, Chilean nitrates, Malaysian rubber or Indian tea brought back extraordinary dividends to European and North American investors. Sometimes these profits were enormous, such as those made by Weetman Pearson, Lord Cowdray, in engineering and oil in Mexico; by Percival Farquhar in Brazil; or by a whole generation of adventurous investors in Cuba. For Britain, income received in various forms from foreign investment before 1914 was much larger than the net export of British capital. Britain owned in that year some £4,000 million of capital invested abroad against a total £5,500 million owned abroad by the US, Germany, France, Belgium and Holland put together[2].

This European free economy, dominated by British commerce, lasted a hundred years between 1815 and 1914. During the last part of this time, travel became easier than ever before. Countries drew even closer to one another so that, for example, the same critiques within those societies were internationally emulated: even French and German socialists felt that they could use the same vocabulary when they criticised capitalism.

A change in the character of private enterprise came as a result of the increase in the nineteenth century of stock dealing and of foreign investment. At the beginning of the nineteenth century China had a banking system but it made, and sought, no international impact. Britain alone had a national bank with a monopoly of state banking, which possessed the only serious reserve of gold in the country, and which looked after the reserves of other banks. It was then the central organisation for nearly 900 private banks, all of whom realised that it was by no means necessary, in order to keep a cash reserve equal to the sum deposited. There was a great diversity of practice and many banks crashed – eighty-nine between 1814 and 1817 alone, though many such were small indeed, with under fifteen shareholders: scarcely more than shopkeepers, who concentrated on holding on to money, in some cases. The banks in London were held together by the clearing houses which most banks supported in Lombard Street. They provided drawers into which clerks from other banks, twice a day, dropped bills or cheques payable by the owner of the drawer. The use of the cheque was already developed, and no London bank (of which there were then sixty) was in the habit of issuing its own notes, nor had it done so for fifty years, since cheques and Bank of England notes met all needs. Country banks in England did issue their own notes, though none smaller than for £5. Gradually this system was modified, so that by 1914 no banks issued their own notes, and the number of banks declined.

Gradually, too, a system comparable to this one was established in most industrial countries. The European continent took some time to recover from the Napoleonic Wars, however, and the size and diversity of the USA prevented the system from spreading fast there. The idea of a US national bank, for example, remained a controversial one for most of the early nineteenth century. On the other hand, France had a national bank from 1800, with an exclusive right to issue notes, although cheques were unknown there till after 1848. The stagnation of French industry in the nineteenth century was partly due to the character of the Bank of France, a private monopoly with close relations with the government. It set itself a target of prudent management of the issue of notes, and little else. The Imperial Bank of Germany, after 1871, served the same purpose as these other ones, also monopolising the issue of notes. Though privately owned, it was managed by officials.

Equally gradually, too, this world banking system began to be supplemented by an expansion of the international organisation of trade in which firms were established whose entire business was the financing of one part or another of foreign trade. Similarly, this system began, during the nineteenth century, to be sustained by a single commodity, namely gold.

England had maintained a gold standard (any citizen could exchange any Bank of England note for gold on demand) since 1718, when Sir Isaac Newton had established the price of gold at £3 17s 10½d per ounce. That price prevailed, save for a short time after the Napoleonic Wars. Gold was affirmed as the basis of the British currency by Sir Robert Peel's Act of 1819. Silver and copper continued to be used but only as token money. The money in circulation did not increase very greatly: in 1789, £10 million was in circulation in England, £24 million in 1870.

Elsewhere, at the beginning of the nineteenth century, Europe retained its ancient silver standard, disorganised though it was, while the US had made gold and silver interchangeable in 1792, at a ratio of fifteen silver pieces to one of gold. (France had the same arrangement in theory. The silver franc was the real unit of exchange there while, in Germany, most states used silver thalers and numerous small coins.) Most of the new gold mined in California, Australia and the Urals, by new industrial processes, in the second half of the nineteenth century went into coinage. By 1870 gold was more abundant than silver was. Thus, during the 1870s, for the first time, a gold standard could be internationally established. The new German Empire turned to gold in 1871. The US announced the gold dollar to be the sole unit of value in 1873. France, and the other European countries which had been using a franc, stopped coining silver in 1878. It was almost as if an international currency had been established. Indeed, a system of that sort was suggested in the 1860s, on the basis of £1 equals $5 equals 25 francs. The discovery of gold on the Witwaterstrand in the Transvaal in 1886 underpinned this civilisation, just as it transformed South Africa. By 1900 South Africa was producing a quarter of the world's gold in large and immensely profitable private companies.

Between 1878 and 1914 this system prevailed. Since 1914 it has not been revived, though in democratic countries, where the free market has been able to survive, national currencies have since 1945 revolved increasingly uneasily round the dollar.

Outside Europe, the Russian experience was characteristic: great fairs of a mediaeval type survived till the end of the nineteenth century. Bills of exchange, letters of credit and joint-stock companies played little part. Cash was short. Commercial banks were founded only in the 1860s (till then, Russia had only state-operated banks), and of the elaborate structure of international commerce, finance and speculation Russia was ignorant. Equally, South America remained insulated from the *grande fête bourgeoise* of the nineteenth century, save in a few temporarily boom areas (for example, the rubber zone of Manaus on the Amazon). Spanish colonial rule had not encouraged the growth of private enterprise or a modern middle class. South American independent states remained poor but were saddled with large bureaucracies and armies paid for by European loans, on the interest on which they usually (except Brazil) defaulted. In India, on the other hand, British rule did stimulate private ownership of agriculture, and Indian capitalism, which after a fashion had existed before the British conquest, led to the achievement of some degree of private prosperity.

Another consequence of industrialisation was to cause all societies within the richer world to become interdependent. In the age of agriculture, crop failures might be made up for by imports from other places. In the nineteenth and twentieth centuries the availability of food and work in the rich communities increasingly depended not on rainfall but on the rise and fall of confidence in the international market. Increasing concentration, and increasing size, of businesses further augmented interconnections. There were many economic crises in the nineteenth and early twentieth centuries (for example, 1819, 1857, 1873, 1893 and 1907) when trade collapsed, unemployment of the workers drawn into factories increased, and prices dropped. Merchants found it hard to sell goods and factory owners found it hard to keep their plants open. Usually, however, agriculture was untouched by these crises. Some even argued that the crisis was a useful purgative, curing high prices, inefficient management and overproduction.

Book Five

Our Times II:

Absolutism and Democracy

The frequent recurrence to fundamental principles is absolutely necessary to preserve the blessings of Liberty.

Constitution of North Carolina

The essence of the argument put forward in the last book is that the five or six generations since 1750 have seen a wonderful series of technical innovations. For a time, there seemed a reasonable chance that these opportunities would be wisely and humanely used. This was largely because the innovations were more frequently conceived and introduced in free countries such as Britain or the United States.

About 1900, there was a general sense of optimism. There was a widespread expectation that representative democracy would become the characteristic form of government in much of the world, within the foreseeable future. But the technical opportunities, though helping to liberate mankind in many ways, exacerbated some of the world's ancient troubles, and the scientific achievements have not been matched by political ones. Even the eighteenth century saw despots making good use of technical innovations. In the nineteenth, those innovations helped even absolute monarchies to become stronger. In the twentieth century, technology has enabled the birth of totalitarian regimes which seek to control not only industrial production and social security but also art and even thought. In consequence of that, and of other maladies, it seemed possible in 1980 that Western civilisation, which had created the

471

possibilities of progress, might fall, either from the onslaught of irrationality without or the failure of nerve within. We have seen great nations losing every shred of humour, all sense of honour, the very idea of decency and fair play. How could it have happened? An English historian, J. H. Plumb, wrote that one truth of history is that 'the condition of man has improved, materially alas more than morally, but nevertheless both have improved'. Has there been a moral improvement? It is hard to see. The country in the world with the best education for longest, the nation with the most serious national preoccupation with learning, the people with the highest rate of literacy in the world in the eighteenth century, were the authors of Auschwitz.

Of course, there has been progress, by any usual definition of the word, in numerous fields, but there has been retrogression in others. The laws of Hammurabi in Babylon in 1800 BC were imperfect. But they guaranteed a more secure life than the code of law which applies in Iraq today. In the earliest Sumerian society, women had a higher status than they have had there ever since. The use of torture for interrogation had disappeared from the practices of powerful states by 1800. The practice has been revived. Punishment of families for the crimes of one of their members survives. 'Compared to most twentieth-century societies,' wrote Richard Pipes, 'the Russian countryside of the imperial age was an oasis of quiet.' Obviously, the qualities of intellectual vigour were more striking in the Renaissance in Italy than they have been there since. No one would use the word 'progress' in respect of art except in limited subjects such as the use of perspective or rhyme or counterpoint. It would be difficult to sustain an argument that people in the twentieth century are on better terms with minorities than they used to be. The idea of Auschwitz and Vorkuta, or of the barrier which divides West from East Germany, would have been unthinkable in the eighteenth century. The nuclear weapon would have been rejected as immoral by most governments in the nineteenth century: Lord Dundonald's scheme for beating Russia (the use of burning sulphur as an asphyxiant) was rejected in the 1850s as ungentlemanly. The dictatorships of the twentieth century, particularly those established in the name of 'the people', would have caused Voltaire and the philosophes, had they known what might happen, to have hesitated before advocating the overthrow of the Bourbons. To read Boswell's Life of Johnson is to become aware of a world more robust and more gentle, more individual if more brutal and more gregarious, more free but more coherent, more literary but closer to nature than is usual in our society.today, formally considerate, liberal, indulgent and responsible though it may seem. The most 'violent' riot in English political history, at Peterloo, Manchester, in the tumultuous days of the first industrial revolution in the world, resulted in nineteen deaths in 1819. There are few industrialising countries in the 1970s where that number are not killed for political reasons every year. The book which follows discusses these setbacks in human affairs. Meantime, J. B. Bury's prediction in the 1920s, that a day would come when the idea of progress would have to be judged as one more star in the intellectual heaven, with its era of rise and wane, seems to many to have arrived already.

42

Modern Absolutism

When Morland was appointed Minister of the Interior, a certain courtier who chanced to witness his arrival at Versailles exclaimed aghast:

'Merciful Heaven! Do you see? No buckles on his shoes.'

'Ah,' returned General Dumouriez. 'Then all is lost.'

Stendhal, *Rome, Naples, Florence*

The urgent consideration of the public safety may undoubtedly authorise the violation of every positive law. How far that or any other consideration may operate to dissolve the natural obligations of humanity and justice is a doctrine of which I still desire to remain ignorant.

Gibbon, *The Decline and Fall of the Roman Empire*, Vol. III

'I do not know how the lust for power is among other rulers,' said Catherine the Great, 'with me it is not very great.'

Quoted by Radishchev, *A Journey from St Petersburg to Moscow*

It is not mere imperfection, not corruption in low quarters, not occasional severity that I am about to describe, it is incessant, systematic, deliberate violation of the law by the power appointed to watch over and maintain it . . . it is the wholesale persecution of virtue when united with intelligence . . . operating on such a scale that entire classes may with truth be said to be its object, so that the government is in bitter and cruel, as well as utterly illegal, hostility to whatever in the nation lives and moves . . . I have seen and heard the strong and too true expression used, 'E la negazione di Dio eretta a sistema di governo.'

W. E. Gladstone, *Two Letters to the Earl of Aberdeen*

1

In the 1750s, at the birth of the age of industry, most of the inhabited part of the globe was ruled by hereditary rulers, among whom succession passed by primogeniture. The enlightened criticism of monarchs in the name of republican humanism which had characterised the Renaissance in Italy had been almost for-

gotten[1]. Several nomadic societies survived: there, monarchy, primogeniture and a settled succession were less frequent, though
the technologically advanced European monarchies encouraged
the creation of tropical versions of their own arrangements in the
remote places with which they came into contact. A few mercantile republics had either limited or abolished the authority of
monarchs. But, despite the execution of Charles of England in
1649, the essential mark of the seventeenth and eighteenth centuries was that monarchies seemed to be becoming stronger not
weaker. Italian cities were every year becoming less and less able
to withstand the power of great nations, and lived in the shadow
of Spain or France. All European monarchs, save the English
one, copied the Sun King, Louis XIV, built palaces in imitation
of Versailles, and sought to find or to train ministers of the executive quality and ruthlessness of Colbert.

The rulers known as the enlightened despots, in Prussia, Naples,
Tuscany, Spain, Austria and even Russia, used their authority
both intelligently and overbearingly. The official known as the
intendant made government more efficient in France and Spain.
For a time, there were some who thought that George III of
England might also turn out to be more than *roi fainéant* and
become 'the common father of all his people'[2].

More and more monarchs sought to establish profitable monopoly companies for trade and manufacturing. Philosophers and
writers looked to the idea of a 'philosopher-king' to bring perpetual peace between peoples and enlightened reforms within
them. Frederick the Great of Prussia was thus the hero of every
thinker in Europe. Diderot described Catherine the Great: 'the
heart of Brutus with the face of Cleopatra'[3]. All these monarchs
were trying their best to abolish privileges, of regions as of classes,
and to remove inequalities within their territories, everywhere
seeking to level disparities of income, replacing landlords and
noblemen by trained civil servants, and a strong central government instead of diverse powers[4].

Naturally, these monarchs or their servants were more repressive than were their predecessors. Canon Antonio Ribeiro dos
Santos wrote of Pombal, the great minister of King João of Portugal, that he wanted to civilise the nation, but 'at the same time
to enslave it'; and, during his thirty years of rule, Pombal im-
prisoned, for longer or shorter periods, the then unheard of number of 4,000 opponents[5].

The enlightened despots were flattered by intellectuals and

those intellectuals in turn were used by the despots. The kings looked on the *philosophes*. Albert Sorel pointed out, as 'a body of auxiliaries or scouts, the *condottieri* of their army'. 'I have made philosophy the legislator of my Empire,' wrote the Emperor Joseph II. He also said: 'In a realm governed according to my principles, prejudices, fanaticism and the slavery of the mind must disappear, before we set out to achieve a unified state of identical atoms in the most disorganised state in Europe'[6].

The *philosophes* and the kings combined to extend governments' power, to annihilate every obstacle, curb or restraint, causing Christian monarchies to become more and more like the Ottoman Empire whose ruler, the Sultan, was only limited by his obligation in matters of law by the *ulema* or 'Muslim institution', part church, part court, part university, the guardian of the Koran, staffed by muftis[7]. These enlightened hereditary rulers had Napoleon I as their real heir. No one believed more strongly than he in absolute monarchy. Every feature of his innovations showed the characteristic marks of the old regime, from the prefect (the *intendant*, in a new guise) to the *conseil d'état* (based on the old *conseil du roi*)[8]. His rule in Italy, abolishing feudal law and laws against Jews, permitting civil marriage and introducing open trials, were those of an enlightened despot *par excellence*. So were the provisions in the *Code Napoléon* giving great power to husbands and fathers, and to masters against servants.

Napoleon's attraction for writers and artists was even greater than that of Frederick the Great: Byron and Stendhal, Balzac and Hazlitt out of free choice admired him as a hero turned ruler because, as Hazlitt put it, 'our vanity or some other feeling makes us disposed to place ourselves in the situation of the strongest party'.

Britain was the exception to this picture of growing monarchical strength since, though her monarchs survived, they were ineffective. As with the Merovingian kings of France, of the seventh century, the power of the British monarch was exercised by a prime minister (or *maire du palais*) – in the British case chosen by the elected representative of a strong, enlightened aristocracy. Nor were the British ministers making any effort to create a centralised government. British colonies were already self-governing before they were independent.

Naturally, the word 'monarchy' gives an inadequate picture of what really constituted government in 1750. Monarchy was everywhere, even in Britain, the apex of a system in which all the lower sections were still run by landed aristocracy. The history of politics in the age of industrialisation is, as John Vincent put it, that of a search for a new system to replace government by those land-owners[9] or, alternatively, the history of how some of those men accepted loss of power gracefully or fought against it, sometimes successfully, usually not.

It would not have seemed in 1750 that the most likely future method of managing rich nations would be democratic. Indeed, except for the recent, apparently exceptional, events in England, democracies seemed in decline. Local freedoms were everywhere being replaced by centralising absolutisms. The eclipse of the oligarchic democracies of Italy, and the substitution of short-term elected men by grand dukes and kings, is a well chronicled, if gloomy, tale. In mediaeval Germany, there was an attempt at creating free clan assemblies and elective monarchies. By the eighteenth century only Württemberg among German territorial states (along with Hungary in the Austrian Habsburg dominions) had an assembly with any influence, and that assembly was a group of burghers whose ancestors had established themselves during a time of anarchy. Oligarchies had taken over the political management of all allegedly free cities, whereas lesser craftsmen had once played a part; while the Imperial Diet, once an assembly which could articulate the interests of electors, princes and cities on the national level, collapsed in the course of the Reformation. The provincial diets of Bohemia, Poland and Lithuania similarly vanished at that time or a little later, since they were dominated by landed interests; their only effect had been to prevent a strong monarchy. Austrian diets were abandoned in 1790, having ceased recently to have a decisive voice in taxation.

These changes were real changes away from dispersion of power. Mediaeval Scandinavia, even if united after 1397, was really, in Geoffrey Elton's words, an alliance of 'aristocratic republics sharing a weak figurehead in a common king'[10]. In mediaeval Catalonia, all social ranks had been represented in a Cortes which met once a year, and no law could pass without the consent of the representatives of a majority of the three estates. The Crown of Aragon also once had a Cortes which limited the power of monarchs in dramatic ways, while the relation between king and vassal in mediaeval Castile obliged the latter, in certain circumstances, to rise against the king: 'If ye swear falsely, may it please God that a vassal slay ye as the traitor Veludo Adolfo slew King Sancho.' The King, it is said, turned pale when the Cid uttered this momentous statement[11]. Even when the Crusaders conquered Byzantium in 1204 the choice of a new Emperor of the East was given to an electoral college of twelve, six from Venice, six from the Franks. For a time in the Middle Ages some thought that kings should be elected as abbots were. But by 1789 the Spanish Cortes, drawn from the whole united country, was feebler. They met for two months in secret. They approved without discussion the son of the king as the heir. They discussed, but did not challenge, royal plans to limit entail and to permit the enclosure of orchards. There was passive opposition to the reforms advocated by the prescient minister Floridablanca, but the most animated discussion concerned the question of how the deputies could obtain seats at a forthcoming bullfight. The assemblies of Castilian cities did not meet after 1665.

Similarly, the French had lost their right to elect municipal councils in 1692 (the King wished to supervise such assemblies in order to raise cash, not to control the people more). In no country did the eighteenth century compare so badly with mediaeval practice as in France: 'I have found much evidence in support of the view that, during the Middle Ages, the inhabitants of each village formed a community independent, in many ways, of the seigneurs,' wrote Tocqueville[12]. Assemblies of clergy, nobility and commons had been common in France in many provinces. At the end of the eighteenth century they survived only in Brittany and Languedoc. (This decay was the result of boredom more than anything else: people preferred to stay at home rather than vote in free elections – just as many in the twentieth century do not bother to vote in elections in trade unions.)

Rudimentary elective institutions even of the Kievan Rus had lingered on into the sixteenth century in Russia. But Ivan the Terrible centralised the structure of the state. Such bodies as the Zémskii Sobor became conferences between a government and its own agents. The Duma, or Tsar's council, ratified decisions taken by the Tsar, though in Viking days it had, in an earlier form, a consultative status. Novgorod had a democracy of all male citizens after it was closed peremptorily in 1477 by the Tsar of Moscow.* Poland had been obliged by conquest to abandon its elective monarchy.

---

* In practice, in the eighteenth century, Russian rulers were often chosen in effect by the officers of the guard and by senior officers. They favoured women, who might give them presents of large estates.

Nor was this decay in free institutions confined to Europe. For example, the slightest knowledge of Indian history suggests that village autonomy in the eighteenth century was less alive than it had been in the eighth. A similar statement, in relation to custom if not law, could have been made among many ancient peoples during the early days of agriculture, though there were few Asiatic countries, or others, which had anything like the self-administration (of villages) to which to look back on that India had, when thinking of village autonomy under the Chola dynasty before AD 1300. The town councils of the Spanish Empire in the Americas had also once been elected by all citizens. By the eighteenth century they had become self-perpetuating and venal oligarchies, if not necessarily incompetent, as John Parry commented, depending for their income on rents from municipal property, not from taxation[13].

The town councils in Portugal, as in the Portuguese Empire, the *camaras*, though elected on the vote of a franchise limited to good or worthy men, had for several generations considerable responsibilities for the fixing of prices of commodities and provisions, the licensing of shops and street-vendors, the provision of police, doctors, gaols, roads, bridges and fountains. They raised money from rents of municipal property, local taxes, fines and occasional capital levies. Everywhere, from Malacca to Recife, in the Portuguese Empire, the same models were followed. Sometimes such municipal councils would make or lend money: the loan which Don João de Castro raised from Goa for the relief of Diu in 1547 on the security of a hair from his beard was an instance. But, by the eighteenth century, in both the Portuguese and the Spanish Empire, meetings of these councils became perfunctory[14].

Continental thinkers did not as a rule regret these declines in representative or consultative government. It was believed by forward-looking Frenchmen in the eighteenth century, for example, that, 'whenever there were assemblies, estates, deliberative bodies, they showed themselves enemies of innovation and jealous guardians of their privileges'. Though Voltaire and others admired England, Rousseau despised the representative system as an absurd inheritance from feudalism[15]. Albert Sorel pointed out that most Frenchmen (and hence Europeans in general) thought 'the English constitution the least rational of conceptions . . . a third-rate piece of work . . . the bizarre relic of the Middle Ages and the English were as incapable of understanding the detail or grasping it as a whole as they were of appreciating the beauty of a Gothic cathedral'[16].

2

Meantime, within regions legally part of one monarchy or another, nomads (as in Spanish and Portuguese America) or tribal authorities (as in central Russia or the Ottoman Empire) sometimes maintained *de facto* supervision of a number of subjects only theoretically subordinate to the higher authority. In vast regions (most of Africa, western North America, Australasia, the South Seas) nomadic or tribal authorities were independent. In other places, such as the Far East, ancient monarchical despotisms, static and stable (fearful that the slightest change, deriving from either conquest or defeat, might cause the collapse of the edifice) survived as they had for generations, sometimes (as in India) making a humiliating obeisance to European or Arab powers in hope of being left alone.

Many of these monarchies made effective use of industrialisation from the very beginning, even if most collapsed because of the inherent difficulty of maintaining such an institution in circumstances increasingly unlike those in which they were founded. Even Brazil boasted an emperor who survived until 1899. The last forty years of that new empire brought great prosperity. The Prussian, Russian, and Japanese monarchies made every adjustment that they could to take advantage of the new benefits which technology could bring to them. Speed and ease of communications made their kingdoms for several generations able to maintain, to expand and to take advantage of military opportunities. The Prussian monarchy became the focus for German unification in the nineteenth century, and the motor of the first of Germany's two 'grabs for world power' in the twentieth. Kaiser Wilhelm II considered his task 'as having been imposed on me from heaven' and sustained that absolutism by militarism[17]. The Italian monarchy had a comparable history, becoming a symbol of Italian unity between 1848 and 1871. The Austrian emperors ceased 'to think the throne an easy chair in which to sprawl', and became more repressive than previously[18]. Though the Austrians 'in their white coats and shakos', in the words of Trevelyan, 'moved unceasingly in their fruitless, mechanical task of repression' over Italy, they ultimately failed to maintain themselves there – and not only because the method of working of Franz Josef had 'the narrow penetration of a gimlet'[19].

The Russian monarchy also devised new methods of repression, from the mid nineteenth century onwards. It combined subsidies to industrialisation with a greater control over its fast-growing population. The railway, the telegraph and then the telephone were all of use. As with Germany, the monarch passed on a centralising repressive tradition, to be subsequently revivified under the totalitarian leaders since that time. The Japanese monarchy had a history similar to that of Germany, with a different outcome: clever enough to transform itself in the 1870s to become the focus for Japanese modernisation, it allowed itself to be used in the 1930s as the inspiration of the militarists seeking to establish the 'Co-Prosperity Sphere'. It survived defeat in 1945, as an institution, shorn of its magical qualities, to become a constitutional monarchy comparable to that of England: an indication of ceremony not of power, such as, indeed, it had been for many hundreds of years before 1868.

The explanation for the collapse of absolute monarchy despite the assistance given to it by technological change was that the attempts at standardisation and modernisation of the enlightened despots often awoke unreason and broke the old consensuses. Under the centralisation imposed by the Habsburg Emperor Joseph II, 'peoples recalled their origins and sought in their national traditions their titles to independence'[20]. The wars of the industrial age let loose forces within nations which could not be contained by treaties between monarchs. Absolute defeat was insisted upon by absolute victors. Increased populations in swollen cities demanded new systems. Then too in the end the incapacity of hereditary rulers for the tasks which they were undertaking became patent: Gian Gastone, the last Medicean Grand Duke of Tuscany, 'out of mere indolence and sloth never dressed for the last thirteen years of his life and scarcely left his bed for another eight'. Surrounded by several hundred *ruspanti* (riff-raff), he invited these individuals to 'pander', as Harold Acton put it, 'in innumerable gross ways to his caprices'[21]. Gibbon's comment seemed more and more appropriate as the state became more and more looked on as the source of all charity, education and welfare: 'Of the various sorts of governments which have prevailed,' he wrote, 'an hereditary monarchy seems to present the fairest scope for ridicule'; adding, 'In the cool shade of retirement we may easily devise imaginary forms of government in which the sceptre shall be constantly bestowed upon the most worthy by the free and incorrupt suffrage of the whole community. Experience overturns these airy fabrics'[22].

It must be said too that the defeat of Germany in 1918 specifically discredited the German dynasties who at that date ruled so many of the major states of Europe. No new throne in the nineteenth century had been raised anywhere (from Bulgaria to Mexico) without a Coburg, a Habsburg, a Hohenzollen or a Wittelsbach coming forward as the candidate and, as Sir Lewis Namier pointed out, 'the German guild of princes had managed to impose on Europe a German theory about the blood of sovereigns having to be uncontaminated by that of non-princely families'.

In the 1980s a few absolute monarchies nevertheless survive, in Morocco and Saudi Arabia, as in the Persian Gulf. Those kings are desirous of putting every modern source of energy at the service of their ancient, almost pre-agricultural, methods of rule. Whether they will survive seems doubtful. Many point to the fall of the monarchy in 1979 in Persia as a good indication of what the future holds for absolutism in general. Yet some Muslim monarchies, though new, have realised that secrecy and control of information can do wonders in modern conditions. Furthermore, as late as 1975 a new King of Spain skilfully chose for himself the mission of providing a 'motor for democracy' in a country which did not see how to descend from the heights of despotism to the valley of freedom; while those democratic states in Western Europe which have retained constitutional monarchies have been able to offer to their peoples the ceremony and carnival which modern industrialised communities require as much as agricultural ones did. Their future looks secure – at least as secure as that of democratic republics. Even in some republics (such as France or the United States) a certain 'democratic royalism', in Robert Nisbet's formulation, lingers[23], while the rationalist intellectuals who believe that the eclipse of monarchy would end people's desires for magical authority have been proved wrong.

3

While monarchy, in the old sense of the word, has all but disappeared, monocracy, or government by a man who was not a monarch by birth but who gained supreme power by his own skill, strength or brutality, has played a larger part than it did in the past. Such monocrats did not play much of a part in the age of agriculture save during the last days of Rome or in Italy during the Middle Ages and Renaissance. On the other hand, monocracy is a good name for what happened in those days, while during the more recent years of the age of industry such tyrants, who have much in common with the mediaeval Italian despots or with Roman emperors, have been frequent. Often these tyrants reached power through the army, as in Spain, Africa or South America. Sometimes, as with the Nazis and Fascists, they did so through the skilful direction of mass movements. Sometimes they have risen through a free political system, whose liberties they subsequently subverted. It is true that the leaders of Fascist or Communist states are often the specific emanations of specific ideologies. But their leaders have much in common, all the same, with traditional despots, even if they use modern methods of communication to protect their egotism, and some superficially modern techniques to persuade people to fawn upon them. The leader of Communist Cuba, for example, and the Duce of Fascist Italy have, and had, much in common with ancient tyrants, while many modern despotisms of both 'left' and 'right' (particularly the new Eastern communisms) have often presided over what Gibbon described as a 'long butchery of whatever was most noble or holy or innocent'[24].

Some despots, it is true, even in the twentieth century, have been mild men. But modern despotism, in order to survive, has usually had to be brutal. Thus General Primo de Rivera in Spain established an easy-going dictatorship and had to resign after seven years, in 1930; the harsher rule of General Franco lasted from 1939 until 1975.

Since 1789 there have often been suggestions that rule by a single man is of great benefit to the state concerned since it makes it more efficient – not a king but a monocrat nevertheless. The best example of this was Napoleon, the first modern tyrant. Napoleon was a man of exceptional quickness of brain, power of decision and capacity for detail. That enabled him to codify the social reforms of the Revolution as effectively as he could win battles. But the myth of Bonapartism has not been of much help to the French. His spiritual successor and nephew, Napoleon III, did not justify the illusion that a single man can accomplish more than a parliament can. The Nazis under Hitler made the myth of the 'hero' a keystone of their system. They might have been served better by the myth of the 'team'. Some Communists have also envisaged, as Trotsky did, a species of heroes: 'Man will become immeasurably stronger, wiser, and subtler, his body will become . . . harmonised, his movements . . . rhythmic, his voice more musical. The average human type will rise to the height of an Aristotle, a Goethe, a Marx.' In Spain, Franco was a cruel but accomplished ruler who, particularly, by skilful management of foreign affairs, was able to keep Spain out of war. But, on the whole, monocrats have not fulfilled the hopes that have been placed in them. Mussolini declared war against Britain and France in 1940 without assuring himself of the whereabouts of his merchant fleet. The consequence was that a third of it was interned in Allied harbours. Nasser, tyrant of Egypt between 1954 and 1970, gave his country a demagogic leadership, but the officers in his wars were afraid to tell him the truth about their defeats. Like Diocletian (according to Gibbon) he saw only 'with his courtiers' eyes: he heard nothing but their misrepresentations'[25]. 'Besides never hearing the truth about anything,' Ottaviano Fregoso remarked of absolute rulers, in Castiglione's *The Courtier*, they 'are intoxicated by that licence which dominion carries with it, and by the abundance of their enjoyments . . . always finding themselves obeyed and almost adored with such reverence and praise . . . they are subject to such boundless self-esteem that they take no advice from others'[26].

Tyrannies are thus hard to justify; can they be explained? Caudillismo prevails in so many Hispano-Portuguese countries, wrote Américo Castro, because 'the will of a few to dominate and the desires of many to be dominated meet in a happy engagement to fill the void caused by the absence of a social culture based on a system of ideas'[27]. A nostalgia for central authority and a love of heroic leadership, however base, plays its part. Thus it is that many countries which are still agrarian have come to be ruled by military officers, engineers, lawyers, businessmen – above all, the first – who often know nothing of agriculture.

In all these societies, which are dominated by despots, life is less stable than it often seems since, underneath an artificial serenity, a work of art achieved by police, each man is haunted by the fear that he may come up against the regulations or arbitrary prejudices that govern the state. Yet the casual traveller only sees the bland smiles.

Unlike monarchs, few modern tyrants have devised a system for a peaceful transition to a like ruler. One reason is that many tyrants begin life as friends of liberty; who would have detected in the friendly country physician François Duvalier the ferocious despot 'Papa-Doc', patron of the Ton-Ton Macoutes? But even under Rome the problem of the succession was never resolved: the greatest Roman emperor, Diocletian, sought a mixture of heredity and adoption. But his successors sought pure heredity. *Coups d'état* destroyed Diocletian's settlement. The single year AD 307 saw seven emperors.

Sometimes the actions of monocrats in the twentieth century directly recall their predecessors of antiquity. Compare, for example, a concert given by Nero to a public speech in the days of Stalin. 'No one was allowed to leave the theatre,' wrote Suetonius, 'during the emperor's recitals, however pressing the reason, and the gates were kept barred. We read of women in the audience giving birth and of men being so bored from the music and the applause that they shammed dead and were carried away for burial'[28]. Solzhenitsyn tells of a speech made by Stalin in a factory at which all the hearers are afraid to be the first person to stop clapping.* All looked round despairingly and clapped on, sweat standing out on their foreheads, exhaustion stealing over them. The man who stopped clapping first, the manager of the factory, suffered.

There are naturally divergencies between the different despotisms in the world. Some, like those in the Communist world, are at the service of an idea. Some are the cynical manifestations of absolute power. But all control, more easily than ever, not a people but simply a disciplined 'multitude of subjects', in Burckhardt's description of the age of the Emperor Frederick II[30]. From the Elbe to Shanghai, that is the characteristic way that most now live. Halévy rightly called the twentieth century the 'era of tyrannies'. Tocqueville erred in thinking that such 'absolute' and 'provident' societies would be 'mild', and would 'not tyrannise but [merely] compass, enervate, extinguish and stupefy a people, till each nation is reduced to nothing better than a flock of timid and industrious animals, of which the government is the shepherd'. For, under the great tyrannies of our day, such supreme powers have often been, indeed usually have been, harsh. Tocqueville could not have imagined how modern technology could devise propaganda which would, in totalitarian states, succeed to a high

---

* Compare also the modern Russian tyranny with remarks allegedly made by a remarkably precocious judge in Russia in the 1770s. He said that all men were equal. When he spoke thus 'everyone turned his eyes away . . . 'It looked as if terror had seized those who stood near . . . they withdrew from me as from one infected by the plague'[29].

degree in making people even think as their rulers want. Robert Ley explained that the Nazi Labour Front realised that 'people are like children . . . they have childish wishes. The State has to care for them and see to it that they get . . . presents if they are to be happy and apply themselves to their work.' In the end, though, the Nazis made their subjects into animals, not children.

Another qualification to Tocqueville's predictions is that many of these new tyrannies are more inefficient and more corrupt (morally and economically) than he supposed would be the case.

Aldous Huxley once remarked: 'The abject patience of the oppressed is perhaps the most inexplicable, as it is also the most important, fact in all history.' The continuing patience of many peoples nowadays has a simple explanation: the sheer size of the police. The late Roman Empire employed 10,000 men with police functions[31]. It is a characteristic of modern times, obsessed though we are with figures, that it is difficult to find exact figures for such organisations as the KGB or the Gestapo. But it is said that even the small Cuban despotism has 10,000 'state security troops'. Russia, now as in the past the most police-conscious state in the world, had in 1895 100,000 police, a corps of gendarmes of 10,000 and a political police of under 1,000. The figure for the KGB in the 1970s was thought to be of the order of 500,000. Of course, some such despotisms have brought the benefits of order in place of chaos. But most have relied for the technological means which preserve them on inventions far away from their own shores; and, as Bertrand Russell put it after his visit to Russia in 1920, 'if a more just economic system is only attainable by closing men's minds against free enquiry, the price is too high'[32].

It is also often obscure whether such and such a government is a despotism or not. Take the case of Mexico. There, a single party has been in power since the 1920s. The last occasion when there was an election in which the opposition had a chance of winning was 1928. Mexicans tell travellers that they live under the dictatorship of a party. And who controls the party? The President. And who chooses the President? The previous President. Does not the press complain? No, because the government controls the supply of newsprint. What about Mexican writers? They do not complain because they too wish to be President. Do they have a chance? They do not. A conversation of this nature might effectively be entertained about countries less sophisticated than Mexico.

43

Modern Democracy

In the eighteenth century, the English, little given to speculation about general principles, were, for that reason, much more guided by strong opinions.

F. A. Hayek, *Law, Legislation and Liberty*, Vol. I

In England, the machine goes on almost of itself and therefore a very bad driver may manage it tolerably well.

Lord Redesdale to Lord Eldon, 19 December 1821

We must plan for freedom and not only for security, if for no other reason than that only freedom can make security secure.

Karl Popper, *The Open Society and its Enemies*

1

The history of democracy during the age of industrialisation begins, like industrialisation itself, with the British and Americans – peoples who, throughout the nineteenth century, were drawn together by what Canning described in 1822 as 'a common language, a common spirit of commercial enterprise and a common regard for regulated liberty'. The management of the British government was then in the hands of a group of landowners who had reduced the power of the monarchs, while allowing them to retain a ceremonial function. The double success of Reformation and Revolution in 1688 meant that, as Raymond Aron observed, the British intelligentsia 'never found itself in permanent conflict with Church and State . . . its polemics were closer to factual experience and less inclined to metaphysics than the intelligentsia of the continent'. The suffrage, however, was tiny, being restricted to those who owned their houses in a limited number of cities and counties. No women played any part, either as voters or as politicians. Electoral activity was sporadic. Between 1700 and 1715 there were eight general elections, more than any ever held since within a similar span of time, the elections in boroughs being difficult for governments to manage. But both borough and county elections afterwards become passive affairs with the system seem-

488

ing to have given control to 'a self-gratifying oligarchy that held power for its own profit'[1].

Despite this, many foreigners looked at the English system with envy. This was not because they admired the electoral process, nor because the last time an English government had ordered torture or had burned a witch was in 1641 and 1684 respectively, but because Britain kept the rule of law. Voltaire and other visitors to England in the eighteenth century realised that, in England, sentences were often harsh,* but three essentials were observed: first, there was nobody so grand as to be able to claim to be above the law. (Voltaire was impressed when Lord Ferrers was hanged in 1760 for murdering his steward, after a trial by the House of Lords. No such fate would have occurred to a nobleman in France.) Second, people could not suffer loss or injury save by breach of the law as established in a properly constituted court – a man might be punished for a breach of the law but for nothing else. Third, King and Parliament were the source of law which ran throughout the land.

At that time, there was no country except England where men were secure from arbitrary power, though there were many governments which were far from oppressive. Law had been considered so important in England that, even in the middle of the Civil War, justices continued to make their bi-annual circuits. By comparison, there were many countries on the Continent where political and judicial decisions were confused while the neglect of many states to interest themselves in affronts by one man against another was worst in Russia, where until 1864 laws did not even have to be made public to be put into effect: even afterwards, laws were often promulgated as confidential memoranda known only to officials.

England was thus an inspiration though foreign admirers often failed to take into account one element of the English experience: that the principles of the constitution (for example, the rights of personal liberty or the right to hold public meetings) derived from judicial decisions determining the right of private persons brought before courts in particular cases. Parliament in England had begun not as a legislature to make laws but as a court concerned to interpret laws. Even the Habeas Corpus Acts, as the great constitutional lawyer A. V. Dicey put it, declared no principles and

---

* For example, there were forty-three executions for robbery in London and Middlesex in 1785.

defined no rights. English civil law was judge-made law in the formation of which the legislature had no part.

Montesquieu considered that the strength of the English constitution derived from the separation of the legislative, executive and the judiciary powers. Those powers were, and are, not divided thus, but Montesquieu's interpretation of them had some effect on the constitution of the United States when they broke away from Britain in the late eighteenth century. Actually the English statesmen in the eighteenth century were concerned primarily 'how best to secure the complete protection of both powers, the judicial and the legislative alike, against the . . . executive', even though the judicature was part of the executive, appointed by the King through the Lord Chancellor; and sometimes the Chief Justice of the King's Bench was a member of cabinet[2]. Law was independent of any private will in England, and was only rarely interfered with by Parliament, and then only to tidy up doubtful points.

There was no code of laws: 'Each trial was in practice a professional conference between the judges and the barristers ". . . to discover how the former decisions of the courts should be applied to the new case". Law was also decentralised – much more so than in France. Magistrates were formally "crown appointments". But in reality the head of the local aristocracy, the Lord Lieutenant, made the appointment. The head of the State was almost powerless'[3].

The question frequently arises as to why it should have been England and Scotland, with their tiny population (seven million in 1750), which initiated the industrial era, rather than France (whose language dominated Europe as much as her art and whose population was twenty-five million in 1750) or Italy, with her intellectual pre-eminence in the Renaissance, or, indeed, one of many other states more or less well placed to set in motion industrial change.

The availability of cheap fuel (coal) was one reason for Britain's success. Coal saved England from a fuel crisis when her supplies of timber, always more modest than those on the Continent, became short during the time of the Tudors. This is the traditional, specifically French explanation for English pre-eminence in the eighteenth century. There is something to that view. Coal led Britain to experiment with all sorts of new manufacturing; for example, Newcomen's pumping machines. But there were social factors: the businessman, within the middle class, was regarded in

France as inferior to the administrator while, in Britain, he was well regarded – because the majority of English noblemen were *nouveaux riches*, in comparison with their continental peers.

The availability in England of cheap labour (from people displaced by the enclosures) used also to be considered a reason for English industrial primacy, particularly by nineteenth-century moralists, such as Marx. That view has been discussed earlier.* Others have argued that the growth of the population played the critical part. Yet growth of population was undoubted everywhere in Europe, even in countries such as Russia which were untouched by industrialisation for a generation or two.

At the beginning of the twentieth century religion seemed to be everywhere in decline. But a religious explanation for England's industrialisation was then, paradoxically, fashionable. Max Weber, and R. H. Tawney after him, argued that 'Puritans encouraged work but discouraged display.' The consequence, they suggested, was the limitation of consumption, and the consequent release of acquisitive activity; hence, the accumulation of capital, through an ascetic compulsion to save[4]. One of the leaders of Britain's second Protestant revolution, John Wesley, wrote in the eighteenth century: 'We ought not to prevent people from being diligent and frugal. We must exhort all Christians to gain all they can, to save all they can; that is, in effect to grow rich.' A century before, another severe Protestant, the 'Leveller' Richard Baxter, had explained that 'waste of time is the first and in principle the deadliest of sins. . . Loss of time through sociability, idle talking, luxury, more sleep than is necessary for health (six or at most eight hours) is worthy of absolute moral condemnation. Every hour lost is lost to labour for God.' Baxter's creed consisted of continual and passionate preaching of the need for hard, continuous, bodily toil: 'Work hard in your calling.' This interpretation of British industrial history receives support from the fact that so many of the early entrepreneurs in Britain (as in the US) were Quakers. The availability of the Bible in print, and in English after 1603, reminded men of the text of Ecclesiastes which told them, 'whatsoever thy hand findeth to do, do it with thy might'. The Puritanical literature of the seventeenth century stimulated literacy. In the third quarter of the seventeenth century nearly forty per cent of the adult male population could read, and they read the Bible and *Pilgrim's Progress* above all.

* See above, page 417.

An interpretation contrary to that of Weber and Tawney is made by Lawrence Stone: 'At the root of all the significant changes in the late seventeenth and eighteenth centuries,' he argues, 'lies a progressive orientation of culture towards the pursuit of pleasure in this world rather than the postponement of gratification until the next.' There was a growing confidence, certainly, during those centuries in man's capacity to master the environment, and a growth of indifference towards the authority of the clergy. The idea spread that the individual pursuit of happiness was desirable: 'the greatest good of the greatest number' was defined as an objective of the social order as early as 1725[5]. Britain in the eighteenth century, too, was beginning to treat children as individuals rather than as objects slightly less valuable than animals, and less so than servants. Tolerance became general: 'Let nothing be done to break his spirit,' Henry Fox instructed the preceptors of his brilliant son, Charles James Fox, 'the world will do that soon enough.' Perhaps the Quaker spirit of accommodation combined with the aristocratic one of optimism to create the peculiar character of easy-going adventurism which marks the late eighteenth century in Britain. Certainly, too, the stimulus to self-help, self-improvement and love of learning encouraged by the Methodist movement gave an extra dimension to Britain's middle class in the provinces, upon which so much depended, long before they had the vote.

Another important difference, however, between Britain and other countries was that the British state, though respected, played no part, to speak of, in economic life. The 20,000 or so civil servants of England, like George Selwyn, or the innumerable clerks, whose fortunes have been so lovingly described by Sir Lewis Namier in his *England in the Age of the American Revolution*, knew, as Boswell did, that it was hard to live luxuriously on less than £2,000 a year. But they knew little more of economics. That was left to bankers, merchants, sea captains and writers. Perhaps indeed, the state of Britain was respected because the state did so little. At all events the government took no interest in, but placed no obstacle before, for example, the building of canals. The central government did nothing to secure the public service, provided no schools, made no roads and gave no relief to the poor. Though Whig England had been compelled to create a standing army, it was small and had no barracks: soldiers were billeted in private houses or in inns. A Board of Agriculture was paid for by the state to assist British farming. But it was not a bureaucracy. Even officers in the British army were financially independent, since they bought their commissions. A lieutenant colonel drew £405 a year, it is true, but he paid the state £3,500 for his commission.

The state had equally no interest, to begin with, in as to how long, or how, children should work. The enlightened laws for work in factories were introduced into Parliament by independent philanthropists. The government concerned itself with law, which touched industrialisation little more than through the upholding of patents. Tariffs did interest governments of the eighteenth century in Britain. But otherwise government was conceived of as ensuring a benign neglect and preventing interference. When English statesmen in the eighteenth century thought of the word 'liberty' they saw in the concept the idea that the pursuit of wealth should be left to the individual. The free market, an invention, as we have seen, of Italians and Dutchmen between the fifteenth and seventeenth centuries, flourished in Britain successfully after 1688. Because it was established before industrialisation, it gave a decisive advantage to British manufacture. On the other hand, in France, a good idea of an economic or technological nature could prosper only if it had the support of the state. The same was true of most German states, with the exception of a few small oligarchic cities. Some of those states were enlightened, such as the Duchy of Saxe-Weimar, which patronised Goethe; but they were, as we now say, *étatiste*.

This commercial liberty underpinned the respect for the rule of law. Indeed, the two concepts were intertwined. When in 1808 the English abolished the Atlantic slave trade, the rich slave merchants of Liverpool changed the pattern of their commerce. In other European countries where the slave trade was abolished (in France in 1818, Spain in 1820 and so on) the traffic continued secretly. Of course, there were in England, as in most countries, distinctions between the legal and the unwritten popular code. There were probably as many acts of mob violence in England than there were elsewhere. Bread riots, cheese riots, meat riots were frequent, and organised. But even so, English law was not usually conceived of as the creation of a ruler, but as a barrier to power.

Despite much snobbery and violence Britain was a robust nation in ways other than in commerce and industry. The modern novel was, in the eighteenth century, constructed by Henry Fielding and was given international renown by Sir Walter Scott, in his series

of books which began to appear in 1814. Moral history was '
founded ·by Gibbon. Modern philosophy was reconstructed by
Hume, and economics invented by his friend Adam Smith. James
Watt's patent for a steam engine ran out in 1800, the year before
Byron went to Harrow, having been extended the year before the
birth of Constable, in 1776. Michael Faraday, the father of electricity, was born in 1791, the poet Shelley in 1792, and Sir Humphry Davy, the grandfather of electricity, in 1778. In comparison,
on the continent of Europe literature and philosophy were servile.
Most writers primarily created what was acceptable at court.
Freedom of expression was to be found, Burckhardt pointed out,
'only among exiles and . . . the entertainers of the common
people'[6].

A special part too was played in Britain's golden age of endeavour by Scotland – particularly in scientific discovery. English
scientific education was inferior to that of France or Germany. In
Scotland that was not so. After the failure of the Jacobite movement, the relations between Scotland and England entered upon
a fruitful era of partnership. Sir Walter Scott's heroes articulate
that. The religious feuds of the seventeenth century helped to
create a society where speculation had become more generally
accepted. Thus the 'scientific revolution' could have a stimulating
effect throughout society.

Still, it was the English who of all people in Europe had a sense
of mission – a sense of the nation almost as a 'new Israel' – and
on to images taken from the Authorised Version of the Old
Testament or the Prayer Book of 1662, Bunyan's *Pilgrim's Progress* or Foxe's *Book of Martyrs* there were imposed romantic views
of Drake and Raleigh, Elizabeth I and Alfred, with Nelson and
Wellington as the modern representatives. The Whigs of the nineteenth century noticed the slow growth of English institutions and
thought, as J. H. Plumb put it, that that gave them 'a moral
message to offer to mankind, as well as a political one'. England
in the eighteenth century was a country where self-reliance, a
sense of local responsibility, successful dependence on voluntary
action and toleration of neighbours' differences all combined to
give, in the words of F. A. Hayek, 'both respect for custom and
tradition, but at the same time a healthy suspicion of power and
authority'[7].

Finally, Britain – England and Scotland living for the first time
in effective unity – gave to the new age a philosophical basis,
particularly expressed by Adam Smith, a lowland Scot whose

Wealth of Nations, published in 1776, demonstrated, in his famous attack on governmental regulation of trade (mercantilism), the interconnection between trade, specialisation and economic growth. This idea began to rule the minds of enlightened people throughout the world.

The principle of political liberty played an important part in ensuring the success of the Industrial Revolution. Not surprisingly, therefore, the countries which copied Britain's example were also democracies: the Netherlands, Belgium, the USA. Only in the second half of the nineteenth century was there an alliance between authoritarian government and innovatory industrialisation, in the cases of France under Napoleon III and Prussia and Germany after 1848. Friederich List realised this important interconnection when he wrote in the 1830s: 'The enormous producing capacity and the great wealth of England are not the effect of national power and individual love of gain. The people's innate love of liberty and justice, the energy, the religious and moral character of the people have a share in it. The constitution of the country, its institutions, the wisdom and power of the aristocracy have a share in it. . . The geographical position . . . nay, even good luck has a share'[8].

Within Europe, among Britain's potential rivals, Portugal's economy was collapsing in the late seventeenth century, for all its surviving great possessions and its discovery of gold in Brazil in the late eighteenth century. Spain also failed to inspire a spirit of innovation. After the unwise abandonment of the Jews and Moors, the King used the Mesta, the convoy which carried sheep up and down Spain, as a model as to how to manage trade with the New World. Trade was organised by civil servants, who ensured the Crown revenue but failed to serve the national economy. Even the trade to the Americas in slaves was farmed out to Genoese contractors (like many other despotisms, the Spanish Crown preferred foreign contractors, since they made less political trouble and could not establish themselves as 'overmighty' subjects). Spain became dependent on them for investment in their mines and plantations. Later, French merchants dominated Seville. Most manufactured goods sold in the Spanish Indies were French in origin. The narrow character of Spanish trade to the Americas, the restriction of commerce to only one port for so long – Cádiz or Seville – the ban on American manufacture (except for sugar), the demand for precious metals (to the neglect of other products of the Americas): all this contributed to the ease with which Spain maintained control over her American empire. Stability and underdevelopment went hand in hand. The epic Spanish conquests were, as has been often pointed out, the last act in the mediaeval crusade of reconquest rather than a break with the past, and after the conquests were complete the conquistadors settled down to become landowners. Cortes' burning of his boats at Vera Cruz was a symbolic act indicating that he wanted to create a new Spain in every sense of the word.

Only in the late eighteenth century did Spain permit an open trade with her colonies in the Americas. In Spain itself theologians thought that business destroyed the mediaeval harmony of the spheres. Lack of roads, poor communications by river, and price-fixing hampered enterprise. Then Spain did not create the naval power needed to protect her empire and failed to supply the cheap goods which the sophisticated in that empire desired. Nor did Spain have a staple. Exports of wool dropped after 1800 and only in iron from the Basque country did the nation find a substitute for the Mexican silver upon which she had relied in the eighteenth century. So it was not surprising that while, between 1789 and 1832, the other countries of Europe grew commercially, after their different fashions, Spain's trade in 1829 fell to a mere third of what it had been in 1785. In Spanish America, owners of capital had no inducement to invest in industry, in the absence of a strong and protected market. It was easier to allow English manufactures to flood in. English merchants, shippers and bankers filled the entrepreneurial gap left by Spain's withdrawal.

In a well-known passage, Tocqueville explained that in France, in the eighteenth century, many had differing views about the ideal state, but all wished to make use, beneficially or malevolently, of the central power as it stood. 'It never occurred to anyone,' he said, 'that any large enterprise could be put through successfully without the intervention of the state'[9]. Spain, under the Bourbons, was, as it were, a dependency of France as much intellectually as militarily.

3

The success of the US experiment in democracy, meantime, made a great impression, perhaps greater than that of England in the nineteenth century. Most continental Europeans believed, after all, that the British monarchs continued to exert some influence on events (a correct assumption until 1885) and the British leadership of the opposition to Napoleon had given her conservative

governments strange bedfellows. Indeed, in the years after 1815
Britain hardly seemed a good advertisement for democracy, being
beset by labour troubles, riots and fears of revolution which were
met by a government more autocratic than democratic. The British system of representative government was astonishingly diverse. In 1815, for example, there was one borough – Preston –
where all the male inhabitants had the vote. There were others
where only one man had it. The demands for a fairer system of
voting, mixed with economic demands, were for a time resisted,
so that universal suffrage was slower to be achieved in Britain
than it was anywhere on the Continent. The US, however, a
country of farmers with a scarcely visible administration, had, as
has been indicated, been self-governing before it was independent.
Its Declaration of Independence spoke of Equality as well as of
Freedom. Knowledge of US legal procedure was communicated
because of the unrestricted entry which the USA allowed to the
adventurous and to the repressed minorities of Europe. The
impact of the US constitution was greater in Latin America
than anywhere else, even if little durable came of that for a
time.

Observers such as Tocqueville in America noticed the extent to
which national self-government grew from local self-government.
Thus, he remarked, taxes were voted by the state but they were
levied and collected by townships. The establishment of a school
was obligatory but each town itself built, paid for and superin-
tended it. In France, the state collector received the local imports;
in the US in contrast, the town collector received the taxes of the
state. The township, it seemed, was organised before the county
in the United States, the county before the state, the state before
the union. The independence of the township was the nucleus
which gave scope to the activity of a political life thoroughly
democratic and republican.

At the same time, those mid-nineteenth-century regimes did
not call themselves democracies, and feared the idea. Disraeli, a
skilful practitioner of parliamentary democracy, hoped in 1867
that 'it will never be the fate of this country to live under a
democracy'[10]. Most educated Englishmen feared that to give the
vote to the masses would risk revolution. Though two new reforms
of the suffrage, in 1867 and 1884, increased the numbers voting
in England to about 4·6 million, the large quantity of servants,
bachelors living with their families, all who had no fixed address,
some other categories and all women, were still excluded from

participation in English democracy before 1914.* Still as a result of other revolutions, several new constitutional states were established in the late nineteenth century, including France, but also, under the patronage of monarchies, an English inspiration, in Spain, Italy, Scandinavia and the Low Countries. The Anglo-Saxon dominions of Canada and Australia (with New Zealand) also founded democracies in the late nineteenth century; and some manifestations of democracy were to be seen in Germany and Central Europe, though the wars of the twentieth century would show them to be modest. In 1910 the three richest states (Britain, the US and France) were representative democracies.

There then seemed good reasons for believing that 'parliamentary institutions would supply the sovereign formula for the coming age', wrote H. A. L. Fisher, 'for no country in the world claiming to be civilised – not even Russia – had been able altogether to withstand the public pressure in favour of responsible cabinets, representative assemblies and democratic electorates'. 'The peoples of Europe,' he went on, 'save for a savage patch in the Balkans, had reached an unprecedented level of comfort and civilisation. Representative institutions, though in many parts of the continent ill rooted, ill practised, and ill understood, were universal. The belief that the world was moving towards unity seemed to be growing in strength. Recourse to arbitration for the settlement of international quarrels was becoming more frequent . . . it seemed as if statesmen had, at long last, learned the lesson that politics is the art of human happiness'[11]. Most great democracies, such as Britain, France and the United States, had acquired colonial possessions but argued that their mission was to prepare the peoples whose government they had assumed for self-government on their own model.

Historians and philosophers alike seemed to believe in progress. For example, Gibbon had written: 'We may, therefore, acquiesce in the pleasing conclusion that every age of the world has increased, and still increases, the real wealth, the happiness, the knowledge and perhaps the virtue of the human race'[12]. Macaulay did not differ: the history of England seemed to him 'the history of physical, of moral and of intellectual improvement'[13]. Much the same point was made by Maynard Keynes, with his accus-

---

* In 1908 there were a little under eight million on the register of voters in England, as opposed to the twelve million who could have been there had there been universal adult male suffrage. There were many ambiguities left behind by the complicated franchises of the past.

tomed grace: 'What an extraordinary episode in the economic progress of man that age was which came to an end in 1914! The greater part of the population, it is true, worked hard and lived at a low standard of comfort, yet were, to all appearances, reasonably contented with this lot. But escape was possible for any man of capacity or character at all exceeding the average, into the upper and middle classes, for whom life offered, at a low cost and with least trouble, conveniences, comforts and amenities beyond the compass of the richest and most powerful monarchs of other ages. The inhabitant of London could order by telephone, sipping his morning tea in bed, the various products of the whole earth, in such quantity as he might reasonably expect their early delivery upon his doorstep . . . he could secure forthwith . . . cheap and comfortable transit to any country or climate without passport . . . and would consider himself much aggrieved and much surprised at the least interference . . . he regarded this state of affairs as normal, certain and permanent, except in direction of improvement. . .

'The projects and politics of militarism and imperialism, of racial and cultural rivalries, of monopolies, restrictions and exclusion,' Keynes continued, 'which were to play the serpent to this paradise were little more than the amusements of his daily paper, and appeared to exercise almost no influence at all on the ordinary course of social and economic life, the internationalisation of which was nearly complete in practice'[14].

Nor was this confidence confined to Anglo-Saxons: Elie Halévy in the preface to his great book wrote that 'representative government bids fair to become part of the common inheritance of mankind'. In the Ottoman Empire, Sultan Abdul Hamid in 1908 could write that 'the intellectual progress of the people having reached the desired standard, we have acquired the conviction that parliament should once more assemble as a guarantee of the present and future prosperity of our country'. Most large Latin American states had then constitutions of a sort: and those states themselves had a consistency and general acceptance of frontiers and conventions more deeply established than much of Europe. Constitutions inspired by European legal theories were everywhere being constructed. Japan had made concessions to the idea of representative government in her constitution of 1889 even if it echoed German rather than Anglo-Saxon prejudices and even if electoral politics in Japan barely concealed the continuing power – particularly after the successful war with China in 1895 – of the military party. Alas, these optimistic hopes for government by consent had many enemies – above all, a pessimistic conviction that human beings had to be protected against themselves for their own good.

44
Democracy's Enemies

Four prophecies of the nineteenth century

1 For a long time I have been aware that we are driving towards
the alternative of complete democracy or absolute despotism
. . . That despotic regime will not be practised any longer by
dynasties. They are too soft-hearted . . . The new tyrannies will
be in the hands of military commanders who will call themselves
Republican.

> Burckhardt, *Reflections on History* (c. 1850)

2 The future smells of Russian leather, blood, atheism and
violence.

> Heine, who advised later generations to acquire thick skins (1842)

3 What the next hundred years will bring I cannot predict; but I
fear we shall not have repose . . . the great are not such that
there will be no abuse of power; the masses are not such that,
in hope of gradual improvements, they will be contented with a
moderate condition.

> Goethe, *Conversations with Eckermann* (c. 1825)

An innumerable multitude of men and women, all equal and
alike, incessantly endeavouring to procure the petty and paltry
pleasures with which they glut their lives. Each of them living
apart is a stranger to the fate of all the rest: his children and his
private friends represent to him the whole of mankind. As for
the rest of his fellow citizens, he is close to them; but he does
not see them; he touches them, but he does not feel them; he
exists only in himself and for himself alone, that is, [he is] an
individual lost in the crowd . . . [Above these men stands] an
immense and tutelary power which takes upon itself alone to
secure their gratification and watch over their fate . . . It would
be like the authority of a parent if its object was to prepare man
for manhood but it seeks, on the contrary, to keep them in
perpetual childhood. For their happiness, such a government
willingly labours, but it chooses to be the sole agent and the only
arbiter of that happiness. It provides for their security, foresees

and supplies their necessities . . . what remains but to spare them
all the care of thinking and all the trouble of living? After having
thus taken successively each member of the community in its
powerful grasp, and fashioned him at will, the supreme power
. . . covers the surface of society with a network of small complicated rules, uniform and minute, through which the most
original minds, and the most energetic characters, cannot penetrate to rise above the crowd. The will of man is not shattered
but softened, bent and guided; men are seldom forced by it to
act, but they are constantly restrained by it from acting.

Alexis de Tocqueville, *Democracy in America* (c. 1835)

1

Few now hope for the establishment of democracies on an international scale. First and foremost, all democracies have met difficulties from within themselves, as the old oligarchic democracy
gave way to mass democracy, with universal suffrage, male and
female, for all over the age of eighteen. Mass circulation newspapers, posters, radio, cinema, gramophone records (of songs and
speeches), symbols, television, polls of public opinion and agencies of public relations imperceptibly affected the working of the
system, never more than during the German elections of 1932,
when the 'black magic of slogans' cast such a spell over the populace. The impact of technology on democracy has been to create
greater and greater expectations, to simplify issues, and to cen-
tralise the issues around the personalities of leaders.

There are also a number of problems in modern democracy
which it would be idle not to notice.

First, the necessity of keeping the rule of law as a principle of
equal importance for the maintenance of democracy as that of the
free vote has occasionally been forgotten. Minority groups have
failed to heed Bertrand Russell's advice (on his return from Russia
in 1920): 'Once the principle of respecting majorities as expressed
at the ballot box is abandoned, there is no reason to suppose that
victory will be seized by the particular minority to which one
happens to belong. . . All groups, communist and others,' he
believed, 'ought to have the patience to set about the task of
winning by propaganda (not force) . . . we take it for granted that
most people will be law-abiding and we hardly realise what centuries of effort have gone to make that possible'[1]. This truth was
known in Greece and in the Renaissance: the Catalan humanist
Vives in 1526 wrote: 'It is no liberty to refuse respect and obedi-

ence to the public magistrates, rather it is an incitement to savagery and an occasion for licence'[2].*

Corrupt judges have also sometimes made nonsense of the ordinary process of law. The movement westwards of the US railroads in the nineteenth century, for example, was attended by a remarkable series of scandals, which make Tocqueville's enthusiasm for the US constitution seem starry-eyed.

Second, some democrats have forgotten not only that liberty assisted the beginning of industrialism but also that a critical part has always been played by free enterprise in maintaining democracy. A good presentation of this point of view was made by John Stuart Mill in his essay *On Liberty*: 'If the roads, the railways, the banks, the insurance offices, the great joint stock companies, the universities, and the public charities, were all of them branches of the government; if, in addition, the municipal corporations and local boards with all that now devolves on them became departments of the central administration, if the employees of all these enterprises are appointed and paid by the government, and look to the government for every rise in life; not all the freedom of the press and popular constitution of the legislature would make this or any other country free otherwise than in name'[4].

From the early days of Greece onwards, free enterprise and democracy have gone hand in hand, with the first usually preparing the way for the latter, even if (as in Nazi Germany and, for a time, in the Communist regimes) sometimes surviving it.

The neglect of some democrats to measure the importance of a flourishing system of private commerce has led, in several countries, to wholesale intervention by the state in the working of the market. The latter may survive since it is resilient, but the universal opinion in the best universities of the West has, for some generations, been that service to the state is a superior undertaking to that of private commerce and manufacture. The spirit of bureaucratic Rome seems to have overtaken that of sceptical Greece, that of Bourbon France seems to have conquered Hanoverian England. Sometimes it has been suggested that people who work in the public service must be more civic-spirited than those in private enterprise. Not surprisingly, in some democracies (Britain among them) the spirit of innovation among entrepre-

---

* Aneurin Bevan, a politician who later became a committed democrat, wrote in 1929: 'There still remains *unfortunately* [my italics] a degree of law-abiding conduct amounting to a broken spirit among the miners of the district[3].

neurs has consequently declined. Exhausted by problems of labour, hampered by taxation, tempted by increasingly corrupt practices, modern entrepreneurs sometimes seem like their equivalents in the last years of Roman civilisation: ignorant, timid, and more likely to appease than to lead.

Third, many modern democrats forget that the strongest free systems have been based on a view of ethics in which natural rights exist. The founders of the constitution of the US, for instance, not only reflected the concept of the separation of powers, but argued that all men had, from God, the right to life, liberty and the pursuit of happiness. It is not always evident that all democratic politicians accept the existence of those 'rights of man', even though they may be doing much for what they believe to be the good of the people of the country concerned.

This partly derives from a difficulty pointed out by A. V. Dicey: 'We have all learned from Blackstone, and writers of the same class, to make such constant use of expressions which we know not to be strictly true to fact that we cannot say for certain what is the exact relation between the facts of constitutional government and the more or less artificial phraseology under which they are concealed'[5]. Much of modern life reflects what Marc Bloch described as the condition of the Middle Ages: 'Although men were not fully aware of the change, old names which were still on everyone's lips . . . slowly acquired connotations far removed from their original meaning'[6].

Fourth, despite a network of local governmental organisations, many complain that for many there is no real participation in politics. The Cubans, in their democratic period, told an American sociologist, Lowry Nelson, 'The government does not remember there are inhabitants living in this town except during elections'[7]. Very often democracies have failed to work out an adequate interrelation between national and local politics. Local government often does not constitute the school of political training which it should, and it is no use telling somebody who wishes to influence, say, educational policy that he should stand for his local council, when he knows that that policy is very often centrally decided and financed.

Thus so many of the more effective democracies are federations with substantial local powers devolved to state governments such as those in West Germany, the United States, Australia or Switzerland. During the last century and a half the chief character of political activity in many countries was the energy and passion at local level and the weakness, superficiality and even unreality of national politics. This was true of Brazil as much of the United States before, say, 1930. The problem is to secure a proper balance between the two spheres.

Fifth, the concept of one man and one woman each having a single vote often awakens, and fosters, a passion for equality which can never be satisfied, nor even properly defined, for, as the Victorian Prime Minister, Lord Salisbury, was quite correct to say, 'Political equality is not merely a folly – it is a chimera'[8], despite its generous citation in the American Declaration of Independence.

Then enormous public meetings commonly carry resolutions by acclamation or by general assent, whilst these same assemblies, as Robert Michels reminds us, 'if divided into small sections of fifty would be much more guarded'[9]. The age of huge public meetings in democracies has declined, but congresses of parties and trade unions, 'demonstrations' and marches often allow crowd psychology to dictate policy; yet, as Lord Halifax put it in the late seventeenth century, the 'angry buzz of a multitude is one of the bloodiest noises in the world'[10]. It was because of this that representative democracy is superior to direct democracy.

Next, it is essential to notice that democratic legislatures, especially if they have only one chamber, can, in the heat of passion, constitute a serious threat to liberty. 'The tyranny of the legislature is really the danger most to be feared,' wrote Tocqueville[11], recalling the dictatorship which the National Convention exercised in the French Revolution between 1792 and 1795, particularly when its powers were concentrated in the twelve members of the 'committee of public safety'. (When the constitution of 1795 was introduced in order to re-establish a semblance of predictable conduct, the most important change was that the legislature should have two chambers.) The first President of the Second Spanish Republic, Niceto Alcalá Zamora, believed to his dying day that the Spanish Civil War would never have occurred if the legislature of Spain had had two chambers between 1931 and 1936.

Democracies have also given inadequate consideration to the fact that majorities can often exercise a tyranny over the minority: whereas the great object of all constitutional restrictions should plainly be to ensure that that does not happen. 'If the free institutions of America are destroyed,' wrote Tocqueville again, 'that event may be attributed to the omnipotence of the majority, which may at some future time urge the minorities to defeatism'[12].

Doubtless Karl Popper was right to argue that it is 'wrong to blame democracy for the political shortcomings of a democratic state. We should rather blame ourselves'[13]. But plainly democracies also have a tendency to be militarily weak. It is not easy, for example, to persuade people who are normally peace loving that such-and-such constitutes a threat to their liberty. This is one of the serious weaknesses of mass democracy as of limited democracy. At the same time, it is also desirable to take notice that democracies have never fought each other in the twentieth century. That experience gives weight, therefore, to Aristotle's belief, echoed in the Middle Ages by Marsilio of Padua, that there is a direct connection between war and despotism as much as one between peace and democracy[14].

But the most important weakness of democracy is that its practitioners take it too much for granted, forgetting how recently democracy in any form has become current; how often democracies have been overthrown even in this century; and how the nervous representative democracy of mass society has a different pattern of behaviour both from that of the limited types of direct democracy practised in Greece, and from the oligarchic system of eighteenth-century England, both of which inspire, by language and memory, present-day systems.

When democracies have failed in this century they have done so for a variety of reasons. Sometimes the democratic politicians have been too inexperienced for, or even afraid of, command. Such was the provisional government in Russia in 1917. Fatalism, optimism or diffidence characterised the democratic politicians in Spain in 1936. 'The Generals are going to rise?' laughed the Prime Minister. 'Well, I for one am going to take a lie-down.' The fledgling democracies of Eastern Europe of 1945 died because, in the course of the Second World War, Russia and Communism came to be regarded as liberators from Germany, and no honest but resilient anti-Communist movement had time to emerge. Italy in 1922 and Germany in 1933 accepted fascism and Nazism for fear of Communist revolution; as well as in the hope of a national regeneration. Democracies in Latin America have been overthrown because their leaders have behaved extravagantly (such as President Goulart in Brazil) or invited parties to share power whose loyalty to democracy was questionable (Chile in 1973; Guatemala in 1954). The overthrow of democracies has often been the work of armies which have regarded themselves as a safeguard for traditional values and a focus for regeneration. Occasionally democratic life has been successfully subverted by radical, revolutionary or Communist parties, though all the instances of that occurring have been in the shadow of prolonged wars, much as occurred after 1917 in Russia, or 1945 in Eastern Europe.

The process whereby democracy gives way to dictatorship has sometimes, in modern times, been as legal as it was in, say, 46–44 BC when Caesar established the Empire in Rome. Caesar captured the state by fraudulent rhetoric as leader of the democrats against conservative senators who, intimidated, gave him all the honours and offices he wanted – dictator for life, Imperator, the right to have a statue to himself named Demigod, the right to have coins in his name and so on. In much the same way Hitler was asked to be chancellor as leader of the largest party, and his Enabling Act, which gave him dictatorial powers, was passed by a majority of the Reichstag, most of whose members had been fairly elected.

In the twentieth century a part in the overthrow of democracies as of other regimes has been played by the conspiracies of other states. Thus the Bolsheviks in Russia received money from Germany in the course of 1917 before mounting their *coup d'état* against the weak democracy established in March 1917: 'It wasn't until the Bolsheviks received from us a steady flow of funds through various channels that they were able to build up their propaganda effort,' wrote the German diplomat Kuhlmann to the Kaiser[15]. That method of conducting war by conspiracy has continued. More often the covert use of international intervention has been a scapegoat for inadequacy. Innumerable small states have now to face the fact, though, that the decisive springs of their politics lie outside their own frontiers. Though they may claim to be independent and legally are so, modern weapons, technology, economics and communications make small states more dependent on large ones than ever before.

From time to time, pessimists predict the end of freedom once more, in terms which suggest that the mass democracy which Western countries have been fortunate enough to experience during the last few generations is comparable to the oligarchic democracies of Italy in the Middle Ages or the early ones of the classical age. But there is a wide range of type. A presidential system, such as exists in the US, is a different matter from the parliamentary one of Britain. Even the presidential system of the US differs, because of the role of the head of government in France and the vice-president in the US, from the French system.

What must strike the relaxed observer of such systems most is the small number of the undertakings concerned. The eastern Mediterranean alone, for example, had in the sixth century BC more than the present thirty or so different democratic systems. They differed, too, substantially. No modern system experiments with those limitations on periods of power to, say, a year or much less the weeks that marked mediaeval Italian states.* Indeed, to suggest that we might have anything to learn from such experiments is to invite ridicule. There are no two-headed systems, despite the increasing equality which the wife has with the husband in determining the business of the family in Western countries. Yet Rome had two annual consulships and Sparta two kings. It is as if many modern democracies have no longer, as Maurice Bowra put it, speaking of Athens in the fated fourth century BC, 'bothered to improve their institutions'[16].

It is not, however, these problems which constitute the most serious challenge to the working of modern democracies – important and perplexing though they are. That most serious challenge derives from an inner pessimism and doubt within democracies themselves. 'A ruling class needs a creed in order to survive,' wrote George Lichtheim in his essay *Imperialism*. A creed is what many democrats do not have. There is no international organisation of democratic states. Yet most people who live in democracies are happy to do so. There has been no instance of the poorest people preferring articulately to live in bondage instead of freedom. But leaders of representative democracies are not always prepared to state that their system, all things considered, with whatever degree of variation introduced to reflect local idiosyncracies, is the right one for the world to follow. Too often Western leaders accept that Arab or the African peoples have not achieved satisfactory free systems and leave it at that, showing a tolerance of iniquity or blatant wrong-doing that betrays

* The constitution of mediaeval Florence: all candidates to the 24-member Priorate had to be enrolled in a guild to prove that they were not aristocrats – a very important point to establish. Nobody leaving office could be re-elected to it within two years, and the prior held his office for two months. Nobody could canvass or ask or intrigue for office, but none could refuse it. Priors had to reside altogether in one house where they lived and ate in common, not accepting invitations or giving private audiences. They received nothing beyond ten solidi a day – a token sum. The Gonfalonier of Justice was chosen every two months from a different section of the city. He was, in effect, the chief of the priorate. His electors were the incoming priors, the captains and guild masters and two men from every section. When in office he lived with the priors.

a lack of confidence in their own systems. Yet democracy is not only more fair, it is, as has been noticed, more pacific. It offers greater chances of experiment in industry, in science and in art. It can lead to self-correction. It provides for an adequate method of succession. Its real history in 'mass societies' may only now be beginning if democratic leaders would only state firmly enough that it is towards it rather than 'development', or 'industrialisation' or other catchphrases that we should seek to guide the poorer countries which now so often suffer under odious despotisms.

45
The Life of Political Parties

As far as the leaders of bourgeois origins in the working class parties are concerned it may be said that they have adhered to the cause of the proletariat either on moral grounds, or from enthusiasm, or from scientific conviction. They crossed the Rubicon when they were still young students, still full of optimism and juvenile ardour. Having gone over to the other side of the barricade to lead the enemies of the class from which they sprang, they have fought and worked. . . Youth has [now] fled. Their best years have been passed in the service of the party or of the ideal. They are ageing . . . and their ideals have also passed, dispersed by the contrarities of daily struggles, often, too, expelled by newly acquired experiences which conflict with old beliefs. Thus . . . many of the leaders are inwardly estranged from the essential conflict of socialism. Some of them carry on a difficult internal scepticism; others have returned . . . to the ideals of their pre-socialist youth. Yet . . . no backward path is open. They are enchained by their own past. . . They have a family. . . Regard for their good name makes them feel it essential to persevere in the old round. They thus remain openly faithful to the cause to which they have sacrificed the best years of their life. But renouncing idealism, they have become opportunists. These former believers, these sometime altruists whose fervent hearts aspired only to give themselves freely, have been transformed into sceptics and egoists whose only actions are guided solely by cold calculation.

Michels, *Political Parties* (English translation), 1915

The life of politics has increasingly become the life of political parties, often seeming to be great new palaces of stone which overshadow the labyrinthine ways of the constitution which they were initiated to serve.

This causes modern politics to be quite different from what they were in, say, the eighteenth century in England, where there were only groups of friends united by common sentiment and the recollection of past loyalties. There were then neither in the Americas nor in Europe large institutionalised parties as we now know them.

In many respects, the struggle of parties seemed at its most creative when representation was not at its fairest but when, as in late nineteenth-century England, in the words of John Vincent, 'the ceremonies, processions, banners, posters, music, bands of "lambs" and supporters, colours, favours, and seating arrangements at the hustings, were much more a drama enacted about the life of the town . . . than a means of expressing individual opinions about the matters of the day to which candidates confined themselves. . . Elections were for the England of 1860 what drama, sport and literature have been for earlier and later times'[1].

Democracy thus became, more than any minor despotism achieved during the Italian Renaissance, a work of art: Burckhardt's phrase about Italian despotisms applies to our modern systems, since modern democracies were conceived in most countries as 'a calculated conscious creation'[2].

Some of this spirit of politics as a great game remains, particularly in the USA, in England and in some new democracies such as Venezuela,* but less in Europe now that ideological parties have become well established. In the US, politics remain much as they were in nineteenth-century England, if more flamboyant. The two parties of the USA since the Civil War have no clear ideological position. From being the party which lost the Civil War, the Democratic party, founded by Jefferson, has matured to become a party more inclined towards collectivism, if led by rich men. The Republicans, who held the Union together in the 1860s, matured to become distrustful of the extension of the power of central government and, at the moment, more inclined towards a decisive international attitude. Essentially, though, both are powerful interest groups unrelated to doctrine, each being primarily organisations in which those who wish to play a part in public life can realise those ambitions, rather than pressure groups whereby a certain ideology can be put into practice.

Within most mass democracies, however, more ideological parties have taken shape. They have been dedicated to the realisation of an idea. Some believe that their long-term designs must be to enthrone a class, others to preserve a Church. The three most important of these groups are the Christian Democrats, the socialists and the Communists. The first derived from a determination to ensure the role of the Christian religion in lay schools, and in a variety of other ways (a corps of military chaplains being con-

---

* A brilliant creation of the 1960s, Venezuelan democracy has about it some elements of plutocracy, but it is a great achievement, causing its architects, such as Rómulo Betancourt and Rafael Caldera, to merit their names carved in gold.

sidered important in one country, a crucifix in state schools in others), but broadened to imply a general recognition of the Church's teaching: the life of the individual soul. Their organisation dates from before the Second World War, during which young Catholic laymen took an important part in the Resistance in France, Belgium and, to a lesser extent, Italy. Since then these parties have been prominent in the political lives of Germany, Italy, France, Belgium, Chile and Venezuela, along with several other smaller countries. Unfortunately, in Italy, they have been corrupt.

The socialist movement is as widely represented. Its roots are in the nineteenth century's dream of a new society organised on a communal basis, partly reformist and progressive, partly, in England, Nonconformist. 'Socialism' was a word coined about 1830 and used, to begin with, by French intellectuals. Between then and 1848 many schemes for ideal forms of reorganising society in the interests of workers – the 'Third Estate' – were put forward. Some of those ideas had roots in the French Revolution, the English Revolution of the seventeenth century or mediaeval dreams of social regeneration. But there was a difference in that many intellectuals were anxious to persuade workers' movements, or to organise them, to take up such concepts and to abandon humdrum efforts to improve living standards. Similar ideas were devised in Spain, Germany, in Britain and in the United States, usually with little reference to each other. In the United States, Robert Owen and others tried unsuccessfully to establish socialist colonies in Indiana and Massachusetts. In 1848 socialists played a modest part in the revolutions, and in 1864 an attempt was made to bring these ideas together in London at a discussion, after which the 'First International' association of working men was founded.

At subsequent meetings, in various cities of Europe, representatives from more and more countries gathered to discuss tactics and aims. Should land after the revolution be divided up or farmed by the community? How would industrial collectivism work? Did terrorism have a part to play? And so on. The organiser of these gatherings was Karl Marx, the German polemicist who then lived in London.

Two distinct trends of thought developed: first, that which led to the formation of the anarchist movement and dominated the early stages of trade unions in Spain and South America; and second, that which led to 'social democracy' which later divided into the movements known as socialism and communism. The first, anarchist, stream of thought believed that it was desirable to destroy the state as it then existed at an early date and proceed to establish a millenarian society organised on an amateur basis by the good, with the support of a benign public opinion. The second school, the socialist or social democratic, argued that that was over-idealistic and that, anyway, while setting up an ideal socialist state, it would be necessary to maintain a powerful, even a dictatorial, bureaucracy. The first school was led by the Russian anarchist Mikhail Bakunin, a dreamer of genius of aristocratic family, and the second by Marx. Personal rivalry, as usual in politics, sharpened the ideological differences. In the end, the International collapsed. Anarchists have been quarrelling bitterly with the subsequently more powerful socialists and Communists ever since.

Within a generation or so, these idealistic views had been articulated. In Spain, the largest workers' organisation was anarchist in its inspiration and that vision of tactics and goal was shared by most of the few workers' leaders in Latin America. Elsewhere, anarchists were few and far between, though their conversion to violence – by the 'propaganda of the deed' – made their presence known everywhere after the murder of President McKinley in the US, the Empress Elizabeth of Austria, several Spanish prime ministers and a few Russian archdukes. Their plan was to destroy the apparatus of the state and to establish a new world of self-supporting communes possibly linked by a statistical apparatus. In theory, they agreed on this matter with Marx and with the socialists or the Communists. But the anarchists did not believe that they should aim at 'a bourgeois revolution' (as the Communists in theory did) and did not think it desirable to maintain a strong state until the real Communist world could be introduced.

The anarchists rejected politics as 'leading to nothing good'. 'The political idea,' said a Spanish anarchist, Anselmo Lorenzo, in Barcelona in 1869, 'whatever the party may be which professes it, is born out of the sphere of privilege'[3]. 'To be governed,' wrote the French revolutionary Proudhon, 'is to be watched, inspected, spied upon, directed, law-driven, numbered, regulated, enrolled, indoctrinated, preached at, controlled, checked, estimated, valued, censured, commanded by creatures who have neither the right nor the wisdom nor the virtue to do so'[4]. Such ideas might now find an echo among *poujadist* shopkeepers, tax rebels in California and Denmark, and perhaps businessmen and others who would prefer the state's role to be 'limited to the narrow functions of protection against force, theft, fraud, and enforcement of contracts', but anarchists disputed the need even for those things. Finally, anarchists looked back to the self-sufficiency of the mediaeval village, in which 'the people control their own affairs, and the daily incidents of their work, by a scheme of voluntary administration, maintained by public opinion, without recourse to the law of the land, and without the expenditure of a single penny . . . whereas latter-day villagers could do no more than cast a vote'[5]. Most workers' leaders in Spain about 1914 maintained views of this sort, especially in the region of Catalonia and in the politically restless and poor agricultural region of Andalusia. But they were a minority of the labour force (if a vocal and militant one) and a small socialist movement also existed. For a time, this anarchist movement operating through the Industrial Workers of the World (IWW) in the US had a following in many states. But in most countries social democrats, as the Marxists called themselves at that time, were dominant. Large and well-organised labour movements on those lines (as will be noticed later) had been founded almost everywhere, always powerful in large and cohesive industries, such as mines and railways, but also always divided as to whether or no to take an active political part in the democratic system and whether or no to negotiate on wages, conditions and hours with employers. For such negotiations would mean parley with the 'class enemy'. In the end, most of these movements did take part in politics and did negotiate, where they could.

The decision of working-class leaders in England, about 1895–1900, to think in terms of an independent party rather than to act through an existing one, either Liberal or Conservative, was a fateful step which altered the old spirit of English politics. The decision may have derived from a failure by the Conservatives 'to do anything about old age pensions', as Robert Blake put it, but the Labour leaders were then men who hoped to capture and to extend, not to destroy, the state as it then functioned and to cause it to work for the interests of the working class[6]. Thus they could have no permanent collaboration with Liberals, for whom the state seemed then by no means the only, nor the best, institution for improving society. The growth of the English Labour movement can be compared with that of the Socialist party in the US, which failed to make any mark on the old system. The chief reason for that is that in the 1890s the US was a nation alive with opportunity, with no very profound sense of class-consciousness; and, as cynics would say, American politics, then as now, required a lot of money. According to Werner Sombart, the German student of labour movements, it was because the people were already in power, that the USA was egalitarian, the American's chances of rising from his class were greater than they were elsewhere, and the US standard of living was high: 'all socialist utopias came to nothing on roast beef and apple pie'[7].

Though Edwardian England was far from egalitarian, there is too a sense in which England was more homogeneous, proud of its constitutional evolution and less bitter than continental Europe. The Labour Representation Committee founded in 1901 had become by 1914 very much like a third parliamentary party, democratic in habit and outlook, even if its constitutional position as the 'parliamentary wing of the trade union movement' made it anomalous. Edwardian England saw a rise in intellectual belief in equality. Why? Was it because differences between classes were growing? No; according to Halévy, the explanation is that there was 'a decay of that Puritan asceticism which made the proletariat ashamed of its poverty as of a crime . . . and the rich regard their own enrichment by work and saving as a fulfilment of a duty. The rich man now wanted to enjoy himself . . . and the revolt of the intelligentsia was a reply to this ostentation'[8].

Before 1914 socialists made little direct impact upon governments, though, in New Zealand, a Liberal–Labour government was formed in 1890, and a French socialist (Alexandre Millerand) joined a coalition government in 1899. A 'Labour' government was also formed in Australia in 1904. Other socialist parties busied themselves with discussions as to how far they should take part in the existing political institutions, which, for a long time, they had despised. In 1914 the German Social Democratic party was the largest one in the German Empire, even if that system stopped it from a chance of gaining power. An Austrian socialist was mayor of Vienna. Several Spanish socialists were members of Parliament. The Russian social democrats, divided though they were between Bolsheviks and Mensheviks, were members of the Duma. In all these parties, there were arguments as to how far it was possible to revise Marx in the light of changing circumstances; and in some of them a 'counter community', in the phrase of Annie Kriegel, already existed as a challenge to 'bourgeois' society[9] – or, as some thought, a utopia so well cushioned against change that nobody felt any need for a revolution.

In Britain, too, the nominally Liberal government of 1906 was in most ways a real foretaste of socialism. To quote Halévy yet again: 'The Election of 1906, on the surface a victory for free trade, and apparently a Nonconformist victory, had been in reality . . . a victory for the proletariat'[10]. Afterwards, in most belligerent countries, the socialist parties supported the First World War. All were divided by the Russian Revolution. Most split in consequence, between Communists who joined Lenin's Third Communist International, and 'socialists' who, though in theory then dedicated to the same long-term cause of international brotherhood and nationalisation of the means of production, distribution and exchange, believed that they could achieve it by democratic politics. The experience of the latter effected changes in most socialist parties and, after 1945 anyway, the socialist parties of Spain, France, Germany (and Britain), with similar groups in smaller democracies, all declared themselves to represent a collective approach to be determined by democratic methods.* The connection which all of them have with trade unions is a complication which, despite appearances, seems unlikely to be to their benefit in the long run. Some democratic socialist leaders become, in the end, as hostile to change as formerly they were in favour of it, 'coming to regard the functions which they exercise', said Robert Michels, 'as theirs by inalienable right'[11].

Unresolved dilemmas remain: do socialists believe that in the end private enterprise should be abolished, only differing, therefore, from Communists about the way that that ideal society is to be realised? Or do they hope for a society in which capitalism and state enterprise go forever hand in hand, circling round each other with suspicion, like the boarhound and the boar in Auden's poem, if 'reconciled among the stars'? Most socialist parties veer backwards and forwards, unsteadily but regularly, towards class consciousness and then towards democratic politics. Nearly all now have a rather modest sense of international brotherhood, in practice if not in theory. Few socialists seriously propose the equal distribution of all the wealth in the world. Instead, they seek to distribute wealth on a national basis. The consequence of carrying out that recipe would be to create rival monolithic states compet-

---

* The question whether this form of humane socialism is a mirage is now a critical one in almost all democracies. On balance, it seems that either the humanity or the socialism will have to be modified. The difficulty about modifying the socialism is that such a modification always seems, or can be made to seem, a betrayal of principle.

ing for the world's resources in a way which would make the competition of capitalists resemble a minuet.

Though well established, even comparatively old and resilient, the socialist parties of Europe have not been much in power in the larger countries save in Germany and Britain. In both those two states, there were socialist governments in the 1920s, in Britain between 1945 and 1951, 1964 and 1970 and 1974 and 1979, and in Germany since 1970. In France, socialists shared power with others in 1936–38 and again often between 1945 and 1958 but have not been in power since and have never led a government composed only of socialists. In Italy, the socialists' taste of power has been as a junior partner in Christian Democratic governments since 1960. In Spain, the socialists' only participation in a government was as part of coalitions in the 1930s, latterly providing the prime ministers during the Civil War. The smaller countries of Europe have often, it is true, had socialist regimes but their failure to dominate politics in Latin democracies has been striking.

Communists (whose philosophy is discussed elsewhere) are also well organised in several democracies: Italy, France, Spain and Portugal. In other democracies, notably Britain, they have the character of conspiracies within the trade union organisations. All these parties were founded in the months following the Russian Communists' *coup d'état* in 1917. They have paid the Russian government a subservience comparable to the Russians' attitude to the Tartars. 'Moderate' policies and competence in managing municipal councils have enabled Italian Communists to appear the equivalent of the Democratic party in the US, or even of the English Liberal party in the nineteenth century. But Communists everywhere still seem slaves to one part of Marx's and Lenin's ideology, if not to its totality; as Oliver Goldsmith wondered: 'Why should we believe that men who are themselves slaves [to a theory] would preserve our freedoms if they should chance to conquer us?' The idea of democratic communism anyway seems as improbable as roast icicles (Solzhenitsyn's phrase). No guarantee exists that modern Communists would preserve freedom should they capture the government in Europe.

The oldest organised political party is the Conservative one in England. Though its structure dates from the 1830s, and though some suggest, ascetically, that 1846 should mark its real beginning, a genealogy of this enterprise can be traced to Pitt the Younger and Burke if not to Dr Johnson, Bolingbroke and before. The constitutional principle which Burke evolved, and which both

Disraeli and Salisbury echoed, was to recognise that change was inevitable (and, therefore, no ideal state could be achieved) and that the test of a good policy was how far the change concerned could be articulated within an accepted series of rules or a constitutional frame. Lord Salisbury put it thus: referring to crusades such as communism, he said that all such 'rest on the false assumption that there is a final and ideal state of affairs in politics which can be aimed at and then fixed. There is not. The spirit of innovation must always exist.' Elsewhere, he said, 'the concessions that were salutary yesterday may be doubtful today and infatuated weaknesses tomorrow'[12]. For Raymond Aron, conservatism is intended 'to prevent the decomposition of eternal moral values'[13]. For others, it is to revive them; for others in England, it is again what it was in the days of Peel: to free society from the shackles which have grown up round it during an age of war, crisis and ignorant 'planning'.*

It is easy to contrast this party with a more anti-constitutional view prevalent on the continent of Europe where the peaceful transition from landowners' rule to democracy was more difficult: no English (or US) conservative would ever have gained applause (as a German conservative did) had he announced, 'The King . . . must always be in a position where he can say to any lieutenant: "Take ten men and shoot the parliament" '[14].

In the early days of representative democracy nearly every country in Europe had a conservative party, with that name. In the twentieth century all, except the English, became fatally marked by association with fascism. Hence the paradox that in Europe the parties of the so-called 'right' are all newer than the radical ones of the 'left'.

---

* 'Only if the state's role in our society is kept to modest dimensions, will respect for it be combined with respect for the large number of private associations which contribute so much to the stability and richness of a society,' said the leader of the British Conservative party in 1978.

46

Syndicalists

Men who have no . . . property except their manual skill and strength ought to be allowed to confer together . . . for the purpose of determining at what rate they will sell their labour.

Sir Robert Peel, 1824

Fanelli [the Italian anarchist] managed to get together [in Madrid, 1868] in the house of Rubau Donadeu, a few workers from the group of El Fomento de las Artes. Fanelli did not speak Spanish and his hearers did not know a word of Italian and very few of them could translate anything even mediocrely from French. . . Fanelli began to speak in French and Italian indifferently. He spoke very vividly. *Cosa horrible! Spaventosa!* when he spoke of the miseries of the workers. In a few minutes, the audience was prisoner of a delicious enthusiasm . . . and those who heard went out, as Don Quixote had gone out, ready to fight evil and to preach the good news.

J. Díaz del Moral,
Historia de las Agitaciones Campesinas Andaluzas: Córdoba

1

Another problem affecting the working or representative democracy in the twentieth century is the power of 'overmighty' associations which have arrogated to themselves corporate power. One example of this is the power gained by trade unions. These organisations are in the forefront of debate in politics in some countries, but the immediacy of the difficulty which they pose should not prevent historical meditation.

Gatherings of workers are among the oldest form of civil organisation. For example, in India under the Maurya Empire, in the third century BC, most artisans worked in guilds, such organisations being to avoid the expense of working alone. As the centuries passed, in a static community dominated by castes, guilds in India assumed many habits comparable to modern trade unions. They not only fixed rules of work, quality and prices but arranged professional education. The behaviour of members was controlled through guild courts, customary usage had the force of law while, since children usually followed their father's professions, guilds could be sure of new blood. Those guilds were not political. They patronised artists. They had property. They acted as bankers and trustees in a modest manner. In different ways, perhaps in emulation of Indian methods, guilds were found later in every mercantile city, under Rome and in mediaeval Europe. In Rome there were trade associations of every sort – bakers, tally clerks, stevedores, firefighters, bargees, carters, masons and lime burners.

Guilds operated as friendly societies, often taking responsibility for the cost of burying their members or of recompensing their losses by fire. They established 'rules of the game' in unpromising circumstances, insisted upon honourable conduct, sought fair conditions, and established codes for apprentices – providing that no one should enter a trade without several years' apprenticeship, that stage to be followed by one as a 'journeyman' in search of work. By the eighteenth century, however, most guilds – and this was approximately so throughout the world – were like those in Spain 'closed monopolies of master craftsmen, hampering the introduction of new methods and of self-made men, and insisting on the minute specification of the nature of processes and products'[1]. As seen earlier, the guild in the English wool trade was both strong and hostile to innovation.

The political transformations of the years between 1780 and 1850 damaged guilds in Europe beyond repair. Populations moved to cities such as Manchester where there were no civic traditions. Apprenticeships collapsed. Some skilled crafts tried to keep rules for admission but, except among a few (naval engineers and cabinet-makers, for example), these attempts were defeated by mechanisation. New machinery simplified processes which had needed special skills and it became out of the question to insist on an apprenticeship of seven years if the use of the new loom could be learned in a month or two. Above all, cities were becoming larger; before 1750 there was no country in the world where most people lived in cities and worked at machinery, but after 1800 a steady growth both in the size of cities and in the proportion of populations within cities began.

By 1900 in Europe only builders, stonemasons and printers maintained a semblance of apprenticeship. At much the same time, serfdom was also finally abolished throughout that continent. Thus a unique situation prevailed. For the first time in history the richest continent had both a swiftly growing population and very few restrictions on its use for labour either of a feudal or any other form. Sir John Clapham pointed out that, in France as elsewhere on the continent of Europe, the revolutionary legislators had had 'one common and keen desire for industry: to rid those who directed it from the surviving mediaeval restrictions and excesses of official control. They abolished the half-decayed guilds and cut down state interference.' But, he added, 'problems of the wage contract' hardly interested them[2]. In addition, efforts to regulate wages previously made by governments, since the Black Death, had been discontinued. It was indeed to try to secure the restoration of a regretted old order that discontented artisans in Britain addressed petitions to their rulers. They wished the state to intervene in an impartial manner between employed and employers in the new conditions.

There were already in being thoughout Europe various organisations or clubs of journeymen which had been founded partly for social reasons, partly for mutual insurance. These 'friendly societies' flourished in the eighteenth century, and were often protected by governments. Already in the eighteenth century the verb 'to strike' work (as in striking or bringing down a sail) had begun to be used in England, while the historian of the English trade union movement Henry Pelling detects a combination to raise wages among the journeymen feltmakers in the 1690s, in the woolcombers of Tiverton around 1700, the knitters of London in 1710, the journeyman tailors in the 1720s and the weavers of Somerset at much the same time. These were held to be illegal but, as in almost every law on the subject until this day, that had little effect. There were strikes by silkweavers in 1763, and by colliers and miners in Newcastle several times about that time. Vast numbers of small clubs were founded in eighteenth-century England and Holland. Thus, in the mid eighteenth century the Union Society of Journeyman Brushmakers had a network of clubs up and down Britain, undertaking to give hospitality for a day to any member 'on the tramp', that is, an unemployed labourer who had set off on foot to seek work. All these clubs were normally limited to those who had served their apprenticeship, though there were exceptions made for sons of members. Most were in a skilled craft. There were also similar undertakings in the US, even during colonial days, particularly in Philadelphia and New York among printers and shoemakers. Such activity was modest because of the large number of slaves and indentured servants.[3]

The history of these associations was transformed by, first, the factory and, second, the French Revolution. The factories demanded disciplined work. Both work and meals were begun by bells. Foremen and managers ruled their new and, in the beginning, young labour force strictly. Many workers hated the new conditions, regretting the days when they worked at home or in the manufacturer's house. From the beginning of factory life, the larger numbers made possible violent clashes in times of dispute – as, indeed, was the case in sugar mills in the West Indies. Thus, as early as 1787 the manufacturers of muslin in Glasgow tried to take advantage of a temporary glut of labour by cutting wages. The workers combined and declined to work for less than a minimum sum. Employers who refused that were boycotted. Many organisations to maintain wages were founded all over Europe, while small manufacturers – ironworkers, knife grinders, papermakers, hatters – also associated because they were afraid of mechanisation. Similar movements were founded in the US, though, since most early cotton factory workers there were either slaves or women and children, they were largely outside the factory system. The early North American trade unions were directed against merchants more than employers. Merchants seemed to be reducing both master and journeyman to a single common level.

The coincidence of the French Revolution with these events was an accident, but its outbreak had an electrifying effect on labour throughout the continent of Europe, particularly in an England beset by labour troubles and awakening political resentments of every sort. Frightened that labour troubles might turn into revolution, the British government, for example, in 1799 passed a law forbidding workers to combine to gain higher wages or shorter hours. William Wilberforce, the friend of the slaves in the West Indies, introduced it. The aim was to make the Royal Proclamation on the subect earlier in the century more effective. Despite this law, thousands of combinations survived. Plans were made to form general unions of workers, particularly in the industrially revolutionary county of Lancashire. Trade and labour clubs were formed which, their organisers claimed, were not specifically combinations to raise wages. Friendly societies could not be made illegal by any British government and their numbers increased. Sentences under the Combination Acts were generally mild: three months' gaol or two months' hard labour. There was then no police in England. Employers asked the government to take the initiative against illegal combinations but they refused.

In 1812 the British law officers were asked to advise about the proposed congress of the illegal woolcombers' union. 'These combinations are mischievous and dangerous,' they said, 'but it is very difficult to know how to deal with them.' So nothing was done. In 1813 and in 1814 Acts were passed which repealed those sections of the old Elizabethan statute which gave magistrates powers to fix wages and regulate apprenticeships. Those measures, resisted by workmen, led directly to the formation of more and more radical combinations. In 1824 the Tory government repealed all the old legislation and finally permitted free combinations in the name of the free market. The following year, magistrates were permitted to appoint mixed panels of masters and men from which both parties would choose referees to decide on the fair wage. If there were no settlement, the magistrates themselves would give an award.

The actual method of organisation of 'unions', as they became known in England about 1818, derived at least in part from the great success enjoyed by the Methodist movement and the lessons that that success seemed to spell for early union leaders who in consequence no doubt devoted a great deal of time to self-education and to study. These details of labour problems in the early industrial age remind us that the labour problems of the twentieth century do not all represent a novelty. Many of the difficulties of our day were faced by our great-grandfathers, with the difference that fewer people were implicated, that the contrasts between rich and poor were greater and that the majority were poor.

In countries other than Britain the same pattern developed somewhat differently, and later. The early labour demands in the US were more political than those in Europe since they included a demand for free schools, the end of gaol for debt, and cheaper courts. The distinction between employer and employee developed gradually in the US since, in the colonial era, most articles were produced at home. In those circumstances, there could be few arguments over prices. In the US, as elsewhere, printers played an important part early on and formed the first national union. In France in 1848 the individual worker still had not become a factory hand. He still had an excellent chance of becoming a master craftsman. Until 1868 the *Code Civil* established by Napoleon was maintained to decide that the master's word should be final in courts of law when a question arose over wages. The *Code Penal* equally forbade combinations and picketing. Indeed, a law of 1803 instituted a pass book (*livret*), in which a workman had to have his employer's name inscribed. No one could be hired unless the history included therein was satisfactory. Napoleon wished to restore apprenticeships, since they so plainly assisted political control but, though he did not legislate for that, the old *compagnonnages* of artisans continued till half-way through the century, when the idea of those peripatetic brotherhoods was ruined by railways. But printers in Paris organised friendly societies and, by the Second Empire, the basis for a trade union movement, despite the power of the *patronat*. In Germany by 1848 journeymen were beginning to call themselves *Arbeiter* (workmen), and to make demands for a twelve-hour day, a minimum wage and the right to travel where they wanted through Germany. Collective bargaining was slow to be adopted since employers were reluctant to abandon the old direct relationship between master and man.

Spanish union organisations were delayed too, despite political agitation from 1808 onwards. The protests of the 1830s against, for instance, an increase in the size of cloth pieces, because the workers were paid by the piece, were more a recollection of mediaeval protests in the cloth trade than a foretaste of modern industrial disputes. A few cooperative associations began to be founded: for example, the society for the mutual protection of cotton workers, founded in 1840. In 1855 Spain had its first strike, over a demand for a legal right of association, and in 1861 a number of Andalusian workers demanded the division of the large estates. Rafael Pérez del Alamo, a vet from Loja, took direct action in a way characteristic of later Spanish working-class endeavours and occupied the valley of Iznájar to establish a 'republic of the poor' there for a few weeks. By 1864 the workers were tacitly permitted to organise at least in the then only important industrial region, Catalonia, and many friendly societies were soon founded.

These early trade union movements usually had political colouring, particularly on the continent of Europe, because they were illegal. But they were not primarily political. They were, on one level, an attempt by the workers, in the absence of either a feudal system or a modern state, to establish a countervailing power to capitalism. They represented also a desire for professional organisations to replace the guilds in a state of affairs where, in Britain, the US and much of Europe, people could, by the 1860s, for the first time in history, follow whatever trade they desired.

2

The history of trade unions since the 1860s is easy to summarise. First, in free countries, they have increased in numbers so as to represent in the 1970s something between twenty per cent (in the US, France or Spain) and fifty per cent (in Britain) of the work force.* Their good organisation in key industries places them at an advantage over an unorganised multitude of individuals. Thus France has only twenty-five per cent of its labour force in unions, but those unions are exceptionally powerful. Both world wars of the twentieth century, incidentally, stimulated union membership everywhere: in the First World War the American Federation of Labor doubled its membership and, in the Second, union membership increased from nine to fifteen millions. Meantime the old functions of unions as 'friendly societies' concerned with funerals, sick pay, compensation for injury, superannuation, have vanished as those activities have been taken over by the state.

The tactics and function of trade unions have also changed. Though the phrase to be 'in union' had for a time a half-sacred meaning to those who used it of themselves, from about 1880 the chief means of protest of labour unions has been the 'strike'. The 1880s and 1890s saw in all industrialised countries a wave of harsh withdrawals of labour: a series of clashes which later assumed almost legendary importance. There were the great British dock strike of 1880, the first big miners' strike in Britain of 1892 and the strike of the British Post Office clerks of 1891. There were the rail strike in the US of 1877, the US steelworkers' strike of 1892, the Pullman car strike of 1894 and the US anthracite coal strike of 1902; and strikes of the vineyard workers in France followed. There were great dock strikes in Australia. In Russia, there was a general strike in the port of Odessa in 1903, and others in Baku and Rostov-on-Don. Railwaymen in Russia – as noticed earlier – struck during the early stages of the revolution of 1905. There were important rail strikes in Brazil in 1891, 1895 and 1901, a strike by stevedores at Recife in 1895 and in 1903 the biggest strike till then in Latin America, in São Paulo in the textile factories. Many strikes in the US were real pitched battles. In the years before 1914, throughout Europe and the US, says Sir John

---

* These figures all depend on the base selected. Thus union members in 1976 in the US were 22,662,000, but the labour force is alternately reckoned as 104 million, 78 million (excluding unemployed, self-employed and 'supervisors') or even 63 million (if part-time and federal state and local government employees are excluded).

Clapham, 'loss of work through industrial warfare became normal': miners, transport workers, railwaymen, woodmen, champagne vineyard workers (in France) and mushroom pickers became engaged in a series of long, often brutal battles in which states sought to hold open 'essential services' and so sided with employers (at that time, most essential services were in private hands). The 'syndicalist revolt' of 1911 was one of the worst challenges to representative government Britain had seen: 'England's two greatest ports [were] threatened with famine or at least were at the mercy of two proletarian dictators'[4].

The First World War brought this era to an end. Trade unionists fought the national enemy with greater ferocity than they had fought employers, while their leaders joined cabinets. After 1918, though, the strikes resumed. Those in Italy in 1919 to 1920 helped to bring the Fascists to power: a socialist paper blamed the 'devaluation of the mighty weapon of the strike' and the 'stupid and ruinous ranting of the irresponsible', for the conditions which led to the march on Rome. Violent strikes and inter-union warfare in Spain, particularly on the railways, helped to lead to the *coup d'état* of Primo de Rivera in 1923. In England, the miners' strike of 1926 (leading to a general strike), the US steel strike of September 1919 and the US General Motors strike of 1937 were formidable challenges. In South America, as in other neutral countries, meantime, the war brought no respite at all to the wave of strikes.

These struggles were particularly violent when, as was usually the case before 1914, unions had limited reserves, and when no charitable assistance was given by the state to strikers or their families. That meant that to be successful a strike had to be short, sharp, intimidatory and damaging. Those conditions changed after the Second World War. In most free countries, unions abandoned the thought of being instruments of revolution and became permanently concerned with better benefits.* The deliberate advocacy of a general strike to paralyse society and ensure the transfer of all means of production to the workers, such as advocated by Eugene Debs in the US or by anarcho-syndicalists in Spain, continued the tactic of a minority.

---

* The significance of the wave of strikes in the winter of 1978–79 in Britain (against the background of which the first edition of this book was written) is that the British unions have abandoned any desire for a privileged moral position in the nation and have joined the American unions in revelling in their place as a powerful pressure group.

Third, labour unions became centralised. Just as the First World War increased combinations in banks, railways and large companies, so it increased unifications among unions. The American Federation of Labor was one of the real victors of the First World War. Though their numbers temporarily declined afterwards, they remained the dominant voice in American labour. Despite those changes, in many countries old rivalries between those who were, or regarded themselves as, superior within a particular industry, which became evident in the nineteenth century, remained to dog the twentieth.

While these tendencies occurred in all countries, every country except Germany (where the movement was refounded from the bottom after 1945) has experienced innumerable anomalies in the method of organising their unions. Some countries have primarily craft unions (as in Britain). Some unions have taken in all skills (for example, the Knights of Labor in the US). Other unions seek to organise all workers in a given industry, or politically motivated ones.

Fourth, there has been a steady growth in trade union law. Lord Randolph Churchill saw the shape of things to come when he asserted: 'Our land laws were framed by the landed interest for the advantage of the landed interest. . . We are now come . . . to a time when labour laws will be made by the labour interest for the advantage of labour'[5]. Thus, after some years of argument, a Bill was introduced in 1906 by a British Liberal government which declared that 'an action against a trade union, either of workmen or masters, in respect of any tortious act alleged to have been committed on behalf of the trade union shall not be entertained by any court'. The Bill placed the trade unions in a privileged position at law. A 'scandal to the lawyers', as Elie Halévy put it, it became law without serious opposition[6]. The consequences began to seem anomalous or wrong, however, only when the unions grew in strength. Equally, that same Trades Disputes Act of 1906 confirmed that people could seek 'peacefully to persuade any person from working' – a provision which has subsequently led to acrimony.*

Courts of law in the US have annulled many labour laws there as infringements of the constitution. Till about 1900 US courts

---

* The Act owed its origin to a strike of railwaymen in Taff Vale, in the Glamorgan coalfields. The strike was carried out in opposition to the wishes of the railwaymen's leaders. The colliery sued the union for damages, and won, had the judgement reversed on appeal, but reaffirmed in the House of Lords.

even held that laws which specified fixed hours of work were unconstitutional. The Supreme Court in the US declared that no worker can be compelled to join a union and to obey its rules. But there are instances, nevertheless, of 'union shops' in which all employed people are automatically members of unions and have to pay fees even if they do not have to accept the union's instructions.

The legal position of unions is one of the most acute problems in democracies of the late twentieth century. The problem which these organisations pose is severe, since their organisers arrogate to themselves a role as first the private protector of as many members of the labour force as they can, as a replacement of the Church, or of the lord in the age of agriculture; and, second, increasingly seek to influence both policy within the industry and legislation within the state. Such actions may have benefits for workers, though that is far from certain. But it is exceptionally difficult to see that such syndicalism can be combined with representative democracy.

Unions have had a long history of opposition to innovations in technology, particularly in the printing industry, but also elsewhere. They have become in this respect comparable to guilds in the past. Since 1945, when unions in Western Europe have had more power than ever, and automation has opened innumerable new possibilities of changes in methods of work, this has become one of the most complicated of questions. Often unions have been less the revolutionaries which the words they use proclaim them to be than arch-enemies of change. They are also disinclined to give a substantial place to women. No female labour leader has yet arisen and unions have never put equal pay between men and women for equal work high on their list of priorities.

Then, as the pattern of employment has changed, so has the character of trade unions to include not only simply men in heavy industry but also those in trade or in clerical work and even professional and public service. In the US in 1900, clerical or office workers numbered fifteen per cent of all workers. In 1980 they numbered forty per cent: the percentage is growing. That is a trend also becoming evident elsewhere.

Finally 'organised labour' has become in nearly every democratic state a third leg in a triad – the state itself and the employers being the other two legs – which has increasingly rivalled the formally sovereign parliamentary institutions. The case for thinking the ensuing corporate state (for the trends are towards corporatism) desirable has been put by Keith Middlemas in a recent work about Britain: 'an original and distinct part in modifying the nature of the state' has been played by the unions, he argues. It would certainly be silly to suppose that role is at an end whatever hopes we may entertain for limiting it.

The achievements of the unions are hard to chart. Certainly, since their inception, wages have risen, hours of work have fallen, conditions of work have improved and, in some countries such as the US, labour unions have exerted effective pressure on governments to introduce free education. But wages among workers who have never been in unions (such as, for example, the special case of domestic servants) have also grown (and the hours of work fallen) and successful employers have always known that good conditions in the twentieth century, as in slave plantations, are an incentive to keeping good workmen. Wages also grew in the nineteenth century before unions were organised, and have risen in countries such as Spain or Russia, between 1945 and 1975, which did not have free trade unions. Wages have grown as fast in the US, with its low proportion of workers in unions, as in any other country.

Most people who have joined unions in the twentieth century have done so in order to benefit, as they suppose, from the system based upon free enterprise and wages rather than to destroy it. Unions which have been opposed to the wage system have failed particularly in the US, where the American Federation of Labor (AF of L), founded about 1886 by Sam Gompers, has now been, for nearly a hundred years, in a dominant but politically aseptic place. It seems probable that the best achievements of unions have been less in respect of securing higher wages than in respect of laws guaranteeing compensation for injury, regulations in mines and so on.

The part of unions outside Europe and North America has been as much the history of collaboration with, as of challenges to, the unrepresentative regimes in power. The Cuban case is instructive. In the 1880s, when Cuba was a Spanish colony, numerous friendly societies were formed. By 1900 many of these had been converted into anarchist clubs (connecting them with Spain). The anarchist connection continued till the 1920s and rendered those unions ineffective, though there were some serious strikes. In the late 1920s the Communists captured the more powerful unions, led them in a revolution in 1933 and, in the late 1930s, secured their legalisation. For ten years, between 1938 and 1948, with nearly twenty-five per cent of the working population in one union or another, the Communists secured a large number of social benefits, such as reduced hours of work, government arbitration in the workers' favour in disputes over wages, holidays with pay and so on. But as a result of the Cold War, the Cuban unions split in 1948 into two. The larger, non-communist union movement dominated labour for ten more years but became associated with the corrupt and, latterly, tyrannical *status quo*. When Castro came to power in 1959 the unions were taken over by the government and subsequently, as in all Communist regimes, became more a ministry of labour concerned to effect governmental policies rather than to represent the employed population. Many other less politically advanced countries now have unions of the same model that Cuba had after 1948: powerful, sectarian and corrupt.

3

The history of labour movements as political parties has been touched upon elsewhere. In both the two world wars, on both sides, the advanced countries became used to the idea that normal union activities could be suspended along with other 'basic rights and privileges'. The attraction of a regulated society has since then never ceased to interest reformers, particularly when faced by the question of how to adjust wages and salaries in nationalised industries and services. But no such society has yet been achieved, save in war, in free societies. Indeed, the idea is a contradiction in terms: a fully regulated society is the negation of freedom.

Today, there are three forms of union: those which dominate the US and Germany and are primarily concerned with material improvements; second, those which dominate the unions in France, Spain and Italy and which are primarily concerned, at least in the long run, to establish a Communist society, positing some prefigurement of their contemporary control of railways and municipal councils; and third, those which exist in Sweden, Israel and Britain, and seem to see the union organisation itself as a precursor of a syndicalist society.

This last attitude of mind has itself had a long history by now. In the 1830s in England there were those who were claiming that 'the unions could solve the problem of political power' and that 'a parliament of the industrious classes could be delegated directly from workshops and mills'. But this last idea, though it has been endlessly embroidered, is not one which seems likely to lead to innovation. Schemes for workers' participation in industry as a rule propose measures which institutionalise private firms, rather than rejuvenate them. Some hoped, in the 1860s, that limited liability might lead to a new type of company, in which worker and capitalist might share profits and risks. Some cooperative mills were established. But the wage earners who were shareholders ceased to look upon themselves as wage earners as soon as they could. Others who stayed where they were put shares into banks, building societies and other enterprises in order to spread their risks.

Yet workers' cooperatives such as those founded in the 1950s at Mondragón in the Basque country offer a good chance of a new form of industrial life, provided, however, that they stand on their own feet; do not expect assistance or favours from the state; and offer the opportunity of turning workers into capitalists. The trouble is that such laudable aims often seem heretical.*

It would be wrong to suppose that the organisations described are characteristic of labour arrangements in all countries. Thus, in many countries with strong governments, Fascist and Communist alike, trade union systems have been devised which bear similarity to free democratic ones, in name and style, but are merely departments within the ministry of labour. Their fine-sounding names, and their attempts to be accepted on their own evaluation by trade unions in free countries, are good examples of hypocrisy paying tribute to what it knows to be a juster, if more disorderly, type of organisation. England has evolved a trade union structure which is 'the merest chaos', in the words of G. D. H. Cole, but it is one which is technically susceptible of reform. Equally, those strong governments which seem to be in no immediate danger of collapse have also drawn on vast numbers of their citizens to work as prisoners on one large project after another. Pious discussions of working conditions, hours of work and payment in our day are out of place in considering such systems. They are referred to as 'slave labour' camps but condi-

---

* The experiment known by the name of Mondragón is a network of industries, agricultural projects and marketing businesses in which all the workers hold a stake. They have received no governmental assistance. There are no trade unionists. There have been almost no strikes. Within twenty years, Mondragón established factories which are among the leaders in Spanish exports of machine tools, washing machines and other domestic objects. Every worker invests the equivalent of £1,000 in the enterprise and expects to take out ten times that on retirement. All plans are carefully managed by the cooperative's bank. Associations of this productive nature are a more promising pointer to the future than the systems of collective enterprise desired by trade unions.

tions of work in sugar mills of the eighteenth century in the West Indies or on cotton plantations of the nineteenth in the US would have seemed paradisaical to those whose job was to build the White Sea Canal. If, in the future, liberal historians survive to write about the labour conditions of the twentieth century, they will concentrate upon these Russian waterworks as Gibbon emphasised the evil rule of the Byzantine Emperor Constantine V or the Roman Domitian. The names of heroic would-be founders of free trade unions in Russia, China or East Europe will then be as well known to the student of comparative labour history as they are unknown to us.*

---

* At the time of writing the demands for free trade unions in Poland have graduated into demands for free parties, and in effect for an end of the Communist state.

47

Our Living Standards

The equivalent of wage rates in terms of consumable goods was higher between 1380 and 1510 than at any time till the late nineteenth century.

Lord Ernle

The question of conditions in early industrial life continues to be debated. Did life get better or did it get worse? J. S. Mill wrote in *Principles of Political Economy*, published in 1848: 'Hitherto, it is questionable if all the mechanical inventions yet made have lightened the day's trial to any human being. They *have* enabled [author's italics] a greater proportion to live the same old life of drudgery and imprisonment.' But even then there can be no doubt that, over all, the conditions in England – then the most industrialised country – had improved, measured, say, by all the indices now used for underdeveloped countries. What statistics did not take into account is that in certain trades, such as mining and lower grade hand-loom weaving, conditions in the mid nineteenth century were worse than they had been in those professions a century before. Some jobs too were more demanding than anything known in the agricultural age: working at a blast furnace, for example; or mining coal, with foul air and inadequate safety conditions; while signalmen and engine drivers have responsibilities heavier than almost any known before.

These are not problems of democracy. Modern industrial life needs different legislation for working conditions from those considered necessary before 1750. The task of governments in modern democracies is to ensure humane laws governing the way that work is carried on; not to carry on the work itself. Most countries where the standard of living has risen so far as to abolish poverty are ones where this limited role of government has been accepted.

The industrial regions of the world remain small in territorial extent in relation to the social changes they have brought. In 1938 the factory workers in the world did not exceed 100 million, or six per cent of the population of working age. In 1938 two-thirds of the world's manufacturing output was still, as in 1870, to be found in the US, Germany and Britain. The position has changed since then. Russia, France, Japan and some other small Eastern countries have industrialised fast. Even so, it seems that not much more than ten per cent of the world's workers are today employed in factories. The percentage is falling because of the increase in the number of persons concerned with services, from transport to entertainment. Workers in factories, after a few generations, have become the aristocrats of labour.

In the late nineteenth century the question of what attitude a state should have towards 'those out of work, able to work and looking for a job', that is, the employable unemployed (as defined by the US in the 1930s) also began to be looked at in a new way.

In ancient Rome in the time of the early emperors a third to a half of the population of the capital is said to have lived on free grain at public expense. When Rome collapsed, those arrangements collapsed too. Unemployment and poverty, along with famine and disease, marked all cities in the Dark Ages of Europe. In the Enlightenment, unemployment was avoided by a large domestic service. In Venice in 1760 the servants numbered 13,000, or ten per cent of the population. 'Stamp your foot on the Paris cobblestones and you can conjure up an army of clerks, runners, secretaries and public writers. Look for one, and a hundred will spring up,' wrote one eighteenth-century traveller. Where they were still unemployed, male and young, those concerned often joined armies. Where they were girls, they became prostitutes. Where they were old, they became beggars, witches or 'pilgrims'. In the late eighteenth century, Madrid convents were giving out 30,000 bowls of soup a day. By that time, with capitals growing, the large class of semi-beggars in so many cities had begun to seem a political, as well as a social, problem. In Madrid, there were numerous riots by 'mobs' in the late eighteenth century. In London at that time, out of a population of nearly a million 115,000 were believed to be 'criminals', though the figure included 50,000 prostitutes. Vast numbers of peasants also were underemployed in the age of agriculture during the winters, as they still are in agricultural countries.

A rough and ready concern for the sick and old marked most peoples. In settled communities, an essential part was the role played by the lord. A typical, if late, feudal provision was that of the Prussian code of 1795: the lord had to see to it that poor peasants were given education; that a livelihood for such of his vassals as had no land was provided; and, if they were reduced to poverty, he had to come to their aid. Cities, of course, had often maintained hospitals. In both Portugal and the Portuguese Empire, the brotherhood of the *Misericordia* assumed numerous spiritual and corporal works, including giving food to the hungry, visiting the sick, burying the dead and so on. In one sense, therefore, here as in other departments, modern nations have simply echoed the behaviour of old cities.

In the countryside, when lords' powers, or other traditional methods, disintegrated, most European communities began to consider laws like those 'Poor Laws' of England established by Tudor monarchs. These laws appointed 'overseers' of the poor charged with levying a poor rate, and making provision for the poor concerned. They destroyed the old system of mutual charity. For the law allowed local authorities to ban alms at the door. The moral duties of householders were henceforth ambiguous. These laws were criticised by continental Catholics, who believed them to be inferior to individual or monastic charity. Nor were continental critics impressed by the provision that English workhouses were later added to the parishes, so that relief could be tied to labour, nor by the melancholy houses of correction (such as Bridewell). Such laws underline some of the resentments which still deface English society. Even so, the English rules provide an interesting general indication of the world's preoccupations. In 1782 a special Act empowered parishes to give 'out-relief' (relief in the form of money given at home) to the 'able-bodied but deserving' poor. Workhouses would be reserved for the old, the crippled and children. Parish officers were enabled to seek work on behalf of the poor in farms and, if wages offered were inadequate, to supplement them. In 1795 another English Act limited expulsions to those who were without means. The same year, a famous meeting was held by the magistrates of Berkshire at the Pelican Inn, Speenhamland, to discuss the increasing pauperism, which seemed to be the consequence of the rising prices of food, itself caused by the rise of population. The magistrates were afraid of revolution in the French style. They decided to help the poor in proportion to bread prices: 'When the gallon loaf of flour . . . cost 1 shilling, every poor and industrious man will have three shillings supplementary weekly and one shilling and sixpence for each of his family.'

A generation later, a new Poor Law in 1834 in Britain established that in every specially prescribed district there should be one workhouse each for children, men, women, and the aged. The aim was to make public charity so disagreeable a deterrent

that any self-respecting person would prefer the meanest independent labour. Still in 1850 about a million people in England were
on relief of one sort or another. All trades were subject to recur-
rent unemployment or underemployment, though, of the larger
trades, only hand-loom weaving had a big permanently redundant
labour force over many years. Was this a 'reserve army of labour',
as Karl Marx thought, to be used to batter down the pay of the
regular troops? Sir John Clapham gives a moderate answer: the
reserve was never strong enough to do all the evils credited to it;
even in weaving, the 'reserve army' did not prevent the steady, if
slow, rise in the power-loom weavers' wages.

At that time, there were numerous schemes for 'self-help' in
most countries. Again, England provides good examples. In the
eighteenth century, as has been noticed, innumerable friendly
societies were established. Many derived from guilds, and provided for relief of sickness and old age. In 1786 John Acland
devised a National Friendly Society, which proposed a contribu-
tory age pension scheme. Nothing came of that. In Germany,
Bismarck, after the unification of the country, began for the first
time to introduce laws which made of the state the supreme
friendly society – with innumerable and fateful consequences.
Regulations were introduced in 1883–85 which provided Germans
with insurance against sickness and accidents. Laws to insure
against old age followed in 1889. Employers, workpeople and the
state all contributed, by a series of intricate provisions (including
the subsequently general use of stamps and cards). These ensured
a modest average pension in old age to all except casual labourers
and wilfully unemployed. Bismarck knew that insurance against
unemployment would be the form of social insurance which German wage earners would like best. But he did not do anything to
that end.

In England, there was much discussion on this matter. Joseph
Chamberlain believed in such legislation, but it was his opponents,
the Liberals, who took the initiative. From 1908 in England every
person not a criminal, or one who had failed to work 'according
to his ability or opportunity, or need', would receive a small
pension at seventy-nine if his income were not above a certain
amount. Embellishments were subsequently introduced. Bismarck's methods, as amended in New Zealand, were imported
for the payment of these pensions (contributions by three parties;
cards; and stamps). Similar schemes for accident, illness and even
unemployment (for which there was still no precedent) were in-

troduced in 1911. A chain of labour exchanges was established throughout the nation in order to administer the arrangements.* These plans worried some reformers. Thus Beatrice and Sidney Webb wrote: 'The fact that the unemployed . . . were entitled to money incomes without any corresponding obligation to get well and keep well, or to seek and keep employment, seemed to us as likely to encourage malingering and a disinclination to work.' Despite such authoritative scepticism, and grumbling about the contributions from the workers that the scheme required, these acts, subsequently to be even more generous, have hence constituted the basis of legislation on welfare in all countries.

During the course of the twentieth century, in Europe and the advanced industrial countries, poverty has changed radically. About 1900 a careful investigator in York, for example, found that 28 per cent of the population were living on incomes insufficient to obtain the minimum food necessary for the maintenance of mere physical efficiency. In 1936, in the same place, he went back and thought that 31 per cent of the population were still in poverty. Using what he considered a better method of analysis, he believed his figure for 1900 should have been 43 per cent. But in 1961 another investigation showed that 3 per cent only of the population of York were destitute. Even if that were an under-estimate for Britain as a whole, it is an appropriate measure of the changes which have characterised a typical industrial country. In 1900 the poor were so because they were paid low wages. In 1936 they were so because they were unemployed. In 1961 the explanation was their age. In the past, riches seemed a scandal in the face of poverty. Now poverty seems a scandal in the face of riches.

A combination of welfare schemes, industrial development and imaginative commerce has meant that this kind of percentage of poverty is a global figure also. The Brandt Report[1] of 1980 estimated that about 600 million or fifteen per cent of the world total population is now seriously impoverished. This is the kind of percentage which characterised Britain in, say, 1935. It seems possible that another generation of inspired development might bring the percentage of the world's poverty down to a really modest figure.

---

* The first unemployment relief was a weekly payment of seven shillings to men in engineering trades, six shillings in the building trades. The payment would begin in the second week of unemployment and last for fifteen weeks.

Some other changes during the twentieth century in respect of poverty were: first, paupers in 1900 were as short-lived as the population had been in 1688 – an average age of thirty – and all working people, even if themselves above the poverty line, had seen poverty close. That is now far from the case in half the world. Second, there have been occasions when popular leaders have reinforced their appeal by saying that they could provide work for millions of unemployed because of the closure of factories or the collapse of exports. The Nazi Hitler and the Democrat Roosevelt, in Germany and the US respectively, were good examples of this. The Nazis' labour front, with their '*Strength through Joy*' holiday camps and cheap cruises, made the regime popular despite the control of labour that it insisted upon. Equally, between 1934 and 1939 huge sums ($14,000 million) were spent on unemployment relief in the US. A third change has been the effect on employment caused by trade unions and the state. Unions have ensured that dismissals are difficult, even impossible. Protection against competition in the labour market created a gulf between those who, in private enterprise or in public, hold an employment and those who, through age or bad luck, have none.

Fourth, all countries outside Europe and North America are the victims of seasonal fluctuation in employment as great as in the age of agriculture. For example, Cuba in the mid 1950s might have an average unemployment of 20·7 per cent from August to October. It would drop to 9 per cent during the sugar harvest. Where people have been unemployed for a long time, initiative dries and they succumb to an inertia which is hard to break away from. 'Job creation' has in the last few years been a preoccupation of all democratic governments; but it is almost always a delusion, since it depends on taxation drawn from genuine or successful employers. Another change has been the increase of secondary benefits to anyone, in any form of employment. The car company Fiat in Italy estimates that every worker who takes home $73 a month costs Fiat $305 in social facilities and arrangements at the factory.

The character of work in rich countries in the twentieth century is utterly different from that which pertains in agricultural countries and which used to pertain in all countries before industrialisation. Yet the received view of what work means in, say, the US today is false. Thus one expert recently wrote: 'of all people who work in the course of a year almost 45 per cent are employed less than full time . . . 55 per cent only fit the stereotype of the conventional worker and 30 per cent of all work is performed by those who are not full-time workers'[2]. Willynilly, the US is likely to dictate the pattern of behaviour elsewhere.

48
Growth and Grossness of the Modern State

[The Webbs] pursued methodically and fanatically the end they had proposed to themselves, to transform the old England of individualism and laissez-faire into an England organised from above.

Elie Halévy,
A History of England in the Nineteenth Century, Vol. VI

All Russian populists were agreed that the state was the embodiment of a system of coercion and inequality and therefore intrinsically evil. . .

Isaiah Berlin, 'Russian Populism', in *Russian Thinkers*

The role of the state can never be spelled out once and for all in terms of specific functions . . . because each day brings new opportunities and circumstances. Government may enable us at times to accomplish jointly what we would find it more difficult to accomplish severally but any such use of government is fraught with danger.

Milton Friedman, *Capitalism and Freedom*

Many practitioners of politics are reluctant to think carefully what should be the role of the state. 'The State is the nation in its collective and corporative character,' wrote Matthew Arnold in *Culture and Anarchy*, 'entrusted with stringent powers for the general advantage, and controlling individual wills in the name of an interest wider than that of the sum of individuals.' 'General advantage': are we sure of it? And what is that mysterious interest 'wider than that of the sum of individuals'? Does not that need very precise definition? 'Society is a garden . . . in continuous need of being tended by wise gardeners lest it be overrun by weeds and pests,' wrote a nineteenth-century Tory radical, Richard Oastler. But what is a weed, socially speaking? Such questions are important to answer intelligently now, when through the capacity of technology a state can make itself artificially more powerful than any of its predecessors. In 1978 the proposal for a 'national data centre', linking together the 11,000 computers working in the US government, was rejected in the name of liberty. We cannot be certain that all countries will do the same if they have the chance.

The relation between nation and state is elusive. If the state seeks to absorb, or become co-terminous with, the nation, the nation recedes, becomes elusive and even hides its identity. An over-active state loses the respect of the nation. That occurred in the later Roman Empire when the state, before it fell, became the largest landed proprietor, the greatest industrialist and the biggest owner of mines and quarries.* But it had long ceased to be respected. In modern times, patriotism has also declined in inverse proportion to the growth of state power. In the eighteenth century Britain had the weakest executive in any country in Europe; but it was the most respected state. When people said, at that time, that they believed England to be a free country what they meant was that it was a country of voluntary obedience and one with a social organisation freely initiated and freely accepted[1].

The character of a state can best be judged by an evaluation of how its civil servants behave. Three things mark the development of bureaucracies since the age of agriculture. First, they have increased in number: Britain had barely 2,000 men in the entire central government in the middle of the eighteenth century, inclusive of sinecures. By 1798 the figure had risen to 16,267 and by 1815 to 25,000; in 1901 the British civil service numbered 116,413 and in 1911, 162,000. By 1980 it employed over 700,000 central government employees and taking into account the armed services, local government, the health services and the education services, employed over thirty per cent of the British labour force[2]. One worker in four depends on the state in the US. Similar figures can be found for many other countries.†

* In the 1926 edition of his famous *Social and Economic History of Rome*, Rostovtzeff argued that the Roman bourgeoisie was weakened by state intervention, peasant revolts and barbarian attacks, just as the Hellenistic bourgeoisie had been weakened by state intervention and Roman attacks. But in the *Economic History Review* in 1930 Rostovtzeff suggested that state intervention was the main, even the only, cause of Roman decline.

† Public-sector employment as a percentage of civilian labour force:

Country	1950	1960	1970	Estimated 1980
Belgium	5·4	6·2	8·5	10·4
France	6·5	9·3	11·4	13·4
W. Germany	n.a.	6·6	8·8	11·5
Italy‡	n.a.	n.a.	11·5	15·6
Britain	12·1	12·6	16·4	20·7
USA	8·7	10·9	14·1	15·3
Japan	n.a.	3·1	3·1	n.a.

‡ Includes regular armed forces.

Yet the Roman Empire at its most flamboyant in the fourth century AD employed only 40,000 civil servants. The increase of civil servants in Spain in the seventeenth century has been regarded by many historians as a cause of its decay: 'Huge sectors were converted from activity to inactivity,' writes Vicens Vives, 'at the cost of productive work'[3]. There were then 150,000 government servants in the country, in a population of ten million.

Beyond most modern bureaucracies in the West, the shade of Rome can be seen. Diocletian's hundred provinces, with their civil and military commands, their city councils and bureaucracies, their judges of first instance and of appeal, their prefects in charge of roads and of sewerage, their urban cohorts and their postal services, form the foundations of the way that our states are managed just as Athens gave the inspiration for our ideals. Equally, behind the vast bureaucracies of Communist China we see the ghost of the old imperial army of 40,000 higher civil servants, 1,200,000 clerks and over 500,000 runners – the product of the Emperor T'ai Tsung's reforms of the early seventh century.

Today, in almost every country, even in every democracy, civil services appear to be vast, uncontrollable organisations without peers. In the past the state was one among a group of institutions to which individuals were loyal. Indeed, a man's loyalty to a great household was, till the sixteenth or seventeenth century in Europe, greater than it was to the state. That has been the case in many countries of Latin America or Asia till recently and is still so in a few. Now bureaucracies give to secular states the support which the Church gave the old system. Nearly all those states which, in the eighteenth century, had the beginnings of a powerful civil service have descendants of them still despite intellectual *mésalliances* (Russia, the Spanish Empire, China, France, Austria-Hungary), sometimes serving a Communist regime, sometimes a democratic president, but all, as a rule, accustomed to intervene in the economic lives of their peoples, usually confidently, often arrogantly, even instinctively.

The exception to this is Germany, whose old system, based on loyalty to the Prussian state, was broken in 1945, and whose subsequent history in Western Europe has come to be constructed on the basis of hostility to hierarchy. In the past a great part of the civil life of Germany was organised from the top. That was one of the reasons for Germany's 'grab for world power', in the phrase of Fritz Fischer. The failure of that 'adventure' led to a strict reversal, at least in West Germany, of the nation's hierarchical arrangements: the only occasion that such a thing has occurred recently.

Bureaucracy exercises such charm over people in search of a competence as to raise a question about their loyalty to ideologies. Could it be that Professor Are of Pisa is correct in suggesting that even the Italian Communist party is interested less in Marx than in letting its friends have a share in the proceeds of bureaucracy[4]? Is it possible that, in that beleaguered society, the Communists have no desire to dismantle the system of economic patronage and political interference built up by the Christian Democrats? In South America, caudillos have behaved primarily as distributors of patronage and benefactions. Independence there inspired the birth of a growth of bureaucrats whom even Bolívar regarded as parasites before the revolution which he planned was complete. 'I can still hear Sidney Webb explaining to me,' wrote Elie Halévy, 'that the future belonged to the great administrative nations, where the officials govern, and the police keep order'[5]. 'The individual ant functions only as part of the ant state,' Burckhardt put it, recalling that insect societies seem 'far more perfect than the human state'[6]. Max Weber reflected: 'It is horrible to think that the world could one day be filled with nothing but those little cogs, little men clinging to little jobs', for that would spell a 'bureaucratisation of the spirit' without precedent[7].

The growth of centralisation has been the second characteristic of the history of bureaucracy – again even in democracies, and indeed in federal democracies. Despite the realisation that centralisation was slow death in such an empire as the Ottoman, it has increased. Wars, revolution and conquests have all promoted it. Centralisation of administration enervates as much as centralisation of government fortifies, a fact confused by people as various as Machiavelli, Bentham, Hobbes, Rousseau, even Marx, who believed that progress meant an escape from localism.

Regulations, of course, are not new. Any mediaeval code contains a number of royal decrees whereby manufacturers, for example, were constrained. In the eighteenth century, innumerable forms circulated in France, with blanks to be filled in by individuals, about the nature of the soil, the means of its cultivation, the livestock and the crops: 'We find the state constantly coming already to the rescue of individuals, in difficulties,' wrote Tocqueville; 'lavish of promises and subsidies . . . and, as there was no danger of publicity, no one felt any qualms about informing it about his personal troubles'[8]. Nevertheless, there was a time, in the nineteenth century, when rules were becoming fewer. In 1791, for example, every French cultivator was allowed to store grain exactly as he wished for the first time. Jeremy Bentham, the reformer who inspired so much institutional change throughout the world in the nineteenth century, believed all government to be one vast evil. He advocated handing over the poor law to a national charity company, and assumed that powerful governments would inevitably be corrupt and inefficient. He suggested that civil servants should tender against each other for those jobs which even he admitted that they should carry out, so that the state would find out which of them would do the work cheapest. Bentham also looked quizzically at laws on apprenticeships, on how things should be measured or made, on sizes and weights, even on those fixing the weight of a loaf of bread in relation to the price of grain, as at the, by then, mostly evaded laws on usury. Even in Germany at that time there were some signs of criticism of the state: 'No other state has ever been administered so much like a factory as Prussia since the death of Frederick William,' complained the poet Novalis, in 1798[9]. Wilhelm von Humboldt, who in the end confirmed the control of education for the state, wrote, in his *Limits of State Action*, that the operation of government ought to be severely limited to what directly and immediately relates to the security of person and property. In France, Ernest Renan believed liberty to be definable as non-intervention by the state, though admitting that 'the very means to remove that idea to an indefinite distance would be precisely that state's withdrawing its action too soon'. Since the middle of the nineteenth century, however, the tendency has been for states to have larger pretensions. But on what principle? Not necessarily that of socialism. Once it is admitted that the state has a role in the economy, it is impossible to decide where that role should end. 'On what principle shall railway rates be controlled? Is the traveller, or sender of goods and messages, to be served at the expense of the same public as the tax payer? Shall one form of transport in the hands of the state subsidise another? In the absence of the vulgar book-keeping test of profit, how shall the utility and efficiency of government enterprises be decided?' All those questions put by Sir John Clapham in the 1930s in his economic history of the nineteenth century are as inadequately resolved now as ever they were. Russia in 1906, for example, was able to persuade herself that 'years of government railway construction began to pay off'. Her strategic railway in 1914 could send a hundred divisions to war within eighteen days. But that meant that one, military, view of what the state should be doing had triumphed, and others (that the state should collect money to provide schools, or that the state should collect less money) had not been successfully put. The problems which might follow from nationalisation were appreciated by some socialists before 1914. Thus a trade union congress in England, in 1913, expressed 'the opinion that the nationalisation of public services such as the Post Office is not necessarily advantageous to the employees and the working class, unless accompanied by a steadily increasing democratic control'.

It seems likely that, if democracy is to be preserved, together with the values of localism and regionalism, the habits of decentralisation, and voluntary, rather than state-sponsored, association, all small-scale operations and commercial endeavour need to be revived.

On these matters, Burke and Kropotkin, Proudhon and Tocqueville, as well as other nineteenth-century political critics of the new state such as Coleridge and Bakunin, conservatives and anarchists, see eye to eye, though the grand error of Bakunin – as of Marx – was to suppose that, in ideal circumstances, the power of the state should 'wither away': a clear indication that those prophets never 'grasped the paradox of freedom', as Karl Popper put it, namely 'that state power is the guarantee of freedom', and that only in law can liberty be obtained.

49

Groaning under Taxes

> My dear departed friend, whose loss is even greater to the public than to me, had often remarked that the leading vice of the French monarchy . . . was in good intention ill directed and a restless desire of governing too much. The hand of authority was seen in everything and in every place . . . and as it always happens in this kind of officious universal interference, what began in odious power ended always, I may say without an exception, in contemptible imbecility.

> Edmund Burke, *Thoughts and Details on Scarcity* (1795)

In the eighteenth century all sovereign states already had elaborate fiscal systems. Some taxes stretched back hundreds of years. A typical tax was that on sheep. When the idea of wandering herds of sheep escorted by herdsmen had become accepted, the fiscal possibilities seemed alluring, both for localities and for national governments. Towns assessed the damage caused. The subsequent fines became taxes. Such taxes were paid in southern Italy in the time of Caesar. In the pastoral hinterlands of Morocco and Tunis, municipalities in the twentieth century still exact from migrating flocks a toll of one sheep for every hundred. The eighteenth century also had developed the idea of taxes on sales, on heads of families and, above all, tolls and customs. Monarchies still also had recourse to loans, including forced loans to pay for wars (a wealth tax of three per cent of entailed capital was raised in this way by the Crown of Spain in 1795). The diversity of ways in which governments raised money in the past was as ingenious as it is in the present. In 1798, for example, municipalities which rented Spanish buildings to private individuals were ordered to sell them to the individuals concerned. The proceeds were to go to the Crown. There were intimidatory requests for gifts, sales of titles, offices, and taxes on servants, horses and carriages, shops and inns, windows and sales. Sometimes taxes were designed to favour domestic industries. Usually they were specific recourses to raise money to serve the state undertakings of which war and the servicing of debts were the most important.* Collection of taxes by tax farming continued because of bad communications. Most governments had property of their own: saltbeds, mines, tunny fisheries, farms, vineyards, and most monarchs depended on those considerably.

In the course of the nineteenth century these taxes were everywhere formalised, 'modernised' and simplified. There was in most countries a movement towards tax on incomes and death duties as the simplest methods of collecting what was needed.

Income tax was invented in Tuscany in the early fifteenth century, echoing certain Roman practices. It was not regularly used until after the beginning of the nineteenth century. During the Napoleonic Wars, income tax was introduced temporarily in England but subsequently abandoned. Nevertheless that first tax introduced to bring the revenue to win the war had within it the familiar graduated element.† In the 1840s in England, Sir Robert Peel appealed for sevenpence in the pound on all incomes over £150 for three years, in 1845, and from then on a modest tax on incomes constituted the basis of finances in England till 1914. Gladstone tried to use the abolition of income tax as a vote winner in 1874 but he failed, though in 1887 he was still denouncing income tax as 'the most demoralising of all taxes', and 'an engine of public extravagance'. John Stuart Mill had thought income tax unworkable because of the low state of public morality but, from the end of the nineteenth century, it has never ceased to grow. By 1906, however, the full tax was only paid on incomes over £700 and even then was only five per cent.‡ Even when Lloyd George in his budget of 1909 made income tax the 'sheet anchor' of British finance, it remained at a maximum of one shilling and sevenpence in the pound for incomes over £18,000.

Here the First World War, in taxation as in other matters, ended an era; people were cajoled by patriotism into paying in England (and, equivalently, in other countries) an income tax of six shillings in the pound and a supertax too. Sir John Clapham,

* The total expenditure of Britain in 1828 was £56 million of which £16 million went to the army and navy; £7 million went to the civil list, bounties and occasional expenditure; £29 million went to collection of revenue. The revenue derived from £36 million customs and excise; £13 million other taxes; and £7 million probate registry.
† It did not affect incomes below £60 and became gradually higher till it reached ten per cent on incomes over £200.
‡ A shilling in the pound.

England's best economic historian, wrote: 'Seldom had there been such tax-paying, or more smoothly working machinery, for the transfer of wealth from the purposes of peace to those of war; and, when the war was over, from class to class'[1]. Since then, taxation has ceased to be simply a source of revenue and become, instead, an instrument of social justice, welfare and economic management.

The part played by excessive taxation in causing the fall of Rome has been discussed. 'The last straw,' wrote C. R. Boxer, of the quarrel between Spain and the Netherlands in the 1570s, 'was the threatened imposition of a sales tax called the Tenth Penny, modelled on the Spanish *alcabala* which [the Duke of] Alva began to impose in 1572.' The English Civil War of the seventeenth century broke out over the government's demand for 'ship money', from which the King hoped to restore the Navy. The revolt of Rio de Janeiro in 1660, the first great revolt of settlers in the New World against European masters, was a protest against a poll tax imposed to build a big ship. The first upheavals of the industrial age, the revolution in the US in the 1770s and that in France in 1789, were both inspired by complaints about taxes: the Stamp Act passed in London in 1765 was the prologue to the American Revolution as surely as was the Finance Minister, Jacques Necker's, attempt to regularise the French system the same to the revolution in 1789. The American Revolution was a tax revolt before it became a war of independence, for the colonists did not only criticise taxation without representation; they did not want taxes at all. In the years since 1945 other tax revolts have spluttered. Perhaps reductions in taxes will be a way of limiting the bureaucracies of Western democracies. 'Proposition 13', adopted in the US in California in 1978, may point the way to new liberalism. Meantime, most democracies are managing their fiscal affairs badly. When taxes are too high, peoples usually devise a dishonest means of evading them. It is said that in Russia, for example, in the late 1970s the 'parallel economy' may account for twenty per cent of the national income. Some have suggested that the British figure may approach that. No wonder governments find it hard to devise effective policies on incomes. The 'psychosis of fraud' which characterised the Spanish-American transatlantic trade, the Portuguese gold trade from Brazil and, indeed, all the seaborne trade of the maritime and colonial powers has been transformed to modern taxes. Smuggling's grandson is tax evasion and it affects democracies and despotisms alike.

Four things need to be said, in conclusion, about the modern state: first, history suggests that the reason for national decline is, as a rule, that the state in the nation concerned has sought to do too much, not too little; that applies as much to the Roman Empire as to the Spanish; second, though the state should seek to provide security, it must also seek to avoid stifling the desire for opportunity and responsibility; third, that centres of power and influence, both public and private, should be diffused so far as is possible throughout the community; fourth, reformers need to bear in mind that the concentration of power in the state places an ever increasing power of patronage in the hands of those who manage it. The only appropriate way to change these arrangements for the better must be to dismantle the state's overweighty pretensions. The state can call on the loyalty of free individuals just as easily as it can on its own servants. Local leaders of communities will flourish in proportion to the extent that they are free of national supervision and interference. Gabriel Hanotaux, in his famous life of Richelieu, praised that statesman as a 'precursor of democracy', since he abolished 'the intermediate powers which imposed themselves dangerously between king and people'. We should now prefer Tocqueville's insistence that those same 'intermediate' authorities, however ancient or apparently illogical, often constitute the real foundations of freedom.

50
Population's Great Leap

Observation tells us that none of the states which have a reputation for being well governed are without some limit of population.

Aristotle, *Politics*

The rural population is a magazine from which the forces of declining mankind are always recruited and refreshed.

Goethe, *Conversations with Eckermann*

The world's population in 1980 was 4·2 billion (4,200 million). The high rate of growth of the years 1960–73 has declined. The world's increase in growth of population came to an end at an unnoticed but momentous turning point between 1960 and 1964. The world's growth rate per year was 1·7 per cent in 1980. In AD 2000 the world's population may be somewhere between 5·8 billion and 6·6 billion with a rate of increase somewhere below 1·6 per cent. The rich countries are now experiencing a decline in fertility, but the diminution in the growth is modest: the growth of population in the seventeenth and early eighteenth centuries was only 0·013 per cent a year, and the 'high growth rate' after 1740 was still only 0·456 per cent. Even so, certain countries may feel threatened in future by shortages, rather than excesses, of population. The German population is apparently in decline and most European ones are static, on both sides of the Iron Curtain. At least one major European political party, the Gaullists, has a conscious policy for encouraging population. Indeed, the French government has tried to encourage the growth of population since 1870, under the Third, Fourth and Fifth republics, a policy upon which, as upon other things, de Gaulle and Pétain saw eye to eye. Michel Debré, a sometime prime minister of France, has proposed a family vote which would give parents an additional vote for each child under voting age. Many Eastern European countries have tried unsuccessfully, it seems, to increase birth rates by financial incentives, as well as by laws forbidding abortion.

A popular prophet, Herman Kahn, has suggested that the population of the world will 'stabilise' between ten and fifty billion.

Colin McEvedy and Richard Jones, in their *Atlas Of World Population History*, make a plausible case for eight or nine billion. At least as good a prediction of stability to come might, however, have been made that the world would have 500 million people at any time between the birth of Christ and AD 1500. A decrease or involuntary stabilisation may occur, before even the figure of six billion is reached. The fall of the population of Germany, both West and East, and in Austria, suggests that political systems make less difference, so far as population is concerned, than do national disasters. A generation ago Germany's anxiety about room to live, *Lebensraum*, was greater than similar ideas felt anywhere else, and had an influence on bringing just such disasters to Germany. Most of the world's richer countries seem to be making their way towards that condition, for in them there has been a decline in the rate of births since about 1880, save for exceptional eras such as the 'baby boom' immediately after the Second World War. One explanation for this change may have been a change in the economic value of children, from being a source of income in agricultural countries to an expense in industrial ones. The economic transformation of these countries also has been accompanied by universal education, and an approach to equality of women.

Another explanation of the change in the pattern of births in rich countries is that until the twentieth century, indeed until the 1970s in some countries, there was always a possibility of emigration. The era of colonisation and adventure-seeking which began in Europe in the sixteenth century came to a head in the early twentieth century (in 1910 a quarter of the population of the USA had been born outside that country). That era has now ended.

Until recently, the encouragement of emigration was the most effective policy towards population. Greek colonisation in the fifth century BC; the German expansion east, beginning in the eleventh century AD; the settlement of Castile at the same time; those were responses to the pressure of population, though some of the more famous emigrations derived from deliberate policies towards minorities; for example, the departure of 200,000 Jews from Spain in the fifteenth century. 300,000 Moors also left Spain in the sixteenth century and 200,000 Huguenots left France in the seventeenth.

Emigration to the Americas stands apart from all others. Though only 100,000 Spaniards went there in the sixteenth century (less than the number of Frenchmen who emigrated to Spain at that time), and only 750,000 Europeans of all nations went to the Americas in the seventeenth and eighteenth centuries, about nine million or more Africans arrived as slaves between 1492 and 1870. The Europeans who emigrated in the nineteenth and twentieth centuries exceed all precedents: seventeen million left Britain between 1825 and 1920 (65 per cent to the US, 15 per cent to Canada, 11 per cent to Australia – 162,000 as convicts – and 5 per cent to South Africa). Nine million left Italy between 1875 and 1925 (though some returned about 1910 to revive the Italian south). Six million Germans, four million Austro-Hungarians, two and a half million Russians, four million Spaniards and over a million Portuguese all left Europe for new worlds. Only the French stayed at home, and received immigrants, mostly on a short-term basis, including Belgians to work in sugarbeet fields and 'child-rich' Poles to work in mines. Thus the New World and, even more completely, Australasia were confirmed for the Europeans. Not only North America beckoned: vast numbers, particularly Italians, went to Brazil – 60,000 to São Paulo alone – to transform the ethnic and social structure of the country.

During the 1920s these places of refuge or opportunity largely vanished. A generation previously, the US had encouraged immigration. Until 1880 there was always unappropriated land, somewhere, for whoever wanted it. Then, in the 1880s, came the first restrictions: a ban on Chinese immigration in 1882 and on contract labour in 1885. Then, with two laws, of 1921 and 1924, the US restricted immigration in proportion to the nations already represented in the US since 1910 and then since 1890. Total immigration was restricted to 150,000 annually. Britain had a right to forty-three per cent and Poland to only four per cent of immigrants. The US laws derived from: fear of unemployment; criticism of those born in, or descended from those born in, Germany during the First World War; and dread that the old US institutions would be ruined by too many Jews and Central Europeans. These laws shattered the dynamism of old America, which had been built on the idea of ceaseless immigration and expansion. The slave trade from Africa to the Americas had also come to an end, for reasons in which economic and moral calculations were balanced. Subsequent laws have altered the character of such immigration as has been permitted. 200,000 'displaced' persons (mostly Germans expelled from East Europe by Russia) were permitted entry to the US in 1948. A law of 1965 fixed the annual quota at 170,000, with no national subdivisions, and allowing specially qualified people – along with 120,000 from the rest of the Americas – beyond the limits. Catastrophes, such as the Cuban revolution of 1959 or the Hungarian revolution of 1956, caused other large immigrations. All in all, sixteen million Germans were expelled from Eastern Europe in 1945–48, while the 500,000 Cubans who left home between 1959 and 1980 were more than those who emigrated there from Spain between 1511 and 1898. Indeed more Cubans fled from their homeland in the course of 1980 than Spaniards emigrated to Cuba in the first two hundred years of the island as a colony.

The legal but large-scale emigration of unskilled and apolitical poor is now at an end for good, never to be repeated, unless, improbably, some new place really offers an attractive haven.

On the other hand, illegal immigration from poor to rich countries seems likely to be one of the major concerns of the future – particularly in the US, but also Venezuela, Italy, Britain, Germany: anywhere where there is a free economy, an easily learned language and a liberal society. The 'undocumented' already constitute a submerged proletariat in rich nations. But the world's attitude to the problem of refugees from political oppression, or the threat of it, may be altered by the vast upheavals caused by the collapse of traditional society in Indo-China: a tragedy too close to current politics to consider with serenity in this book, but one which destroys any illusions that mass movements of population are over.

The second determining fact limiting the growth of population has been the coming of birth control. The idea had been discussed before industrialisation. But first we should notice the Reverend Thomas Malthus. Son of a believer in the perfectibility of man who had been a correspondent of Rousseau's, Malthus became a fellow of Jesus College, Cambridge. In his *Essay on Population*, published in 1798, Malthus argued that, while the supply of food increases in an arithmetical ratio, population does so in a geometric one. Population could only be checked, he believed, by vice or by misery. In a later edition of his book in 1803, he also recognised 'the prudential check' of self-restraint.

This work was much read. When it was translated into German, a certain Professor Weinhold was so alarmed that he suggested a chastity belt should be forcibly applied to all unmarried males who did not have the means to support children. Another German, Robert Mohl, proposed that all states should repeal measures which encouraged early marriage, and embark on propa-

ganda on the subject of prudence. Malthus, meantime, was critical
of contraception: 'I should always particularly reprobate any artificial and unnatural modes of checking the population, both on
account of their immorality and their tendency to remove a necessary stimulus to industry.' But the industrious radical Francis Place,
a tailor with fifteen children, soon suggested that methods of
control were necessary, since moral restraint seemed inadequate.
Nothing happened. Nineteenth-century Europe experienced the
greatest increase in population that it has ever known.

The main argument in Malthus's book, since that time, has
been disproved by events. 'There has only been one man too
many on this earth,' said Proudhon, 'and that man was Malthus.'
The conservative economist Nassau Senior pointed out in 1828
that 'food always increased faster than population. I admit the
abstract tendency of population to increase so as to press on the
means of subsistence. I deny the *habitual* tendency. I believe the
tendency to be the reverse'[1]. So it has turned out: in the 1970s,
food increased by thirty million tons a year. Of these, twenty-two
million only are taken up by the growth of population. The fifty-
seven million inhabitants of Britain of 1980 are better fed than
the eleven million of 1798.

Some claim to be influenced upon these matters by Karl Marx,
whose views on population are, however, inconsistent. At one
point in *Kapital* he argued that 'misery produced population'[2]. At
another, he said, 'population is stagnant when the working day is
very long'. But the increase of population was marked in Marx's
day – above all, in the countries where he was born (Germany)
and where he lived most of his life (England). Marx was born in
1818 and died in 1883. The population of Germany between those
dates rose from about twenty-five million to sixty million. That of
Britain increased from twenty million to forty, without counting
the millions who emigrated in 'almost epidemic proportions'[3].

In both those countries, actually, the rate of growth of population slowed as the working day became shorter: the contrary to
what Marx foresaw. If industrialisation had been as evil as Marx
implied, the demographic 'explosion' would scarcely have happened. At the time of the Napoleonic Wars also, English cotton
manufacturers employed only two per cent of the labour force.
The industrialised villages to which Marx paid such attention also
showed a greater excess of births than did agricultural villages.

As opposed to the muddled preaching by both Marx and Malthus, Annie Besant, daughter of an Irish businessman and the

separated wife of a clergyman, with Charles Bradlaugh, a republican and atheist, tried in 1876 to redistribute an old pamphlet on birth control. They were charged with publishing obscene literature, tried and found guilty, but the sentence was eventually quashed on a technical point. That verdict gave impetus to the idea of education about control of births. By the 1920s there was a national movement under way in England under the inspiration of Marie Stopes, a lecturer in palaeo-botany at University College, London. By 1930 clinics had been set up for the planning of families. A role similar to that of Marie Stopes was played in the USA by Margaret Sanger, a midwife in New York, where her clients were trying incompetently to discover a means of spacing out their children. She travelled to France, gained there some understanding of such matters, and founded a clinic in New York for advice on the control of births, in 1916. She was persecuted, but in 1937 laws banning the sale of methods for the control of births were abrogated. Contraception began to be studied in medical schools. The vulcanisation of rubber soon made possible new methods of contraception. In the 1950s Dr Gregory Pincus, a professor at Boston University, began to develop his pill which prevents ovulation and it came to be used on a mass scale in the 1960s.

Because of the 'pill' and other methods, people can, technically at least, now make love without fear of conception. Along with the prevention of widespread outlets for legal emigration, this has been one of the decisive changes in history. The technology of birth control is still imperfect but richer countries are fast approaching 'the "perfect" contraceptive society in which there will be no unwanted births'[4]. Meantime, as a result, the number of marriages has declined in richer countries, particularly of women who marry young. Partly this is a reflection of couples living together without (or before) marriage. In 1976 a million couples in the US, or two per cent of all couples, were believed to be unmarried, while in Sweden that percentage may be as high as twelve per cent.

A third factor bearing on population in the twentieth century is the increasing number of women in 'prime childbearing years' who are working. The change here has been recent: less than two-fifths of women of that age were working in 1960 in the US. Three-fifths were working in 1977. Other countries are far behind this proportion. Most women in rich countries earn about sixty per cent as much as the average man earns. Plainly, the old purpose of marriage by which a woman offers her childbearing and domestic services in return for economic security is being transformed.

All these innovations in the control of birth were introduced, in the first place, as a result of private initiative, against the desires of governments. Plato would have regarded Annie Besant highly. Gladstone, though educated on the classics, abhorred her. Since 1945 only Japan, after her defeat in 1945 (which showed that any further expansion of population would be difficult), has, among free countries, successfully launched a government-sponsored eugenic programme. The discipline of the Japanese people, the hierarchic character of the society, the elevation of the idea of work above the idea of family, as well as the memory of defeat and the existence of a large market of 110 million people, have combined to make possible a humane policy on the subject of population. In some years as many as eighty per cent of pregnancies in Japan were aborted.

The brutal totalitarian states of the twentieth century also embarked upon policies of population: abortion, contraception, and easy divorce were the three impulses of early Communist attitudes to population. The sexes were announced as equal in law. This careless rapture soon came to an end. In 1936 abortion and contraception were alike forbidden. The old Russian practice prohibiting emigration was reinforced. The free association in Russia of men and women in common-law marriages was no longer recognised. Divorce became harder. Medals were given to mothers of twelve children while paternity summonses were forbidden because of the threat that such things might pose to the family. Since 1945 marriage has become as important a pillar of society in Communist Russia as in any nineteenth-century Russian provincial town.

These changes have been defended on the ground that in the 1920s the priority seemed to be the need to destroy the bourgeois family but that since the 1930s more people have been needed to man the frontiers against fascism and 'imperialism'.

Both Fascist Italy and Nazi Germany had policies for population. In Italy, Mussolini began with a ban on that emigration (except to the Italian colonies) which had relaxed the tensions of liberal Italy. The policy was copied from Russia and was carried out for reasons of prestige. Mussolini's decision merely anticipated the decision taken in the US to limit immigrants. Despite that, Italian legislation was introduced to favour the large family. In

1927 Mussolini launched a campaign for a high birth rate, recalling that the decline of the Roman Empire had been due to a fall in population: Italy's most precious possession, he said, was her 'demographic vitality'. Italy's imperial adventures and her conflicts with the Slavs in the Adriatic could be underpinned by an increase in the numbers of Italians. A generation earlier, in contrast, precursors of fascism, such as Enrico Corradini, thought it desirable to try to find a 'national home' for all Italians who desired to emigrate.

On paper, this programme of Mussolini's was successful. The population of Italy under fascism increased by eighteen per cent, while 'decadent' France, static at about thirty-eight million between 1861 and 1922, still stood at thirty-nine million in 1945. But the rise in the Italian population at this time was due not to an increase in the birth rate (it fell between 1922 and 1944 from 30·8 per thousand to 18·3 per thousand) but to a fall in the death rate made possible by better medicine and better care of babies.

Hitler's Germany learned from Italy, as Italy learned from Russia. The Germans also developed, however, a contradictory attitude towards what, on the one hand, they felt about the size of the population – too large and therefore demanding *Lebensraum* – and their policies on the subject. The Nazi regime in 1933 thus introduced decrees encouraging births, such as loans to young married couples, special allocations to families of five, and the repression of abortion. These latter policies were successful. Unlike what happened in Italy, the birth rate did increase from 14·7 per 1,000 in 1933 to 20·4 in 1939: figures which Germany had exceeded before 1914 and even, to begin with, during the despised years of Weimar, but would never approach again.

One other country under the direction of a determined tyrant has adopted a policy on the subject of population: China. To begin with, Mao Tse-tung followed Marxist orthodoxy: that is, an inactive policy, supposing that an adequate social policy should be able to deal with any conceivable increase in population. In 1953 a movement towards the limitation of births was initiated. In 1957 contraception was allowed, but in 1958 the policy described as 'the great leap forward' in agriculture caused a return to demographic neglect. Afterwards a number of measures were adopted which were designed to limit the population of China. Marriage, for example, is only now officially sanctioned at the age of thirty. As a result of a pill of 'unsurpassed simplicity', the growth of the Chinese population was said to be down to one per cent in many cities and some provinces by 1980. 'Multi-child' taxes have also been introduced. China aims for 'zero growth' by AD 2000, and has insisted upon the control of population in the new constitution.

The growth in the world's population since the eighteenth century has given rise to anxiety that the world is overpopulated. Thus the Western world seems relieved when it hears of measures introduced to reduce the growth of population in China and Japan, or when it hears that German and Russian population rates of growth are falling, or even, as in the case of Germany, falling absolutely. But the record of population projections is not a happy one. It seems likely that by the year AD 2000, though we may still feel alarmed about the overall growth of the world's population, Europeans, North Americans and European Russians will have begun to be more alarmed at the decline in their own fertility.

One solution to this problem might be a policy of encouraging further immigration, as most European countries did in the 1960s and early 1970s. But these immigrants pose social problems. Europeans worried about the future of their national identity, because of a shortage of births, are not likely to interest themselves in recruiting black or brown people to fill the gaps which they detect in their labour force. No country has ever yet chosen immigration for overtly demographic reasons, though it is possible that, in the twenty-first century, with 'zero growth' they will do so. The 'drain' of educated migrants who have left poor countries for rich ones is a foretaste of this. For the Soviet Union there looks like a certainty that Slav workers will decline and have to be replaced by Muslim ones.

Moralists worry more about divorce than they do about population. Here history has a few soothing lessons. At the time when statistics begin to have a basis at all, in the sixteenth and seventeenth centuries, early death meant that few marriages lasted more than fifteen to twenty years. Today even in the US or Sweden (where divorce affects half the marriages) most marriages last longer than that. In the past, as Lawrence Stone points out, marriages were shortened by death, whereas they are today by divorce. Only in the nineteenth century did a combination of a decline in mortality and a respect for the Church's teaching make marriages in Western Europe and North America longer-lasting on average than they have ever been before or since[5]. In 1850 in France, the average marriage lasted twenty-four years.

Further, after a brief period of fashionable unpopularity, the family, though it has scarcely recovered all its old cohesion, is still a very powerful institution, particularly in Latin countries. Emancipation of women, the distinction of business from the family, compulsory education, the flight to distant towns of grown-up children contributed in the 1920s to what appeared to be the 'crisis of the family'. It became fashionable for couples to become engaged without telling their parents. 'Free love' exerted a brief vogue. New constitutions, however, now usually guarantee the 'rights of families'. The universal declaration of human rights of 1948 even asserted the family to be 'natural and fundamental'. Polygamy and concubinage are decreasing, even in Arab countries and in China. In Communist countries, no one has suggested the expensive stratagem of replacing the mother by the state. Juvenile crime has been generally diagnosed, correctly, as deriving from an unsettled family life. In countries which have experienced socialism and those which have not, parents still wish to leave their children their property. All recognise that the family has a part to play in education and 'family allowances' are well established. Despite experiments with communes and 'group living', the family since 1945 has indeed had a new lease of life, because both the television and the telephone, in different ways, keep families closer together, more probably because the state's covetous hands have extended over all other institutions. Tocqueville wisely wrote: 'as long as family feeling is kept alive, the opponent of oppression is never alone'[6].

As people live longer, there has been a cult of youth. Almost all the new radical movements, 'left' or 'right', of the nineteenth and twentieth centuries began, like 'Young Italy', as revolts of youth. Mazzini and his friends, for example, considered men over forty to be too inclined to temporise. The Futurists of pre-1914 Europe believed that parliament should be replaced by 'a committee of twenty specialists none over thirty years old'. When the Nazis entered the Reichstag in large numbers in 1932, the average age of that parliament dropped ten years. Eighty-two per cent of Nazi party members were under forty in 1934. The emphasis on youth characterised Communist movements in the 1920s and 1930s too. One attraction of all these movements was that of an immediate revolution which gave students immediate access to power. But there was also that attraction of the fellowship of struggle, 'the compact columns . . . waving flags, eyes looking straight ahead, the beat of drums and the singing' which, in the words of George Mosse, constituted the appeal of the Hitler youth[7].

Finally, among political movements which have affected population, there has been the women's liberation movement. The movement has been led by determined people. On the face of it, the changes have been less pronounced than seemed likely, despite the achievements of prime ministers in Britain, India, Israel and Ceylon. Women have done heavy work since time immemorial. Women, with children, were decisive in the cotton factories in the Industrial Revolution. Women workers in industry set off the strikes which led to the revolution in Petrograd in 1917. In the upper class in the West women had an inferior status in the past; but the state of affairs among artisans was less clear: women were part for many hundreds of years of the great estate just as if they formed part of the crew of a ship[8]. In the eighteenth century, queens and noblemen had remarkable power: women have never been so powerful in Russia since.

The preparations for allowing women more advantages in public and professional life in democratic countries have had no echo in two-thirds of the world. Islam still recalls the passage in the Koran which states: 'Woman is thy tilth; plough her as thou wilt.' The revival of Islam has meant the end of women's rights in Islamic countries.

Still, the women's movement, which began because of intellectual reasons and not because of women's work in factories, has secured two benefits: the first is that educational opportunity for boys and girls is equal in most countries; the second is that ambitious women can now seek their own fortunes in a limited number of democratic countries without needing a powerful husband or father to help them.

With all these qualifications, the increase in population has been continuous and in many places overwhelming. Since 1750 the population of Europe has gone up from 140 million to 650 million (including Russia-in-Europe); the population of Africa, from say 100 million to 500 million; that of Asia, including Russia-in-Asia, from about 415 million to 2,500 million; the Americas' 17 million in 1750 have risen to 550 million, and even Australasia has increased from under 2 million in 1750 to about 25 million. The Russian population in both Europe and Asia was 50 million in 1750. In 1980 it was 260 million. The global increase has been from 720 million to 4,200 million, a rise of the order of sixfold. Certainly, no such change seems to have occurred before. Obviously, the consequences, political and social, have been remarkable. But what strikes the observer most is that economic and agricultural growth has continued to outstrip the growth of population. The Brandt Report of 1980 suggested that about 600 million people in the world were living in conditions of dire poverty. That is a harsh statistic unless it is realised that that is something like fifteen per cent of the total population of the world: the kind of percentage reckoned as very poor in a rich country like England in 1900. In that year, the world's neglected must have been very much larger.

The statistics indicate after all that on such critical questions as expectations of life and infant mortality recent history has had no precedent for its improvements. The world as a whole had a death rate of 30 to 40 per 1,000 each year in 1750, while today no European country, apart from Albania, has a rate higher than 12·8 per 1,000. China, India and Indonesia have rates of 15, 17 and 20, which are close to Western Europe's rate in 1914. Only Africa has countries with rates over 20 per 1,000.

This naturally brings up the whole matter of medical advances in the industrial civilisation: a subject of importance sufficient to merit a chapter on its own.

Appendix: Turning-points in women's opportunities

The initiative in women's formal political rights was taken in the United States. The states of Wyoming, Colorado, Utah and Idaho enjoyed women's suffrage in 1869, 1893, 1895 and 1896. In England women were permitted to vote for the boards of guardians which administered the poor law in 1834, for municipal councils in 1869, county councils in 1888, and were able to sit on district and parish councils in 1894. New Zealand had women's suffrage in general elections after 1893 and the Australian states of South Australia, Western Australia and New South Wales in 1894, 1899 and 1899 respectively.

Universal suffrage for women was delayed in the US till 1920, in Britain till 1919 (for women over twenty-eight) and 1929 (all adult women), in Spain till 1934, in France till 1944, in Germany till 1918 and in Italy till 1945.

51

The Achievements and Illusions of Medicine

Worth the cost of the war. . .

General Leonard Wood, of the extinction of
yellow fever in Cuba after the Spanish-American War (1898)

1

Industrialisation had profound, lasting and beneficial effects on health and medicine. In the nineteenth century scientifically based medicine transformed health and the expectation of life in the population of rich countries, and subsequently began to do so in poor countries as well. But at the time, and in the places, that scientifically based medicine began to play a part in saving life, the birth rates began to slow down.

Two benefits derive, however, from the eighteenth century. These were, first, the use of mercury, which began to have an appreciable effect on the consequences of syphilis.

The second benefit (and more important than mercury, since syphilis affected fewer people than is often supposed) was inoculation, and then vaccination, against smallpox: an innovation which led to the vast array of preventive injections which characterise modern medicine.

Smallpox is a variety of a mild disease of cattle which appeared in Asia in late classical times. It does not seem to have made much impact in the West till the Renaissance. From then on, in Europe it caused ravages for two centuries. It hit the Americas very hard after the first large epidemic in Santo Domingo in 1519. The disease often affected remote Indian communities before the Europeans arrived.

The Chinese had inoculated themselves against smallpox with a mild dose of the disease since the eleventh century. Perhaps because of a discussion of the subject by the philosopher Li Shih-Chen in the sixteenth century, knowledge of the idea became known in the Middle East by the seventeenth century at least. The idea was brought back to England in 1721 by Lady Mary Wortley Montagu from Constantinople, where her husband was ambassador. Perhaps since inoculation was expensive and risky, it became fashionable. Catherine the Great had herself, and her court, inoculated in 1769. The French began to interest themselves in the technique after Louis XV died of smallpox in 1774. Frederick the Great instructed not only the court but country doctors to take it up. George Washington ordered his army to be inoculated in 1776. Without that order, he might not have won his rebellion against the English.

Twenty years later the English doctor Edward Jenner, in Gloucestershire, became interested in a local belief that milkmaids did not incur smallpox. That turned out to be so. They suffered a milder form, known as cowpox, which they caught from cows. After hesitation, Jenner inoculated a boy with cowpox, which he contracted. When later exposed to smallpox, he did not catch the disease. This use of cowpox marked a decisive change. The commander-in-chief of the British army, the Duke of York, asked Jenner to 'vaccinate' the 85th Regiment of Foot. The plan worked and the Duke of York deserves greater recognition for his farsightedness in that matter than his ill-fame as a commander in Holland gave him. The entire English army was next vaccinated. Napoleon did the same with his forces. The United States took up the idea with enthusiasm. In Spanish America the introduction of vaccine was greeted with fervour: in Caracas, Andrés Bello composed an ode in its honour. By the middle of the nineteenth century, 'vaccination' for all the people, not just those fortunate enough to be able to serve in the army, was compulsory in many countries. By the twentieth century, smallpox was almost eradicated. In 1976 it was reputed to be making its last stand in the southern deserts of Ethiopia. A formal declaration that smallpox had been eradicated was made in 1980.

Mercury and vaccination apart, the Enlightenment brought few immediate benefits to the health of nations. Still great surgeons such as Larrey, Napoleon's chief of the medical service, organised the first effective ambulance service in war, realised the importance of early treatment of wounds and noted the concept of traumatic gangrene. In 1819 René Laënnec invented the stethoscope, in order to listen to chests. He identified the sounds which he heard with certain diseases – making possible diagnoses far more effective than before. Another Frenchman, Marie-François Bichat, had earlier divided the materials of the body into membranes and tissues. He died young, as a result of excessive zeal in dissecting bodies.

The two great discoveries in medicine were those of anaesthesia and the antiseptic method in surgery. Both ideas were simple and, theoretically, could have been discovered at any time. But only in the nineteenth century could the second have been adequately pursued, since it needed precision tools. Paré, in the sixteenth century, might have discovered the antiseptic method, but he could not have ensured its effectiveness. Similarly, only in the nineteenth century were other methods of hygiene understood: for example, that decomposing matter is a danger to health. When asked about drains in 1850, a London woman said: 'Thank God, we have none of those foul stinking things here.' But the growth of big cities made the disposal of sewage the most acute problem.

The standards of private hygiene were higher in mediaeval Europe than during the Enlightenment. There were public baths in most European cities before the fifteenth century. These were abandoned. Even Jews gave up the ritual bath then, because of fear of catching syphilis, or because of the rise in the price of firewood and hence of hot water.* Gilberto Freyre points out that the native Brazilian Indians were accustomed to wash more than their Portuguese conquerors were.

First, however, consider anaesthesia, the first important medical invention deriving from the US. Of course, efforts had long been made to diminish pain during operations. The Chinese had used acupuncture since very early times. The Arabs had tried mandragora, opium and hyoscine, while the use of brandy had been common since the eleventh century. Later on, in the early nineteenth century, Charles Bell, the discoverer of the nervous system, in Scotland suggested that an iron clamp might with advantage compress the nerves during an operation. The apostle of electricity, Sir Humphry Davy, next proposed that laughing gas might be used during operations. A Scottish surgeon, James Escrick, then used mesmerism for operations in India, without pain. Returning to Scotland, he found the Scots less appropriate patients than Hindus. Finally, William Clark, a student of chemistry in Rochester, USA, in 1842 took a tooth out of a woman painlessly with the use of ether.

So began the modern era in surgery. In 1846 William Morton used ether publicly, and successfully, for the excision of a tumour on the neck in Massachusetts General Hospital. Robert Liston, yet another Scot, a surgeon of great dexterity, soon did the same at University College, London. The use of ether spread round the

---

* In the seventeenth century, baths were reintroduced as an Eastern luxury and became synonymous with a brothel (*bagnio*).

world. Sir James Simpson used chloroform for the same purpose. He and two assistants inhaled it in 1847 and fell simultaneously beneath the table. Henceforth pain during surgery could be avoided (though the problems of anaesthesia have not been wholly overcome). Speed was no longer the most important element in any operation. Thoroughness came to be the deciding question.

Major anaesthetics were one thing. Local ones were another. The Incas, for hundreds of years, had known of the anaesthetic character of coca trees. In the late nineteenth century, Austrians began to investigate the properties of leaves of coca, whose crystals they called cocaine. The various valuable uses of this drug came swiftly into being. Intravenous injections began in 1874.

Ordinary surgery, like medicine itself, had few successes before the early nineteenth century, though another French military surgeon, Ollier, introduced the principle of rest, incurring the gratitude of innumerable soldiers: 'Absolute and permanent immobility of the wounded part is essential, in a fixed apparatus.' Sir Joseph Lister and Louis Pasteur were the authors of the decisive innovation. Lister, son of a Quaker microscopist from Essex, had been present as a student at Liston's first operation under ether. He became professor of surgery at Glasgow, and investigated inflammation. He decided 'that the essential cause of suppuration in wounds is decomposition, brought about by the influence of the atmosphere upon blood or serum retained within them and, in the case of contused wounds, upon . . . the tissue destroyed by the violence of the injury'. Making use of the then very recent discovery by Louis Pasteur, that fermentation depended on the presence in the air of living germs, he resolved to use carbolic acid to kill the latter, knowing that the treatment of sewage in that manner at Carlisle had been successful. Lister made a satisfactory operation on a compound fracture in this way for the first time in 1865. He later used catgut or other ligatures which could be absorbed by the body to tie up internal wounds, so preventing the risks of further bleeding inevitable in opening the body up anew. Lister first thought too of lifting limbs upwards prior to an operation so as to render them bloodless before tying a tourniquet, and of tubes for drainage. The use of steam and boiling water, instead of carbolic acid, followed.

These innovations transformed surgery. The first kidney was taken out in 1876. The first operation on the brain was in 1879. The first appendix was removed in 1886. The first gastric ulcer was operated upon in 1892. A lung was removed in 1892. Among innumerable new developments of the twentieth century, successful operations on the heart seem the most daring.

Lister's work would have been impossible, as suggested above, without that of Louis Pasteur, a French genius, the son of a tanner from Dôle, in the Franche Comté. Pasteur believed in hard work, and considered that a good educational system should be based on the cult of great men. Patriotic and authoritarian, he read and admired Samuel Smiles' famous book *Self-Help* when recovering from a cerebral haemorrhage at the age of forty-six. Pasteur explained the mystery of fermentation as being due to the presence of microbes known as 'ferments'. When those are removed, he argued, no fermentation occurs. Similarly, when no germs are present, no inflammation occurs in wounds. The whole world of the micro-organism was thus miraculously, as it seemed, laid bare. At first, these organisms could not be identified. Good microscopes soon showed some of them. Some were dots in shape. Others looked like rods. Bacteria were the most remarkable of these organisms. A quarter of a million of them can sit upon a printed full stop.

Something no doubt was learned by both Pasteur and Lister from the Hungarian doctor Ignaz Semmelweis, who in the 1850s reduced deaths from puerperal fever in the maternity departments of the general hospitals at Vienna and Pest from sixteen per cent of mothers to one per cent, by merely insisting that the surgeons washed their hands. The intellectual climate of the Habsburg Empire prevented Semmelweis from developing his theories further. Driven out of Vienna by the jealousy of his professor, Semmelweis, indeed, was consigned to a lunatic asylum, where he died of neglecting a dirty wound on his right hand.

The work of Lister, Pasteur and the American inventors of anaesthesia was crowned by the development of the first X-ray in 1897, when a student at Harvard medical school, Walter Bradford Cannon, showed that internal organs could be photographed. The X-ray itself had been discovered by Wilhelm Röntgen, professor of physics at Würzburg, in 1895 (he called them X-rays because he did not know what they were).

Following Pasteur's discovery that without life, there is no ferment, Robert Koch, a German bacteriologist, began to designate innumberable bacilli, including that of tuberculosis, in 1882. By 1914 most microbes which harm man and beast had been identified. Some diseases remained unexplained: for example, were the various skin diseases perhaps living organisms? (They turned out to be made by viruses so small as to be indistinguishable through microscopes.) Some old diseases were tracked down to their sources: yellow fever was correctly attributed to the mosquito in 1902 and beriberi to bad diet in 1901. The lonely dreamer Surgeon-Major Ronald Ross finally identified the *anopheles* mosquito as the bearer of malaria, while working in the British army hospital at Begumpett, leading to a long international campaign, managed by others, against that agile carrier.

Medical practice was also assisted by some innovations more simple than these great discoveries. Despite the ideas of Galileo (who saw the uses of such a thing), the clinical thermometer did not exist before the 1850s. The most modern one then was ten inches long, 'like an umbrella'. It took twenty minutes to register. Clifford Allbutt of Leeds, a classical scholar by training who was perhaps a model for 'Lydgate' in George Eliot's *Middlemarch*, made the first short thermometer in 1866. Injections of substances through hollow tubes into veins had occurred since the sixteenth century. But a hypodermic syringe was first used by Alexander Wood in Edinburgh only in 1853. The professional training of nurses began in the 1860s, after following the example of Florence Nightingale in the Crimean War. The whole paraphernalia of modern arrangements of health – ministers, child welfare centres, free distribution of milk to children, and health visits – soon followed.

The medical innovations of the twentieth century have been numerous, beneficial and often startling. Consider two matters: the use of antibiotics; and a more serious attitude to madness.

Alexander Fleming, a Scottish professor of bacteriology in London, made many contributions to the treatment of wounds in the First World War. He still found himself having to argue about the desirability of removing dead tissues from wounds: it was as if Paré had never lived. He also pointed out (and Larrey had realised it long before) that most infections occurred to soldiers *after* they had been admitted to base hospitals. In 1928 he made the observation that microbes were destroyed when in contact with a contaminating mould. The subsequent elaboration of this discovery by Sir Howard Florey and Sir Ernest Chain began the age of antibiotics.

As to madness, Soranus and other Greek writers laid down the principles for a humanitarian attitude. But, under Christianity, the mad, for many hundreds of years, were looked upon as possessed by devils. Lunatics were not killed, it is true. Instead, they were held for public show in institutions such as the Bethlehem Hospital. The Catalan philosopher Juan Vives first suggested, in the sixteenth century, a humane treatment. Johann Wyer wrote, about 1550, that witches were often merely individuals suffering from mental sickness. Paracelsus, a German physician of acute observation,* had first distinguished mania in two sections: neuroses, the products of nature; and psychoses, disorders deriving from fantasies unrelated to life. In the eighteenth century Franz Anton Mesmer, an Austrian fraud, claimed that he could draw madness out of people by a magnet. He told his patients that a hidden force within him enabled him to dominate others: 'animal magnetism'. With this, he had for a time great success: psychosomatic illnesses çan often be cured by charlatans. His contemporary Philippe Puriel, when physician at the lunatic asylum at Bicêtre, Paris, freed lunatics from their chains. Later, while therapy by shock, drugs and electricity was beginning to be used for the mad, Sigmund Freud in Vienna argued that the mind could be divided into several zones – the ego, the id and the libido. The first represented awareness of self. The second stood for the unconscious. The third signified emotional energy. He considered that events which were unacceptable to the first of these were driven by the second into the third. Freud believed that all such events had to be accurately recalled to ensure good health. But they could not be so without using Freud's own methods of encouraging the patient to talk endlessly.

Freud, the most widely cultivated scientist of our times, was determined to give a complete explanation of human life. His disciple Adler thought that desire for superiority was a driving force in most human beings. Another pupil, Jung, believed that the libido might be revealed as, or driven to become, indiscriminately either love, hate or ambition. These views had been previously discussed, equally vigorously, by novelists such as Balzac, also without scientific proof. Freud ignored the varieties in behaviour among people and the changing behaviour of people in different civilisations. But these ideas brought medicine to the centre of intellectual life more than at any time before. Among their

---

* Paracelsus, born Philipp Theophrastus Bombast von Hohenheim, worked in the mines of the Tyrol owned by the Fuggers before travelling through Europe to observe the 'book of nature'. His lectures at Basle in 1527 broke new ground by the fact that they were in German and were more than commentaries on Galen.

effects was to cause it to be supposed that wrongdoing is a disease, not a crime.*

In the 140 years or so following the first use of anaesthesia, medical developments transformed the character of life in the neglected and 'advanced' countries alike. The transformation is obvious, the effect on population less so. A decline in the death rate has never been so important in increasing population as a rise in the birth rate. The changes in medical practice noticed above began to affect the society of Western Europe after the 1870s, just when those countries' birth rates were dropping. Marked improvements even in infant mortality did not occur till after the First World War. The rates of infant mortality for pre-industrial Europe as a whole may have been over 200 per thousand. The figures for 1850 to 1900 did not show much improvement: for example, England's rate was 151 per thousand in 1839 and 163 in 1899. Falls in overall death rates were also slow.

2

It would be foolish to suppose that the history of medicine shows an irresistible forward progress. Man has spread many infections, which were once locally controlled. The industrialisation of the eighteenth and nineteenth centuries caused tuberculosis to become rampant in the new and overcrowded towns. It was much the commonest cause of death in the mid nineteenth century in industrial cities. The spread of Asiatic cholera to the slaves' shanties in Rio de Janeiro, and the ravages of yellow fever among white men in other parts of Brazil, in the nineteenth century were serious setbacks in the history of the Americas. The last generation of European imperial adventurers had numerous immediately destructive consequences. Take, for example, an instance in the Congo. The Senliki valley had been grassland for many hundreds of years. About 1900 the Belgian administrators began to encourage cultivation. The flourishing pastoral population moved down to the valley, establishing contact with tsetse flies which, at that time unknown to science, were the bearers of sleeping sickness. This disease of sleeping sickness has been rampant in Africa since

---

* In an inspired passage, Tocqueville anticipated Freud's view of the importance of childhood: 'We must watch the infant in his mother's arms; we must see the first images which the external world casts upon the dark mirror of his mind . . . we must hear the first words which awaken the sleeping powers of thought . . . if we would understand the prejudices, the habits, and the passions which will rule his life'[1].

the remotest times. Perhaps it was that to which the prophet Isaiah referred when he said 'the Lord shall hiss for the fly that is in the uttermost part of the rivers of Egypt'. Its debilitating drowsiness, high fever and swelling of lymphatic glands were among the main reasons for Africa's failure to advance faster in the past towards sophistication. In consequence, at all events, in the Senliki valley by 1920 the entire population had either fled, were dead or were in hospital.

Similar catastrophes continued in South America. In 1903 the 6,000- to 8,000-strong Cayapo tribe in Brazil accepted a missionary, who deliberately sought to safeguard that people from civilisation and its discontents. But by 1918 there were only 500 Cayapo left, for the missionary had unwittingly carried with him several sicknesses of the cities. By 1950 the tribe had disappeared. In South America in general the population in the eighteenth century was still diminishing in respect of its indigenous peoples. As the white men pressed further and further into the interior along the continent's great rivers, more and more tribes were becoming affected by the devastating diseases of Europe – severe colds and influenza killed many, so did severe catarrh, smallpox and measles. Dysentery was also prevalent. John Hemming, the historian of the Brazilian Indians, estimates that the indigenous population of Brazil fell from two and a half million or so in 1500 to 100,000 by 1960, though perhaps neglecting Indians who passed into the 'white' population by miscegenation.

Nervous diseases are also believed to be on the increase in the twentieth century in advanced countries. The conventional view is: 'the great pressure at which modern commercial and intellectual life is carried on exhausts the nervous system'. Heredity, accidents, syphilis, alcoholism and diabetes also all play a part. It is impossible to say how far these complaints have really increased. Though Hippocrates knew of the anatomy of the brain in the fifth century BC, and though some of his immediate successors made interesting reflections on insanity, little was done in this matter till the Enlightenment. The raising of the expectation of life from thirty years to seventy has obviously affected nervous diseases. Almost certainly it has been the main single reason for the increase in such ills.

Advanced countries have also encountered troubles which they did not have before. Thus the population of Britain, then the richest country in the world, began to suffer seriously from cavities in the teeth during the nineteenth century. The coming of toothbrushes and toothpaste had little effect. The damage was done by worsening diet. Sugar and cheap tinned milk did the harm. The late nineteenth century thus saw a big demand for false teeth. Bad teeth were responsible for the rejection of two-fifths of those who presented themselves for service as volunteers in the South African war. In the late nineteenth century the use of machine-made bread, previously noted, also caused an increase in constipation, piles, and cancer of the bowel. The connection between health and eating habits had been forgotten. Yet in 1289 Arnau de Vilanova the inventor of brandy had pointed out, in a manual of social hygiene, the importance of fresh air, exercise, baths, rest and vegetables.

With the eclipse of older diseases, cancer has become a major cause of death. Since it kills people in their middle or later life, it too was less prominent a threat before the twentieth century. But it is not a new disease: Ramón Lull, the thirteenth-century Catalan man of all talents, suffered a shock, causing his change from the temporal to the spiritual world, when a lady to whom he was attached showed him, to cool his ardours, an ulcerated cancer in her breast. Influenza, too, has at times threatened to become 'the last great plague'. At least ten major epidemics of influenza occurred since the early eighteenth century, above all the epidemic of 1918–19 which killed twenty million people. Influenza derives from diseases of domestic animals and migratory birds. Noticed by Hippocrates, the word 'influenza' was invented in Italy in the fifteenth century to describe something which was believed to be 'influenced' by stars. Its virus was first isolated in 1933, but no adequate defence against it has yet been found.

3

The twentieth century has also seen two major attempts at the distortion of medicine for political purposes, one by the Russian government, the other by the German.

After 1917 Lenin gave instructions that the health of the nation's leaders should be considered an affair of state. Those Platonic instructions were soon used to his own discomfort: Lenin passed the last years of his life as a prisoner of politically directed doctors. He himself was unable to communicate, after his heart attack in 1920, with the outside world. His last strength was consumed by a 'conspiracy of secretaries'[2]. He could not logically complain: earlier, he had written an order to 'the organisational bureau of the communist party': 'I ask that Comrade Krizhirzanovsky be compelled to go, with Krasin, to Riga, there to spend, in a sana-torium or a private apartment, one month of cure and rest.' There was no reference to a medical authority. After 1964 the Russian government began sending its enemies to lunatic asylums, an extraordinary misuse of medicine for which there is, however, some precedent before the Revolution. In 1980 opponents of the Soviet regime seem to be regularly dosed with drugs intended to alter their behaviour.

The Germans under Hitler were even more brutal. Prisoners were used as experimental subjects for every sort of medical enquiry. Even before 1939 the courts set up as a result of the 'Hereditary Health Law' had the power to order compulsory ster-ilisation. The misuse of trust by doctors in concentration camps between 1939 and 1945 was a betrayal of the Hippocratic Oath which has no precedent.

The two regimes, Fascist and Communist, which have so mis-used medicine demand special attention, however, not only be-cause of these disgraceful acts of misconduct, but because their leaders seem, the more they are examined, to be themselves men who might have been classed as mad any time in the eighteenth century. The pathological loathing of Jews felt by Hitler, the extraordinary suspicions of Stalin, the mental debilities shared by so many of their lieutenants, from Himmler to Yezhov, make it possible that those systems will be looked upon as instances in which the lunatic asylum became the centre of government in half the world. The implications of the capture of power in totalitarian states by persons at least temporarily out of control of their senses have, however, been ignored in a world too preoccupied by ide-ology to recognise illness.

4

Still, despite these setbacks in the industrial age, the benefits must be noticed by any balanced judge. The control, if not the con-quest, of malaria is a good example of these benefits.

Malaria's incidence in Africa and elsewhere in the Old World has been noticed. Taken to the Americas by the Spaniards, mal-aria completed the destruction of the indigenous population in the tropical lowlands already begun by smallpox. It dominated the tropical parts of South America till the twentieth century, causing an inertia which explains the ease with which the Spanish Empire maintained itself. Many victims felt that, when they had 'water in the blood', as one of them in Venezuela put it (to one of the pioneers of the campaign against malaria, Dr Enrique Tejera), they might as well give up all attempts at resistance to the problems of maintaining life[3].

In the seventeenth century it became known that malaria could be suppressed, if not cured, by applying to the patient the bark of the chinchona tree, a South American plant first used by the intelligent Condesa de Chinchón, wife of a viceroy of Peru, in 1638. Hence the name of that delightful town of Castile passed to the healing tree. The bark had been used by Indians before but, since it was disseminated in Europe by the Society of Jesus, it was known (and suspected by Protestants) as 'Jesuits' bark'. Since the forests where the chinchona flourished were in the hands of His Catholic Majesty, Protestants had to wait many years before they could assure themselves of a regular supply of this wood: a serious drawback to the Reformation. The Dutch, in the end, established plantations of chinchona in Java in 1854, and after that, with what became known by corruption as 'quinine', Protestant Europeans were able to insulate themselves against malaria. That enabled them to penetrate Africa for the first time.

It was not, however, until the 1880s, as earlier noticed, that the carrier of malaria was identified as the mosquito. Nor was it until the 1940s that the insecticide DDT began to be produced in substantial quantities to enable destruction of vast numbers of the mosquitoes themselves. The spraying of slums, shacks, streets and whole cities with the insecticide has since been undertaken, with immediate consequences for the death rate and the political vitality of the regions concerned: one of the great crusades of this century.

About 1960 it was widely believed that the breeding grounds of malaria had begun to be destroyed for ever. But some mosquitoes have defied DDT; effective measures have to include the repeated spraying of the infected buildings. 850 million people are believed to live in areas where malaria has been inadequately controlled; 350 million where no control has been tried. Today no one believes that 'eradication' of this ancient killer is practicable in the immediate future. 'Control', not elimination, is pursued. It is still in 1980 the world's worst disease. Between a million and two million die of it every year (out of total deaths per year of about 50 million) and perhaps 250 million are continuously affected by it.

52

Urban Man

What can be stable with these enormous towns? One serious insurrection in London and all is lost.

Lord Liverpool to Chateaubriand,
in 1820 (*Mémoires d'Outre Tombe*, 2, ix)

Talking of London, he observed, 'Sir, if you wish to have a just notion of the magnitude of this city, you must not be satisfied with seeing its great streets and squares, but must survey the innumerable little lanes and courts. It is not in the showy evolutions of buildings, but in the multiplicity of human habitations which are crowded together, that the wonderful immensity of London consists.'

Boswell, *Life of Johnson*, Vol. II

1

The age of industry transformed the place of living of the majority of the world's population. This was seen most evidently in the growth of cities. Half the population of England was urban in 1851: a predicament never before found in a great nation. By 1900 agriculture only occupied ten per cent of the English population. All over the world since then the tendency has been the same. As Freyre said of Brazil, 'the city square triumphed over the sugar plantation'[1].

The rise in population, not industrialisation, created modern life. Urbanisation is not the same thing as industrialisation. Egypt is now as urbanised as Switzerland, more so (on the basis of the percentage of the population living in cities of 100,000 or more) than France, but not so industrialised.

The fact that people live in cities has often been regretted as if it were in itself a source of major decline in the quality of life. It is possible to be sceptical about that judgement. Urban life makes for easier access to schools and to professions linked to literacy. In every country those who live in cities are more likely to be able to read and write than those who live in the country. Nor is it wise to feel nostalgic about lost rural serenity. The Elizabethan village was as often as not filled by malice and hatred, the only bond being the occasional outbreak of mass hysteria to persecute the local witch. Village water was also often impure.

The Industrial Revolution found the world's population living in wood, mud, brick and stone. It is leaving it in cement, glass and steel. Improvements may not seem always evident. Yet in the eighteenth century there were places where living conditions were worse than those which obtained in Babylon. Even in Britain, in the early nineteenth century, there were houses with mud floors, many turf houses with squatters. Some farm labourers lived in one-roomed hovels, sometimes below ground, usually damp. In Russia, many houses showed scarcely any improvement on the huts of hunters of the days before 10,000 BC. One of the first observers of Russian life, Radishchev, described a typical house between St Petersburg and Moscow in about 1770 thus: 'the upper half of the four walls and the whole ceiling were covered with soot; the floor was full of dust and covered with dirt at least two inches thick; the oven [was] without a chimney but their best protection against the cold; and smoke filled the hut every morning, winter and summer. Window holes . . . admitted a dim light at noon time; [there were also to be seen] two or three pots . . . a wooden bowl and round trenchers . . . a table, hewn with an axe, which they scrape clean on holidays . . . a trough to feed pigs and calves, if there are any. . . If they are lucky, a barrel of *kvass* [the drink made from fermented bread, much drunk by Russian peasants] that tastes like vinegar and, in the yard, a bath house in which the cattle sleep if people are not steaming in it'[2]. To those who lived in such places, the 'rough brick houses' of Babylon would have seemed a luxury. Of course, those Russians had the countryside in which to breathe; and it is not clear that they would have preferred to have lived in the London of the 1880s with what for Matthew Arnold seemed 'its unutterable external ugliness'. It seems possible that half the population of Asia and Africa still live in conditions worse than those which pertained in eighteenth-century England.

The first impact of the Industrial Revolution on cities and on building was to increase the quantity of brick used. Unless the building was of exceptional importance, stone was only used in regions where it could be quarried. That ruled out much of England and the east of the US. Wood was also scarce because of the need for it in shipyards and in charcoal burning, or because the country concerned had already used up the forests. In 1824 Portland cement was invented (at Wakefield by a builder, Joshua

Aspdin, and given that name since it was intended as a substitute for Portland stone). Cement came into general use after 1850, with demands made for it for sewers in modern cities. How unthinkable modern cities would be without that mixture of limestone and sand! Cast iron was also added as a new building material, first to support columns, then to replace wooden beams, later still to give frames for large buildings, as in the towering new apartment blocks of New York. Reinforced concrete (cement with steel or iron rods embedded, with the strength of steel and stone combined) began to be introduced from the 1850s, after Edouard Coignet showed that such material could be laid under fifteen feet of earth, for sewers. Concrete bridges also began to be made. Steel enabled large buildings, and bridges, to be prefabricated.

The most striking consequence was the skyscraper, the demand for which derived from the rise of land values in New York and Chicago, about 1880. Wrought-iron skyscrapers could be built to the height of fourteen floors, but they had to have greater thickness at the base than at the top. The steel frame could be raised to any height without an increase in the size of the building at the bottom. Thereafter the function of walls was reduced to give privacy and shelter. The first steel skyscrapers went up in Chicago in 1890 and in New York in 1894. There were twenty-nine in the latter city by 1900. Europe was restrained. It was only after 1945 that steel framed skyscrapers began to be built there. London was temporarily saved from these developments by the theory, which turned out to be an illusion, that the ground under it was unsuitable.

Another invention had made the skyscraper a practical, as opposed to a theoretical, possibility: the hydraulic lift was devised in 1852 by Elisha Graves Otis, a Vermont inventor with many other achievements to his credit, such as a steam plough, a steam oven and a turbine waterwheel. Otis's elevator worked by steam and had safety appliances. The passengers were carried in a case with pawls which were forced by springs to engage in ratchets at the side should the rope fail. A hydraulic lift also reached the top of the Eiffel Tower. An electric version was soon introduced.

By the time of the Futurists, about 1910, prefabricated building of ordinary houses had been started in Chicago, where balloon frames, roofs, floors and walls were supplied in factories and put together by amateurs. Ready-made doors and windows were fitted into the prefabricated structures.

Then there was glass. Optical glass had been improving through-

out the eighteenth century. Most glass made for windows, however, consisted of small round sheets, with bulls' eyes in the
middle, constructed from a globe of glass attached by molten
metal to an iron rod. But plate glass had been achieved in France
in the days of Louis XIV (the Hall of Mirrors in Versailles was an
early use of that). From the 1770s, it could be made by steam.
That transformed the history of the window. In the nineteenth
century the demand for window glass in Europe, with so much
new building, exceeded all expectations. 'Great windows open to
the south' (in Yeats' phrase) could be cheaply built while, in a
self-confident and homogeneous society, robberies were supposed
to be likely to be rare. Subsequently in the 1950s and afte. wards
the use of glass, with iron and steel, enabled engineers to make
both roofs and walls transparent.

But it was not only technology which made the modern cities.
As suggested earlier, those conglomerations could not have survived if their supplies had had to come from old methods of
grinding corn, in local windmills or watermills, baking it at home,
bringing meat on foot and gaining milk from suburban cattle
keepers. Railways, refrigeration and tins were needed to ensure
the supply of food for the urban millions.

The modern city saw, too, changes in the commercial exploitation not only of these foods but of everything saleable. In the
seventeenth century some public markets and producers' shops
dating from the Middle Ages were converted into specialised
shops under continuous operation. Kromm invented the department store before the French Revolution in Paris, with several
thousand employees. After 1815 the modern shop came into
being, with fixed prices, low margins of profit, commissions on
sales for the staff, 'sales' at intervals and a social security system
for the employees. This was developed in France with the Bon
Marché, directed by Boucicaut, the Magasin du Louvre, managed
by Chauchard, or the Samaritaine, and in Germany too, after
1830. Street lamps and lighted windows caused a change in the
mid nineteenth century, as did the cheap department store in the
US, invented in 1862 in New York by Alexander Stewart, an Irish
Protestant in origin, but brought to its culmination by John Wan-
amaker of Philadelphia, who began life as an errand boy and first
thought up the one-price system, the marked prices in clear figures
and the money-back guarantees which characterise shopping in
the twentieth century. Mail orders began in 1872 with Montgo-
mery Ward in Chicago, and the chain store with Frank W. Wool-

worth's 'Five and Ten Cent' store at Utica, New York, in 1879.*
These innovations led to the swift end of the old fairs as major
commercial enterprises.

All capital cities grew at the expense of the rest of the country.
Louis XIV tried to check the growth of Paris without success.
Even before the Revolution, provincial printing presses and other
critical small businesses were in decline in France. In the nineteenth century similar efforts to cut the size of cities were more
unsuccessful. In democracies and tyrannies alike, all cities crew.
Big cities grew faster than small ones. In the US in the nineteenth
century, cities of over 8,000 inhabitants grew five times faster than
the country as a whole. The reason was not so much the rise in
population in the towns themselves, though that could not be
ignored, as the influx from country-born workers. In 1851 out of
3,336,000 people aged twenty or over living in London less than
half had been born there. Much the same was true of New York,
Chicago, Barcelona, Essen and Lyons, or other large English or
Welsh towns, and soon would be of Moscow. Then, as the masses
moved into the centre of the cities, the leaders of society moved
out, living more and more in suburbs, often with separate municipal authorities, but linked with the city to which those same
leaders began to 'commute', in order to work, travelling in daily,
on horse or in coaches, before the railways.

The growth of the new industrial cities, particularly in Britain,
where there were few architects of quality and where noblemen
spent their money on building imitation Palladian houses, denoted
a failure of imagination. In most such cities there were, in some
cases there still are, long and dreary streets, street after street
with the same formations, the same alleys filled with rubbish and
the same lack of open spaces for children to play in. Churches
followed specially slowly: despite the increase of population,
London only saw ten new churches in the eighteenth century.
Little effort was made to plan the pattern of the streets according
to sun and wind. The more respectable quarters, where 'artisans'
or clerks lived, were almost as depressing as the straightforwardly
shabby slums.

These cities had, to begin with, no social heritage. All was at
first subordinate to the factory concerned, including public services (police, fire services and water services, not to speak of

---

* When Woolworth died in 1919, he had a thousand 'five and ten cent' stores in
the US and seventy-five in Britain.

hospitals, food inspection, education and church which came later). The factory would be set on the best site, on the river, for it needed water for its boilers, for cooling and for dyeing, and it provided the worst waste (thus ruining the fishing). The factory chimneys, magnificent though they were, polluted air and water. A railway was often driven into the centre of the town, severing natural arteries. Huge piles of waste metal stood untended for years. Workers' houses were built up against the 'works' and so were often bathed in dust. In many pioneering cities of the Industrial Revolution, back-to-back houses opened on to a yard: two rooms out of four had no direct daylight at all. Lavatories were inadequate: Manchester in 1845 had thirty-three per one thousand inhabitants – a proportion which would now be thought bad in a prison. Cellars might sometimes house pigs, a sad reminder of happier rural days, but there was also usually a large human cellar population. Bedbugs, lice, fleas, rats and flies bred in the plaster walls. Plumbing was rotten, drains open and water bad. Even so, the building trades employed more men than any other profession. Reformers concentrated upon the need for good prisons and a state monopoly of sewage, and failed to devote adequate attention to how people were housed. As Lewis Mumford points out, the nineteenth century was an age of rising nationhood, but the municipal councils, on the other hand, did not rise to the occasion and built town halls only[3].

The changes in the size of populations were, of course, unprecedented. The worst conditions were to be found in the boom towns, then as now. Horrible though mid-nineteenth-century London no doubt was, with its fog, tuberculosis and rickets, the expectation of life there was higher than it had been a century before. The errors in planning also showed a failure to think carefully enough what should be the role of the state. Victorian reformers in both the US and Britain, as well as elsewhere, insisted upon a role for the state in such things as the postal service which could have been managed by private companies. They sometimes neglected to give a role to the state in matters such as town planning where the commodity at stake was finite such as land. Finally, many slum cities of the nineteenth century were able to achieve a greater humanity than has proved possible in the futuristic cities of the twentieth century.

In comparison, cities in countries which were slow to industrialise seemed oases of peace. Vienna in 1848 still had walls and a moat. Green slopes lay between it and the suburbs. At night, the gates were closed. Even during the day, they were locked in the event of disturbances. The workers of Vienna lived outside the city, while students, nobility and middle classes lived inside. In general, cities which industrialised later had better services than those which did so early. Still, benefits in the form of better shops, department stores, internal city transport and vast numbers of salesmen followed industrialisation everywhere. Vienna, like other traditional cities, became the battleground of class wars as much as modern ones.

Modern cities of the poorer world, from South America to Africa, are surrounded by shanty towns so neglected as to make nineteenth-century industrial cities seem prosperous. Africa has seen a more rapid industrialisation than anywhere in the world, specially confusing since there is no urban tradition on which to build. Instead, there is a juxtaposition of foreign investment with a population the majority of which are tribal people full of ancient fears, loyalties and prejudices. Usually populated by squatters, the urban areas of Mexico, India and Egypt represent the most complicated of modern political problems. Still, the cities of Europe in the nineteenth century were marked by riots and are now at least politically tranquil; should the pressure of population in Mexico City or Caracas ever be alleviated, the intensity of their difficulties may diminish too.

It is hard to do other than compare unfavourably the lot of those who live in new cities at present with those who lived in Merthyr Tydfil when it was the capital of the British iron trade in 1820. Tough, rough, overworked though the life there must have been, its population, with its four ironworks, was still only 20,000. The city was in walking distance of green valleys.

Though, in many modern cities, history seems remote, the past often remains close in spirit. A comparison between the towns of France and of Britain makes that point clearly. Freed from the likelihood of invasion, England is a country whose towns have outgrown the need for walls. Invaded four times since 1800, France held back her cities at the walls where she could. Thus, where London sprawled, Paris grew upwards. In Britain, only Edinburgh has a tradition of blocks five, six or ten storeys high. Then, in nineteenth-century politics on the Continent, unlike the eighteenth, there were numerous internal troubles. Barricades were easier to put up in old cities. Most streets on the European continent in the days of the great (and nostalgically regretted) street battles of 1830 and 1848 were only six to eight feet wide with tall buildings.

Another tendency in the life of cities was, to begin with, more marked in the US. In the 1950s, in all but Los Angeles of the large US cities, there was a decrease in population. Only in the South in new cities did the urban population keep growing. Yet the countryside also continued to lose population. In place of both, suburbs became, in the 1960s, the preferred living place of the successful family, first in the US, then elsewhere.

In most countries, capital cities have become more and more important, as the pretensions of governments have grown. Networks of communication radiate from capitals often, as with airways, to serve nations' bureaucrats, rather than the vital members of the society concerned.

2

No modern city, however, would be able to survive for a week if it were not for an elaborate system of hygiene beneath it. A modern city may be constructed of stone, steel, glass or brick. But it has to be built primarily upon water: needed against fire, for drinking, cooking, washing, sewage and for industry.

At the beginning of modern times, the water supplies and the hygiene of cities alike had declined not only since *Roma antiqua*, but since the Middle Ages. The ancient Persians never polluted rivers; they worshipped them. The Egyptians bathed twice a day in cold water and washed their clothes often. But, even in a rich country such as England, there was in 1800 rarely a distinction made between sewers and water mains. All rivers were contaminated by domestic and industrial waste. Ditches in cities were used as latrines. Dead animals were left to rot where they lay. The decomposing bodies of the poor in common graves stank. Bed sheets were changed at most three times a year. Women wore quilted petticoats and stays of bone or leather which they rarely washed. The public baths of Rome or Constantinople, the vast *cloaca maxima* and other Roman sewers copied from the Etruscans, the 1,352 public fountains of Rome in the fourth century, the dozen Roman aqueducts – all seemed inconceivable in England, much less in Rome, even in the time of Rome's greatest historian, Edward Gibbon. The hygienic arrangements of Babylon would have strained the imagination of a citizen of eighteenth-century Paris, as they might that of many citizens of Calcutta

today. True, Muslims maintained the tradition of baths as effectively as they did that of mathematics. They had baths of hot air,
hammam baths, most extensively. Steam baths were widely used
in Russia, following Muslim patterns.

In fact, therefore, the most enviable people in the late eighteenth century, so far as hygiene is concerned, seem, from the
point of view of statistics, those who did not live in modern towns.
Yet visitors to old towns would have challenged that view.
Goethe, on his journey in Italy, complained at the absence of a
public cleansing service, of any sort, in Venice. Rubbish, including
excrement, was pushed into corners, and irregularly carried away
in flat-bottomed boats, as manure to the mainland, or thrown into
the sea. Everywhere in Italy, Goethe found majestic colonnades
which were 'made for people to relieve themselves whenever they
felt the urge'. In an inn at Torbole, he found no lavatories: a valet
pointed to the courtyard. 'Where?' 'Anywhere, wherever you
like,' was the reply[4]. But it was not simply the decadent south
which seemed unhygienic. When Charles I's court was at Oxford,
courtiers left behind excreta in every corner of every college. In
Edinburgh, in 1760, there were no latrines, public or private: all
emptied excreta into the street at ten p.m. When Mrs Pepys was
seized with diarrhoea at the theatre, she had no option but to go
to a corner of Lincoln's Inn Fields. Even 'on the marble staircases
of the Louvre, the natural necessities were performed daily'.

Meantime, in Eastern countries, what little water there was
afforded good chances of parasites spreading. The washing pools
of Yemen's mosques were full of snails which carried all sorts of
diseases. Cholera travelled along the pilgrims' routes in spite of
a religion in which washing plays a great part (Muslims were
instructed to wash frequently every day in running water).
Actually, Muslim towns were often more hygienic than Christian
ones, since they were built on hillsides in order to make the best
use of water, from both streams and rain, to carry away rubbish.

It was perhaps too because of the Islamic tradition that towns
in the Spanish world usually retained their fountains. There the
provision of water was an established collective function, arranged
by a spring or a public fountain, and perhaps conveyed in old
Roman lead pipes. The public fountain remained, until the present
generation in many Mediterranean places, a centre of gregarious-
ness, a work of art in construction, an inspiration for poets. As
García Lorca put it:

A village without a public fountain
Is closed, dark; every house is an isolated world.

Or

Who has shown you the road of the poets?
The fountain, and the very old song of the stream[5].

There was in the past no means of keeping water fresh. So, water carriers were essential. Even in the nineteenth century most districts would count themselves fortunate if their population could go to a standpipe at the street corner once a day for an hour or so; though, by then, the rich were starting to be able to obtain running water in their basements.

A few other improvements began in what seemed a dark time. Soap started to be produced in France under Rome, continued to be made spasmodically during the Middle Ages and liquid soap, from potash, was used for laundry from the sixteenth century. Soap from palm oil was the best commercial alternative to the slave trade from Africa for many Liverpool merchants in the nineteenth century. Sir John Harington, a Somerset squire who married an illegitimate daughter of Henry VIII, invented the water closet in 1596, even if for 300 years there were few of them. At Versailles, at the King's court, there were little lavatories made as commodes on wheels. Mass-produced and, therefore, individual plates, knives and forks and cups, the decline of spitting, the custom of shaving heads under wigs, the fashion for changing underclothes every day (defined as elegance itself by Beau Brummell about 1820), all brought benefits. Those who complain of industrialisation need to recall the advantage of cheap cups and saucers.

The problem of sewage became urgent in the nineteenth century, as towns grew yearly so large. The system of the 'privy bucket' meant endless emptying and removal of contents. Even so, where should it be emptied? The first solution found in London was the cesspool, of which there were about 250,000 in London by 1850. But this had an adverse effect on water from wells, at a time when most water in capital cities came from those sources.

Two changes came to rich cities in the nineteenth century and were copied elsewhere. Both were based on the assumption that dirt causes disease. Not for the first time, a false concept – it is not dirt but germs which cause maladies – led to a revolution in habits. The pioneer in most of these changes was a German, Josef

Franach, who suggested, in the six volumes of his *Complete System of Medical Polity*, that states should concern themselves with the preservation of hygiene.

The practical initiative in these matters was, as usual by then, taken in the US. New York was the first great city to arrange for its citizens an ample supply of pure water, by means of a system of reservoirs and aqueducts opened in 1842. By the twentieth century, New York was stretching out in its demands for water into the Catskill mountains a hundred miles away. Huge dams, aqueducts comparable to the Roman ones, fifty-mile-long pure water canals and long tunnels were all soon built. Wild valleys found themselves placed under water to serve the need for water of some distant manufacturing town.

The treatment of sewage had a similar outcome. The career of Edwin Chadwick, a many-sided reformer in England, was illuminating. He insisted in 1837 on the establishment of a sanitary commission. Appointed to head it in 1839, it became, in 1842, a general board of health. Chadwick then recommended that cesspools should be abolished and that sewers should cease to be merely bricked-over water-courses. His scheme was that they should become great arteries in their own right to be cleaned by regular water supplies. Those arteries would carry all rubbish by long underground routes to be disposed of at places remote from the city. Hamburg was the first to build sewers of that sort (because of a big fire there) and Paris began sooner than London, whose problems were affected by a tangled web of local private and political interests. But the realisation that the cholera epidemic of 1850 was connected with pollution by excreta awoke London to a serious appreciation of what should be done. Sir Joseph Bazalgette, a civil engineer of French origin, devised a system based on five sewers running parallel to the Thames which would be capable of dealing with all normal sewage and rain water. Only in stormy weather would it be necessary to use the old sewers connected with the rivers. The sewers discharged their refuse twelve miles from London Bridge at a place where it could be chemically clarified. Here was an effective system of public works plainly superior to the negligent ways of the past.

These improvements spread swiftly throughout the world. For example, the British had four 'sanitation companies' in Latin America by 1880.

At the same time, Europeans and North Americans began to overcome their fear of contact with water in other ways. Swimming began to be again a practical part of education. Public baths began, from the 1840s, to be built again. Slowly, the idea of the private bath captured the imaginations of rich countries. The shower seems to have been devised in the 1880s. All these innovations, or revivals, depended not only upon running water attached to the houses – that immensely important innovation of the mid nineteenth century – but on the availability of heating it too: a possibility made easy after the gas heater of the 1860s and electricity a little later. Enamelled white baths began to be made about 1910 and to be mass-produced in the US and Britain by 1920. By 1939 the compact bathrooms of modern times (bath, basin, lavatory) were everywhere being constructed. The ideal of one such bathroom to every bedroom was beginning to be expressed as a goal by modern builders. These ideals were passed on to a world which was anxious to copy US technology without necessarily copying their political ideals. The achievement of even the first of these aims was, however, far from complete even in rich countries in 1980.

3

By the year 2000 a third of the world's population are expected to be living in cities of over 100,000 inhabitants in size. Tokyo with Yokohama, with about seventeen million in 1980, may by 2000 have twenty-six million. Cairo may have sixteen million, Lagos ten million and Mexico City may be the largest town in the world with over thirty million: it has now (1980) already eighteen million. São Paulo may rival Tokyo. The implications of these developments are unclear. London only reached a million in 1800, and Paris did not join her in that till 1850. Berlin and Vienna did not top a million till nearly 1880, and no Russian city save St Petersburg reached a million before about 1870. Today, however, the cities of the world larger than one million number a hundred. A hundred cities are the size of Rome at her height, many of them larger. Twenty-six cities have more than five million inhabitants. By AD 2000 there may be sixty such cities, forty-five of them in countries now known as 'developing'.

One consequence of this 'urbanisation' has been a vast increase of crime. From the evidence of primitive or hunting tribes surviving into historical memory, crime, among those peoples, was rare and severely punished. Still, the codes of ancient agrarian civilisations make clear that, in those early settled states, urban crime's history had begun. In Rome or Constantinople, or in Eastern cities, the growing, semi-slave, rootless urban proletariat which did not accept, or know, the customs of the dominant people looked on robbery as part of their private war against the occupiers. Where peoples were insecure, or lived in a state of perpetual war, the distinction between crime and self-preservation was ill-marked. Of course, thefts and murders, rapes and minor acts of violence occurred often in the countryside. Figures recently analysed suggest that mediaeval Kent had a worse record than anywhere in the US in the twentieth century. Two-thirds of all convictions in England in some years during the nineteenth century were under the game code.

All the same, crime in modern society seems more and more an urban problem: the Neapolitan *lazzaroni* of the eighteenth century are now to be found all over the world. The absence of rewarding work or stimulating play and its substitution by television, which itself often stimulates violence; the charmlessness of many modern dwellings – above all those provided by the municipality; the loose scale of values in societies richer than those which existed in the past, and the conversion of many who live in cities to a mentality indifferent to the community in which they have rights as citizens, all contribute to shiftlessness. In some cities of the US, murder has been said to have been the most common cause of death among male black people in their prime of life. In other ways too, modern cities recall Juvenal's injunction: 'If you go out to dinner, first make your will.' Cities have been infested with crime since the earliest days. It is the increase in the cities which has offered the new opportunities.

Police have everywhere become essential. As the urban centres multiplied, the inadequacy of the old system of policing became evident. Watch committees, nightwatchmen and footmen outside palaces were not enough. Louis XIV created a police force for Paris; Napoleon developed it through the agency of the skilful Fouché; the Austrians and the Prussians copied it. The Russians had a police force responsible to the Tsar only from the days of Peter the Great, and Tsar Nicholas I invented the modern Russian secret police, the famous Third Department at its head, which became practically supreme in the state and has been a model for totalitarian states, Russia included. In England there was much suspicion of these continental practices: 'They have an admirable police at Paris,' wrote an Englishman in 1811, 'but they pay for it dear enough. I had rather half-a-dozen people's throats should be cut in Ratcliffe highway every three or four years than be subject to domiciliary visits, spies, and all the rest of Fouché's contrivances.' When Sir Robert Peel introduced a police force in London in 1829 it was vigorously opposed as betokening despotism. But it was found nevertheless to reduce the then prevailing high rate of crime. In the twentieth century there are no countries which do not have a police force of some kind.

4

The world of the future seems likely to be a world of cities. Older than nations and states, their history is as long as any other viable organisation of men. The errors of planning of the twentieth century have created worse asphalt jungles than the errors of neglect in the nineteenth. Cities in the new world of communism have tended to be of a mathematical bleakness that causes their inhabitants to feel nostalgia for the slums of capitalism. The new capital of Brazil, Brasilia, created when the water supply of Rio de Janeiro finally began to give out, is a fine collection of monuments but it is not yet a city. There, too, we miss the fountain.

Urban Population
(In order of size in 1750)

1750	c.1980	
Canton 1,236,000	5,000,000	(1973)
London 1,117,000	6,970,100	(1977)
Constantinople 1,000,000	2,534,839	(1975)
Madras c. 800,000	2,470,289	(1971)
Calcutta 700,000 (1814)	3,141,180	(1971)
Paris 547,000	2,317,227	(1975)
Nanking 500,000 (approx. 1843)	2,400,000	(1974)
Ningpo 500,000 (approx. 1843)	250,000	(1973)
Soochow 500,000 (approx. 1843)	598,000	(1957)
Naples 427,000	1,223,927	(1976)
Shanghai 270,000 (approx. 1843)	10,000,000 (estimate)	(1976)
Moscow 250,000	8,011,000	(1979)
Vienna 247,000	1,580,600	(1980)
St Petersburg 220,000	4,588,000 (Leningrad)	(1979)
Amsterdam 201,000	965,246	(1980)
Cairo 200,000 (approx.)	8,143,000	(1975)
Hyderabad c. 200,000	1,215,119	(1963)
Peking 200,000 (approx.)	8,000,000	(1976)
Lisbon 180,000	1,707,500	(1974)
Berlin 175,000	1,909,700	(1978)
Dublin 165,000	567,866	(1971)
Rome 163,000	2,883,996	(1976)

1750	c.1980	
Madrid 160,000	3,146,071	(1970)
Bombay 150,000	5,850,000	(1971)
Delhi 150,000	4,065,698	(1971)
Palermo 139,000	657,326	(1980)
Mexico City c. 137,000	8,941,912	(1976)
Milan 135,000	1,724,819	(1980)
Venice 134,000	367,528	(1980)
Hamburg 130,000	1,664,800	(1980)
Rio de Janeiro 125,000	4,315,746	(1970)
Marseilles 111,000	914,356	(1980)
Lyons 110,000	452,841	(1980)
Cadiz 100,000	135,743	(1970)
Copenhagen 100,000	673,698	(1978)
Valencia 100,000	648,000	(1980)
Warsaw 100,000	1,463,000	(1976)
Florence 78,093	460,944	(1980)
Lima 64,000 (1812)	3,595,000	(1980)
Havana 51,037	1,900,000	(1976)
Philadelphia 42,444	1,949,996	(1970)
New York 33,121	7,895,563	(1970)
Boston 18,028	641,071	(1970)
Alexandria estimated at a few thousands	1,900,000	(1980)

53

Empires

Happy, thrice happy mortals who, situated at the extremity of the
globe amidst the wilds of Africa, formerly so barren and desolate,
can lead a life of content and innocence!

J. S. Stravorinus,
Voyages to the East Indies 1768–1778, of South Africa, 1770

We are still undegenerate in race; a race mingled with the best
northern blood . . . will you youths of England make your country
again a Royal Throne of Kings, a sceptred isle. . . ? This is what
England must do or perish; she must found colonies as fast and as
far as she is able . . . seizing every piece of fruitful waste ground
she can set her foot on and there teaching these her colonists that
their chief virtue is to bear fidelity to their country.

John Ruskin, Inaugural Lecture at Oxford, 1870

It is 'most deplorable that the process of decolonisation is still not
complete'.

Brandt Report (1980)

Readers from outside Europe may wish to point out that their
main criticism of the industrialisation which began in the eighteenth century in Europe and North America is that the Western
Europeans and Anglo-Saxons over the sea, freed by Renaissance
humanists from any theological interpretation of the concept *imperium*, used their superior technology to conquer, or at least to
dominate, most of the rest of the world.

The Western conquests in the sixteenth century have been noticed. They had led by 1750 to the division of all South, all Central
and half of North America between the Spanish, Portuguese,
British and French empires. A few islands lay in the hands of the
Dutch and even the Danes. The division of South America between the Spaniards and Portuguese along the line approximating
to the present frontier of Brazil had been confirmed by a treaty
in 1750. The empires so established sought to isolate themselves.
They tried to ensure that trade to their colonies should be mon-
opolised by shipping of their own. Meanwhile, though the Otto-

man Turks pressed against Europe until 1683, their defeat in that year at Vienna marked the beginning of their real and absolute decline. From then on until the Japanese defeated the Russians in 1905 the European states had matters all their own way in the world.

They had of course quarrels of their own. In the last half of the seventeenth century the British defeated the Dutch and in the eighteenth century beat the French. They thus became the paramount power in North America as in much of the rest of the world. Their great years were 1756–63, when they conquered Canada and much of India. Fifteen years later the British colonists of North America embarked upon their great rebellion against the home country. They carried on too the conquest of the north part of the continent themselves. The Spaniards and Portuguese had conquered their territories in the New World before their independence from the *madre patria* but that independence followed in the 1820s in imitation of North America.

These wars of independence in both North and South America were won by armies led by white men of European origin who were to complete the capture of the Americas for Western European ideals, if not crowns, during the rest of the nineteenth century. They had brought, as has been seen, to both North and South America a slave population of African blood to supplement, or replace, the native Indian labour. In several independent Latin American states some members of the indigenous population later recovered some of their old political control: notably in Mexico. In other parts of Latin America, Indian tribes survived in something close to their pristine conditions. By and large, however, America by 1850 was a Europe-beyond-the-sea. Canada was a British dominion, and the Caribbean was wholly colonial, except for dismal Haiti. But European colonists were pouring into the United States and Latin America to ensure the confirmation there of a Christian God, some notion of European law and the customs of European commerce.

The process of European empire in what the Victorian traveller A. W. Kinglake described as 'the splendour and havoc of the East'[1] differed from what transpired in the Americas because of the survival there of enormous indigenous populations. Still there were some similarities. Thus the oldest European empire, the Portuguese, had been forced to retreat to Timor, Goa and Macao. Their successors, the Dutch, were well established in the thousand islands of the East Indies where they administered a bureaucratic realm as if it was a private estate of immense commercial benefit. They agreed on a division of interests with the British in 1824.

Britain, with her establishment in Malaya,* dominated South-Eastern trade. Various indigenous movements and principalities fought losing battles. The Spaniards held the Philippines, the archipelago of seven thousand islands where Magellan had died and whose first Governor-General had once asked permission of Philip II to conquer China too. (Rudyard Kipling also wondered in the nineteenth century whether 'Britain had conquered the wrong country. Let us annex China'[2].) France, though expelled from India by the British, was established in one or two Pacific islands and in Indo-China. Britain, on the other hand, had been the great inheritor of Portuguese and Dutch initiatives. From the 1850s onwards she managed the Indian subcontinent as an administrative empire. The Mogul emperors who had so impressed the Europeans in the seventeenth century sank into unpitied oblivion, while the British justified their actions, at least to themselves, by arguing that they were rescuing the 'mild Hindoo' from Muslim tyranny. Later they tended to take the Muslim side in arguments within the subcontinent. They had also become the tutelary power in the Persian Gulf.

Meantime in a similar way the only European people to be contiguous to Asia, the Russians, had also expanded steadily eastwards into the half-empty heart of that continent. Beginning to do so in the late fifteenth century, only a generation after Henry the Navigator, the small grand duchy of Moscow had become the nucleus of a large state dominating the other Slav cities by the end of the fifteenth century. Its boundaries were at the Urals before 1550. Ivan the Terrible conquered the Khanate of Kazan in 1552 and that of Astrakhan in 1556. Russians fleeing from the tyrannical Tsars of Moscow drove east into Siberia where there was no serfdom, but during the course of the seventeenth century the Tsars caught up with them. They soon nominally incorporated all of Northern Asia – most of the land being below freezing point for over 200 days a year – into their empire. A Russian city was founded on the Sea of Okhotsk, facing Japan, as early as 1649.

Russian expansion to the south of Central Asia was slower but

* Captain Light established British rule in Penang Island in 1786. The occupation of Dutch possessions in the East Indies during the Napoleonic Wars stimulated British interest which led to Sir Stamford Raffles' foundation of the 'Straits Settlements' and of Singapore.

no less sure. Peter the Great defeated the Khanate of Crimea, which was integrated into Russia in 1783. Caucasia and Georgia were wrested from a dependence on Persia. In the nineteenth century the Tsars established their dominance over Tashkent, Samarkand, Bokhara and Merv. They would have absorbed Afghanistan had it not been for persistent British opposition organised from India.

China and Japan had in the seventeenth century adopted a policy of seclusion. Japan's only contact with the outside world was the Dutch warehouse permitted at Nagasaki. The Celestial Empire of China's only outlet under the Manchu dynasty was a group of Portuguese Jesuits in Peking who were tolerated for their competence in astronomy. Only in the nineteenth century did this isolation come to an end.

The interior of Africa remained for several hundred years untouched by European empires because of the control of its northern coast (including Egypt) by dependencies of the Turkish Empire and because of the sway exercised by malaria and other tropical diseases in the centre and south. Still, Western European merchants established themselves in forts for slave trading and other commerce all the way down the west coast of Africa from Dakar to the Cape, just as the Arabs had been doing for centuries down the east coast. Portuguese merchants and soldiers were a little more deeply established in both Mozambique and Angola. A Dutch colony was set up at 'the tavern of the two seas' – the Cape of Good Hope – in 1652; by the late eighteenth century foreign ships were calling more often than Dutch ones. This colony passed to the British in 1814, but after the Great Trek (in 1835–37) of 'Boer' farmers there were two authorities in South Africa: the British imperial one and the Dutch independent colonists, who after further wars became the heart of the independent republic of South Africa.

France developed trading interests in Algeria after 1815 and established a substantial colony between Oran and Algiers in the 1830s, followed by fierce but eventually victorious wars in which the legendary Marshal Bugeaud was the French hero and Abd-el-Kader (finally surrendering in 1847) the Algerian. By 1841 there were already nearly 40,000 French *colons* there. The British meantime established a zone of interest in the hinterland behind the main trading ports of West Africa chiefly in order to prevent that territory from continuing to sell slaves to South America. Once malaria started to be successfully controlled in the mid nineteenth century, a scramble began first for trade then for administrative control. Some fighting took place between the British and Dutch of South Africa (independent of Holland after 1815), and several disputes and war scares between Britain and France, but there was less fighting in Africa than in any other continent between the Europeans. Some Africans resisted but their fire power was less effective than that of the Europeans, while Christian Africans in certain tribes such as the Fante in what is now Ghana or the Ibo in Nigeria welcomed the estabishment of a *pax Europea*.

Collaboration, negotiation and skilful diplomacy marked 'the grab for Africa' of the late nineteenth century. In the course of a few years the division of the continent was achieved. France succeeded in gaining control of 3·87 million square miles, including the Sahara but also Madagascar, Algeria and Tunisia. After 1904 France also acquired a protectorate over southern Morocco. Britain gained 2 million square miles of Africa with another 1·6 million square miles if the protectorate over Egypt and the Sudan be taken into consideration. Germany, late in interest and late even in securing her own unification, found herself with 900,000 rather unrewarding square miles. The Portuguese, first in the battle for Africa in the sixteenth century, had 787,500 square miles in 1900. The Italians, also late into the 'great game' of colonial empire, acquired 200,000 square miles, failed to capture Ethiopia, but just before 1914 added 400,000 square miles of Tripoli and Benghazi (Libya) to her dominions after a short war with the Turks. Despite the legacy of Isabel the Catholic which suggested that Spain should seek her fortune in Africa rather than in America, that ancient nation had to be content with a mere 80,000 square miles of African empire in 1900. She later acquired an unsure protectorate over north Morocco to balance the French one in the south. Belgium, whose second monarch Leopold II had in a way fired the whole grab for the continent by his personal acquisition of the Congo, had 900,000 square miles. That left a mere 400,000 square miles of territory unconquered: 43,000 in Liberia, the artificial state established for returned slaves; and 350,000 in Abyssinia (which at the end of the colonial era in 1935 succumbed to the Italians). The Dutch republic of Transvaal had been subsumed by 1902 in British South Africa, while occasional Russian interests in Ethiopia in the nineteenth century had been frustrated.

This partition of Africa actually thwarted most countries concerned despite their gains. The Portuguese were thus prevented from linking Angola with Mozambique by the establishment of Rhodesia in the Zambesi basin. The Germans, by their creation of German East Africa, prevented an unbroken line of British possessions from Cairo to the Cape. Contrariwise, the British prevented the French from realising their imperial dream of a belt of French civilisation from Senegal in the west to Djibouti in the east.

As for Australasia, the French, Portuguese, Spanish and Dutch followed the Chinese into Australian waters in the sixteenth and seventeenth centuries – particularly the Dutch. Then the great voyages of Captain Cook in the 1770s led to the British occupation of the main continent of Australia and Tasmania after 1787, and of New Zealand between 1814 and 1840 – a fortunate opportunity for the Anglo-Saxons at the zenith of their ascendancy. As the Australian historian Geoffrey Blainey remarked[3], Australia was first settled with the twin hopes of giving England the naval supplies which it needed (flax for sails, pine trees for masts) and of ridding the country of the people it did not want to keep (convicts). Soon after, the last paradises of indigenous monarchies in the Pacific were also absorbed by European or North American powers: Fiji, Tonga and Gilbert Island were made part of the British Empire; New Caledonia, Tahiti and the Marquesas became part of the French dominions; while the Germans held the Bismarck Archipelago and the Mariana Islands, with part of Samoa. The US absorbed Guam, the rest of Samoa and Hawaii – the latter to become a fully fledged state of the American Union. Drink, religion and European rivalries were the chief reasons for the downfall of the indigenous monarchs such as the Pomare kings of Tahiti.

The 'Europeanisation' of the globe, therefore, seemed almost complete about 1910 – if North, South and Central America with the Caribbean are looked on as Europe-over-the-ocean, and if the Russian capture of Central and East Asia is given a similar definition. Outside the zones of direct European control, the Turkish and Chinese empires were penetrated by paternalist and often patronising European officials and merchants during the nineteenth century; the Persian monarchy was dominated by an Anglo-Russian agreement over zones of interest; and only a very few entities (Japan, Nepal and Thailand; Ethiopia and Liberia; Haiti, the rebel republic of the Caribbean) were without European political direction. Of these only Japan preserved her nationhood and independent strength.

There were some signs, actually, to the far-sighted (including the poet Kipling*) that the age of European domination might be short-lived. Japan beat Russia in war in 1905. The nationalist Chinese revolution of 1911 opened up a new series of possibilities for China mostly directed against European influence. The transfer of authority in 1899 in the Philippines from Spain to the US was resisted violently by the Filipinos, while the Muslim 'Moros' in the Philippines had never been properly conquered by Spain. A long war between the Dutch and Muslims in Sumatra had begun in 1873. Both French and British colonial rulers were constrained to use force to confirm their control over West Africa between 1900 and 1914. Even so, no serious tremors had occurred in the main edifices of European authority and the classically educated (of whom there was no lack in the European empires) recalled that even Tacitus had his doubts as to the permanence of the Roman Empire; yet that Empire had lasted another four hundred years after Tacitus's death.

These structures were maintained as they had been achieved, by superior military power in the hands of the Europeans, although missionary and commercial activities were continuous. Many traditional rulers chose the simple way out of their dilemmas by accepting Western supremacy; others genuinely recognised the value of the Christianity and the civilisation that Europe offered. Commerce subsequently sustained the interlocking unity of all these empires, so that in 1914 it seemed as if the entire world were part of a single 'great international commercial republic' – in Halévy's words: a well-policed and apparently increasingly orderly world, even though under the surface there was much turbulence. Already many, from King Thebaw of Burma to Chinese mandarins, hated the West with violent resentment.

The first effect of the Great War of 1914 was to extend rather than to curtail this European control. Thus most of the Middle East passed from Turkish to direct European rule. The Germans lost their African and other colonies but they lost them to other Europeans. Nevertheless, as a result primarily of other disputes among the Europeans in the Second World War, this 'commercial republic' disintegrated. Since then it has been violently criticised as if it and the last vestiges of it which continue were the cause of

---

* Kipling's 'Recessional' was written in 1897. The elegiac note is obvious: 'Far-called, our navies melt away;/On dune and headland sinks the fire,/Lo, all our pomp of yesterday/Is one with Nineveh and Tyre!'

all the world's ills. The surviving empire, the Russian, is often excluded from this castigation; even so, it should be considered a participant in the adventure of European imperialism; or should we really consider it the great crime?

The following should be considered: first, the real destruction carried out by the Europeans was mostly in the Americas or Australasia, when the indigenous populations were shattered by the Spanish and Portuguese conquistadors and by the Anglo-Saxons – partly by military defeat, partly by 'cultural shock', partly by enslavement and above all by exposure to the diseases of the Old World. The Anglo-Saxon conquest of North America and the Hispano-Portuguese conquest of South America were on a par in this respect if no other. Except in isolated cases – the overworking of Africans in the Belgian Congo in the days of King Leopold (Conrad's *Heart of Darkness*) or of the Egyptians in building the Suez Canal, the destruction of peoples in Central Asia at the hands of the Russians – there were few other instances in which indigenous populations suffered so severely at European hands as to decline absolutely. The experience of European imperialism, indeed, evidently enabled most indigenous populations to multiply – because of the new crops and techniques and because of commerce. The shock of 1492–1550 in the Americas was a special occasion, a turning-point in the history of the world which could not have occurred in a way very different if the then divided New and Old World were ever to be drawn together. Of course there were many other ugly moments: the British repression after the Indian Mutiny, for example.* Asia was, however, no stranger to such times, and the myth of 'Merrie Africa' before the Europeans arrived is as distorting to reality as any other simplification.

Where the Europeans in Africa or in Asia can be reproached is not for their destruction of people in the aggregate but the damage that they did to ancient societies. Europe brought the countries which it ruled within grasp of modern technology, education and mercantile enterprises. Social upheavals followed. Europe also succeeded in destroying many old monarchies and tribal despotisms which, however brutal, might have given continuity, tradition and recollection of art to future political evolution. The Europeans often destroyed the aristocracies or churches

---

* Of which V. G. Kiernan wisely wrote: 'India was never forgiven for what it did in 1857, still less perhaps for what it exasperated the English into doing, or allowed to be done'[4].

which, however barbarous they seemed, might have assisted peaceful evolution in the industrial age – as happened in the European countries and in Japan. The end of empire in, say, Burma or the Belgian Congo left the country with neither a traditional monarchy nor a trained middle class. The natural consequence was chaos and parochiality unredeemed by custom. The British conquest of Burma in the 1880s was a particularly ill-judged manoeuvre, since the conquerors refused to recognise that conquered or free the Burmese are a quite different people to the Indians.

Vietnamese, Cambodians, Indians, Algerians and West Africans also lost land in places where there was substantial European immigration, or where the state or large companies elected to invest. French colonies in Algeria like British settlers in Kenya or Rhodesia occupied the best land. But in the end they were obliged to withdraw. Nor were those places a large proportion of the total areas concerned. On the other hand, a great many Africans were entrusted to carry out compulsory labour service, at the behest of their chiefs, no doubt, but to do the work of the Europeans. There was for the first time a demand for labour for wages and hence the beginning of modern economies. Nearly all the colonies were also divided by differing tribal attitudes towards occupying forces: all colonial empires had their sepoys, *regulares* or other native troops under European officers. Most European empires worked through puppet princes, a method used first by the Dutch in Java and one widely copied by British, French and even Russians in Central Asia. The consequent feuds, the memory of which was to many the most humiliating experience of occupation, made innumerable people educated in the European empires aspire to independence on a basis different from that which the Europeans desired for them. In the formation of those feelings, nationalists often overlooked for a time the fact that the Europeans had created the nations which they set out to try to capture.

A particular characteristic of European expansionism in the nineteenth century was that many European conquests, from Central Asia to the Spice Islands and North Africa, were obtained at the expense of Islam; as Elie Kedourie put it in his *Islam in the Modern World*: 'The long series of defeats at the hands of Christian Europe could not but undermine the self-respect of the Muslims and result in a far-reaching intellectual crisis. For military defeat was defeat not only in a worldly sense; it also brought into doubt the truth of the Muslim revelation itself'[5]. Few of the Muslim countries conquered by the West were really nations. But though for a generation Muslim states interested themselves in Western political ideals, few Muslims accepted Christianity: Christian converts (there were many) were chiefly made from more primitive religions. It was an accepted axiom of British India. that Muslims were impossible to convert[6].

Empire and industrialisation also, of course, had the effects of increasing standardisation and lessening diversity or even, as pre-eminently in the case of the Russian empire since 1917, abolishing it. Even the humblest cultures, Grahame Clark pointed out, were once marked by 'this precious quality of unique identity'[7].

The incorporation of traditional societies within the nexus of a worldwide market has likewise meant that the typical products of particular regions have been made too costly for daily use – and are driven out by standardised, cheaper products. Thus advances of science have gone some way to impoverishing the heritage of many communities. But it may be retorted that the increase in population – itself ensured by matters unconnected with science – necessitated or made such changes inevitable[8].

Technological changes have, however, caused upheavals within free and advanced societies as well as poor and backward ones. In particular they have caused a disruption of the concept of neighbourhood, have destroyed many people's sense of belonging to a local community and have dislocated kinship. Until the eighteenth century, it can be argued, the roots of culture and personality lay everywhere, not just in Africa and Asia, in the neighbourhood as well as in family and religion. But those links which tied the individual to society in the past have everywhere been shaken. Even in so old a world as Western Europe, the nations of the twentieth century, democratic and with universal suffrage, are as unlike the old nations of the eighteenth century as an aeroplane is to an ox-cart. In this respect industrial democracies and poor nations are as one.

There were, of course, two varieties of European imperialism: first, that which led to the permanent conquest of largely empty territories by a race desirious of remaining in those places; and second, that which led to a temporary occupation by soldiers, administrators and merchants of old lands still inhabited by large populations of comparatively sophisticated peoples. The first such occurred in the Americas, in Australasia and in Central Asia and Siberia; the second occurred in Africa and West, South and East

Asia. The Dutch colony at the Cape of Good Hope was in the seventeenth and eighteenth centuries nearer the first of these two categories since the fertile hinterland was virtually unoccupied in 1652 save for wandering Bushmen and Hottentots.

No one knows what would have happened if the Europeans had not arrived in these countries. If Columbus had not arrived in the Caribbean in 1492 the islands then inhabited by the peaceable Arawaks might have been conquered by (and themselves eaten by) the cannibalistic Caribs (just as Islam would have conquered the Philippines had the Spanish not arrived there first). The decay of the Mogul Empire was not initiated by the arrival of the Europeans. The coming of the latter to Africa prevented the conquest of large areas of the Dark Continent by Arabs. The prosperity of the Javanese coastal states was undermined in the seventeenth century after the Dutch capture of Jakata, but because of their conquest by the Sultanate of Mataram – not by Holland. Before that, the Javanese had partly colonised Madagascar and often threatened Malacca. After all, domination over other people had been the rule rather than the exception in all continents. What sort of empire would the Pharaohs have had had they been unable to levy tribute from subject populations?

The Japanese conquest of the Ainus, the Mongol or Manchu conquest of China and the Muslim conquest in the Mediterranean were all acts of imperialism in their way. Before the Europeans reached the East, the Khmers established imperial dominion over Annam and Burma. So were the Hausa-Fulani movements southwards in the nineteenth century in what is now Nigeria. The history of the East suggests that it was the rule, not the exception, for a large indigenous population were ruled by alien minorities which only recently had ceased to be nomadic. Long before the Portuguese reached West Africa, the Negroes moved south and east and began to displace the Bushmen of the south of the Dark Continent. Whether there would have been more or fewer massacres in Asia and Africa if the Europeans had stayed at home is anyone's guess. What is certain is that, both in the New World untouched by contact with Europe and Asia since the opening of the Baring Straits, and in the old Asiatic world of crumbling empires and memories of glory, populations lived as often as not, in the fifteenth century AD, in poverty, misery, prejudice and cruelty. They may have continued so to live – many still do – but Europe and Christianity at least gave them a chance, remote as it often proved, of an escape.

The European empires in some circumstances were also dominated by the indigenous or servile populations. Thus Gilberto Freyre says that Brazil in the eighteenth century was a country where 'Europe was reigning without governing; it was Africa that governed'[9]. European initiatives were also often encouraged by 'natives'. It was Chinese immigrant merchants to Singapore who persuaded the British to expand their control on to the Malayan mainland in the 1860s (Malacca and Penang formed the Straits Settlements in 1867). The creation of British West Africa owed as much to missionary zeal and a determination to bring the slave trade to an end as to the desire for gain or glory – though both the latter did play a part. Equally, the expansion of Russia to embrace most of Central Asia altered the Russian personality. The Slavs had been living in Europe long before most Germans, Franks or Anglo-Saxons. But their ceaseless wars against the Mongols and other Asiatic opponents caused them to turn in many of their reactions into something more comparable to an Oriental despotism than a European empire.

It is also unclear whether the empires were as a rule of benefit to the home countries. West Indian sugar planters and 'nabobs' in India made money in the eighteenth century, but the great imperial adventures of the nineteenth century were largely carried out for reasons of power politics. Britain, though she had expanded her imperial interests in the early twentieth century, had passed her economic peak in the 1890s when the idea of imperialism was at its height. Germany, with scarcely any colonies of substance, was about to become Europe's richest power. The US, with even fewer colonial possessions, was even richer. Even were it to be proven that the pursuit of empire was really a compensation for declining markets in rich countries, it would still be difficult to sustain the argument that economic imperialism was the fount of 'capitalist revival', as was suggested by Lenin in *Imperialism, the Highest State of Capitalism* (written in 1916) or J. A. Hobson in *Imperialism: A Study* (published in 1902). Eric Hobsbawm's argument in *Industry and Empire* was that the empires, particularly India under Britain, provided outlets in excess of anything the home markets could absorb. But that ignores that Britain's largest single trading partner was in the nineteenth century the United States. The loss of the Chinese market was not a serious setback to the United States after 1950.

From the beginning of the European expansion the idea of the conquest of souls was also always present: not much it is true, in the Russian conquest of Asia but a great deal in the Spanish and Portuguese endeavours. The Portuguese in Angola knew themselves to be fighting God's battles and saving Negro souls from heresy when they began to establish themselves in the continent. If the idea of Christian India failed, most Victorian adventurers in Africa at least had more than a touch of the 'muscular Christianity' of Kingsley and of Arnold. There were other ideals beyond religious ones: as late as the 1920s French soldiers engaged in Morocco against Abd-el-Krim fought these colonial wars with a clear conscience, as General André Beaufre put it, 'sure that we were bringing with us civilisation and progress, certain that we would help these people from their backward state'[10].

British administrators had high hopes of creating civil servants with a Roman sense of public duty out of Indians and Egyptians: 'We don't want to stay in your country for ever,' wrote Lord Milner of Egypt. 'We don't despair of leaving you to manage your own affairs . . . [But] if we were to go away tomorrow, you would not succeed in doing so, because you have not shaken off the old tradition. You still require a good deal of training in a better school'[11]. British administrations in West Africa were from the beginning concerned to train Africans for 'self-government'.

Even so unconventional a European as Winwood Reade wrote, in his extraordinary *The Martyrdom of Man* (1872), of what would now be called the underdeveloped world: 'those people will never begin to advance . . . until they enjoy the rights of man; and these they will never obtain except by European conquest'[12].

George Borrow said the same: 'what a crown of glory to carry the blessings of civilisation and religion to barbarians and at the same time beautiful and romantic lands'[13].

Most of the European countries for a time, particularly in the nineteenth and early twentieth centuries, also looked on their empires as giving them a great national mission. The great British Empire in India typified the age. The British not unnaturally saw themselves as immensely powerful, since a hundred million Hindus crouched at their feet. The historian Macaulay when he wrote his famous minute *On Education* in India (1835) was thinking in his own terms of the long-term interests of Hindus when he argued for the superiority of European to Eastern literature[14].

Herman Merivale, a professor at Oxford, summed up the British attitudes in the 1830s, before the age of imperialism had begun: 'The destiny of our name and nation is not here in this narrow island: it lives in our language, our commerce, our industry, in all channels of intercommunication by which we embrace and connect the vast multitudes of states, both civilised and uncivilised throughout the world'[15].

Cecil Rhodes' religious enthusiasm for the British Empire was thus widely shared. In a poem of 1911 D'Annunzio wrote: 'Africa is the whetstone on which we Italians shall sharpen our sword for a supreme conquest in the unknown future'[16]. He was of course merely echoing English or French imperialists. As late as 1939 a Polish government was announcing that it, too, needed its share of Africa[17]. The idea of conquest blended with that of a civilising mission. That Algeria before the French arrived in the 1830s was 'uncivilised' by any reasonable definition is certain.

The impact of European empires upon the continents which they ruled was so great that it is difficult for the one-time rulers and the ruled to make fair assessments. But to call the commercial activities of large American and European businesses by the name of imperialism is a sad misunderstanding. The US, South Africa, Australia and Canada all benefited from foreign investment when they were pastoral nations. So do the still poor countries of the world. Japan did not receive much foreign investment, but the pattern of Japan's military, monarchical, clannish and nationalist industrialism is hard to emulate. In the disputes over the nature of the 'Third World', or the 'underdeveloped world' or the 'developing world' – each few years produces a new euphemism – three things are usually forgotten: first, bad politics cause poverty more often than bad business; second, the rich world was once a poor one and the resources, population and geographical position of many countries now poor are such as could enable them to become prosperous; and third, 'economic imperialism' means, as Jean-François Revel once put it, little more than 'economic activity itself, the distribution of capital, goods and innovations'[18].

The concept of imperialism has also been allowed to play strange tricks in many places – none more so than in Latin America where the main imperialists, Spain and Portugal, were obliged to abandon most of their dominions in 1822 and 1825 respectively, though the former maintained Cuba and Puerto Rico till 1898, and Britain, France and the Netherlands all maintained footholds in the Guyanas till the 1960s. In the early nineteenth century some of these countries were at least as 'advanced', in the sense of producing as much, as the US. In the early twentieth century Cuba and Argentina were better off than many European states. But a combination of nationalism, romanticism, inertia, class consciousness and bad management (admirably described by Carlos Rangel in his brilliant *Du Bon Sauvage à Bon Révolutionaire**) caused Latin America to fall behind the rest of the world's advanced peoples. Latin American intellectuals often blame the North Americans for that and call their businessmen, health inspectors, advisers on education and other philanthropists by the name of imperialists. They do this, it seems, in order to find scapegoats rather than real explanations for their inability over the last few generations to work out for themselves just and enduring political systems.

In any balanced reckoning of European imperialism, its benefits or its disadvantages, the list of crops, techniques and medicine which the advanced world made available between 1440 and 1945 to the isolated and poor peoples is endless. The enthusiasm with which the natives of Tahiti greeted the iron nails made available to them in 1767 by the crew of *The Dolphin* symbolises one side of European expansion. The first hundred years at least of European expansionism must have been wholly beneficial to those with whom they came into contact in Africa and Asia. The control of malaria and cannibalism, the acquisition of the arts of reading and writing and the abolition of human sacrifice and *suttee*† constituted effects of imperialism as much as the overworked jute workers of Bengal constituted another. He who condemns the evils of colonialism must not be allowed to forget the almost daily ritual murder, or the golden stools caked with blood and swarming with flies, which characterised Ashanti in the 1860s. 'Imperialism' drew the neglected parts of the world into the general sweep of human history. The consequent plantations and the mines caused, it is true, vast upheavals of population – Indians and Chinese in particular began to travel to the ends of the earth: Malaya and South Africa became, with rubber plantations and gold mines, the centre of labour colonies for both peoples. Even so, after the initial discoveries had been made and after the initial technologies had been devised, it is difficult to believe that societies other than European would have conducted themselves more humanely: the evidence points to the contrary.

The exception to this comment remains Russia whose zone of effective imperial control, by direct or indirect means, has extended under communism to include such disparate satellites as

---

* Foolishly translated into English as *The Latin Americans*.
† The burning of a Hindu woman on her husband's funeral pyre.

Eastern Europe, Cuba and probably Afghanistan. This Soviet empire is the last of the European empires. It is also the most repressive. Yet is is hard to believe that the eclipse of the 'dismal anarchy of petty despots' in Central Asia before its conquest by Russia was an unmitigated disaster for those who lived there[19].*

* Several Central Asian emirs, like the Emir of Bokhara, lived in fealty to the Tsar till 1917. The character of the Soviet empire is discussed in subsequent chapters, particularly Chapters 42 and 63.

54
Schools and Learning

The French historian Rulhière, now forgotten, said, on being elected to the Academy in 1787, that 1749 was the year when the love of belles lettres was exchanged for philosophy, when the desire to please was replaced by the desire to instruct.

As recalled by Michael Levey, in *Rococo to Revolution*

Here we do not need men who think, but oxen who work.

Spanish Minister in 1850,
when refusing authority to found a school in Madrid

The English were a nation of merchants and manufacturers governed by aristocrats who made it a point of honour to appear ignorant, indeed to be ignorant of the economic foundation on which rested both their national greatness and their own. And it was at Oxford that this aristocracy finished its education. It would have none of a scientific education which it scorned as plebeian and materialist. It demanded an education exclusively classical.

Elie Halévy, *History of England in the Nineteenth Century*

Boswell recalls Dr Johnson asking a boy whom he met, 'What would you give, my lad, to know about the Argonauts?' 'Sir,' said the boy, wisely, 'I would give all I had.'

Two indirect consequences of industrialisation need to be noticed if only briefly: the effect on education and the effect on games. First, education.

We seem to differ from our ancestors, so far as the world of ideas is concerned, in our attention to formal education. Here, surely, is a revolution worthy of the word. Yet there is less novelty in our educational attitudes, as opposed to our institutions, than seems to be the case at first sight. For, in the agricultural age, children were educated as adequately as was necessary to carry out the rhythmic tasks which would await the majority, just as in our times children are educated for the service of industries and factories. The difference is the increase of literacy, not of education as such.

605

In the late eighteenth century most of the adult population of the world was illiterate, even in the richer countries. Then as now, a large number lived on the frontiers of illiteracy, including those who could read but not write, and those who could scarcely write anything, save their name. The incidence of illiteracy is testified to by such statistics as that, in East Yorkshire in the 1750s, two-thirds of bridegrooms could sign their name, only a third of brides. In Britain, at that time, there were only 2,000 schools in the country, all maintained by private charity, one for every fifth parish, and few with more than one teacher attached to it. In 1806 there were said to be two million children in England and Wales who had no education at all, and in 1810 three-quarters of the agricultural population were said to be unable to read. The few 'public schools' of England catered for a tiny minority of sons of aristocrats and merchants. Some rich families educated their children at home, where they learned more classics and literature than they did at the boarding schools which were often (particularly after 1770) turned upside down by open battles between the impoverished, and usually inefficient, schoolmasters and the high-spirited, and often acute, upper-class boys.

France was equally illiterate. A few schools were maintained by the king, and a few more by the Church or lords of manors. The status of teacher was not high. In south-east France, teachers could be hired at fairs. A man willing to teach reading would wear one feather in his hat. One who could teach writing as well wore two feathers. One who could teach arithmetic wore three feathers. As a rule, the pupils paid the teacher, though a few town councils of the *ancien régime* provided buildings in which a *maître d'école* would live and teach. Most countries were much the same. The Chinese and Indians had had for a long time schools at which the children of their noblemen-bureaucrats were taught. The Russians had copied the Europeans after Peter the Great's reforms for those who were between ten and fifteen years old (at fifteen, sons of this service-aristocracy entered the army). In Spain and the Spanish Empire, education was minimal and outside the few big cities non-existent in any formal sense.

The only nation in the world which, in the eighteenth century, did have a policy for education was Germany, though there was no German state. The view that everyone should receive some education was held firmly in Gotha, whose duke, Ernest the Pious, in 1642 ordered that all children should go to school at five years old; and by Prussia, whose king, Frederick the Great, in the eighteenth century decreed that attendance at school should be compulsory between the ages of five and thirteen for six hours. These rules were admittedly not kept. Most teachers even in Germany were unqualified and ill-paid. The school buildings were in bad repair. The curriculum was narrow, attendance was irregular, and few children went to school at all in the summer. Nevertheless it seems that most peasants in Prussia, and perhaps elsewhere in Germany, could read. Merchants and noblemen sent their children to school too and many to universities. But Germany was solitary in the world in these respects.

However, if states were negligent, some churches – notably Protestant churches and, above all, Calvinist churches – had other ideas. The bias towards primary education there at least was strong since the Protestant ethic demanded a knowledge of the Bible. Indeed, as a result Scotland, the Netherlands and Switzerland had in the late eighteenth century something close to universal education, though it was neither free – even if it were cheap – nor compulsory. Every parish in Scotland had to maintain a schoolmaster at the cost of the local landowners, and pauper children were educated free. The Scottish and Dutch universities were the best places of scientific study (including philosophy) in Europe in the eighteenth century. In the early seventeenth century most children in the Netherlands had some kind of schooling – either in village schools attached to the local church, in private elementary schools in towns or in 'Latin schools' in cities for boys between the age of nine or ten and sixteen or seventeen.

Of course, there had normally been good education available and even insisted upon for rulers, civil servants, merchants or even, on occasion, soldiers. During the Roman Empire, literacy was usual for the middle class throughout the Roman world, and the large number of clerks and civil servants led to the increase of educational opportunities, though almost all were the work of Greek teachers. Even Latin literature was taught in Greek. Legionaries were often literate. Roman writing was easy enough and the wax tablet with the metal or wooden 'stylus' was simple to use, too. Children of the rulers and civil servants, like the rich, went from primary school to a grammar school in order to study literature and rhetoric, usually under a Greek.

Rather as occurred in modern European civilisation, fairly late in the day, under Vespasian, the state began to concern itself seriously with education by subsidising teaching from public funds. By the days of Constantine, in the full decline of the Empire, many schools flourished at the cost of cities, though those empty and bureaucratic institutions were too formal to delay the decline of the political system. The Emperor Valentinian nearly approached the idea of universities: every metropolis of every province was supposed to have a school of grammar and rhetoric in Greek and Latin: 'the studious youth were prohibited from wasting their time in feasts', wrote Gibbon[1]. That Roman practice was approximately echoed by the Chinese, Persians and Indians – indeed by all settled empires.

One exception, in this as in most things, was Athens. Most Athenian Greeks in the fifth and fourth centuries BC were literate. The average Athenian's education was limited. It did not include the learning of a foreign language,* there was little science, history or geography, and no economics, but Athenians seem to have been able to read and write. They also learned both poetry and music. Euripides, for example, assumed that his audience could read. (Probably the Ionic Greek alphabet, with each symbol having a different sound and a distinct, simple shape, was an aid to literacy. After all, there are in Greek only twenty-four simply drawn letters.) Schools flourished. Homer was known as 'the schoolmaster of Greece'. The gymnasia, where wrestling and music were taught, were financed by the state (as a preparation for military training).

Mediaeval Italy was a more educated society than was eighteenth-century Italy. Forty per cent of children went to school in Florence in 1338[2] – an exceptional educational achievement at that time. In the sixteenth century the historian Guicciardini also thought, after a journey northwards, that 'the greatest part of the people of the Low Countries master the rudiments of grammar and almost all, even peasants, know how to read and write'[3].

These were exceptional circumstances. Athenians needed literacy because they had grasped the part played in society by law, and there was no professional class of lawyers. Hence, literacy was essential for day-to-day living. Rhetoric, scepticism and arithmetic were also required for survival within, and the management of, that precocious society of ancient Athens. Subsequently the Hellenic system of education based on Alexandria was concerned to ensure that the clever had access to the right materials: hence the great library – and hence education between seven years and

---

* Maurice Bowra tells us that the Greeks believed foreign languages were like the 'twittering of swallows'.

fourteen was a public charge. Roman education, like that of Athens, was concerned with law: 'We learned the law of the twelve tables in our boyhood as a required formula,' wrote Cicero, adding, with a familiarly nostalgic comment, 'though no one learns it nowadays'[4]. Rulers generally sought to pass on knowledge of the governance of their state to their descendants and so always had them educated. Mediaeval education in a few royal or noble families was sometimes admirable.

Such, doubtless, was the basis of education till the eighteenth century, though a few exceptional peoples such as the Jews, after their captivity in Babylonia, attributed greater importance to it for reasons of religion: indeed, the synagogue began as a place for teaching and the instruction of adults and continued as one for boys over sixteen. The modest general educational system of the Middle Ages – the cathedral schools began to teach children intended for the priesthood – was, equally, designed for the needs of a society in which the Church had, for a long time, almost a monopoly of literacy; and where even great rulers such as William the Conqueror, Hugh Capet, Otto the Great and Charlemagne could not write – though the last named could talk Latin. It also suited the Church to propagate a general view that the truth was 'something which had been once known but was now lost'. Priests naturally did their work better if they were literate. So did monks if they were able to read the scriptures – which was not universally the case before 800. Chivalry required horsemanship, swordsmanship and skill with the lance. The guilds needed technical learning, and in later centuries municipal councils began to found lay schools for the sons of burghers – the first since antiquity, though anyone who wanted anything more advanced than the abacus and arithmetic had to go to clerical schools. Girls' education, meanwhile, was minimal. Only if she wished to become a nun was there much chance of a girl learning to read. Otherwise, even in Italy, the most enlightened European country in the late Middle Ages, girls were never taught more than household tasks – to weave, embroider and so on, so that 'when you give her in marriage, men say not that "she cometh out of the wilds" '.

In general in the pre-industrial world there was never any sense that the average peasant or working man had a right to, or a desire for, any general education – any education other than what was necessary for his work. Until the eighteenth century most people did not send their children to schools, even if they could have afforded it, and even if there had been any schools, since they needed them to work at home. Children were needed at harvest time and could be employed from their earliest years. Only in the winter did they have time on their hands. Many were afraid that schools offered hazards to health. Those who managed small farms before the age of universal tax on incomes did not need to read, or even to count, to carry on their main work, even if large farms have always needed elaborate accounting[5]. Those who lived in cities and sought to sell or to exchange commodities had had to read and write for thousands of years – since, indeed, the days of ancient Iraq where, by 3000 BC at the latest, there were schools, mostly in private houses, to enable the children of priests and some soldiers to learn cuneiform and add, as well as to talk clearly[6]; or ancient Egypt, where surviving tablets make it evident that the mathematical problems of 2000 BC were the same as those set in schools today ('What equal areas should be taken from five fields, each of one setat, if the sum of these areas is to be three setats?'). But such urban societies were few.

As late as the eighteenth century there were to be serious doubts as to the benefits of education. Even a nation that made sure that its own children received the elements of education, such as the Dutch, educated a small minority. The attorney-general of King Louis XV wrote in 1766: 'every man who sees further than his dull daily round will never follow it out bravely and patiently', while the president of the Royal Society in England in 1807 opposed the prospect of 'giving education to the labouring class, for it would teach them to despise their lot'. In the sixteenth century the missionary Gregorio López had found it 'damnably dangerous' to teach Indians in Mexico to read and write[7]. Dr Antonio Ribeiro Sanches in Portugal, in the eighteenth century, argued that there was no need to found primary schools in remote provinces since that would result in a shortgage of rural labourers[8].

Some of these attitudes remained for a long time. The Sultan of Oman once even pointed out to Britain in the twentieth century that the reason that they lost India was that they educated the people[9]. Bishop Muzorewa recalled: 'in the 1930s, in colonial Rhodesia, the benefits of an education were still not fully evident amongst my people. . . Many parents regarded time spent at school as time taken away from what they considered more important things'[10].

All these attitudes were swept away after 1800 in industrial countries. The industrial age was served better by literate and educated people than by illiterate ones. 'In most artisan trades,' wrote E. P. Thompson, 'the journeymen and petty masters found some reading and work with figures an occupational necessity'[11]. Germany's education service improved to become a genuinely universal system by 1815, and Holland and Switzerland followed to introduce universal, free and compulsory education. Europe was half literate by 1850, with Italy and Spain rather behind the average, and Germany ahead – indeed, Protestants were everywhere ahead. But most schools still had only one teacher, one room, and England, like Italy, introduced compulsory education only in the 1870s. Professor Cipolla speaks harshly of the English attitude: 'Part of the price England paid for being the first country to industrialise,' he says, 'was that the rapidly growing urban population had no access to schools.' Though the early stages of industrialisation swamped all existing services, private philanthropy and initiative did make many contributions: Robert Raikes founded his famous chain of Sunday schools in 1780, and the Quaker Joseph Lancaster, who so influenced Mexico and Latin America, began his evangelical schools in 1798.

Since that time, in the last three or four generations, education in rich countries has become universal, free, compulsory and, as a rule, coeducational. Even in the thirty-eight poorest countries, the World Bank in 1980 estimated that three-quarters of children of primary school age are now at school, compared with half in 1960. A quarter of the appropriate group are in secondary schools compared with not much more than a seventh in 1960. No greater change has ever occurred in human history. Some qualifications are required. First, there are some countries where the law's provision has never been carried out, however good the system seems to be on the surface. Second, there remains in some countries, such as Britain, a widespread incoherence in the methods of administering education dating from the nineteenth century and only comprehensible because of it. Third, though an industrial society benefits from an educated population, not every country has decided what sort of education that should be. Obviously, it should be more than simply knowing well a series of national classics, such as *The Pilgrim's Progress* or Foxe's *Book of Martyrs*, which was believed to be all that was needed in the English schools of the eighteenth century. Managers of industries in the nineteenth century in much of Europe learned to speak 'of Job or Odysseus, of Catiline or Cicero as if they had lived but yesterday'[12]. Generation after generation throughout the Western world studied one aspect or another of classical civilisation. Bentham complained that at the revised monastic foundations of England, the 'public schools', the children learned nothing which would be valuable to them in an industrial society; but the parents of public schoolboys were indifferent to science. They wanted a classical and philosophical education in their family[13].

That approach to education has now been rejected. In its place, there is more science, but a clear vision is often lacking of Western education in the 1980s, since some teachers are unclear what Western civilisation is. The most recent generation in the West has reacted against Aristotle's concept of a liberal education ('a gentleman must never take too much interest in any occupation, art, or science'), as it has against formal education. Now a reaction against that reaction is beginning. But many societies (particularly the Anglo-Saxon ones) seem caught between two worlds, the world of a good education for a few and that of a mass education, and seem powerless to decide on their aims. In the Communist world a more resolute attitude to education is detectable. It is based on traditional methods: competition, selection, vocational training and nationalism. Probably, however, the muffled voice of contemporary Western education is only a short-term interlude, a halt on the journey. A return to a traditional, disciplined education seems inevitable.

Fourth, the history of education since the late nineteenth century has become inextricably concerned with the history of schools and a national system. This is an extraordinary change from the old method of learning in small villages or colleges, where the teachers carried out themselves the small amount of discipline needed. The modern educational system is the reverse of this desirable parochiality. The conversion of education into one more major national issue in democracies is a challenge to the mood of serenity in which education should be carried out.

There is no doubt, too, that education, like the development of the press and the rebirth of sport, assisted at the birth of nationalism. The versions of history taught in European schools of the 1880s pressed a knowledge of the national past of peoples into the imaginations of schoolchildren that rarely emphasised the 'international republic of letters', nor of commerce. Germans learned anti-Slavism, Frenchmen anti-Germanism. A new consciousness of national literature and history added fuel to aspirations and resentments. The symbolic revival in the nineteenth century in Germany of old Nuremberg, so long neglected, as the centre of the new German culture in place of frenchified cities such as Berlin, was the work of nationalist historians and educators.

A bad education is worse than no education. Gibbon rightly pointed to this when he described the Emperor Valentinian, who nearly founded the university in the Roman world, as being 'unenlightened, but uncorrupted, by study'[14]. One of the first tasks of education is to ensure that verbiage is not mistaken for learning. Yet Western experience shows that teachers, including teachers at universities, have shown themselves, in the age of mass education, to be as inclined to subservience to intimidation as any other group of people. A majority of dons of German universities survived the Nazi capture of power without dismissal or resignation, and a Nazi salute, at the beginning or end of lectures, as required, seemed a small price to have to pay for tenure. A good picture of what German education meant even in 1870 was given by a speech in 1870 of Emil du Bois-Raymond, the most famous German physiologist and Rector of the University of Berlin: 'We, the University of Berlin, quartered opposite the royal palace, are, by the deed of our foundation, the intellectual bodyguard of the House of Hohenzollern'[15]. It was thus not surprising that sixty years later Hans Schemm, the first Nazi minister of culture in Bavaria, could say: 'We are not objective, we are German.'

Communists have worked against the serenity required for true education just as violently. For example, Stalin, in a journal of the central committee of the Communist party of the Soviet Union devoted to history, criticised editors for allowing the publication of an article which had tried to examine with objectivity the attitude of the Bolsheviks to the German social democrats in 1914. He pointed out that the day had passed when 'archive rats' could 'prefer objective facts to history which suited the current policy of the party'[16].

Education in the Middle Ages in Europe was carried out, if at all, with a view to enhancing the power of the Church. In the twentieth century in the same continent it has replaced religion as a prime preoccupation. The library is more important than the chapel in modern universities. Though education is not the good life itself, and though no grants, subsidies and scholarships make up for lack of clear thought as to what the good life should be, education can point the way to the good life as nothing else can: its universal acceptance as being desirable for all is one of the few unquestionable benefits of the last generation.

55

Games

Each and every festival was an occasion for sharpening the loyalty of the people.

Sir Ronald Syme (of Rome under Augustus),
The Roman Revolution

This book, with its multitude of odd and banal facts, arranged so cavalierly, as in a bazaar, has been the history of working hours. But where is the appropriate mention of Callimachus who carried off the prize in the horse race? Where is the special kettledrum set up at Sumer in the temple courtyard? Where is the waltz, first danced at a court ball in 1794? Did not Amasis I, King of Egypt, when reproached for having spent the whole day hunting, reply: 'Bowmen bend their bows when they wish to shoot; unbrace them when the shooting is over . . . so with men. If they give themselves continuously to serious work . . . they lose their senses and become mad, or moody'[1]? Games after all, like war, anticipated agriculture.

Games are more than they seem. That inspired historian of the subject, the Dutch professor Huizinga, pointed out that, according to ancient Chinese lore, 'the purpose of music and the dance is to keep the world in its right course', so as to force nature into benevolence towards man: the year's prosperity in ancient China was held to depend on the right performance of sacred contests[2]. The Greeks' attachment to games, particularly victory in games, was a mark of their appreciation of beauty, their desire to celebrate health, and grace, which played such an important part in their attitude to life. In the earliest days of Sumer, games, music, dancing and religion were part of the same ritual, and the ball games of Crete and Mycenae tell as much about the life of that civilisation as the staircases, the pottery and the estimated figures for the export of wool. The tribes of ancient South America enjoyed log-races, while the rubber ball, unknown to Europe before the Spaniards reached Mexico, enabled the ancient Aztecs to play basketball. At Chichen Itza, there is a court 540 feet by 224 feet, dating back at least a thousand years. The Romans' passion for gambling, for varieties of backgammon and draughts,

614

began the era, it would seem, of real games, and 'the Games', the great chariot races and gladiatorial combats, at their appropriate and fixed times each year in fixed places, reflect, in their prefigurement of modern Mediterranean *fiestas* and *feste*, an historical continuity as strong as the more obvious ones of law or architecture. Modern Italy's *ferragosto* is a memory of the Romans' *feriae augusti*. Under Claudius in Rome, there were, in the first century AD, 159 days of holidays in the year, of which ninety-three were devoted to games at the public expense. The modern tourist with his camera and guidebook stumbles admiringly over the ruins of amphitheatres, where battles were fought between buffaloes and elephants, or Saxon prisoners and Christians, condemning the practices whose institutions nevertheless survive, and perhaps failing to calculate that the 150,000 or so spectators at chariot races in Rome would have exhausted the capacity of all but the largest modern arenas: such temples of entertainment of the twentieth century as the Opéra at Paris seat a mere 2,156.

Sometimes games in the past got out of hand. The rivalries induced by the contests between the 'blues' and 'greens' at Constantinople led to the civil wars and the death of thousands at the hands of what Gibbon described as the 'blue livery of disorder'[3]. 'A happy variation of the natatorial contest,' wrote Huizinga, 'is to be found in *Beowulf*, where the aim is to hold your opponent under water till he is drowned.' Some games such as the tournaments which were the pastime of the European landowners between about the twelfth and the seventeenth centuries acted as substitutes for manoeuvres; and war, for many hundreds of years, was little more than hunting carried on by other means.

The effects of industrialisation on games were several. First, it drew people into cities where natural games of the age of agriculture were less easy to maintain. Children might play in urban streets till the twentieth century but that has been less and less possible in advanced countries because of the automobile. Then the increasing attendance of the majority of the world's children for long periods in schools has combined with a new recognition that exercise is healthy and games beneficial in various ways. The coming of the factory has led also, on the one hand, to the beginning of a cut in hours of work and, on the other, to the provision by companies of fields or courts for athletics. The mass media have concerned themselves with sport too, creating out of good bullfighters, footballers or cricketers heroes of our time.

616 Our Times II: Absolutism and Democracy

The consequence is mass sport. The great ball games of the twentieth century have also their curious histories. Their origins are to be sought in England in the Victorian age, in the unusual structure of English social life, in the existence of a village green, perhaps in the absence of compulsory military training and the spirit of local self-government – even if afterwards they became regimented, scientific, disciplined, highly financed and cut off, as games of the past were not, from the culture of the people.

Then there is gambling – the activity in leisure of thousands of millions of punters and adventurers, housewives and lords, its history unwritten as its transactions are often unrecorded. Its political significance may be considerable. Many good judges attribute the downfall of old Cuba in 1959 to gambling. An American sociologist wrote of Cuba: 'Whether or not they plan in advance for other expenses, there is no doubt that many people on small incomes regularly devote a specified portion of their earnings to lottery tickets. It is useless to argue with them that the same amount placed in a savings account would, in time, provide a competence for old age or for a possible emergency. The lottery is the most potent enemy of any program designed to promote thrift. It encourages a . . . speculative mania, where everyone lives in a bubble which for most investors bursts every Saturday evening'[4]. Perhaps too a history of when a people has holidays tells more than it seems, whether it is the ancient Sumerians who had no weekly holidays but eleven to fifteen days at the New Year's feast, or whether it is the modern 'holidays with pay' desired by workers in factories.

Yet there is a more complicated point to be made. The best form of democracy might have occurred when the system concerned was far from perfect from the point of view of voting but when elections were 'much more a drama about the life of the town' and when the essential preoccupation of politicians was the frame within which the programmes and policies were written; the rules and forms were realised as being of prime importance. Halévy spoke of the rowdy English elections of the early nineteenth century as being explicable only 'if we regard the electoral contests in the light of a national sport, as popular as, indeed more popular than, horse racing'[5]. Perhaps there has been some decline since then. Elections are rarely pure entertainment. The issues have become too grave, it seems. Tocqueville rather gloomily wrote that men living in democratic times 'do not readily comprehend the utility of forms . . . Their chief merit, however, is to serve as a barrier between the strong and the weak, the ruler and the people, to retard the one and give the other time to look about'[6]. Even so, most people concerned to establish or preserve free institutions today appreciate the point. Keynes, writing after the First World War had shocked all civilised spirits, pointed out that his generation had suddenly become aware that Western civilisation was 'a thin and precarious crust erected by the personality and the will of a very few and only maintained by rules and conventions skilfully put across and guilefully preserved' – a democrat, that is, is one who keeps the rules of the game. That is what Plato meant when he said that 'life must be lived as play'[7]. If the rules are kept, policies can be changed. The rules are, therefore, more important than the policies.

Book Six

Our Times III:

Wars of Our Time

Power worship is the new religion of Europe.

George Orwell

Men are usually governed less by interest than by beliefs and passions.

Elie Halévy

56

Modern Souls

In each age of the world distinguished by high activity there will be found at its culmination, and among the agencies leading to that culmination, some profound cosmological outlook, implicitly accepted, impressing its own type upon the current springs of action. This ultimate cosmology is only partly expressed, and the details of such expression issue into derivative specialised questions . . . which conceal a general agreement upon first principles almost too obvious to need expression, and almost too general to be capable of expression. In each period there is a general form of the forms of thought; and, like the air we breathe, such a form is so translucent, and so pervading, and so seemingly necessary, that only by extreme effort can we become aware of it.

A. N. Whitehead, *The Adventure of Ideas*

At first sight, the most curious innovation is that much of the world in the twentieth century lives and dies without religion. This may appear to be a unique condition. Even imperial Rome had its formal deities. Perhaps, it may be thought, here is the explanation for the failure of human beings to benefit from technological advance as they might have been expected to.

But, on examination, this concept of a lay world needs qualification. The last two hundred years have been characterised by revival as well as by disintegration, and by new religious enthusiasm, from messianic preaching to mystical healing. Sceptics in the eighteenth century, such as Gibbon, would have been astonished to find that, two hundred years later, religious conflicts such as those in Ireland, the Middle East, Iran, India, the Philippines and the Sudan were more numerous and more violent than they were in his day. 'Barbarism and religion', whose triumph, during the fifth century AD, Gibbon claimed to be commemorating, have continued hand in hand in the twentieth. The overthrow of the Shah of Persia in 1979 was, on the surface at least, the result of a revolt led by popularly backed conservative holy men in protest against modernisation – an identification of religion with reaction similar to the popular alliance in Spain in 1808 against Napoleon. In the broadest sense, too, of what is desired by religion, the craving for certainty has probably never been stronger (as Isaiah Berlin reminded us in his *Russian Thinkers*[1]) than it is now.

Every form of Christianity has taken numerous new shapes. Thus Roman Catholicism has become 'a refuge from the pressures of mass civilisation', as well as the inspiration of an international political movement of the first importance, while the century of anticlericalism which began with the French Revolution inspired almost as many articulate defenders of the Church as did the Counter-Reformation. To both reforming kings and philosophers the Church of Rome seemed in the eighteenth and early nineteenth centuries the chief obstacle to their designs. Unbowed, Catholic missions redoubled their efforts in Africa, Asia and the Pacific. Alongside them other missions reflecting almost every sect of Christianity fought too for their sacred place in the sun: Evangelicals, Baptists, German Moravians, Anglicans and Methodists were soon to be found in the remotest places, and it was symbolic that it should have been neither a soldier nor an agronomist but a missionary, David Livingstone, who should first have crossed the continent of Africa in the mid 1850s.

Then however debilitated some modern industrial countries may seem, and however deserted their places of worship, there are none where the corruption, negligence and decay are as great as they were in Europe in the eighteenth century. Churches and orders, as a result of anticlerical legislation, have as a rule ceased to be great landowners. They have also lost their freedom from taxation and other exemptions. But disputes about these questions were at the heart of many political problems of the nineteenth and early twentieth centuries. For example, the role of the Catholic Church in culture generally was a determining point of argument before the civil war in Spain, in the *Kulturkampf* in Germany, and in the Dreyfus case in France.

The illusion that religion has declined absolutely derived from the creation of large towns whose citizens seemed to have different outlooks from those held in old villages or settlements. The very metaphors of the Christian liturgy, with its sheep and shepherds, gardens and wildernesses, seemed inappropriate in industrial life; and, in many industrial towns, those who went to church and took communion excluded, in the first generation or two of industrialisation, the factory workers. Anglican opinion at the time of the Industrial Revolution was expressed by Paley when in 1785 he presented Jesus Christ as the first exemplar of the principle of the greatest happiness[2]. Few churches designed after 1750 have been in the first rank among leading examples of architecture. But, taking the word in its broadest sense, religion has fought a good defensive battle. Methodism, for example, was able to an astonishing degree to attract the loyalties of both factory owners and factory workers in much of England, acting as an invaluable source of discipline for work. In a famous passage, Elie Halévy argued that Methodism, indeed, 'the antidote to jacobinism', saved England from revolution in the Industrial Revolution: 'The élite of the working class . . . had been imbued by the Evangelical movement with a spirit from which the established order had nothing to fear . . . In the vast web of social organisation which is one of the dominant characteristics of nineteenth-century England, it would be difficult to overestimate the part played by the Wesleyan revival. . . Thus . . . we can watch between 1792 and 1815 an uninterrupted decline of the revolutionary spirit among the sects'[3]. Methodism amounted, particularly in the US, to a second Reformation, whose emphasis was on popular styles of worship. Partly this was the consequence of inspired sermons by, for example, men such as George Whitefield who could make, it is said, congregations weep merely by pronouncing the word 'Mesopotamia'[4].

In the twentieth century the churches have, if anything, been more active in politics than ever before, even if some of their activities seem questionable, on theological and political grounds. Churches have taken every advantage of every new technique of communication. In the face of overwhelming repression, the churches have also made politically convenient adjustments: thus the Orthodox Church made no serious defence of itself against communism after 1917, and exchanged its loyalty to the Tsar for an almost equally uncritical one to the Secretary-General of the Communist party – though there is a sense now in which religion today forms a real opposition to communism in Russia.

The world wars of the twentieth century placed a strain on religion for two reasons. First, churches in belligerent countries became more explicitly than ever instruments of state. Preachers and priests assumed the roles of recruiting sergeants. One minister of St Giles's Cathedral, Edinburgh, declared in 1917 that anyone who talked of initiating peace negotiations with the rulers of Germany was 'a moral and spiritual leper'.

But at the same time many were so distressed by the suffering which modern war imposed as to contemplate abandoning religion altogether. An English Liberal politician, previously a strong Anglican, C. F. G. Masterman, wrote in March 1918: 'God is a devil who rejoices in human suffering. He may be. There's no evidence to show he isn't'[5]. Winston Churchill in his last speech as Prime Minister in the House of Commons, in March 1955, wondered openly whether God had 'wearied of mankind', after the coming of the atom bomb[6]. Even so, articulate leaders of the Christian Church in the late twentieth century such as Pope John XXIII or John Paul II have demonstrated in an extraordinary way the desire of men and women for religious leadership.

As for other universal religions, neither Buddhism nor Confucianism have made sustained recoveries in the intellectual and moral crises of the twentieth century. But Shintoism did sustain the industrialisation of Japan. It was after, not before, industrialisation that the cult began there of the emperor as a descendant of the sun. The fall of the Ottoman Empire and the Arab awakening caused a 'revolt of Islam' very different from that envisaged by Shelley. In the course of the 1960s and 1970s Muslim leaders have had money available from the oil of the Persian Gulf to finance a world-wide revival of their religion, itself encouraged by the failure of Muslim countries to combine economic progress with Western democratic behaviour. At the time of writing, Muslim fanaticism in the Middle East seems a stronger force than the attractions of either communism or Western liberalism. The 'Muslim revolt', however, is less new than is often assumed.

Meantime, beliefs in charms, spiritualism, ghosts, demons and other mysteries have contrived to exercise a fitful attraction even among educated people. Astrology's followers are increasing. Odd numbers, magpies, four-leafed clovers, black cats, spilled salt, dropped teaspoons still exert despotisms over rational people. The most learned Englishman of the eighteenth century, Dr Johnson, insisted on knocking every post as he walked along Henrietta Street. Burckhardt believed that the religion of the nineteenth century was 'rationalism for the few and magic for the many', while Geoffrey Grigson estimates that today in Britain 'about a quarter of the population . . . holds a view of the universe which can most properly be designated as magical'[7].

'In our country,' wrote Gilbert Freyre, of Brazil, 'fortunes are told with the white of egg in a cup of water; with an ear of corn that is placed below the pillow so that the sleeper may behold in a dream the one who comes to eat it; with a knife that is plunged in the dark to the hilt in a banana tree, the spots or stains being eagerly deciphered early the next morning'[8]. In South America a combination has been made between African (or native Indian) magic and Catholicism in which the Catholic saints are made to seem close to witch doctors. Rosemary and rue are still grown in Brazilian gardens to protect the house against the evil eye. Furthermore there have been few occasions when African or Asian revolt against European rule has not been mixed with religion.

So it can hardly be said that the decline of belief or religion is the chief mark of the world as a whole. This suggests that human nature will never abandon its desire for some general explanation or general scheme which places the day-to-day business of ordinary life in a grand frame.

57

Anti-Churches

The philosophers believed that they had only to hold power for a few hours and, by an operation of the grace of the state, not only the face of the world but the very soul of man himself would be changed. They thought it quite possible for government and quite easy for those who wielded its power to regenerate even Poland, to re-establish the finances even of Spain, even to organise perpetual peace.

Albert Sorel, *Europe and the French Revolution*

One of the most curious aspects of the evolution of some societies, since industrialisation began about 1750, has been the steady substitute of a lay religion for a real one, a lay religion which promises that happiness will (one day) be achieved in this world rather than the next. It has been this conversion of certain ideas, interesting though they might be in themselves as arguments subject to the usual rules of human fallibility, into lay religions which has caused the benefits of industrial development to be misused.

Rousseau was the first to suggest, in the eighteenth century, that even in an atheistic state an organised religion was necessary, though he thought it could not be Christianity, since that divided men from the state. (He did not know much about the Orthodox version of Christianity.) He proposed a civil profession of faith, the articles of which the sovereign people would determine 'not exactly as dogmas of religion, but as sentiments of sociability, without which', he argued, 'it was impossible to be a good citizen'[1].

Once the Revolution had got under way in France after 1789, these ideas began to be put into effect. Civic festivals were organised by the painter David. A movement towards 'dechristianisation' got under way. The Catholic religion in France was replaced not by humanism, or scepticism, but by the worship of Reason. All churches of Paris were consecrated to Reason. Martyrs to that cause soon began also to be worshipped. Reason was depicted with the outward characteristics of a chorus girl. She was soon replaced by a *Culte décadent*, based on a simple belief in republican citizenship and morality. Later still, the worship of the Supreme Being was propagated by Robespierre. That sought to place republican doctrine on metaphysical foundations. Robespierre, educated at a Catholic college, believed in God and the immortality of the soul, and the decrees which he introduced reflected that. Under him, four republican festivals were instituted as days of homage to the revolutionary *journées*, each consecrated to one civic virtue or another. This new religion was introduced by Robespierre himself at the Festival of the Supreme Being in 1794. The ceremony made a great impression on those who were present, but it infuriated the ardent 'dechristianisers', those who thought the state should be secular, and also the Christians. After Robespierre's overthrow, liberty of worship was introduced. Christianity, therefore, returned, first of all in private but subsequently as Napoleon's state religion[2]. Napoleon believed that religion was the vaccine of the imagination:* 'elle la préserve de toutes les croyances dangereuses et absurdes'. So 'the people must have a religion and that religion must be in the hands of the government'.

Actually he believed, rightly, that even Western Catholicism could be turned into the servant of the kind of state which he wished to build.

Meantime, Tocqueville observed that the belief of many living during the French Revolution turned early 'into a species of religion . . . which, like Islam, has overrun the whole world with . . . apostles, militants, martyrs'. 'The French Revolution, though political in origin, functioned on the lines, and assumed many of the aspects, of a religious revolution. Not only did it have repercussions far beyond French territory, but, like all religious movements, it resorted to propaganda and broadcast a gospel'[3]. Jules Michelet wrote: 'The Revolution did not adopt a church. Why? Because it was a church itself'[4]. 'It is with an armed doctrine that we are at war,' Burke had written earlier, in words copied by his political leader William Pitt[5].

The French Revolution excited everyone: 'even the whores ask you about Robespierre', Fr. Pedro Estala wrote from Paris in 1795. But its message was as ambiguous as Rousseau's. Ideas were thrust across the world: such as the Abbé Siéyès' argument that the Third Estate alone represented the nation. Napoleon appreciated that there was a certain emptiness: while *la grande armée*

---

* The metaphor was on his mind since smallpox vaccine had just been introduced. It was echoed by Marx when he said religion was the 'opium of the masses'.

passed him *en route* for Moscow, he remarked, 'Tout cela ne vaut pas des institutions'; and, on another occasion, reflected, 'Well, the future will show whether it would have been better for the repose of the world if neither I nor Rousseau had existed"[6].

The positive elements in the French Revolution were that it introduced rational legislation affecting everything from weights and measures to marriage. It overthrew landlords who would not, because of their dependence on the Crown, have turned their estates into innovating market concerns, as their English colleagues had done.

The French Revolution also had in Western Europe one major negative consequence: it destroyed the organic life of the peoples where its ideas were taken. The great Catalan conservative Francisco Cambó put the matter very well: 'All those organic divisions in political life separating one group from another which had been created over the centuries were cut off from us by the hurricane of the revolution . . . there only remained left the omnipresent state and the solitary individual without resources'[7]. Albert Sorel wrote: 'The Revolution destroyed petty states, diminished frontiers, suppressed feudalism and, after a time of producing anarchy, in the end made states more powerful. . . Each people,' he added, 'in imitation of the French, who had launched these great ideas of the Rights of Man upon the world, conceived of them with notions built up in their own minds. . . So the relatively cosmopolitan Europe of the eighteenth century became the ardently national and divided Europe of the nineteenth'[8]. In the sixteenth and seventeenth centuries the nations of Europe constituted themselves during religious wars because, as George Lichtheim put it in his essay *Imperialism*, 'religious belief defined national identity: When the nation state finally emerged it became possible to do without religious uniformity, but this was promptly replaced by a newcomer: patriotism, the affirmation of unquestioning faith in one's country.' Hobbes made the same point in his *Leviathan*, published in 1651. The lesson of the French Revolution seemed to be that pure democracy would lead in modern Europe, as in ancient Greece, first to demagogry and then to tyranny. For over a hundred years the echoes of events between 1789 and 1801 were regularly detected in other countries and even other continents, Girondins being detected in Spain, an eighteenth Brumaire in Russia: historical parallels falsely evoked on a hundred occasions to deceive.

During the nineteenth century, the consequent nationalism took

on itself many of the attributes of religion. Was Garibaldi a politician or a preacher? Who cared when he was speaking to a crowd
with 'that beautiful voice of his which was part of his fascination
. . . "Make arms of every scythe and axe," he would say. "Come!
He who stays at home is a coward. I promise you weariness,
hardship and battles. But we will conquer or die." They were
never joyful words but, when they were heard, the enthusiasm
rose to its highest. It was a delirium. The crowd broke up, deeply
moved'[9]. Germany followed Italy into this trough of deception, in
spite of her educational system, to articulate strange follies and
hatreds such as those expressed in the historical writing of
Treitschke. For Cecil Rhodes and imperialists of his generation,
the idea of empire also took upon itself the attributes of a religion.
At least Rhodes said that that was so[10].

Compare a similar comment about Russia. 'Russia cannot be
fathomed by the mind or measured by a common yardstick,' said
Tyutchev. 'She has a stature all her own. Russia *cannot but be
believed in*'[11]. Nationalisation overcame many religious attitudes.
In the nineteenth century, men were still primarily distinguished
in the world by their religions. In Jerusalem, a man was a Druse,
a Muslim, a Christian or a Jew. In the twentieth century a man's
ethnic or national loyalties seem stronger. People appreciated the
change as it was happening: 'Yesterday we were an ecclesiastical
community,' proclaimed an Armenian nationalist in 1872, 'tomorrow, we will be a nation of workers and thinkers'[12].

The consequence was the First World War.

A little earlier, Auguste Comte, troubled by what he considered
the 'perennial Western malady', the revolt of the individual
against the species, formulated more clearly than anyone else the
difficulty of rationalism: theology and metaphysics were, he believed, incompatible with positive knowledge. He believed in the
application of scientific canons of explanation in all fields: indeed,
in a cosmic order established by science – cosmic naturally because
scientific laws must be universal in their application and reject the
notion of diversity. But only in Brazil did that rationalism have
any effect. Thus, Comte was the intellectual father of the generation which founded the Brazilian republic, and the national slogan
'Order and Progress' echoes Comte's ideas. Equally Jeremy Bentham's Utilitarianism, which was aggressively anti-religious, also
had a brief appeal as an anti-religion. Ordinary anticlericalism
had also certain fanatical characteristics more usually associated
with religion than with reason.

Communism, however, was nationalism's real successor as a lay religion. The translator of Nietzsche, Oscar Levy, went so far as to argue that in spite of its atheism, communism was a Christian heresy, since it had an international and cosmopolitan faith, and it looked back to a garden of Eden in which strife was non-existent, and in which property was held in common. The Marxist movement in Europe became something very like a 'great religious movement . . . a movement of workers to educate themselves'[13]. There was evidently an echo of such attitudes in the 1870s among Russian populists whose mood, according to Isaiah Berlin, 'can fairly be described as religious. This group of conspirators or propagandists saw itself . . . as constituting a dedicated order'[14], and they it was who invented the compelling idea of the party as a group of professional conspirators with no private lives. Thus it was not surprising that an observer of events in 1917 in Russia wrote, even before the Bolshevik *coup*, that 'the first of May was celebrated in 1917 in Petrograd throughout the length and breadth of Russia as *a great religious festival* in which the whole human race was invited to participate and to commemorate the brother-hood of man'. A year later the same observer, the English jour-nalist Philips Price, wrote: 'My mind went back to 1793, the 20th day of Brumaire, when the great convention did homage to the goddess of Reason in Notre Dame. Today, no formal deity was set up on high and honoured. There were no signs of deism in this carnival of November 8th, 1918. But the new God was every-where. He resided in the heart of every one who took part in the ceremonies of that day and who was inspired by the great impulse to struggle for a new social order. His symbol was seen in the great banner that hung from the House of the Soviets . . . where the gigantic figure of a half naked workman was wielding a sword to defeat the Republic's enemies. Another of his symbols was a great red axe which, in Red Square, lay embedded in a gigantic white block labelled "White Guards" . . . Everywhere his symbols were seen that day denoting struggle, the essence of life, the worship of the "world spirit" '[15].

Thus the new anti-religion was launched, and swiftly recognised as such. Miguel de Unamuno wrote in 1920: 'Lenin is like a prophet of Israel, and what he preaches is a lay religion. Materi-alistic, if you like . . . but a religion. Atheistic, undoubtedly, but a religion. And a religion which will end up in a type of Buddhism. An Asiatic religion in any case'[16]. Maynard Keynes said much the same when, in 1924, on returning from Russia he wrote, 'I feel confident of one conclusion, that if communism achieves a certain success, it will achieve it not as an improved economic theory but as a religion'[17].

This lay religion had its most extreme manifestation in the cult of Stalin. Consider Alexis Tolstoy's poem addressed to Stalin:

Thou bright sun of the nations
The unsinking sun of our times,
And more than the sun, for the sun has no wisdom.

Thus this manifestation of our days has been combined with a revival of idolatry, which the worship of power usually turns out to be. It may be a 'relic of the time of the cave, of human servitude', as Karl Popper says, but our times have shown, in both great and old countries, such as Germany or Russia, and even small and modern ones, such as Cuba, Uganda or the Central African 'Empire', that rulers still wish to be worshipped, at least as much as they have done in the past.

In the US, even, Communists of the 1930s were characterised by 'an impassioned longing to believe' in a collectivist creed which repudiated most of modern American history, which after all has liberated the individual: according to Berdyaev, 'escape from self and a search for a new communion, a new congregation and a semblance of church'[18], but one which also involved a rejection of the world of the spirit.

A similar, conscious and, for a time, successful policy to replace religious emotions with ideological ones approached in a religious manner marked Nazism (though not fascism in Italy, even though Mussolini called his movement a 'church of all the heresies'). Great importance in Nazi Germany was, first of all, attributed to ritual. Hitler thought that the mass meeting was desirable not only because of the ideas transmitted but because it enabled the ordinary man to 'step out of his workshop'[19]. The figure of Hitler, his words and the sound of his voice were blended with startling visual effects, in order to mesmerise the masses of one of the most intelligent peoples into accepting a religious frenzy of patriotism and racism. This frenzy was organised at the 'congress city' of Nuremberg, the Rome of a new paganism, where huge flags flew from tall wooden towers. Eagles and loudspeakers, spotlights, electric organs and neon tube lighting, first used in 1905 and one of the most obviously useful technological devices in politics, granite podiums for the speakers, huge avenues for the parades, all were brought together to support a cult as religious in intent as it was political in effect. One Nazi 'prayer' ran:

Führer my Führer,
Thou hast rescued Germany from deepest distress
I thank thee for my daily bread
Abide thou long with me, forsake me not
Führer my Führer, my faith and my light.

A friend of the great poet Yeats, who was interested in fascism, thought that 'what looked like coming out of Yeats's reflections' in the 1930s was 'Fascism modified by religion'[20], but fascism turned out to be more like communism; a religion for those who accepted it. The fathers of both fascism and communism feared or looked forward to some terrible, or some glorious, catastrophe, a Day of the Lord in which all evil would cease. In the thousand-year Reich, as in the Communist society, immobility would be the rule. It is astonishing that such illusions survive the failure of prophecies to be fulfilled. But so it has been throughout history with prophets.

In Spain, at least the anarchist movement also had for a generation – between 1870 and 1936 – many of the characteristics of a secular religion: 'When will the great day arrive?' an anarchist worker asked a Spanish senator in 1903. 'What great day could that be?' asked the senator. 'The day when all will be equal and the land is divided among everyone,' was the reply[21]. The pursuit of this millenarian belief excited the fascination of many imaginative travellers. In Spain, the belief in the absolute goodness of the anarchist 'idea', and the absolute evil of those who did not partake of it, led to a cult of terrorism which helped to cause both a military dictatorship and then a civil war. 'I fear,' wrote a prominent anarchist, Angel Pestaña, 'that when the critical history of the terrorist days and the establishment of the dictatorship of General Primo de Rivera comes to be written . . . we will appear as the efficient cause of it'[22]. The judgement applies to other ideas sought with religious enthusiasm and ungodly methods.

It has sometimes seemed in the nineteenth or twentieth centuries as if art has been a substitute for God. Modern Christian industrial society devotes its biggest resources in architecture to opera houses, art galleries and libraries. What the cathedral was to the Middle Ages, said Professor Pevsner, the symphony was to the nineteenth century[23]. The regular visits to concerts paid by agnostic Jewish merchants of Germany were actions purely religious in implication. So were the visits to operas of Italians, even if men went to the opera in the nineteenth century in Italy in order to talk politics; and Verdi obligingly included in many of his operas a chorus about 'La Patria'. Yet much of art existed in the age of industry in no-man's-land. Great aesthetic achievements have been carried out but often 'torn out of the common ground of life'[24]. The fact that, in the nineteenth century, easel painting flourished at the expense of wall painting suggests an imbalance between architecture and painting which contrasts sadly with the golden days of the Renaissance. Perhaps music began to lose its way when it became a purely individual performance instead of being related to the carnivals or rituals of society. Dancing did. But Shelley thought 'Poetry is capable of saving us'.

Thus it looks as if the main challenges to the idea of the courteous enjoyment of the benefits of modern life are to be sought in the existence of anti-churches. The three destructive wars of the twentieth century – the First World War, the Second World War and the Cold War – were all consequences of these anti-churches: the first from the anti-church of nationalism; the second from the anti-church of Nazism and racism; and the third from the anti-church of communism and class consciousness.

The next few chapters explore these conflicts which have destroyed so much, including even the idea of progress. It will, however, be necessary first to indicate the interconnection of war and technology which lay at the roots of these conflicts.

58
War in the Nineteenth Century

The history of a battle is not unlike the history of a ball. Some individuals may recollect all the little events of which the great result is the battle won or lost, but no individual can recollect the order in which, nor the exact moment at which, they occurred, which makes all the difference as to their value or importance. . .

Elie Halévy, *History of England*, Vol. I

From the earliest days of the Industrial Revolution technological change affected war and, therefore, the political systems of those actually at war. For example, in the eighteenth century, iron foundries became identified, above all, with the casting of cannon. Could the steam engine have been developed had it not been for John Wilkinson's boring mill, which was first used for cannon? The 'American system of manufacture', that is, the interchange-ability of identical parts, was first used in respect of muskets. The French desire for an assured supply of saltpetre with which to make gunpowder in the eighteenth century led to the transcendental discovery that the soil is inhabited by micro-organisms. Mechanised book-binding began because of the shortage of labour among binders during the Napoleonic Wars, while the high cost of fodder for cattle used to haul coal from the pithead during the same conflict led to Stephenson's *Rocket*. Tinning of food was begun, as was the cultivation of sugarbeet, to serve the French army during the Napoleonic Wars, while dried milk was the response to a quartermaster's demand during the American Civil War. The characteristic material of the age of industry since 1870, steel, has been mostly used for war; and, in the shadow of war, civilised life has continued since then, too – preparing for it, winning or losing it, recovering from it and seeking means to avoid it. Even in Brazil, the war against Paraguay in 1865–70 was, according to a Brazilian historian, 'the major stimulus to . . . modernisation', accelerating the speed of telegraph and railways. The world's first electronic computer, foreshadowing the electronic future, was built at Bletchley Park by British post office engineers to help decipher German codes and tested in December 1943: before the end of the war some 'six or eight models, and some small offspring, were constructed at Dollis Hill with constantly increasing sophistication and brought into operation at Bletchley'.

So it is desirable to consider this military frame against which so much of life has been maintained. Of course, the history of the last two hundred years has also been the history of the novel, of the symphony and of the tractor; but war has probably been its prime mover.

The modern history of war began with the fortress. In the eighteenth century, wars were marked by defence systems inspired by the French engineer Sébastien Vauban. His main idea was a system of polygonal defence, stretched out beyond the city wall, using that wall as a platform for artillery. His fortresses required as great an engineer as he himself was to demolish them. So warfare on land implied the slow assembly of siege batteries. The field gun began its career changing the character of battles on land and sea. Horse artillery was introduced by Frederick the Great. The only guns used by infantry were muskets, with flintlocks which had an effective range of 100 yards at most. They were out-ranged by all artillery – particularly guns firing grapeshot (such as were used so famously by Napoleon at Toulon). Bayonet assaults, as devised by the French in the seventeenth century, kept infantry-men occupied. Rifles were still scarcely used, except for sport.

The field gun undid the fortress. The former could be accompanied by the telescope from the early seventeenth century. That improved the accuracy of artillery fire. Better mobility of supplies (by canals, improved roads and an organised commissariat) gave an impetus in the mid eighteenth century to a mobile army. Meantime, the improved professional armies could be turned, in the event of economic crisis, to control a contrary populace.

Much of the fighting in the world in the eighteenth century was admittedly still being waged by what seemed like the methods of the sixteenth. Wars between Indian tribes and Portuguese gold- and slave-hunters persisted, in Brazil, for example, the bow and arrow still being used sometimes successfully against the arquebus. But artillery gave the Europeans a decisive advantage: at the last great battle with the Indians who refused to move from their old homes in the Jesuit missions (in 1756) at Cabaté, 1,400 Indians were killed in a very few minutes[1].

The largest army in the world in the eighteenth century was that accumulated in Russia by Peter the Great: 200,000 regular troops and 100,000 militia. Peter thought of himself as first and foremost a soldier. When a son was born to him, he told the nation that God had blessed him with another recruit. But when he came to the throne of Russia, his army was still a mere Muscovite horde. It was assembled in the spring – almost every spring – with all available weapons, massed together and let fly on the enemy at an appropriate signal, with scarcely any chain of command or officers trained to guide the men. Peter changed all that. But, though inspired in his organisation by Europeans, he still used Mongol custom to ensure him recruits. Thus, at a time when most European armies were manned by volunteers or foreign mercenaries, the new Russian government demanded that every twenty households annually should provide one soldier. Numerous exceptions cut down the numbers of men available, but this system remained much the same till the First World War. Built round two guards' regiments, Preobrazhenskii and Semenovskii (both composed of nobles), the Russian armies became a match, within a generation, for the professional armies of the Swedes and Turks. A regular navy was similarly established. With these two conscripted forces, the modern state of Russia was created by 1725. In particular, the Russians could prevent the massed hosts of Mongol cavalry sweeping into their country every summer from the Crimea in search of slaves, as they had done for 300 years.

In comparison, the most successful army of the eighteenth century, the British, comprised barely 17,000 regulars in 1770 (Joseph II, the Holy Roman Emperor, required an army ten times that in 1778: but only half, 85,000, could get into the field). No hereditary monarch of the eighteenth century would have dreamed of imposing mass conscription, though the English used the arbitrary press-gang – a system only abolished in 1852. In the mid nineteenth century, even, during the Crimean War, the manager of the Clay Cross works in Derbyshire told Matthew Arnold that, 'sooner than submit to a conscription, the population of that district would flee to the mines and live a sort of Robin Hood life underground'[2]. Conscription had been considered wasteful in the ancient world. Revived during the Dark Ages, all militarily successful states had come to depend on professional standing armies. Spanish infantry in the sixteenth century had depended on conscripting one man in twelve, but he became a professional and was well trained.

Conscription was extended to Western Europe on a regular basis by the French Revolution, when the Convention decreed a *levée en masse*: 'From this moment until that in which our enemies shall have been driven from the territory of the republic, all Frenchmen are permanently requisitioned for service in the armies. The young men will fight; the married men will forge weapons and transport supplies; the women will make tents and clothes and serve in the hospitals; the children will make up old linen into lint; and the old men will have themselves carried into the public squares to rouse the courage of the fighting men'[3]. This characteristic development of the modern world was a return to barbarism, though the philosopher Condorcet thought it a step towards democracy.

The innovation of conscription transformed war in a way almost more critical than gunpowder. For a few centuries before 1789, soldiers had been expensive. Battles were avoided, unless inevitable. 'The object of the campaign,' wrote the historian of the British Army, Sir John Fortescue, 'was not necessarily to seek out an enemy and beat him. . . There were two alternatives . . . to fight at an advantage or to subsist comfortably. . . A campaign wherein an army lived on the enemy's country was . . . eminently successful'[4]. The reign of Louis XIV was described by Albert Sorel as 'a long lawsuit contested with armed might'[5]. Wars of the age of industry consisted of the elimination of the heirs one disliked. After 1789 soldiers became cheap. Napoleon boasted to Metternich in 1813 that he cared 'little for the lives of a million men'[6]. The losses could be made up from new acts of conscription.

A 'nation in arms' has to be fed with violent propaganda. The new means of communication, from newspapers to radio and television, have provided that. Peace thus became more difficult to establish. Treaties became more unreasonable than they had been in the eighteenth century. They were hence often more precarious. By then, too, nations not only conscripted their citizens when they were at war. They did so when they were at peace, on the assumption that a 'trained reserve' was essential. After the 1830s or 1840s the train and then the steamship gave nations a means of transporting millions of fighting men.

The Europeans had by now the largest armies. In 1813, at Leipzig, 539,000 fought. After 1812 Britain had 250,000 in its army and in 1816 had 30,000 troops to occupy France, 25,000 for Ireland, 25,000 in Britain, 20,000 in India – paid by the East India Company – and 49,000 in various colonies, plus 32,000 sailors. At Solferino, in 1859, the battle ranged over sixty square miles and 300,000 men were concerned. More people died there than at Waterloo. Fifteen years later the new Italy, a country of no great military importance, already had 350,000 in its army and 350,000 reservists. Before 1861 the US army was still only 16,000 men strong. In the Civil War both sides began with voluntary enlistment but, as the war lengthened, conscription was resorted to, by the South in 1862, the North in 1863. The South called up ninety per cent of all its men (perhaps 1,400,000) and the North forty-five per cent (2,900,000). In these great engagements, the railway was the package train, the nerve of the new military system and indeed consistently developed by some states for that purpose. Offensively or defensively? In Europe during the nineteenth century it was hard to know.

It is true that some small armies since the French Revolution have won victories: Garibaldi in Naples had only 20,000 volunteers. Kitchener won the Sudan at Omdurman, losing 48 men killed against 11,000 opponents. The twentieth century also would see some examples of small numbers fighting successfully against larger ones. The Cubans in 1895 tied down 50,000 Spanish soldiers with about 6,000 guerillas. A 'handful of pioneers' won great imperial territories, like those who in 1890 conquered Mashonaland for Britain[7]. But the major engagements of the age of industry have been vast undertakings, with millions of men implicated.

These large armies of the nineteenth and twentieth centuries have played an important, even a predominant, part in politics, regardless of war, regardless of the fact that an army successful in war can inspire peace. Thus Spanish America, in her war of independence of the early nineteenth century, replaced the distant king over the Atlantic with armies whose size was out of proportion to their function. European invaders were then improbable. Spain could not hope for reconquest. The army of the US in the 1830s numbered 6,000. The battles of the wars in America of independence against Spain and Britain had been fought with armies of 10,000 or so at most on the two sides. Yet the tiny state of Colombia, in the 1830s, had an army of 25,000 to 30,000. The military budget was three-quarters of the budget of the country. (Peter the Great had gone further, for he spent 80 to 85 per cent of the revenue of the state on the army.) Though justified as providing law and order, armies in Spanish America were usually the cause of anarchy. The wars of independence created warriors, militarism and caudillos. Much the same occurred in Spain in the nineteenth century. There, a network of military forces was organised thoughout the nation, which was divided into eight divisional commands, each with soldiers spread through the region concerned. That system was intended to give stability. Instead, it afforded opportunities for military interventions in politics between 1815 and 1936 on a scale which had never occurred before 1789.

The technological inventions in wars of this age have also been continuous. Of the age of horsedrawn artillery, Napoleon, trained as an artillery officer, was the supreme beneficiary. He always had a large quantity of guns. But better examples of this inventiveness can be seen in the history of the rifle. A regular rifle was in use at the time of the American War of Independence by American 'minute men' – picked marksmen with good eyes who could hit a target up to 1,000 yards away. But they were exceptions. Normally, rifles were used in the eighteenth century to cover a mere 100 yards and were still employed for sport more than for war. In 1807 the Reverend Alexander Forsyth, a Scottish minister from Aberdeenshire, devised percussion priming powder, which led to the percussion cap of steel and copper. Forsyth carried out his experiments in the Tower of London, and Lord Moira, then Master General of the Ordnance, provided a substitute for the discharge of the military inventor's pastoral duties. Napoleon offered Forsyth £20,000 for the secret of his invention. He patriotically refused, though the British government gave him nothing till he was on his deathbed. His system came into use after his death, in 1839, and was of great benefit, because of the impermeability of this cap to wind and rain.

Not long afterwards the bullet was redesigned by Captain John Norton in a cylindrical shape, with a hollow base, on the inspiration of lotus pith arrows which he had seen blown in India.

Again, the British Ordnance took a long time to put the idea into use. The French developed it for Minié's rifle, which had a range of about 500 yards. That outdistanced accurate artillery fire and, along with the precision cap, transformed tactis of infantry.

By the mid 1860s rifle-carrying infantrymen became the rule, not the exception. At the same time the breech-loading 'needle gun', which fired a paper cartridge, invented by J. M. Dreyse in the 1840s, was adopted by the Prussians. It could be mass-produced: 400,000 needle-gun infantrymen were used by the Prussians at the battle of Königgrätz, which effectively, but, for the future tranquillity of Europe, fatally, weakened Austria (still reliant on muzzle-loaded weapons) in her historic role as a bastion of Europe against Russia.

The breech-loading rifle, as opposed to its muzzle-loading predecessor, increased the rapidity with which soliders could fire and enabled them to do so when lying down or from behind cover. Field-Marshal von Moltke was convinced that this rifle made defence stronger than attack and that, therefore, battles would be won by envelopment. Meantime, the Americans were producing pistols in large numbers. After 1846 the revolver, in whose early production Samuel Colt was pre-eminent, was very effective in close fighting, particularly in the Mexican War. A mass demand for it followed among the gold seekers of California in 1849. All these US innovations were distinguished by a full interchange of parts.

The rifle, by methods of 'American manufacture', began to be produced in the same way. It was copied in England by Sir Joseph Whitworth, the Mancunian gunsmith, and the Royal small arms factory at Enfield was producing 1,000 rifles a week by the 1860s. Every rifle needed 700 separate parts, each interchangeable. 'Form, riflemen, form,' adjured the poet laureate, Tennyson, in a poem written in 1859; 'Ready, be ready, against the storm.' The new Enfield rifle used cartridges covered with grease which had to be bitten open before loading. The rumour spread in India that the grease was made from beef or pork fat. For a caste Hindu to bite any fat was a serious sin. Many sepoys in the British Indian service were brahmins and, if they were to bite this fat, they believed that it would take them many lifetimes to get back, through the cycle of reincarnation, to the summit which they believed that they had attained. Hence the Indian Mutiny in 1857.

The French were busy, too. Their *chassepot*, introduced in 1866, and invented by an officer of that name, was superior to both the needle gun and the old musket, since it had an accuracy of 600 metres. Tougher than the needle gun, it could also fire six to seven rounds a minute. But sustained heavy fire with the *chassepot* caused trouble. It had to be well maintained. When put to the test in Franco-Prussian War, it was defeated by the old needle gun (which the French generals assured their men would jam after it had fired a few rounds). The Second Empire fell.

During the rest of the century, the European powers competed to be the most effective producers of firepower, though they had reached by 1871 a high standard of efficiency. Which was better, the French Lebel rifle or the Mauser, the Männlicher or the 303 Lee-Metford? The Martini-Henry used metallic cartridges but Lebel's *poudre B* gave that an advantage. By 1900 all European states had magazine rifles of equal efficiency with calibres ranging from ·315 to ·256, all bolt-operated. All had smokeless powder and could be sighted to 2,000 yards. Machine-guns which could massacre infantrymen had been devised too; for example, the ten-barrel revolving rifle fed by gravity and rotated by a hand-crank, as invented by R. J. Gatling of North Carolina. The French *mitrailleuse* (with twenty-five barrels firing 125 rounds a minute) had been considered a secret weapon when begun in 1865. Excessive secrecy prevented its proper deployment in time for 1870. The machine-gun was only successful after 1884, when Sir Hiram Maxim devised his recoil-operated gun which was to become the crucial weapon in both the last, African stage of European empire-building and in the trenches which were to destroy it. 2,000 rounds could be fired in three minutes – a radical improvement which brought an end to old tribal monarchies and imperial European armies alike. The Matabele war of 1893, for example, was largely won by the British because of their skilful use of their machine-guns.

The American Civil War had constituted a positive laboratory of military invention. Armoured trains, explosive bullets, explosive booby traps and stink bombs all had their first use in that unexpected conflict. So, for the first time for a century or so, did terror used against civilians. Warfare at sea was transformed by the activities of the ironclads *Merrimac* and *Monitor*. Even a submarine (inspired by Fulton in the 1790s) was built. It sank a battleship off Charleston. Sea-mines had first been used by Russians to protect their base at Kronstadt in 1853, while the self-propelled explosive torpedo was produced for the Austrians by a Lancashire inventor, Robert Whitehead, in 1864.

The great French revolutionary wars had been fought by navies in which admirals and captains commanding ships measured in tens rather than hundreds had often played a personal part. Admittedly, the famous British captains such as Nelson or Cochrane had been backed by a navy which after Trafalgar in 1805 numbered more than that of the rest of Europe put together. By 1910, however, a man-of-war had become, in Elie Halévy's words, 'a gigantic factory whose first need was a large number of trained mechanics rather than men skilled in the manipulation of sails: a modern battleship had at least a hundred pieces of machinery'[8].

Propaganda in a modern sense began with the telegraph. But, once established for warlike purposes after the war of 1859 in Italy, it became an essential part of military communications. Telegraph wires also made it possible for events abroad to be reported in hours, not days or weeks. The telephone soon assisted that speed. The war reporter, the official communiqué, the special correspondent, the war photographer and the war artist thus entered battle. Legends have subsequently played as important a part in war as news. Very often what is believed to be the case is more influential on people's imaginations than what is the case.

The nineteenth century was an age during which European statesmen put war to effectual and controlled use: 'between Vienna and Versailles' (in time and space, as Sir Lewis Namier put it[9]), all the great political achievements of that long 'century of peace', 1815–1914, had military implications. Even the two great 'liberal' achievements of the nineteenth century, the unification of Germany and Italy, were the outcome of calculated wars. The unity of the US was achieved by the deliberate decision of the progressive northern states to resist secession by the use of armed force. The creation of the new European empires during that century was the consequence of the deliberate use, or threat, of military might, just as was the assertion of independence by the independent states of South America. This military role of states fortified the unity and strength of states. George Orwell wrote in 1945: 'In the last hundred years, all the developments in military techniques have favoured the state against the individual and the industrialised country against the backward one. There are fewer and fewer foci of power'[10].

The modern state is indeed an institution with many ancestors but its father is war. All states cherish as heroes the leaders in battle in the past, just as the armed services are the final sanction of the laws, and were the creators of the frontiers and unity of the state. The 150 or so states of the world in the late twentieth century have mostly come into being as a result of conflict or the manipulation of military power. Hence, there is a sense in which the historians of the last generation were correct in concentrating on the history of war and its origins. It is against the background of war and the fear of it that the history of our times has been played out. Michael Howard, at the end of a survey of European history, recently drew attention to one critical part of our affairs today which is sometimes overlooked: 'Nothing has occurred since 1945 to indicate that war or the threat of it could not still be an effective instrument of state policy. Indeed, against people not prepared to arm themselves properly it could still be exceptionally effective'[11].

59

The Great War

Life in the old Austria during the last decades of the Emperor
Francis Joseph must have been agreeable . . . tears come to the
eyes of the old who lived through this period when they see it
sentimentally recreated on the screen. Why could it not last? Why
should the disaster which so profoundly changed Europe have
started here, of all places. . . ?

Golo Mann, *The History of Germany since 1789*

1

The First World War broke out because the heir to the Austro-
Hungarian multinational empire was assassinated by a Bosnian
nationalist. This event symbolises the destructive face of nationalism. A multinational Austria-Hungary in the middle years of
the twentieth century would have saved the world much pain. But
the government in Vienna resolved to put an end to Bosnian
nationalism by demanding humiliating concessions from Serbia,
whose government had harboured the murderer. Russia was the
protector of the Serbs. The Austrians found themselves engaged
against that empire also. The German Empire was to Austria
what Russia was to Serbia. Military preoccupations were upper-
most in the German imperial government, which had not tried
unduly hard to work out a harmonious relation between civilian
and military authority: before 1914 no war council had been held
in Germany in which the politicians had a chance to participate
in discussions of military preparations.

The German master class dreamed of world power at Russian
expense. Russia had an alliance with France, who thus also became implicated. The war marked the collapse of the international
system constructed by diplomats; when systems collapse, all the
problems which they have hidden over many generations come to
the surface – the demands of repressed minorities, of underpaid
workers and persecuted sects: above all, in the modern age, the
demands of nationalism at one time seeming reactionary, at the
next revolutionary. The tide of nationalism was rising elsewhere
as well as on the continent of Europe: in Asia, South Africa, the
Middle East – even in Ireland. It was apparent in Latin America:

in Mexico and Cuba, directed against the United States, but in other countries too. This tide, deriving ultimately from the French Revolution, was accompanied by a general romantic disposition to believe that war was glorious. Glory went with nationhood. Nationhood went with the completion of unfinished conquests of the past. The wars were however fought over the consequent unresolved question: 'what national states should arise in Central Europe, and in what frontiers'? Such was Sir Lewis Namier's formulation.

Many, from Fascists in Italy during the First World War to the revolutionary socialists of the 1960s, have spoken of 'the educational value and the ethical aspect of war'[1]. Similar phrases can be found in the works of, respectively, probably the most popular President of the US (Theodore Roosevelt) and the best writer among the Prime Ministers of Britain (Winston Churchill). Roosevelt, for example, told cadets in 1897 at the Naval War College: 'Peace is a goddess only when she comes with a sword girt on thigh . . . No triumph of peace is quite so great as the supreme triumphs of war'[2]. Such romantic views were a contrast to the calculations of strategists, such as Clausewitz, who believed war to be diplomacy carried on by other means; or Bismarck who, when asked if he wanted war, replied, 'Of course not. I want victory.' Even so, that did not prevent the chroniclers of the Great War of 1914 from speaking in terms more appropriate to a tournament. Even during the worst fighting on the western front in the First World War, special correspondents referred to the battle almost as if they had been at Agincourt, not Mons. Even today, in the nuclear age, war colleges are adorned with heraldic emblems and mottoes such as 'Truth, Valour, Duty', 'Stalk and Kill', or 'La Fortune sourit aux braves'. There was, there is, in all this a certain ambivalence. Even in unpromising circumstances, peoples seek historical continuity.

The Great War had been long expected. It was the culmination of two or three generations of crisis, 'splendid little wars', years of acute apprehension and grasping emotions – generations whose diplomatic history has by now been incomparably well documented. 'The Great European war begins,' wrote *The Times* on 7 August, as if to allude to something much talked of, before that date. A disposition, after years of peace in Europe, to suppose that war had its benefits was widely held, not only in the poems of Romantics such as d'Annunzio, but in the speeches of politicians. Europe had had, for a generation, the smell of gunpowder in its transactions. Even the art critic John Ruskin told an audience of cadets at Woolwich that no great art had ever yet risen on earth but among a nation of soldiers. The poetry of the generation of 1914 was heavy with premonition. In 1896 A. E. Housman wrote:

On the idle hill of summer,
  Sleepy with the sound of streams,
Far I hear the steady drummer
  Drumming like a noise in dreams.

Far and near and low and louder
  On the roads of earth go by,
Dear to friends and food for powder,
  Soldiers marching, all to die.

Though the war broke out as a result of miscalculation, the long-term cause was the clash of European nationalism: particularly German nationalism.

Germany was a country, or rather a group of states, which had at the beginning been at a disadvantage in the age of commercial enterprise. No German emperor had been able to establish a common law. All was left to territorial princes, of whom there were until 1789 nearly 300, ranging from kingdoms to bishoprics, countships to lay princes. The hereditary succession to the empire had been only vested in the Habsburg family after 1437, when the electoral princes had whittled away their imperial power. Most German states had elaborate bureaucracies, but Prussia had the only efficient one. Most princes in old Germany had regarded their job as a sinecure. For many generations, there had been no national German currency, no national literature and no national industry. A few French Protestant immigrants had brought some good commercial ideas to Berlin, a quarter of whose population in 1740 were immigrants from France. Kant believed that the only common characteristic of Germans was their 'pedantic inclination to classify themselves in relation to other citizens according to a system of rank and prerogatives'. From a background of diversity and hierarchy, a challenge was mounted which was in the end simplistic. A nation in which the state was non-existent became the supreme advocate of state power. A society supremely conscious of hierarchy in Germany came to demand of the world the acceptance of a view that all Germans, from private to field-marshal, were a superior people. Germany had few colonies. But historians argued that the world was about to be divided into rival empires. Germany, not to be left out, sought an Africa in the Ukraine.

Five other important powers (the word is appropriate, for the European nations brought their empires into the conflict) also became engaged in war in 1914. Britain had had an understanding before 1914 with France which fell short of an alliance. But British statesmen considered that the German invasion of the small state of Belgium was evidence of a bid for world power. Britain could have turned a blind eye to the German entry into Belgium. But it could have done so only as a real surrender of its national will. After all, there was a treaty guaranteeing the frontiers of Belgium which Britain had not only signed, but drawn up.

Italy before 1914 had an alliance with Germany and Austria. She allowed herself to be bought by the French and the British. The Ottoman Empire, whose army had been trained by Germany, became drawn into the conflict out of hatred of Russia and suspicion of both France and Britain. The US entered the war since she feared that a German victory might result in a European military dictatorship: Germany improvidently had also attacked US shipping on its way to provision Britain. Finally, Japan became an ally of Britain in order to seize German colonies.

In the end, in fact, the war became a struggle against Germany more than, as it seemed to be at first, a war of Austro-Hungarian succession. It also became a war of disillusion for the Europeans' colonies: if colonial troops could be used against the Germans, they could also fight, successfully, surely, against Britain and France. Even so the war was essentially fought to decide whether or no Germany was to become the dominant power in Central, Eastern and south-eastern Europe. If the Germans had not sought to fight France, Britain and Russia at the same time (and added the US in 1917) they would surely have won.

Economic motives there were in the dislike of Germany, but all merchants of all nations had thought of themselves as the promoters of peace. They, like Norman Angell, knew war to be a 'great illusion'. The illusion that war was inspired by private manufacturers has taken a long time to die but, as Sir John Clapham reminded us, during the generations when private merchants were most powerful, the world was free from 'general war' for ninety-nine years; nor did anyone suggest that the wage earners accepted the war of 1914 primarily because of the high pay received during it[3].

As for the suggestion that the war was caused by economic

competition between the large states, the truth is that Germany and Britain were on their best terms in the 1890s when the former seemed to be pulling ahead of the latter, on their worst about 1912 when Britain's trade was expanding in its empire, Germany's in Europe. Soldiers and poets were usually more bellicose at that time than merchants. As Lord Grey put it: 'it was the great commercial centres of Great Britain that were most pacific and least anti-German up to the very outbreak of the Great War'[4]. 'Capitalism,' wrote Halévy, 'has no nationality . . . it is a force which makes for peace'[5]. The First World War occurred too at a time when most of the belligerent states had already begun, in the interests of social democracy, to interfere with the working of the free market in a way which would have greatly shocked statesmen of a hundred years before. In those acts, there was a real threat to the internationalisation caused by free enterprise.

The war proper began with Germany's attack on France. In the summer of 1914 France made a feverish effort to finish the grain harvest. She then mobilised her 2,877,000 reservists. That caused much unemployment because of the number of managers and technicians who had gone to fight. By the end of August 1914 half the factories of France were closed. Germany conscripted five and a quarter million men. There, too, there was a rise in unemployment for the same reasons as in France. Russia, far larger than Germany, also mobilised over five and a half million men in 1914, among them four million peasants. Though Russian agriculture had suffered from underemployment before the war, the consequence was similar to what happened in Germany and France. Production from land sown with grain dropped in 1915 to less than two-thirds of what it had been in 1914.

Britain in 1914 relied on volunteers, but otherwise she was no more farsighted than were her co-belligerents. One-fifth of the miners and a quarter of those in chemical industries 'joined up', so damaging industry severely. The US mobilised, in 1917–18, 4·8 million men and women. The likelihood that more millions of Americans were fit, and of the right age, had decisive consequences on events. Even more important was US spending – which totalled $33 billion: twice the expenditure of the federal government during the first hundred years of its existence.

2

All the combatants expected a quick war. Politicians believed that no economy could stand a long conflict. Trade surely would be too greatly disrupted. The contenders had prepared stocks of armaments, not armament industries. They used their arms budgets to buy shells from manufacturers rather than build factories. In addition, officers had been educated to believe that the spirit of attack would triumph.

These predictions proved false. In the past, governments under pressure of defeat made peace before their internal crises became too strong. In this first great war of the twentieth century, governments found the strength to carry on the fight longer than ever before. Hundreds of thousands of recruits were available. They were paid with an endless supply of paper money. The power of states had been greatly enhanced in the preceding generation, by Bismarckian socialism, by social democracy, by centralisation, by mass communication and mass education, by railways and telephones. Was the war a consequence of that *étatisme* more than anything? At all events, people wondered whether the war would ever end: 'I see no end to it . . . it is the suicide of nations,' a German doctor told Philip Gibbs, a British journalist. 'Artillery conquers the ground, infantry occupies it' was the slogan of Foch and repeated as if it were the formula for a great scientific discovery. In practice, it meant that, after throwing thousands of tons of shells and metal at the enemy (107,000 tons of explosive were deposited by the French and British on the first dawn of the third battle of Ypres), masses of men would be ordered forward to exploit the enemy's shock by capturing their guns or their observation points and above all to try to break through their defences of barbed wire, sometimes three belts of thirty strands. (Barbed wire, the American agricultural invention of the nineteenth century, turned out to be the master defensive weapon of the twentieth, making it possible to convert the most unpromising fields into fortresses more resilient than long-prepared stone edifices such as Kovno or Antwerp.)

Of equal importance was the spade. After the first few weeks, it was found that the best defence against artillery was not stone but soil. Hence the tunnels and 'dugouts' by which the war of 1914 is most remembered. 'Dugouts' with ceilings ten metres thick were found to be invulnerable even to heavy shells and, if reinforced by concrete, only three metres were needed. 'In the art of war, it is an axiom that he who remains in his trenches will be beaten,' Napoleon had said[6]. That failed to take into account the character of soil's resilience against big guns. Prefabricated huts invented by Colonel Nissen also made possible the quartering of large numbers of men close behind the trenches. So even if the 'front' were broken, it was easy to insulate the 'bulge' so formed.

What could be done against this stalemate? Cavalry? The early days of that war marked the apotheosis of the horse. Great armies could be taken by rail to the front. But there was nothing mechanical there to make them mobile, particularly once the land became muddy. Neither cars nor lorries were numerous. Neither were effective on rough territory. So horses were essential. The generals used cars to get around, but the field commanders were not able to, even if, as Marc Ferro pointed out, the generals paid obeisance to a bygone era of chivalry by taking victory parades on horseback[7]. Cavalry charges, on the other hand, could no more deal with barbed wire than huntsmen can jump it.

Aeroplanes, the great technological invention of the last few years of peace, seemed one possibility for breaking the deadlock. To begin with, these were used primarily for observation. Then came a stage when there were great air duels between 'aces'. These had little effect on the battles on the ground. There were also bombing raids, on a modest scale. The worst raid was a German one by Zeppelins on London in June 1917, when 162 people were killed and 432 injured. These raids had no effect on industrial production and little on morale. At the end of the war, however, aircraft did begin to play a part on the battlefield. Squadrons of fighters flew low in support of infantry. The success of that tactic persuaded the warring countries to build vast new fleets of aircraft. By November 1918 the US had 3,200 fighters, the British 22,000 (in comparison with 272 in 1914). These aircraft went fast: 140 miles an hour instead of 80 in 1914.

But aviation failed to interrupt the monotony on the ground, useful though it turned out to be once a line had been broken.

Gas was also tried, though all the countries concerned had signed an international convention in 1907, forbidding its use. The Germans experimented in October 1915 with tear gas which they allowed to drift to their enemies' lines. Everyone close to the front choked and panicked. The Germans, interested by that effect, used gas again. It enabled them to advance three miles. But it soon turned out that gas could be countered by masks, by specially treated cloth helmets, or by box respirators. The unpredictable behaviour of the wind could blow the gas back in the users' faces. The weapon was made effective by its use as a gas shell, which could be accurately despatched and, though small, could operate more powerful gases. These shells were used at

Ypres in July 1917, causing 20,000 British casualties, of which the majority survived. The British responded by using chlorine gas. Adolf Hitler, then a corporal, was poisoned by gas in this way. Perhaps that suggested to him that if 12,000 or 15,000 Jews 'had been put under poison gas, as hundreds of thousands of our very best workers from all walks of life had to endure . . . the sacrifice of millions . . . would not have been in vain'[8]. Gas did not, however, turn the fortunes of the war, save on two occasions. In September 1917 General von Hutier was enabled to capture Riga easily by using mustard gas; and in May and June 1917 the Germans were enabled by it to occupy Armentières, with almost no losses. Gas was looked on as atrocious: actually, it was more humane than most modern weapons.

Economic warfare helped to defeat Germany. But it was not the main factor. Britain sought to stop supplies from entering Germany. But many British goods went to Germany through neutral countries, particularly Holland. Holland imported twelve times as much cocoa in 1914–18 as she did in 1910–14, while her exports to Germany rose by the same proportion. The block-houses of the German lines were made, too, from English cement – also bought via Holland. German goods, even shells, continued to be sold to Russia. Still, in 1915 the Germans declared that, in return for the British blockade, they would seal the waters round Britain and Ireland with submarines. Among the ships which they sank was the passenger vessel *Lusitania*. A few days later the British declared all goods going to Germany to be contraband. They thereby established a full blockade. In January 1917 the Germans, in a delayed reply, announced an unrestricted submarine campaign. They sank 540,000, 580,000 and 847,000 tons of shipping respectively in the next three months. England seemed to be cut off from her supplies from the US. Even the entry of the US into the war as a result of that submarine campaign at first made no difference. Then 8,000 warships were brought in to escort the merchant fleets – the main use of navies in the twentieth century – and the sinkings declined.

Germany was, with her allies, seriously short of food. Only her occupation of the Ukraine, with its grain, and her occupation of Romania, with its oil, prevented Central Europe from starving. By 1918 the cattle in Austria-Hungary had dropped from 17 million, in 1914, to about 3½ million, pigs from 7½ million to 200,000. Shortage of fertiliser reduced the German grain harvest by a third, and the decline of cotton imports caused a paucity of clothing worse than that of food. But even so that did not bring victory to the Allies.

The weapon which in the end did destroy the stalemate of the Great War was the tank. The idea of it came to the British and the French at much the same time. Both Winston Churchill and Colonel Estienne thought of developing an armoured engine which by using caterpillar tracks, like the tractor, could move on all sorts of terrain, would by its weight destroy barbed wire as well as enemy machine-gun nests, and so protect advancing infantry. Though considered by Lord Kitchener, the British commander-in-chief, a mere 'pretty, mechanical toy', its production by the British soon began. The secret was kept by the well-leaked rumour that the steel plates used in the production were for petrol tanks: hence the name 'tank'.

About 130 primitive 21-ton tanks were used in September 1916 in an ill-fated Allied offensive, led by General Nivelle. Germany wrecked sixty tanks. The crews inside boiled to death. The supporting infantry were massacred. The Germans were thus convinced that guns would always win such a battle. For a year, the Allies' tanks were used only in driblets, from place to place. Their first effective use in a concentrated manner was at Cambrai in November 1917. 378 Allied tanks led two infantry corps over the Hindenburg line. The Germans broke in panic. By the late afternoon, the British had conquered 10,000 yards – an incomparable day's work. Only lack of reserves to exploit the gap in the offensive (and a German counterattack) made the victory less than complete.

Finally, in August 1918, the Allies combined 462 tanks with aircraft, at the battle of Amiens. Though the tanks could barely travel faster than one and a half miles an hour across the battlefield, they nevertheless inflicted a major defeat on Germany in one day. That persuaded Ludendorff to accept defeat though, oddly enough, the name of that victory, and others in the campaign of which it was part, is scarcely recalled today beside those of terrible stalemates, such as Verdun or the Somme. The coordination of tanks and aircraft was made possible by field radios and telephones.

The difficulty was to make a real peace. Not only had between ten and thirteen million been killed and twenty million wounded – unheard-of figures then – but, in order to cajole men to go to war and to stay there, and to persuade both men and women to work hard in ammunition factories, 'society', says Marc Ferro, 'had to be terrorised by propaganda into giving its last energies'[9]. The legacy of this propaganda was as pervasive for the following generations as were the remains of gas attacks among those who had suffered. Old comrades and industrial workers alike were affected. The Allied propaganda was more effective than that of the Germans; Ludendorff paid tribute to it: 'We were hypnotised by the enemy propaganda as is a rabbit by a snake'[10]. Certainly, British propaganda helped to draw the United States into the war. Two US historians, Commager and Morison, point out that 'one of the appalling revelations of the war was the ease with which modern techniques and mass suggestion enable a government to make even a reasonably intelligent people, with individual backgrounds, believe anything it likes'[11]. Characteristic of the time were the 'four-minute men' in the US, whose task was to infiltrate every public gathering with four-minute celebrations of Wilson and war. The story that the Germans were boiling down bodies of dead Allied soldiers for fat was alleged by *The Times* in April 1918[12]. The subsequent revelation that those stories were false may have been one reason why the stories of the extermination camps of Jews were disbelieved twenty-odd years later.

Propaganda apart, war brought brutality. The western front reflected the rules of war which all the belligerents accepted. The eastern front was different. For example, in 1917 General Brusilov's successful Russian offensive into Austria led to the laying waste of estates, killing of cattle, raping of women, a rehearsal, as Dr Norman Stone comments, for the Russian agricultural atrocities of 1917–18.

The belligerents of 1914 tried to stir up disaffected minorities within their opponents' territories. The Germans and Austrians endeavoured to awaken Russian minorities, preached a holy war against the French and interfered, where they could, in Ireland and in other British, French and Italian possessions overseas. They proclaimed Polish independence, and encouraged Flemish nationalism. In the countries which won, national unity was strengthened. But in the states which lost, disintegration, partly caused by external interference, constituted a reason for defeat and a serious impediment to acceptance of the peace. Myths were created in this war as much as they were in the Dark Ages. Thus in Arab history, as in *Seven Pillars of Wisdom*, there is a legend that the Arabs (led by T. E. Lawrence) freed Damascus. Actually, it was the 3rd Australian Light Horse Brigade. Idealism of sorts caused the victors to see good reasons to speed the break-up of the Austrian and Turkish multinational empires. They failed to destroy German unity, however, while Russian unity was in the end preserved after the end of their own civil war. Only Finland, the Baltic states and the Poles escaped from the fortress of modern Russia, along with Georgia and Armenia, and then in half the cases for only a short time.

The collapse of Austria and Turkey led to the creation of numerous small weak states, which also damaged the chances of lasting peace. The war of 1914 had been in a sense the logical extension of the idea of the self-sufficient 'nation state'. The peace after it, though in theory appreciating that – Wilson's 'fourteen points'* specified among other things an end to the 'great game of the balance of power' – served, through the principle of self-determination, to create many more states. A war which had, technically and in the short term, broken out for similar reasons as those which had caused conflicts in the past (injured pride and the hope of making the best of an opportunity that might not recur) ended with the promulgation of idealistic war aims: 'No peace is possible until . . . the principle of nationality and of freedom of small states is recognised.'

The war left large financial imbalances. All the defeated countries were ruined. That included Russia. But the victors were also half bankrupt. British trade had been in deficit every year since 1822: the gap had been made up by 'invisibles' – profits on insurance abroad, commerce abroad generally. Many of those 'invisibles' were sold. British markets in Asia went to Japan. The war brought to an end the days when there was a balance of gold stocks between industrial countries. The international gold standard, achieved in 1870, never recovered.

At the peace, few were able to be thoughtful. Max Weber had written in Germany: 'This war, with all its ghastliness, is nevertheless grand and wonderful. It is worth experiencing'[13]. Lloyd George in England was an exception for a time: 'We must not allow any sense of revenge, any spirit of greed, and grasping desire to overcome the fundamental spirit of righteousness,' he said on 12 November 1918. But he soon had to make concessions to an intolerant national mood famously expressed by a member of his cabinet, Sir Eric Geddes, when he said, at an electoral meeting in Cambridge: 'If I am returned, Germany is going to pay

---

* 'Quatorze commandements!' exclaimed Clemenceau, 'c'est un peu raide! Le bon Dieu n'en avait que dix.'

restitution, reparation and indemnity and I personally have no doubt that we will get everything that you can squeeze out of a lemon and a bit more'[14]. Hence the harsh peace of Versailles which kept German tempers aflame for another generation.

The First World War had other legacies, one obvious, the other less so. One was the Communist *coup d'état* in Moscow. 'We now face an enemy of a new type,' the last Habsburg emperor Karl wrote vainly but wisely to the Kaiser in 1917, 'more dangerous than the Entente . . . please look beyond its initial advantages to us. These threatening clouds can only be dispelled by immediately ending the war'[15].* The second legacy was the precedent for a new form of half-socialist, half-nationalistic 'statist' society which has subsequently made headway even in peacetime, even in the democratic states.

This latter political innovation was described by Pastor Naumann in Germany in 1915: 'Our self-knowledge is this: we Germans have slipped into this state of socialist or popular [*völkisch*] activity, in the strictest sense of the word . . . When we emerge from the war, we shall no longer be the same economic beings as before . . . upon the basis of wartime experiences, we will demand a regulated economy – regulation of production, from the point of view of the necessity of the state'[16]. To a lesser extent, the same could have been said in every state at war. Germany (which was dominated by Prussia) was ahead and realised what was happening more clearly than others did. The industrialist Rathenau coined the term 'state capitalism' to indicate the industrial reorganisation with which the government went ahead. German industries, he said, 'were doing the work [of providing the necessities of war] without having full liberty, serving the public interest by distributing neither profits nor dividends, their coordinating committees being intermediaries between capitalism and government'. All this constituted 'an innovation that the future may take to'[17]. Rationing was introduced into Germany in January 1915. Price controls came later in the same year. A subsequent regulation insisted that no worker could leave his employment without a licence. In 1916 all male Germans were drafted for war service and a systematic effort was made to increase female labour. Admittedly, this programme was dismantled after 1918. But when the Nazis came to power, and addressed themselves to

---

* Everything points to a deliberate decision by the Kaiser to keep the Bolsheviks in power.

national regeneration, they did little more than draw on these precedents. Ludendorff at one moment thought of mobilising the youth of both sexes in Germany when they reached the age of sixteen. All would be sent to training camps. There would thus be left a society neither civilian nor military. Instead, a truly egalitarian society would emerge, a 'nationalist-aristocratic-corporativist-socialist consciousness', the whole nation in step: a prophecy of both communism and Nazism[18].

The dangers implicit in this were evident at the time. Maynard Keynes in 1915, for example, saw that German economic writers were arguing for the permanent 'militarisation of industrial life'. 'A system of regulations must be set up, the object of which is not the greater happiness of the individual . . . but the strengthening of the organising unity of the state for the object of attaining the maximum degree of efficiency, the influence of which on individual advantage is only indirect. This hideous doctrine is hidden in a cloak of idealism . . . the peace will bring with it a strengthening of the idea of state action in industry . . . in the new Germany of the twentieth century, power without consideration of profit is to make an end of that system of capitalism which came over from England a hundred years ago'[19].

Characteristic of this tendency were three articles in *The Times* in 1916 which suggested the need in England for a national plan – 'a development towards nationalisation . . . a development not by the socialist's panacea of appropriation . . . but by amalgamation, by coordination and by bringing the State into partnership, and an increasing partnership, in the big businesses that result'[20]. Supervision, self-regulation, import controls, rationing of import space in ships according only to the military value of the commodity, a state with an omnipresent role in agriculture, huge taxes, inflation of civil services – these constituted the inheritance of the First World War. The depression and the New Deal, the challenge of Nazism and the Second World War, the establishment of ambitious welfare systems – all this transformed the small-scale states of 1914 into huge 'cold monsters', engaged on a war footing without the stimulus of belligerency.

What gave this new *étatisme* its special effectiveness was its liaison with humanitarianism and the consequent excuse that it had for entering into every detail of everyone's lives. Mr Justice Brandeis gave a good warning when he said: 'Experience should teach us most to be on our guard when the government's purposes are beneficent'[21]. But warnings went astray. The consequence was that, in every country at war, belligerency inspired elaborate new bureaucracies, censors of letters and of newspapers, secret services with larger budgets than ever before, and centralisation. In England a cabinet secretariat was invented. The 130 railways of Britain in 1914 became four in 1918, the forty-three banks also became four. In the United States the government took over the railways, and the Food Administration Board under Herbert Hoover bought food in bulk for the first time. Roosevelt's New Deal, with its national enterprise boards, was a lineal descendant of the political arrangements of the war. The British Labour movement undertook to forgo strikes for the duration of the war in 1915, and in 1917 strikes were prohibited, arbitration of wage disputes became compulsory, profits were limited and in certain war industries all trade union activities were suspended. Here was the modern corporate state of which some statesmen have ever since dreamed.

Russia was not excluded from these developments since, after the failure of British, French, US and German supplies, a great internal Russian thrust forward in 1916 resolved almost all that nation's economic problems. She showed herself capable of substituting her own for imported machinery. The mechanisms inside rifles were all being made by 1916 in Russia. By 1917 she had achieved by her own efforts a superiority of guns and supplies on the eastern front. Where the Kaiser's economic programmes were a direct anticipation of Hitler's, and Wilson's of the New Deal, the Russian war effort of 1915–16 became what Norman Stone provocatively describes as a 'first experiment in Stalinist tactics of modernisation'. So in the summer of 1917, 'most of Russia went on strike'[22].

That breakdown in Russia in 1917 was caused by the great industrial effort of the previous years which occurred in nearly all the belligerent nations. To begin with, the war had been greeted with euphoria, even in Russia. The socialist and labour movements were soothed by increased social benefits. Children were better fed than before. Hours of work were shortened. Women's 'right to serve' meant a breakthrough by women into professions dominated by males till then and to the women's vote in England and the US of 1918. In the US, the war also opened up many jobs to blacks in the North, and gave black servicemen a glimpse of equality.

Most people in most countries believed in the rightness of their cause: the Germans thought that they were defending Europe against Russia, the Russians knew that Holy Russia had to be defended against Teutons. Longuet, Guesde and other French socialists wrote to the Second International to say: 'The workers have no thought of aggression, but are sure they are upholding their country's independence against German imperialism.'

Euphoria lasted till the nations at war began to increase governmental power sharply. In Germany, Ludendorff after 1916 set up something close to a military dictatorship. Only a Kaiser *fainéant* remained. In France, Marshal Joffre and the army almost took power in 1914: 'The prefects are finished, the deputies don't matter, the generals can feed on human flesh.' The deputies, indeed, did not meet between August and December 1914 and, though they then reassembled, 1914 seemed the political *revanche* for which the professional army had been waiting since the days of Dreyfus and Boulanger. Later, Clemenceau ruled in France in the last years of the war as a dictator in the Roman sense of the word.

With the eclipse of Asquith in 1916, the age of the scholar-statesman was over in England. Lloyd George, the successful British war leader, ceased to be leader of the House of Commons, and his parliamentary appearances became rare. Though Britain retained a parliamentary life, opposition to the war coalition was shaken by the splits which the conflict caused in all the parties, including the Labour one, and by the transformation of politics on class lines which the war, despite its nation-building role, increased. Even in the US, Woodrow Wilson, more cautious in his use of presidential power than Lincoln had been in the Civil War, asserted executive authority so much as to cause Charles Evans Hughes in 1929 to wonder 'whether constitutional government as hitherto established in this Republic could survive another great war, even victoriously waged'[23]. In Italy, the war strengthened all anti-parliamentary forces which dreamt of overthrowing the constitutional monarchy and installing a national revolutionary regime, of 'left' or of 'right'.

Such assertions of authority everywhere caused protests. In France, in 1917, there were many strikes, bread riots, even mutinies in the army, after the Nivelle offensive. They were partly inspired by Russia's example but principally by protests against inflation (prices rose eighty per cent in France during the war) and shortages.

One protest against the war seemed to come from the surrealists. But the Dada movement was a challenge to the old bourgeois life as much as to the war. There was also a 'left opposition' to the war, organised by dissident, apparently internationalist, Russian socialists headed by Lenin in Zimmerwald and then at Kienthal. Lenin called for civil wars in order to end the national wars. That call for further confusion did not strike an immediately appealing note.

The defeat of Russia and her replacement by the US among the Allied nations made it easier to suggest that the war had been fought and won for the principles of democracy. Wilson, from that point of view, made a better ally for the English and French than the Tsar did. 'Autocracy is dead, long live democracy and its immortal leader,' cabled Colonel House to Wilson on 11 November 1918, 'in this great hour, my pride goes out to you in admiration and love'[24]. But the leaders of the democrats themselves shared the passions of their peoples. William Archer in *The Great Analysis*, a book published in 1912, thought that 'some great catastrophe', such as the war of 1914 turned out to be, would usher in a happier world order. That optimism proved false. The First World War ushered in a long international crisis which has continued ever since with short intervals.

The war showed that, in the struggles of the twentieth century, there was little chance of the US remaining isolated. All the same, the US decided, through the vote of her Senate, to try to play no part in the postwar world. Russia was divided by a civil war which masked the extent to which she had in 1916 successfully mounted an offensive against the Austrians. Nor did the Germans, temporarily defeated, play any part in the peace. The peacemaking thus enabled the enfeebled imperial powers, Britain and France, to try to freeze the movement of the world against further change.

The consequences of the Great War were four. First, the political experiments of collaboration between industry, labour and government went a long way to inspire that idea of a corporate state desired by Fascists, Communists and some democratic politicians. Second, the bitterness and propaganda left hatred which meant that another war would probably follow soon. Third, the combined effects of war and peacemaking ruined the system of credit upon which the prewar serenity had been built. The German currency was ruined. The stories of banknotes being carried in wheelbarrows, of sandwiches costing 14,000 marks one day and 24,000 the next, and of demented people stating their ages on forms to be '150 million years' are well known. What is less evident is that the war initiated an era of fluctuating, and depreciating, currency which has never come to an end. The fourth consequence was that power in the democratic world shifted to the US. That was reflected first in the change of indebtedness. In 1914 the US owed Europe $6,000 million. In 1918 the US was owed $16,000 million.

The collapse of monarchical despotism in 1917 and 1918 also created new forms of government. Those forms of government were often nervous and aggressive because they were new and ill-established. The pattern had been set after the French Revolution. The governments set up by the French Revolution were less stable than any of those which they overthrew. Yet, 'paradoxically, they were infinitely more powerful . . . This new power was created by the Revolution or rather grew up almost automatically out of the havoc wrought by it.' In those words, Tocqueville summed up what happened after 1918. President Woodrow Wilson, in a speech entitled 'The Four Ends' on 4 July 1918, said that the rulers of Prussia had 'aroused forces they knew little of'; but events were to show that they were forces of which a liberal such as Wilson knew little also.

The world returned to nervous peace in 1919 but its finances continued in a most unsteady state. After a boom, there was a collapse in the stock-market and the near end of the free market. In July 1932 the index of prices of industrial shares was an eighth of what it had been three years before. The US national product was down to half its real value of 1929 and unemployment accounted for twelve million people or about twenty-five per cent of the labour force. This crisis was long-lasting: in 1940 unemployment still accounted in the US for seven million people, in Britain for over a million. It was also world-wide. World trade collapsed. It became barely worth while picking coffee, mining copper or cutting sugar cane. In 1932 every country with any manufacturing industry at all had unemployment of over ten per cent (Belgium had 23 per cent, Denmark 32 per cent, Germany 30 per cent and Britain 22·5 per cent). The more 'advanced' the country, the more severe the crisis. Thus Germany had exported about a third of her manufactured goods in the 1920s. When no foreign country had money to spend on imports, German workers lost their jobs. The consequence was the wreck of the world monetary system, already damaged by the First World War. All countries drew in on themselves. Many believed that free enterprise, and with it democracy, were doomed. Even so percipient an observer as George Orwell thought that the 'period of free capitalism is coming to an end', in 1941[25]. Hence the attraction for extreme 'solutions': Fascist or Communist. Fascists believed that their leaders had effective medicine for the problems of their state.

Some supposed the crisis of the 1930s to be the 'final' one of capitalism. That, however, proved not to be the case. After the revival of the economies of the advanced nations in the late 1930s in the shadow of the Second World War (though Germany was the only advanced country to have cured its unemployment by 1939), capitalism went on to many victories in the 1950s and 1960s. The crisis of 1929–33 now appears to have been the result of great shifts in inter-state indebtedness, the excessive role played by the state in the economies during the war and a sluggishness due to what Walt Rostow has described as 'the process of disengagement from the old leading sectors of the pre-1914 years'[26]. Even so, the crisis was a good opportunity for 'violent men with violent minds'.

3

The First World War was also significant since, for the first time, it brought into international affairs on an equal footing one state which had for many generations turned its back on the world and on Europe: namely, Japan.

Japan had first established contact with Europe, as has been seen, in 1542. St Francis Xavier was at first welcomed as much as Portuguese traders were. 150,000 Christians were soon made. But the era of reunification of Japan and the Tokugawa Shogunate led to the banning of missionaries, the proscription of Christians and the murder of many. The Christian challenge led to the exclusion in 1637–38 of all foreigners, a ban on Japanese travelling abroad and the condemnation of all ships large enough to cross the Yellow Sea. Probably the reason was a fear that some feudal lords would gain too great strength from contact with Westerners. The only exception to this rule was that Dutch merchants were allowed to call once a year at Deshima, an island in the Bay of Nagasaki, and Chinese merchants were allowed to call at Nagasaki. There were also some breaches in the eighteenth century by Russian traders. That system of 'exclusion orders' lasted till Commander Perry's treaty in 1854.

The two hundred years of self-imposed exclusion were the basis of modern Japanese life. The country was run by the Tokugawas – grand viziers. It remained a rice economy. The Emperor was powerless but revered. Confucianism was the religion. Large estates continued to be managed by rich but militarily impotent landlords, whose households protected or were protected by a large number of unemployed ex-warriors or retainers, the Samurai, who had numerous privileges apart from the right to wear two swords.

Japan was prised open again by the insistence of the United States who wished to secure good treatment of shipwrecked sailors and also to trade. Commander Perry gave his ultimatum in 1853: open up, or risk war. Japan gave in. The concession ruined the Shogun. The most conservative forces overthrew the system, after humiliating concessions to other foreign powers. Government was restored to the Emperor Meiji who inaugurated the destruction of feudalism – including the feudal lords who had revived his authority – and the modernisation of Japan. The new government of Japan was dominated by able men of Samurai origin. It was they who ensured the overthrow of the social order, by imperial decree. To a great extent they had run the great estates under their landlords. They realised that Japan had to modernise or be overwhelmed by foreign powers. The former feudal lords were bought out of status and power. They became millionaires instead and helped to finance the railways, the water supplies, the banks and the big trading companies which soon came into being. This modernisation led first to the successful war with China over Korea in 1895 (which gained Formosa and other territory for Japan), then to the equally successful war with Russia in 1904 and finally to the intervention on the Allied side in the First World War. Henceforward Japan was a world power, with a first-class economy which could not be ignored.

Japan was by 1914 not just a modern great power but an imperial one as well (Formosa and Korea had been annexed; she had many leases and rights in south Manchuria, including Port Arthur and Liaotung). At the treaty of Versailles, Japan acquired further the former German port of Tsingtao on the coast of Shantung and all German rights to build railways in that province. Henceforward a strong industrial base coupled with a national psychology deriving from a warrior past drove Japan on to a most aggressive attitude of self-assertion.

This success of Japan stirred many others, in East Asia and beyond. Combined with the patent failures of old Europe in allowing the world war to happen at all, along with the use of colonial troops in the war in Europe, it created Asian and African nationalism. The European powers reacted diversely to the challenges to them; seeking to educate as in the French Empire; to bring in indigenous intellectuals into the civil service, as in the British; to resist any concession, as in the Dutch and Belgian cases. Not much change had come before 1939. The preparations for the end of empire were nevertheless laid.

60

The War of the Nazis I: Races

We got into the Reichstag in order to acquire the weapons of democracy from its arsenal. We become Reichstag deputies in order to paralyse the Weimar democracy with its own assistance.

Goebbels, in *Der Angriff*

1

The Germans' second 'grab for world power' in 1939 was begun in, at first sight, circumstances favourable to them. The Nazi movement institutionalised many of the prejudices of the previous generation. Hitler was a real warlord, not a Kaiser *fainéant*. The Nazis had taken care first to silence, or to force into exile, potential critics (socialists, Communists, liberals, Jews) before the war began. Possibly, the German nation was less united behind its government's quest for world power in 1939 than it had been in 1914. Still, by intimidation, Hitler secured the integration with Germany of the more valuable remains of the Austro-Hungarian Empire (Bohemia and Austria) and dominated the economies of the rest of south-eastern Europe. The German economy in 1939 had recovered from the defeat of 1918 as from the world depression of 1929. In 1939 Germany had Italy, Japan and Spain as likely allies, transformed by fascism or militarism into friends of what they referred to as a 'new order²'. The Italian Fascist dictator wished his country to 'terrify the world for a change rather than charm it with its guitar', as he told his son-in-law, and anyway believed that war was 'to man as maternity is to woman'. As for Japan, the military rulers there had ambitious plans for a Co-Prosperity Sphere in the Far East dominated by herself, which though it had roots in the recent past successes of the country, complemented Hitler's plans for a New German Order.

Germany before 1939 made herself self-sufficient in food, as a result of a four-year plan introduced by Goering. Her investment in synthetic products and access to strategic raw materials from Spain, Sweden and Romania enabled her leaders to be sceptical, to begin with, of the efficacy of another British blockade. The German armed forces had been built up fast since 1933. Their commanders were young, though experienced, survivors from the First World War.

The Nazis also had a great appeal, even among people who, in reflective moments, would have thought better of giving such a brash enterprise the benefit of the doubt. The Nazi state had benefited from the socialists' unwitting preparation for it in the 1920s. In 1928 a little over half of the German national income was in the hands of the central or local authority. The German government drew extensively on the economic and social innovations of the First World War and abolished strikes as well as limited dividends. Labour camps, freely available credit, road building, as well as repression, characterised the policies. Meantime, foreign opposition was slow to grow. The British and French governments distrusted the Russian government under Stalin more than they did the Germans, since most of the Russian governing class, new though it was (including sixty-five per cent of the generals, according to their military attachés), had been recently murdered by their own head of government, many on the patently false charge that they had been working for British intelligence. There were also Frenchmen who wished to recreate a permanent version of Joffre's military dictatorship of 1914 under some semi-fascist auspices.

Nazism had an intimidatory appeal beyond the frontiers of Germany – in 1933 there was no state in Central and Eastern Europe which did not harbour a German minority. George Kennan, then a US diplomat in Central Europe, put the nature of the challenge very well: 'it is hard to visualise the tremendous head of emotional and political steam which the Nazis developed', he wrote. 'Here was a great political movement on the march. We must not let our distaste for Hitler's methods blind us to the fact that this man was one of the greatest demagogues of whom history bears record and, in many ways, an able statesman . . . He was backed up by a party which had fantastic powers of organisation and was inspired by a fanatical stony determination to let nothing stand in its path. It was not easy in those days to know how far this political force was going to carry. Many . . . in Germany and Austria [and elsewhere in Central Europe] who were at first sceptical were finally overwhelmed both by the emotional impetus of the movement and by the success which Hitler had in achieving, by relatively bloodless means, objectives which the Weimar Republic had not been able to achieve in many years'[1].

The Second World War was to some extent caused by a misreading of the reasons for Germany's defeat in 1919. During the nineteenth century, Germany had begun to regard herself as the dominant race of the future. Her swift industrialisation, unification as a modern nation, technological resourcefulness and brilliant creativity seemed to offer support for that view. Historians, good and bad, found justification for such ambitions in the recent, as in the mediaeval, past and the popularisation of these 'Gothic' views sometimes resulted in a cult of barbarism. The German quest for world power had begun before the First World War. Many Germans were anxious to be again on the road to world power after 1918. Their intelligence should have told them that, though they might succeed in war against the other European states, a conflict which involved them against new extra-European powers, Russia and the US, was likely to end in disaster. But the Germans' victory in 1917 caused them to underestimate Russian strength (as did others). Even so, the Germans might have established their hegemony over Europe and the Mediterranean indefinitely, had they not been led by a leader, Hitler, who for all his determination and willpower had an untrained mind dominated by obsessions – above all, as is evident from even the most cursory study of *Mein Kampf* or of Hitler's speeches, his obsession about the evil nature of Jewry. This belief was held by Hitler and his closest associates so strongly that it dominated their entire thinking and planning. It was a concern which demands the preoccupation of historians as much as it failed to secure that of those busy with affairs at the time.

2

However the Second World War is explained, justified or commemorated, it lives as the conflict in which the dictatorship in Germany made use of its absolute power to destroy the Jews. This memory diverts the attention of the student of history from its significance as a final attempt by the Germans to unite Europe by force (resulting in the division of both Germany and Europe into two); but the problem of racial prejudice needs to be examined.

There are five branches of the human species. They are known to anthropologists by the unhelpful names of Caucasoid, Mongoloid, Australoid, Congoloid and Capoid. The Caucasoid group includes Europeans and white Americans, Middle East whites, Arabs and Jews, Persians, Indians and the Ainus of Japan. The Mongoloids are the Chinese, most East Asiatics, Polynesians, Eskimoes, the Indians in the Americas and Indonesians. The

Congoloids are held to include the blacks of both Africa and America, as well as the pygmies. The Australoids include the Aborigines of Australia, some Indian tribes of India and the Negritos of South Asia, while the Capoids are represented by the San (bushmen) and Hottentot tribes of South Africa.

The outstanding question about these species is, did they branch off a single stem 'recently' (say, a million years ago) or did they separate earlier, when long extinct groups, such as apemen, were still alive? A resolution of this uncertainty may one day be found. If the second explanation turns out to be true (as it may, considering the number of diverse languages), the existing races of men will have been shown to have been separately evolving over tens of thousands of years. Such a discovery may inspire some superficial reflections on the nature of racial differences, but a moment's thought would remind the most prejudiced person that the real dislikes between peoples have been those within sub-species: French and Germans; Russians, Germans and Jews; Muslims and Hindus; Arabs and Jews; Chinese and Vietnamese. 'The less we differ the more we hate': George Canning's cynical comment on the history of the British and the Dutch has been the best judgement on the relations between peoples who have quarrelled. Kings and nations alike have gone to war because their interests seemed the same; not because they were far apart.

The evidence of anthropology and history suggests that there are no pure races. This point was made in the 1930s by the Italian professor Orestano, to Alfred Rosenberg (the theorist of race), when the latter was lecturing in Rome. Every nation was a hybrid, Orestano pointed out, including the Chinese and especially the Germans; especially the Prussians, he might have added, since they are half Slav, and were once, when still only citizens of a dukedom, vassals of the King of Poland. They registered themselves as a Slav monarchy at the Congress of Vienna (both the Mark of Brandenburg and Prussia were once German colonies in Slav countries)[2]. Every Slav, too, probably has a dose of some blood from his conquerors between the fifth and thirteenth centuries: Huns, Avars, Bulgars, Magyars, Pechenegs and Mongols. India has assimilated Greeks, Scythians, Turks, Mongols, Parthians and Huns. From the earliest times, England has imported Flemish wool weavers, Italian financiers, Germans, Sephardic Jews, Venetians and Huguenots. From the days of Alexander onwards, every great empire has embraced populations of mixed origin, above all Rome, where, from AD 212, free citizens were

Roman citizens. All distinctions between Romans and provincials vanished, in respect of both opportunities and punishments.

A wholly isolated group of 400 people can perpetuate themselves, if closely grouped on an island, in a valley or ghetto. But anything wider than this makes dispersal inevitable. There have been instances of minor groups being absorbed without trace in a dominant population, within a few generations. The black population of England in the eighteenth century numbered 20,000 in London alone, many becoming beggars and known as Saint Giles's blackbirds. There was a similar, but larger, Arab population in China in the eleventh century. That also has been absorbed.

Almost always, it is true, when two peoples come into contact, one tends to dominate in the end. Had it not been for that, the world would already be khaki in colour since, over the last half million years, the tramp of peoples backwards and forwards has been ceaseless. The Germans were held by Tacitus to have 'never been tainted by intermarriage': hence their 'wild blue eyes, reddish hair and huge frames'. But perhaps the 'red hair' came from a different breed from the one which caused the blue eyes. Cuba is one of the few countries to have a population roughly equal between black or mulatto and white. In the 1940s, the pure Negro was increasing at a slower rate than the native white, and much slower than the mulatto. Essentially, the whites were winning that encounter. The blacks had higher death and lower birth rates in cities than whites, and the black proportion of the population in Cuba dropped continuously between the mid nineteenth century and 1959.

Larger groups, on the other hand, survive indefinitely if they are left alone to thrive, as, for example, the Basques have been or more recently the Germans of the Volga (left alone until Stalin deported them). Other nations have changed their colours imperceptibly. The ancient Egyptians may have been black and became lighter in colour.

Within various groups, indeed within the human race as a whole, certain combinations of factors (climate, religion, diet) have created diversity of custom and priorities. 'Adaptation' can take the form, as with the Alaskans, of developing large chests, lungs, hearts and so on. There are no distinct blood groups, save for the Rhesus factor (which is rare). But those facts invalidate the idea of segregation for natural selection. Nor would any balanced man deny now the influence of both heredity and environment in forming peoples' characters; though probably heredity, as

Professor Sauvy says, has the 'edge' as a decisive influence[3].

Prejudice against half-castes has been continuous in history but is without foundation. The faults attributed to them all derive from environment. But can it be true that Professor Sauvy is right to argue that 'the best way to avoid racial quarrels is to encourage mixed marriages'? Some countries have mixed two peoples of different racial origin so that the mulattoes constitute a majority of the population: but the large number of US citizens who are racially mixed (and would have been known by the words mulatto, quadroon or octaroon in censuses during the nineteenth century) are now classed as black. They also think of themselves as black, are happy to be treated as black, and contribute to a generally false impression of the extent to which the population of the US is characterised by African blood. But many of the most prominent leaders of the US 'black' population have pigments which are more white than black. The position seems odd, and is only to be understood in relation to past attempts by slave owners to avoid a mixture of races by telling strange stories of blacks as maniacs. Furthermore, the 'racial question' in countries where Caucasoids and Congoloids mix is not only a matter of colour: physiognomy plays a part. Tocqueville, incidentally, thought in the 1830s that prejudice of race appeared to be stronger in states of the US which had abolished slavery than in those where it still existed.

Equally important, many discussions which are considered as affecting race should be considered, as they were in the past, matters of language or of religion. For example, in the early Middle Ages the relations between Spaniards and Moors were without extremes of bigotry. Still 'racial prejudice is an aspect of human nature', as Professor Saggs, the historian of Babylon, wrote[4], and with religious and linguistic prejudices it was part of the background of the swift judgements and coarse jokes of the eighteenth century. The Portuguese character, wrote a Jesuit, Padre Francisco de Sousa, in his *Oriente Conquistado* in 1710, 'naturally despises all these Asiatic races'[5]. The English in India kept apart, so far as they could, from Hindu or Muslim women: that was easy enough since those people made a practice of keeping their wives and daughters at home. The new element that has been introduced recently into the problem is the growth of nationalism under the stress of technology and mass sensationalism. As A. J. P. Taylor put the matter in his *The Origins of the Second*

World War: 'Everything which Hitler did against the Jews followed logically from the racial doctrines in which most Germans vaguely believed.' (He might have added, most Europeans.) He went on: 'Hitler took them at their word. He made the Germans live up to their professions or down to them – much to their regret.' It was technology – railways, mass production of Nyklon gas, prefabricated huts and radio propaganda – that enabled Hitler to put into action the ideas of which many nineteenth-century people had idly dreamed.

3

The French Revolution was a fiesta for absurd notions. Like everything else, race came into the discussion. In 1797 a French Jesuit, the Abbé Barmel, argued that the Revolution had been caused by the Knightly Order of the Templars, which had not been exterminated in 1314 (as was believed), but had survived in order to plot against monarchies and afterwards to found a world republic. The revolutionary Louis-Michel Le Peletier,* president of the Constituent Assembly, proposed in 1792 the deliberate breeding of a 'race of revolutionaries'. During the nineteenth century the idea of a good and (by implication) of a bad race was on many lips. Another Frenchman, the Comte de Gobineau, devised a theory of history based on race. Violence and upheaval, he believed, were a consequence of intermixture of races. Even the liberal James Stephen recommended in 1843 against allowing black labour to be taken to Australia, adding, 'We now regret the folly of our ancestors in colonising North America from Africa'[6]. Sir Francis Galton, an Englishman more intelligent than Gobineau and more influential than Le Peletier, argued (with Aristotle) that intelligent people have fewer children than unintelligent ones. The intelligence of a people must, therefore, diminish over the centuries. Decay could only be staved off by organised breeding, or the establishment of a system of castes, such as prevailed in India, which forbids exogamy. Galton, a cousin of Charles Darwin, invented the word 'eugenics' to describe the study of these matters, in 1884. (He also invented the word 'genius', a useful addition to our supply of meaningless superlatives.) A French contemporary,

---

* He proposed the abolition of the death penalty in 1789 but voted for the execution of the King in 1793. He was assassinated before the King died by a member of the royal bodyguard.

Vacher de Lepouge, wrote in the same year that 'in certain conditions a very small number of absolutely perfect males would be
able to fertilise all the women deserving to propagate the race'[7].
   None of these formulations were directed *against* any race,
Jewish or other. The aim was to formulate a superior race (even
though such an idea is almost Jewish in its exclusiveness). But
then: 'It is no use mincing matters,' wrote the historian E. A.
Freeman in 1877, 'but it will not do to have the policy of England,
the welfare of Europe, sacrificed to Hebrew sentiment . . . we
cannot sacrifice our people, the people of Aryan and Christian
Europe, [even] to the most genuine belief in an Asian mystery'[8].
The Anglo-Saxon conquerors of Australia and, later, immigrants
including Labour politicians as well as Liberals were by then
determined to preserve a 'white Australia' by prohibiting the
immigration of Asiatics and Pacific islanders, and deporting labourers on sugar estates. Australia was to be 'saved from the
coloured curse . . . not to be a mongrel nation torn with racial
dissension, blighted by industrial war. Australia was [to house]
the only pure white race'[9].
   A blatant if innocent sense of national superiority thus, in 1900,
distinguished the white nations, astounded at their own technological achievements and the ease with which a few Europeans
seemed to be able to run the world. Kaiser Wilhelm wrote in
1900: 'You should give the name of Germany such cause to be
remembered in China for a thousand years, so that no Chinaman,
no matter whether his eyes be slit or not, will dare to look a
German in the face'[10]. Even Sir Mark Sykes (who was probably
a Zionist in order to rid England of the Jews), like many, could
write of his hero, the proconsul Lord Cromer, as a 'strong dominant figure dreaded by an inferior race, whom he knew and who
knew not him'[11]. That may not sound innocent now but innocent
it was. It was still innocent when Kipling adjured the British to
'take up the White Man's burden', in a famous poem of that
name, and when the *Daily Mail* told English people in the First
World War to refuse to be served by an Austrian or German
waiter: 'If your waiter says he is Swiss, ask to see his passport'[12].
   Germany, meantime, had by 1914 developed a strong sense of
her destiny, based on a romantic view of the Middle Ages and on
a justified view of her industrial achievements. Illusions were
strong. Because the Germans were recently united, they felt more
passionately than others the need to have an enemy, as well as a
master, race. Paul de Lagarde in *Deutsche Schriften*, published in

1878, expressed disillusion with the united Germany which had been achieved and demanded the higher unity of the German *Volk* as it had once been in the Middle Ages. The Jews (recently freed from living in ghettoes) were still pre-eminently town dwellers in Germany, and were naturally reformers. To de Lagarde, Jews seemed the incarnation of decay, modernity, separateness from the national soul. The evangelical pastor Stoecker and the historian Treitschke agreed, though their arguments were religious and nationalist, with less racial animus. Wilhelm Marr invented the word 'anti-semitism' in 1873, and Treitschke gave some respectability to it by saying, in an article in 1879, that 'Jews are our national misfortune.' An anti-semitic deputy was elected to the Reichstag in 1887[13]. *Völkisch* racism soon became appealing to middle-class university graduates and lecturers. These ideas spread to Austria. The *Volk* there began to seem as if it were a mythical church, with its festivals at solstices. The sign of the swastika* was first used in Europe by Lanz von Liebenfels, an Austrian who desired to found a new religious order of the racially pure (and which inspired Himmler's SS). He believed that men were divided into Aryans and apemen[14]. Von Liebenfels was an isolated individual with little following. But the mixture of arrogance and sentimentality, self-confidence and bitterness (particularly at having been patronised by France for so many generations), ignorance and hierarchical authoritarianism, was symptomatic of much of Germany at the hinge of the nineteenth and twentieth centuries. The consequence was much dislike of Germany outside. Winston Churchill looked on Germans as 'carnivorous sheep'. Clemenceau believed Germans 'understand and can understand nothing but intimidation'[15].

The Germans allowed themselves to develop a phobia about the allegedly small space in which they were living. Thus the word *Lebensraum* began to be used as a call to expansion. But the German population had, like others in Europe, ceased to grow fast. This was observable in the figures of German emigration to the US. Between 1850 and 1894 great waves of Germans went across the Atlantic: in 1854 alone, 250,000, and in the 1880s, 100,000 to 200,000 a year. But after 1894 the figures became negligible. 'Germany had no longer men to spare,' commented Sir John Clapham[16]. *Lebensraum* was thus an idea deriving from another set of illusions.

Anti-semitic fantasies were, if anything, stronger in Russia than
* It is Hindu in origin.

in Germany. Among Tartars, Kalmuks and Turks, the Jews, having no connections with land and being among the newest minorities, were specially vulnerable. They had been incorporated into Russia after the partition of Poland in the eighteenth century.

Much of the anti-semitism of the men who subsequently became Nazis derived from the Baltic Germans who had been active in forming the anti-semitic 'Black Hundreds' in Russia before 1914, since *émigrés* from that region played a major part in inspiring national socialism. Rosenberg, the Nazi racist ideologist, was born in Riga, along with Tsarist anti-semitic professionals. Tsarist ex-officers played a decisive part in disseminating the forgery *The Protocols of the Elders of Zion*. This derived from a novel published in 1868 called *Biarritz*, written by Herman Goedsche under the pseudonym 'Sir John Retcliffe'. In it, the Devil appears in the Jewish cemetery in Prague in order to ask representatives of the twelve tribes what they had done during the previous hundred years. They explain how they had begun to dominate stock exchanges, churches, army, artisans, and how, soon, they would take over the world. (The Jews were linked by the Jesuits, in particular, to the idea of masonic conspiracies, particularly in countries where there were few Jews.) The *Protocols* was a document which purported to show how world domination would be achieved and was first published in *Znamya* (in St Petersburg) in 1903. It became well known after 1917, being at first taken seriously even by *The Times* (8 May 1921), which subsequently admitted its error. The forgery was carried out in Paris about 1897 at the height of the Dreyfus affair by Pyotr Rachovsky, then head of the Russian secret police (Okhrana) outside Russia, perhaps with the short-term intention of discrediting the Russian statesman Witte[17].

Innumerable racist theories were thus current in Europe in the childhood of the Nazis. They were no more extremely felt in Germany than elsewhere. There were only 400,000 Jews in Germany in comparison with 700,000 in Hungary, 1,000,000 in Romania, and 3,000,000 in Poland. Most Nazis were, however, brought up in an atmosphere of uncertainty because of the growth of non-German populations, not only Jews, in Central Europe, and were affected by the immigration of Jews into Central Europe as a result of the persecutions in Russia. The collapse of the German Empire in 1918 inspired the darkest thoughts in a nation which had accustomed itself to the idea of world power. It seemed a small step between the views of serious scientists such as Galton and those of zealots such as Hans Gunther, professor of 'racial science' at the University of Jena in 1930, though the step was across a divide between genuine scientific enquiry and prejudiced demagogry.

Hans Gunther himself took that step. His *Short Ethnology of the German People*, which sold 272,000 copies between 1929 and 1943, set an explicit target. The Jews could not be seen as a race, he argued, for they constituted a nation of mixed races – the worst thing possible. Gunther and his friends were encouraged to set up an Institute of Racial Marriage, by whose agencies eugenically selected men and women were supposed to give birth to supreme beings, for whose upbringing the state would be responsible. Hence the boycotts, the burnings of books, the discriminatory Nuremberg laws, the fines and levies on Jewish property and, in the end, the plans for the 'final solution' or the 'desired solution' of the Jewish problem, in order to make Germany 'Jew-free' – a scheme which, to begin with, until 1939, seemed to envisage resettlement (in Madagascar, perhaps) but which became murder on a grand scale after 1941. The ground for this was prepared by a cultural revolution, a real counter-renaissance, as it were, in which the idea of German racial superiority was inculcated into everything, from education to chamber music. The names of Handel's oratorios were aryanised: 'Judas Maccabaeus' became 'William of Nassau', 'Israel in Egypt' became 'Mongol Fury'. The appropriate note was sounded by *Neue Zeitschrift für Musik* of May 1933: 'Soon again German opera houses will give bread to German opera singers and become houses for the cultivation of German music . . . Freed from the alien past . . . German universities and German music schools will give refuge once more to the German scholars and German teachers who may be trusted to guide our German youth to the great German masters'[18]. Mad though this may sound, it was only the obverse to Allied propaganda of the First World War: Marc Ferro quotes a French propagandist who wrote, 'It is now time to draw a veil over those works which recognisably express the spirit of our latter day Huns: the future is to the young hero who will have the courage to banish the works of Handel, Mendelssohn, Wagner, Brahms and Richard Strauss. . .'[19]. It was also unwise. Anti-semitism destroyed German intellectual pre-eminence in the 1930s and drove many Jews and Aryans into exile to work against Germany. Had Hitler used the Jews as the Kaiser had done, he might easily have won the war.

4

Racism was not the only spring of fascism nor even, in the case of all countries other than Germany, its most powerful motive. (The early Italian Fascists included Alfredo Rocco, a Jew, who wrote the Labour Charter of 1927.) 'Those who have never experienced the downfall of their country can hardly realise the grief and suffering which all patriotic Austrians, and especially the young among us, endured when the Monarchy crumbled to dust,' wrote the founder of the Austrian Fascists, Rüdiger von Starhemberg, 'nor can they imagine the rage and bitterness felt by the young soldiers of an old and ever victorious army doomed . . . to a shameful surrender'[20]. Some 'Fascists' formed vigilante groups to protect homes or churches from 'anarchist mischief makers' in 1918–19. Some hankered after the peasant militias of the Napoleonic Wars. Some who were interested in fascism, like W. B. Yeats, longed for what he called 'the despotic rule of the educated – the only end to our troubles'. In politics, Yeats wrote, 'I have but one passion and one thought, rancour against all who, except under the most dire necessity, disturb public order'[21]. Others saw fascism as a movement which would liberate them from the unworthy compromises of party politics or articulate the ethical idea of war, or provide a uniform, or make possible the historic role of the great man, who would enable the nation, above all the young, to live dangerously, and forget the mediocre life of the bourgeoisie. We should also remark upon the cult of physical fitness, and its glorification of an idealised past. In the incoherent anarchy of its ideas and actions, its aspiration to a permanent revolution without limits ('Rebel against everybody: nobody, or almost nobody, is just'), Spanish radicalism, like some other radical movements of the early twentieth century, was an authentic precursor to fascism, just as some socialist or Communist movements have been its bastard sons[22]. The mixed ancestry of this movement, however, needs to be noticed when, as a word, it has taken over in modern politics the role once occupied in theology by evil.

The ancestors of fascism are as difficult to identify and to isolate as are its children. The radicals' violence was one origin. So was Antonio Maura's (conservative) demand for a 'revolution from above'. George Sorel was the ancestor of both Fascist and anarchist violent politics. Among the forerunners of fascism were the agitators of the Futurist movement in art: hitherto, 'literature has tended to exact thoughtful immobility, ecstasy, and sleep, whereas we are for aggressive movement, febrile insomnia, mortal leaps and blows with the fist . . . no masterpiece can be anything but aggressive'[23]. Of all these elements, the demand for a national revolution rather than an international working-class one, as demanded by the socialists, was the strongest. But there was also the desire to avoid being left on the upper shelf of nations as felt by Italian Fascists – 'we don't want to be just a museum, a hotel, a . . . Prussian blue horizon where foreigners come for a honeymoon . . . we must put our stamp on the molten metal of the world'. Pétain's regime in France had the same mixture of regeneration and reverence for the past. The Marshal began his decrees as a monarch ('Nous, Philippe Pétain') and placed a great effort upon his role as moral tutor to the nation. His followers believed that 'thanks to us, the France of camping, of sports, of dancing and of collective hiking will sweep away the France of the aperitifs, tobacco dens, party congresses and long digestions'[24].

The appeal of fascism was not confined to Europe. Brazil, for example, was much influenced by corporatism and even its constitution of 1934 included 'class representatives' from employers' and workers' associations. In 1931 a 'Revolutionary Legion' of Fascists in khaki shirts organised a 'march on Belo Horizonte'.

Another Brazilian Fascist movement, the *Integratistas*, had a profound if indirect effect on the modern history of Brazil, as is evident from noticing the number of those concerned in 1964 in the *coup* against President Goulart who, in the 1930s, were friendly to Fascist ideas[25]. In Mexico, there were 'gold shirts'. In all such movements, foreign influences and national predicaments always combined. Even Dr Getúlio Vargas's *Estado Novo* drew inspiration from European corporatism, despite his alliance with the democracies during the war: a similarity that went even further with Juan Perón in Argentina.

61

The War of the Nazis II: The Fighting

In the French Revolution, both religious institutions and the whole system of government were thrown into the melting pot with the result that men's minds were in a state of utter confusion . . . Revolutionaries of a hitherto unknown breed came on the scene: men who carried audacity to the point of sheer insanity; who balked at no innovation and were unchecked by any restraint . . . who acted with an unprecedented ruthlessness . . . They are still with us.

Alexis de Tocqueville, *L'Ancien Régime*

1

Once the war had begun in 1939, it went well for Germany at first. Hitler made an agreement with Russia to divide Poland, and to re-establish the eastern frontiers of 1914, on lines rather more favourable to Germany. The British and French decision to treat the German invasion of Poland in 1939 as a justification for war, though morally right, was militarily calamitous. They were not strong enough to do anything to help Poland against either Russia or Germany. A British feint to establish themselves in Scandinavia went awry. Germany found herself speedily in control of Norway and Denmark. In May 1940 Germany turned against the Low Countries and France. She again was completely successful.

These victories were won partly for tactical, partly for psychological reasons. Hitler had resolved never again to fight 'long wars of fronts', as he himself had experienced in 1914–18[1]. The German High Command, from Hitler downwards, conceived of modern war as being characterised by swift offensives which would not only surprise, but overwhelm, the enemy at his weakest point. A breach in the enemy's line would be made by tanks and aerial bombing as well as by a judicious use of artillery, as in 1914–18. Once the breach were made, all available tanks would be flung in, and would drive as far as they could, striking in all directions. Motorised infantry, paratroops, bicyclists would be committed, too, to prevent, by 'methodical opportunism', the establishment of a regular front. These ideas had been worked out by several military theorists between the wars, among them Basil Liddell

Hart in England and Charles de Gaulle in France, but it was left to the German General Heinz Guderian (commander of the tank spearhead in 1940) to bring them to perfection. This technique of 'lightning war' used all modern technology, such as radio. The field commanders were instructed to be willing to experiment and not to stick to rules in old order books: as Liddell Hart himself wrote, it was 'one of history's most striking examples of the decisive effect of a new idea carried out by a dynamic executant'[2].

In the early days of the war, too, the idea of a German world mission (not a Nazi one) was shared by all ranks. A hostile witness, Djilas, commented on talks between the Yugoslavs and the Germans in 1942: 'What surprised me more than anything else during these negotiations . . . was how little of the Nazi ideology and mentality was evident in the German army, which did not seem like an unthinking automated machine. Officer-soldier relations seemed less disciplined and more cordial than in other armies. The junior officers ate out of the soldiers' kettle at least here on the battlefield'[3]. Teilhard de Chardin even believed the Germans 'deserved to win because they had more spirit'[4]. Pétain thought the Germans beat the French because the latter had had 'unpatriotic schoolmasters'[5]. The great historian Marc Bloch thought that the German victory over France was 'essentially a triumph of intellect'[6].

Thus, in June 1941, Germany was at first sight in a stronger position than any European conqueror had ever been. Even Napoleon had been less successful. All continental Europe except Portugal and Switzerland were in German hands, or in those of her allies. Even in France, many captured officers relied upon fair treatment after the peace. England, together with a few friends in remote mountains in the Balkans, was holding out with encouragement from the US, but the British bombing of Germany was not effective. Russia had shown every sign of welcoming the German successes and continued to sell her militarily significant materials. The Nazis found the Communists in Russia personally congenial.* The Communist parties of Western Europe accepted Germany as the new paramount power. America was far away. Germany's Japanese ally was proceeding well with her plans for the 'Co-Prosperity Sphere'. Within the German 'New Order' in

---

* Ribbentrop, the Nazi foreign minister, thought 'that, talking with Stalin and the other Kremlin potentates, he had felt that he was among comrades barely distinguishable from his National Socialist acquaintances'.

Europe, there was much support, willing or grudging, for the new state of affairs, notably from traditional conservatives who, despite the Russian alliance, saw fascism as offering protection against communism. Many workers even from France went to work for Germany without much reluctance. The German network of brutal concentration, or labour, camps was less large than the Russian one. The extermination camps for which the Nazis later became infamous had not yet been established.

The first reason for the defeat of this empire was that it sought to expand further at the cost of Russia, a natural ally of Germany at that time more than a natural enemy, since two totalitarian regimes have more in common with each other than with liberal democracies. They were two sides of the same coin. Had Hitler been able to see that, it is doubtful whether the Old World could have been saved from permanent dictatorship. We do not always realise how narrowly we escaped world domination by a Nazi–Communist *entente* nor that it was wrecked by the Nazis not the Communists.

The early days of the German invasion of Russia were successful. It seemed as if the new German aims of establishing a colonial empire in west Russia might be attained. But the German High Command had underestimated Russian industrialisation which had made several advances over the level reached in 1917. The Germans also underestimated the Russians' 'illimitable capacity for obedience and subservience', in Liddell Hart's words, as they did the tenacity of Russian patriotism[7]. Then the German army was not able to cope so easily with the terrain in Russia as they had been in France. The bad Russian roads helped the defence, as the French good roads had been in 1940 a friend to the invaders' motorised infantry. Germany was far behind Russia in numbers of vehicles which could cross rough country. Germany thus became engaged in a long war with an enemy able to use the conflict as a means of national reconciliation. Similar difficulties were met by Japan in her attempt to conquer China. She occupied vast territories of the coast, the Middle Yangtze valley and much of the eastern provinces. The mountainous zones of west China were intractable.

Before Hitler launched the German army against Russia, he should either have negotiated with Britain or, if that were unsuccessful, he should have conquered her. For that he would have received every help from Russia. (Russia would probably have taken advantage of a British defeat to occupy Persia.) But Hitler shied at a direct onslaught on Britain. He failed to destroy the British air force in 1940. For Hitler, what he took to be blood was thicker than ideology. Even in 1941 his admiration for Britain, and his hope for an eventual alliance with the British Empire, triumphed over his strategic sense. Thus he scarcely worked out a plan for the invasion of Britain or a complete blockade by submarine.

The second reason for the defeat of the 'New Order' was that Italy led Germany into difficulties in Africa, where the British and, ultimately, the Americans and French exiles were able to salvage their strategic positions. A *coup d'état* in Italy drew its government out of the war so as to help Germany's enemies at the most sensitive moment. Rebellions thereafter occurred everywhere, even in Germany. In these actions by a 'resistance' against a Europe united by Hitler, the seeds were sown of a democratic Europe: of what the French historians of the movement described as 'a break with the mediocrity of the past, and rejection of conformism, injustice and degradation'[8]. This 'secret war' of murder and ideology, with no rules or hierarchy, of the high-quality radio receiver and of interrogation, of cutting telephone lines and defacement of notices, of a secret press (France had 1,200 resistance papers, selling a million copies an issue), of 7,000 agents dropped by parachute or landed by submarine, had a great psychological effect on postwar politics (and on colonial politics); but the effect on the war was modest.

Finally, Japan miscalculated in their plans for the development of East Asia. The US considered that they had a role to prevent Japanese hegemony over China, and were looking for ways of thwarting them (partly by trying to prevent Japanese access to oil in Indonesia). The Japanese were influenced by junior officers who were themselves moved by Fascist ideas, old-style Japanese ideals and hatred of the rich. These radical revolutionaries inspired a surprise attack on both the US in Hawaii (as they had on the Russian fleet in 1904) and on the other European possessions in the Far East. Once again, as in Germany's attack on Russia, indeed as usual in war, the aggressor won the first battles, and drove out the British, US, Dutch and French from their possessions in East Asia (including Burma, the road through which Britain could help China). The success was overwhelming, above all psychologically, and greatly developed Asian nationalism. But those actions brought the US to full mobilisation, against Germany as well as Japan. A counter-attack began from some Pacific islands which the Japanese had failed to capture, from Australia (which inflicted the first defeat on Japan in New Guinea), and from India, where the British had been for two centuries the paramount power. In the West, counter-attacks could be mounted from Africa and Britain – and, of course, Russia.

The crowning error of the Germans was their quixotic declaration of war on the US immediately after Japan's attack. It was particularly surprising since the German alliance with Japan was superficial. Neither helped each other much and Japan did not even attack Russia in her rear.

Even so, the consequent war was of a more global nature than that of 1914, comparable in its international significance to the wars of the eighteenth century. In this contest, Germany and Japan, even if they were able to dominate much of Europe and East Asia by force, were in a weak position in comparison with the US and Russia, combined with Britain and a few remains of the British and other European empires. Germany and Japan were short of many of the basic products needed for a long war, such as oil, whereas the US and Russia were then the world's largest producers of that fuel. Nor did the Germans and Japanese seek to play with any subtlety on the suspicions which most British and American people had of Russia and communism. Actually, Stalin was at least as much of a tyrant as Hitler was, and had already profited from the war to conquer Bessarabia, half Poland and the Baltic states. The conflict could scarcely be held to be one of democracy against tyranny. But this discrepancy was never exploited successfully by the Germans. The Western democracies were induced to forget temporarily about Stalin's extraordinary crimes. Hitler, whose leadership had been one of the reasons for Germany's early successes, became less and less flexible in retreat, though he continued personally to dominate the generals. His mind became dominated by irrelevant historical parallels.

Hitler's, Mussolini's and Japan's empires were overthrown, at a great cost. Once again, technology played a decisive part in the victory. Thus the German High Command in its wars on all fronts used radio-telephony. That led to a swifter contact between headquarters and field commanders than ever before. The aid to navigation in the air was incalculable. But the use of radio had some unexpected consequences. First, it enabled Hitler, as commander-in-chief, to be in daily contact with generals. Though Hitler's military sense was often effective, it discouraged commanders from thinking for themselves. Second, the use of radio

meant that Allied code-breakers could intercept all their communications. Thus, for the first time in any war, British and
American commanders in the field were able to organise their
battles with their enemies' plans all in front of them. It may well
seem surprising, therefore, that they did not win the war more
quickly.

The German government was offered a computer by the scientists Konrad Zuse and Helmut Schreyer. But the Nazis decided
that they would have won the war by the time it was built. The
British at Bletchley were less optimistic and built the world's first
electronic computer, which began to operate and break codes in
December 1943.

The German leadership had at their disposal a large labour
force. They combed Europe to make it bigger. Perhaps because
they had never had slave colonies in the New World or elsewhere,
not even under Rome, they did not realise that people do not
work well if they are treated badly. At all events, the slave labour
camps of Nazi Germany were much less efficient than normal
factories.

Then there was the Nazi policy to the Jews. The murder of over
three and half million Jews in gas chambers in six main, mostly
Polish, camps of extermination and of nearly a million and a half
by execution in Russia is now one of the best documented as well
as the most atrocious crimes of history. The murders derived from
a cult of an illusion just as did the Russian labour camps. The
men responsible were men of willpower possessed by demons,
though once men join a savage crowd they become part of it, as
the spectators at a gladiatorial show admitted, even in Saint Augustine's recollection. Himmler believed that he was still doing
right after he fainted at the sight of 100 Jewish women being shot
at Minsk. 'To have seen 100 corpses piled up, or 500, or 1,000
. . . and remain decent . . . that has made a glorious unwritten
page in our history'[9]. Yet the carriage of nearly four million people
by railway to Poland was a severe burden on the German war
machine while, if the Germans had used the Russian Jews intelligently, along with other nationalities, they might have won the
war. Far more Jews were, of course, murdered then than the total
numbers killed in most wars. People speculate why the Germans,
the best educated people in the world, should have perpetrated
these crimes. In many ways, however, the connection was logical:
a technologically advanced country alone was capable of carrying
through these plans into action.

Had the war been won by the Germans, others would have suffered similar fates. The Central European gypsies were destroyed, as it was. 'Certain ethnographical tasks' had been begun in 1939 in Poland. Himmler had also conceived of 'consanguine fishing expeditions' to France in order to capture promising blond or blue-eyed men who might become leaders. Himmler in 1941 told a gathering of SS officials that the elimination of thirty million Slavs was an essential prerequisite for German planning in the East. Meantime, the German victories enabled 'various dingy figures, hitherto known only as editors or publishers of the Protocols . . . to be changed', says Norman Cohn, 'into important administrators'[10]; for example, Darquier, commissioner-general for Jewish affairs under Laval, or Endre, who became secretary of state in Hungary and sent 450,000 Jews to Auschwitz. Even the eminently mongrel Spaniards, whose country was not occupied by the Germans, had brief bouts of artificial hostility to Jews whom some of their propagandists discovered, in the absence of Jews in the country since the sixteenth century, to be synonymous with Catalans. In France, laws in October 1940 excluded Jews from responsible positions in culture, the civil service, judiciary and army. Throughout Europe, the yellow star was a badge of persecution. All the half-submerged racial prejudices of Central Europe and western Russia came to a head and gave the richest continent in the world a reminder that the crust of civilisation was thin. There was some illogicality in the thought that Hitler, anxious to preserve purity of blood, wanted to create a German empire. Imperialism, as Gobineau appreciated, renders a mixture of races inevitable. But perhaps, behind Hitler's desire for empire in East Europe and west Russia, was his recognition that he would, thereby, be able to destroy the 'bacteria', the 'abscess', the 'germ carriers' and the 'tropical parasites', in order to preserve the 'host nation'. Hitler compared his task to that of Pasteur and Koch. (Lenin also liked medical metaphors, for he spoke of his movement as an infection which would pass through any wall built against it.)

Walter Laqueur in a recent book, *The Terrible Secret*, asks why the Allied governments did so little to try to save the European Jews. The explanation is that, though most of the information reached the Allied capitals, their officials could not believe it. Laqueur tells how a Polish opponent of the Nazis, Jan Karski, succeeded in reaching the West having observed the murder of many Jews at Belzec. He talked to the liberal judge Felix Frankfurter. Frankfurter told him, 'I can't believe you.' When assured by a third person present that Karski was speaking the truth, Frankfurter said, 'I did not say this young man is lying. I said I cannot believe him.' There is a difference. That perhaps explains why the news from East Europe was not believed for so long.

2

Germany, despite, or because of, her totalitarian leadership, took a long time to awake to the necessity of organising her economy for war. In 1942 the production of civilian goods was only three per cent below the level of peacetime. Germany was still making refrigerators for private buyers in 1942. Road and public building continued till then. There was little redeployment of labour (it was admittedly already controlled) and little use of women, whom the Nazis believed to be best employed at home. Speer's attempt at a national reorganisation for war, in 1943 and 1944, met many difficulties, from the Nazi party in particular. Then, despite some encouragement of local nationalism, the German regime never gave any sustained help to the Flemings, Ukrainians, Slovaks and Croats, all of whom had genuine complaints against the old order of things. Against this, the Allies developed a sound method of compiling statistics, which enabled them, unlike the Germans, to know exactly what they were producing, and what not. They therefore mobilised their resources better than did the Germans. Since their peoples were mainly behind them, in the 'war effort', the Allies did not have to take into account large margins of error, as has been the case with subsequent national statistics.

The Russian defeat of Germany in the East was a triumph for the former's industrial strengths, which Germany had avoided noticing. Russia had had 20,000 tanks (more than the rest of the world put together) in 1941 and produced 100,000 between then and June 1945. The import of many US lorries helped the Russians too, enabling their motorisation and a clever use of mobile warfare. Western bombing tied down Germany's fighters which could have been used against Russia. The Russian production of thousands of fighters (137,000 according to Russian figures) was enough to give them, in the end, command of the air. The building of new industries in the Ural mountains removed Russian industry away from the battle. Even more important, in 1945 over half the industrial workers in Russian factories were women. Meantime, the most strict forms of state control in collective farms diminished. Anti-religious and Marxist slogans declined.

The US organisation for war was even more impressive. While the Russians lost millions, the US lost under 400,000 dead. 14½ million people were, however, successfully mobilised. The US was not touched directly by war, save for the occupation of her dependency, the Philippines, and the bombing of Hawaii. The cost ($330 billion) admittedly necessitated a new structure of taxes which made most US citizens into taxpayers for the first time. But in return, unemployment, high in 1941, was cut by the establishment of new governmental agencies. Industry boomed. A new synthetic rubber industry was created. 300,000 aircraft were produced by 1945. Not only businessmen but scientists and professors were brought into a new collaboration with the government and the military. An espionage service in the US was founded (there had scarcely been such a thing before 1942). Half the national income was devoted to military expenditure from 1942. The constitution remained, however, untarnished and, though the President's power was increased, elections and normal congressional work continued. The leaders of the American trade unions accepted an agreement not to strike in return for an agreement by employers to ban lockouts – the perfect compromise dreamed of by young Fascists in the early 1930s. The US entered the war in 1941 politically parochial, and ended it in 1945 the dominant world power. Few wars have ever been so successful for any nation.

The tank and the aircraft were the distinguishing weapons of the Second World War, both being used as they had begun to be used at the end of the First. All developments in the course of the Second World War were to some extent a response to them. For example, anti-aircraft guns were put on lorries to guard convoys and the motorisation of artillery. Tanks became bigger but later they declined in importance, as first Russia and then Germany invested in mines on the ground. In 1944 the US developed the Sherman tank, with a mine detector in front of it. Names of aircraft replaced those of battleships as emotive marks of military strength – Spitfire, Blenheim, Wellington – mostly harking back to a lost era of limited war. The most significant aircraft was, however, the US's Flying Fortress, which could carry 20,000 pounds of incendiary bombs, flying at 300 miles an hour, with thirteen machine-guns protecting it on all sides. Raids by these fleets of bombers, accompanied by fighters, began from 1944 (though not before, because of inadequate results achieved before photo reconnaissance) to have a devastating effect on German industry, and precision bombing of communications and oil plants in the end was effective.

Then in June 1944, at the invasion of Normandy, the British and Americans had 6,000 aircraft to face 900 German, and were able to use these weapons continuously as a substitute for artillery. The Western use of paratroops (in Sicily and in France), also, was as effective as the earlier German use of such troops had been.

The war in the Far East was won by air power, itself a consequence of the superior industrial system in the US. Aviation was the foundation of General MacArthur's 'Island Campaign' which began in 1943 and which enabled the setting up of bases for the heavy bombing of Japan, from 1944 onwards (from the Mariana Islands, then Okinawa). The consequent raids were few but effective. General LeMay's raid on Tokyo of March 1945 with nearly 500 B29 bombers each carrying six to eight tons of explosive burned about sixteen square miles of land and caused 185,000 killed or wounded. By August 1945 sixty per cent of Japanese merchant shipping was lost, and although she retained most of her overseas conquests, she could not count on getting to them, nor on supplying herself. The atom bombs dropped in August 1945 were extensions of the US bombing policy, and were probably instrumental in persuading the Japanese Emperor to insist on making peace, so enabling the US to avoid a bloody invasion of Japan. On the other hand, they killed 200,000 people. The long-term consequences of Japan's early victories, her designs for a Co-Prosperity Sphere, as of Hiroshima, were considerable.

3

Doubtless, there were aspects of fascism in France, in Italy, even in Germany, which may be described as beneficial. Do we see in Pétain's regime, as argued by Robert Paxton, the beginnings of the efforts to reverse decay, the willingness to give technology a high place, larger factories and economic growth which characterised postwar France[11]? The long digestions and aperitifs of old France have almost been swept away. Do we see even in Nazism the beginning of that destruction of class which, according to Ralf Dahrendorf, characterises modern Germany[12]? Did the necessities of war enforce the modification of the New Order so as to lay the ground for the economic integration of Europe? Some characteristics of fascism will always be with us: above all, the nostalgia for 'action'. Croce wrote about the end of the Risorgimento in Italy: 'Every close of a period of history brings with it the death of something, however much the end may have been sought . . . however essential it may be to the work which was so clearly envisaged and brought to completion . . . no more youthful strivings and heartburnings after an ideal that was new, lofty and far removed from realisation . . . Men even went so far as to regret the dangers'[13]. Fascism was born among those regrets.

The illogicality of Nazi racist theories has not prevented them from having an odd subsequent history. First, they introduced violent political considerations into all discussion of the differences of races. By poisoning the character of that discussion, they have prevented desirable enquiry. It has become impossible to discuss peoples' rational fears of the cultural consequences of intermingling of peoples without inviting the accusation of racism. Second, while the milder version of Nazi racial theories held in South Africa have incurred execration (even though they have been, at least, accompanied by democracy among the ruling white tribe), Jews have continued to be persecuted without exciting a great outcry. Russian anti-semitism, in abeyance for a short time after 1917, grumbles on, and the Jews of the Middle East and North Africa, including the 80,000 Jews of Baghdad, who had lived in that city for a thousand years before the Arabs conquered it, were expelled soon after the formation of the Jewish state.

Thirty years after the Second World War, some of the aims of the vanquished have come about, though not as they would have liked them. Thus Germany, though divided, has no problem of living space, since its population is static. It is also the richest nation in Europe. Japan is the most powerful country in the Far East. Economically it is now the most successful power in the world. Even the corporate state, fitfully put forward by Mussolini, seems increasingly to characterise the economies of many nominally free nations.

Similarly, the concept of national socialism is one which has attracted innumerable African and Asian states. The leaders of these societies would not recognise any link with Nazism. Nor is there any direct one. Yet socialist nationalism turns out, unsurprisingly, to be similar to national socialism. So far from being defeated in 1945, a version of what would have seemed before 1939 to be fascism – vulgar fascism, no doubt, bastard fascism or fascism with a human face perhaps – is with us, unrecognised everywhere, the strongest political movement of the century. Protectionist and nationalist policies by autocratic governments have been followed throughout the world, with often an echo of those gestures rendered infamous by Hitler and Mussolini. Several democracies which the Fascists regarded as decadent in the 1930s also seem almost to be so. Nor has the world been shocked by the triviality and cruelty of what happened in the war into new ways of settling disputes. Several heroes of the 'left', such as 'Che' Guevara, have again elevated violence to a moral virtue. It now seems as if 1945 was, so far from being the end of an era of war, a mere halt on the route in the multinational conflict which has never ceased since 1914. Racial hostility is far from dead: whenever they have the chance, black and brown peoples have shown intolerance for people of other skins on a scale equal to that of whites' ancient distaste for those who differed from them.

Still, 1945 marked the end of an era: when the US and the Russian army met at Torgau in April 1945 not only was the century of German preponderance in Europe at an end. So was the supremacy of Europe in the world[14].

62

The Withdrawal of Europe

All valiant dust that builds on dust. . .

Kipling, *The Recessional*

The European empires withdrew from most of the world during the generation following the Second World War. The elements in the drama were: first, a participation during the war by Indians and Africans as equals and as officers within the European armies, and the quartering in many parts of the European empires of conscripts who plainly were no more 'born to rule' than the local inhabitants; second, the hostility to the idea of empire among some parts of the European 'left', particularly the British: the notion of empire as 'a civilising mission' so characteristic of the past was forgotten; third, the encouragement of the United States at every level – governmental, academic, private and commercial – to nationalist movements everywhere in Africa and Asia: thus it was logical that young Africans such as Kwame Nkrumah or Nnamdi Azikwe in the Gold Coast and Nigeria respectively should have been educated in American or English universities; their views of African development had an American bias against empire; and fourth, the consequent impatience merged with Europeans' sense that their task was to prepare the peoples under their rule for self-government. Nigerians and Ghanaians believed that their time had come. The conviction felt by many in the Second World War that they were fighting a war for freedom meant that the maintenance of empires against the wishes of the peoples concerned was illogical or unacceptable.

In fact the long process of disintegration in the British Empire in India stretched back to the First, not the Second, World War. India became automatically a combatant in 1914, and Indian leaders had responded: India provided over a million troops for the campaigns in Europe, the Middle East and East Africa. During the second half of that conflict, Muslim leaders in India opposed participation in the war; and complaints were made against taxation. Agitation for home rule in India began, and reforms leading to that were introduced in 1919. The death of nearly 400 Indian protesters at Amritsar in March 1918 sharpened Indian demands. From 1919 onwards limited participation by Indians in the government of British India grew. Between 1919 and 1939 Mahatma Gandhi's 'non-cooperation movement' established the Congress party as the main challenge to the British Empire in India. The interwar years were in India years of continuous civil conflict; civil disobedience and non-violent demonstrations had broken the back of the Indian empire before 1939. The interminable conferences and plans for new constitutions would probably have resulted in the establishment of an Indian dominion before the Second World War had it not been for the deepening conflict between Hindus and Muslims. After 1945 this conflict resulted in partition being agreed between Pakistan and India. No colonial war was waged by the British to preserve this jewel in their imperial crown; instead, the partition resulting in independence in August 1948 was accompanied by ferocious acts of violence and the exchange of two million refugees between the two successor states.

This withdrawal from India led to the general disintegration of the British will to preserve the empire anywhere. The eclipse of the old Indian Army marked a fundamental shift in the old order of things in Asia, which that army had guaranteed. The British interest in the Middle East had been acquired as a means of preserving the route to India. East Asia and Africa too were afterthoughts. Thus, despite Churchill's famous remark in the course of the Second World War that he had not become Prime Minister of Britain to preside over the liquidation of her empire, that is what he began to do in his administration between 1951 and 1955; the process was carried to its conclusion by Harold Macmillan between 1957 and 1962. In these acts, Conservative governments carried out what were in electoral terms socialist policies with great efficiency.

The process affected Burma and Ceylon, the Caribbean and Malaysia, West and East Africa, as well as the residual British interests in the east Mediterranean. Britain fought seriously if unsuccessfully to preserve her empire only in two places: Kenya and Cyprus. Victory in both instances could have been possible only with a degree of repression that public opinion at home would have regarded as unacceptable. Britain also tried unsuccessfully in the Suez campaign of 1956 to preserve the Suez Canal Company's ownership of the canal of that name and, much more successfully, against Communists of Chinese origin to preserve an open society in Malaya. In Rhodesia and South Africa, colonists who had established themselves in those zones populated by Africans severed relations with Britain in order to preserve their control: unsuccessfully, in the case of the first, in the end.

Britain had been Europe's premier empire before 1939 and gave an example to the Netherlands and Belgium. Neither country was in a position to commit troops on a large scale to preserve their vast dominions. The Dutch did, it is true, suppress an Indonesian people's army in Java in 1947–48 but a year after their victory they transferred authority to Achmed Sukarno. Belgium moved with haste from a policy based on the maintenance of her presence *ad infinitum* in the Congo to one of independence, resulting in chaos, civil war and international crisis in 1960. Even France followed the British example in respect of most of her African empire and established a network of independent French-speaking African republics usually with close friendship with Paris during 1958–60. Morocco and Tunisia caused much trouble in French politics in the early 1950s but, since there were few French colonists there, there was no overwhelming obstacle to independence in either state.

Four major colonial wars were, however, waged: two by France, two by Portugal. The French fought to preserve their Indo-Chinese dominions from communism in a long war which dragged on continuously between 1946 and 1954. After the French defeat at Dien Bien Phu in May 1954 peace was signed which left the Communists in control of the north of the country and a weak gathering of Confucians, Christians and others in the south – ultimately themselves to be attacked by the Communists and championed by the Americans in a conflict which became a part of the international Cold War of West and East.

The second French war was the worst of all colonial wars, that of Algeria. There could be no swift withdrawal because a million Frenchmen lived there, because the rest of France looked on Algeria as an 'integral part' of their own country and because there never seemed to be *interlocuteurs valables* with whom French administrators could treat. Many Muslims in Algeria lived with and worked with the French with profit. The achievement of France in the years between 1830 and 1954 had been immense, and the French were proud of it. The population had increased from under three million to ten million. Great cities had been built. Road, industries, mines, railways, hospitals and schools accompanied them. 2,000 square miles had been cultivated in 1830, while in 1954 the figure was 27,000.

Still, these benefits were not enough to satisfy the Muslims. Many were neglected and impoverished. Their leaders had been educated to believe that France could be fought, and defeated. The massacre of Muslims at Setif on Victory Day 1945 following a smaller outbreak by Muslims against the French created a sense of outrage which led to the rising against France in the Aurès mountains in October 1954. Eight years later, after innumerable murders and threats of civil war in France, Algeria was independent; the million Frenchmen who had believed that Algeria was France itself were exiles in the motherland.

The Portuguese colonial wars in Mozambique and Angola were of a similar sort. There too there were settlers. There too there were local hatreds within the guerrilla movements. There also in the end the war came to an end in consequence of a political upheaval in the home country; and there also the successor regimes adopted in the first years after the European collapse radical socialist policies in very difficult circumstances.

These events occurred within thirty years of the end of the Second World War. They vastly increased the number of formal centres of authority. In practice they created many zones in which real authority was lacking. The rulers of the new states concerned have often lacked legitimacy. They have sought protection from strong rather than generous powers. Traditions of continuity of government as of law are weak there. They have created large zones where rivalry between great powers is inevitable.

This abandonment of the European position occurred with astonishing speed. Almost everywhere the Europeans handed over to minorities or a minority tribe or a single leader, usually with bitter opponents within the country concerned. The most stable of the countries were those which gave power to those who managed their countries as despots with single parties. Only in India and in Israel, a special case, did representative democracy as practised in Western Europe and North America strike anything like deep roots – though recent events in Nigeria (since 1978) are encouraging in that largest country of Africa. There was thus by 1980 much scepticism as to whether the 'civilising mission' had done its work adequately.

63
The Cold War I: The 'Class Struggle'

> If the Revolution came before the bourgeois revolution, it could result in a political monstrosity similar to the ancient Chinese or Peruvian empire, or, in other words, in a renovated Tsarist despotism, with a communist lining.
>
> Plekhanov

> I'm a Marxist, not a dogmatic one but still a Marxist. I've always believed men were instruments or interpreters of history and that great historical movements were uninfluenced by the charades involved in democratic politics. But after what I've witnessed for a year in Portugal, I'm beginning to believe in Cleopatra's nose. Man counts. He really does.
>
> Mario Soares, Socialist Prime Minister of Portugal,
> *New York Review*, 1975

> We must finish once and for all with the neutrality of chess. We must condemn once and for all the formula 'chess for the sake of chess'... we must organise shock brigades of chess players and the immediate realisation of the 5-year chess plan.
>
> The State Prosecutor of Russia, N. V. Krylenko, c. 1931

1

The 'Cold War' was a struggle between the two powers which emerged victorious over Germany and Japan in 1945, the US and Russia. The appearance of these as the two dominating powers in the world had been foreshadowed, in a famous passage, by Tocqueville a century before.* The difference between them was that, while the US had been constructed on the basis of individual

---

* 'There are, at the present, two great nations, Russia and the US which... started from different points but which seem to tend towards the same end... the American struggles against the obstacles that nature opposes to him... the adversaries of the Russian are men. The former combats the wilderness... the latter, civilisations. The principal of the former is freedom, of the latter servitude. Yet each seems called by some secret design of providence one day to hold in its hands the destinies of half the world' – De Tocqueville (1835)[1].

colonisation, with the encouragement of a lax and open state, the Russian empire had been constructed by a strong, determined, increasingly secretive and jealous central government. Racially both the US and Russia were mixtures, as Peter Struve pointed out in the early 1900s.[2] The US had usually been a defensive power, but had appeared aggressive. Russia had been expansionist, though afraid. The United States was the central power of a conglomeration of allies, most of whom retained the realities of independent sovereignty. Russia's allies retained little more than the trappings. In the formulation of Bergson, one nation represented the 'open society', the other the 'closed society'. One inherited the traditions of the free cities of Babylon and of the Mediterranean, of Greece, the German and Anglo-Saxon habits of consultation and law; the other was the inheritor of an Oriental tradition of despotism, command, regularity, secrecy, conformity, centralised power and Byzantine bureaucracy.

The rulers of Russia were the heirs of the Tsars and a despotism of unprecedented ruthlessness. Those same rulers were dominated by an ideology based itself on the anti-church of Marxist-Leninism. The ethnic European character of most of the population had been overlaid by a despotism whose centralised discipline was essential to ensure the survival of the Communist party in power. That party, minority though it was, had been able to compel admiration from the large number of Russians who admired brutality, force and ruthlessness. Others supported the Russian despotism, either directly or indirectly, out of fear or ambition. Even the more 'humane' Communist leaders such as Bukharin believed that 'proletarian coercion in all its forms from execution to forced labour was, paradoxical as it may sound, the best method of moulding Communist humanity out of the human material of the capitalist period'.[3] The twentieth-century Russians' attitude to truth could best be seen in a remark by Piatakov, an 'old Bolshevik' who, after siding with Trotsky in the 1920s, joined Stalin in 1928 and had a number of posts in the Russian government before being shot in 1937. Piatakov once told an acquaintance, about 1930, in Paris that a true Bolshevik was one who had so submerged his personality in the 'collectivity' that 'he can make the necessary effort to break away from his own opinion and convictions ... and be ready to say that black is white and white is black if the party requires it'.[4]

Not everything evil in Russia could be attributed to communism. From the time of the Decembrist plots of 1825, Russian institutions of repression became steadily worse. In 1826, Tsar Nicholas I founded his Third Section of the imperial chancellery, theoretically to give protection to widows and orphans (hence the handkerchief adopted as its symbol), in practice to control the citizens. His successor, Alexander II, made an effort to curb that body and other police forces, but his murder ended the hope of that. After 1882 the Tsarist police had the right to detain and to send into administrative exile even those merely suspected of political crimes. The police were exempt from any demand to hand over to the judiciary those whom they believed to have committed crimes. Only the approval of the minister of the interior or the chief of the gendarmes was needed to endorse such acts. This attitude to the police was to be found nowhere else in Europe in the late nineteenth century. Thus was established a totalitarian state under the Tsars which the Communists embellished, adding ideology to pan-Slav imperialism, after the confusion of 1917; though the old regime (unlike the new) had respected, as a rule, the families of its victims. Foreign travel was often possible in the past also. But there were chapters of the criminal code before 1917 'which were', as Richard Pipes put it, 'to totalitarianism what Magna Carta is to Liberty'.[5] Even Lenin himself, in the end, accepted that the system which he had established was 'to a large extent the survival of the old one . . . repainted on the surface'.[6]

Russia's evolution from city to world empire had had something in common with that of Rome: the small city state of Moscow, numbering nine to ten million in 1550, expanded by conquest, absorbing nearby Slav city states and taking on much of the colouring of the Central Asiatic despotism of the Tartars to which it was for a long time subject. For 240 years the Russians paid tribute to the Tartar Khan, whose agents were established throughout Russia, checking the correct payment of tribute: the slightest false step brought a summons to the Khan at Sarai: 'In this era,' to quote Richard Pipes again, 'Russians learned that the state was arbitrary and violent, that it took what it could lay its hand on and gave nothing in return, and that one had to obey it because it was strong'.[7]

The despotism in Russia had oriental characteristics. That in China was, of course, *purely* Oriental, with some Western variations. Formally China is still Marxist, Leninist, even Stalinist (for Stalin's name has not been repudiated in China). Doubtless the existence of the vocabulary and argument associated with those names is a matter for confusion, perhaps a means of drawing some of Chinese thinking into Western ways. The Chinese despotism has much in common, however, with the rule of a dogmatic dynasty of absolute emperors. In modern China, as in old, power is controlled by a single ruler advised by mandarins, themselves insulated from contact with ordinary people (despite a show of manual labour *pour encourager les autres*). In Communist China, there is, too, the same ambiguous attitude towards outsiders that there has always been: sometimes warm and welcoming, as in the 1970s; sometimes cold and distant, as in the 1960s. The 'eternal wisdom' of the Chinese often impresses visitors, as they might have been equally impressed by a Benedictine monastery or a militant order in the Middle Ages. The brutality, evident roughness and seething violence of Russia are not apparent. The secrecy of modern Chinese life makes it unknown whether or no there are large slave labour camps. Meantime, unchanged and unchangeable since 2000 BC, the rhythm of the rice harvest, irrigated as in the past according to a remorseless routine, continues, the harvest drawn in by the invaluable water buffalo under Deng as it was under the Han.

For two generations Communism seemed, to its enemies as much as to its friends, a radical means of achieving a new society. This did not happen. Communism in power seemed more like a system of political management which enabled certain countries and people to withstand the innovations and challenges of free enterprise and technological change. Communism offered to many, as Luigi Barzini put it, 'a return to the feudal order', to the security of the man who had his place in society established at birth and could neither regress nor progress from it; it could not be discussed and he could not be promoted by evaluations of merit, or cast down for other reasons.[8] For those who did not have independent thoughts, who liked to be told what to do, who wished their lives to be planned and who had no moral objections to the drabness associated with all dominant bureaucracies, it had for many years an irresistible attraction.

2

The Cold War had many causes. But the main cause was that one of the world's greatest nations, Russia, imposed upon its population and the population of its clients the belief that the determining factor in human history was the conflict between classes. It was an illusion which gave the ideology, or even the religion, to a quarter of the world's population despite the fact that, in the modern world, the most striking thing is, as George Orwell put it, 'the overwhelming strength of patriotism'.[9]

A history of class must embrace much. For example, the most rigid system of differentiation of people was that which has for 2,000 years divided Indians into castes. That system partly derived from conquest by the Aryans, and was also partly based on attitudes of colour: indeed, the Sanskrit word for caste, *varna*, signified colour. The Aryans treated the slightly darker Dasas whom they conquered as inferior and those who descended from mixed Dasa and Aryan as very inferior. The Aryans themselves, meantime, divided into three: warriors or aristocrats; priests; common people. Though, when the Aryans reached India, those divisions were scarcely castes (since there were no rules limiting marriage or social contact between them), they became so. The priests (brahmins) steadily arranged a system in which heredity within professions became normal too. New ethnic groups which occasionally developed were given the status of sub-castes. Elaborate rules as to who one might eat with, or marry, were soon made. By the second or third century BC the functions and limitations of the four castes dominated social activity. The only way to escape from the bondage of caste was to associate with foreigners, and that was far from easy. In India, caste and profession soon became intertwined, so that even sensitive foreign observers confused the two.

Nowhere else probably was so rigid a system of classes established as it was in India. Ancient Egypt approached it with a system deriving from earlier conquest and later from professional distinctions, though men of simple origin could rise to the highest posts and even lower officials could rise also.[10]

The history of class and caste in ancient Rome is treacherous ground. Many historians employ the words 'middle class' when talking of some aspect or other of the Roman Empire, but those people seem to have been far from absolutely differentiated from the poor: rich merchants were held to be middle class, poor ones plebeian, because of their wealth, not their birth. The traditional 'middle class' of republican days had made themselves as rich as the patricians by tax-farming and some other activities. But the history of the Roman Empire is the story of constant struggles by new waves of humble men seeking power to establish themselves and their families. Those waves were led by men who were able to seek their fortunes with the same determination as Napoleon's marshals did. Very nearly all the old patrician families of the Republic had died out by the first century AD. The 'golden age' of Rome was directed by Spaniards of humble origin, such as Trajan and Hadrian, and the revival of the third century was led by equally humble Illyrians, such as Aurelian and Diocletian. Gibbon gave a vivid picture of the Roman nobility during the fourth century AD, walking through the streets, their robes floating in the wind, followed by a train of fifty servants, moving along the pavements with 'the same impetuous speed as if they travelled with post-horses'.[11] But the grandfathers of those splendid noblemen were probably poor. All those imposing adjectives such as *clarissimus, eminentissimus, perfectissimus, egregius*, which prefixed the names of senators, prefects and officials in Diocletian's reign, and whose modern incarnations are our 'right honorables', 'excellencies' and 'highnesses', cloaked a society open to talent.

Earlier, before Rome had been corrupted, as it were, by ideas of conquest, there was even then a far from hard-and-fast all-embracing system of classes. The elementary group in society was the family. The aggregation of families formed the *gens* or the 'house'. The aggregation of 'houses' made the tribe. The aggregation of tribes made the Republic. All ancient peoples regarded themselves not as being part of a 'class' but as having proceeded from one original stock and, in Sir Henry Maine's words, 'even laboured under an incapacity for comprehending any reason save this for their holding together in political union'.[12] People believed in kinship, not class, as is the case to some extent even in sophisticated countries today.

If there are difficulties about any categorisation of society based on the idea of class in Western Europe before industrialisation, how much more difficult it is to see such a society elsewhere. Africa has continued largely tribal. The Aztec and Inca monarchies were served by bureaucrats. Whether it was appropriate to consider the thousands of bureaucrats employed by the Chinese emperors members of an upper 'class' would seem as doubtful as the question whether Egyptian priests can be so 'classified'. The 'class divisions' within the Abbasid caliphate were distinctions between races and religions. The non-Muslim inhabitants of the first Arab empire, Christians, Armenians, Jews, Druses, Copts, Nestorians, were considered primarily as people of a religion different to the paramount one. They were second-class citizens but they were employed by the state, could make money, be admitted to guilds and could fight. Their 'class', such as it was, depended on belief.

Class and caste are also inadequate concepts to grapple with the nature of feudal Europe. For example, in Anglo-Saxon England the word 'thegn' (for which 'lord' is an approximate translation) designated a relation between two people: every thegn was somebody else's thegn. A king's thegn was his free servant but also his companion.

All the dominant families of Carolingian Europe were men of recent riches, descendants of peasants, ostlers or men-at-arms at the court of Charlemagne. The nobility of Castile, at the same time, was divided into *ricos hombres*, who acted as governors of royal lands; and *infanzones* or minor nobility, who lived on their estates. There was antagonism between the two, though both swore fealty to the king whom they recognised as overlord. French society in the eleventh century could, according to Marc Bloch, best 'be conceived of as an essentially vertical structure consisting of innumerable small groups, clustered round superiors, dependent in their turn on others higher in scale'.[13] In the twelfth century, Marc Bloch added, 'human blocks tended to become distributed in horizontal layers'. Has there ever been a real division between nobility, bourgeoisie and working people? It seems improbable. 'Every page of mediaeval history,' wrote Huizinga, 'proves the spontaneous and passionate character of loyalty and devotion to the prince'; the emotional character of party sentiments and of fidelity being heightened by the suggestive effect of liveries, colours, badges and party cries. The bourgeoisie were always urban. They co-existed with, married into, collaborated with and both preceded and outlived what is conventionally known as feudalism.

Distinctions more based on blood than status came to characterise several richer Western European countries from the late Middle Ages and the Renaissance onwards. Perhaps something closer to a class system existed in Europe between the collapse of feudalism and the coming of industrialism than at any other time, though Europe as a whole did not, as has been supposed by some, see a triumph then of the bourgeoisie: 'If any social group bettered its position . . . in those centuries,' says Professor Elton, 'it was the landed nobility'.[14] 'By keeping close to the practical things,' said Marc Bloch, 'which give real power over men, and by avoiding the paralysis which overtakes social classes which are too sharply defined and too dependent on birth, the English aristocracy acquired the dominant position which it retained for centuries'.[15] Italy was another exception: Florence had a social system in which the aristocracy of the early Middle Ages lost their wealth, and rich and poor had an identity of interests by dint of belonging to one of the city's guilds. Thus, if a system of classes existed in mediaeval Europe, it certainly did not do so everywhere; while, from the sixteenth century, it was usually possible for the successful merchant to buy a title or otherwise make his way into the aristocracy, the intelligent poor man to make his way upwards via the Church, or a peer's brother to make money in a warehouse.* In France under the *ancien régime* the king's ministers were almost always of the 'vile bourgeoisie', not the aristocracy.[16]

In 1750 an incoherent series of divisions, cross-sections and radiating systems of prejudice existed everywhere. Had it been possible to plot them on a map, they might have resembled an open field in the days of the high Middle Ages. In some countries such as Britain the aristocracy was financed regularly by good marriages with merchants. In Germany, on the other hand, something like a class system did exist – in a country characterised by extreme territorial subdivisions. There, the peasants, burghers and gentlemen even had their own laws: nobles could not buy peasant land, nor could peasants buy ground rents. Nearly everywhere, in contrast, wrote Jacob Burckhardt of Italy during the Renaissance, even those who might be disposed to pride themselves on their birth could not maintain any superiority in the face of culture and wealth.[17] The Russian nobility were more bureaucrats than aristocrats and so had a different position *vis-à-vis* their sovereigns. Russian society was also complicated by the great number of foreigners among the top civil servants.

Professional divisions were more important: 'the lowest, least educated and uncultivated European believes himself superior to the white born in the New World', wrote the great traveller in South America, Humboldt.[18]

Confusion in social status derived from confusion over landholding. City dwellers had, in the Middle Ages, a series of divisions of their own, based on profession, even if people remained as a rule in the professions of their fathers. Even in France, under the

* In Austria-Hungary, Dr Bruford points out, 'it was always possible to buy titles'. Under Joseph II, it cost 20,000 gelden to be a count, 6,000 to be a baron but 386 to be a 'von' (*Adliger*). Louis XIV in France abolished all titles conferred during the previous ninety-two years but allowed their owners to retain them on paying a further sum. In England, Defoe wrote, 'Antiquity and birth are needless here! 'Tis impudence and money makes a peer.'

old regime, there was plainly, within the world of agriculture, as Sir John Clapham put it, 'perpetual movement from class to class'.[19]

At first sight the Industrial Revolution seemed likely to simplify matters. Into Lancashire and Tyneside, into Glasgow and Belfast, into Lille, Rouen and Saint Etienne as into the Ruhr, Pittsburg and Chicago, vast numbers were drawn by the prospect of regular wages paid in cash. Those and other foci of industrial growth seemed to be creating a new class, the industrial workers, who began a trifle invidiously to be called, and call themselves, 'the proletariat', *die Arbeiter* – as if to suggest that agricultural workers, farmers' boys, domestic servants and soldiers were somehow different.

Between about 1850 and 1914 a coherent culture appeared to take shape in the industrialising nations based on the professional occupation of those who worked within mines, factories and attendant services, such as railways or merchant navies.

The conditions of most of these workers were harsh. The slum cities constructed cheaply to house them became hotbeds of hatred. The thought, or sight, of others living in luxury aroused a bitter wrath against society, even if in some it inspired a desire to rise and to enjoy similar benefits themselves. The fact that iron-masters and cotton kings were usually self-made men stimulated in workers an extra resentment. Large factories generated the possibility of large-scale outbreaks of protest and so justified, or explained, despotic management. That in turn led to political unrest. In mining villages, where nearly all the heads of families worked for mining companies, the combination of residence and place of work, and the danger and the importance of the activity, gave the persons concerned a high morale usually hostile to the political order which the coal produced by them powered.

Meantime, on the other side of the towns concerned, newly rich families, Forsytes or Buddenbrooks, lived in an ample luxury expressed by a cult of music or by long novels, ideally suited to the splendid leisure which new and largely untaxed wealth made possible.

Thus, in the richer, more adventurous countries of the nineteenth century, a period of acute resentments between the different sections of society followed. Of course, these were not the first differences between employees and employed, for disputes on the land and slave revolts had often disorganised agriculture since the dawn of time. The *jacqueries* of the fourteenth century in the countryside of Western Europe had echoes in the developing cities. Low-paid cloth-workers in Florence, the *Ciompi*, once led a violent withdrawal of labour, almost a rebellion, against the merchants. Similar upheavals occurred among weavers in Ghent. The religious quarrels of the sixteenth century caused these protests to be forgotten.

Nor were the quarrels between classes of the nineteenth century confined to factory, mine and railway shed. They had repercussions on the land, where in some countries, in tense conditions – for example, Spain – the battle assumed the character of a competition between landowner and labourer, the first to see how little he could pay, the second to see how little he could work. Still, agricultural disruption was limited since a serious strike could be mounted only during the harvest, and the idea of such a thing seemed so risky and against the long-term interests of everybody that it happened only rarely.

From the beginning of the modern era these problems gave rise to misconceptions. First, most of those who wrote about class during the nineteenth century knew a great deal about antiquity. They remembered the three classes of Lacedaemon – the free inhabitants of the land; the helots, or serfs; and the Spartans who lived in the cities. Had not Plato written: 'God has put gold into those who are capable of ruling; silver into the auxiliaries; and copper into the peasants, and other producing classes'? They knew also that Rome, in its republican days, was divided into three 'classes' (it was then, after all, that the word began its terrible career), the patricians, equestrians and plebeians.

These divisions of society had ceased to apply to Rome during the Empire, when there were as many classes, in fact as opposed to theory, as there are in modern Europe. But economists, social scientists and historians often wrote in the nineteenth and twentieth centuries of peoples as if they had social divisions as strictly delineated as a classical building. In 1869 Matthew Arnold mockingly spoke of the 'Barbarians, Philistines and populace' as being 'the three great classes into which our society is divided'.[20] Arnold's contemporary, Karl Marx, was not only influenced by such a tertiary division, even more important than those between peoples; but being a romantic as much as a revolutionary, he supposed (following the Abbé Siéyès during the French Revolution) that the working class were a chosen class. To Marx, the workers were a class with 'radical claims, a class in bourgeois society which is not *of* bourgeois society', though he was thinking of the *factory* workers who were, when he wrote, a minority even of the workers in England.

Something close to a new religion was based upon this view. Some were attracted to Marxism out of guilt, some out of a desire for discipline. Some desired a complete explanation of human life, but believed that Montesquieu was wrong in attributing it to climate. Some coveted an opportunity to lead a sect, however small. Some were attracted by the accuracy of one of Marx's prophecies – for example, about the inexorable 'march' of industrialisation – to accept his general prognosis. Then the need to belong to a group is, as the German philosopher of history Herder was the first to point out, for many people a need as basic as that for food.

But even if Marx's concepts had validity, in many countries the so-called middle class took a long time to reach power. In Germany before 1914, army, diplomacy, administrators, politicians were dominated by noblemen. The same could be said of other European countries.

The only country where in Europe a bourgeois revolution occurred in the nineteenth century was France. Yet France had the most conservative of all European societies. The French bourgeoisie were possessed of a sense of family, thrift and hard work. But they combined those things with the prudence traditionally possessed by the peasant. The French bourgeoisie had a peasant soul and an aristocratic sense of harmony and permanence, combined with, as Theodore Zeldin put it, scepticism about machines.[21]

An historian of America, Richard Hofstadter, argued that all North American society was middle class in the eighteenth century.[22] While politics were directed by rich men, there was no court, nobility, hierarchy, nor great estates manned by serfs, nor even (until the high days of Victorian industrialism) extravagance in styles of life. Anglo-Saxon America was a middle-class rural world, with no lords of the manor. That classlessness survives to this day. The same has been true of other countries created by Anglo-Saxon colonists, such as Australia and Canada. Those societies, too, were less warlike than most which had preceded them, though the crowding in cities which was caused, or permitted, 'suggested violent solutions to violent minds'. But the selfishness to which these cities gave scope was less threatening to the peace of the world, said Sir John Clapham, than 'the centralised, impersonal, property-controlling and property-owning state-selfishness which' – he wrote in the 1930s – 'shows signs of succeeding it'.[23] Nor did capitalism create a coherent social class. Between the captain of industry in his mock Gothic castle and the village shopkeeper, there was little in common save their appreciation of the profit motive. The two never sought to act in common; certainly not so as to threaten to drench the world in blood in the way that Marx considered 'necessary'.

Sometimes errors of a different sort have been made. Some socialists in Spain in the early twentieth century argued that there was no middle class there before 1917. They thus, to their disadvantage, ignored the shopkeepers, small businessmen and farmers who rejected both collectivism and the radical socialist movement throughout the 1930s, and fought for Franco in 1936. But in Spain, where the poor were always held by observers to have been 'uninterested in the position and the money of the rich', there was an immense array of different grades within society.

Some other questions need to be asked, and not just in Spain. For example, at what stage does the skilled worker cease to belong to the 'proletariat'? Is the manual worker in the public services a proletarian – even though he receives wages from the state, rather than from a private employer? Are wage workers in commerce in the same group as wage earners in industry? A sense of alienation cannot be the only definition of a membership of the working class. For there are many others apart from industrial workers who often feel 'alienated': conscripts, homosexuals, criminals and Jews have sometimes been kept at a distance from a national culture, while many workers at a conveyor belt do not feel so.

Some argue that class distinctions can be measured by money. It has been claimed that, before 1914 in England, the three-quarters of wage earners who were paid by the week, plus the 1.2 million salaried people who earned less than £160 a year, were held to be the working class. The middle class were said to be the 400,000 salaried men earning over £160 a year, the professional men numbering 330,000 and some of the 580,000 farmers. The 620,000 employers and the 60,000 people of 'independent means' were by this definition the upper class. But if class be determined by income, a higher income can presumably make people of a higher class. In that case, why should not the divisions be spoken of as being of wealth, not of class? If that were so, it would presumably be best for a reformer to follow Tom Paine's advice and make available capital subventions to everyone at the age of twenty-one, or to provide a graduated tax on inheritance, rather than to seek the capture of power of a particular class.

Since 1914, conditions in factories have vastly improved, and wages have risen greatly in relation to the cost of living, partly as a result of the realisation of an age-old truth that a contented worker is likely to produce more efficiently than a discontented one. Some members of the so-called 'working class' have now begun to earn higher incomes than those of the 'middle class'. Conditions of work even in mines have also ceased to be demoralising, while some workers at desks, in government departments as in companies, have a more boring day of work than some manual workers. In every country in Western Europe and the US, conditions in the 1990s of factory workers approximated to those of those traditionally regarded as 'middle class'. Factory workers of the 1870s working sixty-three hours a week, protected neither by trade unions nor by social legislation, might have seemed 'departicularised' by misfortune. But that is not the case with the worker in 1990 in Detroit, Milan or Billancourt. Not surprisingly, the old working-class culture of the nineteenth and early twentieth centuries has declined. The libraries formed, for instance, in Welsh mining villages have vanished. With his colour television set and his car, his holiday in the Mediterranean and his materialism, the well-paid European worker of the late twentieth century would seem to Marx to be the epitome of – bourgeois life!

Indeed, the working-class culture of the early stages of the Industrial Revolution now seems to have been as brief a phase in human history as the middle-class one which it was supposed to succeed. True, the two world wars left the populations of the combatant countries unenthusiastic for a repetition of such conflicts. But it also left them nationalistic, a tendency which mass education (which has emphasised a *national* past) and mass media (emphasising the *national* language and *national* issues) exacerbate. Any illusion that classes within one country collaborate naturally with those of the same status within another (upper or lower) was shattered by the events of 1914. Nor is nationalism evident only in time of war, not even in relation to other countries. For example, a Marxist historian has argued that 'Catalanism' (the subject of his particular interest) was not exclusively a representation of bourgeois interests: 'in 1927, the frontiers between peasants, merchants, small business and working class were blurred', wrote Pierre Vilar, and 'à la fin de la dictature [de Primo de Rivera], toutes les classes en Catalogne unissent leur griefs et s'affirment minorité nationalé'.[24] What seemed on the surface a matter of class has also often turned out to be a matter of local prejudice.

All advanced societies have always had in fact more subdivisions than a mere three or four. No theory of class has been of sufficient subtlety to do justice to the differences within the middle class of Europe or the US in the nineteenth century:[25] 'Entre ouvriers, il y a des catégories et un classement aristocratique. Les imprimeurs prennent la tête; les chiffonniers ... les égoutiers ferment la marche'.[26] Instead of a class society, in the eighteenth century, wrote Dr Laslett, 'we should think of a group of some 300,000 families, very various in character ... which several million families were busy imitating unsuccessfully, because they had not enough money to do it well'.[27]

How tiny, too, comparatively speaking, were the enterprises in the nineteenth century when theories of class were being formulated! Large factories of 2,000 strong were exceptional. In most cities of Spain, for example, in 1850, employers outnumbered employees. The small artisan lived on throughout the nineteenth century and only vanished even in the US after 1945. Yet only factories with a labour force of 2,000 or so could provide the conditions of the mass 'alienation' deplored by Marx.

Some of these illogicalities were evident at the beginning. Yet one of the prophets of class consciousness, Engels, could not believe them and complained: 'the most repulsive thing in this country [England] is the bourgeois respectability which has invaded the very blood and bone of the workers. The organisation of society into firmly established hierarchical gradations in which each one has his proper pride ... is taken so much as a matter of course, [and] is so ancient ... that it is comparatively easy for the bourgeois to play his part of seducer'.[28]

One explanation for these illusions is that the leaders of the working classes have often been people of easy circumstances. In 1914, out of 110 social democratic deputies in the Reichstag, only two were ex-workers. Even that symbolic representation was lacking among the French socialists. The French revolutionary leaders were of privileged origin, as were all the precursors of 'socialism' such as Saint Simon, Fourier, Owen, Blanc, Blanqui, Lassalle, Marx, Bakunin, Engels and Lenin. Yet in politics no laws of this sort are valid. The variety of origin of early Fascists and early Nazis puts paid to any serious analysis of politics based on class. For example, in 1932, out of 250 Nazi deputies, 43 had been in industry of some sort, 55 were employees, 12 were teachers, 29 were party officials, 20 had been civil servants, 9 were ex-officers while 50 were farmers.[29]

3

It thus is utterly false to suppose that all history is the history of class struggles. Class systems may have existed from time to time but all have differed. Class consciousness does not give the key to history. Yet the belief that it did so was allowed to dominate for many years the thinking of two great nations: Russia and China, as well as a host of smaller ones and political parties. True, Lenin gave the idea its new cutting edge, in arguing that the Communist party could be a 'revolutionary vanguard' to ensure the capture of power by the proletariat, and might even practise a dictatorship during the transition to the 'true' Communist society. Marx thought that that would be 'less violent' than eighteenth-century changes in society and 'of shorter duration'.

'Imagination to power', students of 1968 wrote on the walls of the Sorbonne, not realising that illusion was already in office. Though denouncing class, the managers of Communist societies assisted the creation of nations rather more sharply divided by class than any which they purport beneficially to have superseded. In Communist societies, at the top, there were managers and party members, neither capitalist nor proletarian, though, in the Russian case, they were the grandchildren of peasants, who reflected, at one remove, the upper class of old Russia, being bureaucrats: men who embarked on a career as formal as any in ancient Egypt, with access to special shops, transport, cars, clothes and travel on certain conditions. These party members, perhaps no more than one per cent of the population on average, were as it were locked into collaboration with the state, since they believed that vengeance would be wreaked upon them if the party ever lost the controlling power.

Beneath them again were the ordinary citizens of the country, factory workers or agricultural workers, whose lives could never flourish unless they joined the élite.

Below them again were the third class, of prisoners or slaves, 'zeks' in camps who made major economic contributions in the country concerned but whose lives vould have made those of helots in Sparta seem Arcadian. They at least knew the meaning of the word 'class'. 'Secure the Soviet Republic against its class enemies,' Lenin instructed his followers in September 1918, 'by isolating them in concentration camps.' Millions died in consequence of that. One can well compare with advantage the 170,000 or so killed throughout the French Revolutionary Terror.[30] During the worst part of the tyranny of Stalin, 'every region and every national republic [in Russia] had to have its own crop of enemies so as not to fall behind the others', wrote Evgenia Ginsburg, 'for all the world as though it were a yearly campaign for deliveries of grain or milk'.[31]

4

Now Marx had written his prophecies for 'advanced' societies such as England, whence his statistics derived. 'Marxism' was conceived as a theory for such places. 'No social order,' he wrote, 'ever perishes before all the productive forces for which there is room in it have developed.' He regarded Russia with contempt for much of his life. Indeed, he quoted forcibly most historians' commentaries on the role of the Mongols or Tartars: 'the bloody mire of Mongol slavery, not the rude glory of the Norman epoch, forms the cradle of Muscovy, and modern Russia is but a metamorphosis of Muscovy. Kalita's whole system may be expressed by the machiavellianism of the usurping slave'.[32] ('Kalita' was Tsar Ivan III, 'the tax collector', who founded the post-Mongol Russian state.) Yet, after the failure of the Paris Commune in 1870, Marx changed his mind. Thereafter, Russia seemed revolutionary to him: when Vera Zasulich, in 1881, wrote asking whether the village commune might not be transformed directly into a socialist commune or whether they, the Russian Marxists, should concentrate on turning Russia into a bourgeois society, Marx replied that the historic inevitability of capitalism was limited to the West, while the village commune was 'the fulcrum of Russia's social regeneration'.[33] Engels agreed: he believed that it was 'one of those exceptional cases when a handful of people can ... bring down a whole system'.[34] The populist revolutionaries were, therefore, able to ally themselves, if not see eye to eye, with Marx. Lenin was the inheritor of both traditions: that which stood for Marxist 'social democracy' and that which represented a Russian millenarian violence, in which the individual will could perform wonders.[35]

The class structure of Russia was specially inappropriate for Marx's ideas. For example, as Pushkin regretted, Russia never experienced feudalism, much less normal capitalism. Though, before the Tartars came, the nobles had some independence of the princes of Russia, they were not linked with them by the intimate relationship known as vassalage. Afterwards, the Grand Dukes of Muscovy built upon their status as supreme tax farmers to the Tartar Khan and adopted the Khan's way of looking at politics. The early Tsars considered Russia to be their own property and saw no distinction between their private property as human beings and the property of the state. These rulers also took over such institutions of the Mongols as the posts and intelligence services, and tried to turn their nobility into a ruling class without territorial roots. All who served the state had a right to land but the Russian nobles never held their estates by freehold. Indeed, they could be made into 'unpersons' overnight, in the nineteenth as well as in the twentieth century. In 1857 this upper class, 'a hierarchy, created entirely by the Tsars, open to all state employees',[36] numbered about one million. A third of these were non-hereditary officials, and held no serfs at all. Between 45,000 and 60,000 landowners held serfs in Russia, of which 18,500 had over 100 and only 1,000 had over 1,000. The 'bourgeoisie' in Russia was, meantime, largely non-Russian – mostly German – and, therefore, debarred from playing any political role. The working class, defined as those working in factories, numbered 679,000 in 1879, two million or so in 1900.

Furthermore, even more interesting, industrialisation in Russia between 1860 and 1914 was not inspired by a national bourgeoisie of restless capitalists anxious for profit. Russian industrialisation was sponsored by the state. It was usually carried out by foreigners. As a rule it had been begun with an eye on military considerations. Russia's industrialisation was thus in keeping with its Mongol past and its old absolutism, but had little to do with the capitalism practised in the countries which Marx had studied.

This Russian industrial process had its curiosities: Russian factories in 1900 averaged ninety men per plant – larger than the contemporary US average; and it had its successes: between 1890 and 1913 the standard of living increased by a third, foreign investment grew, iron ore produced increased from 1.7 million tons to 9.5 million. But this was a capitalist success. Was Marx deceived into supposing a capitalist *class* existed by hearing of the foundries in the Urals which, in the eighteenth century, smelted more iron than anywhere in Europe? By the cotton spinners who in 1850 produced more yarn than Germany did? By the bustling cottage industries? If so, he was wrong: all industrialists in Russia knew that the path to wealth lay not in fighting the authorities but in collaborating with them; that any product which became successful risked becoming a state monopoly; and that, as in ancient China and ancient Egypt, the safest way of becoming rich was to be a foreigner. Isaiah Berlin commented: 'It was not, after all, full grown capitalism that was enthroned in Russia in 1917 . . . but Lenin acted as if the bankers and industrialists were already in control.'[37]

The attachment which Marx had after 1870 to the village community was odd, to say the least, since, though the commune had given peasants identity and a primitive democracy, it was no more than the basic unit of administration in Russia set up in the seventeenth century to ensure an orderly payment of taxes (which it had done), as well as to assign land commensurate with needs while periodically reallocating it. Nor did Marx recognise that Russia, like the US, was a nation which still had much virgin land, even at the time of his own death in 1883. The condition of such a country was very different from that of places in Europe with which Marx was familiar – or which he admired!

The main political problem of Russia, too, was one of nationalities not class. In 1900 the Tsar's empire included 120 million people, in which 56 million 'Greater Russians' dominated 22 million Ukrainians and a lesser number of White Russians, Poles, Jews, Tartars, Lithuanians, Letts, Germans, Armenians, Estonians, Finns, Bashkirs, Georgians and others. This 'prison house of nationalities', to use a phrase employed by Lenin,* has since increased by 100 per cent, with the minority races even more proportionally numerous now than they were then. Events in 1917–18, when Russian state power was temporarily at an end, should have suggested that any 'thaw' in Russia, either of tsarism or of communism, would lead to a revolt of nationalities.

The first explanation for Marx's posthumous success in Russia was that, with the Tsar gone, a new upper class was needed to run the absolute state and to strengthen it. Lenin offered himself as the 'little father' in the Tsar's place and the Communist party instead of the old official class. To begin with largely composed of Jewish intellectuals, the Communist leadership imposed a dictatorship, since anarchy or disintegration seemed the alternative. The old upper class was dead, cowed, in gaol or in exile. The peasants, who formed the majority of the population, preferred absolutism to everything except anarchy, and anarchy they could not obtain. Then the system of soviets, through which the Communist party

* The phrase was probably invented about 1848 to apply to Austria-Hungary.

was managed, ensured that the local party organisations dominated state institutions. The Tsar's old power was vested in the secretary-general of the party, advised by the political bureau of the central committee – the latter being something like a self-appointed parliament. The federal constitution also seemed at first sight to include that right to devolution which Stalin had argued as desirable in 1914. Marx gave to Russia a theory, justifying an indefinite and nationalistic dictatorship by the new leaders.

Another explanation of what happened in Russia is that the situation on the land between 1860 and 1917 had become unstable. Serfs became legal persons in 1861, though they had some dues to pay to the government for their land and had to ask permission to leave the commune. But freedom meant new difficulties: landlords held on where they could to the bulk of the meadow and the forest which previously serfs had shared. The joint cultivation within the communes declined. The increase of population between 1858 and 1897 from 58 million to 120 million bedevilled everything. Even large-scale emigration to the US could not solve that problem. Huge numbers of half-literate peasants were ready for an upheaval: war or revolution or urbanisation. They got all three. In 1917 the millions of peasants in uniform who constituted the Russian army were willing to believe Trotsky's rhetoric and Lenin's comforting assurances. In St Petersburg, a majority of those who rioted against bread queues in the snow were recent immigrants drawn to the capital to work in new factories. By 1930 the sons of these peasants constituted a new urban bureaucracy, the Communist party, ready to destroy those relations of theirs who had remained on the land in the agricultural revolution and delighted to support Stalin in his murderous pursuit of the Jews who had led the Communists in the first years.

Communists never gained power in a free election before 1989. In the first election ever held in Russia, in November 1918, they gained 9.02 million votes (25 per cent), the Social Revolutionaries 20.9 (58 per cent), the Kadets 4.62 (13 per cent) and others 4 per cent. The Communists in Russia then staged their *coup d'état* and established their despotism by means of a victory in civil war. In the end Lenin's triumph, like Tito's and Mao's, was primarily a military one. In the first major victory of 'dialectical materialism', leadership was the decisive factor. Patriotism also counted. By clever exploitation of both, Trotsky transformed his 'flabby panicky mob' of Red guards into an efficient fighting force. Terror played its part: from the very beginning Lenin sanctioned the use of illegal imprisonment, torture, execution and psychological interrogation on a scale never seen before.

5

As for the other combatant in the Cold War, the US, that nation has since 1945 incarnated the Western ideal of an open society with a law independent of the government, with substantial devolution of power to localities and with an appropriate emphasis laid on the uniqueness of the individual. Only in the US, for thirty years after 1945, among even the democracies, was the belief general, as it was in Britain in the eighteenth century, that if a thing were to be done by private action it was liable to be better done than if it is done by the community. The US view of politics and the economy was thus based on an optimistic view of human nature.

Five points in the history of the US are worth recalling: first, independence preceded conquest of the territory. When the *Mayflower* sailed from Plymouth in 1620 with the first English settlers, they were seeking to be free, not to conquer the interior. They and their successors managed their own affairs, elected their own officials and paid the salaries of the English governors. The colonies before they found independence from Britain were free in a way that the peoples of few sovereign states have ever been.

In 1776 the US comprised 400,000 square miles. This doubled when the peace at the end of the War of Independence gave to the thirteen colonies the 492,000 square miles of the Indian Reserve, between the Allegheny mountains and the Mississippi. These 892,000 square miles were then again doubled by the 'Louisiana purchase' of 1803, a transaction with Napoleon I, which cost a mere $15 million. Napoleon knew that he could not hold that territory, save by a long colonial war for which he was unprepared. At that time, the Mississippi region was unmapped, though explorers, such as Meriwether Lewis and William Clark, soon set off for St Louis and reached the Pacific, via North Dakota. Purchase continued: Florida was bought from Spain in 1819 for $6.5 million – another 72,000 square miles. In the course of the nineteenth century, there followed the admission of Texas, which had briefly been independent and, before 1836, a part of Mexico* – another 389,000 square miles (1845); the cession of California, Arizona, Nevada, Utah and parts of Wyoming and Colorada from

---

* Mexico had incorporated Texas in 1721, defeating the Nayarit Indians.

Mexico for another derisory $15 million – 529,189 square miles. This followed in 1846 a war with Mexico which left the latter devastated and deeply pessimistic about its future.

The discovery of gold in California the next year led to the taming of the Wild West in a way which happened so fast that some states, such as Nevada, seemed to be discovered only after they had been founded. The states of Oregon and Washington were negotiated with Canada along the forty-ninth parallel, at no cost, to take in 286,500 square miles; and finally Alaska in 1867 and Hawaii in 1895 were bought for respectively $7.2 million and $4 million. These added another 586,400 and 6,400 square miles to the US. Puerto Rico was absorbed after the Spanish-American War without payment – 3,400 square miles. Subsequent acquisitions, such as Guam, Samoa and the Virgin Islands, caused the land area of the US to exceed 3.7 million square miles, the extra 3.3 million square miles since 1776 being bought for a mere $47 million. No other country has grown so fast, so cheaply and with such relatively little fighting.

The second element in the history of the US has been the increase in the population. In 1700 the population totalled 250,000; in 1750, still only 1,170,000. One can almost understand the reluctance of Britain to take seriously the revolt against her which had the support of only a tiny percentage of these few people. The US population in the late eighteenth century grew wonderfully, however, partly because of the challenge of empty spaces, the demand for labour, the early marriages (men commonly in their mid twenties, women at twenty), the longevity and the small proportion of landless men (twenty per cent only of the rural population of New England in 1750). Chiefly by natural increase, but partly by immigration from Europe, the US population increased between 1780 and 1860 from 2.78 million to 30.1 million, between 1860 and 1910 to 92 million and between 1910 and 1990 to 258 million.

The third element was the transformation of a rural country into urban America. In 1800, 94 per cent of the population was rural. 85 per cent was still rural in 1850. The percentage decreased to 60 per cent by 1900, to 35 per cent by 1950 and could scarcely now be as much as 22 per cent.

The fourth characteristic was the economic success. The manufacturing section of society was stimulated during the revolutionary war. The tariffs of 1791 and 1804 were successful against England. More important, the early North Americans, working alone in a lonely continent, had the moral compulsion of a disciplined community which, as Richard Hofstadter put it, looked on work as having 'a quasi-religious merit'. The fortunate accident of possession of a territory which in 1940 controlled 70 per cent of the world's oil production, 80 per cent of the sulphur, 51 per cent of the copper, 60 per cent of the aluminium, 50 per cent of the zinc and over 95 per cent of the natural gas against only 6 per cent of the population and 7 per cent of the total land area was important too – although the possession of natural resources has never been the decisive element in political or even economic power.

Finally, the US adapted a beautifully written constitution, completed in the 1790s, to the growing nation of mixed origin. The US began as an oligarchic democracy in which the landed aristocracy had been abolished. Old laws, based on English practice, were modified by the rebellion of the 1770s, and by the Civil War of the 1860s.

In the twentieth century the US was both the main 'innovative and creative society in the world' and in many ways also the main disruptive influence among old neglectful and prejudiced peoples. Already by the 1920s, after her military victory in Europe, the US had become the focus of global attention, envy, emulation, admiration and animosity. By 1945, the eclipse of Europe, the declining confidence of the European empires, the political and economic failure in Russia, combined to make of the US the only real source of effective authority on an international plane. The US became a world of its own, one of statistical analysis, technology and electronics, emphasis on education and on innovation, scientific investigation without shortage of money, vast car-ownership and radio-ownership, and instantaneous telephones – the 'world's social laboratory', says Zbigniew Brzezinski, from which the rest of the world learns what may be in store for it.[38] The self-confidence of this society was impaired in the 1970s but, in 1945 when the Cold War was beginning, there were still many who echoed President Wilson's boast: 'My vision is that as the years go on, and the world knows more and more of America' – he was speaking in 1914 – 'it also will drink at these fountains of youth and renewal ... If there will ever be a declaration of independence and of grievances for mankind ... it will be drawn up in the spirit of the American Declaration of Independence'.[39]

In a famous paper written in 1950 by the US National Security Council, the issue between the United States and the Soviet Union was summed up in words which dominated the statements and attitudes of US statesmen from Dean Acheson onwards: 'The Kremlin regards the United States as the only major threat to the achievement of its fundamental design. There is a basic conflict between the idea of freedom under a government of laws and the idea of slavery under the grim oligarchy of the Kremlin . . . The idea of freedom, moreover, is peculiarly and intolerably subversive of the idea of slavery. But the converse is not true. The implacable purpose of the slave state to eliminate the challenge of freedom has placed the two great powers at opposite poles'.[40]

The US constructed its wealth, its nation and its way of life on the basis of free enterprise, free commerce and the free exchange of ideas. Russian began its industrialisation under the despotic power of the Tsar, adopted a millenarian creed, converted its old bureaucratic caste, the *dvoriánstvo*, into a Communist party and expanded its army and its police. The US pursued its goals internationally by limitation and scepticism. Russia since 1917 had the aim of revolutionary world conquest and pursued it by zeal and ruthlessness. In the US, in the 1980s it was still possible to see behind the thin veil of scientific assimilation the shade of Pericles. In Russia, the shadow was that of Darius the Persian.

64

The Cold War II: The Course

'Who, in twenty or thirty years' time, will remember all these storms
in a tea-cup...?' Turgenev asked, about 1870... But the situation
which Turgenev diagnosed in novel after novel, the painful predicament of the believers in liberal western values, a predicament we
thought peculiarly Russian, is today familiar everywhere. So too is
his oscillating, uncertain position, his horror of reactionaries, his
fear of the barbarous radicals, mingled with a desire to be understood and approved by the ardent young... the storm in the tea-
cup blows over the entire world.

Isaiah Berlin, *Russian Thinkers*

1

The first ground for contest between Russia and the US was
Europe. The new conflict began there before the old war ended. In
the last year or two of that war, the great conferences between the
victors were as much concerned with the future of the world as
with the battles being fought. The Russians understood that better
than Roosevelt, better even than Churchill. The Marxist despot,
Stalin, realised that, at such conferences, great men can have a
decisive effect on history. Churchill and Roosevelt, who knew the
history of great men, thought in terms of ideas. Roosevelt was for a
time enthralled by Stalin: he apparently once said of him, 'I think,
if I give him everything I possibly can, and ask him for nothing in
return, *noblesse oblige*, he won't try to annex anything, and will
work with us for a world of democracy and peace'.[1] Churchill,
though a political genius, also gave Stalin the benefit of the doubt
for a long time, for he admired him as a war leader.* Roosevelt
said of Hitler that 'a nation can have peace with the Nazis only at
the price of total surrender'. Peace with the Russians was obtainable at a lower price, but at a price all the same.

At all events, between 1945 and 1948, Russia was able to draw
the line of her influence in Eastern Europe much as she wished,
while the US and Britain were extraordinarily slow to see that the

---

* 'In these general discussions,' Churchill wrote in the last volume of his
memoirs, 'maps were not used and the distinction between the East and
the Western Neisse did not emerge as clearly as it should have done'.[2]

days of tactical wartime collaboration would be over so soon. Stalin knew, as he himself put it at Potsdam, that 'any freely elected government would be anti-Soviet and that we cannot permit' (in Eastern Europe).[3] His own foreign minister of an earlier date, Litvinov, gave a warning when he told an American diplomat in 1946, 'The most we can hope for is an armed truce'.[4]

Arguments about the right attitude to adopt were continuous. This led in the end to the creation of the North Atlantic Treaty, the Warsaw Pact, the acceptance of the division of Germany and, after 1952 (when the Republican party had won a US election on a programme of freeing the Russian 'satellite' states), a general acceptance of a division of Europe between US and Russian spheres of influence. The economic success of the US zone of Europe was made more complete by the formation of a European Economic Community. Efforts to turn that success into another liberal or democratic centre of power have, however, as yet proved incomplete.

2

After 1950 the centre of competition between the US and Russia became first the Far East, and then the Middle East. A Communist party captured power in China in 1949. Combined Chinese and Russian pressure led to the war in Korea, which ended divided, as Germany was. South Korea and Formosa remained, like Japan, part of the US zone of influence. The subsequent history of this competition in the East has primarily been a struggle for influence over the territories which European empires were persuaded to abandon, as a result primarily of their losses, or at least losses of face, in the course of the war; for example, the Chinese in Malaya had been bitterly persecuted by the Japanese. They had bravely attacked the enemy. They could not be treated as they had been before the war, with no political rights.

The roots of Chinese communism are many. First there was nationalism deriving from a sense of outrage at European military intervention in support of commerce during the nineteenth century. There was outrage at the European commerce itself. There was a demand for national renewal after the decadent last days of the Manchu emperors. There was too a recollection of the work of the Confucian philosopher of the eleventh century Chu Hsi, who maintained the nature of man to be good, while evil only appeared through neglect and through lack of the right training and education. The military skill of the Chinese Communists was, however, the determining element in their success. But intellectual enthusiasm for the Soviet regime in Russia also counted a great deal.

After 1949 there were two great centres of authority in the Communist world. Both remained closed countries till the end of the 1970s. The French ex-colonies of Indo-China eventually succumbed to various forms of communism. The French abandoned the civil war in Indo-China in 1955, on the assumption that the already small state would be divided, as Germany and Korea had been. But the southern, capitalist Vietnamese state never established itself. The Communists in the north mounted subversion. The US allowed themselves to become drawn into its defence in the 1960s. A major defensive war then began, even if it was one in which the US dropped as many bombs on North Vietnam as they had on Germany in 1941–45. It was to no avail. The US fought the war more as an administrative bureaucracy than as an army.[5] They decided neither to use nuclear weapons nor to invade the north of Vietnam. The consequence was an ignominious withdrawal.

Since then, the frontiers of the Far East have seemed clearly drawn between Communist and open societies. But the disputes, nominally on doctrinal grounds, between China and Russia increasingly disturbed the Communist world. Outright warfare between Russia's protégé Vietnam and China's, the murderous Cambodia, showed once more how, in the words of Paul Levi, at the Livorno conference of the Italian Socialist party (at which he was the representative of Germany), 'in the history of the proletariat, the time arrives when we must recognise that yesterday's brother is not today's brother, nor will he be tomorrow's'.[6]

After the death of Mao in 1976 and the discrediting of the Cultural Revolution, there were encouraging signs that may yet result in political changes in China. Despotism survived but free enterprise revived. Meantime, most of the ex-colonies of the Europeans in the Far East became independent, at least formally. Australasia, Indonesia, Singapore, Malaysia and the Philippines (a US protectorate from 1899 till 1946) drew, in the end, towards the US, though communism nearly triumphed in 1965 in Indonesia while in the early 1950s in Malaysia, India and Pakistan as well as Iran made the same choice to begin with, though India toyed with a Russian alliance, while seeking to revive an Indian historical past of its own. The emblem of modern India was adopted from the capital on one of the ancient Emperor Ashoka's pillars.

Ashoka's policy of *karma*, a neutral but vague attitude of social responsibility, under the influence of Mahatma Gandhi, characterised the policies of most Indian governments since 1947. After 1979, meantime, the US alignment of Iran was destroyed; the mullahs took over from the company managers.

3

The Middle East became a centre of world rivalry after 1955. In 1945 Britain was still the paramount power there, her influence maintained by a small number of tactically well-placed troops, combined with friendly, traditional regimes. She had established this authority after the First World War, though her interest in the region had been continuous since she began to think of it as a stepping stone on her way to her empire in India. Immediately after 1945, Jewish colonists and new settlers in Palestine re-established the state of Israel, in conditions of ambiguity, as a result of British negligence. Many Arabs fled. Others were expelled, leaving refugees, whose frustrations fed and were fed by nationalism. As many Jews fled to Israel from long-established sanctuaries in the Arab world.

The quarrels in the Middle East between the British and the French, on the one hand, and the Arabs, on the other, had begun before 1939. France was dominant throughout Muslim North Africa. The successful establishment of the state of Israel exacerbated the divisions between the West and the Arabs. The Middle East since 1945 became the world's major source of exportable oil and, therefore, a more important and explosive region than it had been since the Crusades. The Soviet Union began to interest herself in Egyptian nationalism after 1950.

After the failure of an Anglo-French military expedition to keep the Suez Canal international in 1956, and restore their position in the Middle East generally, several Muslim countries fell into the Russian sphere of influence. That ancient region, though, showed itself to be a snare for all outside powers. In the 1970s Egypt expelled her Russian friends. The kings of Saudi Arabia and Jordan, and the tribal leaders in the Persian Gulf, created a new grouping of countries concerned to protect pre-feudal monarchies by means of capitalism and modern weapons. Wars between Israel and her Arab neighbours (one of them intertwined with an Anglo-French expedition to recover control of the Suez Canal) threatened to turn the Cold War there into a world one. But on each occasion, the conflict was contained, though the issues at stake seemed much like those which had led to the world war in 1914. The war in the Gulf against Iraq in 1991 was a nationalist not an ideological one. Despite the 'peace process', which began in 1992, today rivalries in the Middle East still seem the most probable cause of open international war, chiefly because of the continuing dependence of rich countries on oil from the region; partly because the Arabs have been persuaded to look on the Palestinian problem as more important than any other and partly because of the clash between American-led modernisation and Islamic traditionalism.

4

Between 1959 and 1968 the Caribbean and Latin America also became a region for the rivalry of Russia and the USA. Cuba became Communist. The US, by a mixture of intervention, threats and defensive diplomacy, for a long time prevented any other country from succumbing. Skirmishing supported by Cuba (and Russia indirectly) for a time threatened the peace of Venezuela, Guatemala, Bolivia and Peru, while Chile, Brazil and the Dominican Republic experienced short periods when it seemed as if a group friendly to Russia might seize or maintain themselves in power. After 1968 Cuba for a time abandoned her efforts to export her draconian revolution to that part of the world, while the US gave up any attempt to overthrow Castro in Cuba. This balance lasted till the late 1970s, when the Cuban government, unable to make much of a success at home, revived her ambitions in the Central American republics and the Caribbean, resulting in the short-lived Communisation of Nicaragua.

5

Tropical Africa became touched by the Cold War only after the swift disintegration of the European imperial system there following the independence of Ghana in 1957. Britain, Belgium and France then withdrew, fast, from Africa in the 1960s after about eighty years of direct power. The Belgian Congo, or as it became known, Zaire, had nothing in the way of a state established. For months, it constituted an issue for international rivalry. In the end an ex-sergeant-major, Colonel Mobutu, was found to maintain Zaire as a united country.

It subsequently became a matter of policy on the part of the new ex-imperial African states to keep the often arbitrary boundaries of colonial days. These had earlier been drawn without consideration of tribal interests. But a general redrawing was thought certain to promote a general conflict.

Three elements drew Africa deeper into the world conflict: first, the refusal of the minority of English settlers in Rhodesia to accept a transfer of power to the local black Africans, as the British had more or less successfully engineered in other places; second, the determination of the larger minority of settlers of Dutch origin (with some descendants of Englishmen) to maintain a state founded on the dominance of their own number based on Cape Town and Johannesburg; and third, the unexpected revolution in Portugal of 1974, which led to the withdrawal of Portugal from her anciently established (if only recently coordinated) holdings in Mozambique and Angola.

South Africa was of great interest because of her mines, which held vast reserves of gold, diamonds and many other minerals, and because of her strategic position on the hinge of two oceans. The opposition to the Boers was one which seemed to bring together the divided new despotisms in black Africa. The withdrawal of Portugal from Africa, after much fighting, also opened up a chance for Russia and her allies, principally East Germany and Cuba. A *coup de main* by 30,000 Cuban troops led to the establishment in Angola of a tyranny friendly to Russia. A similar regime was established in Mozambique. In 1978 another Cuban expedition, with Russian and East German direction, confirmed yet another primitive Communist regime in power in Ethiopia. It was the only substantial territory in Africa which had withstood the European 'grab for Africa' in the nineteenth century, though Italy had held it between 1936 and 1941.

Meantime South Africa, under its European direction, was the only African state to have carried through a real industrial revolution. It was powered by black labour and managed by the whites. The 'shanty towns' became a magnet for a black African working class comparable to the similar first-generation urban workforces of the world.

6

The theme of the Cold War between 1950 and 1989 was a battle between the US and Russia to control the 'Third World', a formulation apparently coined by the French sociologist Alfred Sauvy in 1952, making a characteristically Gallic reference to the French Revolution ('for this Third World, ignored and exploited and despised exactly as the Third Estate was before the Revolution, would also like to become something').[7] Battle of economic systems? Of power? Begun by the US pre-emptively or aggressively? Really a consequence of Russian determination since 1917? Or the result of a clever manipulation by Russian propaganda of the resentments caused by the collapse of the old empires? A guilt on the part of certain Western nations was not the least important element in this curious story.

7

This conflict lasted for over thirty years till 1989. Its dimensions had all the characteristics of old-fashioned struggles for power, even if they were given a new character by the destructive weapons which the large nations had at their disposal. For the US monopoly of atomic power lasted only from 1945 to 1949, when Russia exploded her first such weapon in a test. The US then began to build a more powerful weapon still, the hydrogen bomb. She successfully tested that in 1952, but the Russians tested a similar one a year later. Britain, France, China and India all entered this perilous field, though none of their equipment had the strength of that held by the US and Russia.

After the competition in bombs came competition in means of delivery. Bombers gave way to rockets and submarines, and to satellites circling the world. Meantime, large conventional armies (carried by vehicles) were maintained by the two most powerful states and all their allies. Ground-to-air and air-to-ground missiles, helicopters, tanks faster and heavier than those in 1945, all made a 'conventional war' possible.

For forty-four years after 1945, all the same, the world lived in what George Orwell in that year described as a 'peace that is no peace'.[8] Orwell rightly considered that the chief consequence of the invention of the nuclear weapon would be to put an end to large-scale wars at the cost of stimulating small ones. Innumerable 'small wars' certainly broke out.

8

The record of democratic countries, in the years since 1945, despite upheavals, was remarkable. Western Europe embarked after 1945 on an age of high mass consumption, of plastics and cars, of electronics and aeronautics. As earlier chapters have shown, the new technology – introduced first in the US, next in Western Europe and then in other capitalist democracies – increased human freedom. The number of enterprises in all capitalist countries grew. In the 1970s in the US, for example, there were well over a million separate operating enterprises, 400,000 of them being born every year, only about 350,000 dying. Enterprises grew in size but so did the market. Large firms, such as the automobile ones, established near-monopolies, but the tendency to monopoly was not consistent while manufacturing accounted for only a quarter of those in employment in the US. It became clear that, despite illusions to the contrary, there was no evidence that large firms in the US were on the increase in the late twentieth century nor that big ones would soon replace small ones. Nearly a fifth of US citizens, too, were self-employed.

The number of stockholders also grew: in 1928 4.7 million people in the US had some kind of stock; in 1989 that figure had risen to 40 million. Finally, in 1972, the year before the beginning of an acute phase of the energy crisis, world trade stood at something like $800,000 million, the bulk of it in democratic capitalist nations ($600,000 million). The increase in these figures since even 1938 is, despite changes in the value of money, what must strike the observer; for the total then amounted to nearly $47,000 million. Even allowing for inflation since 1938, that increase was probably eightfold, a growth far larger than that of population and one unprecedented in the history of commerce.

The Soviet system was far less successful. Communist agriculture has been consistently disappointing. Russian expectations of overtaking the US in industrial performance proved fruitless, despite predictions made in the 1960s. Only in the production of weapons was the Marxist-Leninist state able to match the West.

9

In 1980 there seemed three possible outcomes of the Cold War: first, the continuance *ad infinitum* of the co-dominance of the world by Russia and the US; second, a resolution of the rivalry in favour of one or the other (either from defeat in war, or in 'peaceful competition', or from decay); or third, the appearance of new forces which might cast the old leaders of the Cold War into another or an old mould. What could these be? Anarchism? Regional terrorism? A revived, expansionist, but backward-looking Islam or perhaps some other, some new religion? A 'third way' between capitalism and communism, which did not turn out to be militant Islam? A new co-prosperity sphere in the Far East, based on Sino-Japanese cooperation? A new Europe, in which the golden years of that continent returned?

The stalemate based on the nuclear deterrent and self-control could not have lasted indefinitely. In the short term, these weapons guaranteed peace. But a successful Russian nuclear attack on the US, mounted by a mere five missiles, say, could have launched 800 forty-kiloton warheads and have killed thirty-seven million people. Similar US attacks on Russia could have wreaked similar havoc even if Russian defences were said to be better than the West's. Half the population of the US could have been killed within less time than it took to transmit a declaration of war during the Second World War. Weapons of mass destruction could (and still can) be applied at any point in less time than it normally takes for the police to respond to an emergency in a city. For that present state of affairs to have continued for ever, the world would have to have been governed not only by good luck but by statesmen of will-power, magnanimity, courage and imagination in a way that did not seem to be a reasonable expectation. On the contrary, many political leaders seemed ill-prepared and, in some countries, as ill-disposed as ever in the past. Men with 'hairs on their heart', as King João V of Portugal said his minister Pombal possessed, continued to gain positions of power.

Epilogue

> The writing of history, as Goethe once noted, is one way of getting rid of the weight of the past . . . the writing of history liberates us from history.
>
> Croce

> The future of history and historians is to cleanse the story of mankind from . . . deceiving visions of a purposeful past.
>
> J. H. Plumb

> For it is history alone which, without involving us in actual danger, will mature our judgement and prepare us to take right views, whatever may be the crisis or the posture of affairs.
>
> Polybius

1

There are precedents for many of our manifestations – even the fears which we believe to be uniquely ours. The fear of the destruction of the world as a result of a nuclear war as we approach the year 2000 can be compared to the anxiety which the Christian world felt as it approached the year 1000. It is surprising that some churchmen indeed have not seen, in the history of the twentieth century, the mark of Antichrist, whose dreadful empire, it was supposed in the Middle Ages in Europe, would precede the coming of the kingdom of God. The present world of struggling nation states seems similar, too, to the condition of the eastern Mediterranean in the time of Plato, though transposed to the globe. Then, as now, there were a multitude of states of varying sizes and constitutions, all squabbling amongst each other, with a few large empires in the wings. The rest of the universe is to us what the sands of Africa, the tundra of Russia or the seas beyond the Pillars of Hercules were to the Greeks. Then, as now, as Gilbert Murray put it, in respect of Greece after the Peloponnesian War, the world was 'full of occult superstitions, cults of the anti-rational, faith in chance, and huge audiences attracted by orators who promised all'.

725

But all the same, it is desirable to notice several innovations. First, though the world seems more bitterly divided than at any time since the Renaissance at least, there is already a world society. At least in the non-Communist world, news travels fast, rumours travel faster, fashions and moods cross and recross the earth like waves of quicksilver. The globe is in closer mutual touch than a middle-sized European people were to their own capital fifty years ago. The world is a single strategic stage. Languages may be many but English looks already to be a world one. Measures of time and calendars are already the same in much of the world, while measures of distance, weight and size look like following, in tribute to Napoleon, the metric system. The shadow of a world society is detectable in the increasing willingness of peoples in one state to pronounce authoritatively on the doings in others. This contrasts with the cultural nationalism inculcated by mass media and the commercial nationalism stimulated by domestic collectivist policies, but it is there all the same.

Then some parts of the political condition are new too. Gone are the nomadic tribes, the city states and the majority of the tribal monarchies which flourished in 1750 throughout so much of the world. Gone too is the ambiguity as to whether such-and-such a territory is part of the preserve of this people or that. The land surface of the earth, and much indeed of the sea, is clearly divided up between 170 or so states modelled institutionally on the states which were already in being in Europe in the eighteenth and nineteenth centuries. Even tyrannies have ministries of finance, diplomatic services and national holding companies for a variety of undertakings. The character of these states has absolutely changed too. About fifty of them are democratic. Another thirty are totalitarian,* where the state presumes to control the life of the people in the interests of what the administration argues must be the people's good. The rest are authoritarian, autocratic or still monocratic, in which, though there is as a rule no peaceful way of changing the government, there are some sources of independent authority (such as Churches, rich men, large companies, unions, aristocrats) within the polity. Within a large number of states there are also peoples who have no statehood; indeed, the demands of such people for that modern concept constitute one of the worst problems in the world. Both the democracies and the

---

* The word 'totalitarian' was invented by Mussolini to describe the state which he had founded. However, the survival of monarchy, *monsignori* and Mafia made fascism in Italy less totalitarian than Il Duce desired.

totalitarian states are new since the age of industry began, the former being dependent upon mass education and the latter upon artful use of technology. Before the coming of railways, the telegraph and the telephone, or bad communications generally, prevented the Tsars from imposing a repressive dictatorship in Russia on the scale made possible for the Communists in the twentieth century[1]. Technology has also placed temptations to centralisation and interference before both autocratic and democratic states. We can be sure that, if some autocratic (or democratic) states become converted into totalitarian ones in future, it will be technology which will make that possible, even if ideology may have made it sought after.*

Third, nearly all modern states have written constitutions, comprising a large accumulation of written laws. Here is a striking difference from the condition of life in 1750, when no states at all had such documents, even if some had constitutional laws. Most political arrangements depended then largely upon custom. The irony of this development is that, while the only important country in the world without a written constitution remains Britain, it was British practices which inspired the constitution of the US, which itself has influenced, directly or indirectly, the constitutions of half the world – indeed has influenced the idea that a written constitution is desirable.†

Fourth, the difficulty of making helpful comparisons between rich industrial countries and poor agricultural ones is greater than it ever was. This is not only because the poor agricultural countries are now importing grain from the rich industrial ones. For, while the rulers of rich countries are wondering how to prevent the 'secure, but aimless lower middle class or blue collar workers' (in Dr Brzezinski's formulation[3]) from taking up crime on a larger scale than they are at present, the poor countries are seeking to employ millions of still hopeful agricultural poor who thrust their way into the already overcrowded cities. To both rich countries and poor ones, audiovisual mass communication presents visions of limitless opportunities but, at the same time, puts them at the mercy of magnetic leaders. The greater the possibilities of control offered to governments, the more important the judgement of the

---

* Nor, incidentally, is there 'any automatic stabilising factor', as Henry Kissinger put it, which means that economic improvement makes for greater political stability or freedom.

† As Dicey put it, the US constitution represents a 'gigantic development of ideas which lie at the basis of the political and legal institutions of England'[2].

ruler. Despite that similarity between rich and poor, the preoccupations of the first are now of a different order from those of the second. There is no such thing as a developed world, with no problems to speak of, and an undeveloped one which needs the help of the others. There is no table which can honestly list countries as participants of development or underdevelopment. Perhaps it would be easier if there were. The pressing concerns of the rich countries seem trivial to those of the poor and those of the poor seem incomprehensible, even enviable, to the rich. How often have travellers arrived in remote regions to envy the rural simplicity of some undeserted sweet Auburn in upper Peru! The poor countries do not realise that the rich countries can be ruined by bad government as much as poor ones can be starved by neglect. Cuba, a country which puts herself forward as a leader of the 'developing' world, is a good example of a rich country gone to seed and then to revolution, not of a poor one which has never had a chance.*

Then there can be no doubt than women in the twentieth century have a different life from that which they were as a rule obliged to have in the past. Some of the technical innovations – in the kitchen and elsewhere – which have made this possible have been amply noticed earlier. But the critical change is that women have a greater chance of achieving things in their own right, as opposed to the possibilities that might come to them from the accident of birth or marriage, than ever before.

Another novelty of our time is that most of the politicians who direct modern states are at a loss in the scientific and technical labyrinth which gives the states concerned their power and their opportunities. Hitler was probably the last would-be conqueror to insist on knowing the working of the weapons which he used.† These incapabilities of politicians reflect well the bewilderment of their publics. Every year nowadays brings its new crop of miraculous tales and rumours. Could it be true that, were the sky to be filled at the same time by a small number of supersonic aircraft, the envelope of the earth would disintegrate?‡ Such stories

---

* Cuba had railways before most of Europe, a steam engine before the US and more televisions in 1958 than Italy did.

† It is said he refused to countenance the construction of atomic weapons because he did not know how they worked.

‡ I was assured that this was so by the editor of a Catholic weekly who claimed to have heard it from a grandson of Marconi. I have since ascertained that it is not true.

abound. The average man is as a rule too badly educated scientifically to judge their truth. So it is as if the world were living under a kind of censorship in which a scandal is eagerly passed from person to person. Thus, we are told that the amount of carbon dioxide is increasing: that, indeed, it has increased, from 290 parts in a million to 330 parts per million. By the year 2020, it is said, the amount of carbon dioxide could approach 660. The increase was once believed to be due to the burning of fossil fuels. Now it is said that it is because of the destruction of forests. The layman has always suspected that such things are likely. Where in England, he has wryly but ineffectively asked for generations, are the great forests of Knaresborough, Charnwood, Sherwood, Cranborne Chase, Bere? All are gone, more completely than the mediaeval noble families. The effect, it is said, will be to increase the heat and aridity in the world. Or so it seems. But each man chooses his own evil rumour to believe. This state of affairs differs from the rational nineteenth century, even if it recalls the Middle Ages and even if there is a rational basis to many such fears.

The important developments of the last few years have characteristically been achieved by a science incomprehensible to the layman: namely, microelectronics. The tiny antennae devised as a result have enabled men to land on the moon, build the satellites which circulate the earth and create intercontinental ballistic missiles. Computers and calculators, communication satellites and digital watches are now at the service of all rich societies, even if those societies are incapable of maintaining their sense of continuity. 'Robotics' looks like being a major development of the 1980s. All these schemes derive from the transistor, which replaced the vacuum tube, devised in 1948 in the Bell Telephone laboratories, and the computer, the first peacetime electronic version of which was built at the University of Pennsylvania in 1945, following the successful wartime one built to assist the great code-breakers at Bletchley. The significance of these recent events and the names of the great mathematicians who made them possible (Charles Babbage in the nineteenth century, Zuse, Schreyer, Howard Aiken and Alan Turing among others in the twentieth) will probably in time come to overshadow many of the other happenings in this book.

The prices of these and other such extraordinary systems of calculation, memory and analysis are falling steadily. A computer is already within reach of the pocket of an ordinary man. The Library of Congress may soon be available by computer in every home. Microprocessors are already developing fast. These things will encourage international collaboration: if a computer goes wrong in Zurich the engineer will perhaps telephone a computer in New York to find out the cure. To well-educated people in the arts subjects, it seems, to parody Voltaire, as if one incomprehensible machine after another succeeds each other on the banks of the Hudson River. (To become literate in computer technology will become increasingly important: already all students at Harvard, including those who study literature, are instructed how to write a simple programme for a computer.) Not far away, surely, are man-powered aeroplanes or flying bicycles, the battery-operated car, the typewriter which will type as its master dictates (as already has been marketed for Japanese), the cure for the slightest cold and the cheap desalination plant. Further away, but perhaps within reach, is some way of assuring indefinitely the right atmospheric conditions for the earth's survival in the universe after the sun burns out. Human life itself is almost capable of being invented though that seems one of the inventions least likely to be needed, in a world of over 4,000 million people – the increase in size from 750 million in AD 1700 being one more great novelty. 'The electronics complex during the next quarter of a century will be the pole around which the productive structures of advanced societies will be recognised,' wrote the OECD's 'Interfutures Report' in 1979. Clearly the 'chip' will be an even greater stimulus to invention than it has been hitherto.

We consider all these brilliant opportunities in the future with care. All the more reason, therefore, why states should leave aside the many things that they now insist unnecessarily on managing, in order to give their statesmen time to regulate those more complicated matters with knowledge and wisdom.

The complement of these opportunities is the threat of nuclear war. Here certainly is another novelty. This is a direct threat to most of the world, even if it touches some more directly than others. If nuclear war were to occur, there would be a chance, remote no doubt but undeniable, that the consequence would be the destruction of the human species and of many other species as well. The world might at best return to something close to that stage of evolution where it was after the destruction of the larger reptiles. Byron had a nightmare:

. . . the world was void.
The populous and the powerful was a lump –
Seasonless, herbless, treeless, manless, lifeless.

There are, too, possible setbacks less severe than one which would return the earth to the condition that it was several hundred million years ago. That in a sense happened, after all, in Europe at the end of antiquity. The discoveries of the nature of anatomy which led to a proper awareness of the possibilities of surgery were on the brink of being made before the birth of Christ. Almost every discovery necessary for the achievement of modern Western civilisation was nearly made in ancient Alexandria before AD 200. What was done to analyse plants between Theophrastus, who was born in 370 BC, and the Renaissance? Very little. Aristarchus, in 250 BC, said (in words summed up by Archimedes): 'The earth revolves round the sun in the circumference of a circle, the sun lying in the middle of the orbit.' During the Dark Ages and Middle Ages, most of these and other comparable theories were forgotten. Matthew Arnold in *Culture and Anarchy* suggested that such discoveries were 'unsound at that particular moment of man's development', being 'premature'. He went on: 'The indispensable basis of conduct and self-control upon which alone the perfection aimed at by Greece can come into bloom was not to be reached by our own race so easily; centuries of probation and discipline were needed to bring us to it'[4]. His own comments suggest that he did not think that his own generation was adequately prepared either. On the contrary, he described his countrymen during his own day as living in anarchy.*

Perhaps we are finding it harder than we expected to live in a world which cannot risk another major war. Our states were founded on wars, our national heroes who look down at us from plinths and pillars were all soldiers or admirals. Wars have in the past been the stimulants of technological change, the lever of social change (as much as considered programmes of socialism), and have brought to countries a 'spiritual peace' otherwise rarely obtainable. War and golden ages have often gone together (Athens in the fifth century was continually at war, Britain often so in the sixteenth and eighteenth centuries).

Even during the terrible wars of the twentieth century, the ties established between civilians and soldiers alike created a sense of community apparently unattainable during the piping days of peace. Bringing in the harvest used to be a possible alternative to

---

* Arnold's comments on the working class in Victorian England were: 'body upon body are beginning to assert, and put into practice, an Englishman's right to do as and what he likes . . . meet where he likes, enter where he likes, hoot as he likes, threaten as he likes, smash as he likes'[5].

war, but it is no longer. Could sport be William James's 'moral equivalent' of war? It still seems possible. Or is it an illusion, considering what has been said in an earlier chapter, to suppose that we are indeed still at peace?*

2

With the decline of the absolute authority once established by religion, appeals to history to justify actions have been increasing. Hitler, at his trial after the failure of the *putsch* of 1923, said: 'You may pronounce us guilty a thousand times over, but the goddess of the eternal court of history will smile, and tear to pieces the brief of the prosecutor . . . For she acquits us'[6]. Castro said much the same in 1953: 'Condemn me. History will absolve me'[7].

Modern industrial society sometimes seems free of its past. A modern family, living in a town without history, eats food unknown to its grandfathers, whose names it does not always remember, gains its knowledge of affairs from an invention, the television, undreamt of a hundred years ago, and uses in speech many constructions and words which would have been unrecognised by people nominally talking the same language in the eighteenth century. Nevertheless, history dominates political life: Russian harshness is frequently justified (or explained) by two hundred years of Tartar occupation (which itself ended five hundred years ago), and Russian suspicion of the West is said to have been caused by the efforts at Allied intervention after the First World War.† People make use of words such as 'feudalism' to explain phenomena which would have been unrecognisable to the Cid. The understanding Westerner seeks lines of contact between rural China now and the same nation under the Manchus. The Irish fight daily a new battle of the Boyne. The Arabs fight to recover territory that they lost in 1967, the Jews to confirm their hold over what they lost in AD 70, while their soldiers take oaths of allegiance on the site of the last stand, at Masada, of the old Jewish nation, in their fight against Rome. The Aztecs were lovingly recalled by Mexican revolutionaries of 1911–19, the Incas by the urban revolutionaries (Tupamaros) of Uruguay. Mussolini remembered the Roman legions, and José Antonio Primo de Rivera, the Spanish Fascist leader, revived the symbols of Ferdi-

---

* See above, Chapter 63 about the Cold War.
† Or other invasions, from the Tartars onwards.

nand and Isabella. Kwame Nkrumah, in rechristening the old Gold Coast by the name of Ghana, sought to revive a myth of an ancient monarchy unknown to the grandfathers of modern Ghanaians, while the old controversies over the Atlantic slave trade stimulate, as well as explain, suspicion between black and white. Admittedly, an interest in history can lead to false analogies. The number of times that Hitler in 1945, while his system was in ruins, recalled how Prussia had been saved in 1762 by the death of the Empress Elizabeth of Russia would suggest that here was a man who knew and loved history. But Hitler's knowledge of the past was selective: what was the point of recalling 1762 but forgetting 1918, the lessons of which (avoid a war with the US above all else) were much more relevant to modern Germany?

Revolutions often take the form of resurrections, wrote Lucien Febvre in his introduction to his master Marc Bloch's masterpiece, *Rural France*[8]. The promise of the return of some redeemer-king – Sebastien of Portugal, killed at El-Ksar el-Kebir in 1578, or Emperor Frederick II, or Arthur – has haunted modern societies as well as ancient ones: versions of messianism in which future and past blended. 'Sebastianism' in Portugal, for example, led to an enduring belief that Portugal was a chosen nation, about to be transformed by a startling revival. That belief helped to sustain the enduring national self-confidence which itself explains why the Portuguese maintained their hold over their precarious empire for so long.

Most modern tyrannies, even those which have wished to bring history to an end by a perpetual despotism, have been driven onwards by a strong if misguided view of the past. Hitler sought an empire for Germany in the Ukraine, and dreamed of how the Germans of the future would holiday in the Crimea, driving there along great motorways, thus fulfilling the aspirations of the Germans of 1910, but without realising that the days of the European empires he wished to emulate were already drawing to an end. The whole of the Nazi movement derived from a false view of the past history of races, and of the German and Jewish races in particular. Lenin in 1917 used evidence about the state of Russia which bore some relation to the truth as it had been when he was young, in the 1890s, but which took no account of the transformation of the Russian economy between 1905 and 1917, particularly between 1914 and 1917. The view of the future which dominates Marxism derives explicitly from a series of false comparisons between the behaviour of the world's working classes, merchants and landowners.* Both Nazism and communism have also gone to great lengths to present a distorted view of the past histories of the countries in which they have established their rule.† They have appreciated that one of the most effective ways to capture the mind of the people is to distort its historical imagination, confuse people with new legends and divert them with artificially constructed heroes. Sometimes, these deceiving visions of the past may be embarked upon unconsciously. For example, in the preliminaries to the establishment of the Communist regime in Cuba, Fidel Castro made many speeches denouncing the allegedly overbearing behaviour of the government of the US. What he was saying bore some relation to the conduct of the US a generation or so earlier. It bore little to the prudent international posture of President Eisenhower in 1959.‡

Free countries should learn their history well, too. They should not allow a natural caution to cause them to forget the historic origins of their institutions and ideals. Of course, to all scholars of integrity, the past gives uncertain answers as well as inspiration. The truth of the most straightforward occurrence is elusive. Marc Bloch wrote, in the concluding lines of *Rural France*: 'In the continuum of human societies, the vibrations between molecule and molecule spread out over so great a span that the understanding of a single moment, no matter what its place in the chain of development, can never be attained merely by contemplation of its immediate predecessor'[9]. Free societies sometimes seem today, nevertheless, to have lost their nerve. Lord Clark, at the end of his essay *Civilisation*, seems to have given up the cause for lost[10]. Solzhenitsyn, in his lecture at Stockholm accepting the Nobel Prize for Literature, remarked that he found the civilised world to be 'frightened', with 'nothing better than concessions and smiles to offer to the assault of barbarism'. The French historian Pierre Chaunu suggested, in *Le Sursis*, that the West has 'ten years left to put its house in order' – an activity which he believes to consist in returning to reburnish the ideals which sustained us in the past.

* See above, page 707.
† See Stalin's comment about 'archive-rats' noted above, page 613.
‡ Castro made, for example, a most virulent attack on the new ambassador of the US to Cuba, Philip Bonsal. He spoke of this able diplomat arriving in Havana as if he had been a proconsul of the old Roman Empire. He was really describing the way that Mr Bonsal's predecessor but ten, Sumner Welles, reached Havana in 1933.

That is certainly an admirable aim[11]. The essential task is to place contemporary problems in their right historical frame.

'What constitutes the individuality of a civilisation,' asked Henri Frankfort in 1951, 'its recognisable character, its identity which is maintained throughout the successive stages of its existence?' Here, despite its richness, modern Western civilisation gives often a muffled answer. The identity of all civilisations derives from a 'certain coherence among its various manifestations, a certain consistency in its orientation, a certain cultural "style" which shapes its political and its judicial institutions, its art as well as its literature, its religion as well as its morals'[12]. Tocqueville held strongly the view that 'when the religion of a people is destroyed, doubts get hold of the higher powers of the intellect and half paralyse all the others. Every man then accustoms himself to having only confused and changing notions on the subjects most interesting to his fellow creatures . . . His opinions are all defended and easily abandoned; and in despair of ever solving by himself the hard problems respecting the destiny of man, he ignobly submits to think no more about them.' Such a condition, Tocqueville believed, could not but 'enervate the soul, relax the springs of the will and prepare a people for servitude'. Tocqueville questioned whether man can ever support complete religious independence and entire political freedom: 'If faith be wanting in him, he must be subject: and, if he be free, he must believe'[13].

History since Tocqueville's day has admittedly shown examples of nations who have been both believing and subject, and incredulous and free, as well as sustaining many faiths, not just a national one. Tocqueville also seemed to imply that any religion would serve, true or false, to sustain intelligence. But the moral of his argument is correct. Only societies which have faith in themselves survive. That self-confidence, dependent as it usually is upon simplicity of thought, must derive from the study of that society's past; or, as Grahame Clark has it, 'unless we can hold fast to the values defined by our history, we shall be reduced not to a pristine and, therefore, still hopeful state . . . as to a sub-human condition'[14].

Those who wish to revive the West must also remember that the freedom which we respect, in the form of representative democracy, has only flourished successfully for long in societies which have been inspired at one time or another by the absolute value which Christianity gives to the soul. They should recall Bertrand Russell's dictum, on his return in 1920, that the idea of a society based on law had only been achieved after many centuries of patient struggle and should not lightly be abandoned in the supposed interests of immediate economic benefit[15]. They should also recall that the way that ideals are presented needs naturally to be reconsidered anew by each generation if they are going to survive the fires of the particular time. How much better would it be if we could revive a sense of that conviction felt in the earlier part of this century that representative democracy would provide 'the sovereign formula for the coming age'. We should take comfort from the fact that the vast majority of people to whom such a choice is put rationally and calmly would rather live in a country 'which is poor and weak and of no account than powerful, prosperous and enslaved', as Lord Acton formulated the dilemma in his sonorous manner[16]. The evidence from the poorer parts of the world today does not contradict this confidence. On the contrary, it sustains it. If this is 'democratic narcissism', as a Spanish Fascist journal* accused the author of this book of subscribing to, so be it. Democratic leaders should know that their actions, if they go ill, will be examined, if historians survive at all, by some future personification of Lord Macaulay's New Zealander, who would be puzzled by the fall of a civilisation so rich and so intelligent.† They should notice that the first history to survive antiquity, that of Herodotus, written 'in the hope of preserving from decay the remembrance of what men have been'[18], concerned a battle between free men and tyrants. They should also recognise that one of the benefits of a study of history is that it suggests that it is always possible to reverse, as Plato put it, an apparently fatal tendency towards decay, however late the hour.

---

* *Fuerza Nueva*, 9 September 1980.
† Lord Macaulay's New Zealander appears in the essay on Ranke's *History of the Popes*; he pictured the survival of the papacy even in some remote future when 'some traveller from New Zealand shall, in the midst of a vast solitude, take his stand on a broken arch of London Bridge to sketch the ruins of St Pauls'[17].

Epilogue to the 1989 Edition

The 1980s have been a strange time. They have, to some extent, seen the continuation of attitudes and movements which began in the previous ten years or so. Thus there has been seen the ever greater growth of religion as a political factor of first significance, whether this is an emanation of Islam or of Christianity. Ecological movements have come further forward as significant undertakings in many countries. Despite the worldwide decline in the rate of increase of population, nearly all those states, which have had the means, have introduced even more rigid demographic policies, disguised as 'immigration control'. The rate of crime in countries where statistics can be collected has continued to rise. The ever more sophisticated advances in electronic technology now at the service of scientifically aware societies have continued to transform communications, and hence industry, banking and commerce, in, however, still limited sectors.

Equally, the role of television in domestic politics has increased, as has that of terrorism in international affairs. The former medium appears to have adversely affected the character of political leadership in the United States and, while increasing visual awareness, it must have diminished the reading capacity and reading habits of the world.

None of these things, however, are particularly new in the 1980s. Terrorism has continued to shock but has had few real successes: e.g. the unification of Ireland or the independence of the Basque country.

The great novelty has been the decline of confidence in collectivist, Statist and socialist solutions to the problems of human society. This has been as marked in the great Marxist nations, China and Russia, as in the old Western ones, such as France and, in particular, Britain. The consequence has extended over the frontiers of the nations concerned. Gorbachev, seeking reform at home, has recognised some positive features in the old capitalist regimes, previously castigated roundly by his predecessors. Communism remains the Soviet ideology as far as can be seen, but Gorbachev's moderation in external policy has markedly reduced the threat of a major nuclear war. Good relations between the two great powers, the Soviet Union and the United States as well as the latter's friendly terms with China and Western Europe's renewed relations with the Soviet Union, have combined to create by the end of the 1980s a somewhat more sunny international political climate than was to be seen in the late 1970s. It is true that some have looked on Russia under Gorbachev as being as militarily dangerous as ever. No doubt Russian policy still wishes to exert in Western Europe the hegemony that Stalin obtained in Eastern Europe after 1945. That is a reasonable, imperial, Tsarist but not necessarily a revolutionary aim; even if it may in the end be one as difficult to manage. The events in Russia seem to demonstrate the significance of individual leaders even more than in the recent past, as much in Marxist countries as in capitalist ones.

The disease commonly known as AIDS has made its mark in the 1980s, and appears to be, like the great plagues of the past, something which will last. Fear of it has already affected much of the world in ways which would have seemed improbable in the 1970s. It has affected personal relations, and sex, beyond the limited homosexual world where it is most prevalent.

At the same time, the threat to the environment caused by large-scale industrial growth seems to many now the most serious cause of anxiety. Of course, this is not a new departure. But more than ever before, there is a realisation that the legitimate needs of the world's deprived (who cannot be expected to be concerned by the neuroses of the rich) must be met without damaging further the environment and the long term prospects of the planet. It would seem certain that the adjustment of interests involved here will need substantial concessions on the part of the advanced nations: in particular in respect of their standard of living.

The 1980s have not produced to the mind of this historian works of art and philosophy comparable to earlier years of this century. The future of the novel and of poetry in particular seem uncertain. Human nature in the 1980s may be more interdependent, both within and without the great regional associations. All the same, our steps seem less self-assured. We are making moves towards a real world society for the first time. But how this society will be protected and what sanctions it will have, are unclear.

Epilogue to the 1995 Edition

The Cold War ended in the 1980s. Few people had thought that a possibility. I myself in 1985 dedicated a book, entitled *Armed Truce*, about the beginning of that strange encounter, to my children, with the comment: 'in the hope that they may live to see the end of the conflict whose origins are here described'. I had no real expectation, even in 1985, that an end of an era was at hand. Richard Pipes, professor of Russian history at Harvard, was more far-sighted: 'If the Soviet empire collapses, which one day it will,' he once said to me, I think in 1981, 'I am sure it will happen fast, and will take us all by surprise.'

It did.

That statement of Richard Pipes used a phrase which would not have been generally accepted in the early 1980s. For one success of Soviet propaganda was to insist on the use of a certain language. They wanted people to think that 'the Cold War', in its original form, had come to an end in the days of Khrushchev. Anyone who thought that the Soviet Union constituted, as Reagan put it, an 'evil empire' was dismissed, even by high-minded people, as a 'cold warrior'. Actually all that happened after Khrushchev was that the site of the contest between the West and the Soviet Union, until then played out in Europe, was transferred to the 'Third World'.

A second success of Soviet propaganda was to prevent the use of the expression 'Soviet Empire'. Hugh Seton-Watson, doyen of British historians of Russia, did use it but he was almost alone. The rest of us took the Soviet Union at its face value, and supposed that it was a misuse of words to talk of 'Empire' in relation to Russia. 'Empire' was a word associated with Western European viceroys in Lima or in Delhi, governors-general in Saigon, Accra or Bahia, coaling stations in Bombay or Aden. Kazakhstan or the Caucasus might have been conquered by the Tsars of Russia but, whatever the Soviet Union was it was not an empire in the accepted use of the word: Kazakhstan was a people's republic, not a colony.

Now we know better and see the experience of Soviet power in a realistic light. Russian historians and politicians themselves have, if anything, been more critical of what happened in the

history of their own country between 1917 and 1989 than even
'cold warriors' among Western historians.

The collapse of the Soviet empire was the most important event
of the 1980s. The Soviet catastrophe for once was a turning-point
in world history which appeared to be such at the time.

It happened for several reasons. First, there was a recovery of
Western defences in the early 1980s, as well as the extraordinary
and still most controversial Strategic Defence Initiative – 'Star
Wars'. The two things seemed to show the Soviet leaders that, in
order to keep up militarily with the West, they would have to
devote a colossal effort towards military technology; and even
then, perhaps, they would be incapable of such a thing unless they
freed their thinkers and scientists from the strait-jacket of their
official ideology.

Second, victims of their own propaganda, the Soviet leaders saw
the growing campaign for privatisation, denationalisation and the
withdrawal of the state from the economy (inspired by President
Reagan in the United States, and Mrs Margaret Thatcher in Britain, and then slowly followed elsewhere within the leading Western nations) as evidence that capitalism, so far from being
defeated, was reviving.

There seemed to be a similar revival in the Catholic Church
following the sensation of the nomination of a Pope from Poland.

Third, the leaders of the Soviet Union seemed to have abandoned their belief in the ideology of Marxism-Leninism, after the
death of Suslov in 1981.

Gorbachev, the great moderniser, faced these questions with
imagination and, greatly daring and in the name of modernisation,
lifted the lid from the boiling pot of Soviet politics – a lid so firmly
placed by Lenin and Stalin that no one remembered what was
inside. Gorbachev's catchwords, 'Glasnost', the Russian for Opening up, and 'Perestroika', which means Restructuring, became
words of common usage even in the West.

Once Gorbachev's 'modernisation' began, the subject peoples
of the Soviet empire rebelled, as had always seemed likely in the
event of a real 'thaw' in Soviet political conditions. Some of these
rebellions were outside the formal Soviet borders in eastern
Europe; some occurred within the Soviet Union itself, leading to
the achievement of a degree of independence by numerous new
nations, of which the largest was the Ukraine, which had been
formally a sovereign state since 1917 but now became so in reality
for the first time in history. These rebellions were a sign that

nationalism, which Marxism affected both to despise and to circumvent, was as modern as it was traditional: a combination which seemed confusing to both revolutionaries and conservatives.

All these events occurred as Professor Pipes expected: fast, and taking the West by surprise.

Few in the West thought in terms of celebrating a victory. There were no services of thanksgiving, no military parades. Yet in most senses what occurred was precisely a victory. Further it was just the kind of victory which Lenin, echoing Clausewitz, would have approved: 'the best kind of victory is one where a besieged city surrenders without a fight'.

Charles Bohlen, most intelligent of United States ambassadors to Russia, hoped that, one day, the great empire to which he was accredited in the 1950s would become 'a country, not a cause' (a phrase incidentally picked up by a British White Paper on defence in 1990 without, however, acknowledgement of the source). The cause evaporated, and the country divided into constituent parts.

The West had little idea what to do. One explanation was that most of the initiatives in foreign policy since 1945 had been taken by the Russians and the West had defined their policies simply by responding to them. The President of the United States hoped that the Ukraine would not break away from the Soviet state. But every great Western statesman in the past, from Frederick the Great to Napoleon, would have seen the benefit to Europe of a Russia which was bereft of its richest agricultural land. Chancellor Kohl had the foresight to see that the withdrawal of Russian direction of East German politics provided him with a great opportunity to reunite Germany. That he arranged. It was an event which should have been greeted as a victory. Western statesmen had formally had the reunification of Germany in freedom as a goal of policy for forty years. But in the event they found that this triumph caused them more anxieties than they had supposed possible. One statesman of the West, Margaret Thatcher, indeed changed her posture radically: from being the strongest of Western critics of the Soviet empire in the early 1980s, she seemed to be inspired by President Gorbachev, without realising that he could be no more than an interim figure. (She began to present herself as an opponent not of Communism and Russia, but of German hegemony in Europe.)

By the mid 1990s, with what seemed to be a 'new world disorder' threatening, even sophisticated people began to lose sight of the vast benefits which had flowed from the collapse of communism.

Yet there should be no doubt about that. First, and by far the most important matter, the world is no longer menaced by the prospect of nuclear disaster. Limited nuclear wars may occur. Minor nations may acquire nuclear weapons and threaten their neighbours with extinction if they do not do this or that. Political terrorists or even gangsters may do the same. But the world in the 1990s is not faced by two immensely powerful nations, the United States and the Soviet Union, armed to the teeth, each capable at a moment's notice of inflicting on each other, and so indirectly on the world, such a heavy bombardment that the human race would have been threatened with extinction. The risk of a catastrophe existed for forty years between 1949 and 1989, and the risk was if anything greatest in the 1980s, when the Soviet Union excelled only in its military power. The memory of Austria-Hungary in 1914 recalled to many that often it is the weakest power which causes the cataclysm.

It may seem now that there was never a real risk of catastrophe. But that was far from evident on many occasions: in the 1950s, in respect of Indo-China; in the late 1950s in respect of the Chinese 'off-shore islands', Quemoy and Matsu; in 1962, in respect of Cuba; and, on several occasions in respect of the Middle East. The author of this book was in Washington during the missile crisis of 1962, and believed an adviser of President Kennedy, Richard Goodwin, when he told him that his master thought that there had been a 40 per cent chance of catastrophe. In later days, both Western and Soviet leaders were men less far-sighted and humane than either Kennedy or Khrushchev.

There were, of course, protests against these dangers, but they seemed nihilist or unrealistic. Patriotic people, including the majority of the electorates of most democratic countries, saw no alternative to placing all their expectations in support of policies which in their way were suicidal, but yet were logical.

At least that stage of history, with the world on the nuclear precipice, seems to be at an end, to the great benefit of all life, animal and vegetable as well as human.

The other benefit of the 1990s is that subjection by the totalitarian Soviet empire is no longer possible. No one can predict the future of Russia; an aggressive revival on nationalist lines is possible. Russia, as a country as well as a cause, will always be great, and perhaps again constitute a great threat, but that combination of an intransigent ideology, imperial reach and military power which was offered by Soviet power, with high-minded support from communist parties and from thousands of well-placed secret agents from all over the world, can be ruled out – even if clearly they will attempt, effectively or no, such local measures as the recovery of Chechnya as a part of the Russian federation.

It may be represented that there was never much chance of a global victory for revolution on Soviet lines. That did not seem to be obvious in 1948, when the Sovietisation of the whole of Europe seemed possible, achieved as it no doubt would have been by an astute mixture of internal conspiracy and external bullying, and backed by the use of conventional forces, on the model of what occurred in Czechoslovakia early in that year. Such a Soviet military victory at any time, always a possibility, could have led to the triumph of the Soviet system which in turn might have taken some generations to shake off. The acceptance of Soviet influence over policy even by large, independent countries such as India and Egypt, suggests that a successful Soviet Union could have managed world hegemony quite easily. The memory of the Soviet-Nazi pact of 1939 recalls a time when, for two years, most of the Eurasian land-mass was dominated by an alliance of two totalitarian powers directed by men, Hitler and Stalin, who, though taken seriously in their lifetimes by foreigners as well as their own people, now appear to have had the characteristics of common murderers. That time was a really narrow escape for civilisation. It is no comfort that that civilisation was saved more or less by accident, because of Hitler's attack on Russia in 1941 and his simultaneous and still inexplicable declaration of war on the United States.

The world since the fall of communism has, all the same, seemed an alarming place. On the one hand, the end of the great conflict between the two so-called 'super-powers' (as they were known in the press for many years) relaxed international discipline. Big powers and small acted independently of their once overweening allies. The collapse of the Soviet power led to the eclipse of Russia as a super-power in the sense that she had been before. That eclipse may be a temporary thing. But Russia may also be about to experience a series of civil wars throughout Asia. Other one-time communist powers have experienced violent and apparently unending conflicts. The practice of 'ethnic cleansing' in Yugoslavia has been as brutal as anything that happened in the Second World War; while the use of that bland expression shows that human insensitivity has learned nothing from the knowledge of what the once harmless phrase 'final solution' signified in reality.

On the other hand, the victorious powers in the Cold War have experienced a curious reluctance to devise a new international system. It would be only too easy to contrast the present era with that at the end of the Second World War when the United States at least was full of ideas. A new league of nations? A four-nation college of world policemen? The speeches of Mr Roosevelt, the articles of Mr Lippman, the books of Wendell Wilkie or even the great bridge-player, Ely Cuthbertson, indicated that, at the end of the United States' second experience of global conflict, a generation had arrived who were keen to rebuild the world on a rational basis. That does not seem to be the state of affairs in the late 1990s. On the contrary, even the plans for a reinvigorated United Nations have come to naught.

It is true that an American writer, Francis Fukyama, argued that such planning for reason is unnecessary, since the world has reached the end of its era of political experiment and innovation. *The End of History* (a Hegelian expression in origin, curiously enough, for the moment when the final synthesis was ultimately achieved) insisted that the world could now contemplate the global establishment of representative government, a worldwide network of benign democracies presiding lightly over enlightened capitalism.

Such a conclusion, however much devoutly to be wished, seems premature. Instead we see revival of 'a new tribalism', we see increasing nationalism within even civilised countries such as Britain or France, we suspect that we see, with high rates of violent crime, the birth of what Alan Minc has called the 'new middle ages'. The recent headline in an English newspaper 'Laughing youths slash teacher's throat' might be a subtitle for a whole chapter of anxieties. Even the *laissez-faire* philosophy which inspired President Reagan and Margaret Thatcher in the 1980s, and whose revival seemed to provide one reason for the collapse of Communism, began to look a little tawdry by the mid 1990s.

Some fine political experiments survive: the European Community, for example, has gone from strength to strength. Yet it too has lost some of its capacity to inspire because of the determination of governments to maintain their own outdated priorities. Some important conclusions to great problems have occurred: in the Middle East, in South Africa, in Nicaragua, in Angola, and even, tentatively, in Ireland. Despite the encouragement offered by these settlements, it is too soon to know exactly whether these are triumphant solutions or stages in a process. The international element in each of those concerns does seem, however, to have been removed.

Political institutions seem everywhere in disarray. Appropriately, therefore, the grand surprise of the last years of the century has been the political revival of religion. Islam, both moderate and militant, is a major political force. So is Roman Catholicism, under a Pope, John Paul II, who sought for himself and for the Church a new international standing. Protestant evangelical movements grow every day more important in both the United States and in Latin America. The coming of a new plague in the shape of AIDS has developed human pessimism further than a religion based on the idea of original sin could have anticipated.

Meantime, the revolution in information has threatened to take over rational judgement, and the vast spread of computers, including personal computers, does not seem to have increased the capacity for humane reflection or for good writing. In most democratic countries the power of the Third Estate has grown astonishingly and instant power, if not permanent authority, often seems vested in the hands of television journalists.

Historians should not be expected to be prophets, though on some occasions, as in the case of Richard Pipes and the fall of the Soviet Empire, they are more likely to know the reality of societies more than politicians or officials. I myself believe that the most likely eventuality for the twenty-first century is the realisation of something like the prediction of W. H. McNeill: namely, that by the middle of that time we shall see something like a world empire, managed by a single power, which, without imposing political control on the rest of the world, or wishing to control it, will see its style of government generally copied, as well as its language, its music, its media, its fashion, even its food. It will have a capacity to intervene to prevent 'brutal wrong doing', to quote from Theodore Roosevelt's 'corollary' to the Monroe doctrine, in any country in the world, and quite often it will threaten to do so. It will no doubt take action in the name of the United Nations, but that will be purely formal.

In the 1970s or early 1980s, it did seem as if there were two candidate nations to play this part in the future, namely the Soviet Union and the United States. At that time, the first of these appeared to have a real chance of playing that role, for her leaders had an ideology to support them, they had imperially minded defence forces and they had developed the capacity for international action. Those leaders also seemed to have the self-confidence of intransigence.

That has now changed, and the only candidate for world power appears to be the United States. For, thanks to the surviving ambitions of nation states, it would seem (unfortunately) improbable that the European Union will develop a capacity for decisive action. China seems likely, should any real political relaxation occur, to experience the same internal crises which look as if they will beset the Soviet Union for an indefinite period. The time for an assertion of Japan's imperial capacity, whatever pessimists may assert, is past. The United States is thus the only viable candidate.

The United States has the capacity to apply sustained intelligence, technological preparedness and imagination to such a role; she has the sense of reserve, she has experienced officials capable of playing such a role. She must be the only power in history to have the capacity for empire without the overweening desire for it. The only thing that can hold back the United States from asserting such a place in the world seems likely to be her own spasms of self-doubt. She will probably thus always require the active backing of European allies, such as occurred in the Gulf War of 1991.

A world dominated by a single, restrained yet capable great power would be a far safer place than existed between 1945 and 1989. It would probably be a better world than any other which can reasonably be imagined. It would constitute an end of history indeed, but one surely necessary to secure the happy living-together of the ten billions whom the late twenty-first century is likely to have to accommodate.

References

(Note: these references give the sources for direct quotations and a few other controversial statements only.)

BOOK ONE

1. The Birth of the World

1 Carleton S. Coon, *The Origin of Races* (London, 1968), p. 659.
2 Sherwood Washburn, 'The Evolution of Man', *Scientific American* (September 1978).
3 Marcel Cohen, *Language, its Structure and Evolution* (tr.) (London, 1975), p. 15.
4 Coon, p. 80.
5 Matthew Arnold, *The Scholar Gipsy*.
6 Lewis Mumford, *The Transformations of Man* (New York, 1956), p. 7.
7 J. Z. Young, *An Introduction to the Study of Man* (Oxford, 1971), p. 380.
8 Alexis de Tocqueville, *Democracy in America* (New York, 1948), I, p. 202.
9 André Malraux, *Les Noyers de l'Altenburg* (Paris, 1948).
10 Edward Gibbon, *The History of the Decline and Fall of the Roman Empire* (London, 1869), I, p. 209.
11 Pierre Louis Roederer, *Oeuvres*, 8 vols (Paris, 1853–59), III, p. 461.

2. Hunters

1 Lawrence H. Keeley, 'The Function of Palaeolithic Flint Tools', *Scientific American* (November 1977).
2 John Hemming, *Red Gold: The Conquest of the Brazilian Indians* (London, 1978), p. 220.
3 Coon, p. 39.
4 Jacob Burckhardt, *Reflections on History* (London, 1943), p. 41.
5 Bernard Berenson, *Sketch for a Self-Portrait* (London, 1949).
6 Jean Jacques Rousseau, *A Discourse on the Origin of Inequality* (London, 1952), p. 178.
7 Isaiah Berlin, *Vico and Herder* (London, 1976), p. 53.

3. Farmers

1 Herodotus, *The Histories*, Everyman edition, I, p. 355.
2 H. W. F. Saggs, *The Greatness that was Babylon* (London, 1962), p. 4.
3 Grahame Clark, *World Pre-history* (Cambridge, 1969), p. 80.
4 Christopher Wrigley, in J. D. Fage and R. A. Oliver (eds), *Papers in African Pre-history* (Cambridge, 1970), p. 66.
5 Gibbon, II, p. 212.
6 Karl Wittfogel, *Oriental Despotism* (New Haven, 1957), p. 17.

4. Gods

1 Pierre Montet, *Eternal Egypt* (tr.) (London, 1964), p. 235.
2 Henri Frankfort, *The Birth of Civilisation in the Near East* (London, 1951).
3 Herodotus, I, p. 209.
4 Quoted in Pierre Grimal, *In Search of Ancient Italy* (tr.) (London, 1964), p. 227.

5. Kings and Waterworks

1 Wittfogel, p. 27.
2 Frankfort, p. 81.
3 Romila Thapar, *A History of India* (London, 1966), p. 76.
4 Wittfogel, p. 34.

6. Figures and Alphabets

1 Gordon Childe, in Charles Singer, E. J. Holmyard and A. R. Hall, *A History of Technology* (Oxford, 1954), I, p. 130.
2 Clark, p. 287.
3 Denise Schmandt Besserat, 'The Earliest Precursor of Writing', *Scientific American* (June 1978).
4 John Chadwick, *The Mycenaean World* (Cambridge, 1976), p. 182.

7. Laws and Tablets

1 J. H. Huizinga, *Homo Ludens: A Study of the Play Element in Culture* (London, 1949), p. 11.
2 Tocqueville, I, p. 102.
3 Herodotus, I, p. 355.

8. Pots, Mines and Cloths

1 Sir James Jeans, *The Growth of Physical Science* (Cambridge, 1950), p. 32.
2 Herodotus, I, p. 84.
3 Joseph Needham, *Science and Civilisation in China* (Cambridge, 1954 onwards), I, p. 20.

9. Cities, Trade and Slaves

1 Lewis Mumford, *The City in History* (New York, 1961), p. 38.
2 Carl Ortwin Sauer, *The Early Spanish Main* (Cambridge, 1966), p. 57.
3 Saggs, p. 254.

10. A Short Introduction to War

1 Montet, p. 60.
2 Thapar, p. 126.

BOOK TWO

11. The Masters of the Old World

1 Sir Mortimer Wheeler, *The Indus Civilisation* (Cambridge, 1953), p. 65.
2 Thapar, p. 19.
3 Gibbon, III, p. 141.
4 C. S. and C. S. Orwin, *The Open Fields* (Oxford, 1967), p. 70.
5 Fernand Braudel, *Capitalism and Material Life* (tr.) (London, 1973), p. 18.
6 Marc Bloch, *French Rural History: Its Essential Characteristics* (tr.) (London, 1952), p. 240.
7 José Díaz del Moral, *Historia de las Agitaciones Campesinas Andaluzas: Córdoba* (Madrid, 1929), p. xii.
8 Claudio Sánchez Albornoz, *Spain: A Historical Enigma*, 2 vols (Madrid, 1975), I, p. 322.
9 Tibor Szamuely, *The Russian Tradition* (London, 1974), p. 80.
10 Needham, I, p. 184.
11 Raymond Carr, *Spain 1808–1939* (Oxford, 1966), p. 415.
12 Thorold Rogers, *History of Agriculture and Prices in England 1259–1795*, 7 vols (Oxford, 1866–1902), V, p. 214.

13 E. le Roy Ladurie, *Times of Feast, Times of Famine* (London, 1972), p. 16.
14 Carlo Maria Cipolla, *Literacy and Development in the West* (London, 1969), p. 80.
15 Braudel, p. 58.
16 C. P. Fitzgerald, *A Concise History of East Asia* (London, 1974), p. 54.

12. Master Crops

1   Maurice Bowra, *The Greek Experience* (London, 1957), p. 126.
2   Gibbon, II, p. 416.
3   Fernand Braudel, *The Mediterranean in the Reign of Philip II* (tr.) (London, 1963, 1967), I, p. 329.
4   Sánchez Albornoz, p. 93.
5   Braudel, *Capitalism*, p. 65.
6   Stanley, J. and Barbara H. Stein, *The Colonial Heritage of Latin America* (New York, 1970), p. 34.
7   Gilberto Freyre, *The Mansions and the Shanties*.
8   Quoted in Marc Bloch, *Feudal Society* (London, 1961), p. 294.
9   Jean Jacques Hémardiquer (ed.), *Pour une Histoire de l'Alimentation* (Paris, 1970), p. 93; J. C. Drummond, *The Englishman's Food* (London, 1957), p. 466.
10 Giorgio Vasari, *Lives of the Painters, Sculptors and Architects* (London, 1927), II, p. 182.
11 Michel de Montaigne, *Diary of Montaigne's Journey to Italy in 1580 and 1581* (tr.) (London, 1929), p. 42.

13. Techniques

1   C. R. Boxer, *The Portuguese Seaborne Empire 1415–1825* (London, 1969), p. 98.
2   T. K. Derry and T. I. Williams, *A Short History of Technology* (Oxford, 1960), p. 52.
3   Lynn White, *Mediaeval Technology and Social Change* (Oxford, 1966), p. 53.
4   Gibbon, VI, p. 172.
5   Ramón Menéndez Pidal, *La España del Cid* (5th edn) (Madrid, 1956), p. 74.
6   Marc Bloch, *Rural France*, p. 54.
7   Sir Charles Oman, *A History of the Art of War in the Middle Ages* (London, 1924).

8 Thapar, p. 146.
9 Lynn White, p. 85.
10 Braudel, *Capitalism*, p. 261.
11 Quoted in Mumford, *The City*, p. 258.
12 Montet, p. 281.
13 Dorothy Hollington (ed.), *People and Food Tomorrow* (London, 1976), p. 4.

14. Landlords and Labourers

1 Bloch, *Rural France*, p. 170.
2 John Lynch, *The Spanish American Revolutions* (London, 1973), p. 341.
3 Sarmiento, cited in Lynch, p. 346.
4 Elie Halévy, *A History of the English People in the Nineteenth Century*, 6 vols (tr.) (London, 1924–34), I, p. 69.
5 Bloch, *Rural France*, pp. 75–7.
6 Bloch, *Feudal Society*, p. 218.
7 Anthony Wagner, *English Genealogy* (London, 1972), p. 33.
8 Henri Pirenne, *Mediaeval Cities* (Princeton, 1946), p. 81.
9 Bloch, *Rural France*, p. 77.
10 Bloch, *Feudal Society*, p. 1.
11 Robert Blake, *The Conservative Party from Peel to Churchill* (London, 1972), p. 142.
12 Freyre, p. xxix.
13 Gerald Brenan, *The Spanish Labyrinth* (Cambridge, 1943), p. 97.
14 Quoted in Sir John Clapham, *An Economic History of Modern Britain*, 3 vols (Cambridge, 1926–38), I, p. 22.
15 Isaiah Berlin, *Russian Thinkers* (London, 1978), p. 270.
16 Richard Pipes, *Russia under the Old Regime* (London, 1974), p. 17.
17 Jérôme Carcopino, *Daily Life in Ancient Rome* (tr.) (London, 1941), p. 61.
18 Gibbon, I, p. 55.
19 F. W. Maitland, *Domesday Book and Beyond* (Cambridge, 1921), p. 171.
20 Iris Origo, *The Merchant of Prato* (London, 1957), p. 22.
21 Bernard Lewis, *The Arabs in History* (New York, 1967), p. 104; G. R. Elton, *Europe during the Reformation, Europe 1517–1559* (London, 1963), p. 145.
22 Maitland, p. 35.
23 Richard Herr, *The 18th Century in Spain* (Princeton, 1958), p. 98.
24 Lewis, p. 105.

15. Crops and Cloths

1 Pirenne, p. 155
2 Frederick E. Zeumer, *A History of Domesticated Animals* (London, 1963), p. 198.
3 Lord Macaulay, *Essays and Lays of Ancient Rome:* essay on Ranke, (London, 1903).
4 Julius Klein, *The Mesta* (Cambridge, Mass., 1920), p. 338.
5 Klein, p. 335.
6 James Boswell, *Life of Samuel Johnson*, edited by Augustine Birrell, 6 vols (London, 1904), II, p. 397.
7 J. H. Huizinga, *The Waning of the Middle Ages* (London, 1924), pp. 249–51.

16. Population and its Slow Growth

1 Saggs, p. 4; J. Z. Young, p. 339.
2 C. Cipolla, *The Economic History of World Population* (London, 1962), p. 18; A. M. Carr Saunders, *World Population* (Oxford, 1936).
3 Bloch, *Rural History*, pp. 37–8.
4 D. V. Glass and D. E. C. Eversley (eds), *Population in History* (London, 1965), p. 95.
5 Historical figures in B. R. Mitchell, *European Historical Statistics 1750–1970* (London, 1975).
6 Pierre Chaunu, in *L'Histoire Economique et Sociale de la France*, ed. F. Braudel (Paris, 1971).
7 Lawrence Stone, *The Family, Sex and Marriage* (London, 1977), p. 432.
8 Gibbon, I, p. 101.
9 Gibbon, IV, p. 38.
10 Moses Finlay, *Aspects of Antiquity* (London, 1967), p. 160.
11 Charles Louis Montesquieu, *Lettres Persanes* (Paris, 1897).
12 Quoted in Alfred Sauvy, *General Theory of Population* (London, 1969), p. 412.
13 Jacob Burckhardt, *The Civilisation of the Renaissance in Italy* (New York, 1961), p. 42.
14 Herodotus, I, p. 109.
15 Bloch, *Rural France*, p. 142.
16 Glass, p. 124.
17 Peter Laslett, *The World We Have Lost* (London, 1965), p. 107.

17. Diseases and Doctors

1 W. H. McNeill, *Plagues and Peoples* (Oxford, 1977), p. 120.
2 G. Boccaccio, *The Decameron* (tr.) (London, 1930), p. 24.
3 Saggs, p. 474.
4 Needham, I, p. 204.
5 Freyre, I, p. 134.

18. Swords and Soldiers

1 Sauvy, p. 518.
2 Huizinga, p. 100.
3 Herodotus, I, p. 54.
4 Herodotus, II, p. 170.
5 Thucydides, *History of the Peloponnesian War* (tr. Richard Crawley) (London, 1910), p. 84.
6 Bowra, p. 83.
7 Léon Homo, *Roman Political Institutions from City to State* (tr.) (London, 1929), p. 164.
8 Tacitus, Publius Cornelius, *The Histories* (tr.) (London, 1964), p. 4.
9 Gibbon, I, p. 157.
10 Gibbon, III, p. 271.
11 Gibbon, II, p. 221.

19. The Religious Frame

1 Daniel Cossio Villegas (and others), *A Compact History of Mexico* (Mexico, 1973), p. 41.
2 Bowra, p. 126.
3 Protagoras, quoted in Bowra, p. 182.
4 Bowra, p. 226.
5 Gibbon, I, p. 37.
6 Albert Sorel, *Europe and the French Revolution* (tr.) (London, 1969), p. 177.
7 Américo Castro, *The Structure of Spanish History* (tr.) (Princeton, 1954), p. 321.
8 William Lecky, *The Rise and Influence of Rationalism in Europe* (London, 1863).
9 Gibbon, V, p. 421.
10 Hobbes, *Leviathan*.
11 Gibbon, V, p. 425.
12 Lewis, p. 48.
13 Lewis, p. 58.

14 Sánchez Albornoz, p. 163.
15 Boxer, p. 41.
16 Walter Ullmann, *Law and Politics in the Middle Ages* (Cambridge, 1975), p. 264.
17 Bloch, *Feudal Society*, p. 87.
18 Burckhardt, *Reflections*, p. 46.
19 R. W. Southern, *The Making of the Middle Ages* (London, 1959), p. 189.
20 Burckhardt, *The Renaissance*, pp. 112–13.
21 Freyre, p. 253.
22 Burckhardt, *The Renaissance*, p. 321.
23 Huizinga, *The Waning of the Middle Ages* (London, 1924), p. 62.
24 Lewis, p. 261.

20. Laws and Governors

1 Bowra, p. 86.
2 Thucydides, p. 122.
3 Sir Henry Maine, *Ancient Law* (London, n.d.), p. 31.
4 Gibbon, V, p. 33.
5 Gibbon, V, p. 218.
6 J. D. Fage, *A History of Africa* (London, 1978), p. 47.
7 Boxer, p. 77.
8 Acton, p. 32.
9 J. C. Holt, *Magna Carta* (London, 1965), p. 292.
10 Wittfogel, p. 131.
11 Lewis, p. 210.
12 Maitland, pp. 3–6; V. H. Galbraith, *Domesday Book – Its Place in Administrative History* (Oxford, 1974), p. 175.
13 A. H. M. Jones, *The Decline of the Ancient World* (London, 1966), p. 15.
14 A. Sorel, p. 290.
15 Maitland, p. 156.
16 Burckhardt, *The Renaissance*, p. 42.
17 Lord Acton, *The History of Freedom and Other Essays* (London, 1907), p. 28.

BOOK THREE

21. The Renaissance in Europe

1 Albert Demangéon, *Le Declin de l'Europe* (Paris, 1920), p. 303.
2 Harold M. Edwards, 'Fermat's Last Theorem', *Scientific American* (October 1975).
3 Burckhardt, *The Renaissance*, p. 183.
4 Lynn White, p. 128.
5 Article in *Encyclopaedia Britannica*, 'Pius II'.
6 Arnaldo Momigliano, *Studies in Historiography* (London, 1966).
7 Elton, p. 87.
8 Freyre, II, pp. 229–30.

22. The World Opened Up

1 Braudel, *The Mediterranean*, p. 295.
2 Burckhardt, *Reflections*, p. 176.
3 Freyre, p. 41.
4 Pieter Geyl, *The Revolt of the Netherlands* (London, 1932), p. 257.

23. Commerce Revived

1 Paul Mantoux, *The Industrial Revolution in the Eighteenth Century*, new and revised edn with Preface by T. S. Ashton (London, 1961), p. 15.
2 Maitland, p. 195.
3 Braudel, p. 212.
4 John Hale, *The Medici: The Pattern of Control* (London, 1977).
5 Raymond Dawson, *The Chinese Experience* (London, 1978).
6 John Parry, *The Spanish Seaborne Empire* (London, 1966).
7 C. H. V. Sutherland, *Gold* (London, 1959).
8 Violet Barbour, *Capitalism in Amsterdam in the 17th Century* (Ann Arbour, 1963), p. 43.
9 Geyl, p. 238.
10 Braudel, *The Mediterranean*, I, p. 284.
11 Barbour, pp. 134–42.

24. Slow Journeys by Land

1 Peter Brown, *The World of Late Antiquity* (London, 1971), p. 13.
2 Hugh Trevor-Roper, *The Rise of Christian Europe* (London, 1966), p. 80.

25. A Real Revolution: Printing

1 Keith Thomas, *Religion and the Decline of Magic* (Oxford, 1965), p. 355.
2 Hemming, p. 46.
3 Geyl, p. 82; Elton, p. 18.
4 Halévy, I, p. 457.
5 Irving Leonard, *Books of the Brave* (New York, 1964), p. 13.
6 Needham, I, p. 148.
7 Boxer, p. 345.
8 Bernard Berenson, *Italian Painters of the Renaissance* (London, 1963), p. 212; see also Alejandro Moreno Toscano, in Daniel Cossio Villegas, *Compact History of Mexico*, p. 55.
9 Keith Thomas, p. 184.
10 Boswell, II, p. 262.
11 Mumford, *The City*, p. 550.

26. City Life

1 Alfred Zimmern, *The Greek Commonwealth* (London, 1911).
2 G. M. Trevelyan, *English Social History* (London, 1942), p. 28.
3 James Mellaart, *The Neolithic of the Near East* (London, 1975).
4 Dante, *Inferno*.
5 Hale, p. 26.
6 Quoted in Braudel, *The Mediterranean*, p. 400.
7 Quentin Skinner, *The Foundations of Modern Political Thought*, 2 vols (Cambridge, 1978).
8 Pipes, p. 11.
9 German Arciniegas, *Latin America: A Cultural History* (New York, 1966), p. 88.
10 Quoted in Mumford, p. 246.
11 Elton, p. 25.

27. Gunpowder Wars, Gunpowder States

1 Carlo Cipolla, *Guns and Sails in the Early Stage of European Expansion* (London, 1965), p. 39.
2 T. K. Derry and Trevor I. Williams, *A Short History of Technology* (Oxford, 1960), p. 149.
3 Burckhardt, *The Renaissance*, p. 59.
4 Quentin Skinner, I, p. 125.
5 Mumford, *The City*, p. 363.
6 Burckhardt, *The Renaissance*, p. 102.

7 Quoted in General J. F. C. Fuller, *The Conduct of War* (London, 1961), p. 42.

28. Medicine, Food and People

1 Charles Singer and E. Ashworth Underwood, *A Short History of Medicine* (Oxford, 1962), p. 216.
2 Casanova, *Memoirs*, ed. Matthew Boyd (New York, 1946), p. 7.
3 Benevenuto Cellini, *Life*, 2 vols (London, 1888), p. 178.
4 Freyre, I, p. 262.
5 Figures in Marcel Reinhard, *Histoire Générale de la Population Mondiale* (Paris, 1968), p. 212.
6 Laslett, p. 81.
7 J. Hajnal, in Glass and Eversley, p. 30.
8 Benjamin Franklin, *Autobiography* (London, 1960), p. 28.
9 Stone, p. 6.
10 Carcopino, p. 83.
11 Leonard, p. 46.
12 Franklin, p. 126.
13 J. Trueta, *The Spirit of Catalonia* (London, 1946).
14 Pipes, p. 156.
15 Franklin, p. 231.
16 Philip Curtin, *The Atlantic Slave Trade: A Census* (Madison, Wisconsin, 1969), p. 46.
17 Freyre, I, p. xii.
18 Freyre, I, p. 251.

BOOK FOUR

29. Cotton as King

1 Halévy, I, p. 270.
2 Clapham, I, p. 252.
3 Moses Finlay, *Studies in Ancient Society* (London, 1974), p. 27.
4 Halévy, I, pp. 291–2.
5 Sauvy, p. 126.
6 loc. cit.
7 Halévy, I, p. 243.
8 L. Bogart and D. L. Klemmerer, *An Economic History of the American People* (New York, 1946), p. 445.
9 Theodore Zeldin, *France 1848–1945*, 2 vols (Oxford 1973, 1974), I, p. 65.

30. How Long Did They Work?

1 Clapham, I, p. 565.
2 Paul Mantoux, p. 376
3 Richard Hofstadter, *America at 1750* (London, 1972), p. 97.
4 Sauvy, p. 192.

31. The Power of Steam

1 Braudel, *Capitalism*, p. 274.
2 Samuel Smiles, *Lives of Boulton and Watt* (London, 1865), p. 128.
3 Quoted in Derry and Williams, p. 238.
4 Clapham, I, p. 132.
5 Halévy, I, p. 226.
6 Halévy, VI, p. 239.
7 Denis Mack Smith, *Mussolini's Roman Empire* (London, 1976), p. 160.
8 Halévy, I, p. 227.

32. Iron and Steel

1 White, p. 41.
2 Braudel, *Capitalism*, p. 275.
3 J. Vicens Vives, in C. Cipolla (ed.), *The Economic Decline of Empires* (London, 1970).
4 Herr, p. 28.
5 Lewis Namier, 'Anthony Bacon', *Harvard Journal of Economic and Business Studies*, II, No. 1 (November 1929).
6 Halévy, I, p. 226.
7 Mitchell, p. 399.

33. Revolution by Railway

1 Angel Pestaña, *Lo que Aprendí en la Vida* (Madrid, 1933), p. 284.
2 Sir John Clapham, *The Economic Development of France and Germany 1815–1914* (Cambridge, 1966), p. 154.
3 Milton Friedman, *Capitalism and Freedom* (London, 1963), p. 28.
4 Robert Blake, *The History of Rhodesia* (London, 1977), p. 244–5.
5 Marcel Proust, *A la Recherche du Temps Perdu* (Paris, 1913, etc.), XV.
6 Norman Stone, *The Eastern Front* (London, 1966), p.2.
7 A. J. P. Taylor, *From Sarajevo to Potsdam* (London, 1966), p. 2.

8 Stone, *Eastern Front*, p. 157.
9 Adam Ulam, *Lenin and the Bolsheviks* (London, 1965), p. 126.

34. A New World of Energy

1 Mumford, *The City*, p. 47.
2 Benedetto Croce, *Storia d'Italia dal 1871 al 1915* (Bari, 1928), p. 15.
3 J. B. Kelly, *Arabia, the Gulf and the West* (London, 1980), p. 427.

35. Faster and Faster Journeys

1 Boswell, II, p. 22.
2 Winston Churchill, *The World Crisis 1911–1915* (London, 1923), I, p. 212.
3 Amy Strachey, *St Loe Strachey, his Life and his Paper* (London, 1930), p. 69.
4 Quoted in George Mosse, *Nazi Culture* (London, 1966), p. 48.
5 George Orwell, *Complete Works* (London, 1968), IV, p. 9.
6 James Joll, *Intellectuals in Politics* (London, 1960), p. 163.

36. Another Revolution in Information

1 Tocqueville, *French Revolution*, X.
2 Carmelo Lisón Tolosano, *Belmonte de los Caballeros* (Oxford, 1966), p. 10.
3 Graham Storey, *Reuter's Century 1851–1951* (London, 1952), p. 26.
4 James Joll, *1914, The Unspoken Assumptions* (London, 1968).
5 J. W. Wheeler Bennett, *The Nemesis of Power* (London, 1952), p. 643.
6 Henry Kissinger, *The White House Years* (London, 1979), p. xxii.
7 S. H. Steinberg, *Five Hundred Years of Printing* (London, 1974).
8 Halévy, II, p. 140.
9 George Martin, *The Red Shirt and the Cross of Savoy* (New York, 1969).
10 Halévy, I, p. 149.
11 Zeldin, II, p. 495.
12 Luigi Barzini, in *Encounter* (May 1978).

37. Mass Media

1 John Jewkes, *A Return to Free Market Economics* (London, 1978), p. 21.
2 Zeldin, II, p. 389.
3 Réné Clair, *Reflection Faite* (Paris, 1951), p. 26.
4 Cyril Connolly, *The Unquiet Grave* (London, 1951), p. 117.
5 Raymond Aron, *La Révolution Introuvable* (Paris, 1968), p. 167.
6 Orwell, IV, p. 9.

38. A New Agriculture

1 J. D. Chambers and G. E. Murgay, *The Agricultural Revolution* (London, 1966), p. 8.
2 Halévy, I, p. 222.
3 Pipes, p. 8.
4 E. P. Thompson, *The Making of the English Working Class* (London, 1965), p. 230.
5 R. A. Butler (ed.), *The Conservatives: A History from Their Origins to 1965* (London, 1977), p. 95.
6 Bogart and Klemmerer, p. 212.
7 J. Fred Rippy, *British Investments in Latin America 1822–1949* (Minneapolis, 1959), p. 57.
8 E. John Russell, *The World of the Soil* (London, 1961), p. 81.
9 Peter Flynn, *Brazil: A Political Analysis* (London, 1978), p. 13.
10 Gerald Brenan, *South from Granada* (London, 1952), p. 126.
11 Siegfried Giedion, *Mechanisation takes Command* (New York, 1948), p. 235.
12 Reay Tannahill, *Food in History* (London, 1973), p. 236.
13 Charles Rich, in *Scientific American* (August 1978).
14 Siri von Reis Altschul, 'Exploring the Herbarium', *Scientific American* (May 1977).
15 Lester Brown, in *Scientific American* (September 1975).
16 Albert Soboul, *The French Revolution 1787–1799*, 2 vols (London, 1962), pp. 206–7, 556–7.
17 Leonard Schapiro, *The Communist Party of the Soviet Union* (London, 1960), p. 439.
18 Roy Medvedev, *Let History Judge* (London, 1972); Lord Moran, *Winston Churchill, The Struggle for Survival* (London, 1966).
19 C. P. Fitzgerald, *The Birth of Communist China* (London, 1964), p. 165.
20 ibid., p. 168.

39. The Expanding Stomach

1 Freyre, II, p. 289.
2 J. C. Drummond, *The Englishman's Food* (London, 1957).
3 John Womack, *Zapata and the Mexican Revolution* (London, 1969).
4 Paul Corner, *Fascism in Ferrara 1915–1925* (London, 1975).
5 Redcliffe Salaman, *The History of the Social Influence of the Potato* (Cambridge, 1949), p. 58.
6 Hémardiquer, p. 292.

7   Adam Smith, *The Wealth of Nations*, Everyman edn, 2 vols (London, 1910), p. 199.

40. Industrialisation and Modernisation

1   Burckhardt, *Reflections*, p. 188.
2   Voltaire, *Letters to and from Frederick the Great* (London, 1927), p. 55.
3   Schapiro, p. 282.
4   Jones, p. 33.
5   Clapham, *Britain*, III, p. 466.
6   Sauvy, p. 560.

41. Capitalism in the Nineteenth Century

1   Halévy, I, p. 272.
2   Rippy, p. 17.

BOOK FIVE

42. Modern Absolutism

1   Skinner, I, p. 84.
2   Boswell, II, p. 259.
3   A. Sorel, p. 139.
4   Tocqueville, *L'Ancien Régime*, p. 9.
5   Boxer, II, pp. 190–91.
6   A. Sorel, pp. 140, 150.
7   Elton, p. 145.
8   A. V. Dicey, *Introduction to the Study of the Laws of the Constitution* (London, 1959), p. 400.
9   John Vincent, *The Formation of the British Liberal Party* (London, 1966), p. 10.
10 Elton, p. 126.
11 Menéndez Pidal, p. 26.
12 Tocqueville, *French Revolution*, p. 40.
13 Parry, p. 103.
14 Boxer, pp. 276, 283.
15 A. Sorel, p. 140.
16 A. Sorel, p. 250.
17 Gordon Craig, *Germany 1866–1945* (Oxford, 1978), p. 229.
18 Metternich, quoted in Martin, p. 303.

19 G. M. Trevelyan, *Garibaldi's Defence of the Roman Republic* (London, 1920), p. 8.
20 A. Sorel, p. 165.
21 Harold Acton, *The Last Medici* (London, 1932), p. 301.
22 Gibbon, I, p. 215.
23 Robert Nisbet, *The Twilight of Authority* (London, 1976), p. 261.
24 Gibbon, V, p. 301.
25 Gibbon, I, p. 463.
26 Baldassare Castiglione, *The Book of the Courtier* (tr.) (New York, 1973), p. 248.
27 Américo Castro, p. 650.
28 Suetonius, quoted in Michael Grant (ed.), *Roman Readings* (London, 1958), p. 426.
29 A. Radishchev, *A Journey from St Petersburg to Moscow* (tr.) (Cambridge, Mass., 1958), p. 103.
30 Burckhardt, *Renaissance*, p. 15.
31 A. H. M. Jones, p. 212.
32 Bertrand Russell, *Practice and Theory of Bolshevism* (London, 1920).

43. Modern Democracy

1   J. H. Plumb, *The Growth of Political Stability in England 1675–1725* (London, 1969), p. 9.
2   Halévy, I, pp. 26–7.
3   Halévy, I, p. 26.
4   Max Weber, *The Protestant Ethic and the Spirit of Capitalism* (London, 1930), p. 175.
5   L. Stone, p. 235.
6   Burckhardt, *Reflections*, p. 84.
7   F. A. Hayek, *Law, Legislation and Liberty* (London, 1960), I, p. 159.
8   F. List, *The National System of Political Economy* (tr. Sampson Lloyd) (London, 1895).
9   Tocqueville, *French Revolution*, p. 69.
10 Quoted by A. Southgate, in Butler, p. 163.
11 H. A. L. Fisher, *A History of Europe* (London, 1936), p. 118.
12 Gibbon, IV, p. 242.
13 Macaulay, *The History of England* (London, 1905), I, p. 1
14 J. M. Keynes, *The Economic Consequences of the Peace* (London, 1919), p. 9.

44. Democracy's Enemies

1 Russell, *Practice and Theory*, p. 26.
2 Trueta, p. 126.
3 Quoted in Hywel Francis, *South Wales and the Spanish Civil War* (PhD, Swansea, 1977).
4 J. S. Mill, *Utilitarianism, Liberty and Representative Government* (London, 1910), p. 165.
5 Dicey, p. 11.
6 Bloch, *Feudal Society*, p. 202.
7 Lowry Nelson, *Rural Cuba* (Minneapolis, 1950), p. 215.
8 Lady Gwendolen Cecil, *The Life of Robert Marquis of Salisbury*, 4 vols (London, 1921), II, p. 145.
9 Robert Michels, *Political Parties* (tr.) (London, 1915), p. 25.
10 Lord Halifax, *Complete Works* (Oxford, 1912), p. 403.
11 Tocqueville, *Democracy in America*, I, p. 270.
12 Tocqueville, op. cit., p. 229.
13 Karl Popper, *The Open Society and its Enemies*, 2 vols (London, 1966), I, p. 127.
14 Skinner, I, p. 57.
15 Schapiro, p. 176.
16 Bowra, p. 14.

45. The Life of Political Parties

1 Vincent, p. 15.
2 Burckhardt, p. 41.
3 Anselmo Lorenzo, *El Proletariado Militante* (Mexico, n.d.), p. 17.
4 Pierre Joseph Proudhon, *Qu'est-ce que la Propriété* (Paris, 1966), p. 20.
5 Orwins, p. 6.
6 Blake, *The Conservative Party*, p. 202.
7 Quoted in *New York Review*, 8 February 1979.
8 Halévy, VI, p. 276.
9 Annie Kriegel, *Les Comunistes Français* (Paris, 1968), p. 122.
10 Halévy, VI, p. 12.
11 Michels, p. 208.
12 Quoted in M. Pinto-Duschinsky, *The Political Thought of Lord Salisbury 1854–1868* (London, 1967), p. 81.
13 Raymond Aron, *L'Opium des Intellectuels* (Paris, 1955), p. 100.
14 Quoted in J. Barrington Moore Jr, *Social Origins of Dictatorship and Democracy* (London, 1967), p. 49.

46. Syndicalists

1 Herr, pp. 125–6.
2 Clapham, *France and Germany*, p. 85.
3 Hofstadter, p. 38.
4 Halévy, VI, p. 486.
5 Winston Churchill, *Lord Randolph Churchill* (London, 1906).
6 Halévy, VI, p. 382.

47. Our Living Standards

1 Brandt Commission, *North-South: A Programme for Survival* (London, 1980).
2 *Scientific American* (December 1978).

48. Growth and Grossness of the Modern State

1 Halévy, I, p. 518.
2 *Economist*, 22 November 1979.
3 Vicens Vives, in Cipolla, *Decline of Empires*.
4 *The Times*, 9 September 1977.
5 Elie Halévy, *The Era of Tyrannies* (London, 1965), p. 193.
6 Burckhardt, *Reflections*, p. 35.
7 Max Weber, quoted in Nisbet, p. 38.
8 Tocqueville, *Democracy in America*, II, p. 621.
9 Quoted in Hayek, *The Road to Serfdom* (London, 1944) p. 30.

49. Groaning under Taxes

1 Clapham, *Britain*, III, p. 210.

50. Population's Great Leap

1 Glass, *Malthus*, p. 427.
2 Karl Marx, *Capital*, 3 vols (Moscow, 1961).
3 Glass, *Malthus*, p. 88.
4 Charles Westhoff, 'Marriage and Fertility in the Developed Countries', *Scientific American* (July 1978).
5 L. Stone, p. 62.
6 Tocqueville, *Democracy*, I, p. 328.
7 Mosse, p. 212.
8 L. Stone, p. 36.

51. The Achievements and Illusions of Medicine

1 Tocqueville, *Democracy*, I, p. 35.
2 Ulam, p. 562.
3 Communication from Dr Tejera.

52. Urban Man

1 Freyre, II, p. 26.
2 Radishchev, p. 220.
3 Mumford, *The City*, p. 18.
4 J. W. Goethe, *Italian Journey* (London, 1970), p. 172.
5 F. García Lorca, *Obras Completas*, 2 vols (Madrid, 1974).

53. Empires

1 A. W. Kinglake, *Eothen* (London, 1898), p. 10.
2 Rudyard Kipling, *From Sea to Sea* (London, 1900) I, p. 277.
3 Geoffrey Blainey, *The Tyranny of Distance* (London, 1968), p. 36.
4 V. G. Kiernan, *The Lords of Human Kind* (London, 1972), p. 49.
5 Elie Kedourie, *Islam in the Modern World* (London, 1980), p. 3.
6 Kiernan, p. 65.
7 Grahame Clark, 'Archaeology and Human Diversity', in *Annual Review of Anthropology* (1979), pp. 1–20.
8 Henri Frankfort, *The Birth of Civilisation in the Near East* (London, 1951).
9 Freyre, p. 5.
10 André Beaufre, *The Fall of France* (London, 1967), p. 31.
11 Quoted in E. Kedourie, *England and the Middle East* (Cambridge, 1956), p. 26.
12 Winwood Reade, *The Martyrdom of Man* (London, 1972), p. 415.
13 George Borrow, *The Romany Rye* (London, 1905), p. 162, quoted in Kiernan, p. 89.
14 Quoted in Kiernan, p. 41.
15 Quoted in Henry Sidgwick, *The Development of European Polity* (London, 1903).
16 Quoted in Denis Mack Smith, *Italy, a Modern History* (London, 1960).
17 Galeazzo Ciano, *Diario a Cura de Renzo de Felice* (Milan, 1980).
18 Jean François Revel, *Commentary* (January 1979).
19 Kiernan, p. 104.

54. Schools and Learning

1 Gibbon, IV.
2 C. Cipolla, *Literacy and Development in the West* (London, 1969).
3 James Brown, *History of Education*, 2 vols (London, 1972, 1975), 1, p. 291.
4 Cicero, *De Legibus*, II, XXII, 59.
5 Chadwick, p. 191.
6 Saggs, p. 189.
7 John Parry, *The Spanish Seaborne Empire* (London, 1966), p. 42.
8 Boxer, p. 365.
9 John Boustead, *Wind of the Morning* (London, 1971).
10 Bishop Abel Muzorewa, *Rise Up and Walk* (London, 1978), p. 17.
11 E. P. Thompson, p. 717.
12 J. H. Plumb, *The Death of the Past* (London, 1968), p, 51.
13 Halévy, I, 467.
14 Gibbon, III, p. 82.
15 Quoted in Hayek. *Road to Serfdom*, p. 142.
16 R. Medvedev, *Let History Judge* (London, 1972).

55. Games

1 Herodotus, II, p. 101.
2 J. H. Huizinga, *Homo Ludens: A Study of the Play Element in Culture* (London, 1949).
3 Gibbon, IV, p. 305.
4 Lowry Nelson, p. 262.
5 Halévy, I, p. 134.
6 Tocqueville, *Democracy*, I, p. 57.
7 Plato, *Laws*, VII, p. 803.

BOOK SIX

56. Modern Souls

1 Berlin, *Russian Thinkers*, p. xvi.
2 Halévy, I, p. 344.
3 Halévy, I, pp. 371–7, 514.
4 Hofstadter, p. 36.
5 Arthur Marwick, *The Deluge* (London, 1965), p. 298.
6 House of Commons debates, March 1955.

7 Burckhardt, *The Renaissance*; Grigson, quoted in Keith Thomas, *Religion and the Decline of Magic*.
8 Freyre, II, pp. 152, 255.

57. Anti-Churches

1 J. J. Rousseau, *Social Contract*, IV, viii.
2 A. Soboul, p. 397.
3 Tocqueville, *Democracy*, I, pp. 11–13.
4 Michelet, *Histoire de la Révolution Française*.
5 Edmund Burke, *Letters on a Regicide Peace*.
6 J. H. Rose, *Life of Napoleon I* (London, 1922), p. 21.
7 J. Pabón, *Cambó*, 3 vols (Barcelona, 1952), I, p. 49.
8 A. Sorel, pp. 575, 577.
9 Giovanni Conti Ventosa, quoted in G. Martin, p. 501.
10 Rhodes, in the *Dictionary of National Biography*.
11 Szamuely, p. 60.
12 E. Kedourie, *The Chatham House Version* (London, 1970), p. 300.
13 Karl Popper, *The Open Society*, II, p. 271.
14 Isaiah Berlin, *Russian Thinkers*, p. 231.
15 M. Philips Price, *My Reminiscences of the Russian Revolution* (London, 1921), pp. 21, 347.
16 Quoted in Gerald Meaker, *The Revolutionary Left in Spain 1914–1923* (London 1974).
17 *Collected Writings*, IX.
18 Nicholas Berdayev, *The Meaning of History* (London, 1945), pp. 12, 171.
19 George Mosse, *Nazi Culture* (London, 1966).
20 Frank Tuohy, *Yeats* (London, 1976), p. 202.
21 Díaz del Moral, p. 207.
22 Pestaña, p. 49.
23 N. Pevsner, *An Outline of European Architecture* (London, 1948), p. 146.
24 loc. cit.

58. War in the Nineteenth Century

1 Hemming, pp. 398, 482.
2 Arnold, p. 37.
3 Quoted in Major-General J. F. C. Fuller, *The Conduct of War* (London, 1961), p. 32.
4 Sir John Fortescue, *A History of the British Army*, 13 vols (London, 1899–1902), I, p. 353.

5   Sorel, p. 61.
6   Quoted in Sir Harold Nicolson, *The Congress of Vienna* (London, 1946), p. 42.
7   Blake, *Rhodesia*, p. 68.
8   Halévy, VI, p. 198.
9   L. B. Namier, *Conflicts: Studies in Contemporary History* (London, 1942), p. 7.
10 Orwell, IV, p. 8.
11 Howard, p. 216.

59. The Great War

1   Paul Corner, *Fascism in Ferrara 1915–1925* (London, 1975), p. 24.
2   Address to Naval War College, 2 June 1896, in *Works*, ed. Morrison, XIV, p. 182.
3   Clapham, *Britain*, III, p. 517.
4   Grey of Fallodon, *Twenty-Five Years 1892–1916*, I, p. 134.
5   Halévy, VI, p. 457.
6   Fuller, p. 52.
7   Marc Ferro, *The Great War* (London, 1973), p. 222.
8   Adolf Hitler, *Mein Kampf*, p. 772; Werner Maser, *Hitler's Letters and Notes* (London, 1973), p. 108.
9   Ferro, p. 145.
10 Friederich Wilhelm Ludendorff, *My War Memories 1914–1918*, 2 vols (tr.) (London, 1919), I, p. 358.
11 Samuel Eliot Morison and Henry Commager, *The Growth of the American Republic*, 2 vols (Oxford, 1950), II, p. 479.
12 Marwick, p. 329.
13 Quoted in Marwick, *War and Social Change in the Twentieth Century* (London, 1974), p. 26.
14 *The Times*, 10 December 1918.
15 Ferro, p. 144.
16 Quoted in Marwick, *The Deluge*, p. 45.
17 Ferro, p. 119.
18 Quoted in Ferro, p. 184.
19 Keynes, in *The Economic Journal*, 1915.
20 Marwick, *The Deluge*, p. 176.
21 Quoted in R. Nisbet, *The Twilight of Authority* (London, 1976).
22 N. Stone, p. 310.
23 Arthur Schlesinger Jr, *The Imperial Presidency* (London, 1973), p. 192.
24 Elmer Bendiner, *A Time for Angels* (New York, 1975), p. 56.
25 Orwell, II, p. 135.

26 Walt Rostow (ed.), *The Economics of 'Take-off' into Self-sustained Growth* (Washington, 1963), p. 233.

60. The War of the Nazis I: Races

1 George Kennan, *Russia and the West under Lenin and Stalin* (London, 1961), p. 32.
2 A. Sorel, p. 494.
3 Sauvy, p. 513.
4 Saggs, p. 49.
5 Boxer, p. 147.
6 Quoted in Manning Clark, *A Short History of Australia* (London, 1964), p. 100.
7 Sauvy, p. 510.
8 Quoted in Kedourie, *England and the Middle East* (Cambridge, 1956), p. 84.
9 Manning Clark, p. 212.
10 Michael Balfour, *The Kaiser and His Times* (London, 1975), p. 227.
11 Kedourie, p. 68.
12 A. Marwick, *Britain in the Century of Total War* (London, 1968), p. 50.
13 Quoted in Gordon Craig, *Germany 1866–1945* (Oxford, 1978), p. 154.
14 Karl Bracher, *The German Dictatorship* (London, 1971), p. 274.
15 J. M. Keynes, *Economic Consequences*, p. 26.
16 Clapham, *France and Germany*, p. 209.
17 Norman Cohn, *Warrant for Genocide* (London, 1967).
18 Quoted in Groves, *Dictionary of Music*.
19 Ferro, p. 123.
20 Prince Ernest Stahremberg, *Between Hitler and Mussolini* (New York, 1942), p. 5.
21 Tuohy, p. 204.
22 Pabón, I, p. 236.
23 James Joll, *Intellectuals in Politics* (London, 1960), p. 60.
24 Robert Paxton, *Vichy France* (London, 1972).
25 Flynn, pp. 86, 87.

61. The War of the Nazis II: The Fighting

1 Hermann Rauschning, *The Voice of Destruction* (New York, 1940), p. 27.
2 Basil Liddell Hart, *The Second World War* (London, 1970), p. 66.
3 Milovan Djilas, *Wartime* (London, 1977), p. 234.

4 Paxton, p. 22.
5 ibid., p. 36.
6 Marc Bloch, *L'Etrange Défaite* (Paris, 1957).
7 Liddell Hart, loc. cit.
8 Henri Michel, *The Shadow of War* (London, 1972).
9 R. Hillberg, *The Destruction of the European Jews* (Chicago, 1961), p. 219.
10 Cohen, p. 249.
11 Paxton, p. 231.
12 R. Dahrendorf, *Class and Conflict in Industrial Society* (London, 1959).
13 Croce, p. 3.
14 L. B. Namier, *Vanished Supremacies: Essays on European History 1812–1918* (London, 1962), p. 219.

63. The Cold War I: The 'Class Struggle'

1 Tocqueville, *Democracy*, I, p. 426.
2 H. Seton-Watson, *The Russian Empire 1801–1917* (London, 1967), p. 674.
3 I. Berlin, *Four Essays on Liberty* (London, 1969), p. 137.
4 Schapiro, p. 381.
5 Pipes, p. 57.
6 Lenin, *Works*, XXIII, quoted in Wittfogel, p. 400.
7 Pipes, p. 123.
8 Barzini, *Encounter* (May 1978).
9 Orwell, II, p. 56.
10 Frankfort, p. 90.
11 Gibbon, III, p. 410.
12 Maine, p. 106.
13 Bloch, *Rural France*, p. 104.
14 G. R. Elton, *The Practice of History* (London, 1969), p. 54.
15 Bloch, *Feudal Society*, p. 33.
16 A. Sorel, p. 197.
17 Burckhardt, *Renaissance*, p. 261.
18 Friedrich von Humboldt, *Personal Narrative of Travels to the Equinoctial Regions of the New Continent (1799–1804)*.
19 Clapham, *France and Germany*.
20 Arnold, p. 60.
21 Zeldin, II, p. 26.
22 Hofstadter, p. 18.
23 Clapham, III, p. 518.

24 Pierre Vilar, *La Catalogne dans l'Espagne Moderne* 3 vols (Paris, 1962), I, pp. 136, 138.
25 Reinhold Niebuhr, *The Self and the Dramas of History* (London, 1956), p. 58.
26 Quoted in R. Michels, *Political Parties*, p. 290.
27 P. Laslett, *The World We Have Lost* (London, 1965), p. 218.
28 Quoted in Michels, p. 313.
29 Bracher, p. 401.
30 Schapiro, p. 379.
31 Evgenia Ginsburg, *Into the Whirlwind* (London, 1967), p. 26.
32 Medvedev, p. 216.
33 Schapiro, p. 258.
34 Quoted in Szamuely, p. 19.
35 Quoted in Szamuely, p. 48.
36 A. Sorel, p. 457.
37 Isaiah Berlin, *Russian Thinkers*, p. 237.
38 Zbigniew Brzezinski, *Between Two Ages* (New York, 1970), p. 31.
39 Wilson, 4 July 1914, quoted in Bendiner, p. 19.
40 NSC 68, 14 April 1950, *A Report on the National Security Council by the Executive Secretary on US Objectives and Proposals for National Security.*

64. The Cold War II: The Course

1 Philip Mosely, *The Kremlin in World Politics* (New York, 1960).
2 Winston Churchill, *The Second World War*, VI, p. 360.
3 *Foreign Relations of the United States* (1946), VI, p. 763.
4 See the deposition of US Vice-Consul Claiborne Pell to George Urban, in *Communist Reformation* (London, 1979), p. 228.
5 Guenther Lewy, *The US in Vietnam* (London, 1979).
6 J. Braunthal, *History of the International* (London, 1967), II, p. 216.
7 *L'Observateur*, 14 August 1952.
8 Orwell, IV, p. 10.

Epilogue

1 Pipes, p. 21.
2 Henry Kissinger, in the *Economist*, 10 February 1975.
3 Brzezinski, *Between Two Ages.*
4 Arnold, p. 7.
5 Arnold, p. 44.
6 Alan Bullock, *Hitler, a Study in Tyranny* (London, 1962), p. 120.
7 Hugh Thomas, *Cuba or the Pursuit of Liberty* (London, 1971), p. 851.

8   Bloch, p. xii.
9   Bloch, p. 310.
10 Kenneth Clark, *Civilisation: A Personal View* (London, 1969), p. 216.
11 Pierre Chaunu, *Le Sursis* (Paris, 1979).
12 Frankfort, p. 60.
13 Tocqueville, *Democracy*, II.
14 Grahame Clark, *Annual Review of Anthropology* (1979), 8, pp. 1–20.
15 Bertrand Russell, *The Practice and Theory of Bolshevism* (London, 1920).
16 Acton, *The History of Freedom and Other Essays* (London, 1907).
17 Macaulay, *Essays*, p. 548.
18 Herodotus, I, p. 61.

Index

Aaron, founder of priestly class 157
Abbasid caliphate 697
Abd-el Kader 592
Abd-el Krim 601
Abdul Hamid, sultan 345, 499
absolutism, modern 475ff
Abyssinia 82, 220
Acapulco 216
Achaemenian emperors (Persia) 45,
    162, 163, 187, 222
Achard, Franz Karl 445
Acheson, Dean Gooderham 617, 714
Acland, John 536
Acton, Harold 482
Acton, Lord 190, 197, 736
Adelard of Bath: Arabic numerals
    206
Adler, Alfred 568
Aegina 221
Aeneas Silvius *see* Pius II
Afghanistan 95
Afonso de Albuquerque 214
Africa: agriculture 332, colonisation
    601–2; European 'scramble' for
    593–4, 690–1, 719–20;
    industrialisation 332, 426;
    missionaries 622; Portuguese
    exploration of 212; slave trade
    293–4, 294ff
Africa, North: French influence 596;
    Islamic conquests 210; in Second
    World War 676; slave trade 293–4
Agincourt, battle of 180n, 644
agrarian reform 431–2
Agricola, Georgius 203
Agricola, Michael 247
agricultural implements 24, 51, 86–8

agricultural technology 22, 28, 86–8,
    414ff
agriculture, beginnings of 21, 23, 24,
    61, 301, 315
Agrigentum 109
AIDS 745
aircraft 378–83, 684–5; *see also*
    aviation
air raids 379–81, 649, 684–5
Alamo, Rafael Pérez del 524
Al-Andalus 170, 224, 257
Alaska 13, 20, 421n, 712
Albereda of Bayeux, countess 175n
Alberti, Leon Battista 134, 258
Albigensians 177, 246
Albizzi, Maso degli 255
Albornoz, Claudio Sánchez 67, 81
Alcock, John: Atlantic flight 380
alcohol 82–3, 288–91, 440
Aldrin, Edwin 384
Aldus, Manutius 243
Alesia 109
Alexander II, tsar 694
Alexander the Great 64, 124, 141
    and note 150ff, 186, 222, 252
Alexander Severus, emperor 75
Alexandria 346; library 166, 241
Alfonso, Juan Pablo 362
Alfonso I of Aragon 176
Alfonso III, king 171
Alfred the Great 494
Alfreton, Derbyshire: oil spring 358
Algeria 690–1
al Hajjáj al Thadafí, Muslim general
    210
Alhazen, writer on optics 395
Al Khwarizmi 206
Allbutt, Clifford 567

773